NEIGHBOURS AND SUCCESSORS OF ROME

Traditions of glass production and use in Europe and the Middle East in the later 1st millennium AD

Edited by

Daniel Keller, Jennifer Price and Caroline Jackson

Oxbow Books
Oxford & Philadelphia

Published in the United Kingdom in 2014 by
OXBOW BOOKS
10 Hythe Bridge Street, Oxford OX1 2EW

and in the United States by
OXBOW BOOKS
908 Darby Road, Havertown, PA 19083

© Oxbow Books and the individual authors 2014

Hardcover Edition: ISBN 978-1-78297-397-3
Digital Edition: ISBN 978-1-78297-398-0

A CIP record for this book is available from the British Library

Library of Congress Cataloging-in-Publication Data

Neighbours and successors of Rome : traditions of glass production and use in Europe and the Middle East in the later 1st millennium AD / edited by Daniel Keller, Jennifer Price and Caroline Jackson. -- First edition.
  pages cm
 Papers presented at a conference organized by the Association for the History of Glass, held at King's Manor, York, 19-20 May 2011.
 Includes bibliographical references.
 ISBN 978-1-78297-397-3
 1. Glassware industry--Rome--History--To 1500--Congresses. 2. Glassware industry--Byzantine Empire--History--To 1500--Congresses. 3. Glassware industry--Europe--History--To 1500--Congresses. 4. Glass manufacture--Rome--History--To 1500--Congresses. 5. Glass manufacture--Byzantine Empire--History--To 1500--Congresses. 6. Glass manufacture--Europe--History--To 1500--Congresses. 7. Glassware, Roman--Congresses. 8. Glassware, Byzantine--Congresses. 9. Glassware--Europe--Congresses. 10. Glassware, Medieval--Congresses. I. Keller, Daniel, 1970- compiler of edition. II. Price, J. (Jennifer), Dr., compiler of edition. III. Jackson, Caroline M., compiler of edition.
 HD9624.G553R666 2014
 338.4'7666109409021--dc23
                           2014007701

All rights reserved. No part of this book may be reproduced or transmitted in any form or by any means, electronic or mechanical including photocopying, recording or by any information storage and retrieval system, without permission from the publisher in writing.

Printed in the United Kingdom by Berforts Information Press Ltd, Eynsham, Oxfordshire

For a complete list of Oxbow titles, please contact:

UNITED KINGDOM
Oxbow Books
Telephone (01865) 241249, Fax (01865) 794449
Email: oxbow@oxbowbooks.com
www.oxbowbooks.com

UNITED STATES OF AMERICA
Oxbow Books
Telephone (800) 791-9354, Fax (610) 853-9146
Email: queries@casemateacademic.com
www.casemateacademic.com/oxbow

Oxbow Books is part of the Casemate Group

Front cover images:
Top left: Early Anglo-Saxon claw beaker, 5th/6th century, Ringlemere Farm, Kent; London, British Museum, 2005,1205.1. Top right: Late Sasanian rhyton, 6th/7th century, Amlash(?), Iran; London, British Museum, 1972,0516.2. Bottom left: Early Byzantine lamp, 6th century, Tyre(?), Lebanon; London, British Museum, 1900,0412.1. Bottom right: Umayyad bottle, 8th century, Iran(?); London, British Museum, 1961,1114.1. (All reproduced by courtesy of the Trustees of the British Museum).

Back cover images:
Late Roman gold-glass from the Wilshere Collection in the Ashmolean Museum, Oxford.

Contents

Acknowledgements v
List of Contributors vi

1   Glass from the later first millennium AD: current state of research...1
      Daniel Keller, Jennifer Price and Caroline Jackson

2   The last Roman glass in Britain: recycling at the periphery of the empire...6
      Caroline Jackson and Harriet Foster

3   Opaque yellow glass production in the early medieval period: new evidence 15
      James R. N. Peake and Ian C. Freestone

4   The vessel glass assemblage from Anglo-Saxon occupation at West Heslerton, North Yorkshire............................22
      Rose Broadley

5   Glassworking at Whitby Abbey and Kirkdale Minster in North Yorkshire..32
      Sarah Paynter, Sarah Jennings† and Jennifer Price

6   Glass workshops in northern Gaul and the Rhineland in the first millennium AD as hints of
      a changing land use – including some results of the chemical analyses of glass from Mayen.....................43
      Martin Grünewald and Sonngard Hartmann

7   Campanulate bowls from *Gallaecia*: evidence for regional glass production in late antiquity 58
      Mário da Cruz

8   The Wilshere Collection of late Roman gold-glass at the Ashmolean Museum, University of Oxford....................68
      Susan Walker

9   The "proto-history" of Venetian glassmaking...73
      David Whitehouse†

10   Late Roman glass from South Pannonia and the problem of its origin 79
      Mia Leljak

11   Glass supply and consumption in the late Roman and early Byzantine site Dichin, northern Bulgaria 83
      Thilo Rehren and Anastasia Cholakova

12   An early Christian glass workshop at 45, Vasileos Irakleiou Street in the centre of Thessaloniki............................95
      Anastassios Ch. Antonaras

13 Glass tesserae from Hagios Polyeuktos, Constantinople: their early Byzantine affiliations 114
    Nadine Schibille and Judith McKenzie

14 Successors of Rome? Byzantine glass mosaics 128
    Liz James

15 Glass from the Byzantine Palace at Ephesus in Turkey 137
    Sylvia Fünfschilling

16 Late Roman and early Byzantine glass from *Heliopolis*/Baalbek 147
    Hanna Hamel and Susanne Greiff

17 Changes in glass supply in southern Jordan in the later first millennium AD 162
    Susanne Greiff and Daniel Keller

18 Egyptian glass abroad: HIMT glass and its markets 177
    Marie-Dominique Nenna

19 Continuity and change in Byzantine and early Islamic glass from *Syene*/Aswan and Elephantine, Egypt 194
    Daniel Keller

20 Sasanian glass: an overview 200
    St John Simpson

Acknowledgements

We would like to thank all the authors of the papers in this volume, the referees who reviewed the papers for publication and the contributors to the conference in York for presenting their research in lectures and posters and taking part in the discussion; the Association for the History of Glass Ltd (AHG) for arranging the conference and for funding the colour plates for the volume; and the many other people who have helped this project, particularly Justine Bayley for taking on much of the administration of the conference, Sarah Brown for her generous support during the conference and Tina Jakob for her assistance both in York and in the preparation of this volume.

Daniel Keller, Caroline Jackson, Jennifer Price

List of Contributors

ANASTASSIOS CH. ANTONARAS
Museum of Byzantine Culture
P.O. Box 50047
Thessaloniki 54013
Greece
andonar@physics.auth.gr

ROSE BROADLEY
31 Heathfield Way
Barham, Kent CT4 6QH
United Kingdom
roseclark2@gmail.com

ANASTASIA CHOLAKOVA
Institute of Archaeology
University College London
31–34 Gordon Square
London WC1H 0PY
United Kingdom
sia_cholakova@hotmail.com

MARIO DA CRUZ
Researcher Vicarte, FCT-UNL
Universidade Nova de Lisboa
Associate researcher CITCEM,ICS
Universidade do Minho Braga
Post-doctoral research fellow FCT
Portugal
mariodacruz@hotmail.com

HARRIET FOSTER
Norfolk Museums Service
Shirehall
Market Avenue
Norwich NR1 3JQ
United Kingdom
dr-foster@hotmail.co.uk

IAN C. FREESTONE
Institute of Archaeology
University College London
31–34 Gordon Square
London WC1H 0PY
United Kingdom
i.freestone@ucl.ac.uk

SYLVIA FÜNFSCHILLING
Augusta Raurica
Giebenacherstrasse 17
4302 Augst
Switzerland
sylvia.fuenfschilling@bl.ch

SUSANNE GREIFF
Römisch-Germanisches Zentralmuseum
Forschungsinstitut für Archäologie
Ernst-Ludwig-Platz 2
55116 Mainz
Germany
greiff@rgzm.de

MARTIN GRÜNEWALD
Römisch-Germanisches Zentralmuseum
Forschungsinstitut für Archäologie
Ernst-Ludwig-Platz 2
55116 Mainz
Germany
gruenewald@rgzm.de

HANNA HAMEL
Deutsches Archäologisches Institut
Orient-Abteilung
Podbielskiallee 69–71
14195 Berlin
Germany
hanna.hamel@dainst.de

SONNGARD HARTMANN
Römisch-Germanisches Zentralmuseum
Forschungsinstitut für Archäologie
Ernst-Ludwig-Platz 2
55116 Mainz
Germany
hartmann@rgzm.de

CAROLINE JACKSON
Department of Archaeology
University of Sheffield
Northgate House
West Street
Sheffield S1 4ET
United Kingdom
c.m.jackson@sheffield.ac.uk

LIZ JAMES
Department of Art History
University of Sussex
Falmer
Brighton BN1 9QN
United Kingdom
e.james@sussex.ac.uk

SARAH JENNINGS†
English Heritage
Fort Cumberland
Fort Cumberland Road
Eastney
Portsmouth PO4 9LD
United Kingdom

DANIEL KELLER
Johanniterstrasse 13
4056 Basel
Switzerland
daniel.keller@unibas.ch

MIA LELJAK
Đurmanec 149
49225 Đurmanec
Croatia
mialeljak@gmail.com

JUDITH MCKENZIE
St Hugh's College
Oxford OX2 6LE
United Kingdom
judith.mckenzie@arch.ox.ac.uk

MARIE-DOMINIQUE NENNA
UMR 5189 Histoire et Sources des Mondes Anciens
Maison de l'Orient et de la Méditerranée
7 rue Raulin
69007 Lyon
France
marie-dominique.nenna@mom.fr

SARAH PAYNTER
English Heritage
Fort Cumberland
Fort Cumberland Road
Eastney
Portsmouth PO4 9LD
United Kingdom
sarah.paynter@english-heritage.org.uk

JAMES R. N. PEAKE
European Ceramics and Glass
Bonhams
101 New Bond Street
London W1S 1SR
United Kingdom
peakejrn@gmail.com

JENNIFER PRICE
Garth End
Well Garth
Heslington
York YO10 5JT
United Kingdom
jennifer.price@durham.ac.uk

THILO REHREN
UCL Qatar, a partner of HBKU
Georgetown University Building
Doha
Qatar
th.rehren@ucl.ac.uk

NADINE SCHIBILLE
Arts A121
University of Sussex
Falmer
Brighton BN1 9QN
United Kingdom
n.schibille@sussex.ac.uk

ST JOHN SIMPSON
Department of the Middle East
The British Museum
London WC1B 3DG
United Kingdom
ssimpson@thebritishmuseum.ac.uk

SUSAN WALKER
Sackler Keeper of Antiquities
Ashmolean Museum of Art and Archaeology
University of Oxford
Oxford OX1 2PH
United Kingdom
susan.walker@ashmus.ox.ac.uk

DAVID WHITEHOUSE†
Corning Museum of Glass
One Museum Way
Corning, NY 14830
USA

1

Glass from the later first millennium AD: current state of research

Daniel Keller, Jennifer Price and Caroline Jackson

Introduction

The conference "Neighbours and successors of Rome. Traditions of glass production and use in Europe and the Middle East in the later first millennium AD" was organised by the Association for the History of Glass and held at King's Manor in York on 19–20 May 2011. The geographical range of findspots or origin of the glass presented in the contributions of this volume reaches from north-western Europe with Scotland (James R. N. Peake and Ian C. Freestone), England (Caroline Jackson and Harriet Foster; Sarah Paynter, Sarah Jennings† and Jennifer Price; Rose Broadley), northern Gaul and the Rhineland (Martin Grünewald and Sonngard Hartmann) to the north-west of the Iberian Peninsula (Mario da Cruz), the Veneto in northern Italy (David Whitehouse†) and the Balkans (Mia Leljak; Thilo Rehren and Anastasia Cholakova). Further to the south-east it includes glass finds from the major Byzantine cities of Thessaloniki (Anastassios Ch. Antonaras) and Constantinople (Nadine Schibille and Judith McKenzie) as well as from Asia Minor (Sylvia Fünfschilling), the Levant (Hanna Hamel and Susanne Greiff; Susanne Greiff and Daniel Keller), Egypt (Daniel Keller), Mesopotamia and Persia (St John Simpson). Furthermore, three papers deal with a specific category of glass objects of the late Roman and Byzantine period, gold-glass (Susan Walker), glass mosaics (Liz James) and HIMT glass exported from Egypt (Marie-Dominique Nenna).

The papers in this volume discuss glass finds, their contexts and their archaeological perspective using spatial, typological and compositional approaches to investigate issues of glass production, trade and consumption. Some are mainly concerned with archaeometric studies of glass finds from the later first millennium AD, while others present archaeological glass or glass working finds of this period.

A few provide a synthesis between archaeological and archaeometric research, or include some archaeometric data in otherwise mainly archaeological papers or an overview of the archaeological finds in otherwise mainly archaeometric papers. The integration of archaeology and archaeological science to achieve a better understanding of ancient glass represents a new trend in glass research, as is the synthesis of research of specific glass objects or glass from selected regions in their historical contexts. There is much still to learn about the production, trade and consumption of glass in this period, but the trends combining different facets of archaeologial analysis are becoming firmly established in glass research.

Early/middle Byzantine, Sasanian and early Islamic glass in the eastern Mediterranean and the Middle East

The history of research on Byzantine glass from the studies of the antiquaries and glass historians of the late 19th and early 20th century to the studies with an art-historical focus up to the middle of the 20th century and since then to the increasing dominance of archaeology has recently been summarised (Keller 2010). This overview therefore concentrates on the current state of research, discussing both early and middle Byzantine glass and the early Islamic glass of the later first millennium AD in the eastern Mediterranean and the Middle East. The archaeological study of early Islamic glass has developed only very recently; a chronological division between the Byzantine and early Islamic periods and their respective glass corpora has often been made and sometimes the glass finds from the two periods at the same sites have been studied by different scholars. In the future, it will become important to study the development of Byzantine and early Islamic glass together. So far, only case studies from individual sites have been discussed, as at Tebtynis (Foy 2001), Beirut (Jennings 2006, 123–239), Beth Shean (Winter 2011) and Jabal Harun (Keller and Lindblom 2008; Keller and Lindblom in press). Such case studies can reveal only a limited part of the evidence and regional or inter-regional studies on a larger scale should address this question in more detail. A first step in this direction was made more than ten years ago through the study of the development of glass vessel forms from the early Byzantine to the early Islamic period in Egypt (Foy 2000), and more recently, a regional study of the early Byzantine glass from the Holy Land (Gorin-Rosen and Winter 2010) and a general discussion of vessel types and their uses in the early and middle Byzantine periods (Antonaras 2010) have also been published. The glass of the middle Byzantine period is still not well known from an archaeological perspective and more studies of the chronology based on assemblages from well dated contexts are needed (cf. Price 2010, 260). So far, only the glass finds from the Athenian Agora provide a sequence of glass finds from the early to the middle Byzantine period (Weinberg and Stern 2009, 147–176; Stern 2010).

Research into the development from Sasanian to early Islamic glass is in a similar state. The case studies from sites such as Tell Baruda (Negro Ponzi 1987), Nippur (Meyer 1996) and Kush (Keller in press) provide limited archaeological evidence for sequences of late Sasanian and early Islamic glass, and studies of larger regional or inter-regional assemblages discussing the changes and/or continuity from one period to the next still need to be undertaken. Simpson presents an overview of Sasanian glass and discusses the current state of research of this subject, and similar studies of the early Islamic glass from Mesopotamia, Iran and the Arabian Gulf would be very valuable.

The remaining papers on Byzantine and early Islamic glass in this volume represent the current state of research as they mostly deal with case studies discussing finds and/or chemical analysis of glass from individual sites. The subjects of these papers range from an early Byzantine glass workshop recently excavated in Thessaloniki, Greece (Antonaras) and the chemical analysis of Byzantine glass mosaic tesserae from an important 6th-century church in Constantinople (Schibille and McKenzie) to an overview of the glass finds from the so-called Byzantine Palace at Ephesus, Turkey (Fünfschilling) and a note on the main forms of glass drinking vessels of the early Byzantine and early Islamic periods at the neighbouring sites of Elephantine and *Syene*/Aswan on the 1st cataract of the Nile in southern Egypt (Keller). Late Roman and early Byzantine glass finds from *Heliopolis*/Baalbek, Lebanon are described in their typological and chronological sequence and a short note on their chemical analysis is included (Hamel and Greiff). Studies linking archaeological (*i.e.* contextual and typological) results with the chemical analysis of the finds include the late Roman and early Byzantine glass from Dichin, northern Bulgaria (Rehren and Cholakova) and the typological and chronological development of glass supply in the monastic site on Jabal Harun in southern Jordan with the change from Levantine to Egyptian glass between the 5th/6th and the 8th/9th century (Greiff and Keller).

Two of the papers address wider subjects in late Roman and Byzantine glass, one on Byzantine glass mosaics and their Roman predecessors (James) and the other providing a critical overview of the state of research into HIMT glass and the implications of the export of this late Roman and early Byzantine glass from Egypt to the Mediterranean and north-western Europe (Nenna).

Overall, these papers reflect how our understanding of Byzantine, Sasanian and early Islamic glass is built up step by step with each publication of finds from new sites or new datasets of chemical analysis, but the interpretation of the individual pieces of information in their wider historical context still needs more detailed examination. By bringing together the available evidence for glass production and consumption in the eastern Mediterranean a much broader knowledge of the glass trade, supply and use in the later first millennium AD in this part of the ancient world will be achieved.

Late Roman and early medieval glass in Europe

A longer tradition of archaeological research into glass of the second half of the first millennium AD exists in parts of western Europe, particularly in regions rich in burials with glass vessels, as in Anglo-Saxon England (*e.g.* Harden 1956), but until the 1980s the glass found in settlements received little attention. A conference organised by the *Association Française pour l'Archéologie du Verre* in 1993 (*Le verre de l'antiquité tardive et du haut moyen age – typologie – chronologie – diffusion*) resulted in a multi-authored publication of late Roman and early medieval glass finds from many regions of western Europe and beyond (Foy (ed.) 1995). Since then, research into this subject has increased and expanded very greatly. Typology, chronology and patterns of distribution continue to be very important, but the information now available about the range of glass compositions in use at different times and in different regions has introduced more complex discussions of choice, status, trading networks and variation in local patterns of supply and shortages.

The majority of the papers on late Roman and early medieval glass from Europe study aspects of glass production and use after the end of the Roman empire, while three (Walker; Leljak; Jackson and Foster) look at aspects of glass in the 4th century. Walker shows the potential of the Wilshere collection of late Roman gold-glass at the Ashmolean Museum in Oxford to contribute to discussion about the vessels and their iconography, the quality of the glass used to make them and the status of their owners in late Roman society.

In recent years, the glass finds characteristic of a region and their significance for defining regional glass production have been discussed and explored, focussing less on individual sites and local glassworking and more on regional surveys of glass workshops and their products. Studies of this kind are now being undertaken in regions where late Roman glass and glass working has not previously been well known, such as South Pannonia (Leljak). Regional glass production in the late antique and early medieval period is also recognisable through detailed study of the main forms and products within the context of recorded glass workshops, as is shown with the campanulate bowls from *Gallaecia* (da Cruz). Comparison of assemblages from individual sites with a regional glass corpus can also lead to a more nuanced understanding of the consumption of glass within a region, as assemblages from sites with different social or economic status can be recognised. The case study of the Anglo-Saxon glass finds from West Heslerton, North Yorkshire which is compared to the nationwide corpus of Anglo-Saxon glass from England indicates the potential of such studies (Broadley).

A further approach is the collection and discussion of data on glass working sites from a region over a period of time. The development of glass working and the distribution of the glass workshops in a region can thus be set in their historical context, and also be interpreted as evidence for changes in land use in the region through the time under investigation. This is demonstrated with the study of the glass workshops in the Rhineland and northern Gaul from the Roman to Carolingian periods (Grünewald and Hartmann). Changes of the location of the workshops from major civil and military sites to minor and rural settlements and finally to religious and political centres during the first millennium AD provide valuable evidence for the use of local resources in the context of climatic change and changes in the economic systems. This approach emphasises the potential of studies of glass finds and workshops when they are interpreted in a wider context and used with archaeometric analyses and other archaeological, geographical and historical evidence. On a smaller scale, the proto-history of one of the most famous glass production centres in modern times, Venice, is investigated by collecting and interpreting data on Roman and medieval glass working sites in the Veneto and the Venetian lagoon and postulating a tradition of glass working in this region from the Roman period until the emergence of the golden age of Venetian glass in the Renaissance (Whitehouse).

Late Roman and early medieval glass from Britain is presented mainly in the archaeometric papers discussed in the following section. Their topics are the latest glass from the north-western edge of the Roman empire (Jackson and Foster), Anglo-Saxon bichrome and polychrome glass rods from North Yorkshire (Painter, Jennings and Price), and 9th-century opaque yellow glassworking waste from Scotland, and 5th–7th-century opaque yellow glass beads from Suffolk (Peake and Freestone).

Scientific studies of glass

For the past half century, the technology, origins and distribution of glass have also been researched through chemical analysis of glass finds, which is now of fundamental importance to ancient glass studies (*e.g.* Turner 1956a; 1956b; 1956c). A number of themes pertinent to current approaches in glass studies are seen in the science-based papers in this volume, especially those developing out of the recent rapid advancement of analyses in Roman glass.

The first theme links glass compositions to glass types and vessel styles. The development of stylistic and typological analysis of glasses and our understanding of the distribution of these styles temporally and spatially is very well developed. In comparison, twenty years ago it was assumed that all Roman glass was of a standardised composition, but in the past few years a number of different compositional groups have been identified, predominantly for late Roman and early post-Roman glasses. The most securely identified groups for late Roman glasses are those named Levantine I, Egyptian, 'Roman', HIMT and new groups such as HIT (Freestone *et al.* 2000; 2002; 2008; Foy *et al.* 2003; Freestone 2003; 2005; Rehren and Cholakova 2010). Post-Roman compositions include variations of these late Roman types (*e.g.* Levantine II) and also new types such as Islamic, Byzantine and associated variations and sub-groups. The linking of glass forms with compositions to trace different production groups throws light upon trade networks, glass use and status within the Roman world. For instance, recent research has shown that late Roman and early Byzantine vessels produced in HIMT glass, may be used for more utilitarian items, and this composition displays more signs of recycling. Other compositions, such as Levantine I, appears to be used for higher status vessels (Foster and Jackson 2009). Papers by Rehren and Cholakova, and Jackson and Foster, further advance these observations, suggesting certain primary glasses were chosen by glass workers when producing specific vessel forms. As new analyses are published the number of distinctive categories where form can be linked to vessel style increases. Conversely, other forms appear to be produced in a variety of compositions which change over time (cf. Greiff and Keller).

A second theme emerging from the increased analysis of forms and compositions is that vessel styles and compositions can be mapped across geographical space.

Compositional data suggest that primary glasses used for vessel production were supplied unevenly across the landscape; the relative proportion of compositions within contemporary assemblages can be very different, even in neighbouring locations. This suggests that supply is not dependent upon geographical distance, but that other factors affect what glasses are used. This is observed by Grünewald and Hartmann in northern Gaul and the Rhineland and also illustrated in late Roman and early Byzantine glass in Bulgaria (Rehren and Cholakova) where a mix of compositions are observed, including a relatively new composition HIT, presently seen only at some sites in Bulgaria. Similarly at *Heliopolis*/Baalbek, Lebanon the primary composition is Levantine I, yet compositions such as HIMT, which is thought to be manufactured in Egypt, are surprisingly under-represented in the assemblage despite this geographical proximity (Hamel and Greiff).

The third theme emerging from the scientific papers is the issue of recycling. Successive studies have identified different means of recognising recycling and re-use of glass within vessels, from the declining 'quality' of the glasses, observed as darker colours, glass containing more bubbles and streaks, and potentially the less regular and carefully produced shapes which suggest a more rapid and less skilled production with re-melted glass. This coupled with compositional traits such as the inclusion of certain trace metals indicative of recycling (Jackson 1996; Paynter, Jennings and Price) or the mixing of older and newer technologies (Peake and Freestone; Paynter, Jennings and Price) means that recycling or re-use can now be more confidently identified in glasses and identified where it was not suspected previously. The increase in the number of analysed glasses in the last few years means that compositional and hence stylistic groups of glasses can be identified which have been more or less recycled (*e.g.* Foster and Jackson 2009). This is highlighted here in papers by Rehren and Cholakova, Jackson and Foster, Schibille and McKenzie, Paynter, Jennings and Price, and Peake and Freestone with glasses from late Roman Britain, Anglo-Saxon Scotland and northern England, early Byzantine Istanbul and late Roman/early Byzantine Bulgaria. These papers have all identified an increase in recycling practices, especially in later Roman blue-green glasses and HIMT glasses with the proportion of recycling increasing again in later Byzantine and Anglo-Saxon glasses. In addition to recycling, re-use is also suggested for precious highly coloured glasses such as that for mosaics (Schibille and McKenzie; James 2006, 43; Paynter, Jennings and Price). Similarly the re-use of an earlier Roman base glass with the addition of a locally produced pigment to produce opaque yellow is reported in Anglo-Saxon beads from Scotland (Peake and Freestone) and reworking and remelting of glasses for other alternative uses (Paynter, Jennings and Price). Both procedures suggest, rather than a lack of technological expertise, the clever re-use of existing products with new technologies.

Summary

This volume represents a cross-section of the current state of research on glass from the later first millennium AD in Europe and the Middle East, but it is not a comprehensive overview of the topic such as was presented more than 40 years ago by Donald Harden (1971). An extended update of that paper to include the wealth of archaeological and especially archaeometric data published since then would be a Herculean task. However, the papers in this volume provide useful evidence and ideas for further research. Currently, the principal focus of archaeological and archaeometric glass studies of this period is still concentrated on finds from individual sites, although wider studies in regional contexts are evolving in both disciplines. As already mentioned, another important aspect for future research will be interdisciplinary studies, not only combining archaeological and archaeometric data, but also considering the evidence from other archaeological finds and the archaeological contexts as well as incorporating environmental data and interpreting the historical, social and economic context. Studies in glass of the later first millennium AD illustrate the continuation of some earlier traditions in glass working and use on the one hand, and also show some changes in glass technology. Thus they have the potential to contribute to wider surveys of continuity and change during the transition from the Roman to the early medieval world in Europe, from Byzantium to Islam in the eastern Mediterranean and from the Sasanian empire to the Islamic world in the Middle East.

Bibliography

Antonaras, A. C. (2010) Early Christian and Byzantine glass vessels. In F. Daim and J. Drauschke (eds.) *Byzanz – das Römerreich im Mittelalter. Teil 1: Welt der Ideen, Welt der Dinge.* Monographien des Römisch-Germanischen Zentralmuseums 84.1, 383–430. Mainz, Römisch-Germanisches Zentralmuseum.

Foster, H. E. and Jackson, C. M. (2009) The composition of 'naturally coloured' late Roman vessel glass from Britain and the implications for models of glass production and supply. *Journal of Archaeological Science* 36, 189–204.

Foy, D. (ed.) (1995) *Le verre de l'antiquité tardive et du haut moyen âge. Typologie, chronologie, diffusion.* Guiry-en-Vexin, Musée archéologique départemental du Val-d'Oise.

Foy, D. (2000) L'héritage antique et byzantin dans la verrerie islamique: exemples d'Istabl 'Antar-Fostat. *Annales Islamologiques* 34, 151–178.

Foy, D. (2001) Secteur nord de Tebtynis (Fayyoum). Le verre byzantin et islamique. *Annales Islamologiques* 35, 465–489.

Foy, D., Picon, M., Vichy, M. and Thirion-Merle, V. (2003) Caractérisation des verres de la fin de l'antiquité en méditerranée occidentale: l'émergence de nouveaux courants commerciaux. In D. Foy and M.-D. Nenna (eds.), *Échanges et commerce du verre dans le monde antique*. Monographies Instrumentum 24, 41–85. Montagnac, Monique Mergoil.

Freestone, I. C. (2003) Primary Glass Sources in the Mid First Millennium A.D. In *Annales du 15e Congrès de l'Association Internationale pour l'Histoire du Verre*, 111–115. Nottingham, Association Internationale pour l'Histoire du Verre.

Freestone, I. C. (2005) The provenance of ancient glass through compositional analysis. In P. B. Vandiver, J. L. Mass and A. Murray (eds.) *Materials Issues in Art and Archaeology VII*, 195–208. Warrendale, PA, Materials Research Society.

Freestone, I. C., Gorin-Rosen, Y. and Hughes, M. J. (2000) Primary Glass from Israel and the Production of Glass in Late Antiquity and the Early Islamic Period. In M.-D. Nenna (ed.) *La route du verre. Ateliers primaires et secondaires du second millénaire av. J.-C. au Moyen Âge*. Travaux de la Maison de l'Orient Méditerranéen 33, 66–83. Lyon, Maison de l'Orient Méditerranéen.

Freestone, I. C., Greenwood, R. and Gorin-Rosen, Y. (2002) Byzantine and early Islamic glassmaking in the Eastern Mediterranean, production and distribution of primary glass. In G. Kordas (ed.) *First International Conference Hyalos, Vitrum, Glass. History, Technology and Conservation of Glass and Vitreous Materials in the Hellenic World*, 167–174. Athens, Alphanet.

Freestone, I. C., Hughes, M. J. and Stapleton, C. P. (2008) The composition and production of Anglo-Saxon glass. In V. Evison, *Catalogue of Anglo-Saxon Glass in the British Museum*. British Museum Research Publication 167, 29–46. London, British Museum Press.

Gorin-Rosen, Y. and Winter, T. (2010) Selected insights into Byzantine glass in the Holy Land. In J. Drauschke and D. Keller (eds.) *Glass in Byzantium – production, usage, analyses*. RGZM – Tagungen 8, 165–181. Mainz, Römisch-Germanisches Zentralmuseum.

Harden, D. B. (1956) Glass vessels in Britain, AD 400–1000. In D. B. Harden (ed.) *Dark Age Britain. Studies presented to Edward Thurlow Leeds with a bibliography of his works*, 132–167. London, Methuen.

Harden, D. B. (1971) Ancient Glass, III: Post-Roman. *The Archaeological Journal* 128, 78–117.

Jackson, C. M. (1996) From Roman to Early Medieval Glasses: Many Happy Returns or a New Birth. In *Annales du 13e Congrès de l'Association Internationale pour l'Histoire du Verre*, 289–302. Lochem, Association Internationale pour l'Histoire du Verre.

James, E. (2006) Byzantine glass mosaic tesserae: some material considerations. *Byzantine and Modern Greek Studies* 30, 29–47.

Jennings, S. (2006) *Vessel glass from Beirut. Bey 006, 007, and 045*, Berytus 48–49. Beirut, The American University.

Keller, D. (2010) Byzantine glass: past, present and future – a short history of research on Byzantine glass. In J. Drauschke and D. Keller (eds.) *Glass in Byzantium – production, usage, analyses*. RGZM – Tagungen 8, 1–24. Mainz, Römisch-Germanisches Zentralmuseum.

Keller, D. (in press) Glass vessels. In St J. Simpson *et al.*, *Excavations at Kush: A Sasanian and Islamic site in Ras al-Khaimah, United Arab Emirates II. The Small Finds and Glassware: Catalogue, Discussion and Scientific Analyses*. Oxford, Archaeopress.

Keller, D. and Lindblom, J. (2008) Glass Finds from the Church and the Chapel. In Z. T. Fiema and J. Frösén, *Petra – The Mountain of Aaron I. The Church and the Chapel*, 331–375. Helsinki, Societas Scientiarum Fennica.

Keller, D. and Lindblom, J. (in press) Glass vessels from the FJHP site. In Z. T. Fiema and J. Frösén, *Petra – The Mountain of Aaron II. The Nabataean Sanctuary and the Byzantine Monastery*. Helsinki, Societas Scientiarum Fennica.

Meyer, C. (1996) Sasanian and Islamic glass from Nippur, Iraq. In *Annales du 13e Congrès de l'Association Internationale pour l'Histoire du Verre*, 247–255. Lochem, Association Internationale pour l'Histoire du Verre.

Negro Ponzi, M. M. (1987) Late Sasanian Glassware from Tell Baruda. *Mesopotamia* 22, 265–275.

Price, J. (2010) Concluding remarks. In J. Drauschke and D. Keller (eds.) *Glass in Byzantium – production, usage, analyses*. RGZM – Tagungen 8, 257–260. Mainz, Römisch-Germanisches Zentralmuseum.

Rehren, Th. and Cholakova, A. (2010) The Early Byzantine HIMT glass from Dichin, Northern Bulgaria. *Interdisciplinary Studies* 22–23, 81–96.

Stern, E. M. (2010) Medieval glass from the Athenian Agora (9th–14th c.) and some thoughts on glass usage and glass production in the Byzantine empire. In J. Drauschke and D. Keller (eds.) *Glass in Byzantium – production, usage, analyses*. RGZM – Tagungen 8, 107–120. Mainz, Römisch-Germanisches Zentralmuseum.

Turner, W. E. S. (1956a) Studies in ancient glasses and glassmaking processes, part III; the chronology of the glassmaking constituents. *Journal of the Society of Glass Technology* 40, 39–52.

Turner, W. E. S. (1956b) Studies in ancient glasses and glassmaking processes, part IV; the chemical composition of ancient glasses. *Journal of the Society of Glass Technology* 40, 162–186.

Turner, W. E. S. (1956c) Studies in ancient glasses and glassmaking processes, part V; raw materials and melting processes. *Journal of the Society of Glass Technology* 40, 277–300.

Weinberg, G. D. and Stern, E. M. (2009) *Vessel Glass*. The Athenian Agora 34. Princeton, NJ, American School of Classical Studies at Athens.

Winter, T. (2011) The Glass Finds. In R. Bar-Nathan and W. Atrash, *Bet She'an archaeological project 1986–2002. Bet She'an II: Baysan, The Pottery Workshop*. Israel Antiquities Authority Reports 48, 345–362. Jerusalem, Israel Antiquities Authority.

2

The last Roman glass in Britain: recycling at the periphery of the empire

Caroline Jackson and Harriet Foster

The last glasses found in Roman Britain

The late 3rd to 5th centuries in Britain is very much at a transitional point in time, a point that straddles what is Romano-British and what becomes early Saxon, and this is reflected in the material culture stylistically and compositionally. This transition is very well illustrated by the glass found in the archaeological record. 4th-century glass tends to be dissimilar to that of previous periods in a number of ways. The colour of the glass is dominated by shades of yellow-green and the most common earlier colours such as blue-green and colourless glass are found in much lower quantities in assemblages throughout the British province, and indeed across the north-western Roman empire. The quality of the glass, in terms of its transparency and homogeneity, and the design and skill of execution in forming and decorating tends to be less adept; many more common forms and utilitarian glasses contain seed and are less uniform in shape.

Just as significant as the change in the nature of the glass is the reduction in the range of vessel designs; whereas closed forms such as bottles and flasks often dominated earlier assemblages, there is a move in the 4th century towards more open forms such as dining wares and drinking vessels in the form of cups and beakers. Many of the vessel styles found in Britain are also distributed across the north-west provinces; these include conical beakers and convex cups which are found fairly ubiquitously, also shallow convex bowls, and some of the remaining closed forms, dolphin handled bottles and Frontinus (barrel-shaped) bottles. Other forms appear to have had a more restricted geography, which may possibly be accounted for by a more specific location of manufacture. Two such vessel forms, both globular bodied jugs, one small with one handle and the other with two handles (Price and Cottam 1998, 165–168) are largely unknown outside Britain and so may have been produced within the province.

These production and consumption patterns suggest there were changes occurring within the glass industry itself on at least two levels: the manufacture of glass at the primary production locations and the production of the vessels at secondary workshops throughout the empire, and potentially in Britain. The nature of and the (potential) reasons for these changes, whether they relate to economic, political or social factors, will be explored in this paper using both stylistic and compositional analysis.

Late Roman glass database

The database, discussed very briefly below, forms the basis for the patterns identified in late Romano-British glasses. The data is that published in two papers by Foster and Jackson (2009; 2010) and so is not reproduced or discussed in any detail except where the data is used for illustrative purposes. The glasses selected for analysis, dated to the late 3rd to 5th century, were from 19 sites of varying functions and status throughout Roman Britain and the vessels were of identified forms. Sampling was undertaken to obtain a representative sample of the range of forms in Britain during this late Roman period, in proportion to that found at each site, and to characterise glass which was either naturally coloured (green or blue) or colourless, as these two colour groups represent the majority of glasses found during this period. These two groups also comprise glasses which best illustrate the primary raw materials used in glass production, without considering significant additives. Furthermore, given that these different colours can also broadly reflect differing levels of sophistication in the glass working process (colourless vessels for example being used more commonly for finer wares), sampling of both colour groups also allowed for a full cross-section of glass types from potentially different status groups in late Roman society. Full details of the samples, the methods used to determine compositional data, and their individual compositions can be found in Foster and Jackson (2009; 2010).

Compositionally the glasses studied fall into the two colour groups as may be expected; naturally coloured and colourless. Within these two broad groups the material could be placed into broad compositional groups which are well studied as follows.

- Naturally coloured glass: HIMT, Levantine I and Blue-green material (Freestone 2003; Freestone *et al.* 2005; Foy *et al.* 2003; Jackson *et al.* 1991).
- Colourless glasses: containing either antimony or manganese or a combination of both (Baxter *et al.* 1995; 2005; Jackson *et al.* 2003; Paynter 2006; Silvestri *et al.* 2008).

Many of these compositions have been identified by others, but the glasses analysed from Britain showed distinct variations on these compositions which are discussed in detail below and which highlight many aspects of the island as a discrete consumer of late Roman glasses, a market which was notable for being on the very northern fringes of the Roman empire.

Naturally coloured glass compositions

All the groups identified within this paper are defined through a comparison with earlier glass compositions, a typical example of which is published by Nenna *et al.* (1997, 83, table 2). These compositional groups are described in detail in Foster and Jackson (2009), and all compositions are found in the full range of vessel forms: cups, beakers, bowls, jugs, bottles and flasks.

1. The largest compositional group identified was that classified as HIMT glass – "high iron, high manganese, high titanium" (Mirti *et al.* 1993; Freestone 1994; Foy *et al.* 2003), which represented over 90% of all the naturally coloured vessels sampled (344 of 376 samples). In addition to the compositional characteristics described by the acronym, these glasses are higher in soda and magnesium but lower in lime than naturally coloured glasses from earlier Roman periods. Two related groups were found: HIMT 1 display these characteristics more strongly than HIMT 2 group. This glass is thought to have been manufactured in the eastern Mediterranean, probably Egypt or North Sinai (Freestone *et al.* 2005, 155–156; Leslie *et al.* 2006, 261).
2. Levantine I – These glasses contain higher lime and alumina but lower soda, magnesia and iron than the 'typical' Roman glass composition, and represent around 6% of the naturally coloured glasses sampled. Again the provenance of this glass is thought to be Near Eastern, as with the HIMT glasses, although from a different region (Foy *et al.* 2003). A subgroup within the Levantine I was found in the British material which contained manganese at levels suggestive of its use being for decolourising purposes. Interestingly, several of the Levantine I samples were from vessels with finer decoration, such as wheel or figured cutting.
3. The third major group, represented by around 1% of the naturally coloured glasses analysed, is very similar to earlier Roman compositions, displaying moderate iron, lime, soda, higher potash and alumina, and like the earlier material is termed 'blue-green'. Within this small compositional group, closed forms were the most common form featured.

The different groups all form a continuum of increasing proportions of iron and manganese which can be attributed to the use of different sands (Fig. 2.1) and different manufacturing provenances, amongst other factors, relating to glass trade and consumption which are expanded upon below.

Dating the naturally coloured glasses in Britain

These compositional groups can be dated very broadly based upon the types of vessels sampled and their known periods of circulation. Some samples can also be dated by the chronology of their finds context. Whilst these dates may change as more sites are investigated, they provide a broad chronology at this point in time.

The following list indicates a general timeline for each of these groups.

- The blue-green glasses are an older tradition, certainly in wide circulation by the 2nd century, but in decline by the 4th century.
- Levantine I compositions in the British samples are found amongst glasses which broadly date to the second and third quarters of the 4th century.
- The HIMT material is more complicated – stronger HIMT 1 material appears to be more predominant amongst later, post AD 350 material. If we examine the dates for these samples (Table 2.1), then just over 45% of HIMT 1 material comprises types dating to the mid 4th century to 5th century, compared to just over 9% in the HIMT 2 glass. This observation is supported by the glass from Caister-on-Sea (Foster 2004, 238) a site which was abandoned around AD 350. At this site only a very small proportion of the 77 glass samples analysed was HIMT 1 (5%), strengthening the argument for a progression through HIMT 2 to HIMT 1. Furthermore, no glass specifically dated before AD 350 is found in HIMT 1 glass, compared with a half a dozen examples for the

Table 2.1: Proportions of HIMT 1 and HIMT 2 glasses by broad chronological group.

	HIMT 1		HIMT 2	
	n=	%	n=	%
Early–mid 4th century	0	0.0%	6	2.7%
4th century	67	54.5%	195	88.2%
Mid–late 4th century/early 5th century	55	44.7%	17	7.7%
5th century	1	0.8%	3	1.4%
TOTAL	123		221	

HIMT 2 material, including two shallow convex bowls, featuring figure cut decoration and four beaker fragments from different vessels but found at the same site. The two bowls of the 'Wint Hill' type (Samples COS 48 and BEA 50 from Caister-on-Sea and Beadlam Villa (Foster 2004)) were originally dated quite specifically to AD 320–330 by Harden (1960), yet more recent research based on iconographic evidence suggests they have a production span in the 4th century, but one that did not extend much beyond the second half of the 4th century (Chew 2003, 92; Grünewald 2011, 60–61). The four beaker samples (Samples LUL 369, 370, 371 and 372 from Lullingstone Villa (Foster 2004)), although when published had been separated from their context information, are thought to be those referred to in an earlier report as having come from a pit dated to AD 330–350 (Cool and Price 1987, 118).

The range of HIMT

HIMT glass is not specific to British contexts. It has been found from sites across the Roman empire, both in the east and west, for example by Freestone (1994) from Carthage, Freestone *et al.* (2000) in the eastern Mediterranean and Foy *et al.* from Gaul, the eastern Mediterranean and North Africa (Foy *et al.* 2000; 2003; Freestone *et al.* 2005).

Indeed, the largest study of HIMT glasses published is that by Foy and co-workers (2003), who divided their HIMT glasses into two groups in a similar manner to the Romano-British material discussed here. However, although the groups found by these two studies overlap, they do not completely concur. The HIMT glasses in Foy *et al.* (2003) overlay the range seen in Roman Britain, but many have much higher concentrations of iron, manganese and titanium than the British glasses. None have the HIMT concentrations which are very low in this suite of elements; in essence their 'weaker HIMT' corresponds with our 'stronger HIMT' which therefore represents a middle group in a broad continuum of the composition. The reasons for these differences, and for the groupings amongst HIMT glasses, are many, but the key to this is glass circulation and more importantly recycling which is the theme of this paper.

Colourless glass

Colourless glass has been studied very intensively in recent years (*e.g.* Baxter *et al.* 1995; 2005; Jackson *et al.* 2003; Paynter 2006; Silvestri *et al.* 2008). This is because, as already noted, it tends to be used for finer, higher status vessels; *i.e.* those displaying more decoration, which probably required greater skill and time to produce. They are also less likely to show evidence for recycling of indiscriminate glass of different colours, as the aim was to produce a glass which was 'water-clear' and allowed light to pass through with the least resistance, to allow the contents of the vessel to be studied and to refract light to allow a sparkle in vessels which had undergone cutting or engraving. These vessels are usually pieces associated with dining.

Colourless glasses were found at most of the sites studied, but usually formed a relatively small proportion, less than 10%, of the assemblage, as might be expected of a more valuable high status commodity. Exceptions to this are at Portchester, York Fortress and Caister-on-Sea where they constitute approximately 1/3 of the assemblage, Canterbury and Dorchester where 50% of the assemblage is colourless glass and site A on Shakenoak Farm where they dominate the assemblage at over 50%. This high concentration of colourless glass in these assemblages may reflect the status or function of the site, or may reflect the influx of glass supplied to these sites during key occupation periods.

All colourless groups contained lower concentrations of iron than the naturally coloured glasses indicating specific selection of pure raw materials. Other key distinguishing features of each group include lower alumina, barium and titanium, indicative of a pure, high silica sand.

Colourless glasses also contain a decolouriser which oxidises any iron in the glass to remove the blue or green tinge that is naturally present and produce a colourless matrix. The use of decolourisers provides a basis for forming compositional groups in these glasses, which also link in with the concentrations of alumina, iron and titanium in the base glass; the link between decolourisers and purity of the raw materials used to make the base glass composition also has a chronological pattern which is explored below. Three main colourless compositions could be identified (Foster and Jackson 2010).

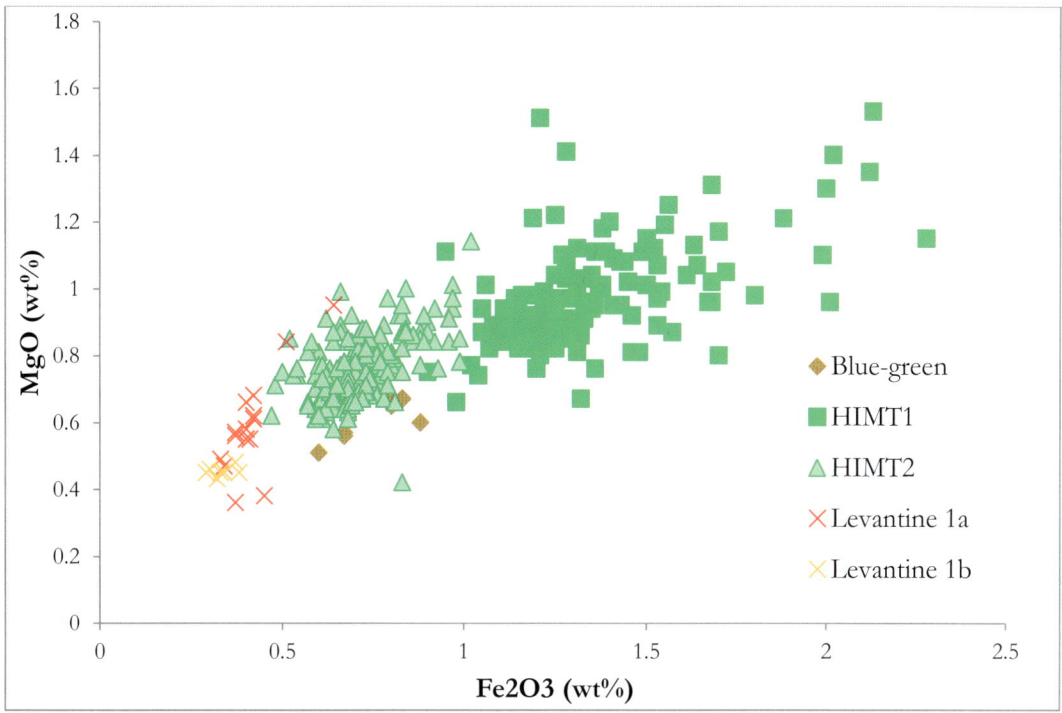

Fig. 2.1: Naturally coloured glasses from sites in Britain.

Colourless 1 was decolourised using antimony, and had very low concentrations of alumina, iron and titanium. These glasses made up around 36% of all the colourless glasses sampled.

Colourless 2 used manganese as a decolouriser, but generally had higher concentrations of iron and associated elements than group 1. Only around 10% of all the colourless glasses sampled were in this group. Two further subdivisions within this group could be made on the basis of alumina, magnesia, lime, potash; one of these groups was found at only one site – Barnsley Park.

Colourless 3 had a mixture of decolourisers in the form of antimony and manganese, the base glass composition is very similar to that seen for Colourless 2, although this was by far the largest colourless group sampled, comprising nearly 54% of the assemblage.

Using the same dating techniques as for the naturally coloured glasses, Colourless 1 appears to have been an older material, more typical of the 3rd century and earlier, although it was still in circulation in the early 4th century. Colourless 2 glasses are characteristic of the 4th century only (in particular the second and third quarters). Colourless 3 glasses date to both the 3rd and 4th centuries.

The range of colourless glasses

These different groups are not unique to British material. What is clear when looking at related material published from various sites around the Mediterranean and Britain is that many of the groups seen in the British material overlap with others seen elsewhere, indicating direct parallels. However, there are also many more compositional groups of colourless glass, dating from much earlier periods too, than is seen in this relatively narrow chronological range of the British material studied here (*e.g.* Baxter *et al.* 2005; Huisman *et al.* 2009; Jackson 2005; Silvestri *et al.* 2008; Velde and Hochuli-Gysel 1996).

Glass recycling: the key to compositional patterning

The key to many of the compositions in this assemblage comes from the recycling of glass. We know the Romans recycled their broken glass as cullet as references in Statius and Martial testify (mentioned in Price 1978, 70; Price and Cool 1991, 24; Fleming 1999, 27; Price 2005, 169). Both authors suggest broken glass was traded, brought together through collection and through exchange, so this information is not new. Archaeologically, this is visible too; the late 2nd–3rd century shipwreck, the Iulia Felix, found off the Adriatic coast was carrying amongst its cargo a barrel of broken glass fragments including colourless cullet (Silvestri *et al.* 2008). Large cullet 'dumps' have also been recovered, for example most recently in Britain at Guildhall Yard and at Basinghall in London (Shepherd and Wardle 2009, 35).

However, identifying recycling in glass is difficult and can only be done chemically by identifying trace elements which would not normally be present as contaminants of the batch raw materials or as additions to the glass batch used for visual effect, such as colourants. These are usually those elements which would act as components of colourants or decolourants in sufficient quantity but are not present as naturally occurring impurities in the glass batch. In recycled glasses one or more of these impurities may be found, but in such small quantities that they would not have been intentionally added, but have derived from the inclusion into the melt of a piece or pieces of decorated or highly coloured/colourless glass entering an otherwise naturally coloured or colourless batch. In strongly coloured glasses these are more difficult to identify as many minerals added to provide strong colours to glass, such as cobalt or copper minerals, contain impurities themselves which therefore can mask 'markers' of recycling, but in naturally coloured and colourless glasses their inclusion can only be accidental through recycling. Foy *et al.* (2003, 49, 56, 83–84, tables 2, 7, appendices 1–2) have provided the chemical composition of naturally coloured 'chunk' or 'raw' glasses, products of primary glass production and therefore glass which has not been recycled. From this material, it is possible to see at what levels any potential recycling 'markers' would be present as natural impurities (*e.g.* Cu ≤ 89ppm, Pb ≤ 0.02% and Sb ≤ 0.01%); in other vessel and cullet glass which belong to the same broad naturally coloured groups, the presence of such markers above these levels, but not in sufficient amounts to indicate intentional addition, then can be suggestive of recycling.

As suggested above, the elements which have been identified most easily as those which indicate recycling when present in small or trace quantities are antimony (not in colourless glass), lead, and copper, as well as tin and cobalt (Jackson 1996; Henderson 1995). It is these elements which give an indication of the recycled nature of many of the glasses studied in this assemblage from Roman Britain.

In the naturally coloured glasses such impurity patterns have been readily identified. The very small group of blue-green glasses do show some evidence of recycling, with higher concentrations of antimony (average around 0.2%) than would be expected in a group which is coloured. However, the glass in this group represents such a small proportion of the total assemblage and is a glass about which no firm conclusions can be made.

The Levantine I glasses do not show any chemical evidence for recycling, suggesting these glasses represent newly manufactured glass which has yet to undergo extensive recycling. These appear to be contemporary in date with the HIMT glasses and have their provenance in a nearby region.

In contrast, the HIMT glasses show extensive recycling with elevated concentrations of copper, lead and antimony compared with those in the newly manufactured glass analysed by Foy *et al.* (2003). Concentrations above those identified by Foy *et al.* (2003) for newly manufactured glass (given above), to cover the *highest* concentrations found in the raw glasses, are used here to give a more *secure* identification of recycling (Cu ≥ 100ppm, Pb ≥ 0.1%, Sb ≥ 0.1%) (Foster and Jackson 2009, 196). Both HIMT 1 and HIMT 2 have concentrations of these elements above this benchmark and show recycling to some extent. Looking at two or more of these elements in combination, HIMT 1 contain around 20% recycled glasses, whilst HIMT 2 is much higher at nearly 40%, although this latter figure is conservative, for example the proportion of HIMT 2 glasses with any one of these elements at the 'recycling marker' levels given above may be as high as 60%. This is surprising as it suggests glasses which occur earlier in the archaeological record in general, *i.e.* HIMT 2, are recycled to a greater extent. Foster and Jackson (2009) suggest this is not because recycling diminished through this time period, but that it is more difficult to distinguish recycled glass when HIMT started to dominate the market. Initially the composition was 'watered down' through recycling with non-HIMT compositions as there were more glass compositions in circulation and HIMT was not so widespread. This produced a composition which showed heavy recycling, but which was a 'weaker HIMT' composition; this is HIMT 2. Subsequently, as more of the glass collected for recycling was of the HIMT composition then the addition of this to HIMT glass would weaken the elemental patterns which are indicative of recycling; this is HIMT 1. In this scenario it may be possible that recycling increased through the period rather than decreased, but it is not possible to detect chemically. By the later 4th century almost all vessels appear to have been manufactured using HIMT glass.

As colourless glasses are generally thought to represent better quality, more high status vessels their recycling would seem to be less likely (Jackson 2005). However, whilst Colourless groups 1 and 2 do not display markers for recycling (with the exception of two samples in the Colourless 1 group), Colourless 3 does. The first indication is the presence of the two decolourisers, one of which, manganese, is often present in such low quantities that it may not be contributing greatly to decolourising the glass, whilst the other, antimony, is. Certainly, the presence of both in the glass is unnecessary. Foster and Jackson (2010), suggest the presence of both decolourisers in this group of glasses may be due to mixing of different groups of colourless glasses or may in fact be the introduction of some HIMT glass to the melt which elevates the concentration of manganese (and iron which is also of a higher concentration in this colourless group). The second indication of recycling in Colourless 3 glass is the presence of copper above 100 ppm in almost 50% of the glasses, and some lead, which itself indicates less careful recycling.

So taking the naturally coloured and colourless glasses into consideration, we have evidence that many of these glasses, indeed for both groups together nearly one third (30%) of samples show evidence of recycling, although this figure may be as high as 46% if indeed we accept that the whole of the Colourless 3 group represents recycled material and the more 'generous' estimate for recycling amongst HIMT 2 material, as given above, is used. However, this clearly varies by compositional type; most of the recycling is seen in the HIMT and the Colourless 3 glasses, although these groups make up the bulk of the total assemblage.

Of the other large groups of glasses the most comparable to these are those by Foy et al. (2003) which are late and post Roman glasses from Gaul and North Africa. Foy et al.'s (2003) most closely related group in terms of date is a HIMT group of glass, mainly dating to the 5th century, which is comparable to the HIMT 1 observed here. Evidence for recycling in this group is less than 15% which is lower than that seen in Britain. This might suggest that in Gaul and northern Africa, where these glasses were found, there were more supplies of fresh glass readily available whereas in Britain there was greater reliance on the use of cullet. Further data to explore this is provided below by a case study from one of the northern-most parts of the empire.

Case study – South Shields (Roman *Arbeia*) – The Commanding Officer's House

The glass from the Commanding Officer's House at South Shields, one of the northern-most forts of the Roman empire up to the late 4th century, is discussed in detail in Jackson and Price (2012). This material represents very late Romano-British glass at an isolated outpost. Most of the vessel glass recovered from the site spanned the early 4th century to the early 5th century and was either colourless or various shades of green, typical of late period Roman glass, and of typical forms seen elsewhere although some forms seem to have a very late circulation compared to the rest of Britain.

What is noticeable from this assemblage is that most glass recovered from the earlier contexts (before AD 350/380) is colourless, whilst the later contexts show glass which is pale or lightly tinted (almost colourless but with a slight green tinge) or green in colour in the vessel wall section. This is not due to vessel wall thickness as glasses of comparable dimensions were sampled.

The colourless glass fits within the groups outlined above, all falling into Foster and Jackson's Group 1. All the 'water clear' colourless glass, which are from earlier contexts, are Group 1, the antimony decolourised group, made with relatively pure sands. This well known group, used for high quality colourless vessels and other colourless vessels, is common from the 1st to the 3rd centuries (Foster and Jackson 2010).

The second 'lightly tinted' colourless group fits within the Group 3 colourless glasses, which have mixed decolourisers (antimony and manganese) and are higher in iron. Group 3 glasses consist of the largest group within the 'colourless' glasses in the late Roman period in Britain (Foster and Jackson 2010). These glasses are all from the later contexts at South Shields. They contain relatively high concentrations of manganese, like the Group 3 glasses, and higher iron. However, although all contain traces of antimony (average 0.05 wt%) only one sample has significant concentrations (0.3 wt%). This indicates they may be a 'hybrid' of the green and colourless glasses. The presence of lead, copper and antimony at higher concentrations in most of these glasses than the 'water clear' colourless glasses suggests recycling.

All the other glasses from the later post AD 350 contexts at the site, are light green or yellow green of varying shades. All are HIMT glasses and fall within the two HIMT groups (HIMT 1 and HIMT 2) described above and discussed by Foster and Jackson (2009). There are no examples of Levantine glasses in the samples analysed. HIMT 2 are lighter in colour and like those seen in other parts of the United Kingdom appear to be the most heavily recycled group. All but one sample in this group has elevated concentrations of copper, antimony and lead. In HIMT 1 approximately 20–30% show evidence of recycling, although the small group size must be accounted for (approx. 10 samples)

Are these groups real?

If the distribution of decolourisers present in all the glasses analysed from South Shields is considered, it can be seen that there is a gradation in the concentrations of antimony and manganese, both elements which were added either intentionally or are present as contaminants of recycling. The earlier water clear colourless glasses are high in antimony which was presumably added intentionally (Jackson 2005). The yellow green HIMT glasses are high in manganese which is a feature of these naturally coloured glasses (Foster and Jackson 2009) and the pale green and yellow green 'lightly tinted' glasses fall somewhere between the two, with the presence of both elements suggesting mixing, probably from recycling. The colourless group 1 is chronologically earliest in this sequence at this site, the lightly tinted glasses and HIMT are all later. These patterns further reinforce those discussed above, although at this site the evidence for recycling of material in later periods is even more evident; the proportion of recycled glass in the lightly tinted and the HIMT 2 groups at South Shields is higher than that seen for Britain as a whole. Of course the HIMT 1 group, which by this time dominated British assemblages, does not demonstrate recycling through elemental composition so clearly, as it would form the bulk of glass for the recycling pool. This suggests these two groups (HIMT 1 and HIMT 2) may not be discrete groups in the archaeological record, but a type which illustrates a continuum of compositions as the pool of raw glass and that of cullet changes through time.

Taking this one step further, the lightly tinted glasses have similar concentrations of iron and manganese as are seen in the HIMT 2 glasses. Therefore is this glass intentionally decolourised using manganese, or is this just another variation of recycled glass, and only 'colourless' because it is a mixture of HIMT glasses and colourless glasses?

This suggests that at this northern frontier site there is a distinct time line which can be drawn between the pre AD 350 glasses and those present in the last phase of occupation. The late 3rd century to mid 4th century is dominated by good quality, antimony glass which shows no evidence for recycling. Clearly glass supply was adequate and high quality glass was in relatively good supply. By the late 4th century two broad groups suggest the assemblage is dominated by HIMT; yellow-green glasses manufactured using raw glass or cullet which was predominantly HIMT 1 glass. The second group, which cannot be differentiated in terms of date at this site, is glass which clearly shows compositional evidence of recycling and consists of HIMT 2 and lightly tinted glasses. By this time there appears to be a greater reliance upon cullet for vessel manufacture. This mimics the patterns seen in glasses elsewhere in Britain suggesting a movement away from the supply of raw glass sources that meant vessel production was more heavily reliant upon recycled material.

Discussion and comments

There are some groups of glasses found within British assemblages which do not exhibit any chemically detectable evidence of recycling. These are the earlier and long lived antimony decolourised colourless glasses and the later Levantine glasses. These two groups co-exist with other groups such as HIMT and lightly tinted colourless glasses which do show recycling to varying extents. Why do some glasses show evidence of recycling and not others? The answer is not entirely clear, but there may be many reasons for these patterns.

Antimony decolourised glasses, those which are water clear, are often represented by highly worked, sophisticated forms and high status glasses. Obtaining a truly colourless glass would require an intimate knowledge of the raw materials and a careful selection of these and associated cullet to maintain the colourless nature of the glass, which would enable high refraction and transparency. It may be that to obtain such a glass, raw glass was preferred as this would be a predictable and highly controlled material in terms of composition. If recycling did take place in glass melting and vessel production, it may be that this is not detectable as colourless glasses would only be recycled with other colourless cullet.

The Levantine composition was also used to produce high quality glassware, and it appears to have been more of a niche product as it is not found in large quantities in Britain when compared with other regions closer to its putative location of manufacture (*e.g.* Foy *et al.* 2003, 85). For these same reasons the glass supply may have been controlled and its use monitored. This may account for the smaller proportion of vessels made in this composition in the late Roman period than HIMT glasses. It may also have been a 'fresher' supply of raw glass to Britain than the HIMT compositions, *i.e.* it was a less recycled material by the time it reached the vessel consumer market in Britain and came by different supply routes. Conversely, HIMT glass may have travelled a preferred route between Egypt, southern Gaul, eastern/northern Gaul and Britain as hinted at by 800 pottery fragments provenanced to these locations which were found on a Gallo-Roman trading vessel found shipwrecked off the coast of Guernsey and dating to the late 3rd/early 4th century (Rule and Monaghan 1993).

Alternatively, an explanation which is not only plausible but may account for the lack of detectable recycling in these two high quality glass groups, is that these vessels were imported from manufacturing centres elsewhere in the empire, rather than being manufactured in Britain from glass cullet or imported raw glass. This is observed by the presence of high status vessels located particularly at sites which were well connected in terms of trade (see Foster and Jackson forthcoming). It has tentatively been suggested that there appears to be less recycled material in assemblages around the Mediterranean (Foy *et al.* 2003) which would support this, although this assumption needs to be tested with more data.

HIMT and Colourless 3 glasses (which it could be argued is a variation on HIMT glass), relied on recycled glass extensively. These compositions were used for more utilitarian, lower status glasses. And these groups of glasses are the most common compositions found from the late 3rd century onwards in Britain. So why is there so much recycled material in British assemblages?

There are probably many answers to this question. The first relates to manufacture. Recycling with HIMT glass was probably easier than with other glasses as it is postulated that it had a lower melting temperature so perhaps lent itself more readily to re-melting/reworking. Its use in more domestic vessels where colour or finesse was not particularly important may have made this easy melting and forming composition convenient, quick and simple to manufacture.

It is also important to bear in mind that stylistically Britain and the north-west become more independent in the 4th century in terms of their glass vessel repertoire. It is possible that by this time 'British' glassworkers had the skills and expertise locally to cater to the market and it was easier to reuse what was readily available in cullet form, rather than import fresh supplies of glass. In this way, in terms of style and production, they became more self-sufficient.

The Roman empire was not a single entity (despite the idea of '*romanitas*') and it is important to recognise that there were regional differences, and identities within these regions, which were organic to some degree and changed over time. For instance, in the 4th century the migration of many Germanic people from beyond the '*limes*' would have affected the 'identity' of societies in the north-west provinces; with the absorption of new cultures comes new ideas. For example, the increased emphasis on drinking vessels in the 4th-century glass vessel repertoire may be accounted for by the influence of more Germanic tastes, and perhaps this served to further accentuate regional differences that were already present and a desire by people to be different, to be independent of Rome. This is mirrored in the pottery industry with the establishment of more local production centres and fewer imports from the continent (Fulford 1989, 196).

However, this supposed 'independence' may not have been something Roman Britons chose; there may have been disruptions to trade, industry and governance caused by social and political changes which did not make it an option but more of a necessity (Faulkner 2004, 221–248). These social and political changes could have influenced trade routes for specific glass compositions and for particular vessel forms from elsewhere in the empire. Glass workers, like others using traded material, would have been directly affected by these disruptions and may have avoided them by changing their patterns of work more regularly and choosing their locations of production more strategically than previously (Fleming 1999, 117–120). These changes cannot be quantified at this time as the exact location of production and the trade routes and consumption/reuse patterns of glass cannot be established. However, we would suggest that the picture relating to vessel production using raw and cullet glass is very complex and encompasses a myriad of these factors, some of which we have presented here. That Britain was at the edges of a rapidly changing empire at this time further accentuates any patterns seen elsewhere in the empire and may suggest that its occupants were making and consuming glass vessels in a very different manner to other surrounding regions.

Acknowledgements

The authors would like to thank the Natural Environment Research Council (NER/S/A/2000/03607) and the staff of the NERC ICP-AES facility at Egham, particularly Jacqui Duffet, Sarah James and Nick Walsh. Thanks are due to the following curators and museums for allowing access to and sampling of late Roman vessel glass: Lauren Gilmour (Oxfordshire Museums Store, Standlake, Oxfordshire), Andrew Morrison (English Heritage, York), Paula Gentil (Corinium Museum, Cirencester), Martin Crowther (City Museums Office, Canterbury), Alan Davies (Norfolk Museums Service, Norwich), Peter Woodward (Dorset County Museum, Dorchester), Bryan Sitch (Leeds Museum Resources Centre, Leeds), Arthur MacGregor (Ashmolean Museum, Oxford), Susan Byrne (Gloucester City Museum and Art Gallery, Gloucester), John Shepherd (Museum of London, London), Jan Summerfield and Maggie Taylor (English Heritage, Dover Castle, Kent), Susan Fox (Roman Baths Museum, Bath), Robert Moore and Paul Robinson (Northampton Museum Store, Northampton), Christine McDonnell and Annie Jowett (York Archaeological Trust, York), Lizzie Pridmore, Louise Hampson and Peter Young (York Minster Library, York). We would also like to thank the Römisch-Germanisches Museum in Cologne, especially Friederike Naumann-Steckner and Christoph Olesch, for allowing us access to the museum library and the Study Collection of Roman glass. Appreciation is due to Hilary Cool and Jennifer Price for assisting with unpublished material from Wellington Row and Coppergate (York) and London.

Bibliography

Baxter, M. J., Cool, H. E. M., Heyworth, M. P. and Jackson, C. (1995) Compositional variability in colourless Roman vessel glass. *Archaeometry* 37, 129–141.

Baxter, M. J., Cool, H. E. M. and Jackson, C. M. (2005) Further studies in the compositional variability of colourless Romano-British vessel glass. *Archaeometry* 47, 47–68.

Chew, H. (2003) La coupe au sacrifice d'Abraham de Boulogne-sur-Mer, Pas de Calais (France). *Journal of Glass Studies* 45, 91–104.

Cool, H. E. M. and Price, J. (1987) The Glass. In G. W. Meates (ed.) *The Roman Villa at Lullingstone, Kent II. The Wall Paintings and Finds*. Kent Archaeological Society Monograph 3, 110–142. Maidstone, Kent Archaeological Society.

Faulkner, N. (2004) *The decline and Fall of Roman Britain*. Stroud, Tempus.

Fleming, S. J. (1999) *Roman Glass. Reflections on Cultural change*. Philadelphia, PA, The University of Pennsylvania Museum of Archaeology and Anthropology.

Foster, H. E. (2004) *Late Romano-British Vessel Glass: Investigating Compositional and Typological Changes to the Assemblage in the Historical Context*. Unpublished Ph.D thesis, University of Sheffield.

Foster, H. E. and Jackson, C. M. (2009) The composition of 'naturally coloured' late Roman vessel glass from Britain and the implications for models of glass production and supply. *Journal of Archaeological Science* 36, 189–204.

Foster, H. E. and Jackson, C. M. (2010) The composition of late Romano-British colourless vessel glass: glass production and consumption. *Journal of Archaeological Science* 37, 3068–3080.

Foster, H. E. and Jackson, C. M. (forthcoming) *A model for glass consumption in late Roman Britain*.

Foy, D., Vichy, M. and Picon, M. (2000) Lingots de verre en Méditerranée occidentale (IIIe siècle av. J.-C. – VIIe siècle ap. J.-C.). In *Annales du 14e Congrès de l'Association Internationale pour l'Histoire du Verre*, 51–57. Lochem, Association Internationale pour l'Histoire du Verre.

Foy, D., Picon, M., Vichy, M. and Thirion-Merle, V. (2003) Caractérisation des verres de la fin de l'Antiquité en Méditerranée occidentale: l'émergence de nouveaux courants commerciaux. In D. Foy and M.-D. Nenna (eds.), *Échanges et commerce du verre dans le monde antique*. Monographies Instrumentum 24, 41–85. Montagnac, Monique Mergoil.

Freestone, I. C. (1994) Appendix: Chemical Analysis of 'Raw' Glass Fragments. In H. R. Hurst (ed.), *Excavations at Carthage II, 1. The Circular Harbour, North Side. The Site and Finds other than Pottery*. British Academy Monographs in Archaeology 4, 290. Oxford, Oxford University Press.

Freestone, I. C. (2003) Primary Glass Sources in the Mid First Millennium A.D. In *Annales du 15e Congrès de l'Association Internationale pour l'Histoire du Verre*, 111–115. Nottingham, Association Internationale pour l'Histoire du Verre.

Freestone, I. C., Gorin-Rosen, Y. and Hughes, M. J. (2000) Primary Glass from Israel and the Production of Glass in Late Antiquity and the Early Islamic Period. In M.-D. Nenna (ed.) *La route du verre. Ateliers primaires et secondaires du second millénaire av. J.-C. au Moyen Âge*. Travaux de la Maison de l'Orient Méditerranéen 33, 66–83. Lyon, Maison de l'Orient Méditerranéen.

Freestone, I. C., Wolf, S. and Thirlwall, M. (2005) The production of HIMT glass: elemental and isotopic evidence. In *Annales du 16e Congrès de l'Association Internationale pour l'Histoire du Verre*, 153–157. Nottingham, Association Internationale pour l'Histoire du Verre.

Fulford, M. (1989) The Economy of Roman Britain. In M. Todd (ed.) *Research of Roman Britain 1960–89*, 175–201. London, Society for the Promotion of Roman Studies.

Grünewald, M. (2011) *Die römischen Gräberfelder von Mayen*. Monographien des Römisch-Germanischen Zentralmuseums 96, Vulkanpark-Forschungen 10. Mainz, Römisch-Germanisches Zentralmuseum.

Harden, D. B. (1960) The Wint Hill Bowl and Related Glasses. *Journal of Glass Studies* 2, 45–81.

Henderson, J. (1995) Le Verre de Dorestad: continuité technologique ou innovation? In D. Foy (ed.) *Le Verre de l'Antiquite Tardive et du Haut Moyen Age. Typologie-Chronologie-Diffusion*, 51–56. Guiry-en-Vexin, Musée archéologique départemental du Val-d'Oise.

Huisman, D. J., De Groot, T., Pols, S., Van Os, B. J. H. and Degryse, P. (2009) Compositional variation in Roman colourless glass objects from the Bocholtz burial (The Netherlands). *Archaeometry* 51, 413–439.

Jackson, C. M. (1996) From Roman to early medieval glasses. Many happy returns or a new birth? In *Annales du 13e Congrès de l'Association Internationale pour l'Histoire du Verre*, 289–301. Lochem, Association Internationale pour l'Histoire du Verre.

Jackson, C. M. (2005) Making colourless glass in the Roman period. *Archaeometry* 47, 763–780.

Jackson, C. M., Baxter, M. J. and Cool, H. E. M. (2003) Identifying Group and Meaning: An Investigation of Roman Colourless Glass. In D. Foy and M.-D. Nenna (eds.) *Échanges et commerce du verre dans le monde antique*. Monographies Instrumentum 24, 33–39, Montagnac, Monique Mergoil.

Jackson, C. M., Hunter, J. R., Warren, S. E. and Cool, H. E. M. (1991) The Analysis of Blue-Green Glass and Glassy Waste from Two Romano-British Glass Working Sites. In E. Pernicka and G. A. Wagner (eds.) *Archaeometry 90*, 295–304. Basel, Birkhäuser.

Jackson, C. M. and Price, J. (2012) Analyses of late Roman glass from the Commandant's House of the Fort at South Shields, Tyne and Wear, UK. In D. Ignatiadou and A. Antonaras (eds.) *Annales du 18e Congrès de l'Association Internationale pour l'Histoire du Verre*, 175–182. Thessaloniki, Association Internationale pour l'Histoire du Verre.

Leslie, K. A., Freestone, I. C., Lowry, D. and Thirlwall, M. (2006) Isotopes in near eastern glass: oxygen by laser fluorination as a complement to strontium. *Archaeometry* 48, 253–270.

Mirti, P., Casoli, A. and Appolonia, L. (1993) Scientific Analysis of Roman Glass from *Augusta Praetoria*. *Archaeometry* 35, 225–240.

Nenna, M.-D., Vichy, M. and Picon, M. (1997) L'atelier de verrier de Lyon du 1er siècle après J.-C., et l'origine des verres "romains". *Revue d'Archaéométrie* 21, 81–87.

Paynter, S., 2006. Analyses of colourless Roman glass from Binchester, County Durham. *Journal of Archaeological Science* 33, 1037–1057.

Price, J. (1978) Trade in glass. In J. du Plat Taylor and H. Cleere (eds.) *Roman Shipping and Trade*. Council for British Archaeology Research Report 24, 70–78. London, Council for British Archaeology.

Price, J. (2005) Glass-working and glassworkers in towns and cities. In A. Mac Mahon and J. Price (eds.) *Roman working lives and urban living*, 167–190. Oxford, Oxbow Books.

Price, J. and Cool, H. E. M. (1991) The Evidence for the Production of Glass in Roman Britain. In D. Foy and G. Sennequier (eds.) *Ateliers de Verriers de l'Antiquité à la Période Pré-Industrielle*, 23–29. Rouen, Association Française pour l'Archéologie du Verre.

Price, J. and Cottam, S. (1998) *Romano-British Glass Vessels. A Handbook*. Practical Handbook in Archaeology 14. London, Council for British Archaeology.

Rule, M. and Monaghan, J. (eds.) (1993) *A Gallo-Roman trading vessel from Guernsey. The excavation and recovery of a Third century shipwreck*. Guernsey Museum Monograph 5. Candie Gardens, Guernsey Museums and Galleries.

Shepherd, J. and Wardle, A. (2009) *The Glass Workers of Roman London*. London, Museum of London.

Silvestri, A., Molin, G. and Salviulo, G. (2008) The colourless glass of Iulia Felix. *Journal of Archaeological Science* 35, 331–341.

Velde, B. and Hochuli-Gysel, A. (1996) Correlations between Antimony, Manganese and Iron content in Gallo-Roman glass. In *Annales du 13e Congrès Internationale pour l'Histoire de Verre*, 185–192. Lochem, Association Internationale pour l'Histoire du Verre.

3

Opaque yellow glass production in the early medieval period: new evidence

James R. N. Peake and Ian C. Freestone

A small assemblage of 9th-century opaque yellow glassworking waste from Tarbat Ness, Scotland, and several 5th–7th-century Anglo-Saxon opaque yellow glass beads from Eriswell, Suffolk, were analysed in the scanning electron microscope (SEM). Microstructural and compositional features indicate that in both groups of glass a common approach was used involving the production of a lead-tin-silicate precursor pigment; this is similar to material produced elsewhere in Europe at about the same time.

Introduction

Although there was a substantial trade in coloured glass in the early medieval period in the form of beads, the origins of the coloured glass materials used in their production are obscure. There is still much that is unknown about the way in which the glass industry was organised, and the links between those glass workshops and the wider world. An understanding of the production technology of various glass colours, and how it varied with space and time, is a first step in distinguishing individual production centres. This paper presents analytical evidence from two British assemblages, which provide some insight into opaque yellow glass production during the period. Opaque yellow is likely to have required specialist skills in its production, as the colour is unstable and fades at high temperatures (Rooksby 1964; Shortland 2004; Tite *et al.* 2008); production in a limited number of locations would therefore be unsurprising.

Recent excavations of the Pictish monastic site at Tarbat Ness (Portmahomack, Scotland) have produced what is thought to be the only known assemblage of glassworking waste from early medieval Scotland (Ewan Campbell, pers. comm.). The site was founded in the late 6th century, and grew to become an internationally important ecclesiastical hub, until its destruction in the early 9th century (Carver 2004). The nature of the glass assemblage, which probably dates to the 8th century, appears to suggest that glassworking was taking place at the site, and it was hoped that analysis could clarify this.

Additionally, an assemblage of opaque yellow glass beads from the 5th–7th-century Anglo-Saxon cemetery complex at RAF Lakenheath (Eriswell, Suffolk) were analysed as part of the ongoing post-excavation work associated with the site. The beads are primarily from female graves and consist of a wide variety of monochrome and polychrome decorated types. The complex is exceptional in that it spans an extensive period of Anglo-Saxon history, and the sheer number of burials places it amongst the largest inhumation cemeteries of the period in the country (Caruth and Anderson 2005). Analysis of these beads is currently underway in the hope of providing further insights into the nature of glass production in Britain during the period.

Materials and methods

The opaque yellow glassworking waste from Tarbat consists of two glass dribbles (approximately 2cm (sample 25/1385) and 3cm (sample 25/1458) in size) and the residue glass from a 'heating tray', which is too decomposed to provide useful analytical information. Additionally, a comprehensive range of approximately 80 samples of opaque yellow glass were analysed from individual beads from Eriswell. Approximately a third of the Eriswell analyses represent samples from monochrome opaque yellow beads, with the remaining having been taken from opaque yellow polychrome decorated bead types and the opaque yellow decoration from beads in

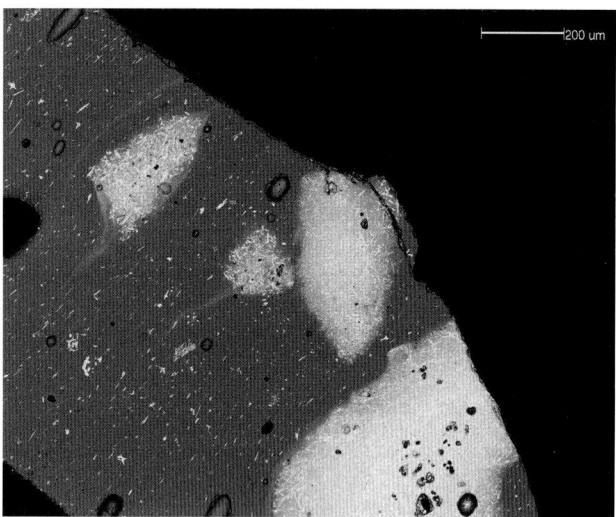

Fig. 3.1: SEM micrograph showing a fragment of opaque yellow glass from Tarbat, taken from dribble 25/1458. Sub-angular aggregates rich in lead and tin, containing acicular lead-tin oxide crystals (white) can be seen in a lead-rich soda-lime-silica glass matrix (grey). Several bubbles are also present.

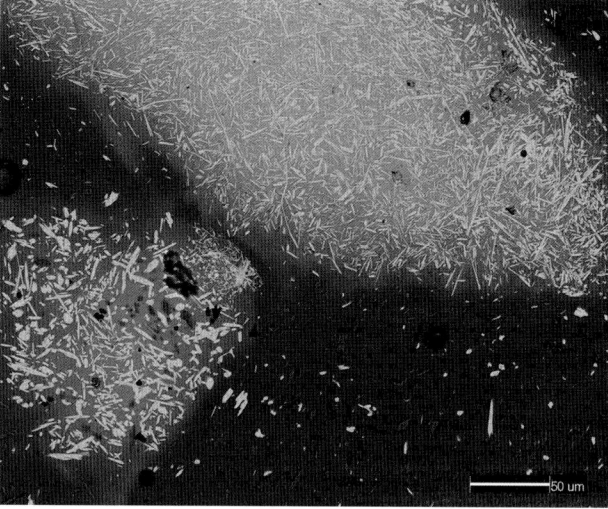

Fig. 3.2: SEM micrograph showing detail of the acicular lead-tin oxide crystals (white) in the large lead-tin aggregates visible in Fig. 3.1. Crystals of wollastonite (CaSiO$_3$) are dispersed throughout the lead-rich soda-lime-silica glass matrix, but these are not easily visible in the image.

other colours (mostly opaque red). These vary considerably in decorative motif, size and shape, being mostly annular, globular, cylindrical, ribbed or segmented. However, it is not within the scope of the present paper to discuss the analyses of colours other than opaque yellow.

Small samples were taken, mounted in epoxy resin and polished in the standard way. They were coated with a thin layer of carbon and examined in the scanning electron microscope (CamScan Maxim). The chemical compositions of the samples were determined using an Oxford Instruments INCA energy-dispersive X-ray analyser (EDXA) attached to the SEM. Relative analytical accuracy is believed to be better than ±2% for silica, and ±5% for other elements present in concentrations greater than 10%, but greater for elements present in lower concentrations. Detection limits were 0.2% for most of the components analysed, 0.3% for lead and tin and 0.4%–0.7% for antimony, depending on the glass matrix. Results were taken from an average of three analyses, and were normalised to 100% to improve comparability.

Results

Oxide compositions (Table 3.1, cols. 1–3) typically show 6–12% Na$_2$O, 28–45% SiO$_2$, and 30–50% PbO, with tin present as 2.5–7.0% SnO$_2$. The opaque yellow glasses are essentially mixtures of soda-lime-silica glass and a component rich in the oxides of lead and tin. All of the glasses analysed are coloured and opacified by lead-tin oxide, visible in the SEM as small crystals dispersed throughout

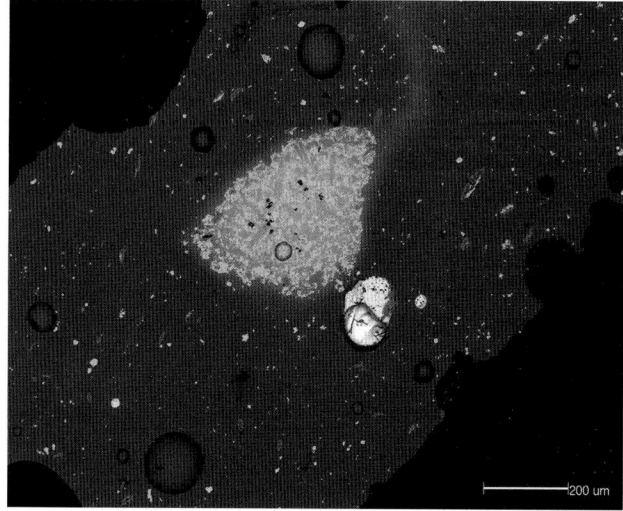

Fig. 3.3: SEM micrograph showing a fragment of opaque yellow glass from Eriswell, taken from a monochrome globular segmented bead. A large irregular region rich in lead and tin, containing an abundance of lead-tin oxide crystals (white), in a lead-rich soda-lime-silica glass matrix (grey) is visible. Within this aggregate, particles of the sodium aluminium silicate mineral nepheline (KNa$_3$Al$_4$Si$_4$O$_{16}$) can be seen (black).

the glass matrix (Figs. 3.1–3.5). In all cases, spot analyses identified these crystals as consisting of approximately 30–35% tin oxide and 60–65% lead oxide, corresponding to the cubic phase PbSnO$_3$ (Moretti and Hreglich 1984;

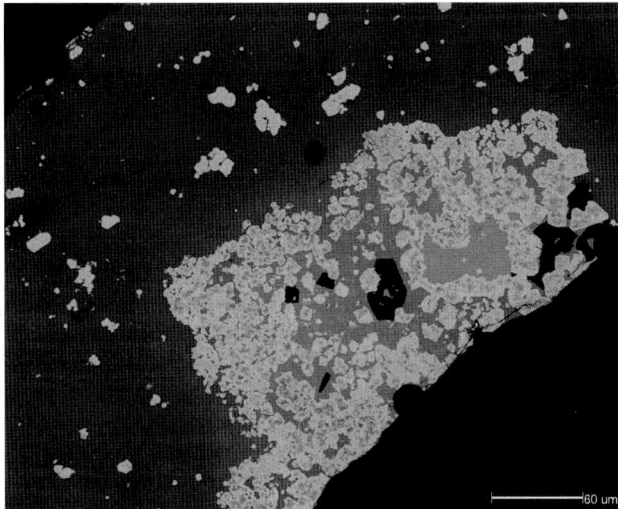 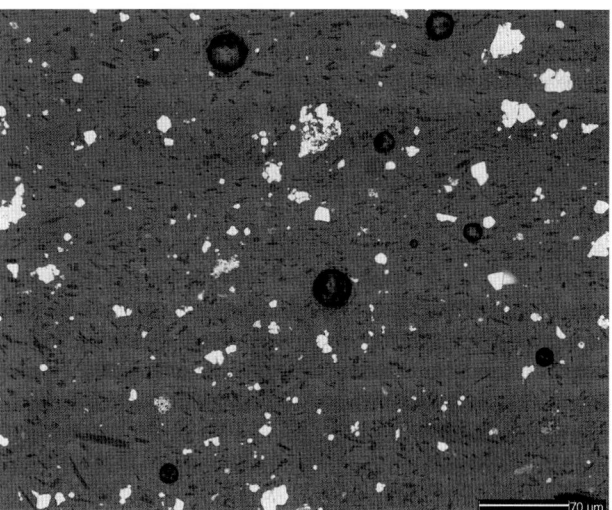

Fig. 3.4: SEM micrograph showing a fragment of opaque yellow glass from Eriswell, taken from a monochrome globular 'ribbed' bead. A large irregular area rich in lead and tin, containing lead-tin oxide crystals (white) is visible in a lead-rich soda-lime-silica glass matrix (grey). Particles of the sodium aluminium silicate mineral nepheline ($KNa_3Al_4Si_4O_{16}$) are also clearly visible (black angular crystals).

Fig 3.5: SEM micrograph showing a fragment of opaque yellow glass from Eriswell, taken from a monochrome cylindrical bead, showing a heterogeneous dispersion of lead-tin oxide crystals (white) within a lead-rich soda-lime-silica glass matrix (pale grey). Throughout the glass matrix a dispersion of acicular wollastonite ($CaSiO_3$) crystals can be seen (dark grey).

Table 3.1: Compositions of some early medieval opaque yellow glasses from Tarbat and Eriswell, alongside those of opaque yellow glasses from elsewhere in northwestern Europe.

Oxide (wt %)[1]	Tarbat: 25/1385[2]	Tarbat: 25/1458[2]	Eriswell[3]	Schleitheim[4]	Dunmisk: 16[5]	Wijnaldum: 22[6]	Maastricht[7]
Na_2O	8.1	5.5	11.3	7.5	9.1	10.3	11.5
MgO	0.4	0.3	0.6	<0.3	0.4	1.0	1.0
Al_2O_3	2.0	2.3	2.2	2.6	2.2	2.1	2.3
SiO_2	36.7	27.9	45.3	30.2	43.6	41.9	44.8
P_2O_5	<0.1	<0.1	0.1	<0.1	2.1	0.1	0.2
Cl	0.6	0.5	0.8	n.a.	0.8	0.6	0.6
K_2O	0.5	0.4	0.5	0.3	1.2	1.0	0.7
CaO	3.5	2.3	4.5	2.4	2.9	4.2	4.9
TiO_2	<0.1	<0.1	0.1	0.3	0.1	0.1	0.1
MnO	0.2	0.2	0.6	n.a.	0.1	0.3	1.1
Fe_2O_3	1.4	3.3	1.0	0.9	0.9	1.1	1.4
SnO_2	2.7	6.9	2.9	4.4	4.7	3.9	4.4
Sb_2O_3	<0.4	<0.4	<0.4	n.a.	0.4	<0.4	<0.4
PbO	42.6	49.3	29.5	51.3	32.9	36.5	30.6

[1] All oxides are in weight percent, normalised to 100%. n.a = not analysed.
[2] Opaque yellow glass dribbles from Tarbat (Scotland), 8th century (new data).
[3] Average of 79 opaque yellow bead samples from Eriswell (SE England), 5th–7th centuries (new data).
[4] Opaque yellow bead from Schleitheim (Switzerland), 7th century (Heck *et al.* 2003).
[5] Opaque yellow crucible glass from Dunmisk Fort (Ireland), 6th–10th centuries (Henderson 1988).
[6] Average of five opaque yellow beads from Wijnaldum (The Netherlands), 6th–9th centuries (Henderson 1999).
[7] Average of four opaque yellow glasses from Maastricht (The Netherlands), 6th–7th centuries (Sablerolles *et al.* 1997).

Rooksby 1964; Tite *et al.* 2008). It is notable that the iron and tin contents of sample 25/1458 are unusually high, corresponding to 3.3% Fe_2O_3 and 6.9% SnO_2 respectively (Table 3.1, col. 2). The iron is likely to have resulted in the slight olive colouration of this sample, whereas the high tin oxide content may have resulted from variations in the quantity of tin added or reflect the heterogeneity of the sample, as will become apparent.

The microstructures of the glasses are coarsely heterogeneous. For example, Fig. 3.1 shows large irregular regions rich in lead and tin, with abundant acicular (needle-like) lead-tin oxide crystals, in a matrix which is richer in soda and silica. There are some notable differences between the yellow glasses from Eriswell and those from Tarbat. The morphologies of the lead-tin oxide crystals in the Tarbat glasses tend to be acicular (Figs. 3.1–3.2), whereas those in the Eriswell glasses are more equant (Figs. 3.3–3.5). The density of the opacifying crystals varies considerably in the samples from Eriswell, which in many cases have a heterogeneous and stratified microstructure with some areas of glass completely deficient in lead-tin oxide altogether. Furthermore, calcium silicate crystals corresponding to the mineral wollastonite ($CaSiO_3$) appear to have formed in the Tarbat glasses (these are not easily visible in the backscattered electron micrographs, but could be resolved in the SEM), as well as in several of the opaque yellow glasses from Eriswell (*e.g.* Fig. 3.5). The sodium aluminium silicate nepheline ($KNa_3Al_4Si_4O_{16}$) is also associated with the tin oxide aggregates in some of the Eriswell opaque yellow glasses (Fig. 3.4), but was not observed in those from Tarbat.

Discussion

We have no direct evidence for glassmaking at either site, and no evidence for its manipulation at Eriswell. However, the glassy residue from the 'heating tray' at Tarbat represents the only sample analysed directly from a refractory ceramic, and may provide evidence for the manipulation of glass. The flat, open shape of this heating tray is paralleled by heating trays associated with potential glassworking debris found elsewhere, for example in early medieval Ireland (Henderson 1988; Henderson and Ivens 1992) and Maastricht in The Netherlands (Sablerolles *et al.* 1997), although the evidence for glassworking is far from unambiguous in many cases. Furthermore, similar lead-tin yellow glassworking waste has been recovered from the late Romano-British site of Catsgore (Biek and Kay 1982), suggesting that this technology may well have been employed during the preceding Roman period. It has been suggested that shallow vessels such as that at Tarbat may have allowed the glass to be scraped out more easily and were used only to soften it prior to shaping, as more closed shapes would have been necessary to melt it completely (Henderson and Ivens 1992; Sablerolles *et al.* 1997). The thinness of these vessels, combined with the shallow shape, would allow for temperature control and the rapid melting of small quantities of glass (Biek and Kay 1982). Whilst the glass dribbles from Tarbat confirm that pre-formed glass was being manipulated in the hot state on the site, they provide no evidence for the manufacture or colouration of the material. However, in spite of the absence of evidence for glassmaking on site, we have good indirect evidence for the glass colouration procedure, as will be seen.

The low potash and magnesia contents of the glasses indicate that the soda-lime-silica base glasses are of the 'natron' type, typical of the glass used during the first millennium AD. The use of lead-tin oxide, lead stannate ($PbSnO_3$), as a colourant was common from about the 4th century onwards, when tin seems to have displaced antimony-based glass colourants. In fact, glass of this type was used in northwestern Europe from the 2nd century BC and continued in use throughout the first millennium AD, and has been suggested to represent the continuity of a Celtic rather than a Roman tradition (Henderson 2000; Henderson and Ivens 1992). During the Roman period however, yellow glasses were more commonly opacified by lead antimonate (Henderson 1999), so the glasses analysed here are characteristically early medieval.

The sub-angular nature of the coarse aggregates of lead-tin oxide crystals in the glass assemblages from Tarbat and Eriswell (Figs. 3.1–3.5) suggest that they were directly added to a soda-lime-silica glass as crushed lumps of a pre-formed material. It appears that the resultant hybrid glass was not heated for long enough to fully disperse these lumps of yellow pigment. As previously stated, the duration of heating would have been kept to a minimum by the craftsperson as lead-tin yellow is unstable and can readily lose its colour at high temperatures (Rooksby 1964; Shortland 2004; Tite *et al.* 2008), which is likely to account for the heterogeneous microstructures. The differences in microstructure observed between samples are likely to have resulted from slight variations in the nature of the raw materials and production technology employed in the manufacture of these glasses; the melting temperature or rate of cooling, for example. Wollastonite probably formed as a devitrification product during cooling (Brun and Pernot 1992), whereas nepheline is likely to have formed due to a reaction between the high sodium oxide content of a soda-lime-silica glass and the aluminous clay-ceramic material of a melting pot; similar inclusions have been noted in the opaque red glasses from Eriswell (Peake and Freestone 2012).

The textural characteristics observed are consistent with the findings of Heck *et al.* (2003) who investigated a crucible and bead of Merovingian date (5th–7th centuries) from Schleitheim, Switzerland (Table 3.1, col. 4), and found that the yellow glass is likely to have been produced in two stages. Here, lead-tin yellow pigment was prepared by heating a mixture of the oxides of lead and tin, which reacted with the crucible fabric to form crystals of lead-tin oxide in a lead-silica glass. This was then mixed with a pre-existing soda-lime-silica glass to form the yellow glass used to make beads. A similar process was used in post-medieval Venice to make yellow glass (Moretti and Hreglich 1984) and it has been suggested that it was widely used throughout the medieval period (Tite *et al.* 2008). Interestingly, small quantities of this lead-tin yellow pigment appear to have been used in the production of the opaque red glass from Eriswell, although the precise reasons for its addition here are unclear (Peake and Freestone 2012).

Evidence for the local working of opaque yellow glass to produce beads has also been produced from the 6th–7th-century Merovingian settlement at Maastricht in The Netherlands (Sablerolles *et al.* 1997). This consisted of a wide range of glassworking waste including crucible fragments predominantly containing residues of opaque yellow glass, but also fragments containing translucent 'colourless' glass. One fragment associated with a granular frit-like material was noted as possible evidence for the manufacture of glass from its raw materials at this site, but considered insufficiently conclusive. However, it does seem certain that glass was being manipulated to produce beads on or near the site, based predominantly upon a supply of glass rods and perhaps also cullet (Sablerolles *et al.* 1997).

Similar glassworking waste has been recovered from 6th–7th-century Merovingian Wijnaldum, The Netherlands, where there is strong evidence for the manipulation of opaque yellow glass to produce beads, including an opaque yellow glass residue fused to a fragment of baked clay (Henderson 1999; Sablerolles 1999). Again, this does not suggest that anything more than the working of opaque yellow glass was taking place. However, it has been suggested that glassworking at the site was based upon imported glass rods (Sablerolles 1999), as at Maastricht. Furthermore, it is interesting to note that at both Maastricht and Wijnaldum the glassworking debris was associated with evidence for metalworking, suggesting that these two industries were practiced together, or even that beadmaking was undertaken as a secondary activity (Sablerolles 1999). This is paralleled at Tarbat, where suspected metalworking waste was also discovered alongside the glass assemblage (Carver 2004). We also have evidence for the direct use of metallurgical by-products in the manufacture of opaque red glass at Eriswell, suggesting that there was a link between the metal and glass industries (Peake and Freestone 2012).

Further potential evidence for the manufacture of yellow glass (also associated with metalworking waste), including crucible fragments and waste glass, was recovered from the early Christian (6th–10th centuries) fort at Dunmisk, Ireland, where it has been suggested that the opaque glass was being directly made from its raw materials, including not only tin and lead, but also soda and silica (Henderson 1988; Henderson and Ivens 1992). This is in contrast to the process proposed by Heck *et al.* (2003), and in the present investigation, where a lead-tin yellow pigment is added to a preformed soda-lime-silica glass. While this inferred technological difference may be real and reflect different practices due the characters and locations of the sites, recent evidence suggests that much of the natron type glass in use in the early medieval period was made in the eastern Mediterranean and imported (Freestone 2006; Freestone *et al.* 2008), so the manufacture of primary glass in the British Isles at this time seems unlikely. However, while there is limited direct industrial evidence for the fusion of glass from its raw materials, soda-lime-silica glass was probably being coloured to produce opaque yellow in early medieval Europe.

The interpretation of opaque yellow glassworking waste from other early medieval sites in Europe is difficult as it is often ambiguous. The glassworking waste from Dunmisk, particularly the yellow glass remaining in a crucible, is potentially the strongest evidence for the production of opaque yellow glass from primary raw materials. However, it may be that the silica grains in this glass, which were interpreted as relicts from primary glassmaking (Henderson 1988; Henderson and Ivens 1992), are in fact relicts from the production of the lead-tin yellow pigment. Indeed, the presence of a small amount of silica is necessary in order to obtain the cubic lead stannate ($PbSnO_3$) which produces the yellow colour (Heck *et al.* 2003; Moretti and Hreglich 1984; Rooksby 1964; Tite *et al.* 2008). They may therefore represent silica grains from the melting pot, or the deliberate addition of a quartz-rich raw material to aid the formation of the colour. The identification of tin oxide within this crucible glass (Henderson 1998; Henderson and Ivens 1992) may represent the remains of tin used in the production of yellow pigment as opposed to yellow glass produced from the fusion of raw materials.

The comparison of the compositions of the opaque yellows from Dunmisk, Tarbat and Eriswell, together with those from Schleitheim, Wijnaldum and Maastricht (Table 3.1), show that they are remarkably similar, particularly given the heterogeneity of the materials. It should be noted that the opaque yellow glasses from Eriswell contain varying amounts of manganese oxide (0.6% on average, but up to 1.7% in some cases); a characteristic which is also seen in the yellow glasses from Maastricht (Table 3.1, col. 7) and seems to relate to the composition of the base glass used in their production. Nevertheless, the compositions strongly suggest that a common technology and similar raw materials were employed in all cases. While there are some textural differences between the Eriswell and the Tarbat glasses (see above), given the similarities in chemistry these differences are likely to reflect local conditions of heating and cooling (crystal shape) and the compositions of the crucibles used to make the pigment (silicate phases) rather than any major differences in technology.

In addition, lead-tin-silica glasses which resemble the inferred precursor material used to colour glass seem to have been used as opaque yellow enamel in Celtic metalwork (Hughes 1987). It is also noted that opaque red enamels were made from a similar material but including copper, and again containing no soda-lime component (Hughes 1987; Stapleton *et al.* 1999). It has been suggested that these red enamels represent the re-use of raffination slags (Stapleton *et al.* 1999), but in view of the yellow glass technology deliberate production by reacting the metal oxides together must be seen as a possibility. Furthermore, the probable addition of small amounts of lead-tin yellow pigment to the opaque red glasses from Eriswell (Peake and Freestone 2012) suggests a strong link between opaque red and opaque yellow glass production during the period.

Conclusions

The current work suggests that opaque yellow glass across early medieval Europe was produced in a two-stage process, as proposed by Heck *et al.* (2003) in their study of Merovingian material from Switzerland. There, lead and tin were reacted in a crucible to produce a lead-rich glass containing abundant lead-tin yellow pigment ($PbSnO_3$). This pigment was crushed and added to a pre-existing soda-lime-silica glass and, depending upon the length of the heating process, the lead-tin yellow dispersed in the soda-lime-silica matrix to form an opaque yellow glass which could be used in bead manufacture. It is likely that the lead-tin-silicate precursor could not be used directly in polychrome beadmaking as its softening temperature, viscosity and expansion coefficient were much lower than other colours. Whether the pigment was mixed with soda-lime-silica glass to save material is uncertain, as the raw glass itself is likely to have been imported, or may represent recycled earlier Roman material collected locally, and it is not clear how its value compared with the lead and tin used to make the pigment.

As with the yellow glass residue on the 'heating tray' from Tarbat, the interpretation of opaque yellow glassworking waste from other early medieval sites is usually very complex; it is not always possible to establish whether glass was being fused from its raw materials or whether pre-made glass was being remelted for manipulation. Furthermore, when inferred relict raw materials are identified (as at Dunmisk, Ireland), it is difficult to determine whether they result from the production of raw glass or of a pigment such as lead-tin yellow. A reconsideration of the evidence suggests that the same colouration technique is likely to have been used at Dunmisk in Ireland (Henderson and Ivens 1992), as well as Maastricht (Sablerolles *et al.* 1997) and Wijnaldum (Henderson 1999; Sablerolles 1999), both in The Netherlands. Analysis of assemblages from elsewhere is required to determine if the colouration technique was widely understood and practiced in local workshops, as opposed to centralised glassmaking centres, or if the pigment or coloured glass was traded widely, or the extent to which both of these apply. In addition, the present data suggest that the relationship between the yellow glasses used in beadmaking and those used in enamelling on decorative metalwork requires exploration.

Finally, the very close similarities in the composition of the yellow glasses from Schleitheim, Maastricht and Wijnaldum with those from Tarbat and Eriswell must raise some questions as to whether the early medieval use of lead-tin yellow is a continuity from an earlier Celtic tradition (Henderson and Ivens 1992), or whether it represents a new technology from the south or east. By the 4th century, lead-tin yellow was used in the Mediterranean (*e.g.* Brill 1976; Brill and Whitehouse 1988) and the technology might have originated there. At present there is only limited evidence, for example at Catsgore in Britain (Biek and Kay 1982), to suggest its continuity through the 1st–4th centuries, when antimony was the commonly used opacifier. The opaque lead-tin yellow glass used to produce beads is therefore likely to represent a distinctively early medieval variant of opaque glass technology.

Acknowledgements

We would like to thank Ewan Campbell, Glasgow University, and Martin Goldberg, National Museum of Scotland, for allowing access to the Tarbat glass assemblage. Our thanks also go to Jo Caruth, Suffolk County Council Archaeological Service, and John Hines, Cardiff University, for making the Eriswell beads available for analysis. Finally, we thank Phil Parkes, Cardiff University, for the production of the reference standards spectra.

Bibliography

Biek, L. and Kay, P. J. (1982) Evidence of glass melting. In R. Leech (ed.) *Excavations at Catsgore 1970–1973. A Romano-British Village*, 132–133. Bristol, Western Archaeological Trust.

Brill, R. H. (1976) Scientific studies of the panel materials. In L. Ibrahim, R. Scranton and R. Brill, *Kenchreai. Eastern Port of Corinth II. The Panels of Opus Sectile in Glass*, 227–255. Leiden, Brill.

Brill, R. H. and Whitehouse, D. (1988) The Thomas Panel. *Journal of Glass Studies* 30, 34–50.

Brun, N. and Pernot, M. (1992) The opaque red glass of Celtic enamels from continental Europe. *Archaeometry* 34, 235–252.

Caruth, J. and Anderson, S. (2005) *An Assessment of the Potential for Analysis and Publication for Archaeological Work Carried Out at RAF Lakenheath Between 1987 and June 2005, Volume I: The Anglo-Saxon Cemeteries ERL 104, ERL 046 and ERL 114*. SCCAS Report No. 2005/94. Unpublished Report, Suffolk County Council Archaeological Service.

Carver, M. (2004) An Iona of the east: the early-medieval monastery at Portmahomack, Tarbat Ness. *Medieval Archaeology* 48, 1–30.

Freestone, I. C. (2006) Glass production in Late Antiquity and the Early Islamic period: a geochemical perspective. In M. Maggetti and B. Messiga (eds.) *Geomaterials in Cultural Heritage*. Geological Society Special Publications 257, 201–216. London, Geological Society of London.

Freestone, I. C., Hughes, M. J. and Stapleton, C. P. (2008) The composition and production of Anglo-Saxon glass. In V. I.

Evison, *Catalogue of Anglo-Saxon Glass in the British Museum*. British Museum Research Publication 167, 29–46. London, British Museum Press.

Heck, M., Rehren, Th. and Hoffmann, P. (2003) The production of lead-tin yellow at Merovingian Schleitheim (Switzerland). *Archaeometry* 45, 33–44.

Henderson, J. (1988) The nature of the Early Christian glass industry in Ireland: some evidence from Dunmisk Fort, Co. Tyrone. *Ulster Journal of Archaeology* 51, 115–126.

Henderson, J. (1999) Scientific analysis of the glass and the glass-bearing artefacts: technique, raw materials used and archaeological interpretation. In J. Besteman, J. Bos, D. Gerrets, H. Heidinga and J. de Koning, *The Excavations at Wijnaldum*. Reports on Frisia in Roman and Medieval Times 1, 287–297. Rotterdam, A. A. Balkema.

Henderson, J. (2000) The production technology of Irish Early Christian glass with specific reference to beads and enamels. In J. Price (ed.) *Glass in Britain and Ireland AD 350–1100*. British Museum Occasional Paper 127, 143–159. London, British Museum Press.

Henderson, J. and Ivens, R. (1992) Dunmisk and glass-making in Early Christian Ireland. *Antiquity* 66, 52–64.

Hughes, M. J. (1987) Enamels: materials, deterioration and analysis. In L. Bacon and B. Knight (eds.) *From Pinheads to Hanging Bowls*. Occasional Paper, United Kingdom Institute for Conservation for Historic and Artistics Works 7, 10–12. London, United Kingdom Institute for Conservation.

Moretti, C. and Hreglich, S. (1984) Opacification and colouring of glass by the use of 'anime'. *Glass Technology* 25, 277–282.

Peake, J. R. N. and Freestone, I. C. (2012) Cross-craft interactions between metal and glass working: slag additions to early Anglo-Saxon red glass. In *Proceedings of SPIE 8422: Integrated Approaches to the Study of Historical Glass*, 842204.

Rooksby, H. P. (1964) A yellow cubic lead tin oxide opacifier in ancient glasses. *Physics and Chemistry of Glasses* 5, 20–25.

Sablerolles, Y. (1999) Beads of glass, faience, amber, baked clay and metal, including production waste from glass and amber bead making. In J. Besteman, J. Bos, D. Gerrets, H. Heidinga and J. de Koning, *The Excavations at Wijnaldum*. Reports on Frisia in Roman and Medieval Times 1, 253–285. Rotterdam, A. A. Balkema.

Sablerolles, Y., Henderson, J. and Dijkman, W. (1997) Early medieval glass bead making in Maastricht (Jodenstraat 30), The Netherlands: an archaeological and scientific investigation. In U. von Freeden and A. Wieczorek (eds.) *Perlen. Archäologie, Techniken, Analysen*, 293–313. Bonn, Rudolf Habelt.

Shortland, A. (2004) Evaporites of the Wadi Natrun: seasonal and annual variation and its implication for ancient exploitation. *Archaeometry* 46, 497–516.

Stapleton, C. P., Freestone, I. C. and Bowman, S. G. E. (1999) Composition and origin of early medieval opaque red enamel from Britain and Ireland. *Journal of Archaeological Science* 26, 913–921.

Tite, M., Pradell, T. and Shortland, A. (2008) Discovery, production and use of tin-based opacifiers in glasses, enamels and glazes from the late Iron Age onwards: a reassessment. *Archaeometry* 50, 67–84.

4

The vessel glass assemblage from Anglo-Saxon occupation at West Heslerton, North Yorkshire

Rose Broadley

Introduction

West Heslerton is an Anglo-Saxon settlement site located near Malton in North Yorkshire, and excavated between 1986 and 1995. The settlement features early and middle Anglo-Saxon activity (c. AD 450–850), while almost all of the glass dates from the middle Saxon period (c. AD 650–850). Vessel glass is an unusual find on occupation sites of this period, and is much less well known than the glass from funerary contexts of the early Anglo-Saxon period (c. AD 450–650). Middle Saxon glass was soda-based and usually of very high quality, with assemblages often exhibiting a wide range of bright colours and decorative techniques. Although the precise significance of vessel glass on a site of this period is still debateable, and depends upon many factors including the quality and quantity found, the very presence of vessel glass is indicative of the relatively high status of the settlement and its people. It also illustrates very specifically that public ('conspicuous') consumption of alcohol was part of the life of the community as this is widely accepted as the main use of glass vessels at the time.

Twenty-two middle Anglo-Saxon sites are currently known to have yielded fragments of vessel glass, and most are concentrated along the southern and eastern coastlines of England, from Southampton in the south-west to Monkwearmouth and Jarrow in the north-east. They can be divided into two categories – the *wic* and non-*wic* sites. *Wics* were large trading centres established on coastlines across northern Europe at this time. The four known in England were Southampton (*Hamwic*), London, Ipswich and York, all of which have produced substantial vessel glass assemblages. The remainder of the sites have their non-*wic* status in common but do not form a cohesive group: some, such as Lyminge in Kent, Barking in Essex and Monkwearmouth-Jarrow in Tyne and Wear, are documented ecclestiastical sites, and others, such as Cheddar in Somerset and Trowbridge in Wiltshire are known to have been centres of secular power, but in the majority of cases including West Heslerton, the precise nature of the occupation is unknown.

The vessel glass assemblage

Thirty vessel glass sherds of Anglo-Saxon date (or 1.2% of all middle Anglo-Saxon vessel glass from settlement contexts currently known) were found at West Heslerton, making it the seventh largest of the eighteen non-*wic* assemblages from England. It is likely that the assemblage represents a minimum of nineteen glass vessels, all of which were used and broken on the site, and deposited nearby. The group includes examples of the majority of vessel forms in circulation in middle Anglo-Saxon England – those present are claw beakers, globular beakers, bowls, cone beakers, palm cups and funnel beakers (Fig. 4.1). The colours are varied, as one would expect from a substantial and good quality middle Saxon vessel glass group. Seven sherds are amber, five are blue-green, five are pale green, four are blue, three are pale blue, three are deep blue-green, one is olive green, one is black, and one is deep pink-purple, appearing black in reflected light. The most common colours for Anglo-Saxon glass in general are the naturally-coloured range including pale blue-green, pale blue and pale green, which in this assemblage totals thirteen sherds and forms the largest sub-group. The more unusual colours are the amber, deep blue-green, black, and deep pink-purple sherds. The methods of decoration include applied trails (*e.g.* Hunter and Heyworth 1998, pls. 4–5) and *reticella* trails (*e.g.* Hunter and Heyworth 1998, pl. 1), which were the principal forms of decoration for middle Anglo-Saxon vessel glass.

4 The vessel glass assemblage from Anglo-Saxon occupation at West Heslerton, North Yorkshire

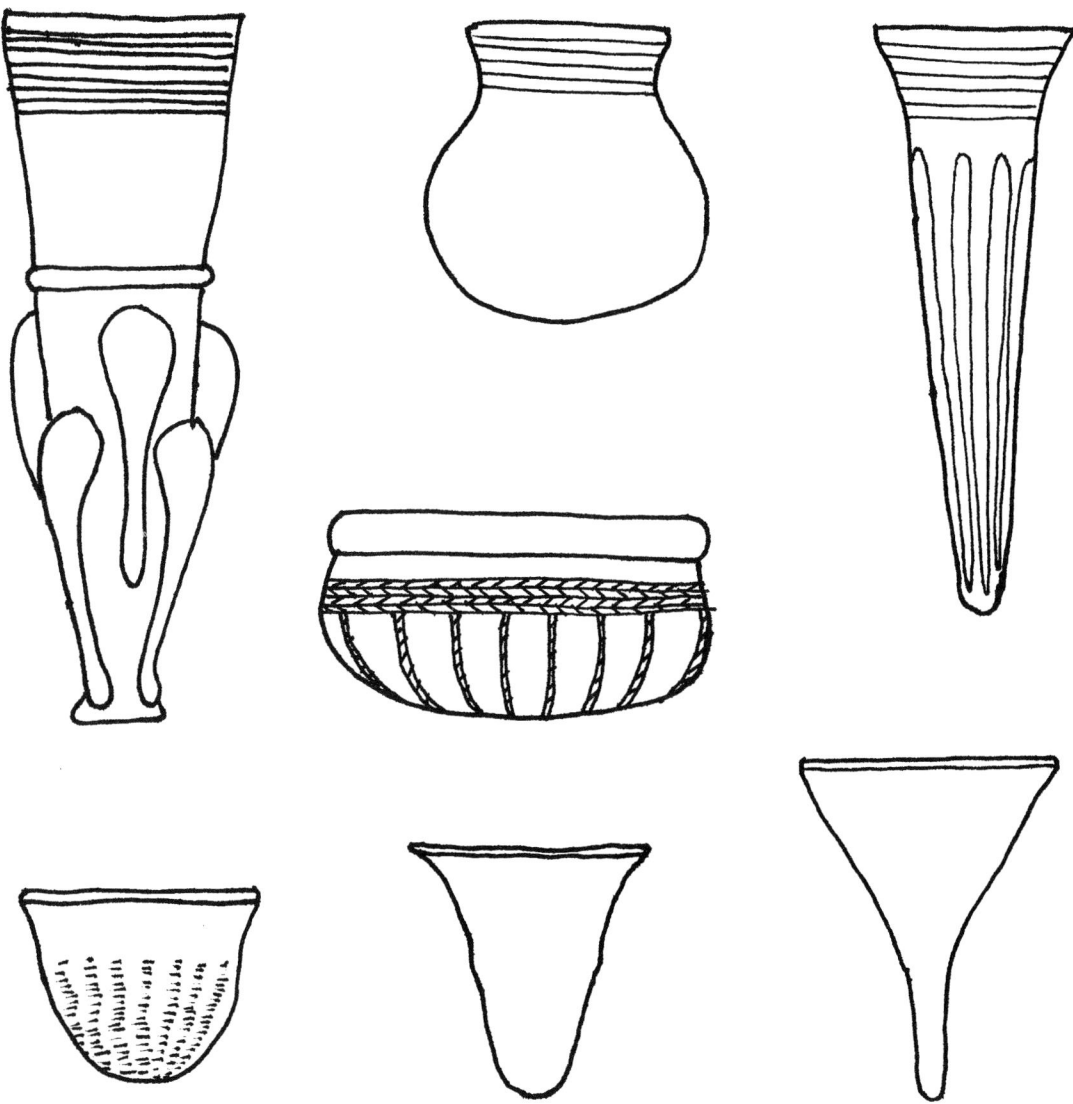

Fig. 4.1: Vessel forms (after Hunter and Heyworth 1998) clockwise from top left: claw beaker, globular beaker, bowl (centre), cone beaker, palm cup, tall palm cup, funnel beaker (scale 1:2.5).

As part of my doctoral research (in progress), I have compiled a national database of 2,848 Anglo-Saxon vessel glass sherds found in twenty-two *wic* and non-*wic* settlement contexts, which enables comparison of the characteristics of site assemblages such as this with the national corpus. For the first time, it is possible to demonstrate quantitatively how typical or atypical an assemblage is, and to identify precisely how particular site groups deviate from the norm. Future work in this area will hopefully lead to a better understanding of issues such as glass use both on individual sites and collectively; the nature of settlements where vessel glass occurs; and the networks of trade and exchange that connected the communities to each other and beyond.

Turning first to the study of vessel forms present at West Heslerton, Fig. 4.2 shows that claw beakers, globular beakers, bowls, palm cups and cone beakers form much higher proportions of the West Heslerton assemblage than at a national level. The most striking difference is seen in the percentage of claw beaker sherds at West Heslerton (33%) compared with the national corpus (1.5%), although it is clear from their distinctive blue-grey colour that four of the five claw sherds from West Heslerton are either from the same vessel or vessels forming a matching set, which helps to explain the elevation here. Similar circumstances may also have contributed to the higher proportions in some of the other groups, such as bowls (17% at West Heslerton,

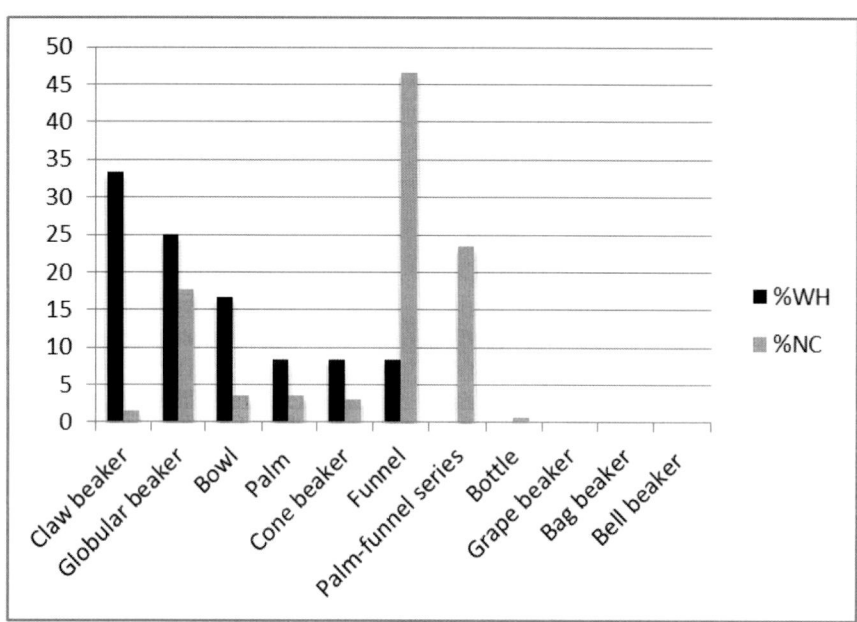

Fig. 4.2: West Heslerton form profile compared to national corpus.

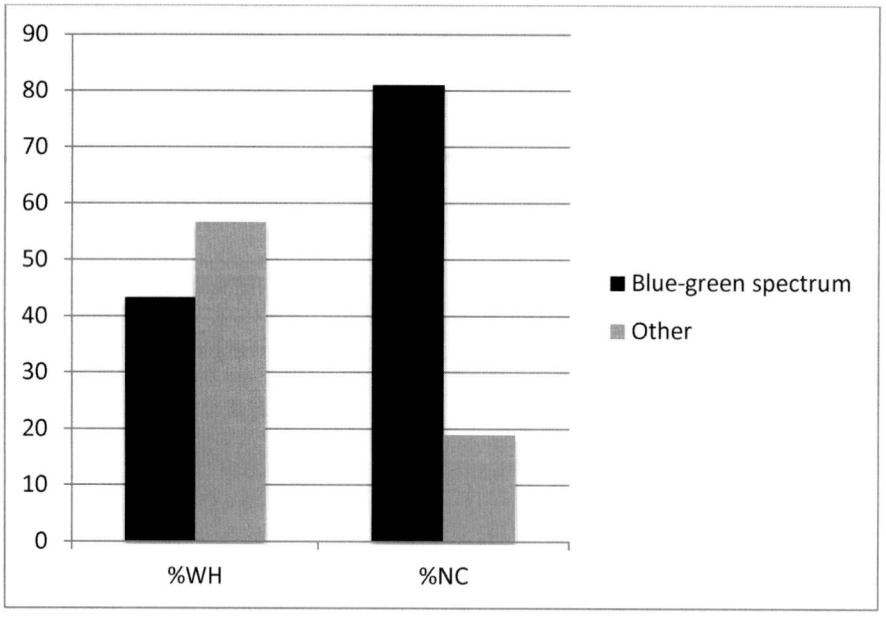

Fig. 4.3: Blue-green glass compared to other colours at West Heslerton and nationally.

3 % nationally) and palm and cone beakers (both 8% versus 3%), although there is little evidence to support this. The proportion of globular beaker sherds is also slightly elevated (25% compared to 18%).

Conversely, the tallest column in Fig. 4.2 represents the percentage of funnel beakers present in the national corpus (47%). Given that funnel beakers would be the largest group within an average assemblage, it is noteworthy that they are almost absent at West Heslerton, where only one possible funnel beaker sherd is present, a pale green heat-softened rim sherd with fine horizontal applied trails. Even if some of the unidentifiable blue-green sherds were from funnel beakers (as is very likely – see Hunter and Heyworth 1998, 20) these forms would still be greatly under-represented at this site. One theory to explain this absence is that the primary causal factor may well be temporal rather than functional – the missing form is late in the series of Anglo-Saxon vessel glass forms, while some of the forms present, such as cone

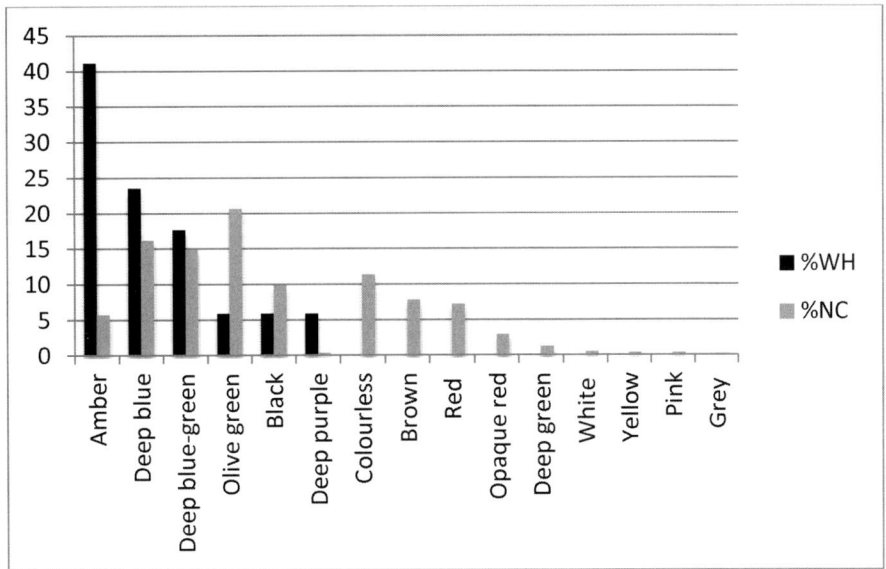

Fig. 4.4: West Heslerton 'Other' colour profile compared to national corpus.

beakers, claw beakers and palm cups, are typically earlier in date. The inflated claw form on the claw beaker (or beakers) supports an earlier date for those sherds within the middle Anglo-Saxon period. This supports the theory that there was a settlement shift in the area in the 9th century when the people of West Heslerton moved their community elsewhere (Dominic Powlesland, pers. comm.), and may even indicate that the settlement or its exchange networks were disrupted earlier than has previously been thought, around the turn of the 9th century.

Another significant way in which the West Heslerton assemblage differs from the national group and the average assemblage is that 'other' glass colours outnumber the usually predominant blue-green spectrum (which includes all shades from pale blue through blue-green and green-blue to pale green). At West Heslerton other colours comprise 57% of the assemblage, with blue-green glass forming only 43%, while nationally the figures are 19% for coloured glass and 81% for blue-green (Fig. 4.3). In Fig. 4.4, the colours are ordered left to right in descending order of size of the groups of sherds at West Heslerton (shown in black), compared with the national corpus (shown in grey). It is clear that at West Heslerton the proportion of amber sherds, which are mainly from globular beakers and perhaps palm cups, is very much higher than is found nationally (41% contrasting with 6%), and that this is a major contributor to the high proportion of coloured glass overall on the site. Part of the explanation of this may be the presence of two or more sherds from a single vessel, as with the blue claw beaker sherds noted above. However, the typological variety of the amber sherds, particularly in the range of decoration (vertical ribbing, looped applied trails and *reticella* trails), does not support this as an explanation and points instead to a genuinely large number of amber-coloured vessels in use on the site. There are also greater percentages of deep blue (24% compared to 16%), deep blue-green (18% compared to 15%) and deep purple (5.88% compared to 0.37%) sherds at West Heslerton than elsewhere, although it has already been noted that the four deep blue sherds are probably from the same claw beaker. The three deep blue-green sherds are identical in colour, but are likely to represent at least two vessels, probably globular beakers, because one sherd has a looped applied trail and another has vertical ribbing – decorative techniques that are extremely unlikely to be found together on a single vessel. The figures for deep purple are based on only two sherds known from Anglo-Saxon England, one of which was found at West Heslerton.

Two other colour groups are present at West Heslerton in smaller quantities than would be expected, based on the national colour profile. They are olive green (6% compared to 21%), and black (6% compared to 10%). It is also noteworthy that no glass from the following colour groups was found: colourless (11% nationally), brown (8%), red (7%), opaque red (3%), deep green (1.3%), or white, yellow, pink, grey (less than 1%). Early impressions suggest that red and opaque red glass may be concentrated in the South East, which may explain their absence here. Although the larger than average presence or indeed the absence of these colours in the archaeological record at West Heslerton may be pure chance, it is likely that they are meaningful to some extent for the study of the supply mechanisms that brought the glass vessels to the site and perhaps also the preferences of the community that lived there. Further research of other assemblages and the expansion of the national corpus may

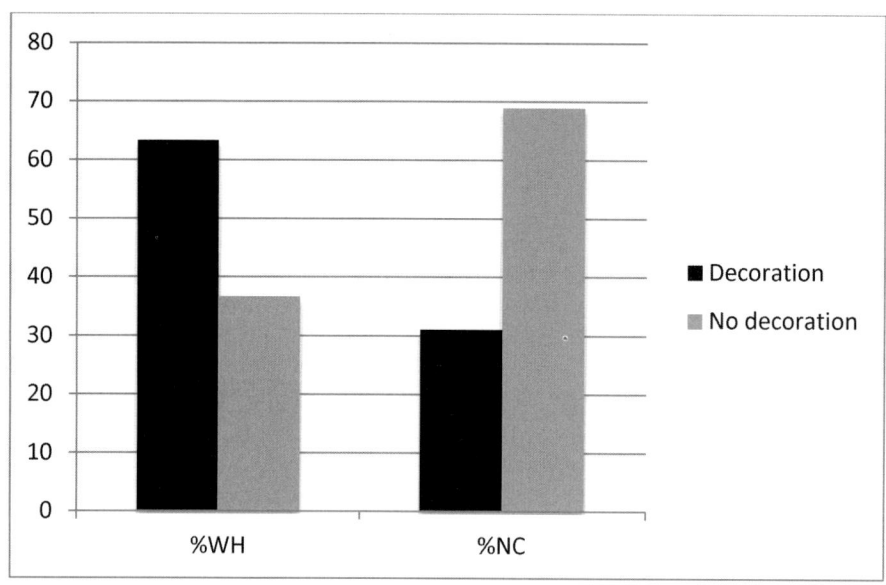

Fig. 4.5: Percentages of decorated and undecorated sherds at West Heslerton and nationally.

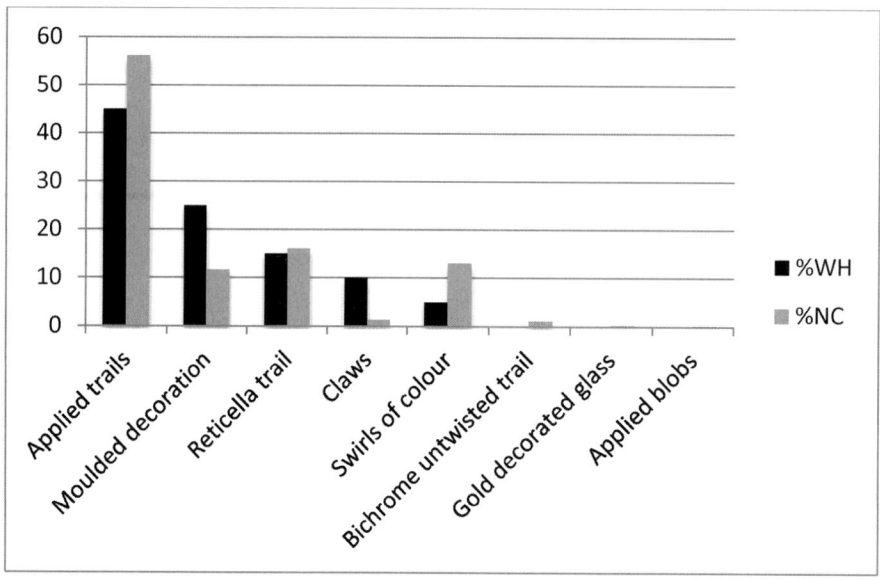

Fig. 4.6: West Heslerton decoration type profile compared to national corpus.

well identify wider patterns and throw more light on this subject. One thing is certain: the chance survival on this site of a rare purple sherd speaks volumes about the connections and wealth of some of the people who lived there.

The final area of comparison considered here is decoration. Firstly it is interesting to notice that 19 of the 30 West Heslerton sherds are decorated (Fig. 4.5: 63%, with 37% not decorated), while nationally the opposite is true (31% and 69% respectively). Such a significant difference cannot be pure coincidence, and must be the result of (probably several) selecting factors. It is likely that the mechanisms by which the original vessels were procured was also a significant factor. The sub-categories that are higher than expected are moulded decoration (25% versus 11%) and claws (10% versus 1.4%). As discussed in relation to form and colour, the elevation in the proportion of claw sherds is related to the fact that four of the five sherds are from either the same or matching vessels. Meanwhile, the group of sherds with moulded decoration, including a group of five ribbed sherds, are all clearly completely different in colour and represent five different vessels. Perhaps there was a local source of ribbed vessels, or possibly a preference for them within the settlement (the former being more likely). Other decorative techniques present in the West Heslerton assemblage include applied trails (45% compared to 56%), *reticella* trails (15%/16%) and swirls of colour in the metal of the glass (5%/13%) which are all present in smaller proportions than at the national level, although in the case of *reticella* trails the difference is only 1% (Fig. 4.6).

The glass vessels in use at West Heslerton were generally both more brightly coloured and more likely to be decorated than was usual, and amber sherds and ribbed moulded decoration were both more common than the national average. There are also significant absences – particularly the funnel beaker form, and colourless and red glass in the colour spectrum. Once other site assemblages are compared with the national corpus in a similar way, it may be possible to see whether any of them exhibit similar patterns, and if so, whether there are any discernible geographical or functional reasons for the patterns.

Key vessel glass sherds

The most distinctive pieces comprise the five ribbed sherds, three *reticella* sherds, two different types of claw fragment (one not blown and deep pink-purple, Figs. 4.7–4.8, and the other hollow and an unusual shade of blue), a sherd featuring a thick tooled trail (in the same blue and probably from the same claw beaker), and a sherd containing red swirls in the metal of the body.

The presence of a 'black' deep pink-purple claw beaker sherd (Figs. 4.7–4.8) is extremely unusual. Glass that appears black is almost always a very dark shade of another colour, usually green, brown or blue, and these are unusual in themselves, but glass of any shade from pink to purple is extremely rare in the spectrum of early medieval glass in northern Europe. Only two sherds, one purple with applied white trails and one pink, are known from Hamwic (Southampton) in England (Stiff 1996, vol. 2, 92, D537, 82, D409; Hunter and Heyworth 1998, 114, item 2649 [described as "dark opaque"], 105, item 420, pl. 5 [described as "opaque clouded red"]), and there are also two, one pink and one purple, from Hedeby, Jutland (Stiff 1996, vol. 2, 203, G140, 213, G324).

Two of the three *reticella* sherds (Fig. 4.10) belong to the usual 'opaque yellow on blue-green body colour' scheme found at many contemporary settlements. Twenty-one sherds are known from Southampton (*e.g.* Hunter and Heyworth 1998, 20), ten from Ipswich (*e.g.* Stiff 1996, vol. 2, 27, B123), nine from Brandon (Evison forthcoming), at least four from Flixborough (Evison 2009, 105), and one each from Whitby (Evison 1991, 143; also in Evison 2009, no. 18 fig. 2), York (Stiff 1996, vol. 2, 10–11, A34), and London (Stiff 2003, 245). The third *reticella* sherd, however has an unusual combination of an opaque yellow and pale green *reticella* trail on an amber body (Fig. 4.12). There are no exact parallels for this colour combination. Only four amber sherds with *reticella* decoration are currently known in England; one has an opaque white on blue-green trail, while the other two have opaque yellow on amber body colour trails. Interestingly, these other three are from York (Stiff 1996, vol. 2, 12, A53–54), showing a regional focus for amber *reticella* vessels. A very similar sherd from Barking Abbey, Essex has a similar opaque yellow on pale green trail, but the body colour is dark brown (Evison 1991, 92).

At least two sherds are from the well-known Valsgärde bowl type (*e.g.* Hunter and Heyworth 1998, 16, 19). One is a rim sherd, and the other, from the middle zone of the vessel wall, shows the classic band of opaque yellow and self-coloured *reticella* trails (Figs. 4.9–4.10). Sherds from these bowls are now known from a number of English sites, including Flixborough (Evison 2009, 105), York (Stiff 1996, vol. 2, 10, A25), Whitby (Evison 1991, 143), Brandon (Evison forthcoming) and Ipswich (Stiff 1996, vol. 2, 27, B123); they are significant finds when assessing the quality and range of an assemblage, as the complete vessels would have been impressive items. One other rim sherd definitely comes from a bowl, but it is an unusual colour for the Valsgärde form. Most frequently, bowl and *reticella*-decorated vessels were made in glass within the blue-green range and have trails with opaque yellow or white threads, as described above. In the last case, however, the rim sherd (Fig. 4.11) has a deep out-folded rim with cavity, horizontal opaque yellow trails within the rim cavity, and an estimated diameter of 123mm, which are characteristic of the bowl form, but the body colour, appearing black, is exceptional. Yellow trails folded into the cavity rim are only seen on Valsgärde-style bowl sherds (Stiff 2003, 245; *e.g.* Evison 1991, 92), so this sherd is likely to be from a bowl of this kind with a very unusual ground colour, as is the body sherd with a pale green and opaque yellow marvered *reticella* trail and amber ground mentioned previously (Fig. 4.12).

Intra-site distribution

The intra-site distribution of this glass is typical of contemporary assemblages in the sense that almost all the glass was associated with other domestic refuse and was found in contexts consistent with this, particularly in the fills of *Grubenhäuser* and peripheral ditches. Very little glass came from the main occupation area, echoing patterns indentified by previous distributional studies, which have showed that areas of habitation were kept scrupulously clean, particularly in the case of items that would have been sharp when recently broken (*e.g.* Campbell 2007, 92–101). As very little work has previously been done in this area, a more detailed assessment of the intra-site distribution both at West Heslerton and at other sites with sufficient

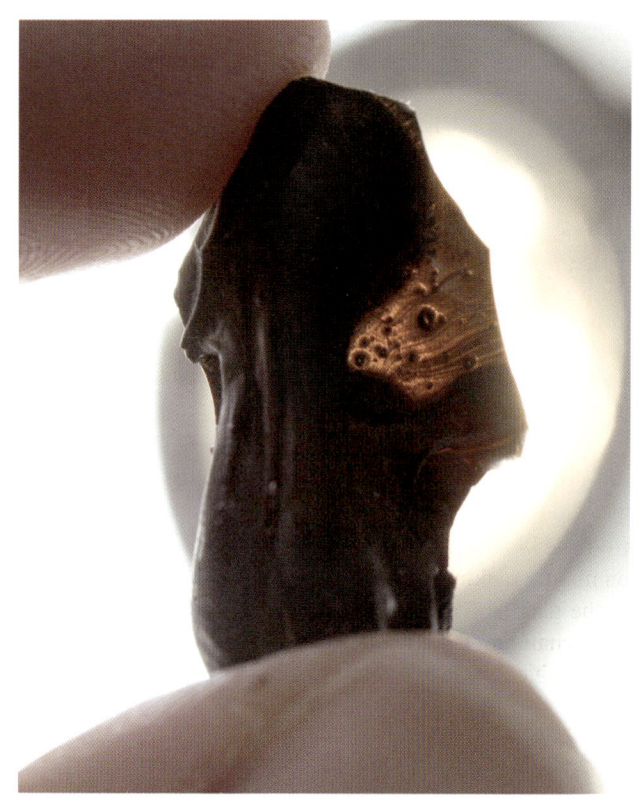

Fig. 4.7: Deep pink-purple claw fragment (HP11AD42AM) in transmitted light.

Fig. 4.8: Deep pink-purple claw fragment (HP11AD42AM), appearing opaque and black in reflected light.

Fig. 4.9: Valsgärde bowl fragment, rim (HP12AD391AB).

Fig. 4.10: Valsgärde bowl fragment, band of reticella decoration (HP12AD650AI).

Fig. 4.11: 'Black' bowl rim sherd (HP12AB782AD).

information to do this will be presented as case studies in my doctoral thesis.

The site and its landscape

This site at West Heslerton appears to be unusual amongst those in England that have produced contemporary vessel glass assemblages of similar size and variety. It is neither a coastal trading settlement nor a suspected monastic centre, which are the main settlement types usually associated with high quality vessel glass in middle Saxon England. Although the settlement was well-organised, with dedicated areas for housing, craft and industry, animal husbandry and crop processing, there are few reasons to define the site as elite. On the contrary, there is a clear shortage of market age cattle in the animal bone assemblage (of c. 900,000 bones) and this has been interpreted as reflecting the payment of cattle as taxes to another higher status settlement (Dominic Powlesland, pers. comm.). The post-hole buildings are comparable in size with others from early and middle Anglo-Saxon settlements such as West Stow (West 1985, fig. 7) and Mucking (Hamerow 1993, fig. 195). With so few excavated examples for comparison one cannot prove at present whether or not the presence of a mill was exceptional. Meanwhile, the presence of Niedermendig Lava quern stones imported from the Rhine is noteworthy, although they are not rare finds on middle-ranking settlement sites of the period. In addition to the glass and quernstones, evidence for imports consists of a small amount of pottery and metalwork and a cowrie shell, which are all of interest. Nonetheless, the calibre of the glass assemblage is still exceptional.

Analysis of the wider context of the site has revealed that within 4.5km to the east of West Heslerton there are seven smaller and two larger Anglo-Saxon settlements (Fig. 4.13), in addition to a small area of settlement to the north and two to the west. Including West Heslerton, this means that there are at least 13 distinct areas of Anglo-Saxon occupation within the valley, and geophysical survey suggests that one may be an early monastery (Dominic Powlesland, pers. comm.). Alongside site evidence such as the organized layout and the animal bone assemblage, this builds a picture of West Heslerton as an upper-middle ranking, rather than high-ranking, settlement within an intricate network of communities. Regarding potential coastal trade routes, West Heslerton is 80km from the sea by river, but only 18km overland to the modern coastline (Fig. 4.14), although conclusions in this area are hampered by the fact that the exact position of the coastline in the area during the Anglo-Saxon period is not known. Proof

Fig. 4.12: Dark amber-brown reticella body sherd (HP11AE438AI).

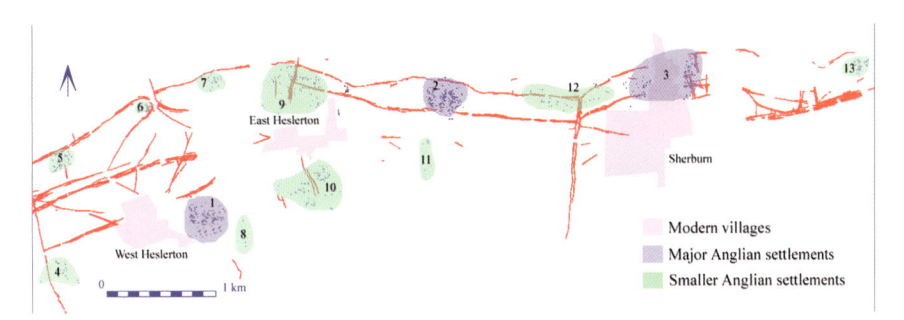

Fig. 4.13: The position of West Heslerton in relation to other known Anglo-Saxon settlements in the Vale of Pickering (©Landscape Research Centre).

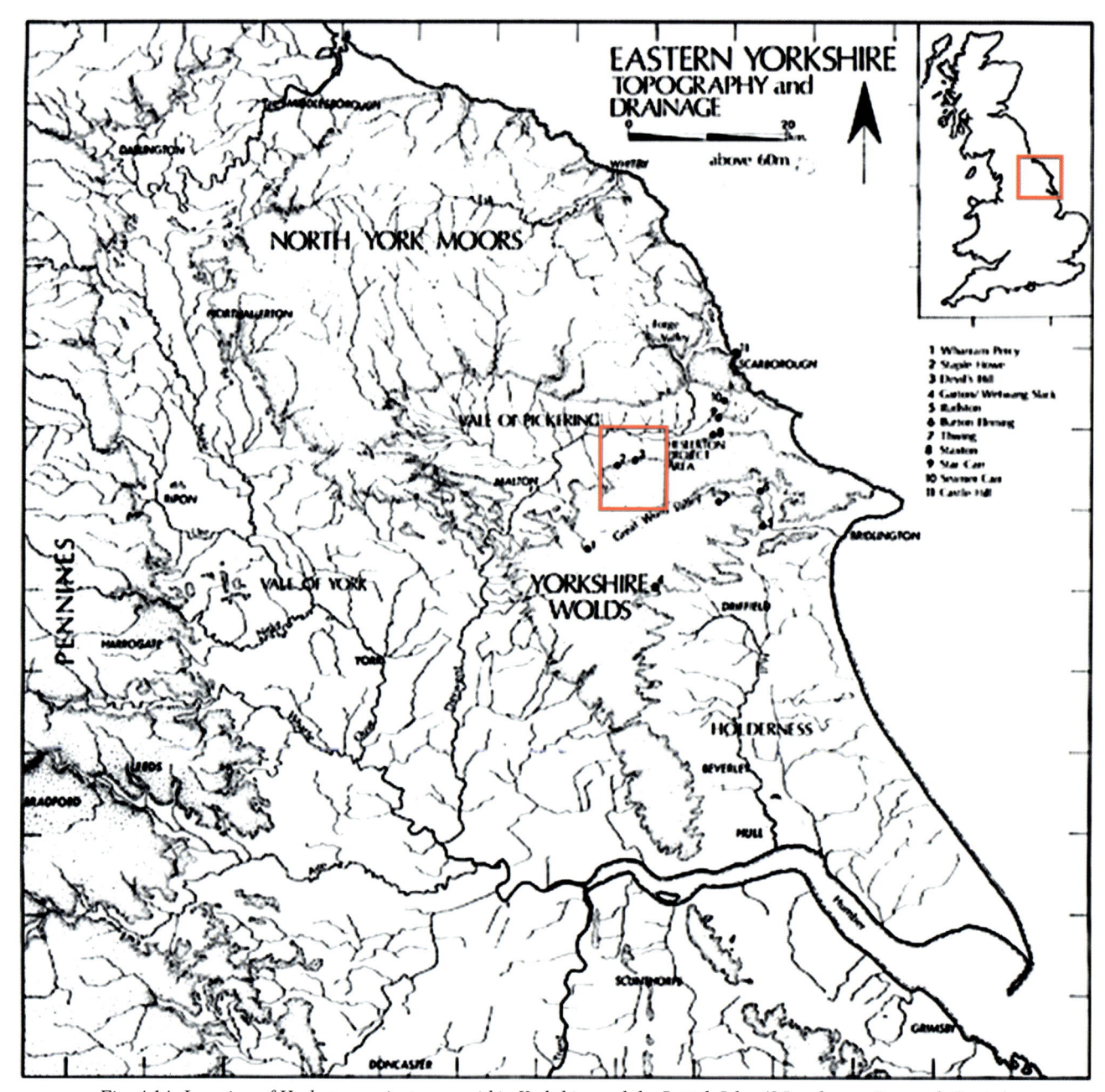

Fig. 4.14: Location of Heslerton project area, within Yorkshire and the British Isles (©Landscape Research Centre).

of proximity to a contemporary monastery or other elite settlement – such as the possible monastic site in the valley – would help to clarify how and why the glass reached the site. Perhaps it was exchanged for the cattle tithe as part of regional socio-political structures, although comprehensive evidence for this is currently lacking.

Summary

Overall, this assemblage has characteristics in common with the national corpus of middle Anglo-Saxon glass groups, including the approximate range of forms, the colours, the decorative techiques, and the deposition in peripheral domestic refuse deposits. However, it also differs from the norm in a number of interesting areas, particularly in the near-absence of funnel beakers, the notably high proportions of deeply coloured and amber sherds, and the high percentage of decorated sherds. The assemblage also contains a few very unusual sherds that stand out from the rest, especially the extraordinary dark purple claw sherd.

The site itself is both undocumented and apparently

atypical amongst contemporary glass-consumption sites in its relative lack of other status markers. It may be that West Heslerton belongs to a group of middle-ranking settlement sites with medium-sized glass assemblages, which is currently scarcely recognised in the archaeological record. Perhaps there was a degree of filtration in which glass imported by elite sites were exchanged or gifted outwards to the mid-level tier of settlements within their sphere of influence, which has hitherto not been noticed simply due to a lack of discovery and excavation in this category of settlement sites. This would certainly help to explain how some rare and high-quality glass vessels reached this site. The planned research to compare glass assemblages and the sites from which they came should yield more information in this area and enable more detailed conclusions on this and other sites and their relationships with each other to be made.

An interesting picture is emerging from this preliminary study. In the future, I intend to include West Heslerton in a comprehensive assessment of all significant groups of Anglo-Saxon glass from settlement contexts and their intra-site and landscape contexts, which will attempt to address key questions about the mechanisms of exchange governing glass vessels and whether vessel glass was the elite commodity it is perceived to have been, and why is vessel glass found on some sites and not others.

Acknowledgements

With thanks to Professor Dominic Powlesland and the staff of The Landscape Research Centre; Emeritus Professor Jennifer Price; and Professor Andrew Reynolds, Institute of Archaeology, UCL. A full report and catalogue of the glass will be published in due course as part of the West Heslerton site publication, currently a work in progress at the Landscape Research Centre.

Bibliography

Campbell, E. (2007) *Continental and Mediterranean Imports to Atlantic Britain and Ireland, AD 400–800*. Council for British Archaeology Research Report 157. York, Council for British Archaeology.

Evison, V. I. (1991) Vessel fragments. In L. Webster and J. Backhouse (eds.) *The making of England. Anglo-Saxon art and culture, AD 600–900*, 90–93, 143. Toronto, University of Toronto Press.

Evison, V. I. (2009) Glass vessels. In D. H. Evans and C. Loveluck (eds.) *Life and economy in Early Medieval Flixborough c. 600–1000. The artefact evidence*, 103–113. Oxford, Oxbow Books.

Evison, V. I. (forthcoming) Glass vessels. In A. Tester *et al.*, *The Middle-Saxon settlement at Staunch Meadow, Brandon*. Suffolk County Council Archaeological Service.

Hamerow, H. (ed.) (1993) *Excvavations at Mucking 2. The Anglo-Saxon settlement*. English Heritage Archaeological Report 21. London, British Museum Press.

Hunter, J. R. and Heyworth, M. P. (1998) *The Hamwic Glass*. Council for British Archaeology Research Report 116. York, Council for British Archaeology.

Stiff, M. (1996) *"Through a glass darkly". Seventh to ninth century vessel glass from 'wics' and 'emporia' in North Western Europe*. Unpublished thesis, University of Oxford.

Stiff, M. (2003) The glass finds. In G. B. Malcolm, *Middle Saxon London. Excavations at the Royal Opera House 1989–99*. Museum of London Archaeology Service Monograph Series 15, 241–250. London, Museum of London.

West, S. (1985) *West Stow. The Anglo-Saxon Village I. Text*. East Anglian Archaeology Report 24. Gressenhall, Norfolk Archaeological Unit/Norfolk Museums Service.

5

Glassworking at Whitby Abbey and Kirkdale Minster in North Yorkshire

Sarah Paynter, Sarah Jennings† and Jennifer Price

Introduction

This paper investigates, using chemical analyses, some unusual finds of Anglo-Saxon bichrome and polychrome glass rods from Whitby and Kirkdale in North Yorkshire, continuing work by the late Sarah Jennings and the late Professor Philip Rahtz.

The archaeological background

Whitby Abbey

The medieval ruins of Whitby Abbey occupy a prominent position on a spur of land, sometimes known as the Whitby Headland, to the east of the town of Whitby in North Yorkshire. The structure visible today dates from the early 13th century but overlies two earlier buildings. The first Abbey at Whitby was founded by King Oswey of Northumbria in AD 655 but was destroyed by the Danes in AD 867 and archaeological evidence suggests that the site was then largely abandoned until the monastery was re-established around AD 1078.

Sir Charles Peers investigated large areas to the north of the Abbey in the 1920s (Peers and Radford 1943). More recently, between 1993 and 2007, English Heritage archaeologists have undertaken a number of excavations on the Headland outside the monastic area (Hunter *et al.* 2005). The majority of these excavations were in response to the continuing rapid erosion of the cliff edge at Whitby. Excavations in 2002 and 2007 included a trench near the cliff edge and to the north east of the Abbey ruins. Although much had been destroyed by medieval ploughing, the surviving archaeological evidence showed that the Headland was occupied in the Anglian period (7th–9th centuries) as well as in the late Iron Age. Some prehistoric and medieval features survived in this area, cut into the natural clay.

Test trench U1 in 2002 and a larger trench U2 sited in the same area in 2007 revealed evidence for a large timber building, measuring 9.2m wide and at least 15m long. A mid 9th-century date has been proposed for this building based on its size and construction. Four equidistantly spaced large pits aligned down the centre, 4.5m from the side walls, were interpreted as the remains of large postholes, from the supports for the central ridge of the building. On abandonment, these pits were back-filled with soil containing debris from various high temperature industries including iron smithing, lead working and glassworking; evidence for domestic occupation was limited.

The glassworking evidence comprised seventeen very small fragments, all less than 25mm long, and all but one was recovered from the residue of samples processed by flotation and sieving (Paynter and Dungworth 2011, Case Study 1; Jennings 2005). The assemblage included angular chips, dribbles and rounded lumps of glass plus two fragments of *reticella* rods, one twisted anticlockwise in bluish green and two opaque white trails with tool marks at one end and the other twisted clockwise in blue glass with three opaque white trails (Fig. 5.1; Jennings 2005).

Kirkdale Minster

Excavations directed by the late Professor Philip Rahtz and Lorna Watts at St Gregory's Minster at Kirkdale in the 1990s (Rahtz and Watts 1997; 2003; Watts *et al.* 1997) produced evidence for a church, probably a small monastery founded in the 7th century, which, according to an inscription on the sundial stone in the south porch of the present church, was 'rebuilt from the ground' between AD 1055–1065. Trench II,

Fig. 5.1: Two twisted glass rods of blue glass with white trails from Whitby (top, SF 36097 and bottom, SF 36099). SF 36099 is just over 20mm long with tool marks at the thicker end.

Fig. 5.2: The small fragment of a twisted glass rod with opaque yellow and white trails, from Kirkdale, about 6mm long.

on the north side of the present churchyard wall, contained a layer of dark earth with evidence for craft-working, including charcoal, slag and other debris, a metal strip inscribed in Old English and a single glass fragment, a very small piece from a *reticella* rod (Rahtz and Watts 1997; 2003, 300–301; Watts *et al.* 1997, 51–52; Paynter 2009).

The glass fragment (KD Tr II AA) is 5.75mm long and 2.9mm in diameter, and is broken at both ends. It comes from a cylindrical rod of pale bluish-green/colourless glass with one opaque white trail and one opaque yellow trail applied to the outside surface, partly marvered and twisted clockwise, which has not been attached to a vessel or formed into an object (Fig. 5.2). It is a most unusual find which, like the metal strip inscribed in Old English, belongs to the 8th–9th century.

Polychrome and bichrome glass rods

Evidence for the production of polychrome and bichrome rods, and unused small fragments of rods, is rare in the British Isles at this period, and appears to be closely associated with monastic complexes. Dr Raleigh Radford's excavations in the monastic complex at Glastonbury, Somerset, found furnaces with evidence for glass working on site, and fragments of drawn trails and twisted rods, one in vivid greenish blue glass with opaque white unmarvered trails, were recorded in furnaces 1 and 4 and may have been made there (Evison 2000, 189–190, 195, cat. no. 54, fig. 1.16).

The formation of similar rods has also been noted at early Christian sites in Ireland, as at Dunmisk, Co. Tyrone, and unused rods, mostly in dark blue with twisted opaque white or opaque yellow unmarvered trails, are known from Armagh and Movilla Abbey, Co. Tyrone (Henderson 2000, 145, fig. 1.5, pl. 2). In addition, fragments of unused rods,

at least two in dark blue glass with twisted opaque white unmarvered trails, were found in association with a Saxon glass furnace excavated in 1990 at Barking Abbey, Essex (MacGowan 1996, 176, 178). The majority of these finds have dark ground colours and twisted trails of one colour, similar to the Whitby rods, but are rather different in details of production from the rod from Kirkdale, which is carefully made, with a very pale ground colour and partially marvered trails in two contrasting colours.

Apart from these pieces, the majority of the twisted rods known at this period occur as decoration on vessels. They have been widely recorded at both ecclesiastical and secular settlement sites in England. By far the largest assemblage was found at Hamwic, Hampshire (Hunter and Heyworth 1998), and a single fragment has been noted as far north as the monastic settlement at Whithorn, Wigtonshire in South-West Scotland (Hill 1997, 314–315, no. 83, fig. 10.12). They occur principally on three vessel forms, Valsgärde-type bowls with folded rims, fine horizontal trails and horizontal and vertical twisted rods applied to the convex body and base, Birka-type beakers with fine horizontal trails and vertical twisted rods applied to the convex lower body, and jars (see Baumgartner and Krueger 1988, 70–73, nos. 12–15; Hunter and Heyworth 1998, figs. 3d, 15 for examples), and also on the rims and bodies of straight-sided palm cups and funnel beakers (see Baumgartner and Krueger 1988, 74–76, nos. 18–23; Hunter and Heyworth 1998, figs. 4–8, 11, 13, 17 for examples). It is, however, often not possible to recognise the original vessel form from the surviving small fragments.

Fragments of the Valsgärde-type bowls have been noted at sites in Yorkshire, as at Whitby (Harden 1956, 152; Evison 2008, 49, no. 18, fig. 2), West Heslerton (Broadley this volume), and Fishergate, York (Hunter and Jackson 1993, 1334, nos. 4636–4639, fig. 644), and at least two of these bowls, plus two globular beakers and a footed beaker were recognised among the seven colourless, blue-green and vivid green-blue vessels decorated with bichrome rods at Flixborough, North Lincolnshire (Evison 2009, 105–107, fig. 2.1–2). Less diagnostic pieces have also been recorded in the region, as at the General Accident Site, York (unpublished).

Very occasionally, the twisted rods were fused to a glass backing to form small flat ornamental plaques. The only one known to the authors was found during excavations at Whitby Abbey in the 1920s (Jennings 2005, 207–208, fig. 1, colour pl. 53; Evison 2008, 49, no. 17, fig. 2, colour pl. 1). It is almost square (dimensions 11.0 × 10.5mm), with seven lengths of rod, yellow-brown with opaque white clockwise twisted trails or blue-green with opaque white anticlockwise twisted trails arranged alternately to produce a herringbone effect, and it may have been held in a metal or leather frame, perhaps as an inlay for a book cover or as a pendant or amulet. Another very similar rectangular object (dimensions 12.5 × 7.0mm) found in the same excavations, was formed from a fragment cut from the wall of a vessel with three bright blue rods with opaque white clockwise and opaque yellow anticlockwise twisted trails arranged to produce a herringbone effect, as seen on Valgärde-type bowls, and this may have had a secondary function similar to the square plaque (Jennings 2005, 207–208, fig. 1, colour pl. 53; Evison 2008, 49, no. 16, fig. 2, colour pl. 1).

Twisted rods sometimes decorated glass beads, and were also used as decorative elements in jewellery in the middle Anglo-Saxon period. Examples of disc beads with twisted rods and glass cabochon insets including short lengths of twisted rods have been studied recently by Evison in her discussion of the beads from Hornby, North Yorkshire and Sleaford, Lincolnshire and of the silver pendant cross from Gravesend, Kent (Evison 2008, 22–23, 25, 70–73, nos. 201–202, 217, map 8, figs. 33, 35, colour pl. 8).

Analytical background

The composition of Roman and medieval glass

Analytical studies (Brill 1999; Foster and Jackson 2009; Freestone 2005; Freestone *et al.* 2008; Sayre and Smith 1961) have established that the great majority of glass found in England from the late Iron Age, Roman and early medieval periods is natron glass. Natron glass is a soda-lime-silica type characterised by low levels of phosphorus, potassium and magnesium oxides. It was made using an evaporitic source of sodium compounds, commonly referred to as natron, combined with sand. In some cases this was beach sand, which contained calcium carbonate in the form of shell (Freestone 2005). In other instances the source of lime is likely to have been limestone.

Large quantities of natron glass were used in Britain during the Roman period for tableware and for windows. The vast majority of this was transparent in various shades of pale blue-green (also known as 'naturally coloured') through to colourless (Price and Cottam 1998, 14–16). Only a small number of distinct natron glass types, each with a subtly different composition and appearance, have been identified and this uniformity across the Roman world is consistent with a large scale production model where large quantities of glass were made at a small number of production sites. The distinctive compositional characteristics of the glass are due to the differences in the raw materials, namely the sand, at each site. There is also archaeological and analytical evidence that this type of model holds true for Byzantine glass (Freestone *et al.* 2002).

The raw glass types most relevant to the Anglo-Saxon period in England are HIMT glass, possibly produced in Egypt, and Levantine I glass, produced in the Syro-Palestinian region (see Foster and Jackson 2009 for a summary). Although some types of 1st to 3rd-century Roman glass contain antimony, Levantine I and HIMT glass are not thought to contain antimony at the point of production.

- HIMT glass has been described by Freestone *et al.* (2005) and is found from the 4th century onwards. It is a soda-rich glass containing around 19wt% sodium oxide (Fig. 5.3). The name given to this glass type derives from the often high iron, manganese and titanium levels in the glass. It also contains elevated levels of zirconium. A range of compositions from weak (referred to as HIMT 2) to strong (HIMT 1), with varying levels of these diagnostic elements, have been noted (for example by Foster and Jackson 2009; Foy *et al.* 2003). This glass often has a greenish or yellowish hue and is very common in later 4th-century assemblages in Britain.
- Levantine I glass has a much lower level of soda (roughly 15wt%) (Fig. 5.3), iron and titanium oxides but higher lime (8 to 10wt%) and alumina (about 3wt%) (Fig. 5.4) and it does not contain manganese. The Levantine I glass characterised by Freestone *et al.* (2000) was produced in the 6th and 7th centuries, but very similar glass with low soda and high lime but also containing manganese has been identified amongst Roman and 4th-century glass (Brill 1999; Foster and Jackson 2009; Foy *et al.* 2003; Silvestri *et al.* 2005) labelled 'Levantine Ia' or 'Group 3'. These glass types containing manganese are likely to be from the same area as Levantine I glass. This glass has a turquoise blue to greenish hue.

In contrast with the Roman period, glass is comparatively rare in Anglo-Saxon England. The recent comprehensive study by Evison (2008) includes a discussion of the composition of Anglo-Saxon glass by Freestone *et al.* (2008). In summary, a manganese-rich glass, similar to the HIMT type, dominated assemblages in England from the mid 4th century onwards (Foster and Jackson 2009), but this supply appears to have been interrupted at some time in the mid 6th century. It was replaced by glass with a low

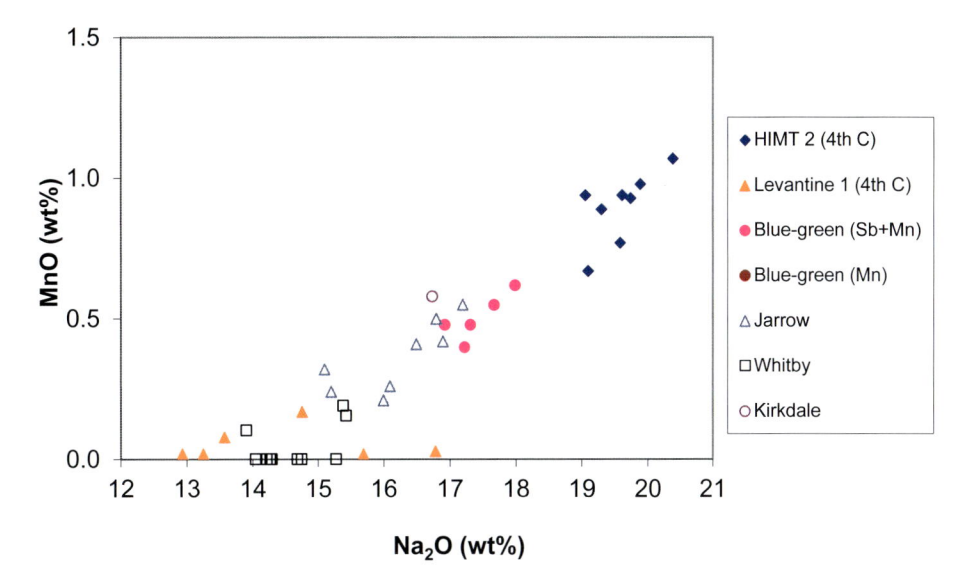

Fig. 5.3: Plot of sodium oxide and manganese oxide showing 4th-century HIMT 2 glass, two types of Roman blue-green glass (one containing manganese and one with manganese plus antimony) and Levantine I glass (data from Jackson 1994; Foster and Jackson 2009) plus the Anglian glass from Whitby and Kirkdale (average composition for each sample in this study except the opaque trails) and Jarrow (Freestone and Hughes 2006). The Whitby glass contains low levels of sodium oxide and manganese oxide, most consistent with Levantine I glass.

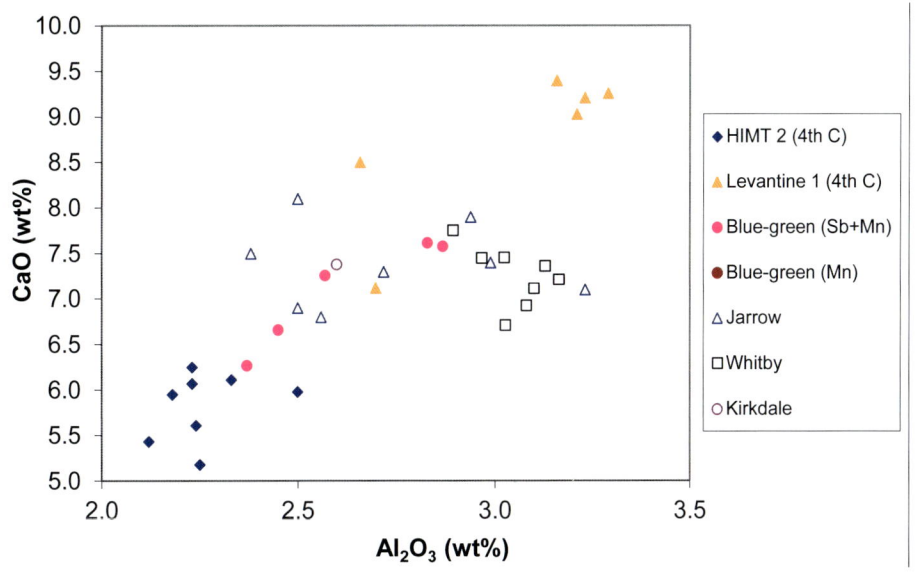

Fig. 5.4: Plot of calcium oxide and aluminium oxide showing 4th-century HIMT 2, two types of Roman blue-green glass and Levantine I glass (data from Jackson 1994; Foster and Jackson 2009) plus the Anglian glass from Whitby and Kirkdale (average composition for each sample in this study except the opaque trails) and Jarrow (Freestone and Hughes 2006). The Whitby glass contains slightly less lime than typical for Levantine I glass but similarly high alumina contents.

manganese content but the dwindling stock of glass had to be extended using a plant ash based vitreous material (Freestone *et al.* 2008). Pale, nearly colourless glass was rare at this time, but reappeared in the late Anglo-Saxon period suggesting that more raw or decolourised glass was finding its way into the country. Some of this glass contains a significant amount of antimony-rich recycled Roman material (Brill 2006). However much of it, including the majority of the analysed glass from Jarrow (7th century) and Hamwic (8th–9th centuries), contained very little antimony and low amounts (around 0.5wt%) of manganese. This glass is compositionally most similar to the 'Levantine Ia' blue-

Fig. 5.5: Small fragments of blue (bottom, SF 36098) and amber (top, SF 36033) glassworking waste from Whitby. The amber fragment is about 20mm long.

green glass of the Roman period, which generally contains manganese, and Byzantine 'Levantine I' glass, both thought to originate in the eastern Mediterranean.

Methods of analysis

From Whitby, the samples analysed comprised olive, amber and blue glassworking waste (Fig. 5.5), chips of red and pale greenish/colourless glass, and two *reticella* glass rods (Table 5.1). One of these was made from white and blue glass twisted anticlockwise with tool marks at one end and the other had a blue glass core with three opaque white trails twisted clockwise (Fig. 5.1). The pale bluish-green/colourless rod fragment with yellow and white trails from St Gregory's Minster, Kirkdale, North Yorkshire, was also analysed (Fig. 5.2; Paynter 2009).

In each case a small sample of glass, a few millimetres in size, was removed, mounted in epoxy resin and polished to a 0.25 micron finish. High magnification images of the glass microstructure were obtained with an FEI scanning electron microscope using back-scattered electron imaging, which shows areas with different compositions as different shades on a greyscale. At the same time, areas of the sample were analysed using an attached energy dispersive spectrometer (EDS) with Oxford ISIS software and a beam voltage of 25kV. The spectrometer was calibrated with cobalt and the accuracy and precision checked by analysing standards of known composition, including Corning Standard A (Brill 1999).

Results

There are a lot of published compositional data for glass contemporary with the Whitby and Kirkdale material. Some comes from primary production sites but other assemblages are from secondary production sites or consumption sites where the glass may have been altered intentionally or accidentally, for example by the addition of colourants, decolourisers or recycled cullet (Hunter and Heyworth 1998; Silvestri *et al*. 2005; Wolf *et al*. 2005). These data have also been collected using a range of analytical methods, so comparison is not always straightforward.

Although glass was being produced on a large scale in the eastern Mediterranean in late antiquity and the early Islamic period, the rarity of glass vessels and windows in England at this time, as well as evidence for extending and recycling glass (Freestone *et al*. 2008) all indicate that raw glass was in short supply in this country. With extensive recycling, a variable degree of mixing and blurring between glass compositions in different assemblages occurs, resulting in compositional data that are difficult to interpret. By contrast, cleaner, less reworked glass will have compositions closer to the raw glass and be more easily identifiable.

The results show that all of the samples from Whitby and the rod from Kirkdale were made of natron glass (Table 5.1), typical of the great majority of glass found in Britain in the late Iron Age, Roman and Anglo-Saxon periods (Freestone *et al*. 2008; Sanderson *et al*. 1998). The glass has been grouped by colour and form for the discussion below.

The glassworking waste from Whitby

Colourless, red and amber glass

The pale greenish/colourless (36054), red (36095) and amber (36033) glass fragments from Whitby stand out because they do not contain any detectable manganese (Fig. 5.3) and red fragment (36056) contains only low levels (0.15wt%). This is most similar to the Levantine I type glass, characteristic of eastern Mediterranean production in the 6th to 7th centuries, as are the high levels of alumina (~3wt%) and fairly low soda (14 to 15wt%), although the lime content is slightly lower than typical (~7wt% as opposed to 8-10wt%) (Fig. 5.4). These Whitby glass fragments are compositionally similar to some 5th or 6th-century yellow-green and amber glass from Sion, Switzerland (Wolf *et al*. 2005) and some approximately 7th-century pale blue windows from Jarrow, Tyne and Wear (Freestone and Hughes 2006).

The Whitby glass also included a rounded lump of greenish/colourless glass with green and red streaks (not analysed) and several small fragments of red glass. Red streaked window and vessel fragments are often found in Anglo-Saxon assemblages. For example, there was a considerable amount of pale green or turquoise window glass with red streaks amongst the assemblage from Monkwearmouth and Jarrow (Cramp 2006) and similar vessel fragments from Hamwic (Hunter and Heyworth 1998).

Table 5.1: The context, small find numbers and SEM-EDS normalised compositional data (wt% oxide except for chlorine) for the analysed fragments of glass from Whitby and Kirkdale. Detection limits 0.1wt% except for SO_3 and P_2O_5 (0.2wt%) and SnO_2 and Sb_2O_5 (0.3wt%), bd = below detection limit. P_2O_5 was sought but not present above detectable limits.

Context	SF No.	Description	Area	Na₂O	MgO	Al₂O₃	SiO₂	SO₃	Cl	K₂O	CaO	TiO₂	MnO	FeO	CuO	ZnO	SnO₂	Sb₂O₅	PbO
Whitby 35125	36056	Blue fragment	Bulk	13.88	0.55	3.02	69.88	bd	0.70	1.08	6.94	bd	bd	1.34	1.63	bd	bd	bd	0.12
			Bulk	13.23	0.53	2.96	69.52	0.25	0.93	2.23	6.78	bd	bd	0.85	1.38	0.12	0.42	bd	0.28
			Bulk	13.26	0.60	3.05	69.21	bd	0.51	2.13	7.03	bd	bd	1.22	1.67	bd	0.34	bd	0.15
			Bulk	13.80	0.60	3.05	69.90	bd	0.53	1.22	6.96	bd	bd	1.26	1.63	bd	bd	bd	0.14
Whitby 35125	36056	Red fragment	Bulk	14.94	0.71	3.04	68.89	bd	0.87	0.89	7.02	bd	0.15	0.90	0.26	bd	0.39	bd	1.18
			Bulk	15.06	0.67	2.91	68.62	bd	0.94	0.86	6.93	bd	0.17	0.89	0.33	bd	0.52	bd	1.26
			Bulk	15.09	0.71	3.03	68.57	bd	0.88	0.86	6.97	0.14	0.13	0.83	0.29	bd	0.45	0.39	1.11
Whitby 35016	36099	Blue core of rod	Bulk	14.27	0.53	3.12	69.71	bd	0.97	1.02	6.97	0.11	bd	1.23	1.23	bd	bd	bd	bd
			Bulk	14.27	0.64	3.10	70.02	bd	0.90	0.98	7.12	0.10	bd	1.15	1.06	bd	bd	bd	bd
			Bulk	14.34	0.53	3.10	70.69	bd	0.94	1.01	7.13	bd	bd	0.92	0.93	bd	bd	bd	bd
Whitby 35016	36099	White trail on rod	Bulk	13.46	0.54	2.80	65.04	bd	0.95	0.60	6.54	bd	bd	0.40	0.00	bd	5.40	bd	3.95
			Bulk	13.51	0.51	2.93	65.78	bd	0.97	0.62	6.75	0.13	bd	0.70	0.04	bd	4.52	0.37	2.75
			Bulk	13.57	0.50	2.87	67.02	bd	0.97	0.59	6.94	0.11	bd	0.37	0.03	bd	2.91	bd	3.44
Whitby 35034	36097	Blue core of rod	Bulk	14.85	0.56	2.83	67.94	bd	1.04	0.68	7.08	bd	bd	0.55	3.85	bd	0.32	bd	0.35
			Bulk	14.83	0.53	2.83	68.73	bd	0.98	0.69	7.06	bd	bd	0.47	3.19	bd	bd	bd	0.44
			Bulk	14.79	0.46	2.96	69.57	bd	1.03	0.65	7.11	bd	bd	0.48	2.79	bd	bd	bd	0.28
Whitby 35034	36097	White trail on rod	Bulk	14.53	0.69	2.83	66.77	bd	0.93	0.84	7.30	bd	0.21	0.62	0.16	bd	3.88	bd	0.84
			Bulk	14.67	0.62	2.67	66.50	0.26	0.86	0.80	7.41	0.18	0.15	0.56	0.16	bd	4.20	bd	0.64
Whitby 35125	36098	Blue fragment 1	Bulk	8.07	0.68	2.85	67.55	bd	0.85	10.70	6.56	0.10	bd	0.61	0.87	bd	0.41	bd	0.19
			Bulk	9.30	0.63	2.94	67.80	bd	0.53	9.25	7.30	0.11	bd	0.54	0.22	bd	0.37	bd	0.13
			Bulk	5.38	0.52	2.96	66.58	bd	0.92	14.40	6.41	bd	bd	0.54	0.69	bd	0.58	bd	0.30
Whitby 35125	36098	Blue fragment 2	Bulk	13.95	0.65	2.85	70.49	bd	0.93	0.84	7.29	0.10	bd	0.79	1.36	bd	bd	bd	bd
			Bulk	13.88	0.59	2.85	70.28	0.20	0.93	1.08	7.27	bd	bd	0.82	1.37	bd	bd	bd	bd
			Bulk	13.88	0.58	2.97	69.86	bd	0.96	0.86	7.23	bd	bd	1.00	1.45	bd	bd	bd	0.13
			Bulk	13.16	0.53	2.92	69.81	bd	0.94	1.84	7.30	bd	bd	0.88	1.29	bd	0.30	bd	0.13
Whitby 35211	36054	Colourless fragment	Bulk	15.16	0.56	3.03	71.90	bd	1.05	0.64	6.68	0.10	bd	0.36	0.00	bd	bd	bd	bd
			Bulk	15.26	0.51	3.01	71.79	bd	1.06	0.66	6.67	bd	bd	0.34	0.00	0.13	bd	bd	bd
			Bulk	15.15	0.47	2.99	72.07	bd	1.06	0.69	6.66	bd	bd	0.33	0.00	bd	bd	bd	bd
Whitby 35246	36033	Amber working waste	Bulk	14.67	0.58	2.99	72.18	bd	0.96	0.64	6.90	bd	bd	0.45	0.00	bd	bd	bd	bd
			Bulk	14.61	0.53	3.11	72.18	bd	0.97	0.63	6.83	bd	bd	0.40	0.05	bd	bd	0.29	bd
			Bulk	14.45	0.54	3.08	72.27	bd	0.99	0.59	6.89	bd	bd	0.44	0.00	bd	bd	bd	0.16
Whitby 35085	36095	Red fragment	Bulk	14.40	0.53	3.13	72.27	bd	0.92	0.87	6.53	bd	bd	0.67	0.54	0.13	bd	bd	0.16
			Bulk	14.29	0.54	3.11	72.16	bd	0.98	0.93	6.55	bd	bd	0.60	0.84	bd	bd	bd	0.35
			Bulk	13.74	0.55	3.24	71.62	bd	1.00	0.94	6.45	bd	bd	0.84	0.95	0.13	0.35	bd	0.65
Kirkdale		Yellow trail on rod	Dark matrix	10.03	0.61	2.46	45.82	bd	0.60	0.90	4.35	0.18	0.31	0.81	0.22	0.12	0.95	bd	32.64
			Bulk	9.92	0.62	2.41	43.09	bd	0.54	0.79	4.16	0.14	0.30	0.87	0.22	bd	2.23	bd	34.71
Kirkdale		Colourless core of rod	Bulk	16.79	0.86	2.64	68.58	0.25	0.84	1.03	7.35	0.12	0.62	0.83	bd	bd	bd	bd	0.24
			Bulk	16.64	0.80	2.60	68.54	0.29	0.97	0.96	7.41	0.14	0.55	0.75	bd	bd	bd	bd	0.25
			Bulk	16.69	0.85	2.56	68.40	0.27	0.95	0.97	7.34	0.16	0.58	0.83	bd	bd	bd	bd	0.24
Kirkdale		White trail on rod	Bulk	15.23	0.96	2.39	67.92	0.44	1.12	0.58	6.78	bd	0.43	0.87	bd	bd	1.69	bd	1.23

One of the red fragments from Whitby (SF 36095) contained a large metallic inclusion (Fig. 5.6), which was predominantly copper with some metallic lead and tin oxide. There were also greenish/colourless areas and red regions; copper sulphide droplets, also containing some lead, were present in the red areas but the red colour was due to very fine dendrites of cuprite throughout the glass. Elevated copper was also present in the red streaked glass from Jarrow, often with elevated levels of tin and lead (Brill 1999).

The composition of the streaked red glass from Whitby and other sites, such as Jarrow, is different from those of contemporary red enamels. The red streaked glass is made from a typical natron glass to which a copper-rich colourant was added. The presence of a metallic copper-, lead- and tin-rich inclusion in one of the Whitby samples supports the suggestion of previous authors that the colourant may have been derived from bronze (Brill 2006). The heterogeneity, partial oxidation and dissolution of the colourant appear to be intentional in order to obtain the streaky marbled effect. In contrast, published analyses of Anglo-Saxon enamels show that these tend to be very lead-rich, with in excess of 40wt% lead oxide, and are probably metalworking slag. Roman opaque red glass varied compositionally but was produced by adding a copper and lead-rich colourant to a natron glass base (Stapleton *et al.* 1999). In this sense the Anglo-Saxon red glass owes more to Roman glass technology than to contemporary enamelling although the colourant levels are very much lower; less than 1wt% each of copper and lead oxide were detected in the Whitby glass. Enamels were intended to be opaque so that their appearance was not affected by the substrate beneath, whereas the marbled glass was used for windows as well as vessels, where transparency was necessary to show the decorative pattern and colour.

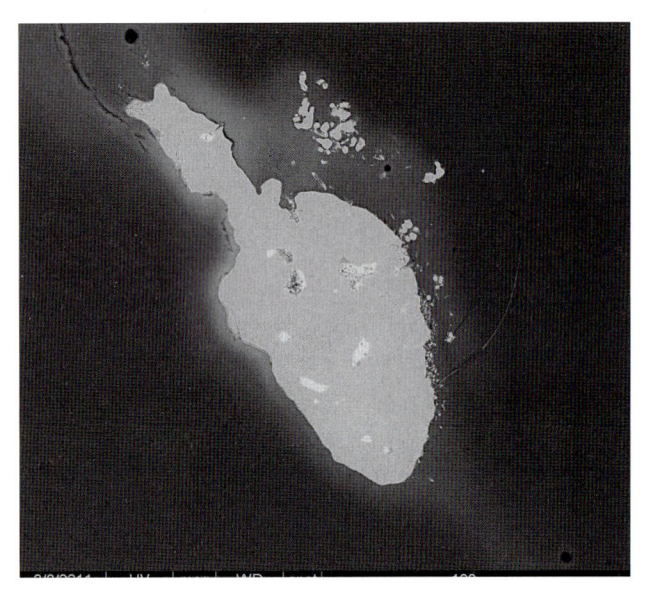

Fig. 5.6: Back-scattered electron SEM image of a metallic inclusion in the red Whitby glass (SF 36095). The inclusion is metallic copper (light grey) with some metallic lead and tin oxide (white) in a surrounding natron glass (dark grey).

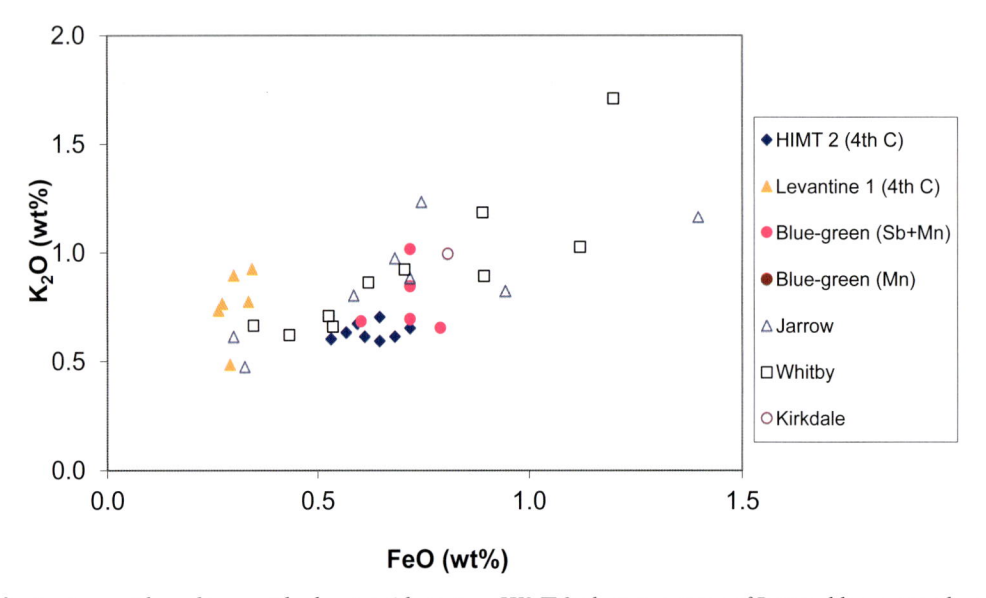

Fig. 5.7: Plot of potassium oxide and iron oxide showing 4th-century HIMT 2 glass, two types of Roman blue-green glass (one containing manganese and the other containing both manganese and antimony) and Levantine I glass (data from Jackson 1994; Foster and Jackson 2009) plus the Anglian glass from Whitby and Kirkdale (average composition for each sample in this study except the opaque trails) and Jarrow (Freestone and Hughes 2006) (Paynter 2009). The Whitby glass and some of the Jarrow glass, particularly blue colours, contain elevated levels of potassium and iron oxides.

Blue glass

The potassium content in the blue glass from Whitby was variable and reached high levels (14wt%) in some of the working waste. Sometimes high potassium levels indicate that plant ashes have been added to the glass. Some glass with a significant plant ash component is known to have been made at this time, particularly for deep blue colours (Wolf *et al.* 2005; Hunter and Heyworth 1998); however, this results in diagnostically increased levels of magnesium, aluminium and phosphorus in the glass (Freestone *et al.* 2008). The Whitby fragments do not share these characteristics despite containing significantly higher levels of potassium.

It is more likely that the composition of the Whitby glass has been altered by potassium-rich waste gases from the wood fuel used to fire the glassworking furnace. This effect has been noticed previously in archaeological and experimental glassworking waste from wood-fired glass furnaces (Paynter 2008) and from many other industries where wood fuel was used. The wood burns to produce ash and, although the composition of wood ash is very variable, compounds of calcium, potassium and magnesium generally make up a large proportion of it. These compounds undergo transformations and reactions in the heat of the fire. Potassium carbonate decomposes to form volatile potassium oxide, which is carried through the furnace where it comes into contact with the surfaces of the structures, crucibles and the glass itself. As a result, glassworking waste is often enriched in potassium and sometimes also alumina and iron, derived from ceramic pots or furnace structures; additional iron oxide may be introduced as iron oxide scale from blowing irons. Enrichment of these elements is more likely to be encountered in glass that has been repeatedly recycled.

Alternatively, since bluish green copper oxide coloured glass from other sites of this period, such as Hamwic, England (Hunter and Heyworth 1998) and Sion, Switzerland (Wolf *et al.* 2005) also tend to have raised levels of potassium and iron oxides (Fig. 5.7), then another possibility is that these compositional traits derive from how blue glass was being coloured at this time. For example did the copper-rich colorant also contain potassium and iron compounds? The melting and recycling of glass during this period may have been centralised in few places resulting in a fairly standardised product, particularly for certain colours.

The *reticella* rods from Whitby and Kirkdale

The blue glass in one of the *reticella* rods from Whitby (SF 36097) contains more copper oxide than the rest of the blue glass in the assemblage and does not have the elevated levels of potassium and iron described above and so this rod may have been brought to Whitby preformed. The other *reticella* rod (SF 36099) is more crudely made and has tool marks at one end. The blue glass in this rod matches the working waste from the site, so it is very likely to have been formed at Whitby.

The very pale bluish-green-colourless glass in the Kirkdale rod is slightly different again, containing more manganese, titanium and sodium oxides but less alumina than the Whitby glass (Table 5.1). This is a similar glass composition to the broadly contemporary glass from Jarrow and Hamwic, England, and Sion, Switzerland, which contain small amounts of manganese (around 0.25–0.5wt%) and antimony (0.3wt%), as well as lead (0.5wt%) and copper (up to several wt%) (Freestone and Hughes 2006; Hunter and Heyworth 1998; Wolf *et al.* 2005). These elements may have been introduced accidentally, for example through recycling, or intentionally, to modify the glass colour. The levels of major oxides, such as soda, lime and alumina (Figs. 5.3–5.4) are comparable to types of Roman blue-green glass (Paynter 2010). As explained above, blue-green glass was extremely common in the Roman world, when it was used to produce tablewares, bottles, jars and windows, and this old glass is likely to have been a resource for glassworkers in the Anglo-Saxon period. In particular, significant recycling may have occurred in the mid Anglo-Saxon period, when new glass appears to have been difficult to obtain. So the core of this rod may be made from recycled Roman material, though the applied trails contain opacifiers typical of the Anglo-Saxon period and whether the rod was shaped at Kirkdale or elsewhere is unknown. Alternatively, a similar composition to the glass core might result from mixing glass types, for example Levantine I and HIMT 2.

The compositional data for the opaque white trails on the glass rods from Whitby and Kirkdale show that this glass was produced by adding a mixture of lead and tin oxides to a natron glass. The lead oxide dissolved but the tin oxide (SnO_2) remained as small particles throughout the glass, scattering light and rendering the glass opaque white. The white glass contained slightly higher levels of tin oxide than lead oxide.

The rod from Kirkdale also had an opaque yellow trail, which was again produced by adding a mixture of lead and tin oxides to a natron glass but with considerably more lead oxide (around 30wt%) than tin oxide (around 2wt%). Whilst some lead oxide had dissolved, crystals of lead stannate ($PbSnO_3$) persisted throughout the glass rendering it opaque yellow.

The types of opacifier used in glass have varied chronologically and regionally. Calcium antimonate was used from a very early date, for example in Egypt and Mesopotamia, to make white glass, and continued to be used in Roman glass. In contrast, tin compounds were used to opacify glass in some areas of northern Europe around the 2nd to 1st century BC (Tite *et al.* 2008) but their use did not become widespread until later, from about the 4th century. Tin oxide was used for white and lead stannate for yellow. It is, however, not uncommon for white glass, opacified

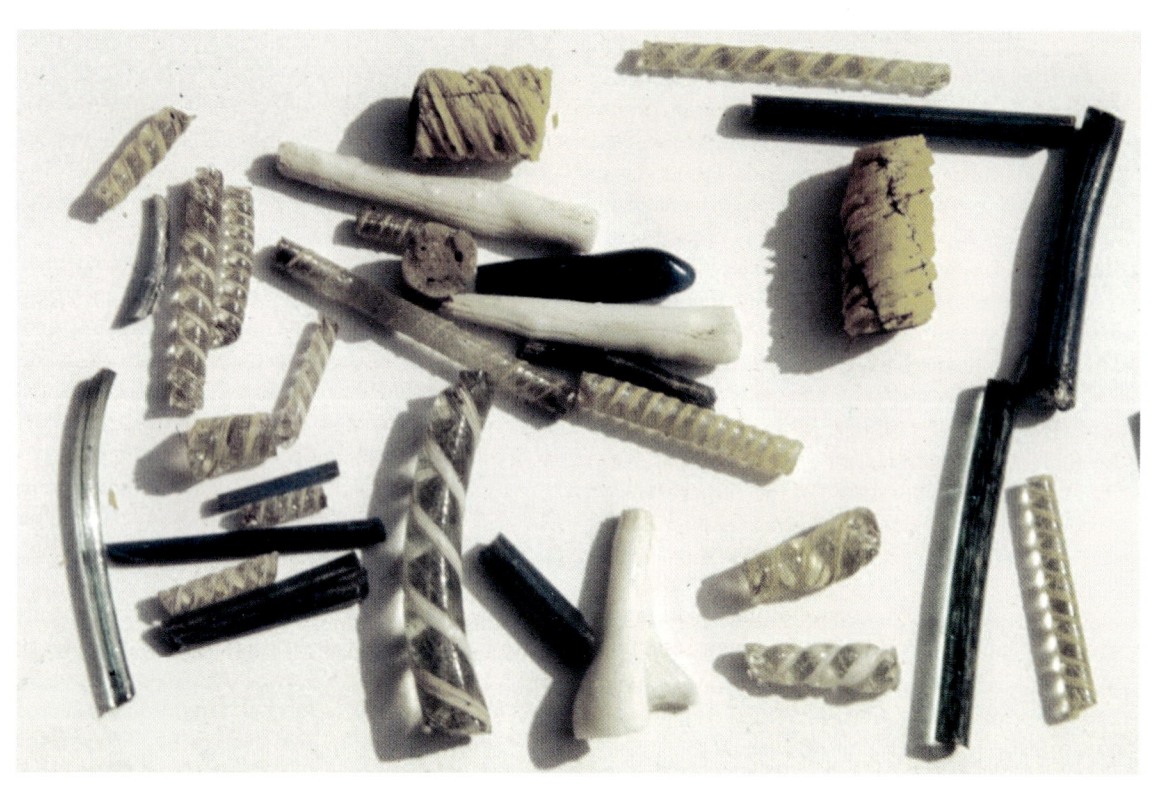

Fig. 5.8: A selection of twisted glass rods, many with opaque trails, from the 9th-century glassworking assemblage from San Vincenzo, Italy; the shortest are approximately 10mm long.

with tin oxide, also to contain a substantial amount of lead oxide as well, but in solution in the glass rather than as part of the opacifying crystals.

The coloured trails in the *reticella* decoration of the contemporary Hamwic glass were nearly always opaque yellow or white and Henderson (1998) confirmed that the opacifiers were similarly tin oxide for the white glass and lead stannate for the yellow. As with the Whitby and Kirkdale material, some lead oxide was detected in the white Hamwic glass but the ratios of lead oxide to tin oxide were considerably higher in the yellow glass. This type of glass decoration is common for the 8th to 9th centuries and the distribution is discussed in more detail by Hunter and Heyworth (1998, 37–38).

Conclusions

The small assemblage of glass from the recent excavations at Whitby demonstrates that glass was being worked in the Anglian settlement near to the Abbey. The glass is typologically and compositionally consistent with that in other glass assemblages of the 7th to 9th centuries. Fragments of window and vessel glass were found, and the assemblage includes small amounts of turquoise blue, amber and red streaked glassworking waste, plus two bichrome *reticella* rods, one of which was probably made at the site, but there was no evidence of glass blowing amongst the waste. The highly unusual small decorative glass plaque with *reticella* decoration from earlier excavations may have been made on the site, and the similar piece cut from a vessel could also have been reworked there.

The glass from Whitby is notable for its very low manganese content, which is consistent with Levantine glass types. Some of the Whitby glass, for example the amber and greenish/colourless fragments and the blue core of one of the *reticella* rods, contained very little lead suggesting that it had not been heavily recycled.

The blue glass from Whitby was compositionally similar to contemporary glass from other sites, mainly in blue or green colours, which raises the possibility that the production of particular glass colours during this period was reasonably standardised and perhaps took place in fairly few places on a Europe-wide basis.

The glass from the Anglo-Saxon Minster at Kirkdale is slightly different and is more likely to be made from recycled Roman pale batch of blue-green glass. It is a very small piece from a carefully formed rod of a type applied to vessels in England and elsewhere in northwestern Europe and also further afield, as at the monastery of San

Vincenzo in southern Italy, where many closely comparable rod fragments (Fig. 5.8) have been recorded in association with production of glass vessels, lamps and windows at the monastery in the early-mid 9th century (Dell'Acqua 1997, 34–35; Rahtz and Watts 2003, 300–301). The piece came from a deposit with debris from other craft production at Kirkdale, but no other glass was found, so it is not known whether the rod itself, or vessels or objects decorated with such rods, were produced at the Minster.

The quantity of glass from the two monastic sites in North Yorkshire is very small. At Whitby, the material was recovered from soil samples taken during the excavations, and at Kirkdale only one tiny piece was found. Nevertheless, the Whitby evidence shows that some glassworking took place there and the fragments from both sites were large enough for their compositions to be analysed, using modern scientific techniques. Recycling was common practice at all periods, and particularly in England in much of the later first millennium, so archaeological evidence of glassworking is often sparse and difficult to detect but thorough sampling strategies provide a means of addressing this problem.

Bibliography

Baumgartner, E. and Krueger, I. (1988) *Phönix aus Sand und Asche. Glas des Mittelalters*. Munich, Klinkhardt und Biermann.

Brill, R. H. (1999) *Chemical analyses of Early Glasses*. Corning, NY, The Corning Museum of Glass.

Brill, R. H. (2006) Chemical analyses of some glasses from Jarrow and Wearmouth. In R. Cramp, *Wearmouth and Jarrow Monastic Sites 2*, 126–142. Swindon, English Heritage.

Cramp, R. (2006) *Wearmouth and Jarrow Monastic Sites 2*. Swindon, English Heritage.

Dell'Acqua, F. (1997) Ninth-century window glass from the monastery of San Vincenzo al Volturno (Molise, Italy). *Journal of Glass Studies* 39, 33–41.

Evison, V. (2000) The glass fragments from Glastonbury. In J. Price (ed.) *Glass in Britain and Ireland, AD 350–1100*. British Museum Occasional Paper 127, 189–199. London, British Museum Press.

Evison, V. I. (2008) *Catalogue of Anglo-Saxon Glass in the British Museum*. British Museum Research Publication 167. London, British Museum Press.

Evison, V. I. (2009) Glass vessels. In D. H. Evans and C. Loveluck (eds.) *Life and Economy at Early Medieval Flixborough, c. AD 600–1000. The artefact evidence*, 103–113. Oxford, Oxbow Books.

Foster, H. E. and Jackson, C. M. (2009) The composition of 'naturally coloured' late Roman vessel glass from Britain and the implications of models of glass production and supply. *Journal of Archaeological Science* 36, 189–204.

Foy, D., Picon, M., Vichy, M. and Thirion-Merle, V. (2003) Caractérisation des verres de la fin de l'Antiquité en Méditerranée occidentale: l'émergence de nouveax courants commerciaux. In D. Foy and M.-D. Nenna (eds.) *Échanges et commerce du verre dans le monde antique*. Monographies Instrumentum 24, 41–85. Montagnac, Monique Mergoil.

Freestone, I. C. (2005) The provenance of ancient glass through compositional analysis. In P. B. Vandiver, J. L. Mass and A. Murray (eds.) *Materials Issues in Art and Archaeology VII*, 195–208. Warrendale, PA, Materials Research Society.

Freestone, I. C., Gorin-Rosen, Y. and Hughes, M. J. (2000) Primary glass from Israel and the production of glass in late antiquity and the early islamic period. In M.-D. Nenna (ed.) *La route du verre. Ateliers primaires et secondaires de verriers du second millénaire av. J.-C. au Moyen-Age*. Travaux de la Maison de l'Orient Méditérranéen 33, 65–83. Lyon, Maison de l'Orient Méditérranéen.

Freestone, I. C. and Hughes, M. J. (2006) Origins of the Jarrow glass. In R. Cramp, *Wearmouth and Jarrow Monastic Sites 2*, 147–155. Swindon, English Heritage.

Freestone, I. C., Hughes, M. J. and Stapleton, C. P. (2008) The composition and production of Anglo-Saxon glass. In V. I. Evison, *Catalogue of Anglo-Saxon Glass in the British Museum*. British Museum Research Publication 167, 29–46. London, British Museum Press.

Freestone, I. C., Ponting, M. and Hughes, M. J. (2002) The origins of Byzantine glass from Maroni Petrera, Cyprus. *Archaeometry* 44, 257–272.

Freestone, I. C., Wolf, S. and Thirlwall, M. (2005) The production of HIMT glass: elemental and isotopic evidence. In *Annales du 16e Congrès de l'Association Internationle pour l'Histoire du Verre*, 153–157. Nottingham, Association Internationale pour l'Histoire du Verre.

Harden, D. B. (1956) Glass vessels in Britain, AD 400–1000. In D. B. Harden (ed.) *Dark Age Britain*, 132–167. London, Methuen.

Henderson, J. (1998) Appendix Three. Electron microprobe analysis of the Hamwic glass. In J. R. Hunter and M. P. Heyworth, *The Hamwic Glass*. Council for British Archaeology Research Report 116, 97. York, Council for British Archaeology.

Henderson, J. (2000) The production technology of Irish early Christian glass with specific reference to beads and enamels. In J. Price (ed.) *Glass in Britain and Ireland, AD 350–1100*. British Museum Occasional Paper 127, 143–159. London, British Museum Press.

Hill, P. (1997) *Whithorn and St Ninian. The excavation of a monastic town, 1984–1991*. Stroud, Sutton Publishing.

Hunter, D., Baker, P., Campbell, G., Daulby, M., Graham, K., Jennings, S. and Paynter, S. (2005) *Whitby Abbey Headland Project Heritage Lottery Funded Work 1998–2004*. Centre for Archaeology Report 1/2005. Swindon, English Heritage.

Hunter, J. R. and Heyworth, M. P. (1998) *The Hamwic Glass*. Council for British Archaeology Research Report 116. York, Council for British Archaeology.

Hunter, J. R. and Jackson, C. M. (1993) Glass. In N. S. H. Rogers, *Anglian and other finds from 46–54 Fishergate*. The Archaeology of York 17.9, 1331–1344, 1452–1458. York, Archaeological Trust.

Jackson, C. M. (1994) Tables A1 and A2. In M. J. Baxter, *Exploratory multivariate analysis in archaeology*, 228–231. Edinburgh, Edinburgh University Press.

Jennings, S. (2005) Anglian glass from recent and previous excavations in the area of Whitby Abbey, North Yorkshire. In *Annales du 16e Congrès de l'Association Internationale pour l'Histoire du Verre*, 207–209. Nottingham, Association Internationale pour l'Histoire du Verre.

MacGowan, K. (1996) Barking Abbey. *Current Archaeology* 13.5 (no. 149), 172–178.

Paynter, S. (2008) Experiments in the reconstruction of Roman wood-fired glassworking furnaces: waste products and their formation processes. *Journal of Glass Studies* 50, 271–290.

Paynter, S. (2009) *St Gregory's Minster, Kirkdale, North Yorkshire. Analysis of a glass rod.* Research Department Report Series 18–2009. Swindon, English Heritage.

Paynter, S. (2010) Analyses of colourless Roman glass. In I. Ferris (ed.) *The Beautiful Rooms are Empty. Excavations at Binchester Roman Fort, County Durham 1976–1981 and 1986–1991*, 333–338. Durham, Durham County Council.

Paynter, S. and Dungworth, D. (2011) *Archaeological Evidence for Glassworking. Guidelines for best Practice.* Swindon, English Heritage.

Peers, Ch. and Radford, C. A. R. (1943) The Saxon monastery of Whitby. *Archaeologia* 89, 27–88.

Price, J. and Cottam, S (1998) *Romano-British Glass Vessels. A handbook.* Practical Handbook in Archaeology 14. York, Council for British Archaeology.

Rahtz, P. A. and Watts, L. (1997) Kirkdale Anglo-Saxon Minster. *Current Archaeology* 13.11 (no. 155), 419–422.

Rahtz, P. A. and Watts, L. (2003) Three ages of conversion at Kirkdale, North Yorkshire. In M. Carver (ed.) *The Cross goes North. Processes of conversion in northern Europe, AD 300–1300*, 289–309. Woodbridge, York Medieval Press.

Sanderson, D. C. W., Hunter, J. R., Warren, S. E. and Heyworth, M. P. (1998) Appendix two. Scientific analysis of the Hamwic glass. In J. R. Hunter and M. P. Heyworth, *The Hamwic Glass.* Council for British Archaeology Research Report 116, 71–96. York, Council for British Archaeology.

Sayre, E. V. and Smith, R. W. (1961) Compositional categories of ancient glass. *Science* 133, 1824–1826.

Silvestri, A., Molin, G. and Salviuolo, G. (2005) Roman and medieval glass from the Italian area: bulk charcaterization and relationships with production technologies. *Archaeometry* 47, 797–816.

Stapleton, C. P., Freestone, I. C. and Bowman, S. G. E. (1999) Composition and origin of early medieval opaque red enamel from Britain and Ireland. *Journal of Archaeological Science* 26, 913–921.

Tite, M., Pradell, T. and Shortland, A. (2008) Discovery, production and use of tin-based opacifiers in ancient glass, enamels and glazes: a reassessment. *Archaeometry* 50, 67–84.

Watts, L., Rahtz, P., Okasha, E., Bradley, S. A. J. and Higgitt, J. (1997) Kirkdale – the inscriptions. *Medieval Archaeology* 41, 51–99.

Wolf, S., Kessler, C. M., Stern, W. B. and Gerber, Y. (2005) Coloured window glass from Sion (Valais, Switzerland). *Archaeometry* 47, 361–380.

6

Glass workshops in northern Gaul and the Rhineland in the first millennium AD as hints of a changing land use – including some results of the chemical analyses of glass from Mayen

Martin Grünewald and Sonngard Hartmann

Introduction

This paper is a result of two areas of research carried out in the *Römisch-Germanisches Zentralmuseum* (RGZM), the *Forschungsbereich Vulkanologie, Archäologie und Technikgeschichte* in Mayen (VAT) and the *Kompetenzzentrum für Archäometrie* in Mainz (archaeometry). Through mapping the distribution of glass workshops in northern Gaul and the Rhineland in the first millennium AD, some links with the changes in land use can be established (cf. project of the *Deutsche Forschungsgemeinschaft "Zur Landnutzung im Umfeld eines römischen 'Industrierevieres'"*, FI 805/6-1). A large number of glass vessels found in late antique graves

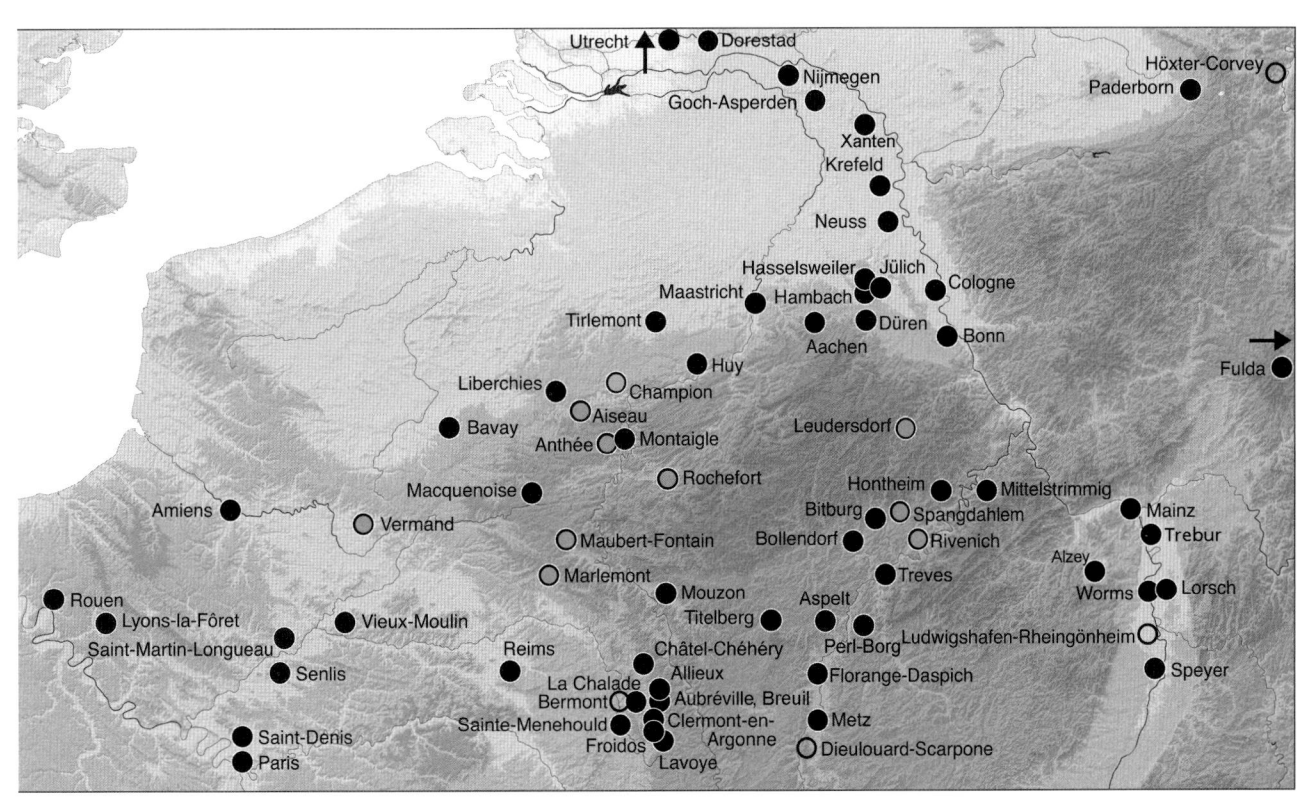

Fig. 6.1: Glass workshops from the first millennium AD between the Rhine and the English Channel. Circles indicate either doubtful workshops or workshops not precisely datable to the periods of study (Martin Grünewald, graphic conversion Vera Kassühlke, RGZM).

at Mayen have been studied by Martin Grünewald (VAT, see Grünewald 2011), and chemical analyses of the glass were undertaken by Susanne Greiff and Sonngard Hartmann at the RGZM (archaeometry). The analyses of 62 well dated glass fragments have made it possible to identify two different groups: one with a traditional Roman composition and another, usually called HIMT glass, which is characterized by higher levels of iron, manganese, and titanium. Together with a positive correlation of these elements it indicates the use of sands from sources different from the traditional Roman composition. The HIMT glass also has higher levels of sodium and magnesium than the Roman composition.

This overview presents the glass workshops attested in the regions between the Rhine and the English Channel during the first millennium AD. A preliminary article about the first half of the first millennium AD has already been published (Grünewald and Hartmann 2010), and the maps in the earlier article have been adjusted for this paper. More than 70 glass workshops in the region have been recognised from finds of furnaces, crucibles or working waste. In addition, sites marked by circles on Fig. 6.1 are further workshops, not definitely dated to the first millennium, as, for example, Höxter-Corvey. Recent research suggests that Kordel (*Landkreis* Trier-Saarburg/Germany) dates from the 12th or 13th century (Clemens 2012, 40) rather than from the Roman or early medieval periods, so it has not been included. In other cases, the evidence is not sufficient for production sites to be identified, as at Winningen (Kiessel 2009, 377–378, fig. 168) and Martberg (Nickel *et al.* 2008, 181, no. 03.02.018.01 and 188, no. 03.02.164.01), where scoriae have been found.

The beginning of Roman glass workshops

There was huge production of glass bracelets and beads in the region in the Latène period (Wagner 2006), but until the beginning of the 1st century, glass vessels were nearly unknown, although some have been found in southern France, Portugal and Spain (Feugère 1989, 29–62) and in the region north of the Alps, as at Manching (*Landkreis* Pfaffenhofen/Germany) and Basel/Switzerland (Feugère and Gebhard 1995, 504–511 with further references). Apart from a very few examples, such as the fragment of a core-formed vessel from Preist (4th or 3rd century BC, *Eifelkreis* Bitburg-Prüm/Germany; Zeitler 1990, 64; Nortmann 2012, 15), the first vessels were brought to the region from Italy by Roman soldiers. Almost all of the glass in the region in the Iron Age were beads and bracelets. The distribution of these objects hints at regional production of glass jewellery, for example in the Lower Rhine area and the Main-Rhine-region (Haevernick 1981, 299–301; Wagner 2006, 147–153; Gebhard 2010, 10–11). Wagner (2006, 39) suggests that glass working was concentrated in *oppida* and other important Celtic settlements. Raw glass is known from several Celtic contexts, as at Bad Nauheim and Manching

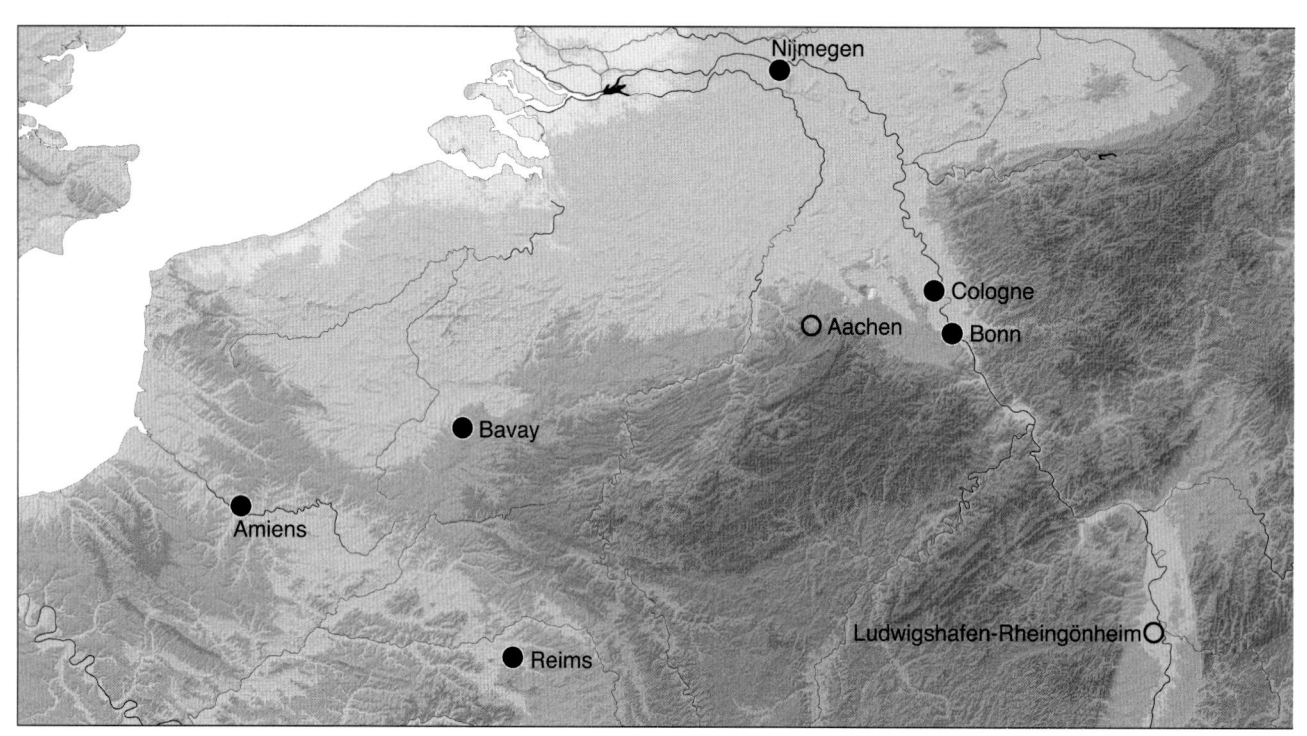

Fig. 6.2: Glass workshops from the 1st century (Martin Grünewald, graphic conversion Vera Kassühlke, RGZM).

(Wagner 2006, 35–36). Wagner has also suggested Celtic raw glass production using regional sands and halophytes, but the chemical analyses of Celtic glass from Zarten (*Landkreis* Breisgau-Hochschwarzwald) do not show any evidence for a use of organic alkali (Andreas Burkhardt in Wagner 2006, 324).

From the 1st century onwards (Fig. 6.2), glass workshops producing vessels are known in northern Gaul and the Rhineland. The first Roman workshops were established in Cologne Eigelstein and Cologne Praetorium in the second quarter of the 1st century (Follmann-Schulz 1991, 35–36; Höpken and Schäfer 2006, 74–77). The pillar-moulded or non-blown ribbed bowl (Isings 1957, 17–21, form 3) is very common in the 1st century, and fragments found in Eigelstein may indicate that the form was produced there (Höpken and Schäfer 2006, 77, fig. 6). Significantly, nearly all 1st century workshops between the Rhine and the English Channel are situated in major urban centres such as Cologne and Amiens and in the legionary fortresses, as at Bonn and Nijmegen (Follmann-Schulz 1991, 36–37). The demand for glass was concentrated in the areas inhabited by soldiers from the Mediterranean and other wealthy Romanised glass users.

The civil character of the settlement and the indigenous burial customs may explain why comparatively few of the glass vessels known from Mayen graves belong to this early period. Among these, two dark blue fragments have been examined analytically. Their glass owes its intense blue colour to the high content of cobalt (CoO 0.14 and 0.18%), and one of the two fragments has a high iron content (Fig. 6.5, left). Cobalt is a well-known colouring agent for blue glass in 1st century, when brightly coloured glass was often used (Fischer 2008, 83). Neither of the dark blue fragments has a significantly high content of decolorant such as antimony. One explanation might be that the raw glass has been intended to be used as coloured glass (cf. Jackson *et al.* 2009, 154) and therefore no intentional effort was made to decolourise the glass.

Glass workshops in the 2nd and 3rd centuries

In the 2nd and 3rd centuries (Fig. 6.3) more glass workshops are known, as at Treves, but the overall distribution pattern does not change. In Gaul some glass workshops were sited in secondary and rural settlements, but none are known outside the larger settlements and *castra* in the Rhine region. The principal workshops in the northwestern provinces of the Roman empire were established in Cologne (Höpken and Schäfer 2006, 74–85). Certain vessels decorated with coloured threads (*e.g.* Harden *et al.* 1988, 124), for example, are well represented in the cemeteries of Cologne and are assumed to have been made in the city. From the 1st to the 3rd centuries most glass workshops of the Rhineland were sited in the political and economic centres. The majority of glass vessels were made of blue-green glass typical

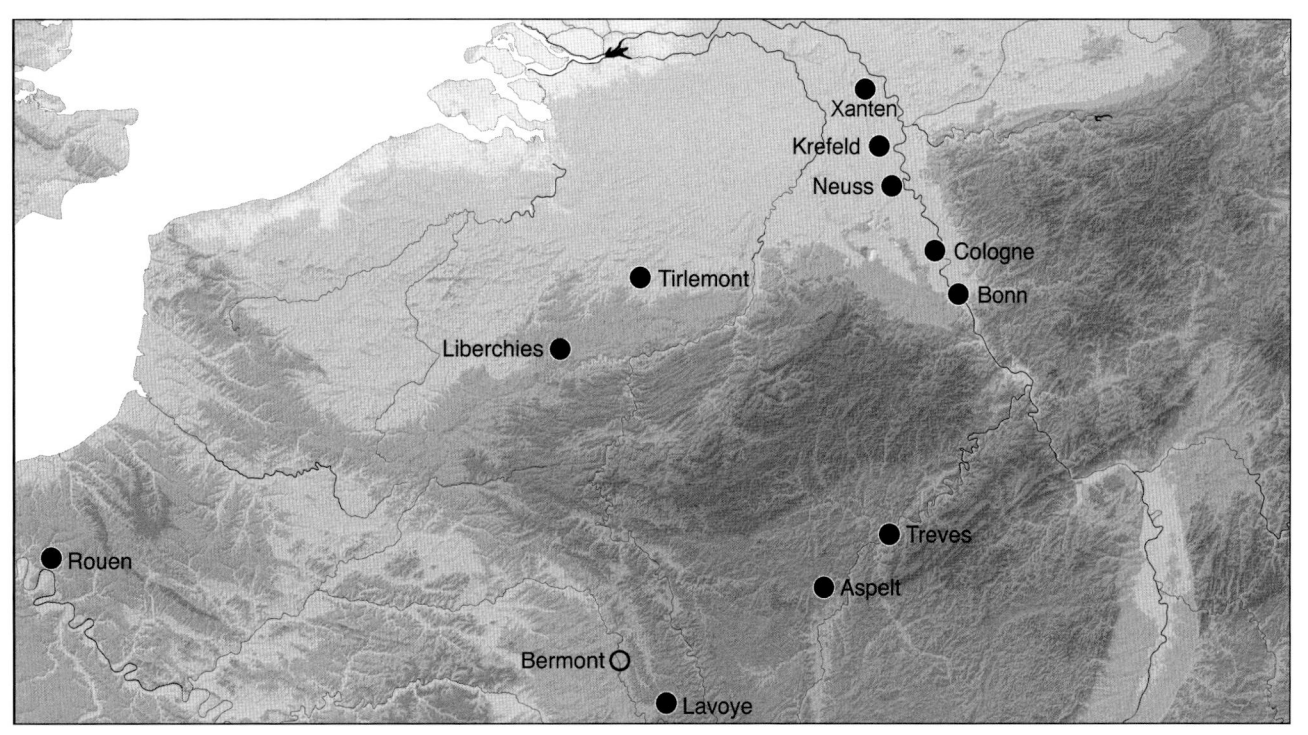

Fig. 6.3: Glass workshops from the 2nd and 3rd centuries (Martin Grünewald, graphic conversion Vera Kassühlke, RGZM).

for the 2nd and 3rd centuries with the traditional Roman composition with relatively low iron content, below or around 0.6% (*e.g.* Foster and Jackson 2009, 190, table 1: 0.62% Fe). Among the mostly naturally coloured blue-green or greenish/bluish fragments analysed from Mayen, there seems to be no other glass composition until the 4th century.

Subgroups of the traditional Roman composition have been suggested for northern Gaul and the Rhineland. Based on analyses of glass in the Rhineland, Komp (2009, 216) has suggested seven groups of Roman glass production, though the sources have not been located. Further analyses of better dated objects may show whether those groups have chronological significance as discussed by Komp for her group 4 (1st century) and group 1 (late antiquity, Komp 2009, 202 see below). A group of Belgian glass vessels dating from the second half of the 1st and beginning of 2nd century with a composition different from Levantine I, Egypt I and HIMT was published by Fontaine-Hodiament and Wouters (2002). In isotopic analyses of glass associated with a 2nd century furnace in Tienen (Belgium) the Nd signature shows a source of primary glass production in the western Mediterranean or northern Europe (Ganio *et al.* 2012, 752). According to British and French researchers the other raw glass groups mentioned were produced in Egypt and Levantine. Using the Strontium values, the current discussion favours Sinai as the provenance for HIMT glass (Freestone *et al.* 2005).

There is no direct archaeological evidence for local raw glass production in the first centuries in northern Gaul and the Rhineland. Elsewhere in the northwestern provinces, however, objects from the different stages of raw glass production are known from *e.g.* Sulzburg (*Landkreis* Breisgau-Hochschwarzwald/Germany) and York (United Kingdom) (Martin-Kilcher *et al.* 1979, 187; Jackson *et al.* 2003).

Late antique glass workshops (end of 3rd to mid 5th century)

In late antiquity numerous glass vessels were produced in minor and rural settlements as well as in major towns (cf. Louis and Gazenbeek 2011, 36 for northeastern Gaul). The number of known glass workshops increases from eleven to 23 at this time (Fig. 6.4). It is significant that many of the glass workshops were set up in regions with poor soil quality, as in the Hambach Forest (*Landkreis* Düren/Germany; Brüggler 2009, 6) and in the upland areas in the Eifel. In many of the late antique rural settlements of the Eifel region there is evidence for metal working (Luik 1999, 215), in contrast to the agricultural activity of earlier periods. In the Eifel (*Landkreis* Daun/Germany) there is a significant decline in the formation of rural settlements and after the second half of the 3rd century only the more

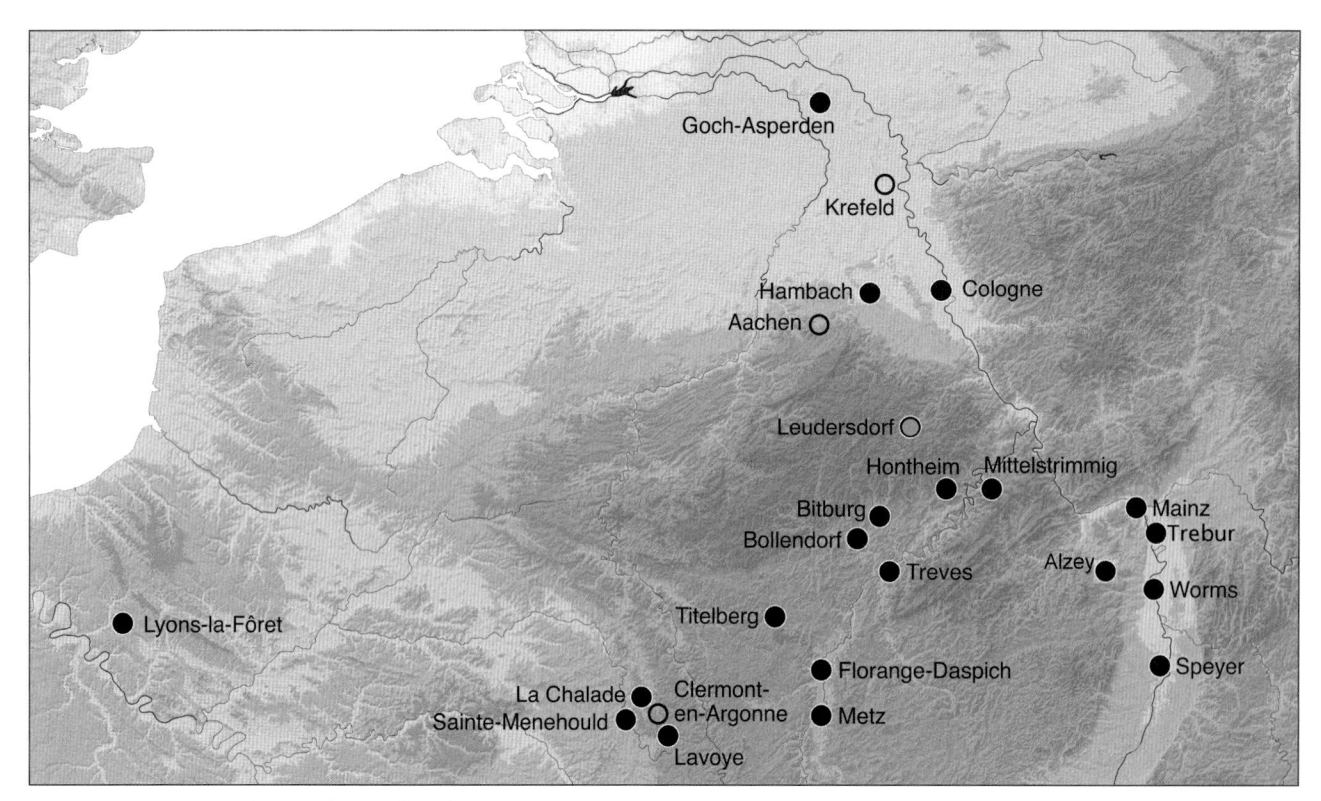

Fig. 6.4: Glass workshops from late antiquity (Martin Grünewald, graphic conversion Vera Kassühlke, RGZM).

fertile soils were used for cultivation (Henrich 2006, 117). The economic base of the former *villae rusticae* changed from the 3rd to the 4th century. At the same time, there was a rise in the exports of the Eifel pottery industry *e.g.* in Mayen (*Landkreis* Mayen-Koblenz/Germany; Redknap 1999, 133–138; Glauben *et al.* 2009, 137–138; Hunold 2012, 293–297). The pottery, metal and glass workshops in this region all needed a plentiful supply of wood.

Between the 1st and the 3rd centuries the Hambach Forest area was used for agricultural purposes (Brüggler 2009, 208–209). Between c. AD 50 and c. AD 220 there was a peak of grain pollen, as at Jülicher Börde, while in later periods, and specifically at the beginning of the 5th century, agricultural use of the land in this area had nearly stopped At the same time the forested areas expanded (Bunnik 1995, 344–345; Fischer *et al.* 2005, 306, 309–313). A similar pattern has also been recorded for the Eifel. In these regions, the analyses show a significant increase of the beech pollen counts in late antiquity (Hunold and Sirocko 2009, 146). The increasing availability of wood may have been a reason for the establishing of the glass workshops in regions where agriculture was no longer profitable and forests were regenerating. The climatic conditions in late antiquity, with cooler summers, may have been less suitable for agriculture (Büntgen *et al.* 2011, 581). Thus, the distribution pattern of glass workshops and the changes in land use seem to be related to climatic decline.

In the Hambach Forest a large workshop with several production sites in former villae has been located (Brüggler 2009, 226–227). The graves belonging to this community make it possible to date the workshop to the 4th and 5th centuries. Chemical analyses of the glass shows significantly high iron values for some objects although others have the traditional Roman composition. This was interpreted as an argument for local raw glass production by Wedepohl (Follmann-Schulz *et al.* 2000, 134), but according to Freestone and others these high iron values occur in many late antique glasses (HIMT glass) in different regions of the Roman empire (Freestone *et al.* 2005). However, by contrast with the HIMT glass from *e.g.* Mayen, the material from Hambach does not show a distinct correlation between iron and titanium (Fig. 6.5). According to Wedepohl (Follmann-Schulz *et al.* 2000) the higher vanadium values and similarities between the elements of the sand of the local river Rur and the glass from Hambach provide an additional argument for raw glass production in Hambach. In more recent publications these arguments are discussed as a sign of a more regional glass production in late antiquity, which may suggest increased use of local raw materials (group 1 according to Komp 2009, 179). In this connection it is noteworthy that the furnaces and crucibles in Hambach were heated to a temperature of c. 1100° C (Brüggler and Daszkiewicz 2004, 806, 817) which is necessary for raw glass production but not glass working. In summary, there are some hints, but no compelling evidence, for raw glass production in Hambach (Brüggler 2009, 86–90).

Unlike much of the Mediterranean region, there was a plentiful supply of wood in northern Gaul and the Rhineland, which would have assisted production of raw glass. Many late antique glass workshops were sited in woodlands. The amount of wood needed to produce raw glass was definitely higher (50kg wood for 1kg raw glass, according to Brüggler 2009, 215), than to remelt it. Glass working is possible at temperatures from 630°C and higher, while raw glass production needs temperatures higher than c. 1100°C (Brüggler and Daszkiewicz 2004, 806, 817), and the transport of wood to the workshops would have been expensive.

The changes in the distribution pattern of the glass workshops and the change in the range of forms of glass vessels (van Lith and Randsborg 1985, 463; Brüggler 2005, 155) may be contemporary with the introduction of the new HIMT composition (cf. Freestone *et al.* 2005) of glass in the 4th century, and this is considered for Britain by Jackson and Foster (this volume). The chemical analyses of closely dated glass vessels from the cemetery of Mayen show that some vessels from the last third of the 4th century to the second half of the 5th century were made with the new HIMT composition (Fig. 6.6), and it can be demonstrated that regional vessel forms such as conical beakers with diagonal ribs and cylindrical flasks with funnel mouths (Isings 1957, 127–129, 160–161, forms 106b, 132; Grünewald 2012) were only made of the HIMT composition (Fig. 6.5). Production at Hambach is suggested for the barrel jug (Isings 1957, 158, form 128) from Mayen, because of the basal design with ECVA (Fig. 6.5). A base fragment with an identical design was found in a pit near a glass furnace in Hambach 111 (Follmann *et al.* 2000, 124). Local manufacture of vessels in the region of Mayen is suggested by the distribution pattern of regional glass types (Grünewald 2011, 191–194; Grünewald and Hartmann 2010, 18–20).

Merovingian glass workshops (second half of the 5th to first half of the 8th century)

In the Merovingian period (Fig. 6.7) only a few glass workshops are known and their distribution pattern is difficult to interpret. The production sites at Macquenoise and Hasselsweiler (Päffgen and Wedepohl 2004, 840–842) may point to continuity of glass working in rural landscapes, close to their Roman predecessors. In many cases only the production of glass beads has been documented, as at Wijnaldum and Rijnsburg, to the north of the mapped area (Götzen 1999, 48). There is strong continuity with late antiquity, and significant reduction of vessel types such as beakers, bowls and tumblers. The contrast between the relatively large number of late antique workshops and the

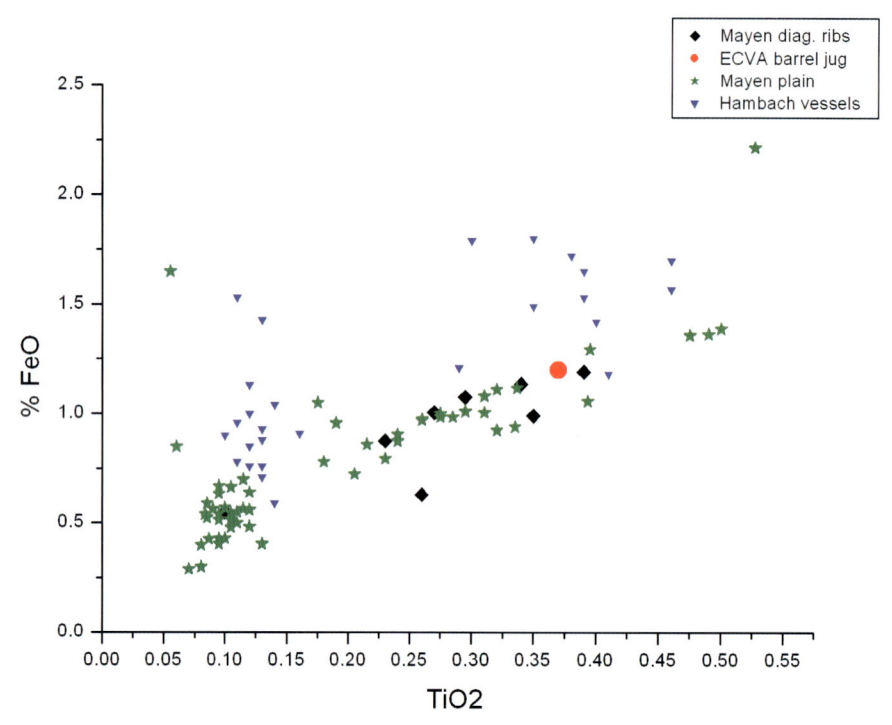

Fig. 6.5: Comparison of Mayen and Hambach compositions (FeO/TiO2) with highlighted typical vessels (Sonngard Hartmann, RGZM).

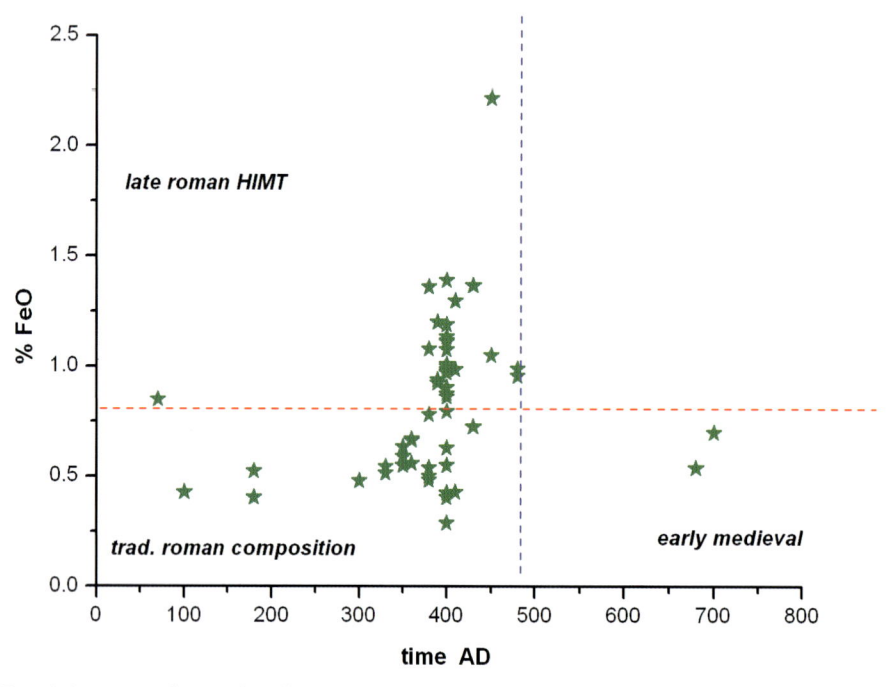

Fig. 6.6: Mayen glass with different compositions over timeline (Sonngard Hartmann, RGZM).

small number of Merovingian workshops is paralleled by a general reduction of glass use and is not simply a reflection of the current state of research.

Merovingian glass compositions in the Rhineland are known from sites like Hasselsweiler and Gellep (Päffgen and Wedepohl 2004, 842–847; Wedepohl et al. 1997). To some extent they are similar to the late Roman HIMT composition but there seems to be wider variation than during the late Roman period, as it has been shown when comparing the iron values of the later Gellep and the Roman

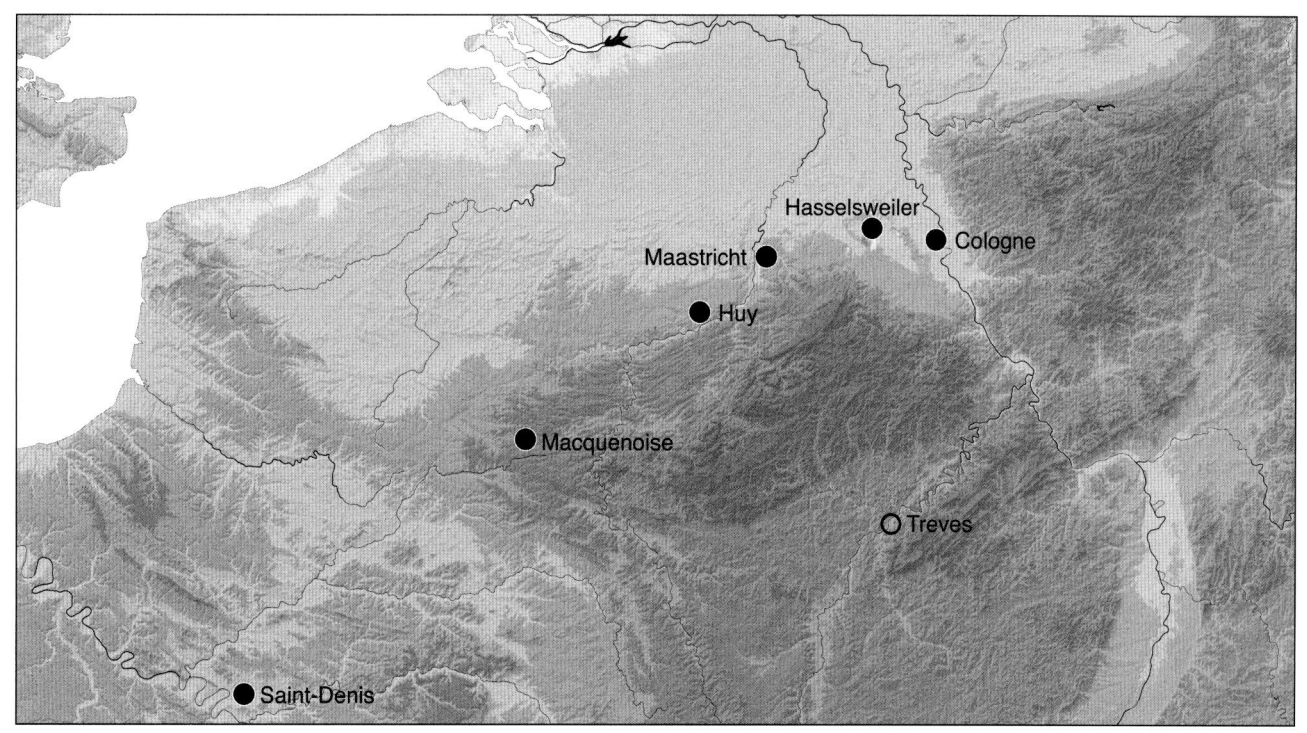

Fig. 6.7: Glass workshops from the Merovingian period (Martin Grünewald, graphic conversion Vera Kassühlke, RGZM).

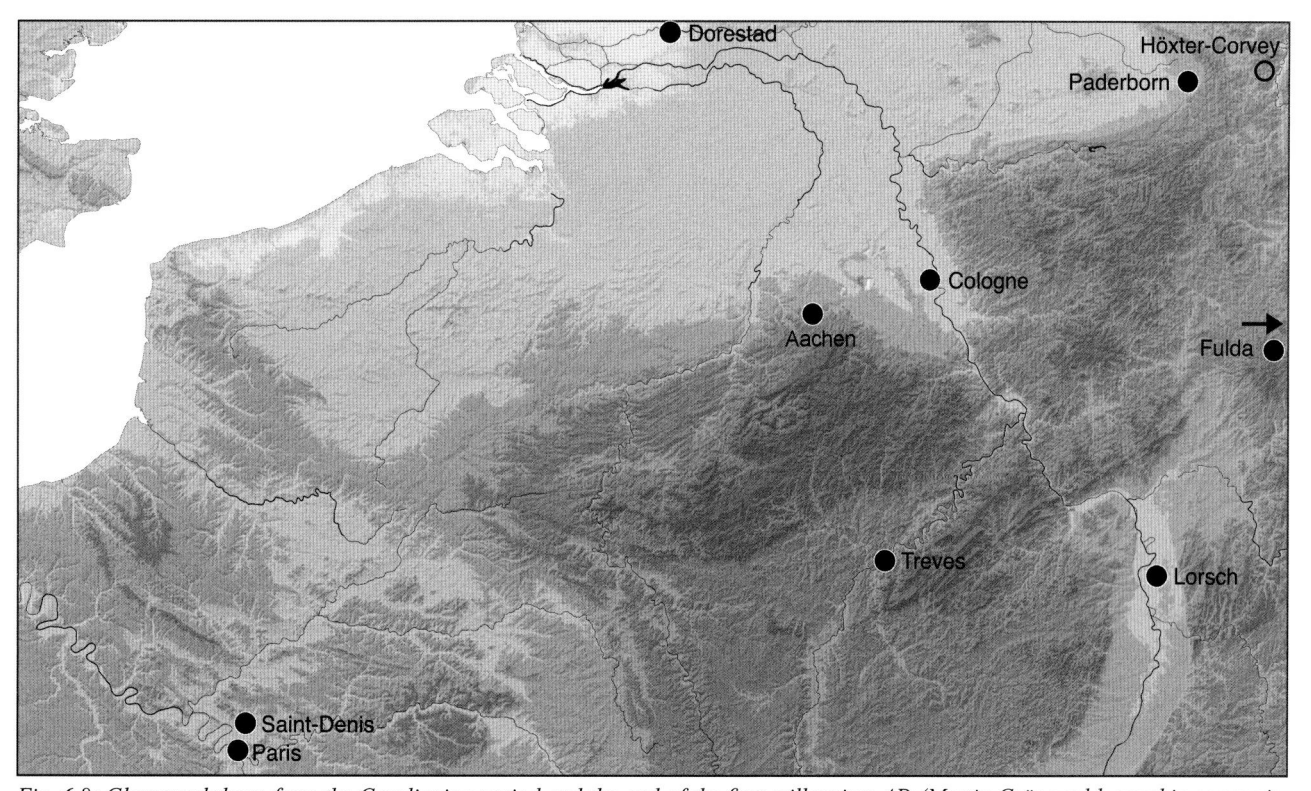

Fig. 6.8: Glass workshops from the Carolingian period and the end of the first millennium AD (Martin Grünewald, graphic conversion Vera Kassühlke, RGZM).

Mayen compositions (Grünewald and Hartmann 2010, 22, fig. 14). Recent analyses show that the glass from the second half of the 5th century (Fig. 6.6) found in Mayen is also of HIMT composition Only two later Merovingian objects from Mayen were made in a different type of soda-lime-glass. In general Merovingian glass compositions seem to be similar to the main group of Roman soda-lime-glass. The existence and importance of the production of this raw glass in the Roman and Merovingian periods in the northwestern provinces is still under discussion (Zimmermann 2011, 109–124).

Carolingian and later glass workshops (second half of the 8th to 10th century)

Carolingian glass workshops (Fig. 6.8) have been found in religious and political centres such as palatinates and monasteries like Lorsch, Aachen and Fulda (Päffgen 2003, 20–23; Giertz and Ristow 2013; Wedepohl 2003). An important example is known in the well-dated palatinate at Paderborn of the end of the 8th century. A secondary workshop using late soda-lime-glass is attested there as well as glass objects made of wood ash glass, a new composition in which potassium substitutes sodium as the alkali. The new glass composition has been thought to be related to difficulties in the importation of soda or soda-lime raw glass from the east after the confrontation between the Carolingians and the Arabs (Stephan and Wedepohl 1997, 706), but the Arabs also used a different glass composition with plantash after this time (Freestone 2006, 203). Hence it is more likely that the demand for natron outstripped the supply because the changed climatic conditions caused no new soda to be formed in *e.g.* Wadi Natrun. This shortfall may have been further accentuated by the increased scale of glass production at this period (Freestone *et al.* 2006, 521–530). The demand in the monasteries and palatinates for *e.g.* window panes might explain a change in the distribution pattern, the glass workshops returning to the economic centres. An improvement in climate connected with increased use of land for agriculture is also significant at this time (Schreg 2009, 157–158; Bunnik 1995, 345).

Summing up

The Carolingian renaissance is comparable to the 1st century in the concentration of glass working sites in economic centres. A different distribution pattern is common in the later medieval period, starting in the 12th–14th centuries, which may be in some respects comparable to late antiquity. There are many different reasons for the changing patterns of distribution of glass working in the first millennium AD. The siting of the workshops is a complex phenomenon connected with demand and resources such as the materials for production and the wood for firing the furnaces. Comparison with other workshops with high consumption of wood for fuel, such as pottery or metal production, and the similarity of the distribution patterns of those workshops in late antiquity may indicate a connection with changing land use and have close links with climatic change. In late antiquity and the Merovingian period there was climatic deterioration, and a similar phenomenon is well known from AD 1300 until 1850 during the little Ice Age (Alt and Sirocko 2009, 170). In both periods secondary glass workshops were far removed from the economic centres (see Clemens and Steppuhn 2012, with further literature about later glass workshops).

A long list of find spots with hints of glass working, which at the current stage of research cannot be either interpreted or dated exactly, are also listed in the catalogue and shown on Fig. 6.1. More knowledge about those glass workshops will probably change the present picture. Furthermore the current overview does not provide an answer to the question of where the raw glass used in Gaul and the Rhineland was produced. Further research will be necessary to explore these issues.

Catalogue of glass workshops of the first millennium AD between the Rhine and the English Channel

Question marks (?) indicate either doubtful workshops or workshops not precisely datable to the period. The workshops of Evreux (*département* Eure/France), Sorel-Moussel (*département* Eure-et-Loir/France) and Troyes (*département* Aube/France; cf. Foy 2010, 27) are outside the mapped area (Fig. 6.1). Further evidence for glass workshops in Germany have also been found in Augsburg, Haithabu (*Landkreis* Schleswig-Flensburg), Hiddenhausen-Oetinghausen (*Landkreis* Herford), Gross Köris-Klein Köris (*Landkreis* Dahme-Spreewald), Mühlberg (*Landkreis* Gotha) and Oldendorf-Melle (*Landkreis* Osnabrück; cf. Päffgen 2003, 13, 21).

Glass workshops from the 1st century

- Aachen, Minoriten-Grosskölnstraße (Germany)?: the traces of glass working mentioned by van Geesbergen (1999, 120) are probably connected with metal working, because the chemical analyses of nine small crucibles indicated processing of nonferrous metal (Strauch 1996, 96; Keller 2004, 44).
- Amiens, rue du Maréchal-de-Lattre-de-Tassigny (*départment* Somme/France): remains of finished products and working waste; end of 1st century (van Geesbergen 1999, 117; Foy and Nenna 2001, 47).
- Bavay (*départment* Nord/France): furnace (van Geesbergen 1999, 117; Foy and Nenna 2001, 47).

- Bonn (Germany): three complexes each with two furnaces, glass working waste, limestone mould fragments from the production of square bottles (Isings 1957, 63–67, form 50). The glass furnaces were abandoned during the last third of the 1st century (Follmann-Schulz 1991, 36; Follmann-Schulz 2010, 235–237).
- Cologne, Eigelstein 14 (Germany): more than five furnaces, glass working waste; Cologne, Praetorium (Germany): three furnaces (Follmann-Schulz 1991, 35–36; Höpken and Schäfer 2006, 74–77).
- Ludwigshafen-Rheingönheim (Germany)?: early chemical analyses suggest that one of three crucibles may have been used for glass working. Comparison with more recent analyses shows that the chemical composition is not a conclusive argument for glass working (Roller 1957, 60–61; Ulbert 1969, 57–58, pl. 61.8–10).
- Nijmegen (Netherlands): fragments of glass and pottery, glass scoriae; 1st century (Follmann-Schulz 1991, 37).
- Reims (*département* Marne/France): glass working waste, such as raw glass, glass drops, etc. (Cabart 2003, 44).

Glass workshops from the 2nd and 3rd centuries

- Aspelt (*Kanton* Esch-sur-Alzette/Luxembourg): crucible (Niederbieber 104), furnace, but it is unclear whether this was used for glass working (Dövener 2003, 44).
- Bermont (Moiremont, *département* Meuse/France)?: possible crucibles may indicate glass working (Gazenbeek 2003, 293).
- Bonn (Germany): two fragments of crucibles (Niederbieber 104) probably indicate glass working in the 3rd century (Follmann-Schulz 1991, 37).
- Cologne, Eigelstein 35–39 (Germany): eleven furnaces, raw glass, glass working waste; Cologne, Helenenstraße: furnace with three parts, basin, crucible, glass working waste; Cologne, Gereonstraße: raw glass, fragments of furnace; Marienburg: raw glass deposit for production of melon beads (Höpken and Schäfer 2006, 83).
- Krefeld (Germany): small glass furnace, probably for production of coloured glass jewellery (Reichmann 1995, 132).
- Lavoye, La Clairière (*département* Meuse/France): furnace of the second half of the 3rd century (Polfer 2005, 125; Gazenbeek 2003, 293 mentioned seven further furnaces without dating in Lavoye and several pits with crucibles of the 2nd and 3rd centuries in two nearby findspots in Argonne: Verrières, La Haie-Guérin and Varennes, La Gruerie).
- Liberchies (Pont-à-Celles, *province* Hainaut/Belgium): crucibles, glass working waste, fragments of furnaces covered with melted glass; AD 180 to 260 (van Geesbergen 1999, 118; van Geesbergen 2000, 3; Hanut 2006, 12).
- Neuss (Germany): glass working waste; first half of 2nd century (Sauer 1991, 560).
- Rouen (*département* Seine-Maritime/France): some evidence for glass working in the 3rd century (Foy and Nenna 2001, 53).
- Tirlemont (Tienen, *province* Vlaams-Brabant/Belgium): furnace, raw glass; 2nd century (Hanut 2006, 12).
- Treves, Hohenzollernstraße (Germany): fragments of crucibles; 2nd century and 3rd to early 4th century (cf. late antique workshops, Goethert-Polaschek 2011, 106).
- Treves, Hopfengarten, Heiligkreuz (Germany): furnace for crucible, annealing furnace, crucible; black glass with high iron content may be an evidence for production of jewellery; second half of 2nd century (Pfahl 2000, 53–54; Goethert-Polaschek 2012, 25).
- Xanten (Germany): some evidence for a glass workshop; 2nd or 3rd century (pers. comm. Bernd Liesen).

Glass workshops from late antiquity (end of 3rd until mid 5th century)

- Aachen, region of the cloister of the Münster (Germany)?: fragment of crucible; probably 4th century (Päffgen 2003, 10; Päffgen and Wedepohl 2004, 837).
- Alzey (Germany): two fragments of crucible (Alzey 27), glass cullet for recycling; mid 5th century (Oldenstein 2009, 219–220).
- Bitburg (Germany): fragments of crucibles; 4th century (van Geesbergen 1999, 120).
- Bollendorf (*Eifelkreis* Bitburg-Prüm/Germany): crucibles, raw glass (Steinhausen 1932, 51; Luik 1999, 215).
- Clermont-en-Argonne (*département* Meuse/France)?: crucibles, waste, wall of furnace, the late antique dating is not surely attested (Polfer 2005, 72).
- Cologne near Waidmarkt (Germany): two fragments of crucibles. Kattenbug: fragment of crucible (Höpken and Schäfer 2006, 84).
- Florange-Daspich (*département* Moselle/France): a crucible covered with melted glass inside probably indicates a workshop in late antiquity (Polfer 2005, 123–124).
- Goch-Asperden (*Landkreis* Kleve/Germany): two furnaces, possible blowpipe, glass for recycling, moils, fragments of crucibles, raw glass chunks, glass waste indicates the production of vessels as well as jewellery (black bracelets); around AD 400 and in the first third of the 5th century (Brüggler 2008, 110–111; Brüggler 2011).
- Hambach (*Landkreis* Düren/Germany), eight find spots: Hambach 59: four to six furnaces. Hambach 75: nine furnaces, glass working waste, moils, raw glass, glass for recycling. Hambach 111: three furnaces, glass working waste, fragment of crucible. Hambach 127: production waste. Hambach 132: 12 or 13 furnaces, glass working

waste, fragments of crucibles, moils, glass drops and threads, glass for recycling, etc. Hambach 382: seven furnaces, fragments of crucibles. Hambach 488: more than two furnaces, fragment of crucible. Hambach 500: two furnaces, crucible (Follmann-Schulz *et al.* 2000, 153, 162–165, 177–178; Brüggler 2009, especially 65–92, 210–215).
- Hontheim, Entersburg (*Landkreis* Bernkastel-Wittlich/ Germany): fragments of crucible (Alzey 28), glass fragments of the 2nd and 3rd centuries for remelting, pottery fragments mostly dating from the first half and mid 4th century (Gilles 1985, 131–133).
- Krefeld (Germany)?: fragment of crucible (Alzey 28) (Follmann-Schulz *et al.* 2000, 109).
- La Chalade/Le Plagneux (*département* Meuse/France): fragments of crucibles may indicate glass working (Polfer 2005, 143).
- Lavoye-Les Tannières (*département* Meuse/France): furnace, crucibles, glass working waste; 3rd to 4th century (Polfer 2005, 125; further evidence for late antique glass working: Gazenbeek 2003, 293).
- Leudersdorf (*Landkreis* Vulkaneifel/Germany)?: fragments of round discs of green, turquoise and reddish brown glass, intended for use as raw material for mosaics (Luik 1999, 214–215; Henrich 2006, 84).
- Lyons-la-Forêt (*département* Eure/France): forty fragments of crucibles with melted glass inside; 3rd and 4th centuries (Foy and Nenna 2001, 56–57).
- Mainz, Bauhofstraße (Germany): glass waste and raw material; late 3rd and 4th centuries (Witteyer 1999, 11).
- Metz, quartier Saint-Marcel (*département* Moselle/ France): scoriae, tile covered with melted glass, glass drops, etc. (van Geesbergen 1999, 117; Foy and Nenna 2001, 56).
- Mittelstrimmig (*Landkreis* Cochem-Zell/Germany): fragments of crucibles; mid 4th century (van Geesbergen 1999, 121).
- Sainte-Menehould-Houis (*département* Marne/France): furnace, fragments of crucibles, glass working waste, metal tools, material of the 3rd and the 4th centuries (Gazenbeek 2003, 291; Polfer 2005, 72).
- Speyer, Domplatz (Germany): fragments of crucibles, remains of furnace; first half of 4th century (Grünwald 1989, 42–43).
- Titelberg (*Kanton* Esch-sur-Alzette/Luxembourg): a few remains of a furnace, crucibles, raw glass, scoriae, glass drops and threads, etc. Thill (1968, 523) dated this to the 3rd and beginning of the 4th centuries, but later production is possible, as some coins on the site date from the end of the 4th century and some possible remains of later glass vessel forms are present (Thill 1968, 521–528; Grünewald 2011, 188–190).
- Trebur (*Kreis* Groß-Gerau/Germany): production of glass beads is attested by raw glass fragments, a mould, semi-finished and finished beads of the 4th and beginning of the 5th century (Knöchlein 2002, 105–114).
- Treves, Kesselstadt (Germany): fragments of crucibles, jewellery (rings) from the first third of the 4th century (Goethert-Polaschek 2012, 25).
- Treves, Dom (Germany): furnace, fragments of crucibles, raw glass, probably for production of inlays for *opus sectile* wall decoration (Goethert-Polaschek 2011, 107).
- Treves, Barbarathermen (Germany): fragments of crucibles with reddish brown glass inside, probably for production of inlays for *opus sectile* wall decoration (Goethert-Polaschek 2011, 107; 2012, 25).
- Treves, south-western neighbourhood (Germany, three findspots close to each other): Töpferstraße: fragments of crucible (Speicher 2/Alzey 28), glass waste (Goethert-Polaschek 1983, 316, fig. 274a; Goethert 1984, 249; Goethert-Polaschek 2011, 70).
- Treves, Lintzstraße: furnace(?), fragments of crucibles, fragments of burnt clay covered with melted glass (Goethert-Polaschek 1983, 316, fig. 274b; Goethert 1984, 249; Goethert-Polaschek 2011, 72–76).
- Treves, Hohenzollernstraße: two furnaces from the end of 3rd to beginning of 4th century and after the mid 4th century respectively, remains of older furnaces from the end of 3rd century, fragments of crucibles from the second half of 3rd to mid 4th century, glass working waste, raw glass, moils, drops, threads, etc. (Goethert-Polaschek 2011, 76–143; 2012, 19–24).
- Worms (Germany): furnace, glass working waste, two fragments of crucibles (Päffgen and Wedepohl 2004, 836; Grünewald and Vogt 2001, 18–20).

Glass workshops from the Merovingian period (second half of the 5th until first half of the 8th century)

- Cologne, Heumarkt (Germany): two furnaces, fragments of glass vessels, production of vessels and beads is attested (Päffgen 2003, 18; Päffgen and Trier 2001, 27).
- Hasselsweiler (*Landkreis* Düren/Germany): fragments of glass vessels, fragments of two crucibles; second half of 5th century (Päffgen and Wedepohl 2004, 840).
- Huy, Aux ruelles and rue Sous-le-Château (*province* Liège/Belgium): remains of four furnaces, many crucibles, glass working waste such as glass drops, threads, etc.; mid 5th to mid 6th century (de Bernardy de Sigoyer *et al.* 2005, 29–33; Fontaine 2005, 72–73).
- Maastricht, Jodenstraat (*province* Limburg/Netherlands): fragments of crucibles, glass working waste, production of glass beads; 6th to 7th century (Päffgen 2003, 18; Päffgen and Wedepohl 2004, 841–842).
- Macquenoise (near Chimay, *province* Hainaut/Belgium):

two furnaces, fragments of crucibles, production of beakers dating c. AD 530–580/610 (Päffgen 2003, 18; Päffgen and Wedepohl 2004, 842).
- Saint-Denis (*département* Seine-Saint-Denis/France): fragments of crucibles found in the waste near the Merovingian cemetery (Foy and Nenna 2001, 58).
- Treves (Germany)?: mapped by Päffgen and Wedepohl 2004, 841.

Glass workshops from the Carolingian period and the end of the first millennium AD (second half of the 8th until 10th century)

- Aachen, three findspots in the vicinity of the palatinate: Büchel-Straße, Dom Quadrum and Hof (Germany): raw material for gold-glass tesserae, crucibles, raw glass chunks, tesserae; around AD 800 (Giertz and Ristow 2013).
- Cologne (Germany): probable glass furnace; 9th or early 10th century (Päffgen and Trier 2001, 30; Päffgen 2003, 20).
- Dorestad (*province* Utrecht/Netherlands): fragment of crucible (Päffgen 2003, 23).
- Fulda (Germany): melted chunk of blue glass, fragments of crucible; second half of 8th until second half of 9th century (Kind *et al.* 2003, 73–74; Päffgen 2003, 22).
- Höxter-Corvey (Germany)?: fragments of crucibles(?), raw glass (for enamel or glass); 9th to 11th or 12th century (Stephan and Wedepohl 1997, 676, 706, 715; Stephan 2000, 349, 791).
- Lorsch (*Landkreis* Bergstraße, Germany): moil, glass tesserae, Carolingian (Kronz *et al.* 2002, 50, 60–61, fig. 8.32).
- Paderborn (Germany): fragments of furnace covered with glass, melted glass, glass tesserae; AD 776/777 (Winkelmann 1977, 123–125; Päffgen 2003, 22).
- Paris (France): fragments of crucibles; 9th to 10th century (Foy and Nenna 2001, 59).
- Saint-Denis (*département* Seine-Saint-Denis/France): fragments of crucibles with glass inside, scoriae (Foy and Nenna 2001, 60).
- Treves, St. Irminen (Germany): evidence for glass working: tesserae with gold foil for remelting, painted fragments of window glass, etc. (Clemens 2001, 48–52; Päffgen 2003, 20).

Further sites mapped in Fig. 1 which are not precisely datable to the periods of study

- Aachen, Katschhof (Germany): fragments of three crucibles may indicate a glass workshop (Strauch 1996, 30; Keller 2004, 44).
- Aiseau (*province* Hainaut/Belgium)?: doubtful fragment of crucible (van Geesbergen 1999, 119; Polfer (2005, 25 note 72) excluded this site because of the lack of evidence for a workshop).
- Allieux (Vauquois, *département* Meuse/France): furnace, glass blocks (Gazenbeek 2003, 293; Polfer 2005, 148).
- Anthée (*province* Namur/Belgium)?: glass rods and powdered remains of glass found in the region of a Roman villa (van Geesbergen 2000, 3; Brüggler 2009, 218).
- Aubréville (*département* Meuse/France): furnace (Gazenbeek 2003, 293 also mentioned further evidence for glass working at Pont-Verdunois west of Aubréville).
- Breuil (*département* Marne/France)?: possible crucibles may indicate glass working (Gazenbeek 2003, 293).
- Champion (*province* Namur/Belgium)?: two furnaces, the interpretation as glass furnaces is doubtful (van Geesbergen 2000, 3; Brüggler 2009, 218).
- Châtel-Chéhéry (*département* Ardennes/France): furnace and block of glass (Polfer 2005, 139).
- Dieulouard-Scarpone (*département* Meurthe-et-Moselle/France)?: doubtful glass working waste (van Geesbergen 1999, 118; Polfer (2005, 25 note 72) excluded this site because of the lack of evidence for a workshop).
- Düren (Germany): fragments of raw glass and furnace, moils, glass drops and threads, probably Roman (Komp 2010, 73–74).
- Froidos-Berthaucourt (*département* Meuse/France): furnace, crucibles (Foy and Nenna (2001, 57) said this was late antique; Polfer (2005, 125) and Gazenbeek (2003, 293) have accepted dating in the 3rd century).
- Jülich, Kölnstraße (*Landkreis* Düren/Germany): fragment of crucible (with different dating: Päffgen and Wedepohl 2004, 837: 3rd–4th century; Follmann-Schulz *et al.* 2000, 112: early type Niederbieber 104, 2nd or early 3rd century; Perse 1995, 127: without dating).
- Lavoye, Parc Saillet (*département* Meuse/France): furnace, fragments of furnace covered with glass, fragments of crucibles, unknown dating (Polfer 2005, 125; further evidence: Gazenbeek 2003, 293).
- Macquenoise (*province* Hainaut/Belgium)?: crucibles(?), scoriae, glass working waste, the mould for production of a grape flask (Isings 1957, 108–109, form 91a) is a fake; Roman (van Geesbergen 1999, 119; van Geesbergen 2000, 3).
- Marlemont (*département* Ardennes/France)?: „quelques fouilles qui ont déterminé l'emplacement d'une verrerie gallo-romaine", not mentioned in more recent French literature (Albot 1906, 210; Götzen 1999, 247).
- Maubert-Fontain (*département* Ardennes/France)?: traces of a furnace; Roman (3rd century), not mentioned in more recent French literature (Albot 1906, 210; Götzen 1999, 246).
- Metz (*département* Moselle/France)?: glass droplets may be evidence for glass working; mid 1st to 3rd century (Foy and Nenna 2001, 53).

- Montaigle (Onhaye, *province* Namur/Belgium): crucible covered with block of melted glass (Hanut and Mignon 2012, 263).
- Mouzon (*département* Ardennes/France): crucibles (Polfer 2005, 126).
- Perl-Borg (*Landkreis* Merzig-Wadern/Germany): possible raw glass, glass working waste, fragments of crucibles, clay and mortar fragments of furnace covered with melted glass; Roman (Birkenhagen and Wiesenberg 2013, 149–150, 169).
- Rivenich (*Landkreis* Bernkastel-Wittlich/Germany)?: glass scoriae and melted glass may indicate glass working (Polfer 2005, 133).
- Rochefort / Jemelle (*province* Namur/Belgium)?: furnace, the interpretation as a glass furnace is doubtful (van Geesbergen 1999, 119; van Geesbergen 2000, 3–4; Brüggler 2009, 218).
- Rouen, abbey Saint Ouen (*département* Seine-Maritime/France): antique furnace, discovered in 1853 (Foy and Nenna 2001, 60).
- Saint-Martin-Longueau (*département* Oise/France): indications of glass workshops (Woimont 1995, 425–426, no. 587; Polfer 2005, 127).
- Senlis (*département* Oise/France): Roman furnace (Polfer 2005, 113).
- Spangdahlem-Unterm Rohr (*Landkreis* Bitburg-Prüm/Germany)?: glass scoriae, Roman and medieval pottery fragments, glass workshop doubtful (Jahresbericht 1939, 68–69; Polfer 2005, 134).
- Utrecht (Netherlands): fragments of crucibles were found in the Roman camp, but are not stratified (Isings 1957, 12).
- Vermand (*département* Aisne/France)?: glass fragments formerly interpreted as glass working waste (van Geesbergen 1999, 118; Polfer (2005, 25, note 72) excluded this site because of the lack of evidence for a workshop).
- Vieux-Moulin, pré Tortu (*département* Oise/France): glass workshop; Roman to medieval (Woimont 1995, 498, no. 674; Polfer 2005, 148).

Acknowledgements

We would like to thank the organisers of the conference for the very friendly support; Daniel Keller, Susanne Greiff, Julius Grünewald and the reviewer for their suggestions for this paper.

Bibliography

Albot (1906) La verrerie et les verriers italiens dans les Ardennes. *Revue Historique Ardennaise*, 209–273.

Alt, K. W. and Sirocko, F. (2009) Die kleine Eiszeit – Leben und Sterben im Schatten klimatischer Extremereignisse. In F. Sirocko (ed.) *Wetter, Klima, Menschheitsentwicklung. Von der Eiszeit bis ins 21. Jahrhundert*, 170–175. Darmstadt, Wissenschaftliche Buchgesellschaft.

de Bernardy de Sigoyer, S., Peters, C., Mathieu, S. and Fontaine, Ch. (2005) Vestiges de fours de verriers d'époque mérovingienne à Huy aux Ruelles (Belgique). *Bulletin de l'Association Française pour l'Archéologie du Verre*, 29–33.

Birkenhagen, B. and Wiesenberg, F. (2013) *Zirkusbecher und Rippenschalen. ROMAN GLASSMAKERS Mark Taylor & David Hill. Werkschau 1989–2012*. Schriften des Archäologieparks Römische Villa Borg 5. Merzig, Kulturstiftung Merzig-Wadern.

Brüggler, M. (2005) Glas und Glasproduktion in der Spätantike. In Badisches Landesmuseum (ed.) *Imperium Romanum. Römer, Christen, Alamannen. Die Spätantike am Oberrhein*, 155–163. Stuttgart, Theiss.

Brüggler, M. (2008) Burgus und Glashütte bei Goch-Asperden. In *Archäologie im Rheinland 2007*, 109–111. Stuttgart, Theiss.

Brüggler, M. (2009) *Villa rustica, Glashütte und Gräberfeld. Die kaiserzeitliche und spätantike Siedlungsstelle HA 132 im Hambacher Forst*. Rheinische Ausgrabungen 63. Mainz, Philipp von Zabern.

Brüggler, M. (2011) Spätantike Glasherstellung am Niederrhein – Eine Glashütte am Burgus von Goch-Asperden. In J. Drauschke, R. Prien and S. Ristow (eds.) *Untergang und Neuanfang. Studien zu Spätantike und Frühmittelalter 3*, 163–189. Hamburg, Dr. Kovač.

Brüggler, M. and Daszkiewicz, M. (2004) Spätantike Glasherstellung im Hambacher Forst. Ergebnisse der Laboranalysen vom Fundplatz HA 132. *Kölner Jahrbuch* 37, 805–818.

Büntgen, U., Tegel, W., Nicolussi, K., McCormick, M., Frank, D., Trouet, V., Kaplan, J. O., Herzig, F., Heussner, K.-U., Wanner, H., Luterbacher, J. and Esper, J. (2011) 2500 Years of European Climate Variability and Human Susceptibility. *Science* 331, 579–582.

Bunnik, F. P. M. (1995) Pollenanalytische Ergebnisse zur Vegetations- und Landwirtschaftsgeschichte der Jülicher Lössbörde von der Bronzezeit bis in die Frühe Neuzeit. *Bonner Jahrbücher* 195, 313–349.

Cabart, H. (2003) Une activité verrière à la fin du Ier siècle à Reims (Marne). In D. Foy (ed.) *Cœur de verre, production et diffusion du verre antique*, 44–45. Gollion, Infolio.

Clemens, L. (2001) Archäologische Beobachtungen zu frühmittelalterlichen Siedlungsstrukturen in Trier. In S. Felgenhauer-Schmiedt, A. Eibner and H. Knittler (eds.) *Zwischen Römersiedlung und mittelalterlicher Stadt. Archäologische Aspekte zur Kontinuitätsfrage*. Beiträge zur Mittelalterarchäologie in Österreich 17, 43–66. Wien, Österreichische Gesellschaft für Mittelalterarchäologie.

Clemens, L. (2012) Hochmittelalterliche Glasproduktion auf der Kordeler Hochmark (Lkrs. Trier-Saarburg). In L. Clemens and P. Steppuhn (eds.) *Glasproduktion. Archäologie und Geschichte. Beiträge zum 4. Internationalen Symposium zur Erforschung mittelalterlicher und frühneuzeitlicher Glashütten in Europa.* Interdisziplinärer Dialog zwischen Archäologie und Geschichte 2, 29–42. Trier, Kliomedia.

Clemens, L. and Steppuhn, P. (eds.) (2012) *Glasproduktion. Archäologie und Geschichte. Beiträge zum 4. Internationalen Symposium zur Erforschung mittelalterlicher und frühneuzeitlicher Glashütten in Europa.* Interdisziplinärer Dialog zwischen Archäologie und Geschichte 2. Trier, Kliomedia.

Dövener, F. (2003) Neues zur römischen Villa in Aspelt – „op der Stae". Musée Info. *Bulletin d'Information du Musée National d'Histoire et d'Art* 16, 42–44.

Feugère, M. (1989) Les vases en verre sur noyau d'argile en Méditerranée nord-occidentale. In M. Feugère (ed.) *Le verre préromain en Europe occidentale*, 29–62. Montagnac, Monique Mergoil.

Feugère, M. and Gebhard, R. (1995) Die Glasgefäßfragmente von Manching. *Germania* 73, 504–511.

Fischer, R. (2008) Naturwissenschaftliche Untersuchungen an römischen Gläsern aus Hellingen. *Annuaire du Musée national d'histoire et d'art (Luxembourg)* 1, 76–84.

Fischer, T., Gruhle, W., Schmidt, B. and Zimmermann, A. (2005) Mögliche Schwankungen von Getreideerträgen. Befunde zur rheinischen Linienbandkeramik und Römischen Kaiserzeit. *Archäologisches Korrespondenzblatt* 35, 301–316.

Follmann-Schulz, A.-B. (1991) Fours de Verriers romains dans la provinces de Germanie Inférieure. In D. Foy and G. Sennequier (eds.) *Ateliers de verriers de l'Antiquité à la période pré-industrielle*, 35–40. Rouen, Association Française pour l'Archéologie du Verre.

Follmann-Schulz, A.-B. (2010) Formen für Vierkantgefäße aus dem römischen Legionslager in Bonn, 1. Jahrhundert n. Chr. In Ch. Fontaine-Hodiament (ed.) *D'Ennion au Val Saint-Lambert. Le verre soufflé-moulé. Actes des 23e Rencontres de l'Association française pour l'Archéologie du Verre*. Scientia Artis 5, 235–240. Bruxelles, Institut Royal du Patrimoine artistique.

Follmann-Schulz, A.-B., Gaitzsch, W., Hartmann, G., Tegtmeier, U. and Wedepohl, K. H. (2000) Spätrömische Glashütten im Hambacher Forst – Produktionsort der ECVA-Fasskrüge. Archäologische und naturwissenschaftliche Untersuchungen. *Bonner Jahrbücher* 200, 83–241.

Fontaine, Ch. (2005) Fragments de verres plats d'époque mérovingienne trouvés à Huy (Belgique): une production locale? In D. Foy (ed.) *De transparentes spéculations. Vitres de l'Antiquité et du Haut Moyen Âge*, 72–73. Bavay, Conseil Général Département du Nord.

Fontaine-Hodiament, Ch. and Wouters, H. (2002) Ensemble de sept verres gallo-romains provenant de tombes diverses et appartenant au Musée d'Archéologie et d'Arts décoratifs (Musée Curtius) Liège. Deuxième moitié du Ier s. - début du IIe s. *Bulletin de l'Institut Royal du Patrimoine Artistique* 28, 1999–2000, 267–271.

Foster, H. E. and Jackson, C. M. (2009) The composition of 'naturally coloured' late Roman vessel glass from Britain and the implications for models of glass production and supply. *Journal of Archaeological Science* 36, 189–204.

Foy, D. (2010) *Les verres antiques d'Arles*. Paris, Éditions errance.

Foy, D. and Nenna, M.-D. (2001) *Tout feu, tout sable. Mille ans de verre antique dans le Midi de la France.* Aix-en-Provence, Edisud.

Freestone, I. (2006) Glass production in Late Antiquity and the Early Islamic period: a geochemical perspective. In M. Maggetti and B. Messiga (eds.) *Geomaterials in Cultural Heritage*. Geological Society Publication 257, 201–216. London, The Geological Society.

Freestone, I., Schachner, L., Shortland, A. and Tite, M. (2006) Natron as a flux in the early vitreous materials industry – sources, beginnings and reasons for decline. *Journal of Archaeological Science* 33, 521–530.

Freestone, I. C., Thirlwall, M. and Wolf, S. (2005) The production of HIMT glass: elemental and isotopic evidence. In *Annales du 16e Congrès de l'Association Internationale pour l'Histoire du Verre*, 153–157. Nottingham, Association Internationale pour l'Histoire du Verre.

Ganio, M., Boyen, S., Fenn, Th., Scott, R., Vanhoutte, S., Gimeno, D. and Degryse, P. (2012) Roman glass across the Empire: an elemental and isotopic characterization. *Journal of Analytical Atomic Spectrometry* 27, 743–753.

Gazenbeek, M. (2003) L'Argonne dans l'antiquité. *Gallia* 60, 269–317.

Gebhard, R. (2010) Celtic Glass. In A. Hilgner and B. Zorn (eds.) *Glass along the Silk Road from 200 BC to AD 1000*. RGZM – Tagungen 9, 3–13. Mainz, Römisch-Germanisches Zentralmuseum.

van Geesbergen, D. (1999) Les ateliers de verriers dans le nord de la Gaule et en Rhénanie (1er – 4e siècle après J.-C.). In M. Polfer (ed.) *Artisanat et productions artisanales en milieu rural dans les provinces du nord-ouest de l'Empire romain*. Monographies Instrumentum 9, 105–124. Montagnac, Monique Mergoil.

van Geesbergen, D. (2000) Les ateliers de verriers des époques gallo-romaine et médiévale découverts en belgique (synthese des données et bibliographie). *Bulletin de l'Association Française pour l'Archéologie du Verre*, 3–5.

Giertz, W. and Ristow, S. (2013) Goldtesellae und Fensterglas. Neue Untersuchungen zur Herstellung und Nutzung von Glas im Bereich der karolingerzeitlichen Pfalz Aachen. *Antike Welt* 44, 59–66.

Gilles, K.-J. (1985) *Spätrömische Höhensiedlungen in Eifel und Hunsrück*. Trierer Zeitschrift Beiheft 7. Trier, Rheinisches Landesmuseum Trier.

Glauben, A., Grünewald, M. and Grunwald, L. (2009) Mayen am Übergang von Spätantike zu frühem Mittelalter. In O. Wagener (ed.) *Der umkämpfte Ort – von der Antike zum Mittelalter*. Beihefte zur Mediaevistik 10, 135–156. Frankfurt, Peter Lang.

Goethert, K. (1984) Glasfabrikation in Trier. In Rheinisches Landesmuseum Trier (ed.) *Trier. Kaiserresidenz und Bischofssitz*, 249. Mainz, Philipp von Zabern.

Goethert-Polaschek, K. (1983) Glasfabrikation. In *Die Römer an Mosel und Saar*, 316. Mainz, Philipp von Zabern.

Goethert-Polaschek, K. (2011) Spätantike Glasfabrikation in Trier. Funde aus dem Töpfereiviertel und an der Hohenzollernstraße. *Trierer Zeitschrift* 73/74, 67–146.

Goethert-Polaschek, K. (2012) Glasfabrikation im römischen Trier. In L. Clemens and P. Steppuhn (eds.) *Glasproduktion. Archäologie und Geschichte. Beiträge zum 4. Internationalen Symposium zur Erforschung mittelalterlicher und frühneuzeitlicher Glashütten in Europa.* Interdisziplinärer Dialog zwischen Archäologie und Geschichte 2, 17–28. Trier, Kliomedia.

Götzen, D. (1999) *Die Glasproduktionsstätten des 1.–9. Jahrhunderts im Rheingebiet, Frankreich, Benelux, Schweiz und Österreich.* Unpublished master thesis, Humboldt-Universität zu Berlin.

Grünewald, M. (2011) *Die römischen Gräberfelder von Mayen.* Monographien des Römisch-Germanischen Zentralmuseums 96, Vulkanpark-Forschungen 10. Mainz, Römisch-Germanisches Zentralmuseum.

Grünewald, M. (2012) Etudes typo-chronologiques du verre de l'Antiquité tardive trouvés à Mayen: Les bouteilles Isings 132. In V. Arveiller and H. Cabart (eds.) *Le verre en Lorraine et dans les régions voisines. Actes du Colloque International, 26e Rencontres de l'Association Française pour l'Archéologie du verre.* Monographies Instrumentum 42, 197–210. Montagnac, Monique Mergoil.

Grünewald, M. and Hartmann, S. (2010) The Late Antique glass from Mayen (Germany): First results of chemical and archaeological studies. In A. Hilgner and B. Zorn (eds.) *Glass along the Silk Road from 200 BC to 1000 AD.* RGZM – Tagungen 9, 15–28. Mainz, Römisch-Germanisches Zentralmuseum.

Grünewald, M. and Vogt, K. (2001) Spätrömisches Worms. Grabungen an der Stiftskirche St. Paul in Worms III. *Wormsgau* 20, 7–26.

Grünwald, U. (1989) Töpferöfen des 1. Jahrhunderts. In H.-J. Engels (ed.) *Unter dem Pflaster von Speyer,* 35–44. Speyer, Zechnersche Buchdruckerei.

Haevernick, Th. E. (1981) Gedanken zur frühesten Glasherstellung in Europa. In Th. E. Haevernick, *Beiträge zur Glasforschung. Die wichtigsten Aufsätze von 1938 bis 1981,* 299–301. Mainz, Philipp von Zabern.

Hanut, F. (2006) La verrerie dans la cité des Tongres au haut-empire: un aperçu général. In P. Cosyns, G. Creemers and B. Demarsin (eds.) *Roman Glass in Germania Inferior. Interregional Comparisons and recent results.* Atvatvca 1, 10–28. Tongeren, Provinciaal Gallo-Romeins Museum.

Hanut, F., Mignon, Ph. and Lauwens, G. (2012) La verrerie de la forteresse de l'Antiquité tardive à Montaigle (province de Namur, Belgique). In V. Arveiller and H. Cabart (eds.) *Le verre en Lorraine et dans les régions voisines. Actes du Colloque International, 26e Rencontres de l'Association Française pour l'Archéologie du verre.* Monographies Instrumentum 42, 247–268. Montagnac, Monique Mergoil.

Harden, D. B., Hellenkemper, H., Painter, K. and Whitehouse, D. (1988) *Glas der Caesaren.* Cologne/London/Milan/New York, Olivetti.

Henrich, P. (2006) *Die römische Besiedlung in der westlichen Vulkaneifel.* Trierer Zeitschrift Beiheft 30. Trier, Rheinisches Landesmuseum Trier.

Höpken C. and Schäfer, F. (2006) Glasverarbeitung und Glaswerkstätten in Köln. In P. Cosyns, G. Creemers and B. Demarsin (eds.) *Roman Glass in Germania Inferior. Interregional Comparisons and recent results.* Atvatvca 1, 74–85. Tongeren, Provinciaal Gallo-Romeins Museum.

Hunold, A. and Sirocko, F. (2009) Klimagunst und die Blütezeit des Römischen Reiches. In F. Sirocko (ed.) *Wetter, Klima, Menschheitsentwicklung. Von der Eiszeit bis ins 21. Jahrhundert,* 144–149. Darmstadt, Wissenschaftliche Buchgesellschaft.

Hunold, A. (2012) Mayen und sein Umland zur Zeit des Gallischen Sonderreichs. In Th. Fischer (ed.) *Die Krise des 3. Jh. n. Chr. und das Gallische Sonderreich.* ZAKMIRA-Schriften 8, 275–306. Wiesbaden, Reichert.

Isings, C. (1957) *Roman Glass from dated finds.* Archaeologica Traiectina 2. Groningen/Djakarta, J. B. Wolters.

Jackson, C. M., Joyner, L., Booth, C. A., Day, P. M., Wager, E. C. W. and Kilikoglou, V. (2003) Glass-making at Coppergate, York? Analytical evidence for the nature of production. *Archaeometry* 45, 435–456.

Jackson, C., Price J. and Lemke Ch. (2009) Glass production in the 1st century AD: insights into glass technology. In K. Janssens, P. Degryse, P. Cosyns, J. Caen and L. Van't dack (eds.) *Annales du 17e Congrès de l'Association Internationale pour l'Histoire du Verre,* 150–156. Brussels, University Press Antwerp.

Jahresbericht 1939 (1940) Jahresbericht des Rheinischen Landesmuseums Trier für 1939. *Trierer Zeitschrift* 15, 35–104.

Keller, Ch. (2004) *Archäologische Forschungen in Aachen.* Rheinische Ausgrabungen 55. Mainz, Philipp von Zabern.

Kiessel, M. (2009) *Die römische villa rustica „Auf dem Bingstel", Gemeinde Winningen, Kreis Mayen-Koblenz. Untersuchungen zu Befunden, Fundmaterial und Besiedlungskontinuität.* Berichte zur Archäologie an Mittelrhein und Mosel 15. Koblenz, Direktion Landesarchäologie Koblenz.

Kind, Th., Kronz, A. and Wedepohl, K. H. (2003) Karolingerzeitliches Glas und verschiedene Handwerksindizien aus dem Kloster Fulda. *Zeitschrift für Archäologie des Mittelalters* 31, 61–93.

Knöchlein, R. (2002) Gewerbliche Betätigung in einer Ansiedlung der späten Kaiserzeit bei Trebur, Hessen. *Archäologisches Korrespondenzblatt* 32, 105–116.

Komp, J. (2009) *Römisches Fensterglas. Archäologische und archäometrische Untersuchungen zur Glasherstellung im Rheingebiet.* Aachen, Shaker.

Komp, J. (2010) Ein römischer Glasmacherofen in Düren. In *Archäologie im Rheinland 2009,* 73–74. Stuttgart, Theiss.

Kronz, A., Sanke, M. and Wedepohl, K. H. (2002) Karolingerzeitliches Glas aus dem Kloster Lorsch. *Zeitschrift für Archäologie des Mittelalters* 30, 37–75.

van Lith, S. M. E. and Randsborg, K. (1985) Roman Glass in the West: A Social Study. *Berichten van de Oudheidkundig Bodemonderzoek* 35, 413–532.

Louis, A. and Gazenbeek, M. (2011) La production du verre sous l'Antiquité. In L. Ayache (ed.) *Musée de la cour d'or – Metz métropole. Archéologie et usages du verre,* 31–37. Metz, Editions Serpenoise.

Luik, M. (1999) Gewerbliche Produktionsstätten in Villen des römischen Rheinlandes. In M. Polfer (ed.) *Artisanat et productions artisanales en milieu rural dans le provinces du nord-ouest de l'Empire romain.* Monographies Instrumentum 9, 205–212. Montagnac, Monique Mergoil.

Martin-Kilcher, S., Maus, H. and Werth, W. (1979) Römischer Bergbau bei Sulzburg «Mühlematt», Kreis Breisgau-Hochschwarzwald. *Fundberichte Baden-Württemberg* 4, 1979, 170–203.

Nickel, C., Thoma, M. and Wigg-Wolf, D. (2008) *Martberg. Heiligtum und Oppidum der Treverer I. Der Kultbezirk. Die Grabungen 1994–2004*. Berichte zur Archäologie an Mittelrhein und Mosel 14. Koblenz, Direktion Landesarchäologie Koblenz.

Nortmann, H. (2012) Eisenzeitliche Glasfunde aus der Moselregion. In L. Clemens and P. Steppuhn (eds.) *Glasproduktion. Archäologie und Geschichte. Beiträge zum 4. Internationalen Symposium zur Erforschung mittelalterlicher und frühneuzeitlicher Glashütten in Europa*. Interdisziplinärer Dialog zwischen Archäologie und Geschichte 2, 9–16. Trier, Kliomedia.

Oldenstein, J. (2009) *Kastell Alzey. Archäologische Untersuchungen im spätrömischen Lager und Studien zur Grenzverteidigung im Mainzer Dukat*. Mainz, http://ubm.opus.hbz-nrw.de/volltexte/2009/2070/pdf/diss.pdf.

Päffgen, B. (2003) Glasherstellung spätrömischer und frühmittelalterlicher Zeit im Rheinland und dessen Nachbargebieten. In A. Eibner, S. Felgenhauer-Schmiedt and H. Knittler (eds.) *Auf gläsernen Spuren. Der Beitrag Mitteleuropas zur archäologisch-historischen Glasforschung*. Beiträge zur Mittelalterarchäologie in Österreich 19, 9–28.

Päffgen, B. and Trier, M. (2001) Köln zwischen Spätantike und Frühmittelalter. Eine Übersicht zu Fragen und Forschungsstand. In *Zwischen Römersiedlung und mittelalterlicher Stadt. Archäologische Aspekte zur Kontinuitätsfrage*. Beiträge zur Mittelalterarchäologie in Österreich 17, 17–42.

Päffgen, B. and Wedepohl, K. H. (2004) Frühmerowingische Glasherstellung in Hasselsweiler bei Jülich. *Kölner Jahrbuch* 37, 835–848.

Perse, M. (1995) Archäologie vor den Toren – Bodendenkmalpflege in Jülich 1989–1994. In H. G. Horn, H. Koschik and B. Trier (eds.) *Ein Land macht Geschichte. Archäologie in Nordrhein-Westfalen*. Schriften zur Bodendenkmalpflege in Nordrhein-Westfalen 3, 127–130. Mainz, Philipp von Zabern.

Pfahl, St. F. (2000) Die Ausgrabung Trier „Hopfengarten". Wasserversorgung und Glasherstellung in einem „Handwerkerviertel" der römischen Stadt. *Funde und Ausgrabungen im Bezirk Trier* 32, 43–54.

Polfer, M. (2005) *L'artisanat dans l'économie de la Gaule Belgique romaine à partir de la documentation archéologique*. Monographies Instrumentum 28. Montagnac, Monique Mergoil.

Redknap, M. (1999) Die römischen und mittelalterlichen Töpfereien in Mayen, Kreis Mayen-Koblenz. In *Berichte zur Archäologie an Mittelrhein und Mosel* 6, 11–401. Trier, Rheinisches Landesmuseum Trier.

Reichmann, Ch. (1995) Stadtarchäologie in Krefeld 1990–1994. In H. G. Horn, H. Koschik and B. Trier (eds.) *Ein Land macht Geschichte. Archäologie in Nordrhein-Westfalen*. Schriften zur Bodendenkmalpflege in Nordrhein-Westfalen 3, 131–133. Mainz, Philipp von Zabern.

Roller, O. (1957) Eine römische Glashütte in der Pfalz. *Pfälzer Heimat* 8.2, 60–61.

Sauer, S. (1991) Neuss Gnadental. *Bonner Jahrbücher* 191, 560.

Schreg, R. (2009) Siedlungsverdichtung und Stollenbau – der Mensch gestaltet die Landschaft nach seinen Vorstellungen. In F. Sirocko (ed.) *Wetter, Klima, Menschheitsentwicklung. Von der Eiszeit bis ins 21. Jahrhundert*, 154–159. Darmstadt, Wissenschaftliche Buchgesellschaft.

Steinhausen, J. (1932) *Archaeologische Karte der Rheinprovinz. Ortskunde Trier-Mettendorf*. Geschichtlicher Atlas der Rheinprovinz 3.I.1. Publikationen der Gesellschaft für rheinische Geschichte. Bonn, Peter Hanstein.

Stephan, H.-G. and Wedepohl, K. H. (1997) Mittelalterliches Glas aus dem Reichskloster und der Stadtwüstung Corvey. *Germania* 75, 673–715.

Stephan, H.-G. (2000) *Studien zur Siedlungsentwicklung von Stadt und Reichskloster Corvey*. Neumünster, Wachholtz.

Strauch, D. (1996) Römische Fundstellen in Aachen. *Zeitschrift des Aachener Geschichtsvereins* 100, 7–128.

Thill, G. (1968) Une verrerie gallo-romaine au Titelberg. *Hémecht* 20, 521–531.

Ulbert, G. (1969) *Das frührömische Kastell Rheingönheim. Die Funde aus den Jahren 1912 und 1913*. Limesforschungen 9. Berlin, Mann.

Wagner, H. (2006) *Glasschmuck der Mittel- und Spätlatènezeit am Oberrhein und den angrenzenden Gebieten*. Remshalden, Greiner.

Wedepohl, K. H., Pirling, R. and Hartmann, G. (1997) Römische und Fränkische Gläser aus dem Gräberfeld von Krefeld-Gellep. *Bonner Jahrbücher* 197, 177–189.

Wedepohl, K. H. (2003) *Flach- und Gefäßglas der Karolingerzeit*. Nachrichten der Akademie der Wissenschaften zu Göttingen 2. Mathematisch-Physikalische Klasse. Göttingen, Vandenhoeck & Ruprecht.

Winkelmann, W. (1977) Archäologische Zeugnisse zum frühmittelalterlichen Handwerk in Westfalen. *Frühmittelalterliche Studien* 11, 92–126.

Witteyer, M. (1999) *Mißratene Götter. Der Terrakottenfund aus Mainz. Dokumentation der Ausstellung 2. Februar bis 26. März 1999*. Mainz, Landesamt für Denkmalpflege Rheinland-Pfalz/Archäologische Denkmalpflege/Amt Mainz/Commerzbank.

Woimont, G.-P. (1995) *L'Oise*. Carte Archéologique de la Gaule 60. Paris, Académie des Inscriptions et Belles-Lettres/Ministère de la Culture.

Zeitler, J. P. (1990) Zwei hallstatt-frühlatènezeitliche Fremdfunde von der Ehrenbürg, Ldkr. Forchheim, Oberfranken. Bemerkungen zur kulturhistorischen Interpretation des sog. Südimports. *Archäologisches Korrespondenzblatt* 20, 61–73.

Zimmermann, M. (2011) Technische Abhängigkeiten des frühmittelalterlichen Glasmacherhandwerks. Eine Zusammenfassung archäologischer Hinweise zum Transport von Rohstoffen und *know how* aus dem Orient nach Europa. *Zeitschrift für Archäologie des Mittelalters* 39, 109–124.

7

Campanulate bowls from *Gallaecia*: evidence for regional glass production in late antiquity

Mário da Cruz

Introduction

Roman secondary glass production in the north-west of the Iberian Peninsula is finally coming to light (Fig. 7.1). Several workshops have been identified in recent years, not only in the main towns such as *Asturica Augusti* and *Lucus Augusti* (Astorga and Lugo, Spain) or *Bracara Augusta* (Braga, Portugal), but also in smaller settlements like *Vicus Helleni* and *Tude* (Vigo and Tui, Spain). *Bracara Augusta* in particular plays an important role in the region from the end of the 3rd century, as capital of the Roman province of *Gallaecia,* to the late 6th century, as the capital of the Swabian kingdom. This period is likely to be the peak of glass production when at least three glass workshops operated in the town. With the annexation of the Swabian kingdom by the Visigoths in AD 586 *Bracara Augusta* started to decline and glass production seems to have been interrupted. From the 7th century onwards, glass vessels are almost absent from the archaeological record. The Roman province of *Gallaecia* was created by the Emperor Diocletian around AD 284–288 and corresponds to modern Portugal to the north of the river Douro and the Spanish autonomous territories of Galicia, most of Asturias and the northwestern part of Castile-Leon.

Within the Gallaecian glass production campanulate bowls stand as the most popular glass vessels, being found in almost every late antique archaeological site. Such bowls can be related to other European vessels from the same period, and thus form part of an "international" late antique style. The Gallaecian bowls, however, have some particular details of production that allow us to identify a regional style and consequently local glass production, from the end of the 4th century to the middle of the 6th century or beyond. The standard Gallaecian campanulate bowl is of simple design, although there are many variations in shape, size, colour and decoration. The name "campanulate" comes from their general shape which resembles an inverted bell. It is preferred to "campaniforme" to avoid confusion with the prehistoric campaniforme culture used in the Latin languages (Bell-Beaker culture in English, *Glockenbecherkultur* in German).

The present study is a first essay in identifying and classifying a specific group of glass vessels, but it does not pretend to investigate all available data or to suggest that all the campanulate bowls found in *Gallaecia* were of local production. Even if the evidence points in that direction there is a possibility that some of the examples presented here have their origin in other Roman provinces.

Main forms

The campanulate bowls form a cohesive group of glass vessels with shared features. Apart from the general shape they all have a very distinctive "match head" rim profile with a thick fire-rounded edge, which is more symmetrical in the deeper versions and slightly in-turned or thicker inside on the shallower versions. The body tends to be conical but with slightly curved walls. The wall of the body is significantly thinner than the rim and the base, and is often very thin indeed. The base is flat or concave, and usually very thick without a clear angle between the body and base. All examples show a central mark left by the pontil.

The bowls have been classified as four main forms according to the shape of the body (Fig. 7.2), though some examples do not fit exactly into the standard forms. Let us not forget that they were blown, rather than cast or mould-blown, which means that no two bowls are completely identical. However, the variation in shape, size and capacity

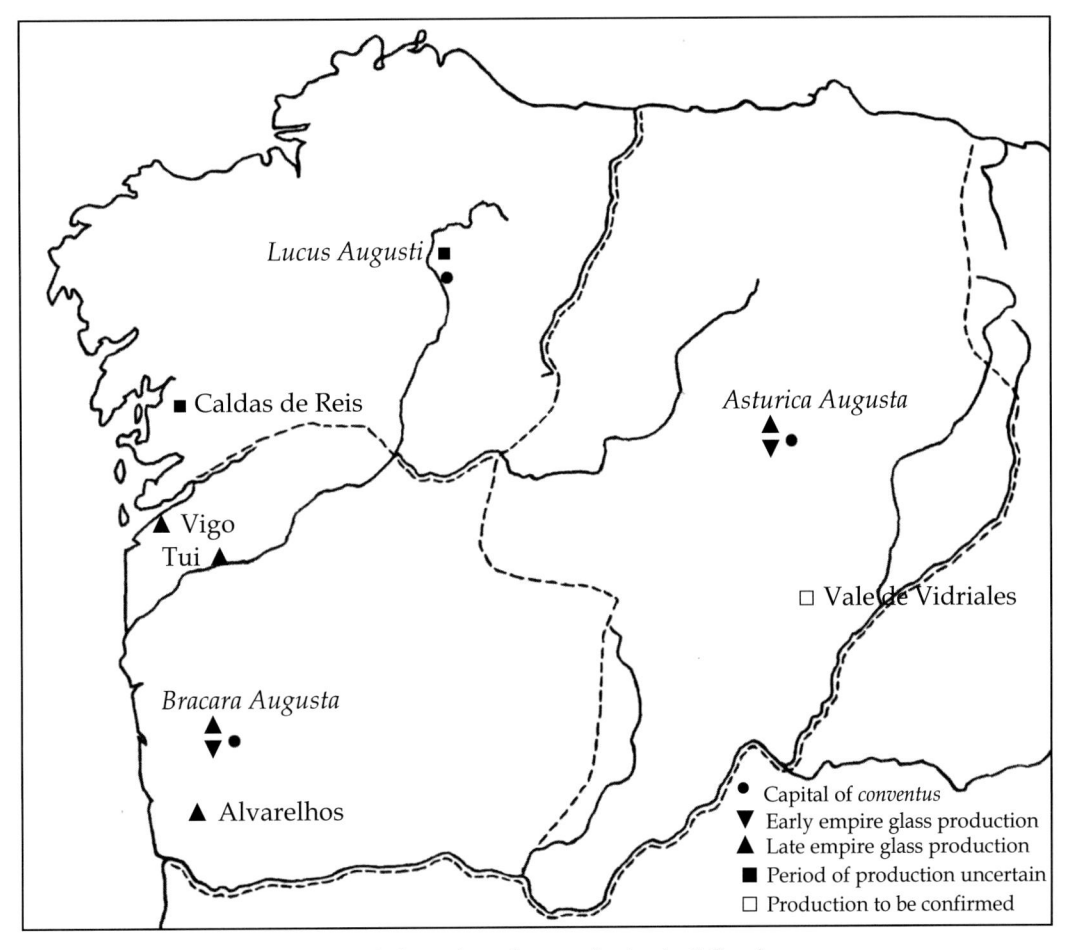

Fig. 7.1: Secondary glass production in Gallaecia.

reflects an intention to comply with standard sizes and it may be that these reflect different purposes or functions. We can assume that the beakers and the deep bowls were meant for drinking, the shallow bowls for eating or serving food and that the intermediate bowls could have had various uses. The rim diameter alone provides a fairly accurate identification of the different forms (see captions in Fig. 7.2).

Of the four main forms, Figs. 7.2.1 and 7.2.4 are the most easily recognised as belonging to an international style, while Figs. 7.2.2 and 7.2.3 illustrate the Gallaecian style. If we compare these forms with the Merovingian examples from northern France, illustrated by Jean-Yves Feyeux (1995), we note that they all differ in some details. Our beaker (Fig. 7.2.1) resembles Feyeux types 51 and 57, but is shorter and has a wider and better developed concave base. The cup/deep bowl (Fig. 7.2.2) resembles Feyeux type 55 but again has a better developed concave base. The bowls and shallow bowls (Fig. 7.2.3–4) are equivalent to Feyeux type 81 but in most cases they show some unique features that distinguish them as typical of the Gallaecian style.

Beakers are the least common of the four forms. They are so rare that we had some reservations in including them in this study. The only complete example illustrated here (Fig. 7.2.1) comes from a necropolis in Paredes, Asturias (Requejo Pagés 1999) and the closest parallel comes from another necropolis in La Olmeda, Palência (Abásolo *et al.* 2004, 53). Either they are imports from northern Europe or a speciality of some other workshop in central or northeastern Iberia. By contrast, cups and deep bowls (Fig. 7.2.2) are the most common of all the campanulate bowls, which is remarkable for a regionally specific form. They define the shapes and decorative techniques of the production from Gallaecian workshops. Bowls and shallow bowls (Fig. 7.2.3–4) are clearly an evolution of the earlier deep bowls but interestingly they match the "international" design, Feyeux type 81, most closely.

Unsurprisingly, the bowls were predominantly made in the late Roman colours: different shades of yellow/green, dark green and brown, as well as some in greenish colourless and blue/green.

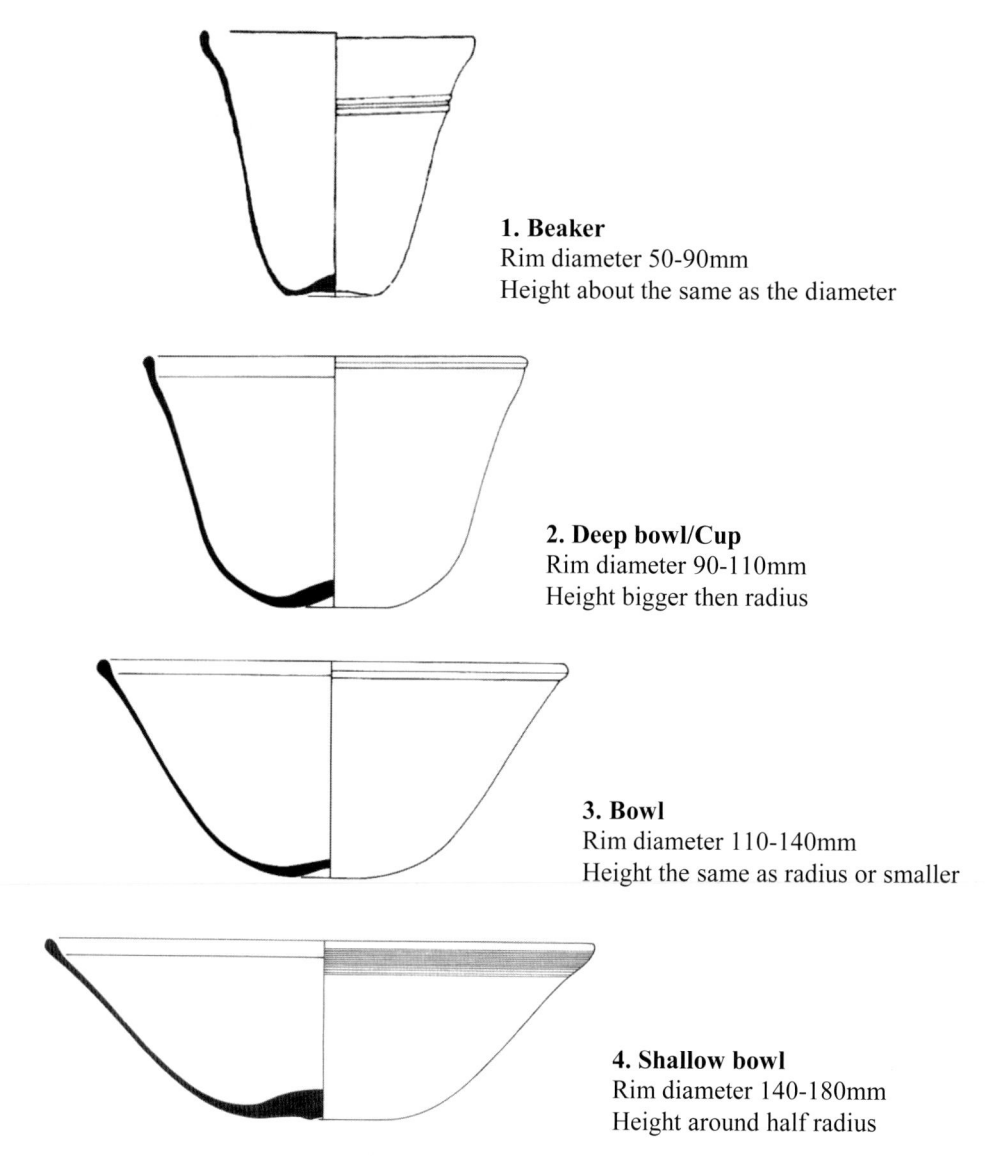

1. Beaker
Rim diameter 50-90mm
Height about the same as the diameter

2. Deep bowl/Cup
Rim diameter 90-110mm
Height bigger then radius

3. Bowl
Rim diameter 110-140mm
Height the same as radius or smaller

4. Shallow bowl
Rim diameter 140-180mm
Height around half radius

Fig. 7.2: Main vessel forms (scale 1:2).

Form and decoration

The dominance of the campanulate bowls in the 5th and 6th centuries is presumably explained by their design. The vessels are elegant, functional and, despite their simple lines and soft colours, individually they all differ in some details. Some were undecorated while others had wide range of decoration (Fig. 7.3, Table 7.1). Most of the decoration was formed when the vessel was hot, with the exception of the abraded vessels, and almost all of the decoration was produced with either spiral threads or pattern-blowing.

Spiral threading is a decorative technique involving the application of threads, also called trails, around the rim, neck or body of the vessels. The threads might be left standing proud of the surface or melted flush with the surface (Stern 2001, 30). Self coloured threads applied to the upper body to produce the effect of a ribbed horizontal band are very common (Fig. 7.3.2). The threads were applied at a relatively early stage, before the final reheating, and were partially melted into the surface. This produces a wavy surface effect, rather than standing proud as sometimes occurs on 1st century vessels, or melting flush with the surface. Self coloured festooned threads are very rare (Fig. 7.3.3). In this case the threads are pinched and pulled down the body to produce the festoons. These festooned threads are left more clearly in relief than the horizontal ones. Examples with translucent dark blue/green threads with blobs are also rare, but they are characteristic of local production in *Gallaecia* (Fig. 7.3.4).

Opaque white threads, usually associated with bowls

Table 7.1: Decoration versus vessel form.

Decoration versus form	1 beaker	2 cup/d.b.	3 bowl	4 s. bowl
Plain	√	√	√	√
Spiral thread and blobs				
Same color as the vessel				
Horizontal/spiral threads	√	√	√	
Festooned threads		√		
Translucent dark blue/green				
Horizontal/spiral threads		√	√	
Blobs		√		
Opaque white				
Horizontal/spiral threads			√	√
Festooned threads and others			√	√
Pattern-blowing				
Expanded vertical ribs	√	√	√	√
Expanded oblique ribs		√	√	√
Fish-bone pattern			√	√
Geometrical patterns and Christian symbols		√	√	√
Mixed techniques				
Expanded ribs and threads		√	√	√
Expanded ribs and other pattern-blowing		√		
Indents		√		
Decoration formed when the vessel was cold				
Abrasion			√	√

and shallow bowls, are the second most popular form of trailing (Table 7.1). They were used in the decoration of the campanulate bowls from the second half of the 5th century and are associated with the latest forms of the bowls. The designs using opaque white threads were more elaborate than the self coloured designs and were usually melted flush with the surface. However it is possible to distinguish two groups; the ones applied on an early stage, stretching and spreading with the blowing of the vessel into the final shape (Fig. 7.3.12), and the ones applied on a later stage and keeping their thickness (Fig. 7.3.11). The first ones are called *threaded* and the second ones *thread-wound*, according to Marianne Stern (2001, 30).

Pattern-blowing is a decorative technique used predominantly in combination with free blowing (Stern 2001, 27). The inflated gather was blown into a patterned mould and blown again outside the mould to expand and shape the vessel. Ribs are the most popular expanded patterns, usually left vertical (Figs. 7.3.5, 7.3.7–8), but also twisted obliquely (Fig. 7.3.6). Some examples have geometric or Christian symbols on the base (Fig. 7.3.8–9). The bowls with herringbone pattern are very unusual (Fig. 7.3.13), as a matter of fact we only know two bowls and one flask, all found in the same archaeological site in Vigo, Spain (Cruz 2009b, vol. III, 375) in association with raw glass, which suggests that a local workshop may have produced these vessels for which no parallels are known.

Vessels with spiral threads and pattern-blowing are also known, showing an overlap between these comparatively simple decorative techniques. The commonest is the application of spiral threads, either self coloured or opaque white, on pattern-blown bowls (Figs. 7.3.7, 7.3.13). In these cases the threads stand proud because the spiral threading is one of the latest finishing stages. There are also cases where ribs are combined with geometric patterns on the base (Fig. 7.3.8) but it is not clear whether they have used single or multiple moulds.

As well as the two main decorative techniques mentioned above, another form of hot decoration, vertical indents on the body, sometimes occurs on campanulate bowls (Fig. 7.3.10). This decoration is more common on beakers and bowls with cracked-off rims than on ones with fire rounded rims.

Decoration formed when the vessel was cold is also present. There are a few examples with abraded decoration. The rarity and poor quality of the designs suggest that this may not have been a very popular method of decoration, perhaps because the thin walls of the campanulate bowls were not strong enough to support the technique. The best preserved example is a bowl with an inscription found at Vigo, Spain (Fig. 7.3.14). The inscription is incomplete but there is a good parallel from Holme Pierrepont, Nottingham (Price 2000, fig. 3.9, pl. 7) which reads from the inside: *SEMPER* (always). The bowl from Vigo is generally comparable with the one from Holme Pierrepont in form

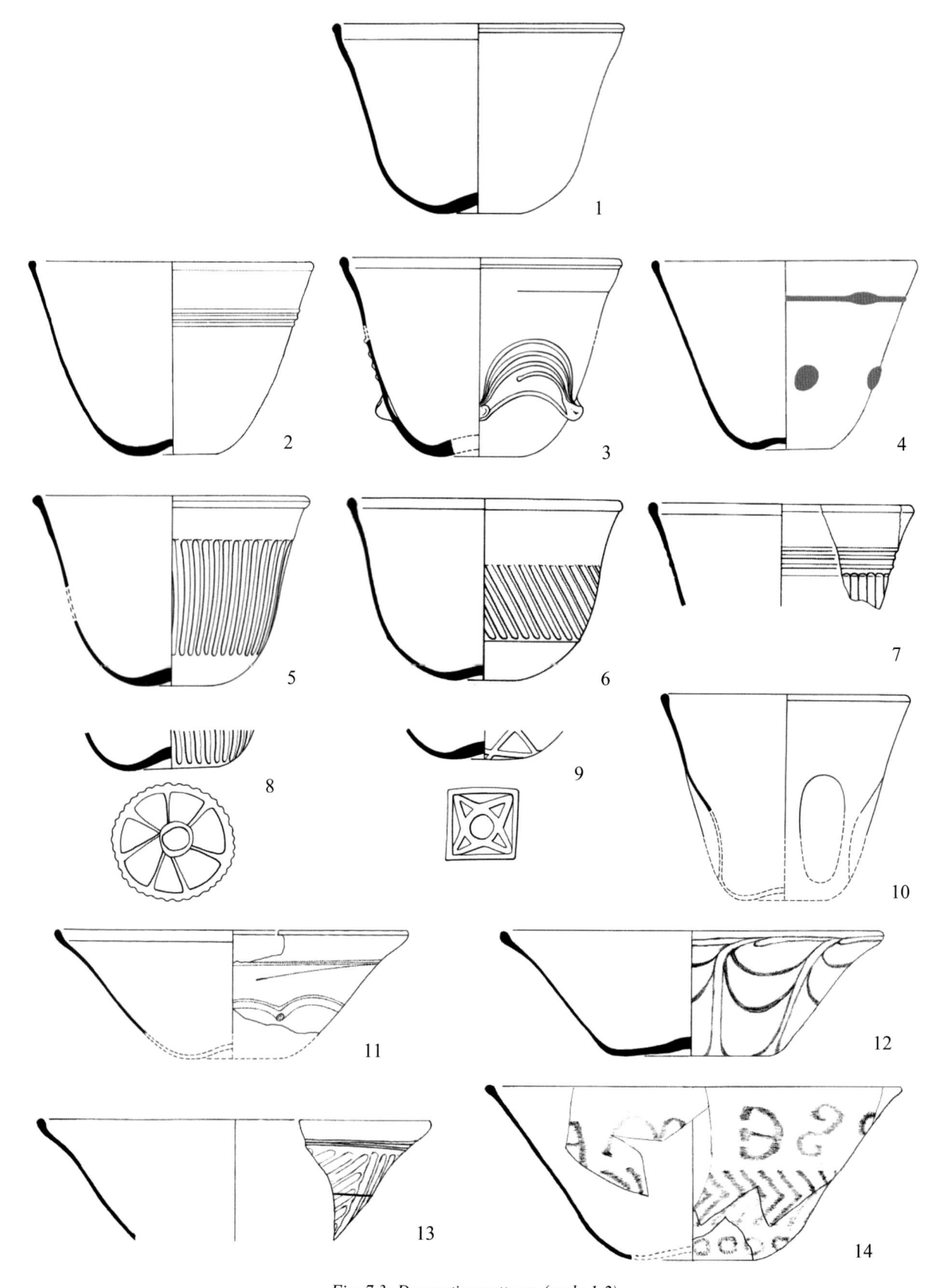

Fig. 7.3: Decorative patterns (scale 1:2).

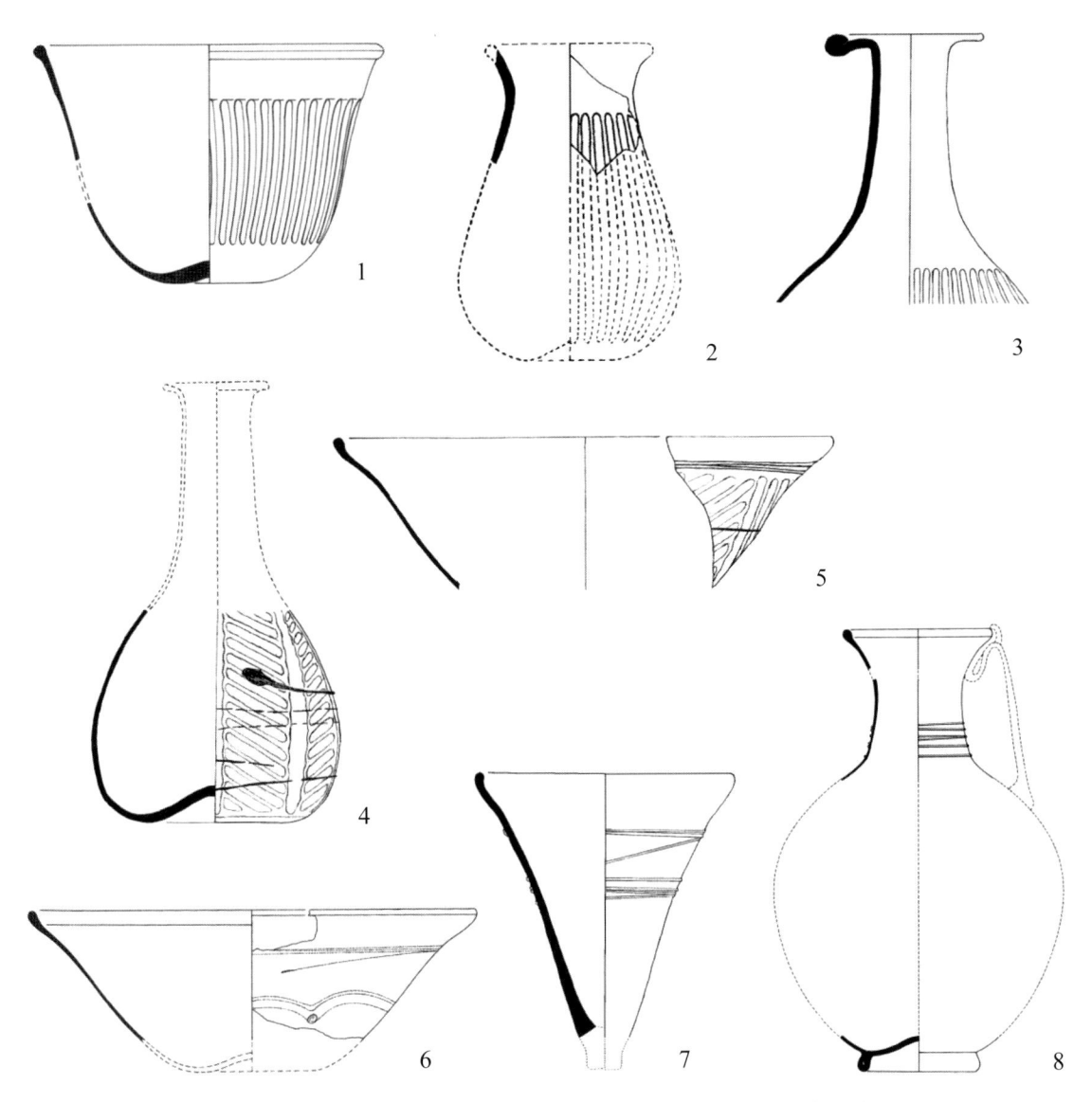

Fig. 7.4: Similar decoration on different vessel forms (scale 1:2).

and decoration. Both have a fire-rounded rim and shallow body and three horizontal zones of abraded decoration, of which the top (inscribed letters) and bottom (small circular rings) are very similar, though the middle zone on the Vigo vessels is a band of herringbone motifs, while the Holme Pierrepont fragment shows a longtailed bird and vegetal motifs. Another parallel for the Vigo bowl is a lower body fragment found in Trethurgy, Cornwall, UK (Price 2000, pl. 8), with the same central and lower motifs. The three pieces are clearly from the same workshop, if not the same artist, but the available data is not yet sufficient to pinpoint exactly where they were produced. Vigo is a possibility not only because it was an important trading port in late antiquity but more importantly because there is evidence for secondary glass production there (Cruz 2009b, vol. I, 244). In addition to the bowl shown here, at least eight more fragmentary examples with abraded designs are known from Vigo, including five found amongst glass waste and raw glass in a glass production context in Rosalia de Castro Avenue.

Campanulate bowls are the focus of this study in part because they are found in abundance and are representative of the region, and also because there is not yet enough information to produce a satisfactory study of all late antique Gallaecian glass. This does not, however, mean that campanulate bowls were the only glass vessels produced in the local Gallaecian workshops. The spectrum of Gallaecian glass production is likely to have included a wider range of glassware, such as cups and bowls with cracked-off rims, and some bottles, jugs, jars, flasks and even lamps. Despite the lack of data we can construct an overview based on stylistic comparison, and in some cases, can suggest the existence of sets of glass tableware (Fig. 7.4).

Fig. 7.4.1–5 show the variety of pattern-blown designs and help us to understand that these moulds were used to blow both open and closed vessels, such as jars and flasks. Observation of the ways that the patterns expand on jars and flasks suggests that the mould was probably cylindrical rather than conical. The flask and the bowl with herringbone patterns (Fig. 7.4.4–5) came from the same archaeological context and are good examples of a local glass blowing style, the special "signature" being the opaque white spiral thread overlying the herringbone pattern. In the case of the expanded ribs and the opaque white spiral threads (Figs. 7.4.1–3, 7.4.6–8) it is more difficult to point to a single glass blowing or workshop tradition because the decoration is quite common and may have been produced in different places.

Chronology

Accurate dating of the different forms and styles of decoration is a serious difficulty, as few examples are known from stratified and well-dated archaeological contexts, and most of the chronology proposed is taken from parallels found elsewhere. As a general rule, the shallowest bowls appear to be the latest in date, but the more detailed picture, combining the form and the decoration, is much more complex.

The beakers (Fig. 7.2.1) are so scarce that we can only suggest that they were in use in the second half of the 4th century or the beginning of the 5th century, based on the chronology of the necropolis at Paredes, Asturias, where the only complete example was found (Requejo Pagés 1998, 269).

The deep bowls (Fig. 7.2.2) probably appeared in the second half of the 4th century, were in use throughout the 5th century and disappeared in the first half of the 6th century. As well as the finds from the necropolis of Paredes (Requejo Pagés 1998; 1999), where they are quite common, they are dated within the 4th and 5th centuries in Galicia, Spain (Xusto Rodrigues 2001, 347), in the "Meseta" necropolis (Fuentes Dominguez 1990, type IIIc) and in *Conimbriga*, Portugal (Alarcão *et al.* 1976, 196). Deep campanulate bowls were, however, still being produced in Braga, Portugal, at the end of the 5th century or beginning of the 6th century in a local workshop excavated recently (Cruz 2009b, vol. I, 217). All the dating evidence in Iberia appears to be earlier than the chronological horizon accepted for Feyeux type 55 in northern France (mid 6th century–beginning of the 7th century), although the Iberian data may need some revision.

The bowls and shallow bowls (Fig. 7.2.3–4) are later forms, even though they overlap in time with the earlier deep bowls. They probably appear in the first half of the 5th century and continue in use until the end of the 6th century or later. Bowls (Fig. 7.2.3) seem to be a transitional form between the deep bowls and the shallow bowls, and are more common during the 5th century, while the shallow bowls (Fig. 7.2.4) are more common in the 6th century. Alarcão dates these bowls to the 4th and 5th centuries (Alarcão *et al.* 1976, 193) but the 4th century may be too early since they are absent from the necropolis of Paredes, which dates from the second half of the 4th century to the beginning of the 5th century (Requejo Pagés 1998; 1999). Patrick Perin dates Feyeux type 81 found in northern Gaul from the mid 5th century to the mid 6th century (Perin 1995, fig. 5).

Turning to the development of the decoration, self coloured spiral threads were in fashion at the beginning, that is, the end of the 4th century and the 5th century, and seem to have been gradually replaced by opaque white threads in the second half of the 5th century. Self coloured spiral threads are very common on deep bowls and bowls and virtually absent on shallow bowls. In turn, opaque white threads appeared and became dominant at the end of the 5th century and the beginning of the 6th century (Foy 1995, 204). With pattern-blowing, expanded ribs are the most common pattern, being present on all the main forms at all periods, though the ribs tend to be sharper on the deeper bowls and more blurred on the shallow ones. Geometric patterns and Christian symbols on the base are typical of the end of the 5th century and the beginning of the 6th century in southeastern France (Foy 1995, 202), whereas the Gallaecian designs are more geometric and less explicitly Christian, and are found with and without the expanded ribs.

Secondary glass production sites in *Gallaecia*

The campanulate bowls are the most abundant and widespread of all the glass vessels on archaeological sites in northwestern Iberia in late antiquity. It is not an exaggeration to say that for every two glass fragments found one is probably from a campanulate bowl. This alone is good evidence for secondary glass production in *Gallaecia* (Fig. 7.1), but further information can now be presented based on recent finds, or in some cases rediscoveries, of evidence for glass production such as glass waste, raw glass, crucibles and glass-working structures.

Glass-working was probably introduced into the region during the 1st century from the military camps such as *Asturica Augusta* or *Petavonium* (Astorga and Rosinos de Vidriales). The latter camp is situated on a valley in the Spanish province of Zamora with the evocative name of "valley of the glassworks" (a free translation of "Vale de Vidriales"). There is strong evidence for glass production in the military camp of *Petavonium* itself and elsewhere in the valley, in a place called "Teso de los vidrios" ("hilltop of the glasses") near the village of Granucillo de Vidriales, two furnaces have been found by chance but not yet excavated (Cruz 2009b, vol. I, 253). All three of the *conventus* capitals had glass workshops at some point of their history but *Bracara Augusta*, the capital of *Gallaecia*, is the one that has produced most information, with three glass-working sites being identified so far, at least two of which were in operation in late antiquity. The latest to be identified and excavated, the CTT workshop, is thought to have been dismantled by the end of the 5th century or beginning of the 6th century and campanulate bowls were one of the main products there (Cruz 2009a, 27; 2009b, vol. I, 217).

Secondary glass production seems to have increased greatly in the region in the 4th and 5th centuries, spreading from Braga and Lugo to smaller towns, such as Tui, Vigo and Caldas de Reis. These, along with Alvarelhos and *Bracara Augusta*, are particularly interesting because they are part of the trend towards regional late antique glass production. The establishment of glass workshops along the western Atlantic coast and particularly along the main terrestrial and maritime routes seems to indicate an intention to reach markets beyond the local and regional level. Vigo is a good example of this trend as it was a dynamic seaport in late antiquity and an important centre of glass production, with at least two glass-working sites (Cruz 2009b, vol. I, 244). A similar situation on a smaller scale can be seen in the neighbouring town of Tui where one glass-working site has been reported (Vilaseco Vásquez 2003), as it is strategically located at the crossroads of two important land and river routes. The occurrence of similar types of abraded campanulate bowls in Vigo and in Britain also implies contacts between the two regions (see above for the discussion of Fig. 7.3.14 and the parallels from Britain).

Chemical analyses of the compositions do not yet distinguish between the different "chemical signatures" of local workshops considering the specificity of Roman glass production (Price 2005, 168). At present we can recognise with relative security the origins of the raw glasses, that is, the glasses produced from raw materials in the primary glass production sites (Picon and Vichy 2003). Surprisingly, the chemical analysis of three of the campanulate bowls from Braga shows the presence of all of the three groups of glass (Table 7.2), available to glass blowers during the period of production of these bowls.

Two of the samples, Bra 15, a yellow/green bowl with self coloured spiral threads, and Bra 16, brown/green bowl with expanded ribs, belong to group 1, a glass from the 5th century, the first of the two HIMT glasses (High Iron, Manganese and Titanium) with a probable origin in Egypt (Foy *et al.* 2003, 47). The third sample, Bra 17, analysed both glasses of a pale yellow/green bowl with opaque white threads, Bra 17I being the transparent yellow/green glass and Bra17W the opaque white glass. These analyses showed that the yellow/green glass belonged to group 2 and the opaque

Table 7.2: Composition of three campanulate bowls from Bracara Augusta *(Braga, Portugal) by Bernard Gratuze (IRAMAT, Orleans, France). Major values by weight per cent.*

	G 1		G2	G3
	Bra 15	**Bra 16**	**Bra 17I**	**Bra 17W**
Na2 O	19,0%	20,3%	18,0%	17,5%
Mg O	1,07%	1,24%	1,23%	0,66%
Al2 O3	2,99%	3,03%	2,68%	2,12%
Si O2	65,2%	62,4%	63,9%	64,6%
P2 O5	529	0,09%	0,16%	0,08%
Cl	0,44%	0,76%	0,86%	0,95%
K2 O	0,72%	0,75%	0,70%	0,63%
Ca O	5,69%	6,10%	9,24%	5,85%
Ti O2	0,31%	0,41%	0,20%	0,10%
Mn O	2,07%	2,28%	2,05%	0,99%
Fe2 O3	1,61%	2,43%	1,16%	0,72%
Sn O2	7	25	35	3,35%
Sb2 O3	1,42	7,34	109	82

white glass to group 3. Group 2 is the second HIMT glass, in use from 6th–8th centuries and also probably originating in Egypt (Foy *et al.* 2003, 47), while group 3 was produced on the Syrian-Palestinian coast between the 3rd century BC and the 9th century AD (Picon and Vichy 2003, 22). This is usually transparent blue/green, that is, natural coloured glass, but was also used to produce artificial colours, such as the opaque white on our campanulate bowl. In this case the colourant and opacifier was probably lead stannate ($PbSnO_3$) known to be used for opaque yellow (Page *et al.* 2001, 137) or tin oxide (SnO_2), hence the high percentage that we see as a major value in the composition (Table 7.2, Bra17W).

Analyses of other campanulate bowls have been made in a different laboratory, but unfortunately the results, despite being very informative, cannot be directly compared with the ones above due to discrepancies in the techniques used (Cruz 2009b, vol. I, 37 and vol. III, 15). These unpublished analyses show that of the 13 campanulate bowls examined, 3 belong to group 3, 4 to group 1 and 6 to group 2.

Conclusions

The campanulate bowls from *Gallaecia* are a remarkable and somewhat paradoxical "family" of late antique glass vessels. They are remarkable because they are unpretentious and popular as well as being the most representative and recurrent of all the late antique glass vessels found in the northwestern part of the Iberian Peninsula, and paradoxical because they are at the same time both international and local. The general shape is comparable with examples from other parts of the Roman empire, hence the international style, but there are also particularities that result into a regional style not found outside *Gallaecia* and the neighbouring regions of the northern and central Iberian Peninsula. For example the deep bowls, so common in Braga, have not yet been found (or perhaps have not yet been recognised) elsewhere, not even in other parts of the Iberian Peninsula. By contrast, the bowls and shallow bowls are found all over the western Roman empire including southern Portugal, as at Torre de Ares, Algarve (Nolen 1994, vi-88–vi-94), Spain, as in the eastern part of Cartagenensis (Sánchez de Prado 2009, figs. 6–8), and south-west France (Foy and Hochuli-Gysel 1995, fig. 14.9–15). This particularity of the campanulate bowls, which are both local and international, is very informative about late Roman glass working, showing how the local glass blowers were aware of the contemporary techniques and fashions from elsewhere, but at the same time linked into the local styles and traditions.

The campanulate bowls are good evidence for a prolific and novel tradition of late antique glass production in a remote part of the ancient world which has not hitherto been recognised in glass studies. The eight secondary glass production sites, and at least twelve glass workshops identified so far, demonstrate that the north-west of the Iberian peninsula deserves recognition in the late Roman glass industry, as a region able to supply its markets with everyday, good quality glass vessels.

Catalogue

Fig. 7.2: Main vessel forms

1. Yellow/green beaker with self coloured spiral thread below rim. From Paredes necropolis, Siero, Asturias, Spain. Museo de Asturias, inv. no. PAR 97 T28-2 (drawing provided by the Museum of Asturias).
2. Complete profile of a brown/green deep bowl. From Braga, Portugal. MDDS, inv. no. 1999.2734 (drawn by the Museum of Braga).
3. Complete profile of a dark yellow/green bowl. From Braga, Portugal. MDDS. inv. no. 1999.2098 (drawn by the Museum of Braga).
4. Complete profile of pale yellow/green shallow bowl with opaque white spiral thread below rim. From Braga, Portugal. MDDS. inv. no. 1999.2674 (drawn by the Museum of Braga).

Fig. 7.3: Decorative patterns

1. Brown/green deep bowl without decoration (Fig. 7.2.2).
2. Brown/green deep bowl with self coloured spiral thread below rim. From Paredes necropolis, Siero, Asturias, Spain. Museo de Asturias, inv. no. PAR 97 T6-3 (drawn by the author).
3. Complete profile of a dark green deep bowl with self coloured festooned thread on upper body pinched down at regular intervals. From Braga, Portugal. MDDS. inv. no. 1999.2725 (drawn by the Museum of Braga).
4. Yellow/green deep bowl with a translucent dark blue/green thread and blobs. From Paredes necropolis, Siero, Asturias, Spain. Museo de Asturias, inv. no. PAR 97 T9-4 (drawn by the author).
5. Almost complete profile of a yellow/green deep bowl with vertical expanded ribs. From Braga, Portugal. MDDS. inv. no. 1999.2677 (drawn by the Museum of Braga).
6. Complete profile of a pale green deep bowl with oblique expanded ribs. From Braga, Portugal. MDDS. inv. no. 1999.2695 (drawn by the Museum of Braga).
7. Rim and body of a dark yellow/green deep bowl with self coloured spiral thread and vertical expanded ribs. From Braga, Portugal. MDDS. inv. no. 1999.2011 (drawn by the Museum of Braga).
8. Base of a pale yellow/green deep bowl with vertical expanded ribs and floral pattern-blown motive on the base and a central pontil mark. From Braga, Portugal. MDDS. inv. no. 2007.0383 (drawn by the Museum of Braga).
9. Base of a yellow/green deep bowl with a pattern-blown motive on the base. From Braga, Portugal. MDDS. inv. no. 2007.0010 (drawn by the Museum of Braga).
10. Rim and body of a pale yellow/green deep bowl with vertical indents on the body. From Braga, Portugal. MDDS. inv. no. 2007.0373 (drawn by the author).
11. Rim and body of a dark yellow/green bowl with opaque white spiral threads on the upper body and festoons on lower body. From Braga, Portugal. MDDS. inv. no. 1999.2111 (drawn by the Museum of Braga).
12. Almost complete yellow/green shallow bowl with festooned opaque white threads on the body and base. From Braga, Portugal. MDDS. inv. no. 2008.0580 (drawn by the author).
13. Rim and body of a pale yellow/green bowl with expanded herringbone pattern and opaque white spiral thread on upper body. From Vigo, Spain. ADRO, inv. no. UARCII.05/8118 (drawn by the author).
14. Complete profile of a pale yellow/green bowl with abraded decoration. From Vigo, Spain. ADRO, without inv. no (drawn by the author).

Fig. 7.4: Similar decoration on different vessel forms

1. Yellow/green deep bowl with vertical expanded ribs (Fig. 7.3.5).
2. Upper body of a blue/green jar with oblique broad rim and vertical expanded ribs on the body. From Lucenza, Orense, Spain (Xusto Rodriguez 2001, 392) (drawing provided by Xusto Rodriguez).
3. Rim, neck and upper body of a dark blue/green pyriform

flask with vertical expanded ribs. From Astorga, Leon, Spain. Museo Romano, inv. no. AA/EA-JC/94/67/9 (drawn by the author).
4. Body and base of a pale yellow/green pyriform flask with expanded herringbone pattern and a spiral opaque white thread on the body. From Vigo, Spain. ADRO, inv. no. UARCII.05/6996.7000 (drawn by the author).
5. Rim and body of a pale yellow/green bowl with expanded herringbone pattern and opaque white spiral thread on upper body (Fig. 7.3.13).
6. Rim and body of a dark yellow/green bowl with opaque white spiral threads on the upper body and festoons on lower body (Fig. 7.3.11).
7. Brown/yellow conical lamp with opaque white spiral thread on the body. ADRO, inv. no. AC/00-V88.1013 (drawn by the author).
8. Rim, neck and base of a pale yellow/green oval jug with opaque white spiral thread on the neck. From Braga, Portugal. MDDS, inv. no. 2007.0369 (drawn by the author).

Bibliography

Abásolo, J. A., Cortes, J. and Marcos, F.-J. (2004) *Los recipientes de vidrio de las Necrópolis de La Olmeda*. Palencia, Diputación de Palencia.

Alarcão, J., Delgado, M., Mayet, F., Moutinho Alarcão, A. and de Ponte, S. (1976) *Céramiques diverses et verres. Fouilles de Conímbriga VI*. Paris, De Boccard.

Cruz, M. (2009a) *Vita Vitri. O vidro Antigo em Portugal*. Lisbon, Museu Nacional de Arqueologia, Museu de Arqueologia D. Diogo de Sousa.

Cruz, M. (2009b) *O Vidro Romano do Noroeste Peninsular. Um olhar a partir de Bracara Augusta*. Braga. Unpublished thesis, Universidade do Minho.

Feyeux, J.-Y. (1995) La typologie de la verrerie merovingienne du nord de la France. In D. Foy (ed.) *Le verre de l'antiquité tardive et du haut moyen âge. Typologie, chronologie, diffusion*, 109–137. Guiry-en-Vexin, Musée archéologique départemental du Val-d'Oise.

Foy, D. (1995) Le verre de la fin du IVe au VIIIe siècle en France méditerranéenne, premier essai de typo-chronologie. In D. Foy (ed.) *Le verre de l'antiquité tardive et du haut moyen âge. Typologie, chronologie, diffusion*, 187–242. Guiry-en-Vexin, Musée archéologique départemental du Val-d'Oise.

Foy, D. and Hochuli-Gysel, A. (1995) Le verre en Aquitaine du IVe au IXe siècle, un état de la question. In D. Foy (ed.) *Le verre de l'antiquité tardive et du haut moyen âge. Typologie, chronologie, diffusion*, 151–176. Guiry-en-Vexin, Musée archéologique départemental du Val-d'Oise.

Foy, D., Picon, M., Vichy, M. and Thirion-Merle, V. (2003) Caractérisation des verres de la fin de l'Antiquité en Méditerranée occidentale: l'émergence de nouveaux courants commerciaux. In D. Foy and M.-D. Nenna (eds.) *Échanges et commerce du verre dans le monde antique*. Monographies Instrumentum 24, 41–85. Montagnac, Monique Mergoil.

Fuentes Domínguez, Á. (1990) Los vidrios de las "Necrópolis de la Meseta". Ensayo preliminar de clasificación. *Cuadernos de Prehistoria y Arqueologia Universidad Autonoma de Madrid* 17, 169–201.

Nolen, J. U. S. (1994) *Cerâmicas e Vidros de Torre de Ares. Balsa/Lisbon*, Instituto Português de Museus/Museu Nacional de Arqueologia.

Page, J.-A., Pilosi, L. and Wypyski, M. T. (2001) Ancient Mosaic Glass or Modern Reproductions? *Journal of Glass Studies* 43, 115–137.

Perin, P. (1995) La datation des verres mérovingiens du nord de la Gaule. In D. Foy (ed.) *Le verre de l'antiquité tardive et du haut moyen âge. Typologie, chronologie, diffusion*, 139–151. Guiry-en-Vexin, Musée archéologique départemental du Val-d'Oise.

Picon, M. and Vichy, M. (2003) D'orient en occident: l'origine du verre à l'époque romaine et durant le haut Moyen Âge. In D. Foy and M.-D. Nenna (eds.) *Échanges et commerce du verre dans le monde antique*. Monographies Instrumentum 24, 17–31. Montagnac, Monique Mergoil.

Price, J. (2000) Late Roman Glass Vessels in Britain and Ireland from AD 350 to 410 and Beyond. In J. Price (ed.) *Glass in Britain and Ireland AD 350–1100*. British Museum Occasional Paper 127, 1–31. London, British Museum Press.

Price, J. (2005) Glass-working and glassworkers in cities and towns. In A. Mac Mahon and J. Price (eds.) *Roman Working Lives and Urban Living*, 167–190. Oxford, Oxbow Books.

Requejo Pagés, O. (1998) Vaso de vidrio de la tumba nº 10 de la Necrópolis de Paredes (Siero). *Nuestro Museo* 2, 267–271.

Requejo Pagés, O. (1999) Noticia sobre el yacimiento Tardorromano de Paredes (Siero). Primera Necrópolis Romana de Asturias. In J. González-Echegaray et al., *De Oriente a Occidente. Homenaje al Dr. Emilio Olávarri*, 305–319. Salamanca, Publicaciones Universidad Pontificia.

Sánchez de Prado, M. D. (2009) La Vajilla de Vidrio Durante la Antiguidade Tardia en el *Conventus Carthaginensis*. *Boletín del Seminario de Estudios de Arte y Arqueología* 75, 159–200.

Stern, E. M. (2001) *Roman, Byzantine and Early Medieval Glass. 10 BCE – 700 CE*. Ostfildern-Ruit, Hatje Cantz.

Vilaseco Vásquez, X. I. (2003) Algunhas consideraçôes sobre a presencia dunha àrea de fundición de vidro no *Tude* Romano (Tui, Pontevedra), *Gallaecia* 2, 253–265.

Xusto Rodriguez, M. (2001) *O Vidro Provincial Galaicorromano*. Vigo, Universidade de Vigo.

8

The Wilshere Collection of late Roman gold-glass at the Ashmolean Museum, University of Oxford

Susan Walker

In 2007 the Ashmolean Museum acquired, with the help of the Art Fund, the Victoria and Albert Museum Purchase Grant Fund, the Friends of the Ashmolean Museum and private donors, the Wilshere Collection of late Roman gold-glass, funerary inscriptions and sarcophagi.

Charles Willes Wilshere (1814–1906) was a prominent supporter of the 19th-century "Oxford" or "Tractarian" Movement, reviving an Anglicised version of Catholicism. A lawyer by training and the independently wealthy son of a Hertfordshire landowner, Wilshere collected antiquities energetically in Rome from about 1860 to 1890. Salvaging some artefacts at risk from the rapid expansion of the city at the time of the unification of Italy, Wilshere gave significant objects to Pope Leo XIII (Kraabel 1979, 42, note 6). On Wilshere's death in 1906 his collection was bequeathed to Pusey House, built on St Giles in 1884 and named after Edward Bouverie Pusey (1800–1882), leader of the Oxford Movement from 1845. Pusey House remains today the centre of Anglo-Catholic worship in Oxford. Wilshere's aim was to provide public access to the collection, which illustrated the origins of Christian worship in Rome, and Christianity's Hebraic roots.

In the course of the 20th century the collection was loaned to the Ashmolean Museum of Art and Archaeology, located just to the south of Pusey House in Charles Cockerell's University Art Galleries on Beaumont Street. By the early 20th century the galleries had been considerably enlarged to the north, in a new building commissioned to accommodate the Ashmolean's archaeological collections by Sir Arthur Evans, Keeper from 1894–1908.

By the 1990s, some inscriptions from the Wilshere Collection were displayed upstairs in the Evans Building on a wall of the Beazley Gallery, a room otherwise devoted to classical Greek and Hellenistic art and archaeology; some of the gold-glass was displayed with the Byzantine collections in showcases set along the wall of a corridor leading to the western stairs on the ground floor. In 2006, the Evans building was demolished and replaced with a new building designed by Rick Mather Architects, which opened to the public in 2009. In the new space it was possible to lay out the collections under the rubric "Crossing Cultures, Crossing Time", emphasising the often surprising connections between peoples, principally from Asia and Europe, from prehistory to modern times. The "Crossing Cultures" galleries are arranged on the lower ground floor, while the "Crossing Time" floors follow a chronological sequence akin to archaeological stratigraphy, moving later in time up from the ground floor to the top of the new building. The first floor covers the period from late antiquity to early modern (roughly AD 300–1500), and focuses on links developed along the over-ground trade routes between Central Asia and the Mediterranean region. A new gallery explores the Mediterranean world from AD 300, looking at personal connections across the Mediterranean region, principally made by traders, soldiers and pilgrims. Around its walls are displayed objects from key cities in the region, shown in relation to the large map dominating the centre of the room. One short wall is occupied by 4th-century Rome and Italy after the fall of Rome; nearly all the gold glass and six of the inscriptions from the Wilshere Collection are displayed here (Fig. 8.1). Beyond distinguishing the religious affiliations of the Christian, Jewish and possibly pagan owners of the glass vessels, the fragments are arranged by iconographic theme.

In the course of the 20th century, the objects within the Wilshere Collection were published by category: the glass by C. R. Morey in his posthumous corpus (Morey 1959); the inscriptions by O. Marucchi (1912) and H. Leon (1960); while the sarcophagi have found their way into various studies of early Christian sarcophagi from Rome (*e.g.* Bisconti and Brandenburg 2004). A considerable amount of work has been done more recently on the Jewish material, largely inscriptions commemorating individuals buried in the slots (*loculi*) within the catacombs, which were sealed by the slabs (Kraabel 1979). The gold-glass fragments include one unusual menorah with polychrome enamel decoration from the base of a plate (Fig. 8.2); another fragment of the same plate is surrounded by the injunction "Pie, zeses!" ("Drink, live!") in the Latinised Greek commonly used in late antiquity. Kraabel's work has revealed an origin for the *loculus* slabs and possibly the other Jewish artefacts from the collection in the Randanini Catacomb, located on the Via Appia opposite the church of San Sebastiano, from which uncontrolled sales of antiquities were made in the 1860s (dello Russo 2011).

A brief report of some highlights of the Wilshere Collection was made by T. B. L.Webster (Webster 1929), whose manuscript catalogue remained otherwise unpublished. Recent archival research by Vattuone (2000) points to the acquisition of twelve pieces from the collection of the Baron Recupero of Catania, Sicily, via the antiquarian dealers Vincenzo and Tommaso Capobianchi in 1861–1862. Some of these pieces were previously recorded in the early 19th-century archive of the Vatican prefect Gaetano Marini (Rini 2006). It is now planned to publish the Wilshere Collection as a whole, tracing the origins of as many pieces as possible and using scientific analysis to examine the chemical composition of the glass, to recover any surviving organic compounds in the traces of ancient mortar on the glass and surrounding the inscriptions, and to review the marbles used for these and for the sarcophagi.

Many questions may be asked of this interesting and significant array of 37 pieces of sandwich gold-glass, the third most important collection of the genre after those of the Vatican and British Museums. For the preparation of the Ashmolean catalogue, the gold-glass is divided into three broad categories by iconography and associated text:

1 Glass with portraits of private individuals and/or biblical scenes and/or text reflecting a desire for personal salvation (18 pieces, of which eight are the bases of large cups or bowls, eight are uninscribed blue glass "blobs", and two are the bases of narrow-walled beakers with simple inscriptions and limited or no images).
2 Glass with images of Christ and/or martyrs (13 pieces).
3 Glass from a range of other categories (6 pieces). This last category comprises a fragment of inlay or revetment; part of an inscription perhaps from a 3rd-century portrait; a fragment of border decoration from the base of a vessel; a fragment of a complex, blue glass vessel with inlaid roundels of gilded clear glass set in coloured frames; a fragment of an inscribed rim of a dish and another rim with gilded decoration.

Drawing on a recent study of the care of the dead in late antiquity (Rébillard 2009), the question is posed as to whether the first category of glass was used at *refrigeria* (funeral feasts) and *parentalia* (commemorative feasts) of private individuals, and the second at commemorative feasts of the martyrs and/or private burials associated with the martyr shrines (Grig 2004).

The nature of the greenish and decoloured glass itself conforms to Roman standards rather than the light blue "Levantine" and highly coloured "HIMT" of the mid first millennium AD (Freestone *et al.* 2009). The surviving lamp on the menorah is of Roman rather than late antique type. Although a visual inspection suggests that both greenish ("natural") and intentionally decoloured glass are present (Figs. 8.3–8.4), chemical elemental analysis of twenty glasses undertaken in the 1980s for Dr Marlia Mundell Mango by Professor Julian Henderson of the University of Nottingham suggests widespread use of the decolouring agents manganese and antimony. This work remains unpublished and the samples will be reanalysed in the coming year; meanwhile I am most grateful to Professor Henderson for discussing his results with me. While full interpretation must await a second analysis, it is worth noting that the remarkably consistent results of the 1980s examination imply that at least the analysed glasses (from catalogue groups 1 and 3) were deliberately decoloured. They thus correspond to the higher quality mentioned in the contemporary edict on maximum prices issued by the Emperor Diocletian in AD 301, if the designations of "Judaean" and "Alexandrian" glass have been correctly interpreted as (cheaper) greenish and (twice as expensive) decoloured glass (Stern 1999, 461–462). Examination under microscope of the glass plate decorated with a menorah reveals the use of an extra layer of glass (Fig. 8.5). The blue glass blobs are better termed "lenses", since both sides are convex. They offer simple, uninscribed vignettes capturing moments of complex narratives of salvation also found on some clear glass bases (see group 1 above and Fig. 8.6). Very similar glass is known from 4th-century graves excavated in Cologne, where the vessels were buried intact (Harden 1987, 277–279).

Iconographically, it is clear that the gold-glass pieces in catalogue group 2 reflect a growing focus on the cults of Christian martyrs, and, in a funerary context, their role as intercessors on behalf of the deceased (Grig 2004b; Fig. 8.7). As suggested above in the characterisation of group 1, carefully selected Biblical scenes recall divine deliverance (Grig 2004a; Fig. 8.8). The single representation of the hero Hercules in the Wilshere Collection may have been commissioned for a pagan burial: pagans regarded Hercules as the conqueror of the underworld (Harden 1987, 280; Fig. 8.9).

Like the pilgrims' bottles produced later in Jerusalem, most gold-glass appears to have been made in Rome

Fig. 8.1: The Gallery of the Mediterranean world from AD 300, with the display of the Wilshere Collection of inscriptions and gold-glass background left.

Fig. 8.2: Detail of a menorah on a fragment of gold-glass (AN2007.6a).

Fig. 8.4: Decoloured "Alexandrian" glass used for sandwich gold-glass (AN2007.38).

Fig. 8.3: Greenish glass used for sandwich gold-glass (AN2007.7).

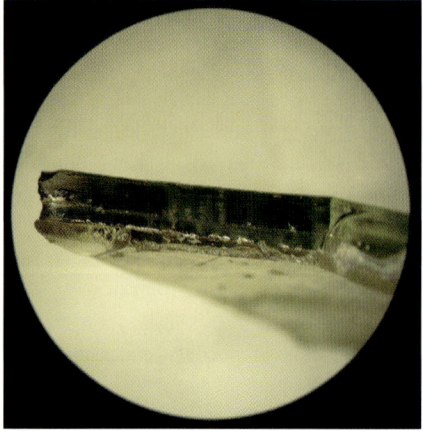

Fig. 8.5: An extra layer in the sandwich of the Jewish gold-glass with a menorah (AN2007.6a) beneath the microscope.

Fig. 8.6: Daniel with a cake (AN2007.28).

Fig. 8.7: Pope Sixtus (AN2007.8).

Fig. 8.8: A couple surrounded by five biblical scenes: clockwise, from above their heads, Christ heals the paralytic; Christ raises Lazarus from the dead; Adam and Eve in the garden of Eden; Abraham and Isaac; Moses and the rock.

Fig. 8.9: Hercules kills the Kerynian stag in his third labour (AN2007.16).

Fig. 8.10: A couple praying, the man dressed in a late antique tight-sleeved tunic, the bejewelled woman in a dalmatic with elaborate decoration (AN2007.26).

for a local market of Romans, whatever their faith or ethnic origin. The frames of the images and some of the preferred themes are closely comparable to those used by contemporary Roman makers of engraved glass who, however, do not use text (Paolucci 2002). Text cut into the gold leaf is another key subject for research: detailed study of the letter forms may help identify individual workshops (Claudia Lega, pers.comm.). Such locally focussed design may well reflect the edict of the Emperor Constantine II, issued on August 2, AD 337. The emperor enjoined glassmakers and engravers, among other skilled craftsmen, to stay at their place of work and pass on their skills to their sons in return for tax ememption (*Codex Theodosianus* 13,4,2 = *Codex Justinianus* 10,66,1).

It is difficult to establish the status of the ancient owners of gold-glass. Many scholars would agree with Alan Cameron (1996) that they were not at the elevated social level of the commissioners of ivory diptychs and grand silver services. The world of gold-glass does not lie above ground in the grand new basilicas commissioned by emperors and patronised by the senatorial aristocracy. Rather it finds an underground home in the catacombs where these pieces were found cemented into the walls, retrieved from breakage after funeral or commemorative feasts (*refrigeria* or *parentalia*) to serve as a permanent gift to the deceased. However, the recipients were not poor: the individuals portrayed on gold-glass are elaborately dressed in the newly fashionable dalmatic, a generously sleeved tunic decorated with increasingly elaborate bands (Walker 1999), and interestingly from the Oxford Movement's perspective the forerunner of modern clerical dress (Fig. 8.10). Few other than Christ and the martyrs are named, and the identification of names on gold-glass, whether of popes or individual users, remains controversial (Cameron 1996).

As to its date, the gold-glass appears to run from the beginning of the 4th century through at least its middle decades. The increasingly influential church fathers railed aginst expendıture on such feasts, taking the reasonable view that the money could have been better spent on the poor; another concern was the apparently frequent occurence of louche, drunken behaviour at funerary and commemorative banquets, even those celebrated at the shrines of martyrs (Rébillard 2009, 142–153).

These preliminary observations will surely be modified by research to be undertaken in the coming year, and no doubt many new questions will be raised. However there can be no question of the Wilshere Collection's interest and significance for our understanding of late Roman gold-glass and the nature of the people who used it.

Bibliography

Bisconti, F. and Brandenburg, H. (2004) *Sarcofagi tardoantichi, paleocristiani e altomedievali. Atti della giornata tematica dei seminari di archeologia cristiana*. Monumenti di antichità cristiana, serie 2.18. Vatican City, Pontificio Istituto di Archeologia Cristiana.

Cameron, A. (1996) Orfitus and Constantine: some notes on Roman gold-glasses. *Journal of Roman Archaeology* 9, 295–301.

Dello Russo, J. (2011) The Discovery and Exploration of the Jewish Catacomb of the Vigna Randanini in Rome. Records, Research and Excavation through 1895. *Roma Subterranea Judaica* 5, 1–24.

Freestone, I. C., Wolf, S. and Thirlwall, M. (2009) Isotopic composition of glass from the Levant and south-east Mediterranean region. In P. Degryse, J. Henderson and G. Hodgson (eds.) *Isotopes in Vitreous Materials*. Studies in Archaeological Science 1, 31–52. Leuven, Leuven University Press.

Grig, L. (2004a) Portraits, Pontiffs and the Christianization of 4th-century Rome. *Papers of the British School at Rome* 72, 203–230.

Grig, L. (2004b) *Making Martyrs in Late Antiquity*. London, Duckworth.

Harden, D. B. (1987) *Glass of the Caesars*. Milan, Olivetti.

Kraabel, A. T. (1979) Jews in imperial Rome: more archaeological evidence from an Oxford collection. *Journal of Jewish Studies* 30, 41–58.

Leon, H. J. (1960) *The Jews of Ancient Rome*. Philadelphia, PA, The Jewish Publication Society of America.

Marucchi, O. (1912) *Christian epigraphy. An elementary treatise, with a collection of ancient Christian inscriptions, mainly of Roman origin* (translated by J. Armine Willis, Cambridge). Cambridge, Cambridge University Press.

Morey, C. R. (1959) *The Gold-Glass Collection of the Vatican Library, with additional catalogues of other gold-glass collections*. Vatican City, Biblioteca Apostolica Vaticana.

Paolucci, F. (2002) *L'arte del vetro inciso a Roma nel IV secolo d.c.* Florence, All'Insegna del Giglio.

Rébillard, E. (2009) *The Care of the Dead in Late Antiquity*. Translated by E. T. Rawlings and J. Routier-Pucci. Cornell Studies in Classical Philology 59. Ithaca, NY, Cornell University Press.

Rini, D. (2006) "Serra Lignea" alle origini dell'iconografia martiriale del Profeta Isaia. *Annali della Pontificia insigne accademia di Belle Arte e Lettere* 6, 257–276.

Stern, E. M. (1999) Roman glass-blowing in a cultural context. *American Journal of Archaeology* 103, 441–484.

Vattuone, L. (2000) I vetri dorati della Collezione Wilshere nella Pusey House di Oxford. In *Annales du 14e Congrès de l'Association Internationale pour l'Histoire du Verre*, 132–136. Lochem, Association Internationale pour l'Histoire du Verre.

Walker, S. (1999) Porträts auf Leichentüchern aus Antinoopolis. Einige Anmerkungen zu Kleidung und Datierung. In K. Parlasca and H. Seeman (eds.) *Augenblicke. Mumienporträts und ägyptische Grabkunst aus römischer Zeit*, 74–78. Munich, Klinkhardt und Biermann.

Webster, T. B. L. (1929) The Wilshere Collection at Pusey House in Oxford. *Journal of Roman Studies* 19, 150–154.

9

The "proto-history" of Venetian glassmaking

David Whitehouse†

Introduction

The "Golden Age" of Venetian glass began about AD 1450 when the Venetian *cristallo* was developed as a luxury glass product (Tait 1979, 25–28). How did it come about? Was it built on a foundation of skills accumulated over centuries; did Venetian glassmakers develop their skills quickly in the late 1400s and early 1500s; did they acquire them from abroad (*i.e.* outside the Veneto region); or did all these processes come together when Venice emerged as one of the richest powers in the Mediterranean and nurtured glassmaking – just as it nurtured printing, textiles, painting, and other luxurious arts and crafts?

Here, without denying for a moment the spectacular innovations of Venetian glassmakers in the Renaissance, or their borrowings from abroad, I want to focus on just two of the ingredients in the Golden Age: the continuity of glassmaking in the Veneto between Roman times and the Renaissance which Rosa Barovier Mentasti (1995, 845) called the "proto-history" of Venetian glassmaking and in particular the continuity throughout this period of commercial relations with the eastern Mediterranean. The reason I refer to the Veneto instead of Venice is that (unlike Rome, Florence, Milan, Naples or dozens of other Italian cities) Venice did not exist in Roman times (Brown 1996); it was born in the 8th century. And so we must look at the early history of glassmaking in the Veneto if we want to understand the nature of the continuity of glass working in the central Middle Ages.

The earliest evidence for glassmaking in medieval Venice is documentary. In AD 982, *Domenicus fiolarius* witnessed the deed of donation of the church of San Giorgio on the Venetian island of San Giorgio Maggiore to the Benedictine order (Barovier Mentasti 1995, 847). *Fiolarius* means "glassblower" and Domenicus is the first Venetian glassmaker whose name has come down to us. One hundred years later, two other Venetian glassmakers appeared in Benedictine documents: *Petrus fiolarius* in AD 1083 and *Petrus fiolarius Flabianicus* in AD 1090 (Barovier Mentasti 1995, 847). A fourth glassmaker, *Johannes fiolarius* who lived or worked near the church of Sta Margharita, was noted in a document of AD 1158 (Zecchin 1987, 5; Barovier Mentasti 1995, 847). Although none of these documents concerns glassmaking, they do indicate the presence of glassworkers in Venice between the 10th and 12th centuries. I assume that, once established, glassmaking continued in Venice without a break although, after AD 1158, the documents are silent until AD 1224, when 29 members of the guild of glassmakers – not a handful by any means – were punished for ignoring the rules of the *Ufficio di Giustizia*, which regulated trade practices (Barovier Mentasti 1995, 849).

Glassmaking and glassworking, AD 1–800: the Mediterranean and northern Europe

This is a very short summary of information that is widely known (cf. Freestone 2003; 2005; Shortland *et al.* 2006). Roman and early medieval glass made in the Mediterranean region and northern Europe contains three principal ingredients: silica, usually in the form of sand, soda and lime. The soda was in the form of the mineral natron, the largest source of which is the Wadi al-Natrun, between Alexandria and Cairo in Egypt. After about AD 800, however, soda was largely replaced by ash derived from either halophytic plants (in the Mediterranean region) or ferns and beach trees (in northern Europe). We are confident about the replacement of natron by plant ash because each is associated with different quantities of three elements:

potassium, magnesium and phosphorus. Similarly sands from different regions may be associated with different trace elements. Thus, glass containing either natron or plant ash and sand from a specific source may have a distinctive chemical "fingerprint" that indicates the origin of the raw materials and perhaps the region in which they were melted. The application of this knowledge has transformed our understanding of the Roman glass industry.

In the 1960s, discovery and excavation at two sites in Israel, Bet She'arim (Brill 1967) and Jalame (Weinberg 1988), followed by excavations at other sites (Gorin-Rosen 2000, 52–56), led to the realisation in the 1990s that making glass from raw materials (primary production) and making objects from raw glass (secondary production) took place in different locations (Freestone and Gorin-Rosen 1999, 105–108; see more recently: Foy et al. 2003; Freestone 2003; 2005; Nenna 2008). Moreover, chemical analyses of fragmentary vessels from sites all over the Roman empire revealed just a handful of strikingly similar compositions. In other words, either natron and sand or raw glass were traded over very great distances. Finds at numerous terrestrial sites and in shipwrecks confirm what common sense would suggest: that the item of trade was raw glass (Foy et al. 2000; Freestone 2003; Nenna 2008).

Raw glass continued to be an item of trade in the early medieval period (Whitehouse 2003). For example, when the monastery at Jarrow in north-east England was founded in AD 675, the glassworkers came from France and the glass used to glaze the windows of the church contained natron (Bede, *Historia Abbatum* 5; Freestone and Hughes 2006; Cramp 2006, 56). Indeed, most of the analysed fragments had compositions similar either to that of raw glass ("Levantine I") from Apollonia, Dor and Bet Shean in Israel, or to that of another type of raw glass from the eastern Mediterranean ("Egypt I"; cf. Gratuze and Barrandon 1990; Freestone et al. 2000).

Elsewhere in Italy, finds from the Crypta Balbi in Rome include a huge late 7th-century dump containing some 10,500 fragments of raw glass, workshop debris and finished objects, samples of which were shown to contain natron (Mirti et al. 2000). Incidentally, some 26 percent of the 7th-century glass at the Crypta Balbi in Rome consisted of broken windowpanes, some still attached to fragments of plaster frames (Mirti et al. 2000, 360). Evidently, they had been collected for recycling, supporting the view that, tesserae apart, perhaps the majority of Roman glass collected for recycling in early medieval Europe was window panes from the ruins of Roman public buildings. Whilst the evidence for the reuse of glass is extensive, other new glasses were still being produced, probably in the East (Freestone et al. 2008). Certainly glasses analysed from Glastonbury Abbey and from Jarrow, both used for glazing, were manufactured using late antique glass, not recycled Roman material (Freestone and Hughes 2006).

In the 8th century, too, despite the evidence of the imported ceramics and coins, which point to a contraction of long-distance trade, the glass at the Crypta Balbi contained natron rather than plant ash, pointing towards continuing contact with Egypt or the Levant (Mirti et al. 2001) – or the continuing substantial re-use of Roman glass.

Roman and early medieval glassworking in the northern) Adriatic

For students of glassmaking in Venice, AD 1224 is a watershed. Before this date, very little written evidence of glass workers exists, and we must piece together our knowledge of earlier glassmaking in Venice and the Veneto from archaeological and archaeometric sources. Archaeologists face formidable obstacles in the Venetian lagoon: few of the key sites in Venice are accessible because they are beneath buildings that are still in use; and, when they are accessible, the earliest deposits are two metres below sea level. Nevertheless, excavations in Venice and on the islands of Torcello and San Francesco del Deserto, have revealed how settlers from the mainland began to colonise the lagoon, beginning in the 2nd or 3rd century (Leciejewicz 2002, 56). At the same time, we have a better understanding of how the political and economic focus shifted through time: from the Roman city of Aquileia, through the early Byzantine cities of Heraclea, and Altinum, all of which are on the mainland, Torcello and Malamocco on the edge of the lagoon (Cantino Wataghin 1992, 356–357; Pavan and Arnaldi 1992, 420–423, 436–447) and finally Venice itself, which expanded in the 8th century and in AD 811 became the seat of the doge (Castagnetti 1992, 582–583).

Aquileia was the first of these regional centres. Parts of Roman Aquileia have been excavated and the finds include pieces of crucibles coated with glass, and droplets and other by-products of glass working. The clearest evidence of glassworking at Aquileia consists of two 2nd-century mould-blown bottles found at Linz in Austria, one of which is inscribed SENTIA SECVNDA FACIT AQUILEIAE and the other SENTIA SECVUNDA FACIT AQ VITR (Glöckner 2006, 190, 199, nos. AUS 68–69; cf. another base fragment from Ribnica, Slovenia: Lazar 2006, 246–247, 253, no. SI 67). The abbreviated last word in the second Linz inscription may refer either to glass (*vitrum*) or to the glassmaker Sentia Secunda (*vitraria*). At least one other glass workshop may have existed at Aquileia, for bottles inscribed with the name C SALVIVS GRATVS occur there and at other sites in northern Italy, Slovenia, Austria and southern Germany (Calvi 1968, 13; Lazar 2006, 247–248; Glöckner 2006, 189–190; Rottloff 2006, 146; Höpken 2011, 171), and numerous tombstones at Aquileia indicate that the Salvii was a prominent local family (Calvi 1968, 13).

Glassworking, therefore, was already established at

the head of the Adriatic no later than the 2nd century. We know of at least one other glass workshop that operated in the region in the 4th century: at Sevegliano, 16km north of Aquileia (Termini Storti 1994; Buora 1997). The continuity of glass working after the 4th century is documented at several sites, notably the hilltop fortress of Ibligo, 120km from Venice. Here, excavations revealed a modest settlement of the 1st to 4th centuries, with evidence of glass working: not melting raw materials, but re-melting chunks of imported glass (Bierbrauer 1987, 285–286). Between the 5th and the 7th centuries, Ibligo expanded and the presence of imported amphorae, and North African tableware and lamps suggests that the community was not only larger but also wealthier than it had been (Bierbrauer 1987, 305). These exotic items were used side by side with glass vessels. Again, the glassware was produced on the spot probably using raw glass imported from the Levant, although there are no published analyses of the glass yet to corroborate this.

In the lagoon, evidence for the use of glass in late Roman and early medieval times has been recovered from excavations on the islands of Torcello and San Francesco del Deserto (Ferri 2006). The settlement on Torcello grew in importance after AD 639, when the bishop of Altinum retreated from the mainland and began to build the cathedral of Sta Maria Assunta (Leciejewicz 2002, 55; Ferri 2006, 188). The most recent excavations on the island yielded more than 1,000 fragments of glass, consisting almost entirely of drinking vessels (goblets with a bell-shaped bowl, short stem and a conical or disk-shaped foot, and simple conical beakers), together with a few bottles, lamps and, only in the 7th century, crown windowpanes. Excavations on the neighbouring island of San Francesco del Deserto furnished a similar collection of about the same date.

Such is the background, against which glassmaking arrived in the Venetian lagoon: the familiar pattern of importing raw glass from the eastern Mediterranean and remelting it locally. During the first seven centuries AD, glassmakers in Egypt and the Levant supplied glass workers all over the Mediterranean region and farther afield in Europe. What happened to transform this entirely ordinary pattern of glass working into the extraordinary industry that developed in Venice?

Venice between east and west

The answer, I suggest, is embedded in the precocious development of Venice as a city, which emerged as an economic force in the 8th century (McCormick 2001, 526–528). Already a regional power in the 730s, Venetian merchants were operating along the west coast of Italy and selling slaves to the Muslim world by AD 750 (McCormick 2001, 871, no. 157). No later than AD 795 Venetian ships were sailing regularly to the Levant (McCormick 2001, 526, 885, no. 230). In AD 797, Charlemagne's ambassadors to Harun al-Rashid stopped at Treviso, 30km north of Venice, and so presumably sailed from Venice (McCormick 2001, 527, 887, no. 238). According to Jacoby (2009, 371–372), "Venice's commercial and maritime expansion in the eastern Mediterranean was underway and its basic patterns were already established by the late eighth century." Even at this early date, Venice belonged to the commercial and diplomatic world of Damascus and Alexandria. When, in AD 828, Venetian merchants stole the body of St Mark from Alexandria, they sailed in a fleet of no fewer than 10 ships (McCormick 2001, 527, 913–914, no. 406). By AD 852, the Venetians were building *chelandie*, large Byzantine-style galleys (McCormick 2001, 405, note 61). As a result of this surge in maritime activity, the wealth of Venice grew. The numbers of newly built churches tell the story: 12 before AD 800, but 23 between AD 800 and 900 (McCormick 2001, 530–531). By the time of the Crusades, Venice was virtually a colonial power (Prawer 1973).

The eastern Mediterranean

Thanks to the meticulous excavation of an early 11th-century shipwreck, we have a vivid insight into the way in which raw glass continued to the traded around the Mediterranean in the Middle Ages (Bass *et al.* 2009). Forty years after Domenicus witnessed the document at San Giorgio Maggiore and 60 years before Petrus witnessed his document, disaster struck a small cargo ship off the south coast of Turkey. The ship sank at Serçe Limanı, opposite Rhodes, and its underwater wreck was excavated by Bass between 1977 and 1979. The hold contained three tonnes of cullet in the form of raw glass and broken glass vessels, which were already in pieces and stowed in baskets when they were brought on board. Other finds show that one or more of the ship's last ports of call were in the Levant and that the ship sank in or soon after AD 1025. However, the glass from the shipwreck at Serçe Limanı was predominantly plant-ash glass, *i.e.* only four out of 103 analysed samples were natron glasses and another four were silica-lead glasses, whereas the remaining analysed samples were plant ash glasses (Brill 2009, 463–468).

We do not know the destination of the Serçe Limanı ship, although some of the crew may have come from Byzantium or the Black Sea. Was the ship sailing north to Byzantium, whose glass industry in the 11th century existed but is almost completely unknown to us? Was it heading west to Greece, about which we are almost equally ill-informed, now the "Middle Byzantine" glass workshop at Corinth has been re-dated to the years around AD 1300 (Whitehouse 1991; 1993)? Or was it travelling even farther afield, perhaps to Italy?

In any case, if a glass drinking vessel weighed 100

grams, three tonnes of cullet was sufficient to make 30,000 glasses and the cargo illustrates that, in the 11th century, just as in pre-Roman and Roman times, glassmaking and glass working were still separate activities in the eastern Mediterranean and that somewhere north or west of the Levant and Egypt glassware was being produced in fairly large quantities.

Medieval glassworking in Venice

Our knowledge of glassworking (as distinct from glass using) in the Venetian lagoon begins on Torcello. In 1961 and 1962, more than 30 years before the excavations mentioned above, archaeologists from the Polish Academy of Sciences excavated a glass workshop (Leciejewicz *et al.* 1977). The remains included a circular feature, which they interpreted as a furnace. Whether or not it was a furnace (the interpretation is debatable: see, for example, Barovier Mentasti 1995, 847), the whole area was strewn with droplets of glass, broken crucibles and lumps of frit. Evidently a glass workshop existed in the vicinity and the excavators believed that its activities included both primary production of raw glass (indicated by the frit) and secondary production of glass vessels. Chemical analyses showed that the glass was a natron glass (Leciejewicz *et al.* 1977, 164–165; Brill 1999, vol. 1, 108, 134, vol. 2, 227, 317–319). Originally, the workshop was attributed to the 7th century, but radiocarbon dates now indicate that it should not be dated earlier than the 9th century (Leciejewicz 2002, 58).

The availability of natron glass after AD 800 would be remarkable in most parts of Europe. But in Venice this is not the whole story. Verità and Toninato (1990) published a series of analyses of medieval glass from the Venetian lagoon and from Ferrara, which is on the mainland, 85km from Venice. The glass was made at several dates between the 8th or 9th and the 13th centuries and it has two fundamentally different compositions. The first composition was fluxed with natron. In the second composition, the fluxing agent was plant ash and the chemistry resembled that of glass made in Venice in and after the 15th century. Verità and Toninato (1990) point out that some of the latter samples are similar in composition to glass from the Serçe Limanı wreck, indicating a common origin for the raw glass or plant ash. The transition from natron to plant ash in the region, they suggested, took place in or about the 12th century. Evidently, before that date, Venetian glassmakers were receiving supplies from more than one source in the Levant.

Just outside the Venetian lagoon, near Malamocco, are the remains of a shipwreck, explored in 1980 (Molino *et al.* 1986). The ship carried a cargo that included raw glass. The glass had been stowed in wooden tubs containing chunks weighing up to 15kg (Molino *et al.* 1986, 185–186). Two chunks were shown to contain about 16% of sodium, 2.7% aluminium, 8.1% calcium, 0.6% potassium and 0.65% magnesium (Molino *et al.* 1986, 192, note 9): in other words, they are natron glasses from the Levant or Egypt. Among the finds from the sea bed was a late medieval cannon, but it is not certain that it came from the wreck, which (according to Barovier Mentasti 1995, 845) may date from any time between the 10th and the 14th centuries.

Regardless of the date of the Malomocco wreck, we know that, when the written sources resume in the 13th century, the Venetian glass industry was dependent on materials imported from the Levant or Egypt. The earliest surviving Venetian reference to the importation of cullet is in a document of AD 1233 and the importation of *vitrum in massa* (chunks of raw glass) and *alumen album* ("white alum") from Alexandria is recorded in AD 1255 (Zecchin 1980). In AD 1277, Doge Jacopo Contarini entered into an agreement with Bohemond VII, prince of Antioch, which exempted Venetians from paying duty in the port of Tripoli (in present-day Lebanon) except when they exported broken glass (Lamm 1929/30, 491, no. 47; Tait 1979, 10). By this time, Venetian glassmakers were importing Syrian plant ash and shortly afterwards its use became mandatory, as part of the government's effort to preserve the high quality of Venetian glass (Zecchin 1980).

The "proto-history" of Venetian glassmaking: a suggestion

Chemical analyses of 9th to 13th-century glass from the Venetian lagoon and from Ferrara, 85km south-west of Venice, have revealed two fundamentally different compositions: one containing natron and the other containing plant ash. The chemistry of the second group resembles that of glass made in Venice in and after the 15th century and, in some cases, it is similar to the composition of glass from the Serçe Limanı wreck, indicating a common origin for the raw glass or plant ash. The transition from natron to plant ash in Venice seems to have taken place in or about the 12th century. Although, Torcello apart, no medieval glass workshop has come to light in Venice or the lagoon, documents of AD 982, 1083 and 1090 establish the presence of glassblowers. Thus, although the evidence is slight, we have reason to believe that glass containing natron continued to be available to glassworkers in Venice until after the end of the first millennium AD. The most likely explanation for the continuous production of natron glass by the Venetian glassmakers is the recycling of glass from other sites in Italy, although the possibility of the acquisition of natron glass from Egypt until the 9th century cannot be ruled out (cf. Greiff and Keller this volume).

In short, circumstantial evidence exists for expecting continuity of glassmaking in the Venetian lagoon between Torcello in the 9th century, *Domenicus fiolarius* in the 10th century and the guild of glassmakers in the 13th century. Throughout this period, Venetian merchants were a constant presence in the eastern Mediterranean. Indeed, between AD 1124 and 1291, Venice occupied and governed one-third of Tyre, which had been and still was a major primary and secondary producer of glass (Aldsworth et al. 2002; Carboni et al. 2003). Throughout the same period, Venetian glassmakers used either glass that contained natron from Egypt or glass fluxed with plant ash that in some cases was similar to glass from Serçe Limanı. Rather than a new initiative, I suggest, the treaty between the doge of Venice and the prince of Antioch in AD 1277 may have codified centuries-old practices, which were already in place when glassworkers set up shop on Torcello in the 9th century and which continued to supply the likes of Domenicus, Petrus, Petrus Flabianicus, and Johannes between the 10th and the 12th centuries.

Editorial note

David Whitehouse sadly died before the paper was edited. Therefore certain sections have editorial amendments, but the paper has not been substantially changed.

Bibliography

Aldsworth, F., Haggarty, G., Jennings, S. and Whitehouse, D. (2002) Medieval Glassmaking at Tyre, Lebanon. *Journal of Glass Studies* 44, 49–66.
Barovier Mentasti, R. (1995) La vetraria veneziana. In R. Pallucchini (ed.) *Storia di Venezia. Temi, L'Arte, Part 2*, 845–905. Rome, Istituto dell'Enciclopedia Italiana.
Bass, G. F., Brill, R. H., Lledó, B. and Matthews, S. D. (2009) *Serçe Limanı II. The Glass of an Eleventh-Century Shipwreck*. College Station, TX, Texas A&M University Press.
Bierbrauer, V. (1987) *Invillino – Ibligo in Friaul I. Die römische Siedlung und das spätantik-frühmittelalterliche Castrum*. Münchner Beiträge zur Vor- und Frühgeschichte 33. Munich, C. H. Beck.
Brill, R. H. (1967) A Great Glass Slab from Ancient Galilee. *Archaeology* 20, 88–95.
Brill, R. H. (1999) *Chemical Analyses of Early Glasses*. Corning, NY, The Corning Museum of Glass.
Brill, R. H. (2009) Chemical Analyses. In G. F. Bass, R. H. Brill, B. Lledó and S. D. Matthews, *Serçe Limanı II. The Glass of an Eleventh-Century Shipwreck*, 459–496. College Station, TX, Texas A&M University Press.
Brown, P. F. (1996) *Venice & Antiquity. The Venetian Sense of the Past*. New Haven, CT/London, Yale University Press.
Buora, M. (1997) Una produzione artigianale di un vetraio a Sevegliano (Agro di Aquileia, Italia Settentrionale) nel IV sec. D. C. *Journal of Glass Studies* 39, 23–31.
Calvi, M. C. (1968) *I vetri romani del Museo di Aquileia*. Pubblicazioni dell'Associazione Nazionale per Aquileia 7. Aquileia, Associazione Nazionale per Aquileia.
Cantino Wataghin, G. (1992) Fra tarda antichità e alto medioevo. In L. Cracco Ruggini, M. Pavan, G. Gracco and G. Ortalli (eds.) *Storia di Venezia. Dalle origini alla caduta della serenissima I. Origini-età ducale*, 321–363. Rome, Istituto dell'Enciclopedia Italiana.
Carboni, S., Lacerenza, G. and Whitehouse, D. (2003) Glassmaking in Medieval Tyre: The Written Evidence. *Journal of Glass Studies* 45, 139–149.
Castagnetti, A. (1992) Insediamenti e "populi". In L. Cracco Ruggini, M. Pavan, G. Gracco and G. Ortalli (eds.) *Storia di Venezia. Dalle origini alla caduta della serenissima I. Origini-età ducale*, 577–612. Rome, Istituto dell'Enciclopedia Italiana.
Cramp, R. (2006) The Anglo-Saxon window glass. In R. Cramp, *Wearmouth and Jarrow monastic sites II*, 56–80. Swindon, English Heritage.
Ferri, M. (2006) Reperti vitrei altomedievali dagli scavi di Torcello e San Francesco del Deserto-Venezia. *Journal of Glass Studies* 48, 173–189.
Foy, D., Picon, M., Vichy, M. and Thirion-Merle, V. (2003) Caractérisation des verres de la fin de l'Antiquité en Méditerranée occidentale: l'émergence de nouveaux courants commerciaux. In D. Foy and M.-D. Nenna (eds.) *Échanges et commerce du verre dans le monde antique*. Monographies Instrumentum 24, 41–85. Montagnac, Monique Mergoil.
Foy, D., Vichy, M. and Picon, M. (2000) Lingots de verre en Méditerranée orientale (IIIe siècle av. J.-C. – VIIe siècle apr. J.-C. Approvisionnement et mise en oeuvre. Données archéologiques et données de laboratoire. In *Annales du 14e Congrès de l'Association Internationale pour l'Histoire du Verre*, 51–57. Amsterdam, Association Internationale pour l'Histoire du Verre.
Freestone, I. C. (2003) Primary Glass Sources in the Mid First Millennium AD. In *Annales du 15e Congrès de l'Association Internationale pour l'Histoire du Verre*, 111–115. Nottingham, Association Internationale pour l'Histoire du Verre.
Freestone, I. C. (2005) The provenance of ancient glass through compositional analysis. In P. B. Vandiver, J. L. Mass and A. Murray (eds.) *Materials Issues in Art and Archaeology VII*, 195–208. Warrendale, PA, Materials Research Society.
Freestone, I. C. and Gorin-Rosen, Y. (1999) The Great glass Slab at Bet She'arim: An Early Islamic Glassmaking Experiment? *Journal of Glass Studies* 41, 105–116.
Freestone, I. C., Gorin-Rosen, Y. and Hughes, M. J. (2000) Primary glass from Israel and the production of glass in late antiquity and the early Islamic period. In M.-D. Nenna (ed.) *La route du verre. Ateliers primaires et secondaires du second millénaire av. J.-C. au Moyen Âge*. Travaux de la Maison de l'Orient Méditerranéen 33, 66–83. Lyon, Maison de l'Orient Méditerranéen.
Freestone, I. C. and Hughes, M. J. (2006) Origins of the Jarrow glass. In R. Cramp, *Wearmouth and Jarrow monastic sites II*, 147–155. Swindon, English Heritage.
Freestone, I. C., Hughes, M. J. and Stapleton, C. P. (2008) The composition and production of Anglo-Saxon glass. In V. Evison, *Catalogue of Anglo-Saxon Glass in the British Museum*. British Museum Research Publication 167, 29–46. London, British Museum Press.
Glöckner, G. (2006) Signs, inscriptions and other designs on Roman vessels in Austria. In D. Foy and M.-D. Nenna (eds.)

Corpus des Signatures et Marques sur verres antiques 2, 187–208. Aix en Provence/Lyon, Association Française pour l'Archéologie du Verre.

Gorin-Rosen, Y. (2000) The ancient glass industry in Israel. Summary of the finds and new discoveries. In M.-D. Nenna (ed.) *La route du verre. Ateliers primaires et secondaires du second millénaire av. J.-C. au Moyen Âge*. Travaux de la Maison de l'Orient Méditerranéen 33, 59–63. Lyon, Maison de l'Orient Méditerranéen.

Gratuze, B. and Barrandon, J.-N. (1990) Islamic Glass Weights and Stamps: Analysis Using Nuclear Techniques. *Archaeometry* 32, 155–162.

Höpken, C. (2011) Bodenmarken eckiger Glasgefässe aus Straubing, Raetien (Deutschland). In D. Foy and M.-D. Nenna (eds.) *Corpus des Signatures et Marques sur verres antiques 3*, 171–174. Aix en Provence/Lyon, Association Française pour l'Archéologie du Verre.

Jacoby, D. (2009) Venetian commercial expansion in the eastern Mediterranean, 8th–11th Centuries. In M. Mundell Mango (ed.) *Byzantine Trade, 4th–12th centuries: the archaeology of local, regional and international exchange*. Papers of the Thirty-eighth Spring Symposium of Byzantine Studies, 371–391. Farnham, Surrey/Burlington, VT, Ashgate Publishing Limited.

Lamm, C. J. (1929/30) *Mittelalterliche Gläser und Steinschnittarbeiten aus dem nahen Osten*. Forschungen zur islamischen Kunst 5. Berlin, Reimer, Vohsen.

Lazar, I. (2006) Base marks on glass vessels found on the territory of modern Slovenia: commentary and catalogue. In D. Foy and M.-D. Nenna (eds.) *Corpus des Signatures et Marques sur verres antiques 2*, 245–261. Aix en Provence/Lyon, Association Française pour l'Archéologie du Verre.

Leciejewicz, L. (2002) Italian-Polish researches into the origin of Venice. *Archaeologia Polona* 40, 51–71.

Leciejewicz, L., Tabaczyńska, E. and Tabaczyński, S. (1977) *Torcello: Scavi 1961–62*. Rome, Istituto Nazionale di Archeologia e Storia dell'Arte.

McCormick, M. (2001) *Origins of the European Economy: Communications and Commerce, A.D. 300–900*. Cambridge, Cambridge University Press.

Mirti, P., Davit, P., Gulmini, M. and Saguì, L. (2001) Glass Fragments from the Crypta Balbi in Rome: The Composition of Eighth-Century Fragments. *Archaeometry* 43, 491–502.

Mirti, P., Lepora, A. and Saguì, L. (2000) Scientific Analysis of Seventh-Century Glass Fragments from the Crypta Balbi in Rome. *Archaeometry* 42, 359–374.

Molino, A., Molino, P., Socal, A., Turchetto, E. and Zanetti, P. (1986) Il relitto del vetro. Relazione preliminare. *Bollettino d'Arte, Supplemento 37–38, Archeologia Subacquea* 3, 179–194.

Nenna, M.-D. (2008) Nouveaux acquis sur la production et le commerce du verre antique entre Orient et Occident. *Zeitschrift für Schweizerische Archäologie und Kunstgeschichte* 65, 61–66.

Pavan, M. and Arnaldi, G. (1992) Le origini dell'identità lagunare. In L. Cracco Ruggini, M. Pavan, G. Gracco and G. Ortalli (eds.) *Storia di Venezia. Dalle origini alla caduta della serenissima I. Origini-età ducale*, 409–456. Rome, Istituto dell'Enciclopedia Italiana.

Prawer, J. (1973) I Veneziani e le colonie veneziane nel regno latino di Gerusalemme. In A. Pertusi (ed.) *Venezia e il Levante fino al secolo XV*, 625–656. Florence, Leo S. Olschi.

Rottloff, A. (2006) Bodenmarken auf halbformgeblasenen Gläsern aus Raetien. In D. Foy and M.-D. Nenna (eds.) *Corpus des Signatures et Marques sur verres antiques 2*, 145–185. Aix en Provence/Lyon, Association Française pour l'Archéologie du Verre.

Shortland, A., Schachner, L., Freestone, I. and Tite, M. (2006) Natron as a flux in the early vitreous materials industry: sources, beginnings and reasons for decline. *Journal of Archaeological Science* 33, 521–530.

Tait, H. (1979) *The Golden Age of Venetian Glass*. London, British Museum Publications.

Termini Storti, A. R. (1994) Una produzione vetraria tardoantica a Sevegliano (Agro di Aquileia). *Aquileia Nostra* 65, 209–224.

Verità, M. and Toninato, T. (1990) A comparative analytical investigation on the origins of Venetian Glassmaking. *Rivista della Stazione Sperimentale del Vetro* 20, 169–180.

Weinberg, G. D. (1988) *Excavations at Jalame: Site of a Glass Factory in Late Roman Palestine*. Columbia, MO, University of Missouri Press.

Whitehouse, D. (1991) Glassmaking at Corinth; A reassessment. In D. Foy and G. Sennequier (eds.) *Ateliers de verriers de l'antiquité à la période pré-industrielle*, 73–82. Rouen, Association Française pour l'Archéologie du Verre.

Whitehouse, D. (1993) The date of the 'South Centre' Workshop at Corinth. *Archeologia medievale* 20, 659–662.

Whitehouse, D. (2003) Things that Traveled: The Surprising Case of Raw Glass. *Early Medieval Europe* 12, 301–305.

Zecchin, L. (1980) Materie prime e mezzi d'opera dei vetrai nei documenti veneziani dal 1233 al 1347. *Rivista della Stazione Sperimentale del Vetro* 10, 171–176.

Zecchin, L. (1987) *Vetro e vetrai di Murano. Studi sulla storia del vetro I*. Venice, Arsenale Editrice.

10

Late Roman glass from South Pannonia and the problem of its origin

Mia Leljak

Unlike Roman glass from northern Pannonia, the material from southern Pannonia (today northern Croatia) is not well known (Fig. 10.1). This is mostly due to a long-term lack of interest in this subject and to the fact that the majority of finds have not been published, giving rise to many unknowns about the Roman glass industry in this territory. At present, glass vessels dated to the late Roman period appear to be much more numerous than those of earlier periods. It is difficult to say whether this is the result of a lack of imports in the early Roman period, or to the general state of research and the lack of information about the unpublished material. Vessels from the earlier periods were mostly imported from Italy, while those from later periods may have been produced locally. However, the latter assumption has not yet been

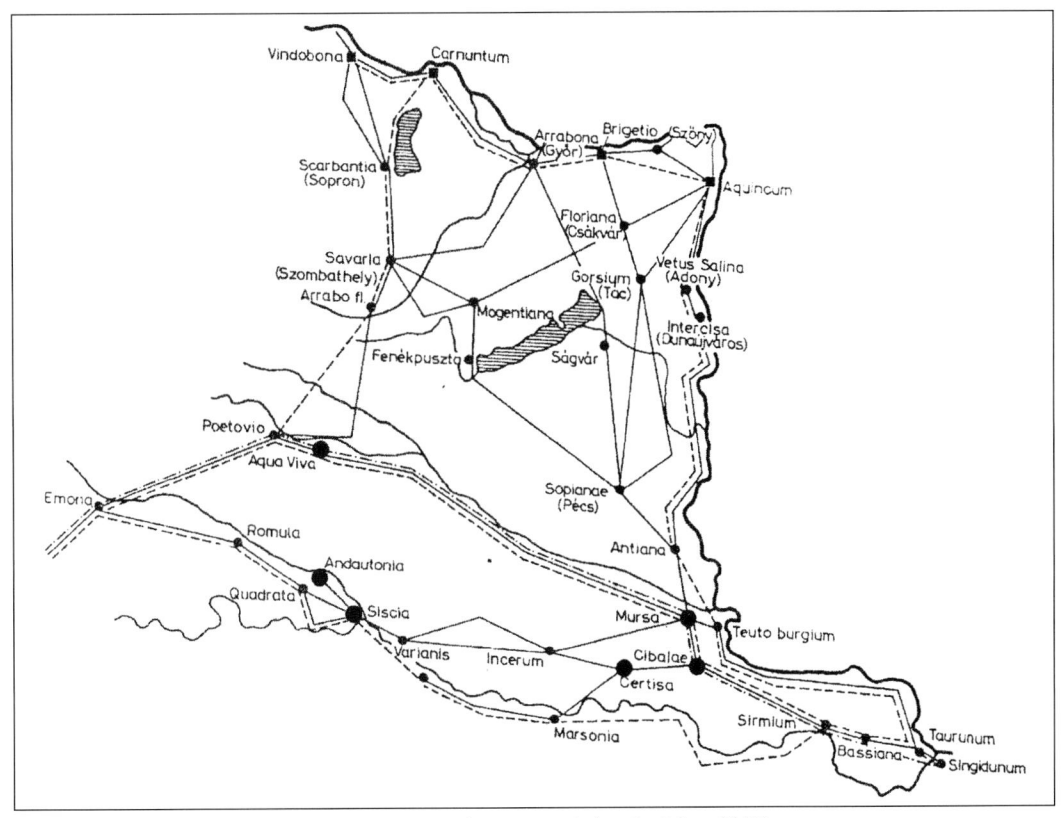

Fig. 10.1: Map of Pannonia (after Barkóczi 1988).

securely substantiated by archaeological evidence, and is therefore unproven.

So far, two furnaces hypothetically interpreted as glass-making facilities have been found, although, this interpretation is not secure. The first furnace was found in 1998 in Sisak (Roman *Siscia*), with only its lower circular section preserved (Fig. 10.2). We can only speculate about the form of the upper part of the furnace, that is, whether it was rectangular and domed, or some other shape. The diameter of the furnace was 85–90cm; it was constructed in brick, including a brick-paved floor, and was covered with a layer of lime plaster. In the relevant publication, it was not mentioned if there were any remains of molten glass attached to the floor of the furnace (Lolić and Petrinec 2000, 42). When it was found, the structure was filled with rubble containing fragments of glass vessels and molten glass, which gave rise to the assumption that it was used for the production of glass vessels (Vidošević 2003, 12).

In its shape, size and the material of construction, the furnace from *Siscia* fits the general appearance of Roman glass furnaces. However, the evidence for this identification is far from certain. Curiously, neither the site itself nor its neighbouring area yielded any other finds to establish that the structure was indeed a glass furnace. In other words, there was no glass waste or raw materials, or tools and equipment for the production of glass, or a large quantity of

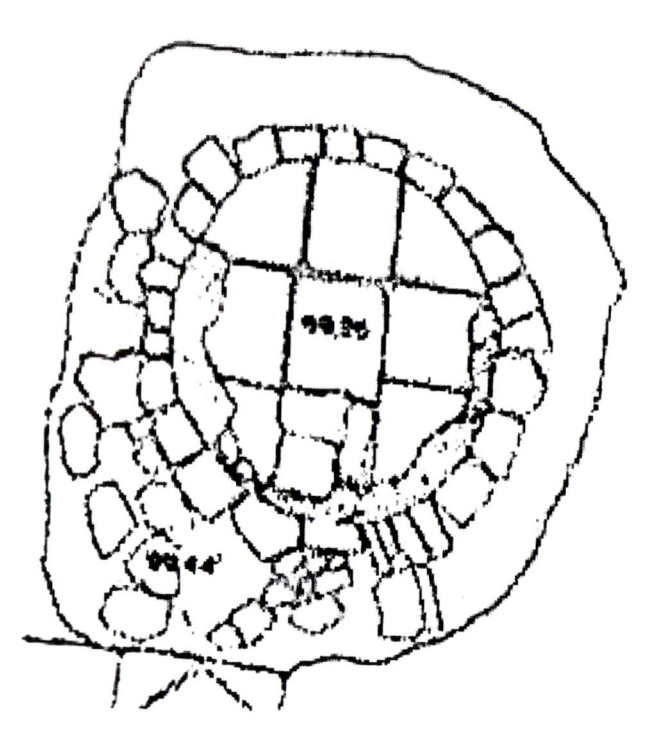

Fig. 10.2: Furnace from Siscia *(after Vidošević 2003).*

Fig. 10.3: Remains of the furnace from Cibalae *(photo archive of the city museum in Vinkovci).*

fragments, let alone entire vessels. It is almost certain that glass working took place in *Siscia* but it is not clear when this happened. The furnace described above has been dated to the 1st century on the basis of coins found in its immediate vicinity, and it is possible that it was also in use in the 2nd century. It is usually assumed that the local Pannonian

Fig. 10.4: Vessels from Cibalae *(photo Mia Leljak).*

workshops were active in the late Roman period (Šaranović Svetek 1986, 53). However, *Siscia* was an important trading centre throughout the Roman period receiving the status of colonia (*Colonia Flavia Siscia*) in the reign of the Emperor Vespasian (AD 69–79), and the town becoming the capital of the province of *Pannonia Savia* during the reign of the Emperor Diocletian (AD 284–305), so there is little doubt that glass workshops existed there before the 3rd and 4th centuries. However, at this point there is no evidence to confirm this assumption.

The second furnace was found in 2008 in Vinkovci (the Roman town of *Cibalae*). The excavators concluded that it was used for making glass vessels, as molten glass was found inside the furnace (Vulić 2009, 100). The furnace had been damaged by a recent burial and only its lower section was preserved, measuring 2.36 × 0.68m, which was roughly half of its original size (Fig. 10.3). The surviving lower part is rectangular in shape and consists of two separate, probably square, areas built of brick, now measuring 1.28 × 0.68m and 1.08 × 0.4m. Due to poor preservation of the

Fig. 10.5: Vessels from Štrbinci (photo Mia Leljak).

remains, the purpose of the structure cannot be determined with certainty. It has been assumed that one section was used for the melting of glass, since several lumps of molten glass were found, while the other part was probably used either for cooling the finished vessels or also for glass melting. The firing chamber and the upper part of the furnace have not been preserved, although it is probable the later had a rectangular and domed shape. The remains of collapsed Roman bricks found on the site may come from the dome of the furnace or from the architecture surrounding the furnace. Alternatively, however, these finds may belong to some other structure on the site, and not the furnace.

As in the case of the furnace from *Siscia*, no glass fragments (such as glass waste, raw materials, tools for the manufacture of glass, or the remains of ceramic pots in which glass was melted) were found on the site or in the vicinity. Moreover, there was no other material finds, such as architectural fragments, ceramics or any other small finds to provide further knowledge of the furnace. Therefore, on the basis of the structure of the furnace alone, it is impossible to form conclusions about its date and/or precise function. What we can say is that the glass workshop in *Cibalae* appears to have been active in late antiquity, as glass vessels dated to the 4th century have been found (Fig. 10.4) and both the quality of glass and the techniques of manufacture point to local production. The glass contains a lot of bubbles and vertical streaks and the vessels are incorrectly shaped. Comparing them with the admittedly small amount of similar examples from other parts of the Roman empire these differences are more than apparent (Burger 1966, 137, fig. 122.335.4; Kunina 1997, 325, no. 365), as the lack of analogies as well. The jug (Fig. 10.4) does not have direct analogies in the literature only approximate, both for the shape and the decorations (Marijanski-Manojlović 1987, 153, pl. 57.7; Barkóczi 1988, 189, no. 462, pl. 46.462; Prammer and Möslein 2008, 226–227; Migotti 2009, 220, pl. 36.103.11).

If a workshop was located in the area of the furnace, it is difficult to say whether it functioned as a single structure, or as one of a group; the evidence is insufficient. The furnace was found on a site in the suburb of the Roman city, that is, in an area suitable for the location of glass workshops.

The greatest quantity of late Roman glass vessels in southern Pannonia was found in the late Roman cemetery on the site of Štrbinci (perhaps Roman *Certissia*) near the town of Đakovo. This cemetery has yielded a wide variety of late antique and early Christian finds. The majority of the vessels found served for everyday use, like oval plain or fluted jugs, conical beakers, spherical bottles and various balsamaria (Fig. 10.5). Their dominant colour was various shades of green. The vessels at Štrbinci were probably produced locally, judging by the large quantity found, and their poor quality, characterized by their irregular shapes, and the bubbles and vertical streaks in the glass. In addition, there is a lack of close other analogies for a large number of those vessels elsewhere in Pannonia, which gives rise to a presumption, not yet confirmed, for their manufacture in the locality or at least in South Pannonia. There had been given some assumptions about the possible glass production at Štrbinci, based on some finds and remains found at the site (Migotti 1998, 14; 2009, 164), but unfortunately they are not substantiated by further analysis, so at this point there is no secure evidence for such interpretations.

In any discussion about the Roman glass industry in northern Croatia, a long-neglected subject, lots of unknowns should be confronted. It is therefore not surprising that the discoveries of the furnaces in *Siscia* and *Cibalae* were rather sensational. However, it seems that the conclusions reached were premature and insufficiently grounded. It is arguable that glass workshops in major cities in the Croatian part of Pannonia must have existed in late antiquity, but the archaeological evidence presently available is insufficient, and without further finds the existence of such workshops cannot be proved and the types of vessels possibly produced in them cannot determined. In conclusion: whereas glass workshops are clearly recognisable in the Serbian and Slovenian parts of southern Pannonia, as at *Sirmium* and *Poetovio*, the production of glassware in the Croatian part of southern Pannonia remains uncertain.

Bibliography

Barkóczi, L. (1988) *Pannonische Glasfunde in Ungarn*. Budapest, Akadémiai Kiadó.

Burger, Sz. A. (1966) Late Roman cemetery at Ságvár. *Acta Archaeologica Academiae Scientiarum Hungaricae* 18, 99–234.

Kunina, N. (1997) *Ancient glass in the Hermitage collection*. St. Petersburg, The State Hermitage.

Lolić, T. and Petrinec, I. (2000) Lokalitet privatni poslovni prostor Autoposavina vlasnika. In Z. Burkowsky, A. Bugar *et al., Pregled zaštitnih arheoloških istraživanja 1990–2000*, 42. Sisak, Gradski Muzej.

Marijanski-Manojlović, M. (1987) *Rimska nekropola kod Beške u Sremu*. Posebna izdanja/Vojvođanski muzej 8. Novi Sad, Vojvođanski Muzej.

Migotti, B. (1998) The production of glass jewellery at Štrbinci (NE Croatia). *Instrumentum* 8, 14.

Migotti, B. (2009) Kasnoantičko groblje na Štrbincima kod Đakova-iskopavanja u 2004. i 2005. *Arheološki radovi i rasprave* 16, 107–224.

Prammer, J. and Möslein, S. (2008) The Necropolis of Straubing (Germany). In J.-J. Aillagon (ed.) *Rome and the Barbarians. The birth of a new world*, 226–227. Milan, Skira.

Šaranović Svetek, V. (1986) *Antičko staklo u jugoslovenskom delu provincije Donje Panonije*. Posebna izdanja/Vojvođanski muzej 7. Novi Sad, Vojvođanski Muzej.

Vidošević, I. (2003) Rimska keramika s lokaliteta Starčevićeva ulica 37 u Sisku. *Godišnjak Gradskog Muzeja Sisak*, 3/4, 11–74.

Vulić, H. (2009) Vinkovci-Ulica bana Josipa Jelačića 11. *Hrvatski Arheološki Godišnjak* 5, 99–100.

11

Glass supply and consumption in the late Roman and early Byzantine site Dichin, northern Bulgaria

Thilo Rehren and Anastasia Cholakova

Introduction

The late Roman and early Byzantine site at the centre of this study is situated near the present day village of Dichin, Veliko Tarnovo district, northern Bulgaria (Fig. 11.1). It was excavated in 1996–2003 by a British-Bulgarian team under the terms of a joint project of Nottingham University, National Institute of Archaeology, Bulgarian Academy of Sciences and Veliko Tarnovo Regional Museum (Poulter 2007; Dinchev *et al.* 2009).

The site is located on a small hill in the plain of the river Rositsa, part of the Danube catchment basin (Fig. 11.2), in the vicinity of the Roman and early Byzantine town *Nicopolis ad Istrum*. The ancient settlement near Dichin is not particularly large, but remarkable with its defensive system with solid stone-brick curtain and *proteichismata*, gates, and towers, now partially excavated. The buildings inside the walls have stone foundations with mud-brick superstructures, and a dense planning of the settlement is revealed, as typical for such kind of sites in the Balkans during late antiquity (Fig. 11.3). The Dichin site combines both military and agricultural functions. The chronology of the settlement consists of two main periods of occupation, the first from c. AD 410 to 490 and the second from c. AD 540 to 580, although a certain disagreement exists about the sub-periods of its occupation (see Dinchev *et al.* 2009, 15–18). According to the Bulgarian authors the site suffered from devastating fires first at around AD 470 (the end of the first phase of the main period I) and again around AD 490 (the end of the second phase of the main period I) with no significant cultural differences between the two sub-phases. However, this detailed stratigraphy is not recognised by the British team excavating elsewhere in the site, and the first period is considered as continuous until AD 490 when the settlement is destroyed and abandoned. After a hiatus lasting for most of the first half of the 6th century, the settlement is partly reconstructed. Certain distinctions can be seen between the first and the second main periods. The 6th-century settlement has less dense habitation and less carefully constructed buildings. During the second period also some parts of the defences are not maintained anymore, and the general repertoire of archaeological materials shows less diversity and nearly no imported goods. That gives us reason to see the 6th-century occupation of the site as markedly poorer in cultural and economic characteristics. The settlement is finally devastated and abandoned in the last quarter of the century.

The glass vessel fragments from Dichin were studied as part of wider post excavation research on the finds from the site (Cholakova 2009a). In total, there are about 270 identifiable glass fragments (predominantly from vessels) from the site; 119 of them, based on their degree of preservation, were selected for the final archaeological publication (Cholakova 2009b). This assemblage is divided into several main groups according to the techniques of manufacture and decoration, colour and quality of the glass; when possible, the vessel type was also considered, following, where appropriate, the typology originally developed by Clasina Isings (1957). The well established chronology and relatively tight dating of the Dichin site is important as it enables insight into the chronological distribution and changes of this material throughout the nearly two centuries represented here. The possibility to identify imported and regional glass artefact production also provided the incentive for a more detailed chemical study of glass vessel supply and its interpretation in a broader context of cultural and economical exchange and processes during the late Roman and early Byzantine periods.

Ongoing parallel programmes for chemical analyses of

Fig. 11.1: Map of the Balkans with the location of Dichin (modified from Dinchev et al. 2009).

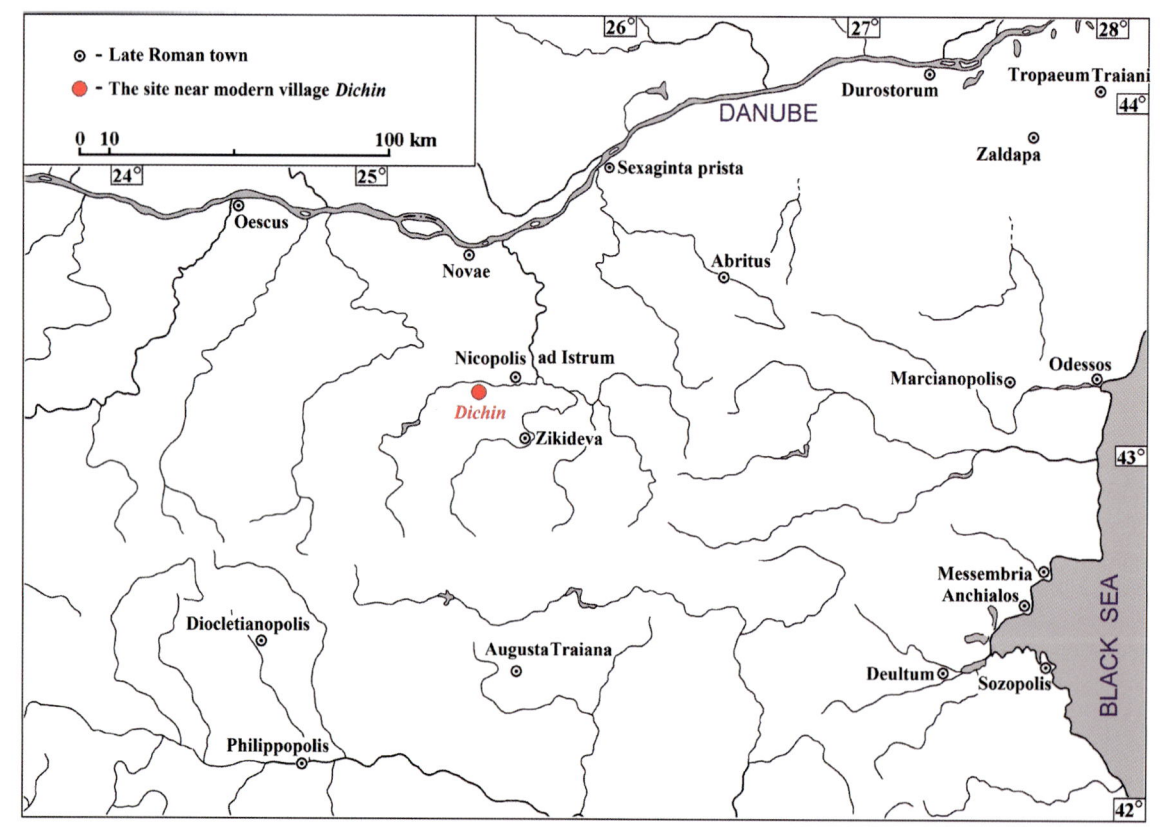

Fig. 11.2: Map of the region south of the Lower Danube with the location of Dichin (modified from Dinchev et al. 2009).

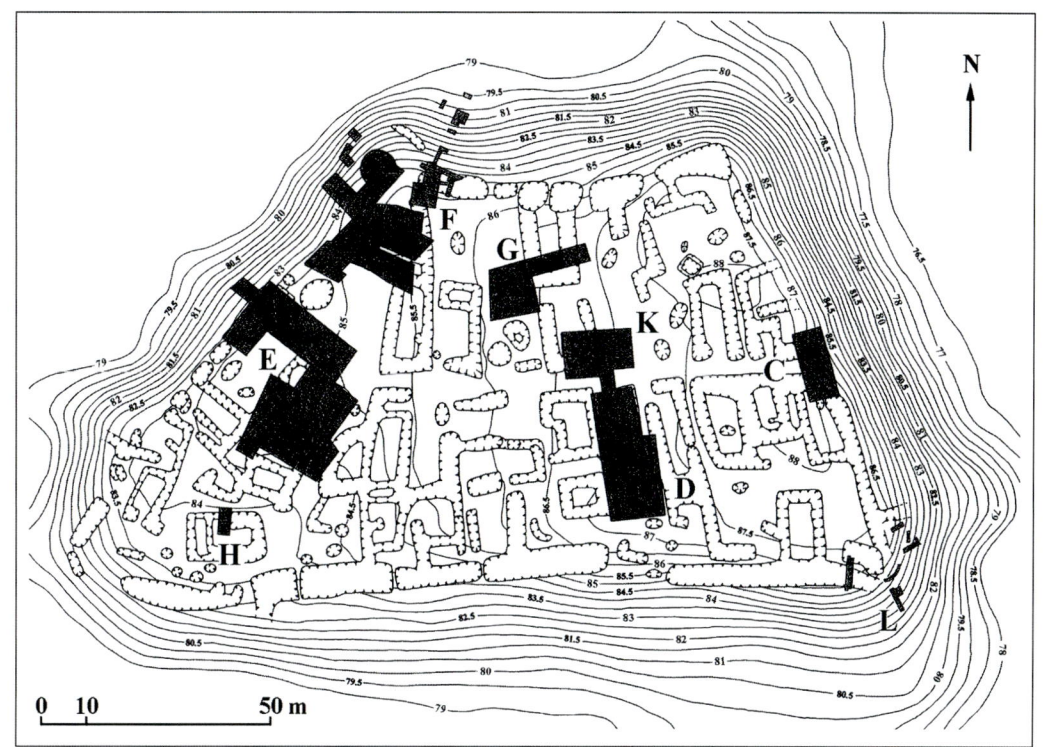

Fig. 11.3: Topographic plan of the site of Dichin with the location of areas excavated in 1996–2003 (modified from Poulter 2007 and Dinchev et al. 2009).

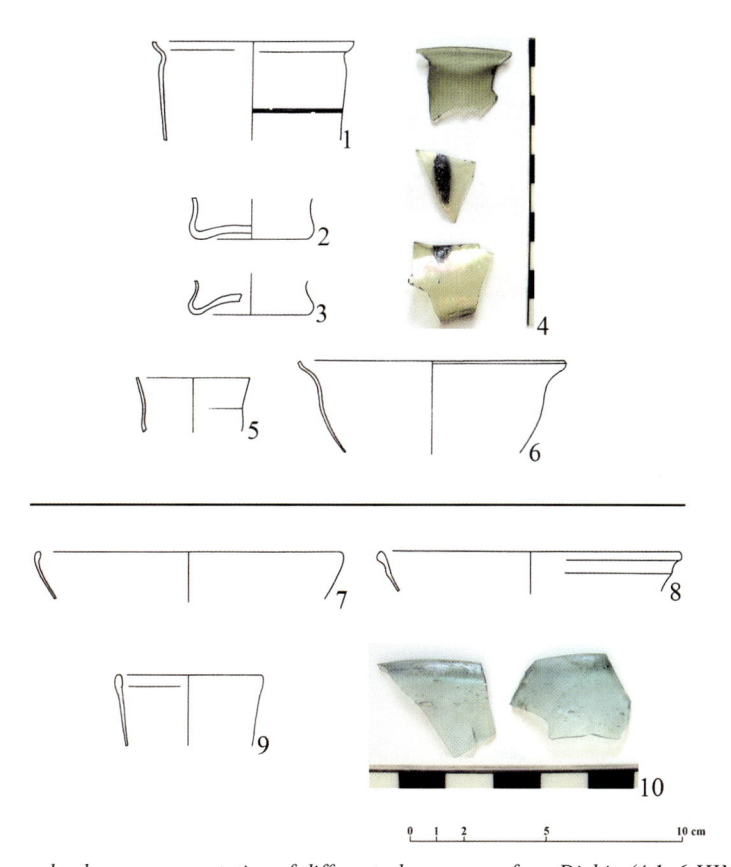

Fig. 11.4: Vessel shapes and colours representative of different glass groups from Dichin (4.1–6 HIMT, 4.7–10 HIT glasses).

the glass from Dichin are currently being performed at the UCL Institute of Archaeology and Nottingham University, respectively (for analyses performed in Nottingham see Smith 2011), and this paper can therefore only give an interim report. In preliminary papers (Rehren and Cholakova 2009; 2010) two iron-rich groups of glass artefacts were identified, one consistent with the well-known HIMT group, and the other showing the same iron- and titanium-rich composition, but no elevated manganese (dubbed HIT glass). Here, we now present the entire assemblage analysed by us, without a bias towards a particular glass type or form.

The present paper is based on the results obtained from the analyses of the glass finds from the NW Area F of the site (Fig. 11.3) excavated by the Bulgarian researchers. Consequently, their conclusions about the chronological development and periodization of the settlement are followed here, acknowledging that there is a slight misalignment with the periodization used by the UK excavation elsewhere in the site. The aim of this paper is to look more closely at the overall range of compositions of glass from Dichin in relation to known European, Near Eastern and North African production and consumption groups. Furthermore different aspects of consumer choice, mechanisms of supply and demand, and the role of recycling in the provision of glass objects outside the main centres of the empire are touched upon. It is hoped that in the long run, an integrated approach of the interpretation, *i.e.* the attempt to link the main compositional glass groups to particular vessel types or groups of vessel types, will allow revealing the specifics of the imported and regional/local production, as well as their chronological distribution. Identifying similarities between the techniques of workmanship of the vessels belonging to different compositional groups could also help to reconstruct some features of the secondary glass working industry and its relations to the primary raw glass supply; these are research questions currently under investigation as part of an ongoing doctoral project.

Methods and materials

The corpus of glass samples analysed as part of this project includes 80 of the approximately 270 fragments, including approximately one third of the fragments published in the catalogue (Cholakova 2009b). It is believed that this is a fairly representative group in which we can recognize 71 particular vessels and 3 window glass pieces, even though we cannot exclude the possibility that specific glass types are underrepresented due to their preferential weathering, disintegration during burial, or other reasons. The results presented here are based on an initial set of electron microprobe analyses conducted on polished cross sections of the fragments, using established procedures at the UCL Institute of Archaeology's Wolfson Archaeological Science Laboratories. A refinement of these procedures is currently being developed, and the revised dataset will form part of Cholakova's forthcoming PhD thesis. To avoid future confusion we are not reporting the individual measurements here, but restrict the data presentation to binary scatter plots and a summary table. As such, the results are to be understood as preliminary; however, we do not anticipate significant changes in the final numbers, and are confident in the usefulness of the current data and interpretation.

Results

There are several chemically distinct groups visible among the 80 analysed fragments. We had already identified the more strongly-coloured HIMT and HIT glass (Rehren and Cholakova 2009; 2010); of these, there are now a total of 16 HIMT glasses and 6 HIT glasses. They all have more than 1.4 wt% FeO and more than 0.4 wt% TiO_2, reaching 3.6 wt% FeO and 0.7 wt% TiO_2. They also show a good correlation of iron oxide and alumina, the latter ranging from c. 2.5 wt% to more than 4 wt% in the extreme. These glasses are visually easily identified by their specific yellow/yellow-amber (HIMT) and saturated aqua green (HIT) colours (Figs. 11.4.4, 11.4.10).

The HIMT vessels (mainly beakers and cups Isings 1957, 127–130, 137–138, forms 106b, 106c, 109c, and very few examples of convex bowls Isings 1957, 113–114, 143–147, forms 96a, 116), have cracked-off and polished or unworked rims, no pontil marks on the bottoms, often decoration of wheel-engraved lines or/and blobs and trails of blue glass, and their manufacture does not seem very skilful (Fig. 11.4.1–6). According to the stratigraphy of Dichin these fragments come from 5th-century contexts, probably from the very beginning of the settlement. A certain concentration of these vessels can be seen during the first phase of the first period (c. AD 410–470), while such fragments are not present in well dated 6th-century contexts. Chemically, these glasses show a considerable variation in their iron oxide, magnesia and alumina concentrations (Fig. 11.5, see also Table 11.1), suggesting that they come from different batches within the larger HIMT group. Numerous parallels of this distinct chemical group dated to the 4th and 5th centuries are found across the late antique world (*e.g.* Golofast 2009, fig. 1; Foy *et al.* 2003, 48–50, figs. 3–4), and Freestone *et al.* (2009b, 42) call it even 'arguably the most abundant glass type' in this period. A few of the HIMT pieces at Dichin could be interpreted as glass blowing waste – *i.e.* direct evidence for their regional production or at least for the local collecting of cullet, such as a single misshaped fragment, and possibly a moil.

In contrast, HIT glasses are not as much present as HIMT fragments, but that group is remarkably homogeneous in its composition (Table 11.1) and also in the typological

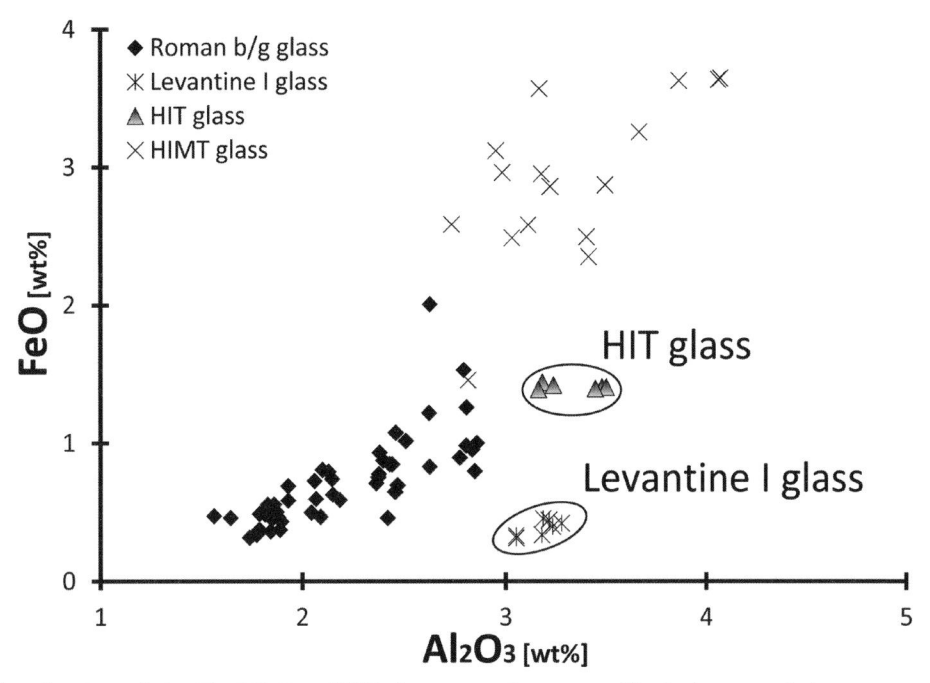

Fig. 11.5: Scatterplot of FeO vs Al₂O₃. The HIMT and HIT glasses are characterised by high iron and alumina contents. Note the tight clustering of the six HIT and seven Levantine I samples.

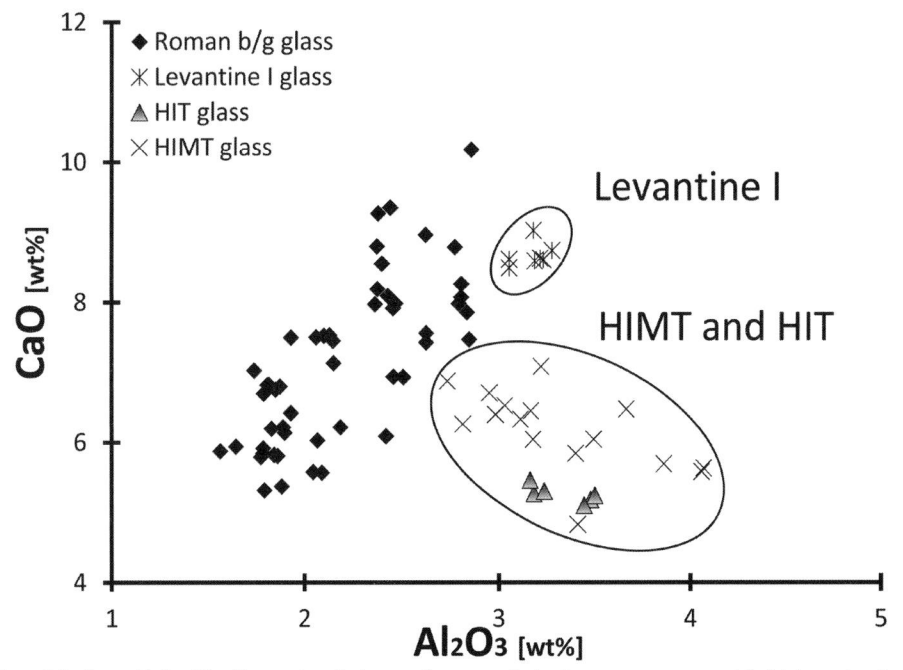

Fig. 11.6: Scatterplot of CaO vs Al₂O₃. The Levantine I glasses form a relatively narrow group with higher alumina than the main glass group.

and technical features of the vessels. Due to the degree of fragmentation it is not possible to reconstruct entire shapes, but cups and bowls can be identified (Fig. 11.4.7–10). They are of high quality, with carefully fire rounded and polished rims, and pontil marks on the bottom. In general they come from 5th-century contexts, and several well dated contexts point more closely to the second phase of the first period (c. AD 470–490). At the same time this group of vessels is not found in some earlier closed contexts; hence, it can be concluded that HIMT and HIT glass types at Dichin are not exactly contemporary, although the types overlap, while HIT glasses continue a little longer. It seems that

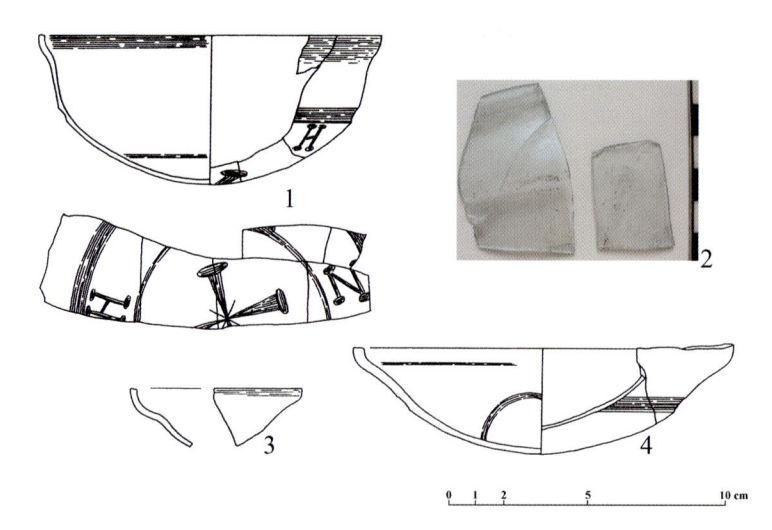

Fig. 11.7: Vessel shapes and colours representative of Levantine I glass finds from Dichin.

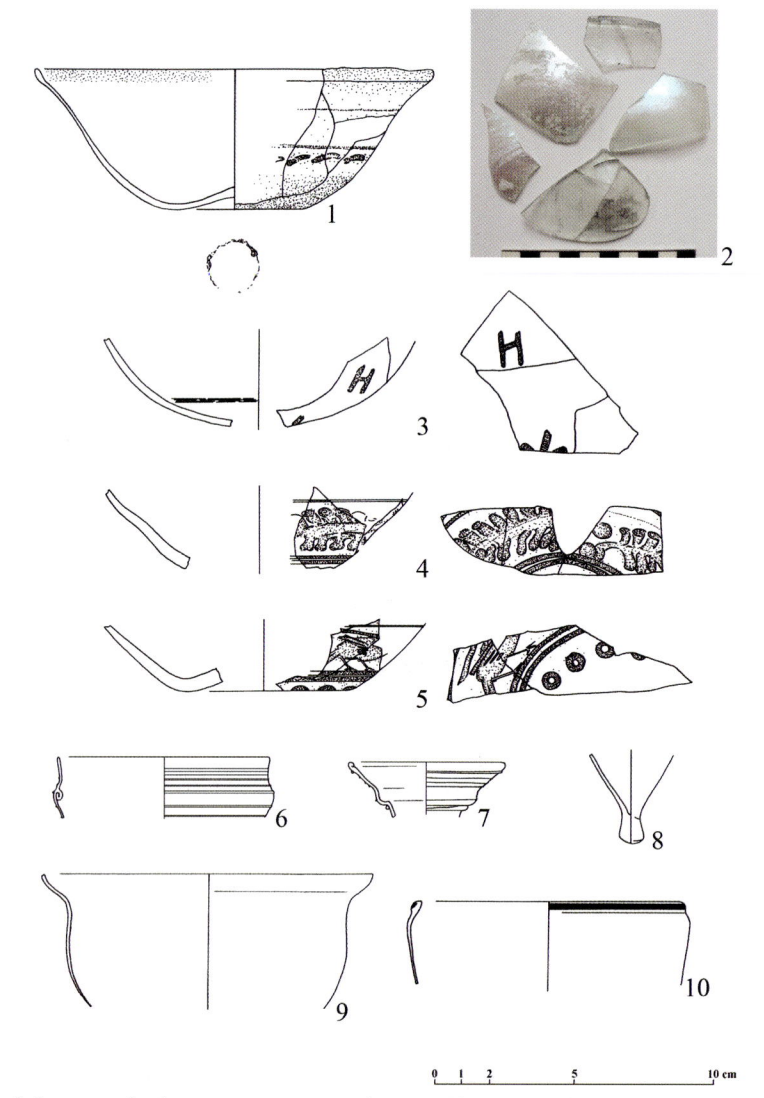

Fig. 11.8: Vessel shapes and colours representative of Roman blue-green glass ('clean' sub-group) from Dichin.

Table 11.1: Summary of EPMA data of the glass assemblage from Dichin, organised by groups as defined in the text. The first group (clean) is similar to Roman blue/green glass, while the medium and dirty groups are either varieties of Roman blue/green glass, or related to a variety of weak HIMT glass as defined by Foster and Jackson (2009). The first row for each group gives the average values for each oxide, followed in the second row by the standard deviation. Oxides with a star (*) indicate those where a correction factor had been applied to the measured data following the assessment of measurements of reference glasses (Corning A and B).

	SiO_2	Na_2O	CaO*	K_2O	MgO	Al_2O_3*	FeO	TiO_2	MnO*	P_2O_5	Cl	SO_3	∑ IMP
clean	**70.0**	**18.6**	**6.22**	**0.40**	**0.48**	**1.89**	**0.47**	**0.08**	**0.72**	**0.02**	**1.10**	**0.13**	**3.65**
n=26	0.9	0.8	0.57	0.06	0.09	0.18	0.10	0.02	0.25	0.02	0.09	0.09	0.40
medium	**66.0**	**19.0**	**8.12**	**0.59**	**0.91**	**2.34**	**0.78**	**0.12**	**1.34**	**0.05**	**0.89**	**0.21**	**5.27**
n=14	0.4	0.4	0.65	0.06	0.14	0.17	0.08	0.02	0.38	0.03	0.08	0.11	0.26
dirty	**66.7**	**18.0**	**8.08**	**0.69**	**1.01**	**2.72**	**1.16**	**0.16**	**1.23**	**0.07**	**0.82**	**0.21**	**6.44**
n=11	1.1	1.1	0.96	0.13	0.18	0.14	0.35	0.06	0.47	0.04	0.12	0.10	0.21
Lev I	**70.3**	**15.0**	**8.67**	**0.94**	**0.54**	**3.17**	**0.38**	**0.06**	**0.05**	**0.06**	**0.83**	**0.06**	**5.40**
n=7	0.4	0.5	0.17	0.04	0.02	0.09	0.06	0.01	0.04	0.01	0.08	0.03	0.18
HIT	**68.2**	**18.2**	**5.26**	**0.38**	**1.03**	**3.33**	**1.41**	**0.59**	**0.03**	**0.02**	**0.92**	**0.26**	**9.12**
n=6	0.9	1.0	0.12	0.02	0.07	0.15	0.02	0.03	0.03	0.01	0.12	0.07	0.32
HIMT	**65.5**	**17.3**	**6.17**	**0.41**	**1.11**	**3.32**	**2.90**	**0.53**	**1.64**	**0.09**	**0.89**	**0.23**	**10.50**
n=16	1.2	1.6	0.57	0.06	0.22	0.42	0.59	0.14	0.49	0.04	0.14	0.09	1.27

these vessels represent a separate import to the site; if their chemical homogeneity is confirmed through more sensitive trace element analyses then one can decide whether they are likely to come from a single batch, suggesting that they were imported as a single group.

Another tight group is formed of seven samples characterised by very low soda (c. 15 wt%) and relatively high potash levels (nearly 1 wt%). These samples are also very low in titania (800 ppm or less) and iron oxide (half of one percent or less), cluster tightly around 0.5 to 0.6 wt% magnesia and 8.5 to 9.0 wt% lime, and are high in alumina, with just over three percent (Fig. 11.6, Table 11.1). As a group, these are very close to Levantine I as defined by Freestone (2006), and very similar to each other, suggesting that as with the HIT glass objects, they could possibly come from a single production, even though they are clearly from different vessels, and probably made by different artisans.

All the fragments are identified as bowls Isings 116 (Isings 1957, 143–147, form 116), a well known late Roman type, widespread in Europe and the Mediterranean (*e.g.* Price and Cottam 1998, 124–126; Jennings 1997/98, fig. 9.5–7), probably being produced longer in the east (Dussart 1998, pls. 4.25, 4.31). In Dichin these vessels come mainly from closed contexts of the first phase of the first period (c. AD 410–470) and the type certainly is not found beyond the end of the 5th century. Fragments are clearly distinguished by their typical cold worked rims, cracked off and then polished, and with wheel-cut decoration on the body. The glass is pale or more saturated blue/blue-green (Fig. 11.7.2). Even though the group seems stylistically very tight, some differences separate shallow plain bowls with thicker walls and more crude manufacture (Fig. 11.7.3–4) from finer vessels decorated with engraved Greek inscriptions and Christian symbols (Fig. 11.7.1–2). All finds are certainly imported production. The reconstructed bowl which belongs to the latter variety has very close parallels in the eastern Mediterranean and North Black Sea region (Iliffe 1934; Harden 1949; Kunina 1997, N433), mostly thought to date to the 4th century. These finds now extend the distribution of this ornamental pattern up in to the 5th century. There are several other very similar and contemporary fragments with such inscriptions known from Dichin and other sites in the region (Cholakova 2009b, 260). This confirms the ongoing use of these vessels at such a late date, making an explanation of the reconstructed bowl as an heirloom preserved in a later context unlikely. Interestingly all Isings 116 (Isings 1957, 143–147, form 116) fragments analysed here belong solely to the Levantine I glass type.

This leaves 51 samples, or nearly two thirds of all analysed finds, which form the main group of glass fragments from the site. Among them a range of vessel shapes, types and techniques of decoration can be observed (Figs. 11.8–11.9), in contrast to the typologically tight glass groups discussed above. All three window glass pieces belong to this group, as well.

Chemically, this main group forms a relatively broad

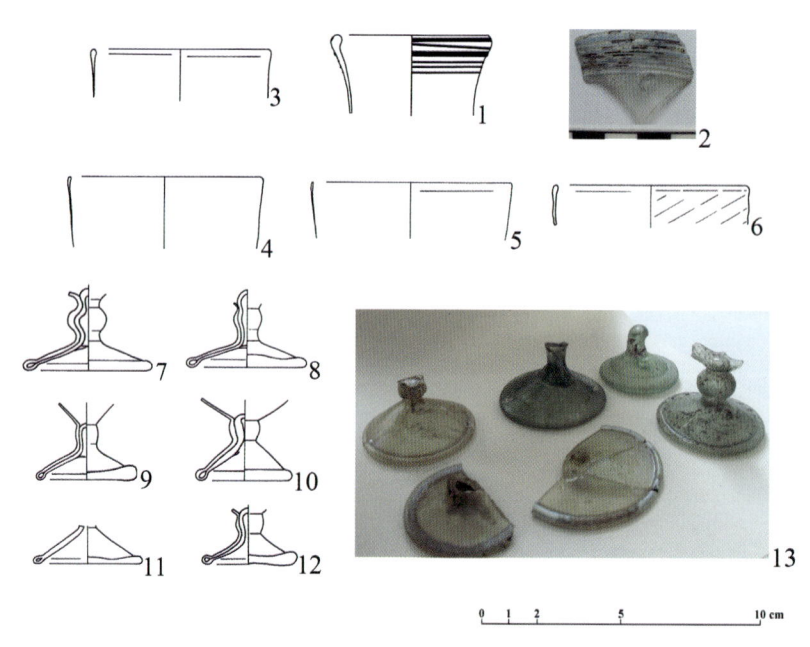

Fig. 11.9: Vessel shapes and colours representative of Roman blue-green glass ('medium' and 'dirty' sub-groups) from Dichin.

continuum, with soda ranging mostly from 17 to 20 wt% and lime mostly from 5.5 to 9.0 wt%. The minor oxides have a wider relative variability, such as alumina (1.8 to 2.7 wt%), magnesia (0.4 to 1.2 wt%), iron oxide (0.3 to 1.2 wt%), and potash (0.3 to 0.8 wt%). Taken together, there is a strong impression that these minor oxide levels are positively correlated with each other, leading to the definition of 'cleaner' and 'dirtier' compositions within the main group (Table 11.1). We interpret the consistent correlation of these oxides to indicate that the sand used for these glasses comes from a single geological source, while the different absolute levels indicate that the quality of this sand differed between different glass melting episodes. Thus, we see these oxides as specific indicators for the geological origin of the sand used to produce the glass, and as such as a broad geographical provenance characteristic of this glass type. In order to explore the chemical variability of this group more closely, we have added the weight percentage concentrations of potash, magnesia, alumina, iron oxide, phosphate and titania (the latter times five) to an overall impurity measure. We have omitted lime from this measure as it can derive from both geological limestone and current marine biota, thus mixing geological and marine signatures. The increased weighting of titania was used to compensate for its relatively low absolute concentration compared to the other impurities, giving it a similar effect on the impurity index as those, and to further emphasise the separation between this main group, and the HIMT/HIT glass. Using this overall impurity measure, we can identify three clearly distinct subgroups within the main compositional group; the clean subgroup has total impurities from 3 to 4.4 wt%,

the medium subgroup has 5.0 to 5.9 wt% total impurities, and the dirty subgroup has 6.1 to 6.7 wt% total impurities (Fig. 11.10). The relatively clear gaps between the otherwise continuous impurity levels suggest to us that these three groups have some real meaning, and are not arbitrary. For comparison, the HIMT and HIT glasses have total impurities of 8.3 to 13.2 wt%, with the high values driven of course by the five-fold weighting of their titania levels.

The cleaner subgroup is compositionally similar to the Roman blue-green glass, previously mostly known from the north-western provinces where it is a dominant glass type until the early 5th century. Here, the Dichin samples from this sub-group date almost all to the 5th century (mainly to the first phase: c. AD 410–470); significantly, none of the Isings 111 goblets (Isings 1957, 139–140, form 111) – an indicative 6th-century type at the site – is included in this clean sub-group.

As mentioned above, vessels identified among the cleaner sub-group belong to a range of shapes/ types produced and are decorated using different techniques (Fig. 11.8). A few fragments of bowls with engraved and abraded decoration are of particular interest. They bear simple geometric patterns, zoomorphic and floral ornaments, inscriptions and Christian symbols. The last decoration (Fig. 11.8.3) seems contemporary with and influenced by the engraved bowls Isings 116 (Isings 1957, 143–147, form 116) found at Dichin made of Levantine I glass type, discussed above. Some of the finds represent skilful manufacture and are certainly produced in workshops outside the Lower Danube region (Fig. 11.8.4–5); their analogues have an East Mediterranean origin (Kunina 1997, NN 431, 432; Price 2000, fig. 9/3).

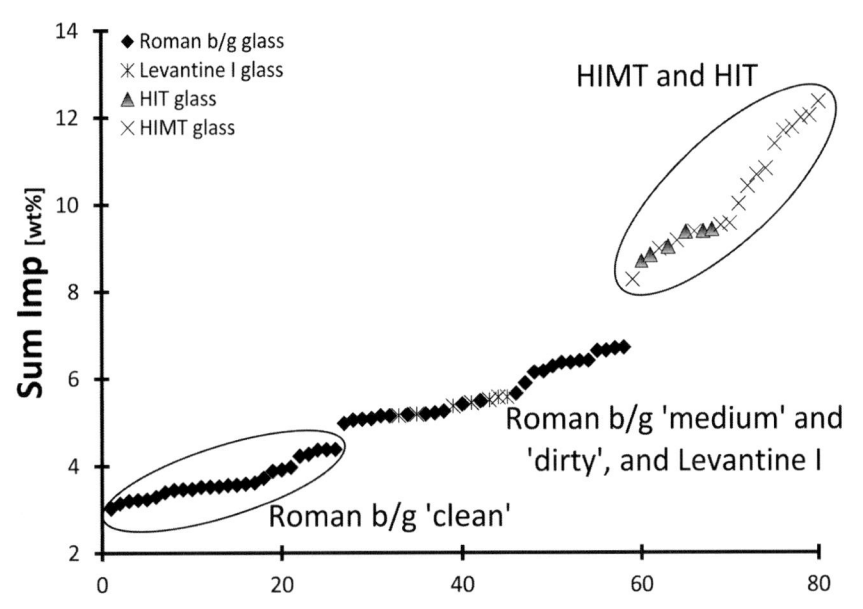

Fig. 11.10: Graph presenting the sum of impurities (see text for definition) of all 80 analysed glasses from Dichin, sorted along the x-axis by increasing total impurity level (y-axis). The HIMT and HIT glasses are clearly separated from the rest of the samples. The main group shows several discrete sub-groups, here defined as 'clean', 'medium' and 'dirty'. Despite their low iron concentrations (see Fig. 11.5), the Levantine I samples fall among the 'medium' sub-group; this is mostly due to their higher alumina concentrations (see Fig. 11.6).

Other bowls show a lower level of finishing and not so elaborate patterns (Fig. 11.8.1–3), and this probably characterises them as products of secondary glass workshops of only regional significance. According to the stratigraphy of the site they are dated to the first phase of the first period (c. AD 410–470). The reconstructed shallow bowl with fire rounded rim (Fig. 11.8.1–2) belongs to a well known type of late antique glass which has a wide distribution (*e.g.* Ortiz Palomar 2001, fig. 88.1; Fünfschilling 2009, fig. 3.12). We have analysed several fragments which appear visually similar enough to potentially come from this particular vessel, and these cluster also in their composition very closely indeed, supporting our hypothesis.

The cleaner sub-group includes also other typical late antique shapes, such as bowls with cracked-off rim Isings 96a (Isings 1957, 113–114, form 96a), a few jug fragments, vessels with trail decoration, oil lamps with pointed base (Fig. 11.8.6–10), and bottom fragments with and without pontil marks. Several fragments with a specific ornament of blue trails on the rim form a separate range of bowls and cups (Figs. 11.8.10, 11.9.1–2), even though the quality of glass and its manufacture are not very consistent. Our analytical results confirm this diversity – two samples belong to the chemical sub-group of dirtier Roman blue-green glass (Fig. 11.9.1–2). The fashion of such decoration is certainly influenced from the East Mediterranean (*e.g.* Jennings 1997/98, 118–119, fig. 24); vessels of a higher quality probably represent imported production which was used at the same time together with regional imitations. The finds belong to the 5th-century contexts, and are probably more characteristic for the second phase of the first period (c. AD 470–490).

The medium and dirtier sub-groups are dominated by fragments of Isings 111 stemmed goblets (Fig. 11.9.3–13; Isings 1957, 139–140, form 111), which make up nearly one third of glass finds across Dichin, and are the only fragments found in secure 6th-century contexts in the Bulgarian-excavated part of the settlement. In our set of samples stemmed goblets constitute c. 60% of the medium and dirtier sub-groups. The type appears only occasionally in 5th-century contexts at the site, but during the second period (c. AD 540–580) it is abundant. During this second period the settlement characteristics of Dichin have changed, with an overall decline in cultural development. The large presence of stemmed goblets could be a reflection of these changes towards the end of the 6th century. This predominance of Isings 111 goblets (Isings 1957, 139–140, form 111) is a widespread phenomenon of the 6th century in the Balkans and in the eastern Mediterranean. More general, these vessels are quite popular during the early Byzantine period and numerous variants from different regions can be observed. The finds from Dichin are very close in their technique of manufacture to some goblets from Asia Minor (Gill 2002, fig. I.5), which indicates similarities in the production traditions. Remarkably a variety of tints of naturally coloured glass are present in this group – from yellowish to blue-green and darker green (Fig. 11.9.13). The majority of these stemmed goblets were possibly made regionally, considering the limited quality of their manufacture, and since only few imported items are found in the 6th-century layers. We may assume that they were produced predominantly from recycled glass and cullet, rather than from freshly-made glass imported from one of the primary production centres.

The concentrations of minor oxides in the medium and dirtier sub-groups have similarities not only to Roman blue/green glass, but also to glasses which Foster and Jackson (2009) dubbed HIMT 2, and to 'Group 2' of Foy *et al.* (2003). However, these groups are not well defined in the literature, and the increased concentrations of minor oxides could also result from increased recycling. Future research will focus on discriminating more clearly between these various compositional groups from the literature, and through trace element analysis of these glasses to test whether they have systematically elevated levels of base metals such as lead or copper, often seen as indicators of recycling (Jackson 1997), through the incorporation of decorative elements (blobs, trails – for example Figs. 11.8.10, 11.9.1–2) into the glass cullet.

The rest of the samples in the medium and dirtier sub-groups of the Dichin main glass consist of window glass pieces, fragments decorated with blue trails, discussed above, and a few more bottom and rim fragments which do not form a specific archaeological set.

Discussion

The site of Dichin represents a relatively small fortified settlement which has the typical features of late antique and early Byzantine culture to the south of the Lower Danube (Dinchev *et al.* 2009). It existed for much of the 5th and 6th centuries, and suffered at least one destruction event before its final devastation. The 6th-century occupation here is marked by a significant decrease in the cultural and economic status of the population.

The glass assemblage consists of mostly relatively crude glass vessels of a typical late Roman and early Byzantine spectrum of predominantly open shapes. Only a few finds of glassblowing waste can possibly indicate some limited local glass working at the site. This is in line with the model of a small settlement, not particularly wealthy, but sufficiently connected to the early Byzantine economy to have access to and demand for modest luxuries such as glass vessels and windows.

Of interest to us is the make-up of the glass assemblage in terms of compositional groups; the majority is very similar to the slightly earlier 'Roman blue-green' glass well known from Britain (*e.g.* Jackson *et al.* 1991), occurring here in nearly two thirds of all analysed fragments. Particularly the later glass of this type falls in the subgroups with increased impurity levels, and has similarities also with glasses which other scholars link to HIMT glass (Foster and Jackson 2009). This indicates either an increasing impurity of the primary glass of this type, as one would expect if the quality of the primary glassmaking sand deteriorates over the life time of the glass factory, or the change to another later glassmaking centre which used dirtier sand. Alternatively, it could be due to an increasing uptake of contaminants during recycling. Ongoing research tries to address this question through trace element analysis and comparison to analysed glass fragments from elsewhere.

In addition to this dominant group there are three smaller groups present among the finds from Dichin. A set of seven samples match the Levantine I composition, with relatively low soda and high potash levels. These samples are chemically so similar to each other that they could well come from a single delivery of glass. Freestone and co-workers (Price *et al.* 2005; Freestone *et al.* 2009a) have recently suggested criteria to identify single glass batches through chemical analysis, and as in their case study, we find the potentially related fragments to be chemically identical within the analytical uncertainty of the electron microprobe used. The vessels in question are Isings bowls 116 (Isings 1957, 143–147, form 116) discussed above which most probably have reached the site not routinely but as one-off supply.

Sixteen samples fall in the group of HIMT glass, while another six are high in iron and titania, but have hardly any manganese ('HIT' glass). The HIMT glasses are amber-coloured and of relatively crude craftsmanship, while the HIT glass is strongly green-transparent, and of a high standard of finish. As the Levantine I group, it seems likely that the HIT glass fragments all originate from a single delivery of glass, possibly even from a single batch.

Overall, it appears that during the lifetime of the settlement the population of Dichin had access to a range of glass types. The bulk of the glass seems to be the Roman blue-green which is well-known from the north-western provinces, and which seems to show some gradual change in composition over time. Noteworthy is the observation that the dominant glass types of the early Byzantine eastern Mediterranean, Levantine I and II (*e.g.* Freestone *et al.* 2002, Kato *et al.* 2009, Rehren *et al.* 2010), are present here only at less than ten percent of the total analysed finds, with several fragments apparently coming from not more than three or four vessels. The good correlation of most of the compositional changes to chronological horizons indicates that this was at least partly driven by a change in glass supply, if not customer's demands and preferences. The link of specific vessel types to specific and less common compositions could indicate the procurement of a particular set from further afield, even as a single acquisition which could reflect certain social relations and the position of its owner, rather than through typical trade connections (such a scenario has been demonstrated earlier by Price *et al.* 2005). Logically, the compositional groups present in Dichin as tight clusters of few samples, identified with some probability as single batches of glass (*i.e.* Levantine I and HIT glass), demonstrate also an archaeological homogeneity which is not found in the larger glass groups (*i.e.* the Roman blue-green glass). This observation can be helpful for understanding different levels of secondary glass working in the provinces and their raw material supply. Some secondary workshops may have had regular access to fresh raw glass from one or more of the primary producers, while others, probably smaller workshops, may have been entirely dependent on recycled cullet. In Dichin we found that tight chemical groups are linked to vessels from glass ateliers with higher artistic standard of production, probably also higher level of organisation and located outside the Lower Danube region, and which have better access to fresh primary glass compared to the supply available to the smaller scale regional and local workshops.

A preliminary attempt to look into the chronological distribution of the glass types in Dichin reveals that during the 5th century HIMT, Levantine I and the cleaner sub-group of the Roman blue-green glass are all in use, as well as some examples of the dirtier Roman blue-green sub-group. Toward the end of the century HIT glass is in use as well, even though not very abundant. Following the hiatus in the first decades of the 6th century the overall pattern is completely different, probably as a result of general changes in the settlement's fortunes and in parallel to a broader decrease of the living standards. This period is dominated by the dirtier sub-group of the Roman blue-green type, worked in local or regional workshops of moderate artistic skill. Further research has to address whether this change in glass supply is specific to Dichin, or reflects a broader trend in the eastern provinces of the empire.

Conclusion

The analysis of a large number of glass finds from the archaeological site of Dichin in northern Bulgaria has identified a complex pattern of changing compositional preferences. The dominant glass type is very similar to the Roman blue-green glass, represented by three sub-groups throughout this 5th–6th-century assemblage. These results expand the chronological and distributional frameworks of the Roman blue-green glass previously well known mainly from earlier complexes from the north-western provinces. Furthermore, the Dichin samples provide evidence for compositional development of that type over nearly two centuries, explained either by gradual shift of the composition of the raw materials used in glass making, a change in production centre, or by intense recycling. Interestingly, the medium and dirtier sub-group have similarities to glass groups which in the literature have been linked to HIMT glass (Foster and Jackson 2009). However, the complex relationships between these major compositional groups, and how they develop over time and space, are not well understood. Three more compositional groups are also confirmed at the site – HIMT and HIT glasses, and Levantine I. The two last groups, *i.e.* HIT and Levantine I, are only present with just a few samples, but form tight sets which allow their possible identification as single batches of glass, potentially suggesting a special meaning of their acquisition. An attempt to study analytical glass groups in relation to particular ranges of vessel types demonstrates certain relationships between vessel morphology and techniques of manufacture, and primary raw glass composition, giving an insight into the different levels of secondary glass working. The well established stratigraphy of the site helps to see the changes in supply during the 5th and 6th centuries connected with general processes in the cultural and economic development. The first period of the settlement is remarkable for the diversity and quality of glass types (Roman blue-green, HIMT, HIT and Levantine I), while the second period is marked by a strong dominance of the dirtier sub-group of the Roman blue-green glass, and generally limited manufacturing skills.

Acknowledgements

The excavations in Dichin were funded by the joint project of Nottingham University, Bulgarian Academy of Sciences, Institute of Archaeology with Museum and Veliko Tarnovo Regional Museum. We are very grateful for the Bulgarian Ministry of Culture for granting permission to export selected glass samples for analysis by EPMA in London. The chemical analyses were done by Philip Connolly at the Wolfson Archaeological Science Laboratories, UCL Institute of Archaeology. We gratefully acknowledge discussions with Professor Ian Freestone and Dr James Lankton; any remaining errors are ours.

Bibliography

Cholakova, A. (2009a) Glass from Late Roman/Early Byzantine Dichin, Northern Bulgaria (summary). In E. Laflı (ed.) *Late Antique/Early Byzantine glass in the Eastern Mediterranean*. Colloquia Anatolica et Aegaea 2, 261–262. Izmir, Hürriyet Matbaası.

Cholakova, A. (2009b) Part VI. Glass vessels from Gradishteto. In V. Dinchev, G. Kuzmanov, P. Vladkova, A. Cholakova and Ts. Popova, *Bulgarian-British archaeological excavations of Gradishteto near the village of Dichin, Veliko Tarnovo region, 1996–2003. The results of the Bulgarian team*. Excavation and reports 39, 257–307. Sofia, National Institute of Archaeology/Bulgarian Academy of Sciences (in Bulgarian).

Dinchev, V., Kuzmanov, G., Vladkova, P., Cholakova, A. and Popova, Ts. (2009) *Bulgarian-British archaeological excavations of Gradishteto near the village of Dichin, Veliko*

Tarnovo region, 1996–2003. The results of the Bulgarian team. Excavation and Reports 39. Sofia, National Institute of Archaeology/Bulgarian Academy of Sciences (in Bulgarian).

Dussart, O. (1998) *Le Verre en Jordanie et en Syrie du Sud*. Bibliothèque Archéologique et Historique 152. Beirut, Institut Français d'Archéologie du Proche-Orient.

Foster, H. and Jackson, C. (2009) The composition of 'naturally coloured' late Roman vessel glass from Britain and the implications for models of glass production and supply. *Journal of Archaeological Science* 36, 189–204.

Foy, D., Picon, M., Vichy, M. and Thirion-Merle, V. (2003) Caractérisation des verres de l'Antiquité tardive en Méditerranée occidentale: l'émergence de nouveaux courants commerciaux. In D. Foy and M.-D. Nenna (eds.) *Échanges et commerce du verre dans le monde antique*. Monographies Instrumentum 24, 41–78. Montagnac, Monique Mergoil.

Freestone, I. (2006) Glass production in late Antiquity and the early Islamic period: a geochemical perspective. In M. Maggetti and B. Messiga (eds.) *Geomaterials in Cultural Heritage*. Geological Society London Special Publications 257, 201–216. London, Geological Society of London.

Freestone, I., Ponting, M. and Hughes, M. (2002) The origins of Byzantine glass from Maroni Petrera, Cyprus. *Archaeometry* 44, 257–272.

Freestone, I., Price, J. and Cartwright, C. (2009a) The batch: its recognition and significance. In K. Janssens, P. Degryse, P. Cosyns, J. Caen and L. Van't dack (eds.) *Annales du 17e Congrès de l'Association Internationale pour l'Histoire du Verre*, 130–135. Brussels, University Press Antwerp.

Freestone, I., Wolf, S. and Thirlwall, M. (2009b) Isotopic composition of glass from the Levant and the south-eastern Mediterranean Region. In P. Degryse, J. Henderson and G. Hodgins (eds.) *Isotopes in Vitreous Materials*. Studies in Archaeological Sciences 1, 31–52. Leuven, Leuven University Press.

Fünfschilling, S. (2009) Special relationship between the glass finds from Carthage and Rome and comparisons with finds north of the Alps. In K. Janssens, P. Degryse, P. Cosyns, J. Caen and L. Van't dack (eds.) *Annales du 17e Congrès de l'Association Internationale pour l'Histoire du Verre*, 143–149. Brussels, University Press Antwerp.

Gill, M. A. V. (2002) *Amorium Reports, Finds I. The Glass (1987–1997)*. With contributions by C. S. Lightfoot, E. A. Ivison, M. T. Wypyski. British Archaeological Reports International Series 1070. Oxford, Hadrian Books.

Golofast, L. (2009) Early Byzantine glass from the Tauric Chersonesos (Crimea). In E. Laflı (ed.) *Late Antique/Early Byzantine glass in the Eastern Mediterranean*. Colloquia Anatolica et Aegaea 2, 301–335. Izmir, Hürriyet Matbaası.

Harden, D. (1949) Tomb-groups of glass of Roman date from Syria and Palestine. *Iraq* 11, 151–159.

Iliffe, J. (1934) A Tomb at El Bassa of 396 AD. *The Quarterly of the Department of Antiquities in Palestine* 3, 81–91.

Isings, C. (1957) *Roman glass from dated finds*. Archaeologica Traiectina 2. Groningen/Djakarta, J. B. Wolters.

Jackson, C. (1997) From Roman to Early Medieval glasses – many happy returns or a new birth? In *Annales du 13e Congrès de l'Association Internationale pour l'Histoire du Verre*, 289–302. Lochem, Association Internationale pour l'Histoire du Verre.

Jackson, C., Hunter, J., Warren, S. and Cool, H. (1991) The analysis of blue-green glass and glassy waste from two Romano-British glass-working sites. In E. Pernicka and G. Wagner (eds.) *Archaeometry '90*, 295–305. Basel, Birkhäuser.

Jennings, S. (1997/98) The Roman and early Byzantine glass from the Souks excavations: an interim statement. *Berytus* 43, 111–146.

Kato, N., Nakai, I. and Shindo, Y. (2009) Change in chemical composition of early Islamic glass excavated in Raya, Sinai Peninsula, Egypt: on-site analyses using a portable X-ray fluorescence spectrometer. *Journal of Archaeological Science* 36, 1698–1707.

Kunina, N. (1997) *Ancient glass in the Hermitage collection*. St. Petersburg, The State Hermitage ARS Publishers.

Ortiz Palomar, M. (2001) *Vidrios procedentes de la provincial de Zaragoza. El Bajo Iimperio Romano. Catalogo: Fondos del Museo de Zaragosa*. Publicacion num. 2009 de la Institucion "Fernando el Catolico". Zaragoza, Institucion "Fernando el Catolico".

Poulter, A. G. (2007) The transition to late Antiquity on the Lower Danube: the city, a fort and the countryside. In A. Poulter (ed.) *The transition to late Antiquity on the Danube and beyond*. Proceedings of the British Academy 141, 51–97. Oxford, Oxford University Press.

Price, J. (2000) Late Roman glass vessels in Britain and Ireland from AD 350 to 410 and beyond. In J. Price (ed.) *Glass in Britain and Ireland AD 350–1100*. British Museum Occasional Paper, 127, 1–31. London, British Museum Press.

Price, J., Freestone, I. and Cartwright C. (2005) 'All in one day's work'? The colourless cylindrical glass cups found at Stonea revisited. In N. Crummy (ed.) *Image, Craft and the Classical World. Essays in honour of Donald Bailey and Catherine Johns*. Monographies Instrumentum 29, 165–171, Montagnac, Monique Mergoil.

Price, J. and Cottam, S. (1998) *Romano-British glass vessels. A handbook*. Practical Handbook in Archaeology 14. York, Council for British Archaeology.

Rehren, Th. and Cholakova, A. (2009) The Early Byzantine HIMT glass from Bulgaria (abstract). In E. Laflı (ed.) *Late Antique/Early Byzantine glass in the Eastern Mediterranean*. Colloquia Anatolica et Aegaea 2, 263. Izmir, Hürriyet Matbaası.

Rehren, Th. and Cholakova, A. (2010) The Early Byzantine HIMT glass from Dichin, Northern Bulgaria. *Interdisciplinary Studies* 22–23, 81–96.

Rehren, Th., Marii, F., Schibille, N., Stanford, L. and Swan, C. (2010) Glass supply and circulation in early Byzantine Southern Jordan. In J. Drauschke and D. Keller (eds.) *Glass in Byzantium – Production, Usage, Analyses*. RGZM – Tagungen 8, 65–82. Mainz, Römisch-Germanisches Zentralmuseum.

Smith, T. (2011) Interdisciplinary studies of ancient glass from Dichin, Bulgaria. In I. Iliev (ed.) *Proceedings of the 22nd International Congress of Byzantine studies III*, 36. Sofia, Bulgarian Historical Heritage Foundation.

12

An early Christian glass workshop at 45, Vasileos Irakleiou Street in the centre of Thessaloniki

Anastassios Ch. Antonaras

Introduction

Thessaloniki, an important port and a big urban centre in the north-eastern Mediterranean, was the main commercial hub for trade with the Balkan hinterland. During the Roman imperial period the city grew in size and importance and in the late 3rd century was chosen by Galerius for his imperial capital. He enhanced its appearance with an extensive programme of public building, and Constantine the Great spent almost a year and a half there, constructing further public buildings, water reservoirs and a new fortified port, before choosing the ancient Greek colony of Byzantion (known for eleven centuries as Constantinople) as his future capital, leaving Thessaloniki in second place among the Balkan cities. Many kinds of craft activities are known in Thessaloniki, especially during the late Roman and early Byzantine periods (Antonaras in press a).

Several forms of glass vessels have been ascribed to local production (Fig. 12.1), a few in the late 1st century (Antonaras 2010a), but the vast majority in the 4th, 5th and probably 6th centuries. The main products were tablewares (pitchers, flasks and beakers), unguentaria and lamps (Antonaras 2009a, 75–84; 2010b; 2010c).

Glass workshops or evidence for glass working have been located in at least four sites in Thessaloniki (Fig. 12.2). Three of them were already known before the discovery of the workshop at 45, Vasileos Irakleiou Street (no. 1 on Fig. 12.2). They are in the Roman forum (no. 2 on Fig. 12.2), where several craft workshops operated in the 4th or 5th century after it ceased to have an official function, in the ruins of a public bath house over which an early Christian basilica was built in the mid 5th century (no. 3 on Fig. 12.2), and in the eastern necropolis close to the city walls (no. 4 on Fig. 12.2), in a workshop used by clay lamp makers for a time, probably in the 4th century, and by a glass worker in the late 5th or early 6th century (Antonaras 2009a, 61–75; 2009b; 2010b; 2010c; 2010d).

The glass workshop at 45, Vasileos Irakleiou Street

The first firmly identified glass workshop has recently been unearthed at the centre of the city in a salvage excavation in 2010 at 45, Vasileos Irakleiou Street (Figs. 12.3–12.5). Parts of two intersecting streets and two *insulae*, mainly built in the Tetrarchic period, were found (Akrivopoulou in press; Antonaras in press b). The present paper will focus on the finds from the corner workshop at the southern end of the eastern *insula*. This was constructed during a 5th or 6th century phase of building activity and was used as a glass workshop for a period between the late 5th and the 7th centuries. It is rectangular (9 × 11m), built with cut stone and rubble with plaster, and has two entrances (1.20m and 1.25m wide) in its western wall, leading to the street. The thick walls and a vertical water pipe found in one wall indicate that it was a two-storied structure, as were the *ergasteria* (workshops) in Byzantine Thessaloniki, according to the written sources (Dagron 2002, 396, 422–423; Antonaras in press a). The level of the floor of the workshop was a little lower than the threshold, and probably on the same level as the adjacent street. Parts of the floor on the north east side were covered with ashes, pieces of coal and small fragments of glass.

A circular glassworking furnace, (furnace C on Figs. 12.4–12.5) c. 1m in diameter externally, which was repaired and slightly repositioned four times, was located at the south-west corner of the workshop (Figs. 12.6–12.9). Two earlier furnaces (furnaces A and B on Figs. 12.4–12.5) of similar dimensions, and obviously closely similar in date,

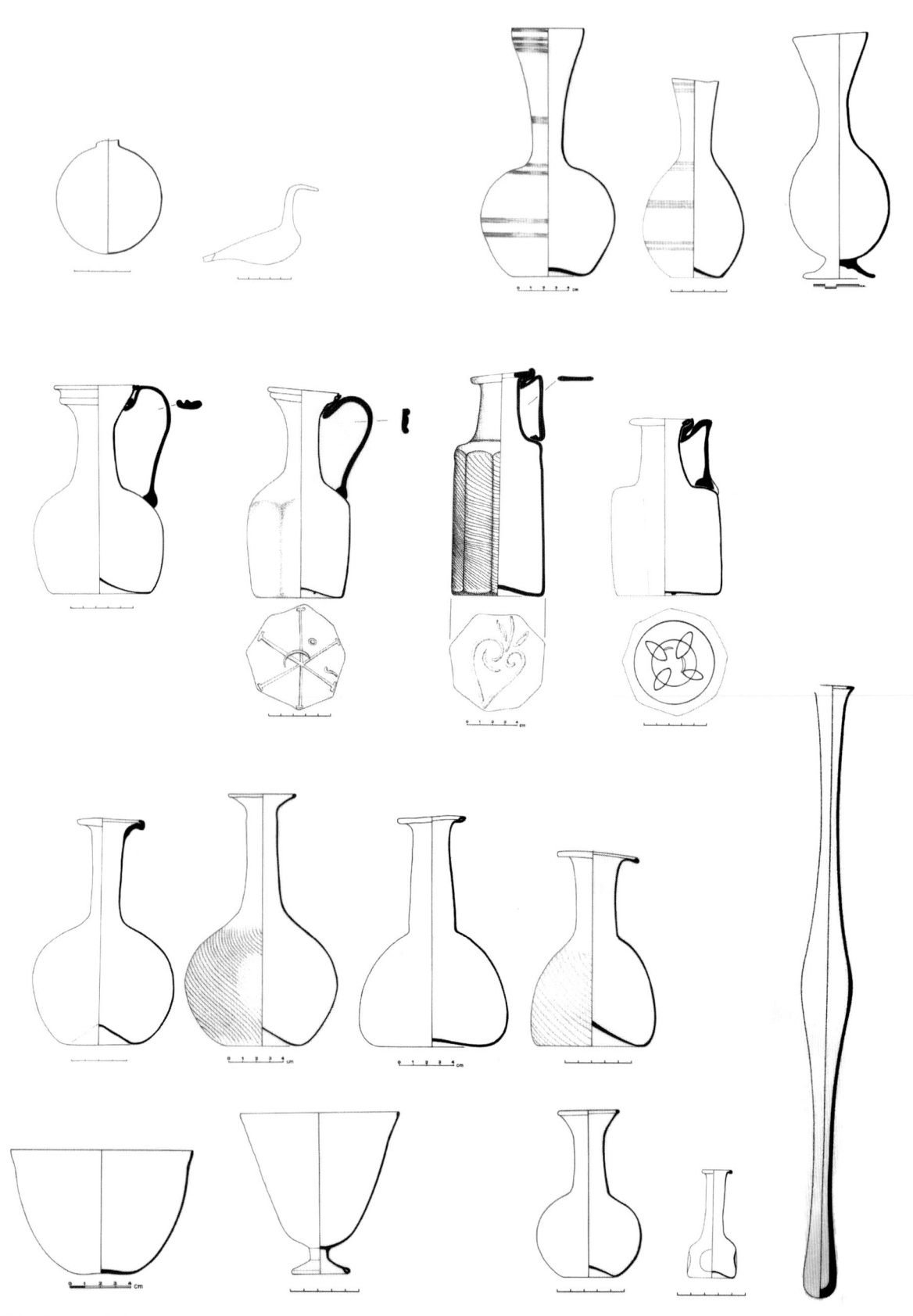

Fig. 12.1: Forms of glass vessels of the 1st–6th centuries attributed to Thessalonean glass workshops (drawings Chrysoula Mallia, digitally generated by the author).

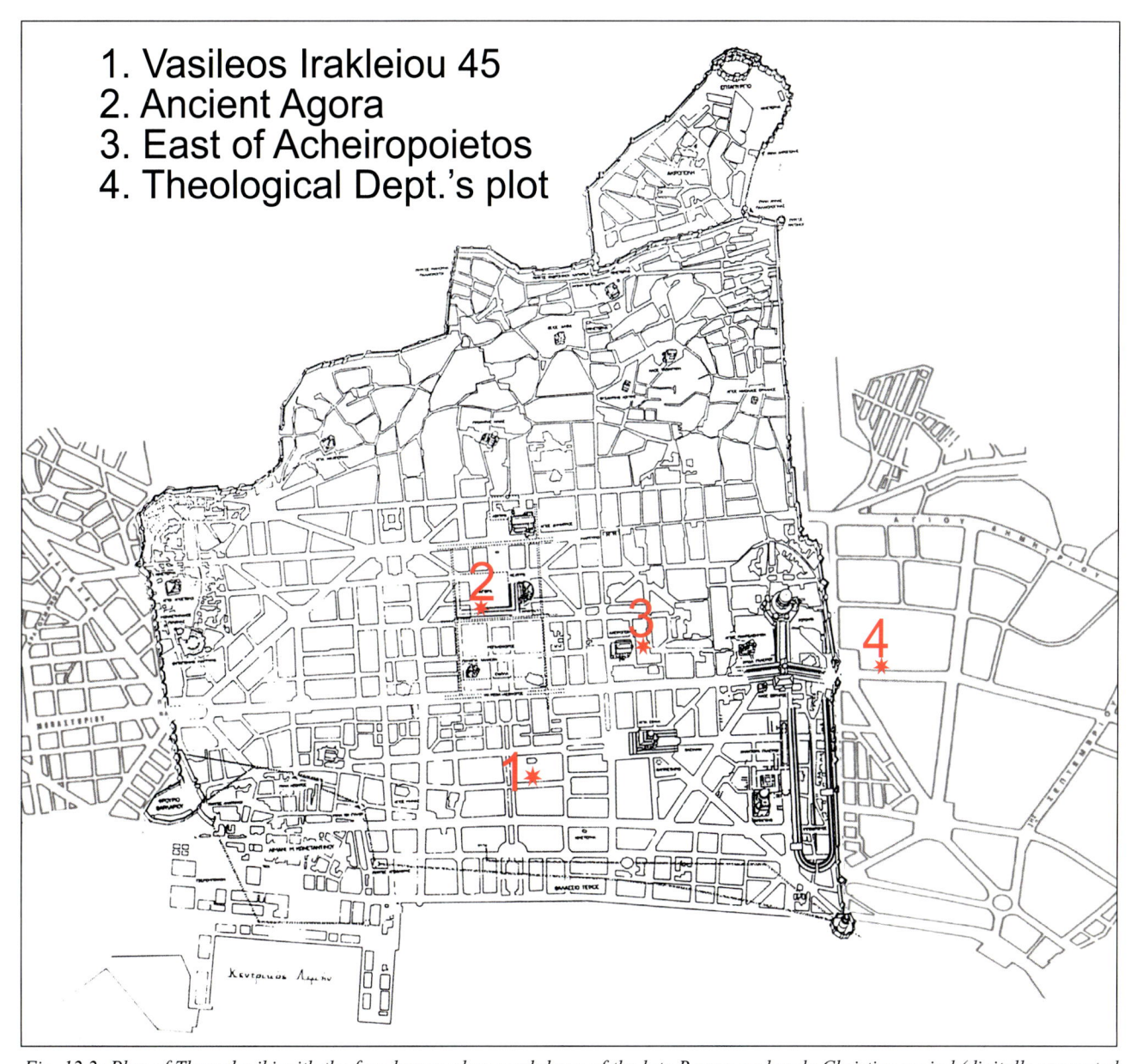

1. Vasileos Irakleiou 45
2. Ancient Agora
3. East of Acheiropoietos
4. Theological Dept.'s plot

Fig. 12.2: Plan of Thessaloniki with the four known glass workshops of the late Roman and early Christian period (digitally generated by the author).

were found close by to the north and 20cm below the level of furnace C. Only a small part of the burnt soil and few pieces of brick from the foundation of the firing chamber of furnace A are preserved. The estimated external diameter is c. 1m and it was constructed around 15cm lower than furnace B. This furnace was placed in front of the southern opening of the workshop blocking it, which suggests that the door was already sealed by the time the furnace was built. No sign of the stoke hole is preserved. Furnace B is sited approximately 30cm to the south of furnace A. Part of the burnt soil and several pieces of brick from the foundation of its firing chamber are preserved (Figs. 12.6–12.7). The walls are c. 20cm thick, and constructed from pieces of brick which measure c. 10 × 17 × 3cm. Its estimated external diameter is c. 70cm and it is built at approximately the same level as the first phase of furnace C. It may be contemporary with, or slightly younger than furnace A. No sign of its stoke hole has survived.

Furnace C, which is approximately 30cm south of furnace B, has a sequence of five furnaces which were built almost on top of each other (Fig. 12.8). It is well known that glass furnaces were regularly repaired, and sometimes completely rebuilt, because of their exposure to high temperatures, which created the characteristic sequence of overlapping and

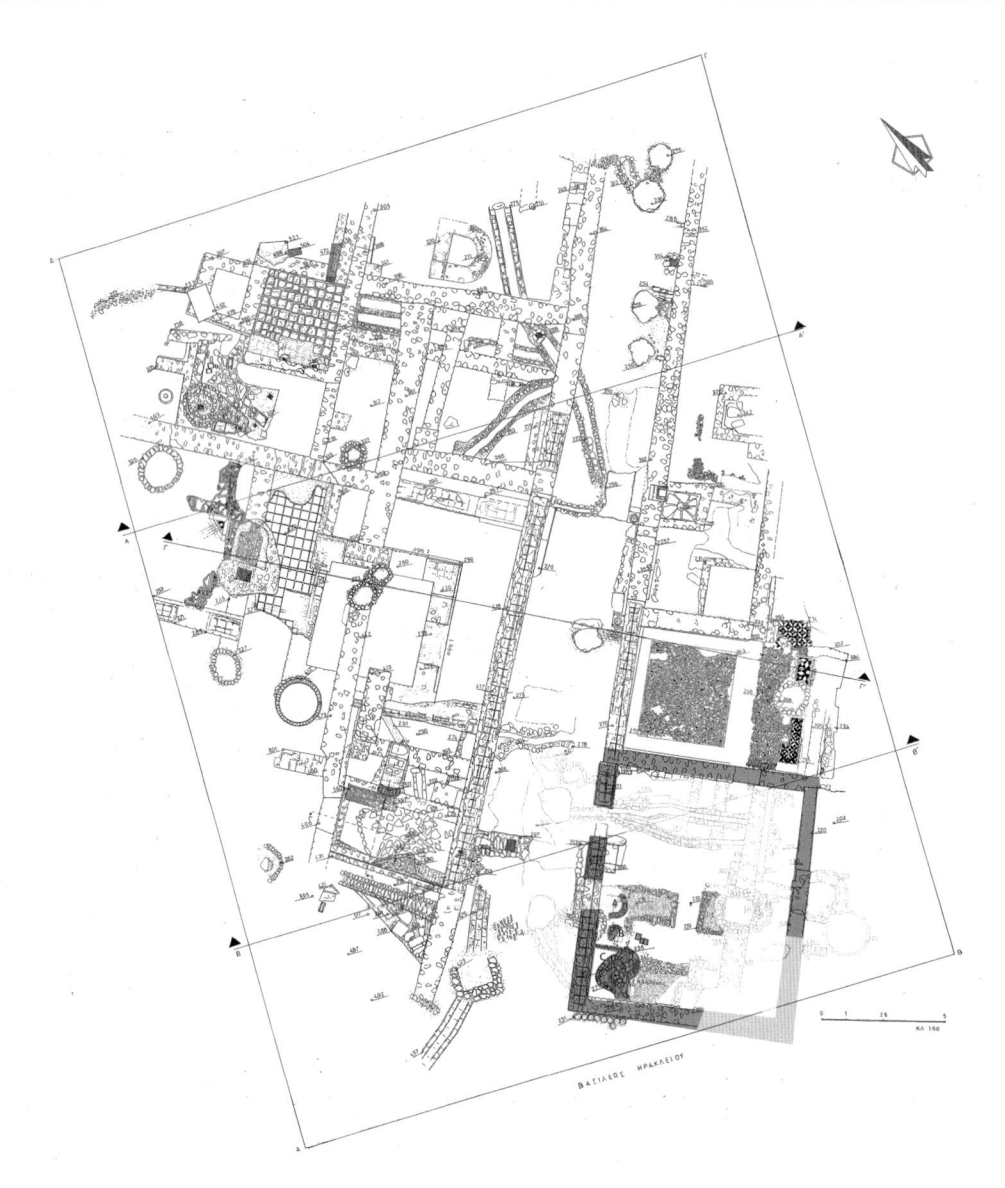

Fig. 12.3: General plan of the excavation at 45, Vasileos Irakleiou street, with the glass workshop highlighted (courtesy of 9th Ephorate of Byzantine Antiquities).

intersecting circular structures seen here. These furnaces are circular or ovoid and their estimated external diameters range between 85 and 100cm. The lowest two, *i.e.* the two oldest (phases 1–2 on Fig. 12.8), have a diameter of 100cm, the two following ones (phases 3–4 on Fig. 12.8) have a diameter of 90cm and the top one, *i.e.* the youngest (phase 5 on Fig. 12.8), has a diameter of 85cm. No sign of the stoke holes and information about the orientation of the furnaces has survived. Between each furnace a layer of dark red soil, c. 10–15cm thick, is found on top of which a layer of bricks bonded with mud has been set to form the floor of the combustion chamber of the next furnace (Fig. 12.6). Only between the second and the third furnace from the top (phases 3–4 on Fig. 12.8) a thin layer of red burnt soil, c. 2–3cm thick, is found. In every

major phase of reconstruction the furnace appears to have been totally demolished and the building material removed and most probably reused. A layer of clayey soil was placed over the remains of the former furnace and on the leveled surface the new furnace was constructed, following more or less the size, the shape and the position of the previous one. In the floor of the fourth and fifth furnace from the top (phases 1–2 on Fig. 12.8) faint traces of lime plaster are visible. The walls of all five furnaces are c. 20cm thick and built of small (15–25 × 7–14cm) pieces of brick, which are almost exclusively late antique, 3cm-thick ones, with a few thicker (c. 5cm) Roman ones. The only visible, almost intact brick in a floor was found in the top most, *i.e.* latest furnace (phase 5 on Fig. 12.8); it measures 30 × 25 × 3cm.

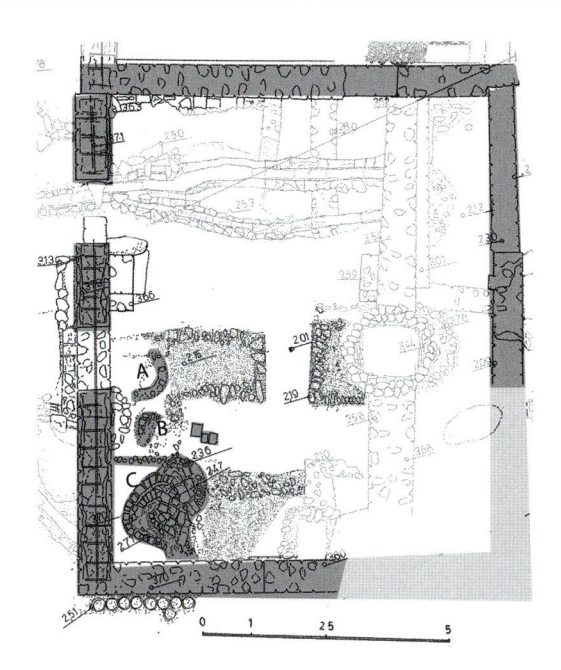

Fig. 12.4: Plan of the glass workshop at 45, Vasileos Irakleiou street with the furnaces A, B and C (courtesy of 9th Ephorate of Byzantine Antiquities).

Fig. 12.5: General view of the glass workshop with the furnaces A, B and C (Sofia Akrivopoulou).

Fig. 12.6: Glass furnaces B (right) and C (left) from the south (Sofia Akrivopoulou).

Fig. 12.7: Glass furnaces B (top) and C (bottom) top view (Sofia Akrivopoulou).

Fig. 12.8: Glass furnaces B (top) and C (bottom). The five phases of furnace C (1–5) are outlined (Sofia Akrivopoulou).

Many pieces of burnt clay, *i.e.* furnace walls, and moils, distorted masses of glass, droplets and dark green chunks were found in the layer of debris covering the upper phases of furnace C. No molten glass is visible on the surfaces of the bricks in the walls and floors or in the spaces, as might be expected if free standing crucibles were in use in the furnaces, as small amounts of molten glass would drip to the floor of the firing chamber. Furthermore, the presence of dozens of pieces of clay or mortar covered with a flat and smooth layer of glass (0.5–1cm thick) on them quite probably indicates that the furnaces were tank furnaces and these pieces belong to the upper part of the furnace. No traces of crucibles were found among the workshop debris. The only curved clay find associated with the area of the furnaces that is thick enough does not have any vestiges of glass on it. Some dislodged bricks, which have become extensively vitrified on their surfaces because of the high temperature, but do not show any traces of glass, are probably connected with the lower part of the furnace. Finally, the only indication for lime plaster in the interior of the furnaces is preserved in the lowest one (phase 1 on Fig. 12.8) where a layer of plaster 6cm thick is well preserved (Fig. 12.9).

No physical remains of an annealing chamber or furnace have been found on the site although it should be noted

Fig. 12.9: Detail of a glass furnace C, phase 1, coated with plaster (Sofia Akrivopoulou).

though that the rectangular features (c. 1.5 × 2m; noted on Fig 12.4 with stippling) adjacent to the furnaces A and C may possibly have served this purpose, using the heat of the furnaces (see Figs. 12.4–12.5). They have thin walls (20cm) made of small stones and mud. A similar feature partly

Fig. 12.10: Raw glass of different colours (the author).

Fig. 12.11: Raw glass and deformed glass (the author).

Fig. 12.12: Raw glass and deformed glass (the author).

Fig. 12.13: Testing droplets and deformed glass (the author).

12 An early Christian glass workshop at 45, Vasileos Irakleiou Street in the centre of Thessaloniki 103

Fig. 12.14: Moils (the author).

Fig. 12.15: Distorted bases of stemmed beakers (the author).

Fig. 12.16: Dip-mould blown stemmed beakers (the author).

Fig. 12.17: Base of a free blown stemmed beaker-like lamp with a long handle (left) and a rim of a flask decorated with dark-coloured trail (right) (the author).

preserved in the central part of the workshop, is severely damaged by more recent disturbance that prevents us from seeing whether it was with another furnace. These features seem to be the foundations of taller structures. Similar rectangular structures adjacent to circular glass furnaces have been reported from the 4th-century glass workshop of Philippi (Gounaris 1995–2000, fig. 3, plan 3) and have been identified as annealing furnaces by Maria Skordara

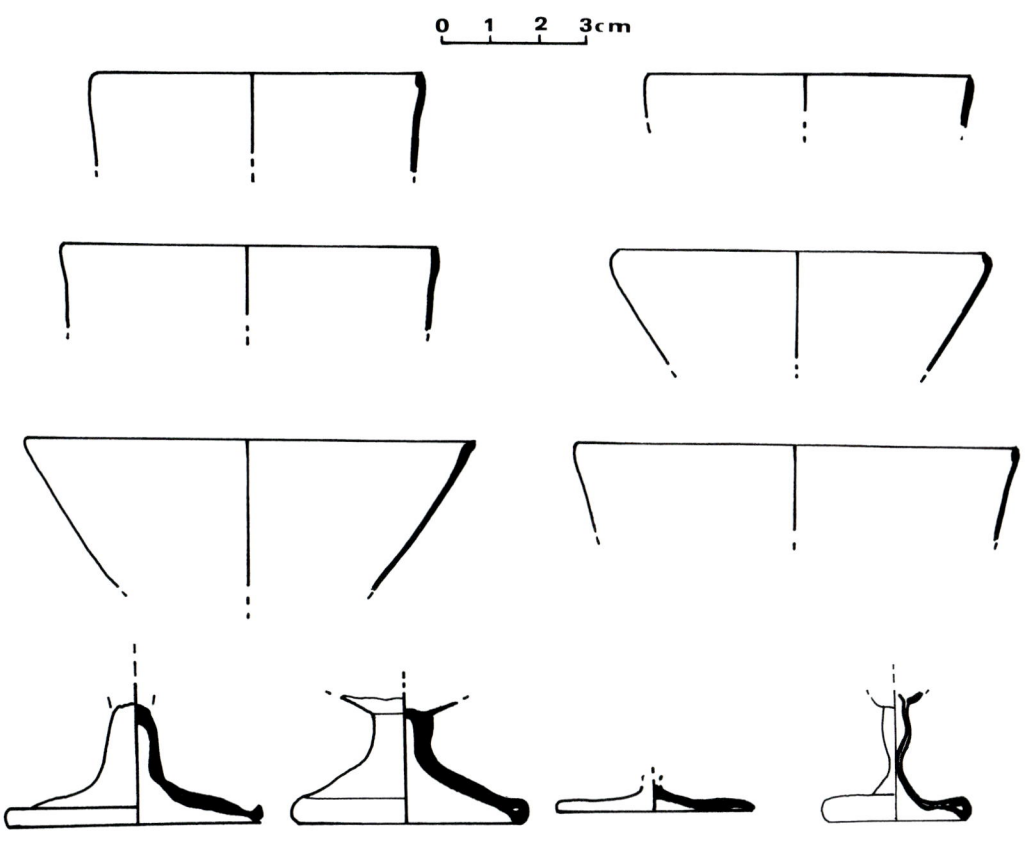

Fig. 12.18: Drawings of bowls and stems of stemmed beakers (Chrysoula Mallia).

Fig. 12.19: Base of a stemmed beaker-like lamp with long handles (the author).

who is preparing a doctoral thesis on them (personal communication, 21-6-2012). Furthermore, they may be compared to structures in France, Switzerland and Germany that have also been identified as annealing furnaces (see Foy and Nenna 2001, 64; Nenna 2008, 62–63 for further references). Pieces of a marble slab found next to the furnace at the level of the workshop floor might be associated with glass production, and could possibly have been used for marvering. A few pieces of glass from the workshop, chips, and distorted pieces and vessels, were also found in and around the street outside of the workshop.

Fig. 12.20: Bases of stamped stemmed beakers (the author).

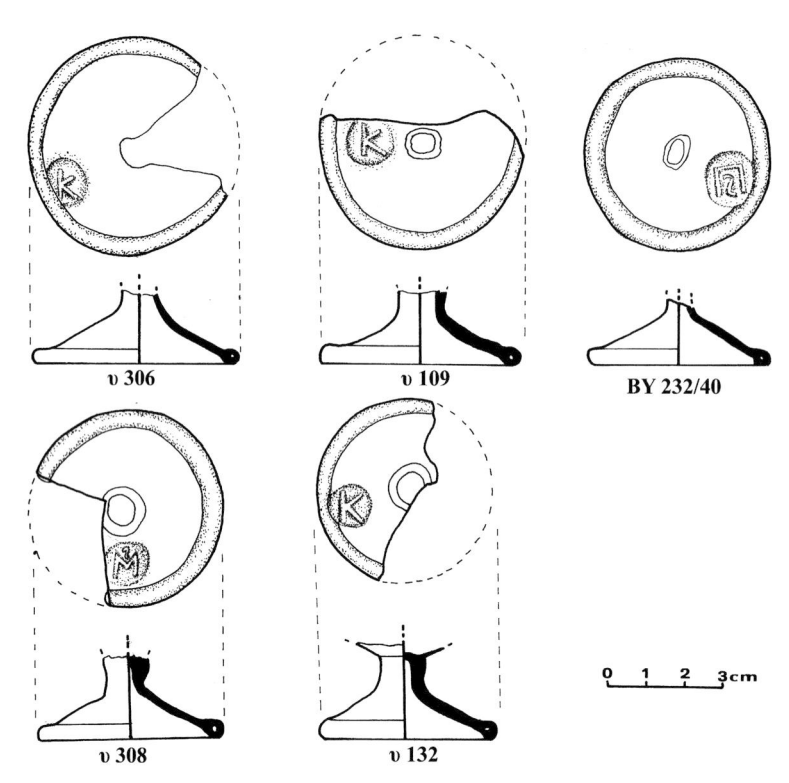

Fig. 12.21: Drawings of stamped stemmed beaker bases (Chrysoula Mallia).

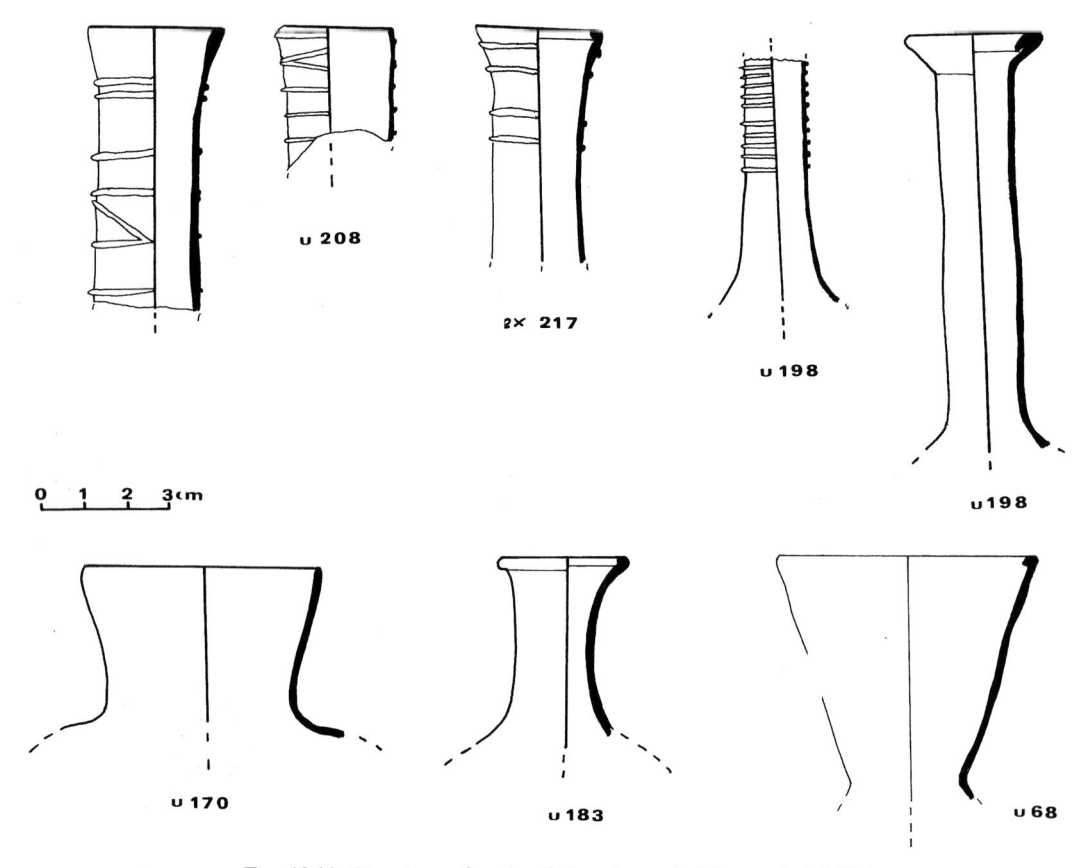

Fig. 12.22: Drawings of necks of closed vessels (Chrysoula Mallia).

Fig. 12.23: Closed vessels/flasks and stemmed beakers (the author).

Fig. 12.24: Base of a deformed stemmed lamp (the author).

The shape of the furnace structures are comparable with what is generally known about glass working furnaces elsewhere in the ancient world (as in France, at Troyes: Foy and Nenna 2001, 53; or Cesson-Sévigné: Foy and Nenna 2001, 55) and they, and the presence of glassworking debris indicate that blown vessels were produced in this workshop. Furthermore, it is clear that dip mould blowing was employed at the site, as faint vertical ribbing is visible on some fragments. As is well known, the mould blowing technique after being in vogue during the 1st century went out of fashion until the 4th century when it was revived in a new version, dip mould blowing, which involved blowing the gather of glass in a mould and further inflation and the shaping of the vessel by free blowing outside the mould, so that the decoration on the vessel expanded and covered larger areas, being partially distorted and less sharp.

Wasters and glass working remains

The quantity of wasters and other glass working material from this excavation is substantial and offers important information about the production processes and the products of the site. The material was mainly discarded in a small

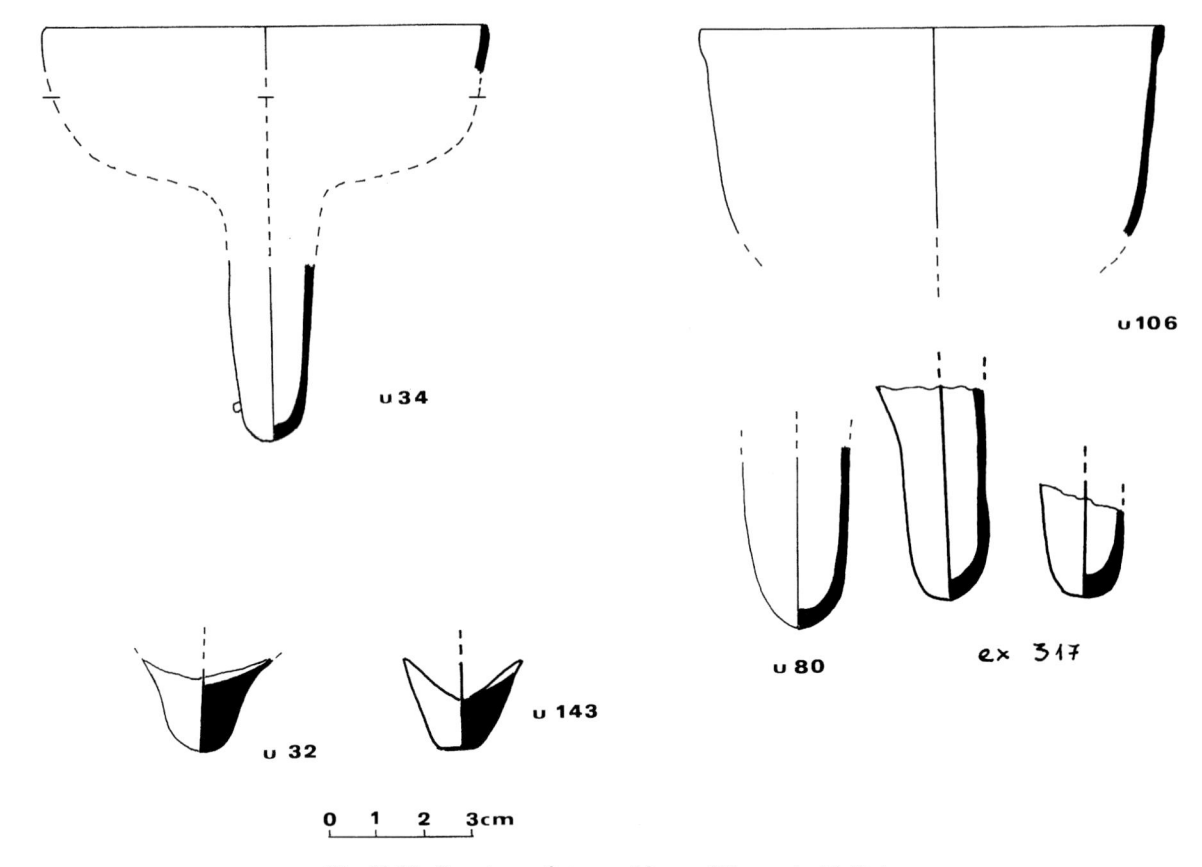

Fig. 12.25: Drawings of stemmed lamps (Chrysoula Mallia).

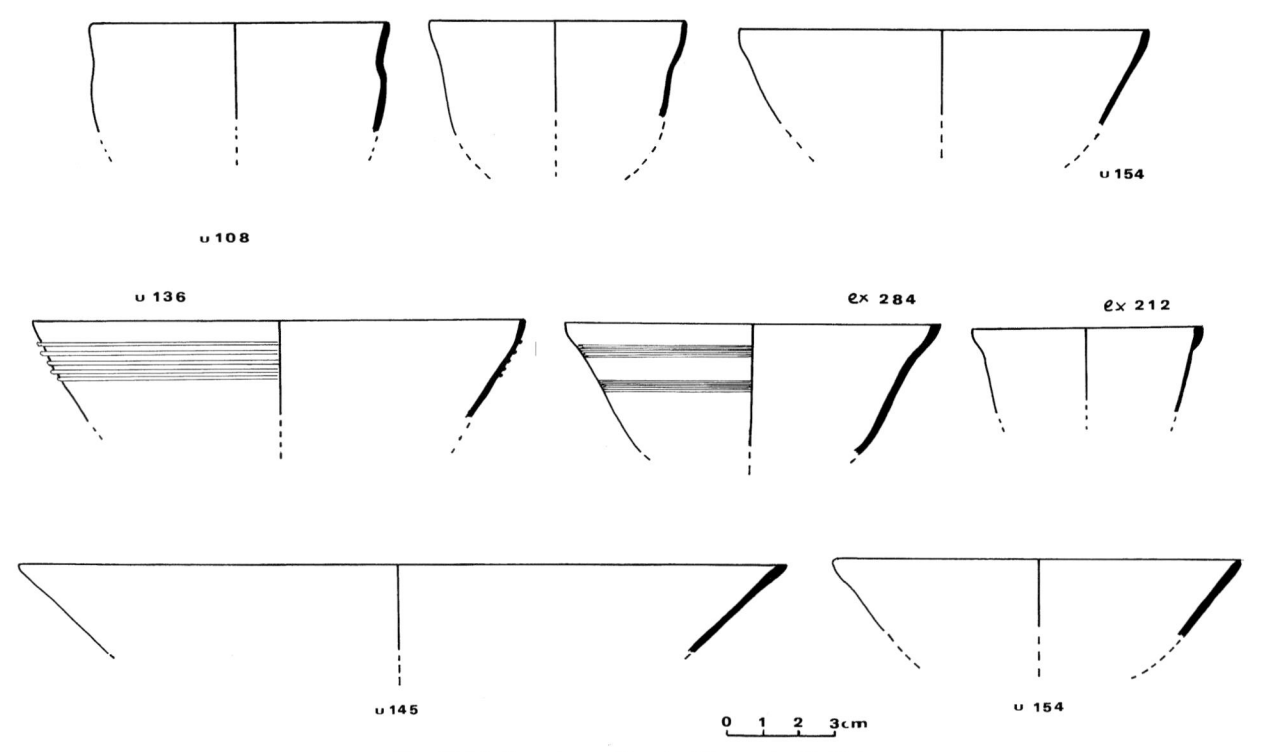

Fig. 12.26: Drawings of bowls (Chrysoula Mallia).

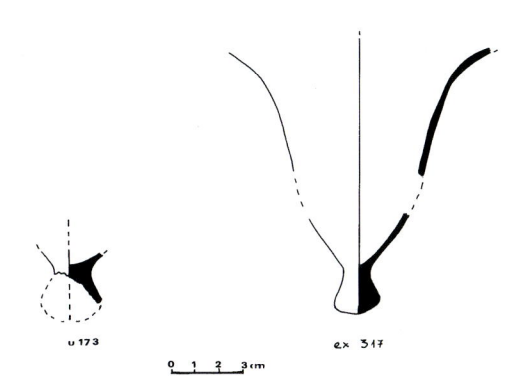

Fig. 12.27: Conical or cylindrical lamps with heavy knob-bases (Chrysoula Mallia).

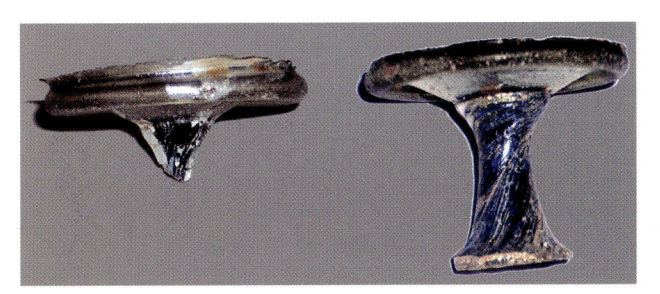

Fig. 12.28: Bicolored stemmed beakers (the author).

Fig. 12.29: Cup-like conical base of a stemmed beaker (the author).

Fig. 12.30: Cup-like conical base of a stemmed beaker from the American School of Classical Studies excavations in the area of Gymnasion at Corinth, MF 71-190 (the author).

Fig. 12.31: Deformed fragments of window panes (the author).

pit at the north west part of the workshop, where ashes and raw clay were also found. The presence of raw clay might be connected to the need to repair the furnaces frequently.

Raw glass produced in large-scale primary workshops in the Levant and Egypt was transported in the form of big chunks to remote areas of the empire where secondary glass workshops, like the one under discussion, operated in most urban centres (Stern 1999, passim, esp. 472–478; Price 2005, 167–172). In the secondary glass workshops, the raw glass was reheated and melted in small crucibles or tanks, along with fragments of broken vessels and window panes which were comprehensively recycled from the 1st century onwards. Lumps of colourless greenish and dark green raw glass weighing 2682g and dark blue glass weighing 90g have been found in the Vasileos Irakleiou workshop (Figs. 12.10–12.12).

Testing droplets (tear-shaped threads) are another common residue from glass production. The viscosity or even the colour of the batch was tested with them. As well as these, other distorted pieces and threads of glass were found, often with tooling marks, or the outline of the surface they landed on while still hot and viscous. In total a little less that 2.5kg of them have been found on the site, all of a greenish tinge (Figs. 12.11 upper left, 12.13).

An equally important group of finds are the tubular endings from the blown glass gathers, the ring-shaped moils (Fig. 12.14). Almost all of them (c. 0.5kg) were greenish, which was obviously the principal glass colour used in the workshop, while only a very few were bluish (23g). From their texture and their size it can be concluded that the glass blower used an iron pipe with a gathering end 2.5cm wide.

Distorted vessels

Pieces of vessels have been located in the remains of the workshop, the greenish ones weighing 326g and the bluish ones 35g. Among them the following forms have been identified.

Stemmed beakers

These are one of the most widespread forms of glass vessels in the region in late antiquity (Antonaras 2008, 24; 2009a, 162–169, forms 35–36). Several dozen stemmed beakers were recorded in this excavation, mainly with smooth, long or short stems, although some beaded stems were also present (Figs. 12.15–12.21, 12.23 middle row), and several examples were severely distorted. They were used as drinking vessels, mainly with fire polished rims, and also as lamps, mainly with cut off rims and with the addition of three small handles around the rim. These handles are very rare among our finds and the rim fragments found are all fire polished (Fig. 12.18). However, some of the base fragments show traces of the long handles that were attached to the rim and continued in the form of a fine thread down the body to the stem of the base (Figs. 12.17 left, 12.19). Hence, it can be accepted that the majority of the locally produced stemmed beakers were intended to be tableware, while a few are recognisable as lamps. Almost all of them are made of greenish glass, which, as explained above, was the main type of glass used in the workshop although some were made in the rarer blue glass. Some pieces show shallow vertical, dip-mould ribbing (Fig. 12.16). All the pieces were made from a single gather of glass folded and tooled to create the body, stem, and conical base.

Five base fragments from stemmed beakers (Figs. 12.20–12.21), found among other workshop waste are unique because they have stamped inscriptions (Antonaras 2011). On three of them a capital "K" is visible, on a fourth part of the sunken field is preserved, while the fifth is stamped with "Ms". These letters may possibly refer to the capacity of the vessel, that is, a 20, 40th or 46 of an unknown unit of liquid measurement. One other find of this type with the ligature «Πς», which might be deciphered as an 80th or 86, was found nearby in a salvage excavation in Agias Sofias Street (Marki 1994, 511–515), and is now in the Museum of Byzantine Culture, Thessaloniki. This interpretation of the letters would mean that there are three vessels with single, one with double and another with quadruple units of capacity. However, the fact that the vessels all have almost identical dimensions does not support this hypothesis, since a beaker with four times the capacity of another would have a wider and more massive base. It is, however, difficult to think of another, more meaningful, explanation. The stamps cannot refer to the content, as they are open, rather than sealed, vessels. Also, they are unlikely to refer to the workshop, because it is assumed that a single stamp would be used, rather than three entirely different ones. Moreover, the small size of the workshop and the small number of the finds do not support the suggestion that three different craftsmen were active in it, each of them with his/her own stamp, but as the bases were found among the wasters from the workshop, it seems logical to ascribe this peculiar production to the activity of the workshop.

Funnel-mouthed, closed vessels

Funnel-mouthed, closed vessels were the second largest group of vessels identified among the workshop wasters (Figs. 12.22, 12.23 upper row). These have concave bottoms and funnel-shaped mouths with fire polished rims, or simple necks with infolded tubular rims, and are all made in the colourless greenish glass used for the vast majority of the locally produced vessels.

Stemmed lamps

Stemmed lamps, which were widely distributed in this region between the 5th and the 7th centuries (Antonaras 2008, 26; 2009a, 170–173, form 38) are another vessel form probably produced in the workshop (Figs. 12.24–12.25). At least ten examples were found, one with a quite distorted base, and all were made in the same greenish glass as the two forms previously mentioned as possible local products.

Other glass vessels

A few hemispherical bowls (Fig. 12.26), wide, conical lamps ending in a massive knob (Fig. 12.27), a flask base and a few small handles of lamps have been identified among the early Christian finds from the excavation but they were not among the workshop waste. In addition, two forms of stemmed beakers appear to have been made from two different gathers, one for the bowl and the other one for the stem and the base. There are two examples of the first form. The bowl was made in greenish glass with a characteristic fold at the lower edge, while the long smooth stem was made in dark blue glass, as, presumably, was the discoid base, now missing (Fig. 12.28). The second form is identified from one or two small fragments of conical, cup-like bases (Fig. 12.29). These finds resemble a form that appears in 6th-century contexts in Corinth, where better preserved examples show a vessel with a deep conical body, attached to a conical base with vertical standing ring at the edge that gives it this cup-like shape (Fig. 12.30: MF 71-190, unpublished; from the area of the gymnasium at Corinth, excavated by the American School of Classical Studies at Athens to be published by the author). Similar finds dated to the 6th–7th centuries are known from Kourion and Salamis on Cyprus as well as from Sardis (Young 2007, 495, no. 45 with further references therein). Other finds include a 1st-century aryballos (Isings 1957, form 61), a late 2nd/3rd-century bowl (Isings 1957, form 85), found in the same context as blue raw glass chunks of the workshop, and a bowl and some long, clumsy, dark green stems of beakers probably belonging to the middle Byzantine period (9th–12th centuries). Finally, a few fragments of 17th/18th-century tableware were found in a cesspit on the site while several other cesspits yielded late 19th or early 20th-century glass vessels, mainly bottles and tablewares distorted by fire.

Window panes

Several fragments of window panes, weighing 235g were also found among the workshop waste (Fig. 12.31). They are made by the cylinder technique, typical for late antiquity. These fragments are made in greenish glass similar to that used in the workshop, and some have imperfections like folds or severe/acute tooling marks. Therefore, they could be waste from local production, although in that case a far bigger quantity would be expected. Window panes are heavy products, compared to glass vessels, and it is known that they were meticulously collected and recycled, so the finds might also be interpreted as fragments collected for remelting and reuse.

Gems

The three rectangular, dark green gems found in the area of the workshop may be a slight indication of another kind of production in this workshop. They are known as ὑέλια in Greek sources, and were used to adorn precious objects, such as gem-studded religious metal objects and books, or similar objects with secular functions. One of them, which is partly preserved, was found in the debris of the upper phases of furnace C. They are quite rare – to my knowledge there are only two other identical finds in the wider region of Thessaloniki, from the early Christian *Solinos* basilica at Chalkidiki (unpublished) and the early Christian quadriburgium *Louloudies* in Pieria (unpublished), and since they have been found in connection with a glass workshop, they were probably also local products (Fig. 12.32).

Conclusions

The material found suggests that the glass workshop was in operation between the 6th and the 7th centuries, possibly in the late 6th century, when an adjacent small storeroom of amphorae was established in part of the southern street of the quarter (Akrivopoulou and Slambeas in press). The stemmed beakers and funnel-mouthed flasks are also dated to the same period. Some of the applied decorative elements among the finds, such as the blue blobs occur in the 4th and the 5th centuries in the eastern Mediterranean, while the fine threads, often of dark blue or red glass, wound around the neck or the rim of the flasks in the workshop (Figs. 12.17 right, 12.22 upper left, 12.33) suggest connections with Syro-Palestinian workshops, particularly in the late 6th and 7th century (Stern 2001, 269–270, 299–302, nos. 162–165; Arveiller-Dulong and Nenna 2005, 474–475, 478–479, nos. 1303–1305). In addition, the numismatic evidence of a coin hoard found in the period of use of the workshop, indicates that the period of operation extended at least until the middle of the 6th century (the coins of the excavation will be published by Dr E. Maladakis).

The location of the workshop seems strange at first, since it is known that according to Roman law, workshops, especially those using open fires, were not allowed within the walls of cities. In particular, they were prohibited in densely inhabited areas, such as the area of our find, for two reasons: to minimize the possibility of setting the city in fire by an accident, and to avoid everyday annoyance to the neighbours (Pitsakis 1971, λη'–λθ'; Pitsakis 2002, 246, note 54). Nonetheless, archaeological finds show that, despite the law, glass workshops were quite frequently sited in the central areas of cities, in shops or abandoned public buildings, because, as it appears, they were at the same time production and retail units (Price 2005, 172–174; Antonaras 2009a, 61–66; in press a; Gorin-Rosen and Winter 2010, 177–178, pls. 10–11).

The glass workshop was added to an important late 3rd – early 4th-century building at some time in the 5th or 6th century when that building was reconstructed, and possibly also changed its original use. The commercial character of this area was probably already established by then, so the craftsman could turn to advantage the site of the workshop, on one of the principal streets of the city, very close to the market place and the *Mesē*, the *decumanus maximus* of the Roman times, which throughout the Middle Ages remained the main commercial street of the city. The two entrances to the shop allowed both free access for the buyers to the interior and the undisturbed operation of the furnace. It seems likely that at least part of the merchandise was sold on the street, where a short bench was built on the pavement in front of the shop.

To sum up, this find is very important for the study of the history of glass working in Thessaloniki, as it presents the first early Christian glass workshop to be archaeologically investigated in the city. The location offers further evidence for the functioning of workshops using open fire and at the same time selling their own products in the city centre. The portable finds include glass vessel forms already known from other sites in the city, which belong to the eastern Mediterranean glass repertory and have strong ties with Syro-Palestinian production, but also include some products peculiar to the workshop. Indeed some of them

Fig. 12.32: Glass gems (the author)

Fig. 12.33: Flask decorated with dark blue applied trails (the author).

are distinguishable from the rest of the early Christian production of glass vessels in Thessaloniki and they provide important information about a group of otherwise unknown form of vessels, the stemmed beakers with stamped letters on their bases.

Bibliography

Akrivopoulou, S. (in press) Η ανασκαφή στην οδό Βασιλέως Ηρακλείου 45 στη Θεσσαλονίκη [=The excavation at 45 Vaslileos Irakleiou street, Thessaloniki]. *To Archaeologico Ergo ste Makedonia kai Thrake* 24.

Akrivopoulou, S. and Slambeas P. (in press) Late Antique Coarse Ware from a rescue excavation in Thessaloniki. In *4th International Conference on Late Roman Coarse Ware, Cooking Ware and Amphorae in the Mediterranean: Archaeology and Archaeoetry. The Mediterranean: a market without frontiers*.

Antonaras, A. (2008) Glass Lamps of the Roman and Early Christian Periods. Evidence from the Thessaloniki Area. In C.-A. Roman and N. Gudea (eds.) *Lychnological Acts 2. Acts of the 2nd International Congress on Ancient and Middle Age Lighting Devices. Trade and Local Production of Lamps from the Prehistory until the Middle Age*, 23–30. Cluj-Napoca, Mega.

Antonaras, A. (2009a) Ρωμαϊκή και παλαιοχριστιανική υαλουργία. Αγγεία από τη Θεσσαλονίκη και την περιοχή της.[=Roman and Early Christian Glassworking. Vessels from Thessaloniki and its region]. Athens, I. Sideris.

Antonaras, A. (2009b) Glass Vessels from Roman and Early Christian Thessaloniki and its surroundings (1st cent. BC – 6th cent. AD). In K. Janssens, P. Degryse, P. Cosyns, J. Caen and L. Van't dack (eds.) *Annales du 17e Congrès de l'Association Internationale pour l'Histoire du Verre*, 74–79. Brussels, University Press Antwerp.

Antonaras, A. (2010a) Glass Doves and Globes from Thessaloniki.

North Italian Imports or Local Products? In *Quaderni Friulani Di Archeologia* 19 = *Atti del Convegno Intorno all'Adriatico. La diffusione e la produzione di vetro sulle sponde del mare Adriatico nell'antichità*, 27–33. Udine, Società Friulana di Archeologia.

Antonaras, A. (2010b) Glass-working activities in Late Roman and Early Christian Thessaloniki. Local Workshops and vessels. In J. Drauschke and D. Keller (eds.) *Glass in Byzantium – Production, Usage, Analyses*. RGZM – Tagungen 8, 93–105. Mainz, Römisch-Germanisches Zentralmuseum.

Antonaras, A. (2010c) Glassware in Late Antique Thessalonikē. In L. Nasrallah, Ch. Bakirtzis and S. J. Friesen (eds.) *From Roman to Early Christian Thessalonikē. Studies in Religion and Archaeology*. Harvard Theological Studies 64, 301–334. Cambridge, MA, Harvard University Press.

Antonaras, A. (2010d) Υαλοποιία και υαλουργία στο ρωμαϊκό και παλαιοχριστιανικό κόσμο. Υαλουργική δραστηριότητα στη Θεσσαλονίκη [=Glass-making and Glass-working in Roman and Early Christian world. Glass-working activity in Thessaloniki]. *Archaiologikon Deltion, Meletes*, 57, 237–260.

Antonaras, A. (2011) Stemmed beakers with stamped bases from an Early Christian glass workshop at the centre of Thessaloniki. In D. Foy and M.-D. Nenna (eds.) *Corpus des signatures et marques sur verres antiques 3*, 239–242. Aix-en-Provence/Lyon, Association Française pour l'Archéologie du Verre.

Antonaras, A. (in press a) Artisanal Production in Byzantine Thessaloniki. In *Hinter den Mauern und auf dem offenen Land. Neue Forschungen zum Leben im Byzantinischen Reich*.

Antonaras, A. (in press b) Βασιλέως Ηρακλείου 45, Θεσσαλονίκη. Το παλαιοχριστιανικό υαλουργείο [= 45, Vaslileos Irakleiou street, Thessaloniki. The early Christian glass workshop]. *To Archaeologico Ergo Ste Makedonia kai Thrake* 24.

Arveiller-Dulong, V. and Nenna, M.-D. (2005) *Les verres antiques du Musée du Louvre II. Vaisselle et contenants du Ier siècle au début du VIIe siècle après J.-C*. Paris, Somogy.

Dagron, G. (2002) The Urban Economy, Seventh–Twelfth centuries. In A. Laiou (ed.) *The Economic History of Byzantium. From the Seventh through the Fifteenth century*, 392–461. Washington D.C., Dumbarton Oaks Research Library and Collection.

Foy, D. and Nenna, M.-D. (2001) *Tout feu, tout sable. Mille ans de verre antique dans le Midi de la France*. Aix-en-Provence, Edisud.

Gorin-Rosen, Y. and Winter, T. (2010) Selected insights into Byzantine glass in the Holy Land. In J. Drauschke and D. Keller (eds.) *Glass in Byzantium – Production, usage, analyses*. RGZM – Tagungen 8, 165–182. Mainz, Römisch-Germanisches Zentralmuseum.

Gounaris, G. (1995–2000) Πανεπιστημιακή ανασκαφή Φιλίππων 1997–1999, *Εγνατία* 5, 323–356.

Isings, C. (1957) *Roman Glass form Dated Finds*. Archaeologica Traiectina 2. Groningen/Djakarta, J. B. Wolters.

Marki, E. (1994) Αγίας Σοφίας 52. *Archaiologikon Deltion* 49, B2, 511–515.

Nenna, M.-D. (2008) Nouveaux acquis sur la production et le commerce du verre antique entre Orient et Occident. *Zeitschrift für Schweizerische Archäologie und Kunstgeschichte* 65, 61–66.

Pitsakis, K. G. (1971) *Κωνσταντίνου Αρμενοπούλου, Πρόχειρον Νόμων ή εξάβιβλος*. Athens, Dodoni-E. K. Lazos.

Pitsakis, K. G. (2002) Η σημασία του νομικού έργου του Κωνσταντίνου Αρμενόπουλου. In Th. Zeses, P. Asemakopoulou-Atzaka and V. Katsaros (eds.) *Η Μακεδονία κατά την εποχή των Παλαιολόγων*, Θεσσαλονίκη 14-20 Δεκεμβρίου 1992, Θεσσαλονίκη, 239–258. Thessaloniki, Aristoteleio Panepistimio Thessalonikis.

Price, J. (2005) Glass working and glassworkers in cities and towns. In A. Mac Mahon and J. Price (eds.) *Roman Working Lives and Urban Living*, 167–190. Oxford, Oxbow Books.

Stern, E. M. (1999) Roman Glassblowing in a Cultural Context. *American Journal of Archaeology* 103, 441–484.

Stern, E. M. (2001) *Roman, Byzantine and Early Medieval Glass 10 BCE – 700 CE. Ernesto Wolf Collection*. Ostfildern-Ruit, Hatje Cantz.

Young, S. H. (2007) Glass. In A. H. S. Megaw, *Kourion Excavations in the Episcopal Precinct*, 485–525. Washington, D.C., Dumbarton Oaks Research Library and Collection.

13

Glass tesserae from Hagios Polyeuktos, Constantinople: their early Byzantine affiliations

Nadine Schibille and Judith McKenzie

Introduction

The site of the ruined 6th-century church of Hagios Polyeuktos at Saraçhane in Istanbul was rediscovered during excavations in 1960 and identified on the basis of fragments of a monumental inscription, the text of which is preserved in the *Palatine Greek Anthology* (*AP* 1.10; Conner 1999; Harrison 1986; 1989; Mango and Sevcenko 1961, Sodini 1993, Whitby 2006). The church had been commissioned by the noblewoman Anicia Juliana and at the time of completion (before AD 527), it was the largest, most impressive and unusual ecclesiastical building in the Byzantine capital (Bardill 1994, 67; 2004, 62–64, 111–116; Harrison 1986, 221–222, 225). Hagios Polyeuktos is believed to have significantly influenced the subsequent architectural developments in Constantinople, most notably the grand Justinianic foundations (including Hagia Sophia) that it predates by only a few years (McKenzie 2007, 332–339, 344). The building and its location had fallen into oblivion after its collapse sometime in the 12th or 13th century and was known only from written sources.

The main body of the church (excluding the narthex and the projecting apse) was laid out as a square of nearly fifty-two metres in length and width and divided into a central nave and aisles (Harrison 1989, 52, fig. 48). As such, the plan and dimensions (100 royal cubits square) of Hagios Polyeuktos emulated the biblical description of Solomon's Temple in Jerusalem (Harrison 1984; 1986, 410; 1989, 137–144; Ousterhout 2010, 243–246). The type of roofing of Hagios Polyeuktos is controversial, but judging from the substantial foundations and walls as well as the drainage arrangements, the excavator Martin Harrison (1986, 410–414; 1989, 60, 131–132) and Sheila Gibson, the architect who prepared his reconstructions (Harrison 1989, figs. 167, 171), suggested that it might have been vaulted (Conner 1999; Mango and Sevcenko 1961; McKenzie 2007, 334; Sodini 1993), while it has also been argued that it had a timber roof (Bardill 2006). The decorative programme, particularly the exquisitely carved marble decoration, is unique in its own right and has been linked with Sasanian (Harrison 1986, 414–417; 1989, 122–124) and Egyptian influences (McKenzie 2007, 335–339), while parallels are also found in the church of San Vitale in Ravenna (Italy), consecrated in AD 547 (Deichmann 1976, 96–99, fig. 22).

The excavation of Hagios Polyeuktos yielded a large number of window glass fragments and glass mosaics, both in the form of loose tesserae as well as small pieces of mosaic still embedded in plaster (Harrison 1986, 182–196, 204–206; 1989, 78–80). The evidence suggests that the church essentially followed a Roman system of fenestration and glazing. The fragments of figurative mosaics (groups of 3–6mm wide tesserae embedded in plaster) were nearly all found in the area of the apse, where they had a gold ground. As these fragments are dated stratigraphically to the original 6th-century construction according to the excavator (Harrison 1989, 80), they had escaped 8th-century iconoclastic obliteration. The poem mentioned (*AP* 1.10, lines 70–73) seems to indicate that there was a mosaic depicting the baptism of Constantine above the west entrance (Fowden 1994, 275; Milner 1994, 74, 78–81). In the rest of the church, geometric and abstract motifs (circles, triangles, arcades) seem to have predominated, with dark blues and shades of green being the most common colours. If vaulted, the ceiling probably would have been covered with gold-glass tesserae (Mundell Mango 1992, 125–126).

Given the church's historical and architectural importance, the edifice is a valuable testimony of architectural design and decoration in 6th-century Constantinople. The analytical study of the glass mosaic tesserae from Saraçhane can

Table 13.1: EPMA results of the 28 tesserae from the church of Hagios Polyeuktos in Istanbul, giving the mean of repeated measurements for each sample ($n \geq 5$) in wt% of the oxides. The window glass fragment was measured by LA-ICP-MS.

	colour	Na_2O	MgO	Al_2O_3	SiO_2	P_2O_5	SO_3	Cl	K_2O	CaO	MnO	FeO	CuO	SnO_2	PbO
Sb-tesserae															
Poly_005	blue opaque	14.58	0.39	2.13	70.50	0.12	0.24	0.85	0.40	7.25	0.13	0.74	0.09	0.02	0.24
Poly_006	blue opaque	15.27	0.44	2.28	65.51	0.16	0.36	0.77	0.52	7.17	0.41	1.19	0.35	0.04	0.41
Poly_007	blue opaque	13.87	0.49	2.37	69.24	0.13	0.31	0.71	0.49	7.97	0.26	0.51	0.07	0.03	0.98
Low Mn-tesserae															
Poly_008	turquoise	14.93	0.59	2.78	67.67	0.24	0.13	1.02	0.72	8.30	0.06	0.39	2.28	0.28	0.35
Poly_009	turquoise	14.96	0.61	2.87	69.48	0.20	0.12	1.03	0.77	8.84	0.04	0.38	0.86	0.07	0.30
Poly_010	turquoise light	15.63	0.61	2.81	69.97	0.18	0.12	1.12	0.68	8.46	0.02	0.41	0.50	0.05	0.05
Poly_011	turquoise light	15.08	0.81	3.10	69.94	0.32	0.10	1.19	0.61	8.76	0.10	0.53	0.10	0.02	0.09
Poly_012	green bluish	16.40	0.74	2.57	65.93	0.14	0.26	0.98	0.66	8.14	0.39	0.72	1.12	0.30	1.67
Poly_013	green	13.18	0.50	2.61	62.68	0.11	0.13	1.01	0.63	7.60	0.05	0.34	1.85	1.12	7.49
Poly_014	green	13.90	0.52	2.73	65.56	0.13	0.07	1.04	0.73	8.11	0.05	0.36	1.51	0.42	5.11
Poly_015	green	13.70	0.54	2.58	65.08	0.10	0.09	0.95	0.64	7.55	0.04	0.42	1.29	0.50	6.33
Poly_016	green	13.87	0.53	2.52	64.59	0.11	0.05	1.00	0.63	7.66	0.03	0.39	0.45	0.80	7.07
High Mn-tesserae															
Poly_001	purple/black	18.31	0.96	2.30	64.99	0.14	0.32	0.90	0.62	8.22	2.17	0.76	0.07	0.01	0.19
Poly_002	blue translucent	18.51	0.94	2.39	64.33	0.15	0.37	0.86	0.67	8.32	1.34	1.43	0.18	0.01	0.47
Poly_003	blue translucent	18.75	0.93	2.34	64.82	0.10	0.36	0.91	0.61	8.19	1.47	1.04	0.20	0.02	0.61
Poly_004	blue translucent	18.72	0.92	2.34	65.30	0.22	0.35	0.88	0.64	8.34	1.40	1.02	0.04	0.02	0.26
Poly_018	turquoise bluish	19.52	0.79	2.17	66.98	0.17	0.29	1.17	0.47	7.47	0.13	0.61	0.92	0.14	0.25
Poly_019	yellow opaque	13.85	0.81	1.88	54.18	0.10	0.22	0.85	0.50	6.56	1.71	0.54	0.03	1.63	16.25
Poly_021	purple/black	18.55	0.92	2.32	65.04	0.15	0.34	0.90	0.66	8.33	2.32	0.77	0.05	0.03	0.22
Poly_024	red opaque	18.40	0.95	2.28	63.76	0.11	0.30	0.88	0.61	7.96	1.39	2.74	0.95	0.09	0.28
Poly_025	amber opaque	16.31	0.87	2.07	57.92	0.08	0.32	0.90	0.57	7.57	1.88	0.61	0.05	0.85	8.74
Poly_026	amber opaque	16.61	0.90	2.05	58.16	0.09	0.28	0.91	0.57	7.58	1.94	0.62	0.05	0.94	8.65
Poly_027	colourless	18.60	0.83	2.15	64.97	0.05	0.28	1.15	0.53	8.99	2.38	0.54	0.05	0.01	0.00
Poly_029	colourless	18.54	1.07	2.45	64.71	0.09	0.36	0.91	0.64	9.02	1.71	0.87	0.02	0.03	0.03
Poly_030	colourless	18.89	0.79	2.11	66.26	0.07	0.34	1.07	0.50	8.26	1.95	0.52	0.03	0.02	0.02
Poly_031	colourless/gold leaf	17.48	1.10	3.01	65.59	0.12	0.22	0.93	0.55	6.51	1.99	2.57	0.06	0.02	0.07
Poly_window	colourless transp.	18.41	0.98	2.18	66.65	0.09			0.57	8.76	1.44	0.83	0.01	0.00	0.01
Plant Ash-tesserae															
Poly_017	green	13.75	2.09	1.90	66.11	0.25	0.18	0.65	1.54	8.95	0.82	0.97	2.28	0.14	0.30
Poly_022	red opaque	11.61	2.81	1.81	65.89	0.31	0.14	0.75	2.24	9.12	1.24	2.17	1.90	0.00	0.14

Table 13.2: Measured (EPMA) and published values of the Corning ancient glass standards.

	Na$_2$O	MgO	Al$_2$O$_3$	SiO$_2$	P$_2$O$_5$	SO$_3$	Cl	K$_2$O	CaO	MnO	Fe$_2$O$_3$	CuO	SnO$_2$	PbO
Corning Ancient Glass Standard A														
Average of n=18	14.11	2.62	0.93	66.29	0.11	0.13	0.10	2.89	5.17	1.14	1.06	1.27	0.24	0.05
Published values	14.30	2.66	1.00	66.56	0.13			2.87	5.03	1.00	1.09	1.17	0.19	0.12
Absolute deviation	0.19	0.04	0.07	0.27	0.02	-0.13	-0.10	-0.02	-0.14	-0.14	0.03	-0.10	-0.05	0.07
Relative deviation	1.35	1.40	7.12	0.40	18.00			-0.78	-2.76	-14.25	2.93	-8.80	-25.01	56.81
Corning Ancient Glass Standard B														
Average of n=34	16.78	1.02	4.23	61.45	0.86	0.51	0.19	1.07	9.19	0.27	0.35	2.91	0.04	0.53
Published values	17.00	1.03	4.36	61.55	0.82	0.54		1.00	8.56	0.25	0.34	2.66	0.04	0.82
Absolute deviation	0.22	0.01	0.13	0.10	-0.04	0.03	-0.19	-0.07	-0.63	-0.02	-0.01	-0.25	0.00	0.29
Relative deviation	1.29	1.25	3.06	0.16	-4.99	5.51		-7.22	-7.41	-9.51	-1.93	-9.48	9.21	35.76

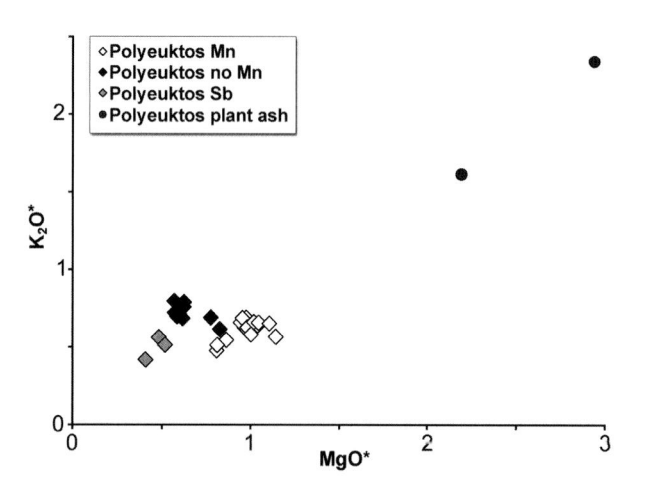

Fig. 13.1: Potash and magnesia levels of the Hagios Polyeuktos tesserae (reduced EPMA data indicated by asterisks). Potash and magnesia concentrations identify most of the tesserae as natron-type soda-lime-silica glasses, with the exception of two samples with compositions typical of plant ash glasses.

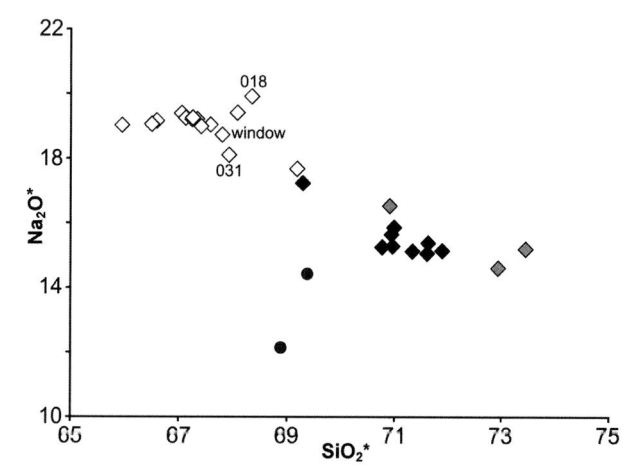

Fig. 13.2: Soda and silica concentrations of the Hagios Polyeuktos tesserae (reduced EPMA data). The ratio of soda relative to silica separates the tesserae into three groups that correlate with the presence or absence of manganese and antimony. The lower soda levels in the low manganese samples may reflect a chronological development of declining soda in glass from the Roman to the Byzantine and early Islamic periods. However, the tesserae that contain antimony and that display a similarly high silica to soda ratio (~4.5) do not fit this model, as they are assumed to be of Roman origin, due to the presence of antimony.

provide crucial insights into Byzantine mosaic making during one of the most prolific artistic and architectural periods in the history of Constantinople, especially in light of the limited data of Byzantine mosaics available to date. It is of great interest, for instance, how the mosaic tesserae from this major ecclesiastical foundation in the capital relate chemically to contemporary mosaics in the Byzantine provinces (*e.g.* Ravenna, Sagalassos). Through the chemical characteristics of the glass mosaics, both in terms of base glass compositions and additives (colourants, opacifiers), a clearer understanding of the manufacture of mosaics in the Byzantine world can be gained.

From the middle of the first millennium BC through to the late 8th or the 9th century AD, raw glass in the Mediterranean region and Europe was typically produced from a mineral sodium carbonate collected from lake deposits in the Wadi Natrun in Egypt (so-called *natron*) and a locally available silica source (*e.g.* Sayre and Smith 1961; Henderson 1985; Freestone *et al.* 2002; Gratuze and Barrandon 1990; Wedepohl *et al.* 2011). The only primary production installations active during the period in question (*i.e.* 4th to 8th century) have been excavated in Syro-Palestine on the Levantine coast (Gorin-Rosen 1995; 2000). The glasses produced from Levantine coastal sands and mineral soda from Egypt have been identified among glass assemblages from all around the Mediterranean, Europe and possibly even Mesopotamia (Foy *et al.* 2003; Freestone *et al.* 2000; 2002; Mirti *et al.* 2000; 2001; 2008; Picon and Vichy 2003; Schibille 2011). Natron was eventually replaced by potassium rich wood ash in Carolingian Europe (the earliest wood ash glasses date to before AD 780) and by soda rich plant ash in the Islamic Near East (Freestone and Gorin-Rosen 1999; Gratuze and Barrandon 1990; Henderson

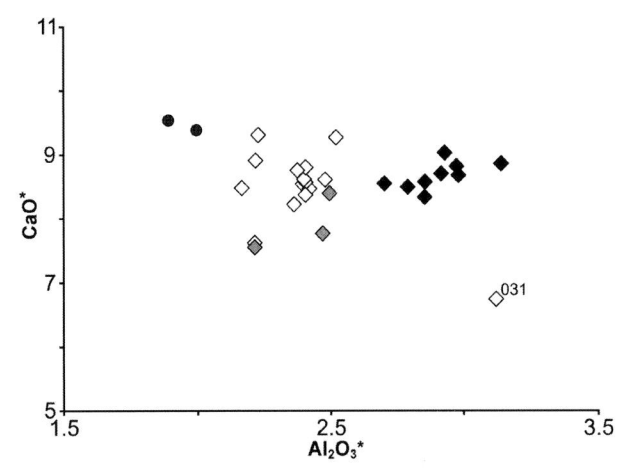

Fig. 13.3: Lime and alumina concentrations of the Hagios Polyeuktos tesserae (reduced EPMA data). Lime and alumina are the two most abundant elements incorporated into the glass as part of the sand source, and illustrate that the three groups of natron-type glasses were produced from different silica sources.

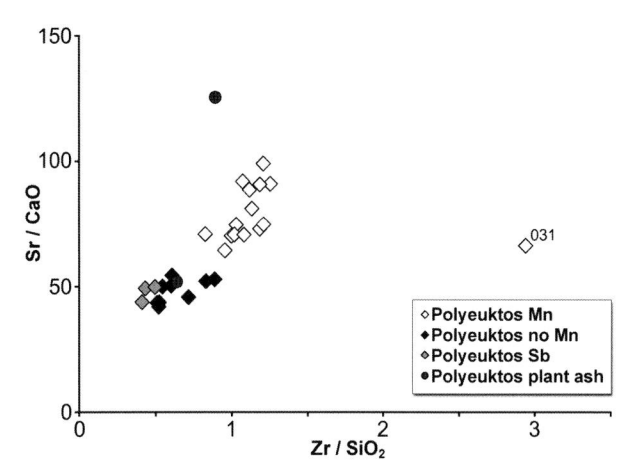

Fig. 13.5: The comparison of the strontium and zirconium concentrations (LA-ICP-MS) of the glasses as a function of their lime and silica contents (EPMA), respectively, clearly separates the two main groups of glass represented in the Hagios Polyeuktos assemblage. Different raw materials (lime and silica) have evidently been used for the production of the low manganese and the manganese-rich tesserae.

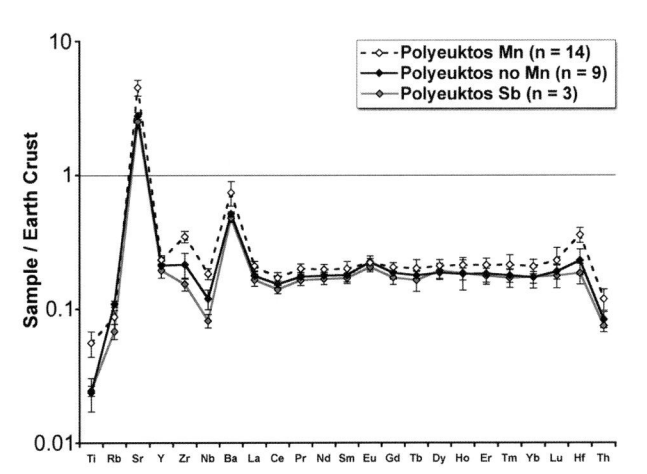

Fig. 13.4: Trace element patterns (LA-ICP-MS data) of the Hagios Polyeuktos tesserae. Average abundance of selected trace elements associated with the silica source, normalized to the composition of the Continental Earth's Crust (Kamber et al. 2005). The three groups of natron-type tesserae have comparable light rare earth element (REE) distributions, but differ in some of the heavy elements such as Ti, Zr and Hf. For all three groups silica sources were used that are depleted in mineral contaminants.

et al. 2004; Wedepohl and Simon 2010; Wedepohl et al. 2011). Aside from analytical studies of mainly non-coloured glasses, only limited attention has been paid to the analyses of strongly coloured and often opaque mosaic tesserae and the secondary working processes involved in their production (Andreescu-Treadgold and Henderson 2006; Arletti et al. 2010; 2011; Fiori et al. 2003; Freestone et al. 1990; Gedzevičiūtė et al. 2009; Marii and Rehren 2009; Schibille et al. 2012a; van der Werf et al. 2009). Little is known about the production of Byzantine mosaics, how the mosaicists obtained their raw materials or how the supply of glass and/or tesserae was organised during the Roman and Byzantine period (Dunbabin 1999; James 2006; 2010). No glass furnaces for the secondary workshops for the manufacture of mosaics of Byzantine date have so far been found. A recent analytical study of late Roman and early Byzantine mosaics from Sagalassos (Turkey) has identified changes in the organisation of mosaic making from a centralised model (Roman) to a diversification of the supply during the 5th or 6th century (Schibille et al. 2012a).

In order to shed light on the production of Byzantine mosaic tesserae and the relationship between mosaics of geographically different sites in terms of base glass composition and colour palette, this study reports the analysis of 28 glass tesserae from the church of Hagios Polyeuktos in Constantinople. The data were compared to established primary glass production groups (Freestone 2005) and other 6th-century mosaics, most notably data from Hagia Sophia (Brill 1999), San Vitale at Ravenna (Fiori et al. 2003) and Sagalassos (Schibille et al. 2012a). In this way, the compositional data can potentially reveal the provenance of the raw glass and establish how the mosaics of Hagios Polyeuktos relate to contemporary mosaic assemblages.

Materials and methods

The 28 glass tesserae analysed in this study were collected during the excavations at Saraçhane and are now held in the Institute of Archaeology, University of Oxford. Their

Table 13.3: LA-ICP-MS elemental data of the average trace element distribution (n = 4) expressed in ppm.

	Li	Be	B	Sc	Ti	V	Cr	Ni	Co	Zn	As	Rb	Sr	Zr	Nb	Ag	In	Sb	Cs	Ba
Sb-tesserae																				
Poly_05	2.89	0.40	159.80	2.45	185.43	6.77	7.45	21.58	546.38	21.96	3.75	4.63	317.25	28.85	1.12	0.71	0.34	10085	0.02	173.74
Poly_06	3.22	0.49	77.80	2.53	193.66	9.94	7.00	19.16	631.26	40.77	0.00	5.91	353.97	28.14	1.23	0.73	0.68	24277	0.05	196.84
Poly_07	3.50	0.53	114.15	2.28	218.40	10.35	8.46	9.90	120.81	19.08	0.00	5.71	397.29	34.34	1.40	0.69	0.10	14565	0.03	198.00
Low Mn-tesserae																				
Poly_08	3.48	0.47	85.87	2.70	169.70	7.89	9.64	29.58	4.66	29.53	45.08	8.24	363.06	35.43	1.53	9.49	0.00	16.48	0.06	194.62
Poly_09	3.70	0.72	78.49	2.90	175.99	8.15	11.41	10.50	4.70	13.51	19.23	9.15	370.99	36.17	1.74	4.44	0.05	6.27	0.06	194.04
Poly_10	3.61	0.42	84.04	2.67	167.92	7.66	10.46	7.76	2.52	21.54	11.33	8.51	367.76	35.69	1.50	2.53	0.18	3.62	0.05	198.65
Poly_11	3.59	0.66	96.55	2.95	253.85	9.65	12.40	5.50	3.13	14.14	6.92	8.19	401.15	50.22	1.95	0.90	0.04	2.82	0.05	199.05
Poly_12	4.82	0.58	137.78	3.32	309.54	16.88	17.04	19.76	31.77	32.71	35.97	8.26	429.94	58.68	2.48	6.34	0.00	58.83	0.09	204.07
Poly_13	2.77	0.47	70.52	2.36	148.82	7.09	9.74	20.41	9.42	24.58	91.25	8.92	379.63	34.14	1.62	20.67	0.57	151.26	0.05	202.72
Poly_14	2.68	0.42	66.07	2.24	162.18	7.20	10.89	14.78	3.60	15.27	117.50	8.60	408.53	39.51	1.72	10.35	0.00	176.28	0.07	213.17
Poly_15	2.59	0.46	65.72	2.68	194.23	7.14	16.18	20.04	4.12	13.92	65.02	8.60	393.98	54.17	2.02	15.46	1.20	95.07	0.06	206.60
Poly_16	2.62	0.71	74.62	2.66	153.66	7.37	9.70	8.40	2.43	32.13	41.97	9.58	417.25	39.27	1.82	14.03	0.00	83.61	0.08	216.08
High Mn-tesserae																				
Poly_01	6.79	0.69	167.82	3.20	512.21	33.67	13.98	26.83	119.38	22.79	4.90	6.72	613.46	66.91	2.54	0.21	0.31	60.20	0.05	353.64
Poly_02	7.47	0.58	161.58	3.36	525.32	26.20	17.15	110.53	883.64	45.78	0.00	7.60	583.93	64.12	2.74	0.17	0.92	65.08	0.07	297.40
Poly_03	7.12	0.48	161.00	3.18	523.71	25.82	14.65	69.27	454.94	33.06	6.85	7.25	579.44	65.98	2.74	0.18	1.04	61.67	0.06	295.11
Poly_04	7.51	0.49	161.79	3.26	529.97	24.92	15.49	45.47	418.67	26.32	0.00	7.20	588.81	70.64	2.75	0.10	0.65	61.71	0.06	295.39
Poly_18	7.00	0.71	186.07	2.95	281.83	13.87	12.57	13.48	23.72	32.20	18.29	6.22	481.40	63.93	2.48	4.60	0.15	14.14	0.25	156.82
Poly_19	3.58	0.59	106.85	2.60	248.68	21.89	10.81	9.98	5.58	53.74	51.68	7.14	649.56	65.60	3.03	37.11	0.00	230.65	0.13	319.66
Poly_21	6.53	0.96	155.35	3.71	352.43	42.29	16.48	35.10	146.62	40.45	11.46	9.09	758.44	81.64	3.26	0.92	0.24	113.35	0.12	413.09
Poly_24	5.86	0.41	141.34	3.79	523.86	24.32	15.45	19.94	24.38	25.19	9.12	6.98	580.44	75.57	2.84	5.96	0.04	57.46	0.07	258.62
Poly_25	4.80	0.47	127.00	3.40	454.04	25.32	12.53	8.83	5.98	24.09	39.28	6.59	686.68	68.78	2.86	10.79	0.26	158.11	0.07	315.87
Poly_26	5.32	0.48	130.78	3.14	453.34	26.56	13.40	8.48	6.13	23.76	31.12	6.55	671.15	64.95	2.88	6.38	0.00	149.46	0.07	304.48
Poly_27	6.64	0.52	140.15	3.13	483.91	24.60	13.00	6.62	4.26	11.71	0.00	6.18	827.04	69.60	2.65	0.67	0.01	75.11	0.04	268.66
Poly_29	5.65	0.46	168.81	3.35	584.38	27.02	16.63	12.08	5.58	21.08	0.00	6.87	675.19	78.41	3.02	0.36	0.02	166.79	0.04	337.94
Poly_30	5.28	0.47	158.95	3.21	422.82	21.86	11.53	5.77	3.67	11.50	0.00	5.59	585.83	54.79	2.27	0.04	0.02	4.12	0.03	217.06
Poly_31	5.01	0.62	156.05	5.58	1635.73	66.03	50.07	27.95	17.99	52.24	0.00	6.68	432.12	192.74	5.36	0.73	0.04	6.34	0.04	349.23
window	6.87	0.54	164.29	4.51	482.43	26.35	15.08	8.22	5.13	19.79	5.46	7.12	710.02	75.61	3.12	0.06	0.01	239.87	0.21	270.92
Plant Ash tesserae																				
Poly_17	113.19	2.39	648.68	3.24	334.32	19.54	23.03	24.54	59.86	106.68	66.28	20.19	1121.71	59.03	2.73	14.22	0.24	78.95	10.38	273.86
Poly_22	6.20	0.84	64.23	3.23	268.07	15.75	11.76	13.43	7.58	164.44	105.75	14.90	473.18	42.17	2.28	8.13	2.12	151.33	0.16	231.02

	La	Ce	Pr	Ta	Au	Y	Bi	U	W	Mo	Nd	Sm	Eu	Gd	Tb	Dy	Ho	Er	Tm	Yb	Lu	Hf	Th
Sb-tesserae																							
Poly_05	4.84	9.30	1.29	0.08	0.05	5.67	0.06	0.76	0.08	0.93	5.05	1.14	0.29	0.95	0.13	1.01	0.18	0.57	0.08	0.45	0.07	0.87	0.74
Poly_06	5.27	9.76	1.34	0.09	0.57	5.80	0.28	1.03	0.11	3.87	5.36	1.08	0.33	1.12	0.16	1.10	0.21	0.53	0.08	0.62	0.09	0.90	0.85
Poly_07	5.94	10.73	1.51	0.10	0.06	7.05	0.05	0.94	0.07	0.95	6.03	1.28	0.34	1.19	0.19	1.29	0.29	0.68	0.10	0.61	0.10	1.18	0.91
Low Mn-tesserae																							
Poly_08	5.41	9.90	1.35	0.12	0.37	6.77	2.70	0.43	0.73	0.54	5.22	1.13	0.36	1.09	0.16	0.96	0.21	0.58	0.09	0.48	0.10	0.94	0.75
Poly_09	5.39	10.60	1.42	0.16	0.09	6.19	1.57	0.48	0.13	0.64	5.61	1.19	0.33	1.12	0.18	1.12	0.23	0.57	0.09	0.51	0.10	1.03	0.81
Poly_10	5.38	10.47	1.34	0.12	0.05	6.17	0.52	0.49	0.10	0.50	5.55	1.17	0.35	1.03	0.18	0.98	0.21	0.59	0.08	0.53	0.08	1.02	0.83
Poly_11	5.85	10.87	1.50	0.12	0.11	7.05	0.21	0.48	0.08	0.31	6.09	1.19	0.35	1.20	0.17	1.16	0.22	0.59	0.09	0.55	0.09	1.32	0.89
Poly_12	5.77	11.05	1.47	0.14	0.22	6.42	3.34	0.89	0.28	1.15	5.61	1.14	0.33	1.14	0.18	1.02	0.21	0.52	0.08	0.55	0.09	1.57	1.10
Poly_13	5.32	10.57	1.40	0.09	0.36	6.27	23.19	0.69	0.61	0.64	5.70	1.11	0.34	1.06	0.16	0.97	0.19	0.55	0.08	0.56	0.08	1.02	0.90
Poly_14	5.93	10.88	1.53	0.12	0.28	6.80	16.34	0.50	0.81	0.56	5.95	1.37	0.35	1.28	0.19	1.13	0.22	0.63	0.09	0.56	0.09	1.12	0.91
Poly_15	6.40	11.43	1.64	0.15	0.53	7.59	18.31	0.56	0.31	0.54	6.27	1.54	0.40	1.40	0.19	1.34	0.27	0.77	0.11	0.61	0.11	1.68	1.05
Poly_16	6.27	11.98	1.59	0.15	0.15	7.25	19.23	0.60	0.59	0.72	6.21	1.24	0.35	1.30	0.18	1.15	0.24	0.73	0.11	0.67	0.10	1.22	1.09
High Mn-tesserae																							
Poly_01	6.41	10.81	1.60	0.17	0.29	7.05	0.13	1.01	0.22	4.28	6.28	1.28	0.34	1.33	0.18	1.26	0.23	0.67	0.11	0.62	0.11	1.83	1.19
Poly_02	6.54	12.29	1.68	0.16	0.19	6.97	0.17	1.21	0.26	6.92	6.55	1.42	0.33	1.39	0.20	1.18	0.26	0.73	0.11	0.67	0.12	1.95	1.33
Poly_03	6.79	12.30	1.70	0.19	0.12	7.03	0.17	1.28	0.22	3.87	6.74	1.49	0.35	1.23	0.19	1.24	0.26	0.71	0.10	0.65	0.13	2.01	1.40
Poly_04	6.82	11.81	1.68	0.19	0.06	7.54	0.14	1.19	0.21	4.45	6.74	1.48	0.38	1.42	0.22	1.47	0.26	0.77	0.11	0.68	0.11	2.15	1.33
Poly_18	6.56	11.27	1.62	0.15	0.11	7.18	1.27	0.99	0.14	0.55	6.35	1.36	0.33	1.26	0.19	1.23	0.25	0.72	0.10	0.72	0.10	1.96	1.19
Poly_19	6.80	12.34	1.75	0.27	0.88	7.19	63.80	1.30	0.45	3.46	6.57	1.47	0.41	1.39	0.27	1.31	0.31	0.82	0.16	0.82	0.19	2.11	1.34
Poly_21	8.08	14.41	2.07	0.25	0.03	8.83	0.47	1.53	0.78	6.02	7.91	1.79	0.45	1.35	0.25	1.47	0.35	0.91	0.14	0.82	0.14	2.41	1.58
Poly_24	6.43	10.68	1.58	0.16	0.16	7.72	1.17	0.95	0.24	2.49	6.08	1.28	0.30	1.30	0.18	1.09	0.24	0.65	0.10	0.60	0.09	1.65	1.63
Poly_25	7.01	12.42	1.70	0.20	0.28	7.53	40.17	1.24	0.26	3.20	6.46	1.44	0.35	1.34	0.21	1.24	0.26	0.73	0.10	0.71	0.11	1.87	1.42
Poly_26	7.35	13.32	1.69	0.18	0.06	7.15	27.79	1.14	0.30	3.05	6.61	1.32	0.33	1.25	0.19	1.21	0.24	0.72	0.10	0.68	0.09	1.78	1.74
Poly_27	6.80	11.83	1.69	0.16	0.04	8.06	0.02	0.98	0.14	3.08	6.38	1.38	0.35	1.37	0.19	1.22	0.27	0.71	0.11	0.71	0.11	1.77	1.10
Poly_29	6.52	12.14	1.64	0.18	0.06	7.06	0.04	1.13	0.24	3.80	5.93	1.15	0.32	1.12	0.17	1.08	0.23	0.65	0.09	0.62	0.10	1.90	1.06
Poly_30	5.61	10.29	1.37	0.12	0.05	6.42	0.02	0.89	0.08	1.48	5.18	1.03	0.29	1.08	0.14	0.96	0.21	0.52	0.09	0.52	0.08	1.33	0.85
Poly_31	11.34	14.74	2.70	0.30	0.07	12.95	0.14	0.96	0.37	3.62	10.85	2.35	0.57	2.32	0.33	2.02	0.45	1.19	0.17	1.15	0.18	4.45	1.66
window	7.24	13.35	1.76	0.16	0.02	7.86	0.02	1.14	0.18	3.00	6.74	1.30	0.33	1.37	0.19	1.27	0.26	0.67	0.11	0.59	0.10	1.91	1.27
Plant Ash tesserae																							
Poly_17	5.89	11.59	1.40	0.17	0.44	5.69	2.77	0.97	1.21	2.14	5.42	1.19	0.31	1.05	0.14	1.04	0.24	0.60	0.10	0.69	0.12	1.76	1.37
Poly_22	6.84	12.55	1.81	0.17	0.29	8.03	15.59	0.52	1.27	3.98	7.35	1.43	0.40	1.55	0.21	1.32	0.30	0.72	0.11	0.70	0.10	1.32	1.12

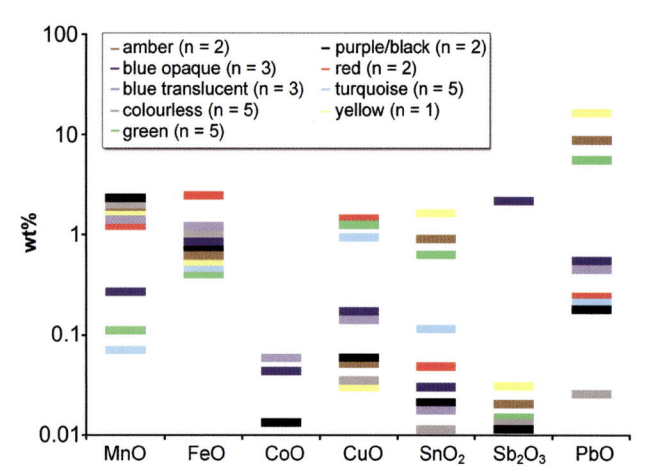

Fig. 13.6: Colour palette of the Hagios Polyeuktos tesserae as a function of transition metals in the glass. The colours of the Hagios Polyeuktos tesserae are caused by the addition of transition metals, predominantly Mn (black and colourless), Fe (red), Co (blue), Cu (green, red and turquoise) and Pb-Sn (green and yellow). The opacity of many of the tesserae is the result of antimony (Sb) and tin (Sn) based opacifiers.

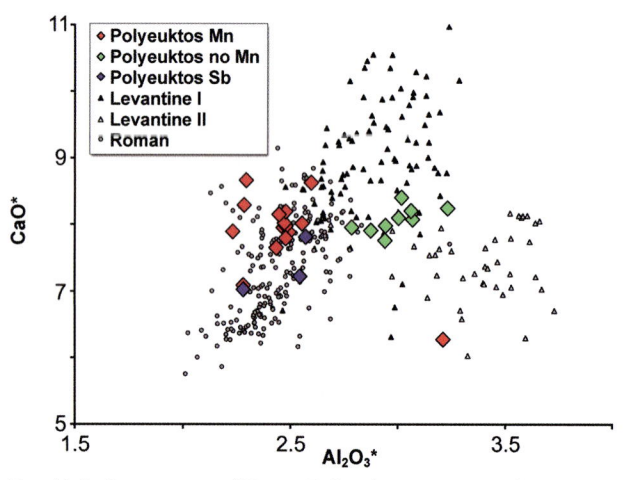

Fig. 13.7: Comparison of Hagios Polyeuktos tesserae with Levantine I and II and Roman glass types. Lime and alumina levels (reduced data) of the manganese-rich and antimony containing tesserae from Hagios Polyeuktos are consistent with 1st to 4th-century Roman glass compositions from Italy (Arletti et al. 2005; Mirti et al. 1993; Silvestri 2008; Silvestri et al. 2005; 2008). The tesserae low in manganese are more closely associated with Levantine I glass from Jalame, Beit Shean, Apollonia and Dor (data from Ian Freestone).

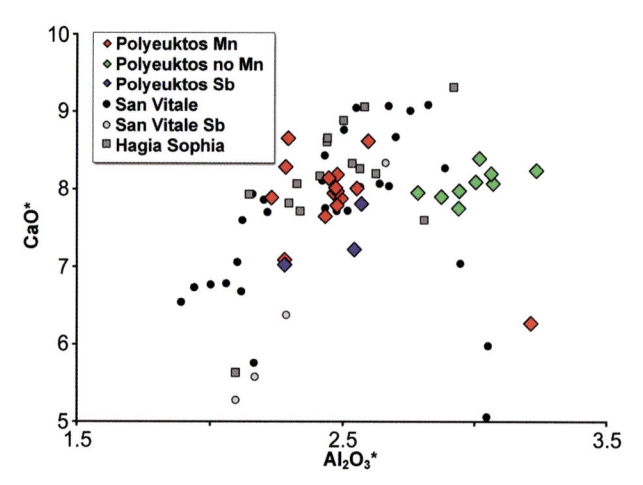

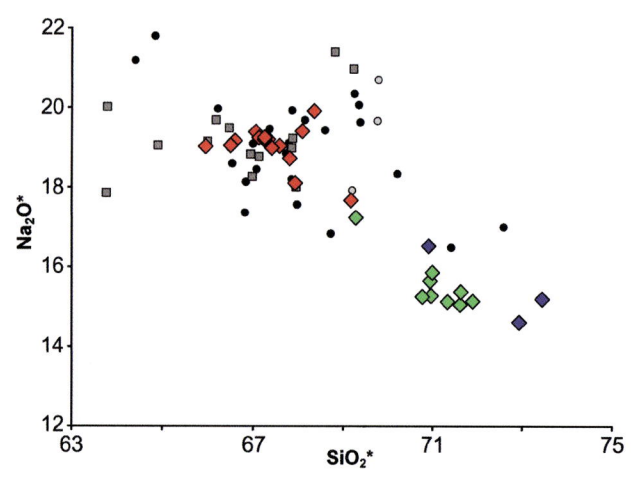

Fig. 13.8: Comparison of Hagios Polyeuktos tesserae with 6th-century mosaics from San Vitale (Ravenna) and Hagia Sophia (Istanbul) (Brill 1999, section IX; Fiori et al. 2003). Compositional parallels were found between the manganese- and antimony-rich tesserae from Hagios Polyeuktos and the mosaic tesserae from San Vitale in Ravenna and Hagia Sophia in terms of their lime and alumina concentrations (reduced data), indicating a single silica source for all these 6th-century mosaics. No close match was identified between the low manganese samples from Hagios Polyeuktos and any of the contemporary mosaics.

Fig. 13.9: Comparison of Hagios Polyeuktos tesserae with 6th-century mosaics from San Vitale (Ravenna) and Hagia Sophia (Istanbul) (Brill 1999, section IX; Fiori et al. 2003). The Polyeuktos manganese-rich samples display similarities in the soda to silica ratio (reduced data) with the mosaics from the other Byzantine ecclesiastical contexts. Again, the low manganese tesserae from Hagios Polyeuktos are distinct from the other assemblages.

colours consist of various shades of blues and greens, as well as amber, red, purple-black and yellow. Some almost colourless transparent samples might originally have been gold leaf tesserae and one of these is still identifiable as such (Table 13.1). Additionally, one virtually colourless window glass fragment was included in the analysis (Poly-window). The tesserae are relatively regular in shape, small in size with sides usually ≤10mm long and they weigh between

0.4g and 1.4g. Unfortunately, the archaeological contexts of the tesserae do not provide an unequivocal date for the samples as some layers were disturbed and the individual tesserae must necessarily predate their deposition (Harrison 1986, 182–196). However, it is thought that in selecting the assemblage of tesserae sampled here, Harrison chose examples which he thought dated to the original 6th-century decorative programme of the church or not long thereafter (Elizabeth Harrison, pers. comm.).

Samples were taken from each of the tesserae by means of a diamond-coated saw, mounted in epoxy resin, and polished down to 1μm grade. The chemical analyses of the major, minor and trace elements were performed by wavelength-dispersive microprobe analysis (EPMA, Jeol 8600) and by laser ablation-inductively coupled plasma-mass spectrometry (LA-ICP-MS) (for detailed analytical conditions see Schibille 2011). For the microprobe analyses Corning ancient glass standards A and B were used as secondary reference materials to monitor the accuracy of the measurements (Table 13.2). The analyses were carried out with an accelerating voltage of 15kV and with a beam current set to 6nA and defocused to 10μm diameter. Counting times of 30s on peak and 15s on background were used and the elemental concentrations then converted into weight percent (wt%) oxides using the PAP correction programme. Several measurements (n ≥ 5) were taken of each sample to obtain more representative results (Table 13.1). For the graphical representation of the major and minor oxides based on the EPMA results (Figs. 13.1–13.3), the compositions were reduced to the seven main constituents (SiO_2, Na_2O, CaO, MgO, K_2O, Al_2O_3, FeO) and normalised (according to Brill 1999, 9). LA-ICP-MS analyses were carried out in the Field Museum at Chicago following the same protocol as described in (Dussubieux *et al.* 2009), and the average of the elemental concentrations (n = 4) are given in Table 13.3.

Results

Base glass compositions

Most of the analysed samples are of the soda-lime-silica type and display low magnesia and potash concentrations (Table 13.1, Fig. 13.1) with the exception of two tesserae (Poly-017 and 022) that have the chemical signature of plant ash glasses. The assemblage can be divided into two main groups based on the presence or absence of manganese. These glasses differ in the mixing ratio of silica to soda (Fig. 13.2). The group of tesserae containing none or low levels of manganese oxide (< 0.5%) have on average more silica (~ 67% non-reduced data) and lower soda (~ 15%) than the samples that have considerable amounts of manganese (> 1%), which have high soda (~ 18%) and somewhat lower silica (~ 63%) contents (Table 13.1, Fig. 13.2). The ratio of silica to soda levels is accordingly about 4.5 and 3.5 for the low manganese and manganese-rich glasses, respectively. The window glass fragment Poly-window with a manganese content of about 1.4% was assigned to the high manganese group. An exception is bluish turquoise sample Poly-018 that has no manganese but seems to be more closely related to the manganese-rich group. Consequently, this sample has been assigned to the manganese-rich group throughout the manuscript. The gold leaf tessera Poly-031 on the other hand differs significantly from the other samples, despite the presence of manganese at high levels (~ 2%) (Fig.13.1). Additionally, there are three opaque blue samples that are low in manganese but with elevated levels of antimony (Table 13.1). As with the low manganese group, these samples have high silica and relatively low soda concentrations (Fig. 13.2).

Apart from the different ratio of soda and silica, the two groups also differ in the silica source used for their production. While all the samples have comparable lime contents with an average of 8%, the two groups differ in the mineral contaminants that are typically introduced with the sand source (*e.g.* Al, Ti and rare earth elements). The low manganese group has on average higher alumina concentrations (~ 2.7%) than the manganese-rich samples (~ 2.2%) (Fig. 13.3). Titanium, zirconium and all rare earth elements (REE), on the other hand, are marginally higher in the tesserae that contain high manganese (Fig. 13.4). The difference becomes more pronounced when the amount of silica is additionally taken into account. If, for instance, zirconium is normalised against the silica content and compared to strontium as a function of the calcium concentration, the two groups separate into well-defined coherent clusters (Fig. 13.5). This illustrates clearly that the two groups derive from different silica and lime sources. The sand used for the production of the low manganese samples was slightly more depleted of mineral contaminants than the sand employed for the manufacture of the manganese-rich tesserae. The iron oxide contents of the latter are equally higher compared to the low manganese group (Table 13.1) which may indicate that manganese in fact served as a decolouriser to counter the effects of the iron in these glasses (see for example Schibille *et al.* 2012b and references therein). The three dark blue tesserae that contain considerable amounts of antimony have on average relatively low lime contents (~ 7.5%), alumina concentrations comparable to those of the manganese rich group (~ 2.2%) and the lowest levels of any of the mineral contaminants (Figs. 13.3–13.5). In contrast, the two plant-ash glasses have the lowest levels of alumina (< 2%) and highest lime contents (~ 9%), while the trace element distribution is not so different to the natron type glasses (Fig. 13.3, traces not shown). The manganese-rich outlier (Poly-031) with a high zirconium to silica ratio was produced from yet another sand source (Fig. 13.5). Judging from its high zirconium contents together with its elevated levels of iron, manganese and titanium, this not intentionally coloured sample can probably be classified as an HIMT glass (Degryse and Shortland 2009; Freestone *et al.* 2002; Schibille *et al.* 2012b).

Colourants and opacifiers

The colour palette of the tesserae differs between the two groups. The low manganese group consists exclusively of various shades of green and turquoise, whereas the high manganese group is a hodgepodge of translucent blues and purple black, opaque amber, red and yellow samples as well as the almost transparent colourless tesserae that might have once been gold leaf tesserae, but that have since lost their *cartellino* (thin glass cover) and gold layer. All three samples that contain considerable levels of antimony are of a dark blue colour (Table 13.1). The colouration and opacification of the tesserae are caused by the addition of metals, namely Mn, Fe, Co, Cu, Sn, Sb and Pb (Fig. 13.6). Manganese, for instance, serves as the main colourant only in the purple black glasses and might have been added to some of the other glasses where it was found at elevated levels as a decolouring agent. In the strongly coloured tesserae (red, yellow, blue) manganese has probably no specific colouring effect. Excess amounts of iron oxide (> 2%) are found only in the deep red tesserae (Poly-022 and -024), while cobalt was detected in the blue (both opaque and translucent blue) tesserae and to a lesser extent in the black tesserae. The cobalt colourant appears to be associated with slightly elevated levels of iron and manganese (Table 13.1), reflecting the trace elements commonly found in cobalt ores (Shortland *et al.* 2006b). All green, red and turquoise tesserae are based upon copper colouration (Fig. 13.6), with the exception of sample Poly-011 that has only traces of copper and accordingly only a faint tinge of turquoise (Table 13.1). The colour red in these glasses is produced under reducing conditions, forming either metallic copper or cuprous oxide (cuprite Cu_2O) particles. The elevated concentrations of iron in these samples may thus serve as reducing agent. Copper in its oxidised divalent state (CuO) in contrast imparts a translucent light blue colour to the glass (Barber *et al.* 2009; Gedzevičiūtė *et al.* 2009; Weyl 1953).

Together with lead-tin (or lead-antimonate) yellow these glasses can turn various shades of green (Heck *et al.* 2003; Lahlil *et al.* 2008; Moretti and Gratuze 2002; Moretti and Hreglich 1984; Paynter and Kearns 2011; Shortland 2002). Accordingly, the green tesserae show high concentrations of lead oxide (> 5% except sample Poly-012) and tin oxide. The high ratios of SnO_2 to CuO (> 1:3) exceed at least in three cases (samples Poly-013, -015, -016) the proportion of tin in high tin bronze. Hence, whereas in the red and turquoise specimens low traces of tin were most certainly incorporated into the glass as a by-product of a copper-tin alloy, the high levels of tin in the green tesserae strongly suggest a deliberate addition independent of copper (Table 13.1) (Freestone *et al.* 2003). The green tesserae are then opacified by lead-tin particles. Considerable concentrations of tin and lead oxides also characterise the yellow and amber coloured tesserae (Fig. 13.6), where they serve as both the colourant as well as the opacifier in the form of lead-tin yellow. There is no notable difference between the yellow and amber samples in terms of base glass composition or colouring transition metals. The difference in colour (*i.e.* bright yellow versus dull amber) is presumably the result of different redox conditions during firing (Green and Hart 1987). Calcium antimonate is most certainly responsible for the opacity of the opaque dark blue samples (Poly-005, -006, -007) and the red tesserae are opacified by metallic copper or cuprite. All other tesserae are of a more or less translucent quality.

Discussion

The analysed mosaic tesserae from Hagios Polyeuktos fall into two distinct groups of low magnesium and low potassium soda-lime-silica glasses, with the exception of two samples that have relatively high levels of magnesium and potassium (> 2% and 1.5%, respectively) and that indicate the use of a soda-rich plant ash (Fig. 13.1). These two plant-ash tesserae, however, are not further discussed here. Suffice to say that they provide evidence for some additions to or restoration of the mosaics in Hagios Polyeuktos sometime after the 9th century, when plant ash began to be used as the fluxing agent in glass production (Shortland *et al.* 2006a).

The two groups of natron-type glasses might have been part of the original decorative programme of the edifice and seem to belong to the initial building period or shortly thereafter. The two groups of tesserae are fairly homogeneous in terms of their base glass compositions, disregarding two outliers (samples Poly-018 and -031). The two groups separate clearly on the basis of elements typically associated with the silica source, such as aluminium, titanium, zirconium and hafnium, as well as a different soda to silica ratio (Figs. 13.1–13.5, Tables 13.1, 13.3). The declining soda levels combined with higher alumina concentrations of the low manganese glasses compared to the manganese-rich tesserae may well be a reflection of a chronological trend that has been observed at other sites (Fischer and McCray 1999; Freestone *et al.* 2008b; Freestone 2005; 2006). However, the three opaque blue tesserae that contain considerable amounts of antimony (Poly-005, -006, -007) must be excluded from this chronological model. They represent yet another glassmaking tradition with low alumina and lime contents together with low soda to silica ratio similar to the low manganese samples (Figs. 13.2, 13.4, 13.5). This difference in attribution is confirmed when comparing the chemical data of the Polyeuktos tesserae to those of the established Levantine I and II primary production groups as well as to those of Roman glasses from mainland Italy (Fig. 13.7). Whereas the glasses from Hagios Polyeuktos containing either manganese or antimony show a good degree of overlap with the cluster of 1st to 4th-century Roman glasses as regards their lime and alumina contents, the tesserae with low levels of manganese seem to be more closely associated with Levantine I glass, albeit with overall lower lime concentration than commonly found in the Levantine I reference group. This interpretation is in line with the trace element patterns of the Polyeuktos and Levantine I glasses (Fig. 13.4, Freestone *et al.* 2008a). Sample Poly-031, having high alumina and low lime is a clear outlier and assumed to be related to HIMT glass.

The higher levels of mineral contaminants in the manganese-rich glasses, most notably elevated concentrations of iron, may have necessitated the use of manganese as a decolourant and may possibly point to the inclusion of recycled late Roman glass in the 6th-century mosaics of the church of Hagios Polyeuktos. Given the presence of tin as an opacifier (lead stannate yellow) in the yellow and amber samples of this group (Poly-019, -025, -026), it is unlikely that these tesserae predate the 4th century, as it was only during that time that tin-based opacifiers started to replace antimony-based opacifiers in Mediterranean and European glass production (Freestone *et al.* 1990; Shortland 2002; Tite *et al.* 2008; Turner and Rooksby 1959; Heck and Hoffmann 2000; Heck *et al.* 2003; Moretti and Hreglich 1984). The three blue tesserae opacified by antimony (Poly-005, -006, -007) may be genuine Roman tesserae that were re-used in the 6th-century mosaics as opposed to recycled, *i.e.* re-melted, Roman glass. The main arguments for this are the presence of antimony that was no longer used after the 4th century (Sayre 1963; Tite *et al.* 2008; Turner and Rooksby 1959), the low level of contaminants as well as the fact that they are all dark cobalt blue samples that may have been more interesting for re-use. That Roman tesserae had been stored and re-used has been observed, for instance, with respect to opaque red glass tesserae from Beit Shean in Israel (Shugar 2000). The samples not containing any significant manganese or antimony levels on the other hand are not consistent with typical Roman base glass compositions, but might be related to the Levantine I glass type and more or less contemporary with the secondary production of the tesserae (*i.e.* 6th century) (Fig. 13.7). These tesserae are of different shades of turquoise and green and typically semi-opaque due to the presence of air bubbles, while some lead-tin opacification is seen in the green specimens (Table 13.1, Fig. 13.6).

It seems then that the tesserae assemblage from the church of Hagios Polyeuktos comprises varying soda-lime-silica raw glasses (at least 3) and different opacifying traditions (antimony and tin). Since antimony as an opacifier largely ceased to be used from the 4th century on (Sayre 1963; Tite *et al.* 2008; Turner and Rooksby 1959), the antimony-based samples are probably re-used Roman tesserae. The use of tin-based opacifiers prevailed from the later Roman and throughout the Byzantine and Islamic periods, hence does not allow for an unequivocal chronological attribution, except that tin-based opacification most likely post-dates the 4th century (Tite *et al.* 2008). A similarly eclectic mix of tesserae within an early Byzantine ecclesiastical context has been found also in 6th-century Ravenna (Brill 1999, section IX; Fiori *et al.* 2003) and Sagalassos, although in the latter no tin-based opacification has been identified and none of the mosaic tesserae from the Byzantine church there show comparable compositions (Schibille *et al.* 2012a). There is good agreement between both the manganese-rich tesserae and the antimony-rich tesserae from Hagios Polyeuktos and the 6th-century mosaics from San Vitale in Ravenna in terms of lime and alumina concentrations (Fig. 13.8). In addition to the base glass composition, the Ravenna assemblage shows remarkable similarities with the colour palette and the use of colourants and opacifiers of the high manganese tesserae from Hagios Polyeuktos. For instance, the San Vitale mosaics include different shades of blues and greens, amber, purple, red and turquoise as well as gold and silver leaf tesserae, with Fe, Cu, Mn and Co as the main chromophores and both antimony- as well as tin-based opacified samples alongside translucent glasses (Fiori *et al.* 2003). Some exceptional antimony-rich white tesserae are present at Ravenna that possibly point to the re-use of Roman tesserae, as tin-based opacifiers were more systematically used also in Italy from at least the 5th century on, even though antimony-opacified tesserae continued to be used (or more likely re-used) in Italy until the 13th century (Uboldi and Verità 2003). Other than that, the tesserae containing manganese at significant levels and those without manganese from Ravenna do not form separate groups and are thus not distinguished here. Some of the published data of mosaic tesserae from the church of Hagia Sophia in Istanbul (Brill 1999, section IX) are also consistent with these groups (*i.e.* Ravenna and manganese-rich Polyeuktos). Unfortunately, no information about the context of the Hagia Sophia tesserae is given by Brill.

A number of features are clearly common to all three 6th-century glass tesserae assemblages (*i.e.* San Vitale, Hagia Sophia, Hagios Polyeuktos). A large proportion of tesserae from all three sites have alumina levels between 2.2% and 2.7%, lime concentrations in the range from 7.6% to 9% as well as virtually identical silica to soda ratios (~ 3.5) (Figs. 13.8–13.9). Similar values are found in many of the Roman glasses from Italy dating to the 1st to 4th century, save for a trend of elevated lime concentrations in the 6th-century mosaics compared to the Roman glasses (Fig. 13.7). It seems then that many of the 6th-century mosaic tesserae from northern Italy as well as from the Byzantine capital are based on raw glass produced in the Roman tradition and from very similar silica sources. What is more, the tesserae were evidently produced from the same base glass independent of their colours. There may have been some recycled Roman glass used in the production of these 6th-century tesserae, given their similarities with Roman base glass compositions together with their relatively high levels of contaminants. However, contamination levels of transition metals commonly seen as indicators of recycling cannot be extrapolated to coloured glass that contain high levels of colourants such as mosaic tesserae, and a more conclusive working model for glass recycling is hence required for strongly coloured glasses (*e.g.* Freestone and Hughes 2006; Freestone *et al.* 2002; 2008a). Taken together, the evidence points to a certain centralisation of the manufacture of early Byzantine mosaic tesserae (including colouration and opacification). This, at least, seems to be true for major ecclesiastical foundations and decorative projects in Byzantine urban centres in the 6th century.

The situation at the church of Hagios Polyeuktos is more complex, however, because its assemblage includes a further type of soda-lime-silica glass. The tesserae from Hagios Polyeuktos without any manganese at significant levels have a close compositional relationship with Levantine I glasses from Apollonia-Arsuf and some from Jalame (Fig. 13.7), whereas none of the other available 6th-century mosaic tesserae show similar characteristics (Figs. 13.8–13.9). Hence, mosaic tesserae of a different primary glass type were also used in the decoration of Hagios Polyeuktos and not in the other chronologically and/or geographically related sites (*i.e.* Hagia Sophia, Ravenna, Sagalassos). Given that the Levantine I type glass was produced as late as the early Islamic period (Freestone *et al.* 2008b; Henderson *et al.* 2004), this second group of glass tesserae might represent a different *i.e.* later decoration campaign of the church, although it is equally possible that they are contemporary with the manganese-rich tesserae. The colour palette could provide indirect evidence that they were part of the 6th-century decoration because the low manganese samples exclusively comprise shades of green and turquoise (Table 13.1). If the different tesserae recovered from Hagios Polyeuktos were contemporary, the colour restriction of the low manganese glasses could be considered proof for the specialised production of green and turquoise coloured glasses. Such colour specialisation seems feasible in light of the fact that copper oxide in its divalent state (CuO) is responsible for both green and turquoise colours.

Although the dates of the individual tesserae tested from Hagios Polyeuktos are not provided by recorded archaeological contexts, their chemical compositions indicate a certain chronological span of the assemblage. The presence of antimony-based opacification in three cobalt blue samples may indicate the re-use of genuinely Roman (dark blue) tesserae, while the presence of plant-ash glasses testify to changes (repairs, redecoration or additions) to the mosaics of Hagios Polyeuktos sometime between the 9th and the late 12th or 13th century when the edifice fell into disrepair. Furthermore, it can be noted that the two main glass compositions identified among the set of tesserae tested from the church of Hagios Polyeuktos can be classified as late antique Roman type glasses (manganese-rich tesserae) also found in Hagia Sophia and at Ravenna, but in addition Hagios Polyeuktos has Byzantine Levantine I type glasses (low manganese samples).

Conclusion

The compositional data of glass mosaic tesserae unearthed at the 6th-century church of Hagios Polyeuktos at Saraçhane in Istanbul have shed new light on a number of key issues related to the manufacture of late antique and Byzantine glass mosaic tesserae. The analysis of 28 glass tesserae plus one window glass yielded three different natron-type glass groups plus two plant ash samples. The larger group of fourteen samples containing manganese in excess of 1% have low alumina, moderate lime and high soda levels consistent with 1st to 4th-century Roman glass from Italy. This suggests the possible inclusion of recycled Roman glass in the manufacture of some of the 6th-century tesserae. Contemporary mosaic assemblages from Hagia Sophia (Istanbul) and San Vitale (Ravenna) show similar compositional characteristics, which is interesting also in light of artistic parallels between San Vitale and Hagios Polyeuktos. Due to the similarities in the base glass composition it seems highly likely that the mosaic tesserae from all three sites were produced from the same raw material, which in turn suggests a certain centralisation of the production and trade of mosaic tesserae during the 6th century, similar to the Proconnesian marble capitals found in numerous Justinianic churches (McKenzie 2007, 336, 339, 343–344). A constant supply of mosaic tesserae was ascertained at least for major artistic campaigns in important Byzantine urban centres. At the same time, Roman tesserae were selectively re-used. For example, antimony-based tesserae were identified among the Hagios Polyeuktos assemblage that typically show low levels of alumina, lime and trace elements and are, as we have suggested, re-used Roman tesserae, despite their relatively low sodium concentrations. However, this is limited to one specific colour, namely dark cobalt blue. The San Vitale mosaics also yielded some antimony-opacified tesserae, but these are exclusively white and pinkish samples that differ in their overall composition from the antimony samples from Hagios Polyeuktos. These re-used tesserae have different base glass characteristics, implying that antimony was used as an opacifier in glasses of varying provenance. This selective re-use also indicates that some colours were highly priced and more difficult to produce or no longer produced in the 6th century, maybe due to shortages in the raw materials (*i.e.* cobalt, antimony) or the lack of technological skills (opacification through calcium antimonate).

Of particular note is the discovery of a further compositional group at Hagios Polyeuktos, which has no parallels among the other 6th-century mosaic tesserae analysed to date. The low manganese tesserae are relatively tightly clustered with high alumina and low soda and trace element concentrations. These tesserae were certainly produced from a silica source different to the high manganese specimens and may be related to the Levantine I primary glass production group. At this point it is impossible to tell whether these samples are contemporary with the manganese-rich glasses or later. What is noticeable is the restriction in colour of the low manganese group from Hagios Polyeuktos to only shades of green and turquoise and the fact that neither of the other sites (San Vitale, Hagia Sophia) display similar chemical compositions. This may be indicative of a colour specialisation along with a diversification in the manufacture of mosaic tesserae during the Byzantine period. In line with this interpretation, mosaic tesserae from other Byzantine ecclesiastical contexts have been found to have a wide compositional spread, reflecting a more diversified supply of tesserae than during the Roman period (Schibille *et al.* 2012a).

Acknowledgements

We wish to thank Elizabeth Harrison for her efforts in tracking down these unique samples, and to Marlia Mango for granting us access to the archive material at the Institute of Archaeology, University of Oxford, and John Hayes, for some helpful observations. We also thank Norman Charnley who has kindly provided technical help with the EPMA analyses and Laure Dussubieux for conducting the LA-ICP-MS analyses at the Field Museum of Natural History in Chicago. This research was supported by a Marie Curie Intra-European Fellowship within the 7th European Community Framework Programme (to NS).

Bibliography

Andreescu-Treadgold, I. and Henderson, J. (2006) Glass from the mosaics on the west wall of Torcello's Basilica. *Arte Medievale* 5, 87–140.

Arletti, R., Conte, S., Vandini, M., Fiori, C., Bracci, S., Bacci, M. and Porcinai, S. (2011) Florence baptistery: chemical and mineralogical investigation of glass mosaic tesserae. *Journal of Archaeological Science* 38, 79–88.

Arletti, R., Fiori, C. and Vandini, M. (2010) A study of glass tesserae from mosaics in the monasteries of Daphni and Hosios Loukas (Greece). *Archaeometry* 52, 796–815.

Arletti, R., Giordani, N., Rarpini, R. and Vezzalini, G. (2005) Archaeometrical analysis of glass of Western Emilia Romagna (Italy) from the imperial age. In *Annales du 16e Congrès de l'Association Internationale pour l'Histoire du Verre*, 80–84. Nottingham, Association Internationale pour l'Histoire du Verre.

Barber, D. J., Freestone, I. C. and Moulding, K. M. (2009) Ancient copper red glasses: investigation and analysis by microbeam techniques. In A. Shortland, I. C. Freestone and Th. Rehren (eds.) *From Mine to Microscope. Advances in the Study of Ancient Technology*, 115–127. Oxford, Oxbow Books.

Bardill, J. (1994) Brickstamps and the date of St Polyeuktos. *Bulletin of British Byzantine Studies* 20, 67.

Bardill, J (2004) *Brickstamps of Constantinople*. Oxford, Oxford University Press.

Bardill, J. (2006) A new temple for Byzantium: Anicia Juliana, King Solomon, and the gilded ceiling of the church of St. Polyeuktos in Constantinople. In W. Bowden, A. Gutteridge and C. Machado (eds.) *Social and Political Life in Late Antiquity*. Late Antique Archaeology 3.1, 339–370. Leiden, Brill.

Brill, R. H. (1999) *Chemical Analyses of Early Glasses*. Corning, NY, The Corning Museum of Glass.

Conner, C. L. (1999) The epigram in the church of Hagios Polyeuktos in Constantinople and its Byzantine response. *Byzantion* 69, 479–527.

Degryse, P. and Shortland, A. J. (2009) Trace Elements in provenancing raw materials for Roman glass production. *Geologica Belgica* 12, 135–143.

Deichmann, F. W. (1976) *Ravenna. Hauptstadt des spätantiken Abendlandes II. Kommentar Teil 2*. Wiesbaden, Franz Steiner.

Dunabin, K. M. D. (1999) *Mosaics of the Greek and Roman World*. Cambridge, Cambridge University Press.

Dussubieux, L., Robertshaw, P. and Glascock, M. D. (2009) LA-ICP-MS analysis of African glass beads: Laboratory inter-comparison with an emphasis on the impact of corrosion on data interpretation. *International Journal of Mass Spectrometry* 284, 152–161.

Fiori, C., Vandini, M. and Mazzotti, V. (2003) Colour and technology of mosaic "glazes" in the Justinian and Theodora's panels of the Basilica of San Vitale in Ravenna. *Ceramurgia + ceramic acta* 33, 135–154.

Fischer, A. and McCray, W. P. (1999) Glass production activities as practised at Sepphoris, Israel (37 BC–AD 1516). *Journal of Archaeological Science* 26, 893–905.

Fowden, G. (1994) Constantine, Silvester and the church of St Polyeuctus in Constantinople. *Journal of Roman Archaeology* 7, 274–284.

Foy, D., Picon, M., Vichy, M. and Thirion-Merle, V. (2003) Caractérisation des verres de la fin de l'Antiquité en Méditerranée occidentale: l'émergence de nouveaux courants commerciaux. In D. Foy and M.-D. Nenna (eds.) *Échanges et commerce du verre dans le monde antique*. Monographies Instrumentum 24, 41–85. Montagnac, Monique Mergoil.

Freestone, I. C. (2005) The provenance of ancient glass through compositional analysis. In P. B. Vandiver, J. L. Mass and A. Murray (eds.) *Materials Issues in Art and Archaeology VII*, 195–208. Warrendale, PA, Materials Research Society.

Freestone, I. C. (2006) Glass production in Late Antiquity and the Early Islamic period: a geochemical perspective. In M. Maggetti and B. Messiga (eds.) *Geomaterials in Cultural Heritage.* Geological Society Special Publications 257, 201–216. London, The Geological Society.

Freestone, I. C., Bimson, M. and Buckton, D. (1990) Compositional categories of Byzantine glass tesserae. In *Annales du 11e Congrès de l'Association Internationale pour l'Histoire du Verre,* 271–279. Amsterdam, Association Internationale pour l'Histoire du Verre.

Freestone, I. C. and Gorin-Rosen, Y. (1999) The great glass slab at Bet-She'arim, Israel: An early Islamic glassmaking experiment? *Journal of Glass Studies* 41, 105–116.

Freestone, I. C., Gorin-Rosen, Y. and Hughes, M. J. (2000) Primary glass from Israel and the production of glass in late antiquity and the Early Islamic period. In M.-D. Nenna (ed.) *La route du verre. Ateliers primaires et secondaires du second millénaire av. J.C. au Moyen Âge.* Travaux de la Maison de l'Orient Méditerranéen 33, 65–83. Lyon, Maison de l'Orient Méditerranéen.

Freestone, I. C. and Hughes, M. J. (2006) The origins of the Jarrow glass. In R. Cramp (ed.) *Wearmouth and Jarrow Monastic Sites* 2, 147–155. Swindon, English Heritage.

Freestone, I. C., Hughes, M. J. and Stapleton, C. P. (2008a) The composition and production of Anglo-Saxon Glass. In I. V. Evison, *Catalogue of Anglo-Saxon Glass in the British Museum.* British Museum Research Publication 167, 29–46. London, British Museum Press.

Freestone, I. C., Jackson-Tal, R. E. and Tal, O. (2008b) Raw glass and the production of glass vessels at late Byzantine Apollonia-Arsuf, Israel. *Journal of Glass Studies* 50, 67–80.

Freestone, I. C., Ponting, M. and Hughes, M. J. (2002) The origins of Byzantine glass from Maroni Petrera, Cyprus. *Archaeometry* 44, 257–272.

Freestone, I. C., Stapleton, C. P. and Rigby, V. (2003) The production of red glass and enamel in the Late Iron Age, Roman and Byzantine periods. In C. Entwistle (ed.) *Through a Glass Brightly. Studies in Byzantine and Medieval Art and Archaeology presented to David Buckton,* 142–154. Oxford, Oxbow Books.

Gedzevičiūtė, V., Welter, N., Schüssler, U. and Weiss, C. (2009) Chemical composition and colouring agents of Roman mosaic and millefiori glass, studied by electron microprobe analysis and Raman microspectroscopy. *Archaeological and Anthropological Science* 1, 15–29.

Gorin-Rosen, Y. (1995) Hadera, Bet Eli'ezer. *Excavations and Surveys in Israel* 13, 42–43.

Gorin-Rosen, Y. (2000) The ancient glass industry in Israel – summary of the finds and new discoveries. In M.-D. Nenna (ed.) *La route du verre. Ateliers primaires et secondaires du second millénaire av. J.C. au Moyen Âge.* Travaux de la Maison de l'Orient Méditerranéen 33, 49–63. Lyon, Maison de l'Orient Méditerranéen.

Gratuze, B. and Barrandon, J. N. (1990) Islamic glass weights and stamps – analysis using nuclear techniques. *Archaeometry* 32, 155–162.

Green, L. R. and Hart, F. A. (1987) Colour and chemical composition in ancient glass: An examination of some Roman and Wealden glass by means of ultraviolet-visible-infra-red spectrometry and electron microprobe analysis. *Journal of Archaeological Science* 14, 271–282.

Harrison, R. M. (1984) The church of St. Polyeuktos in Istanbul and the Temple of Solomon. In C. Mango and O. Pritsak (eds.) *Okeanos. Essays Presented to Ihor Sevcenko on his Sixtieth Birthday by his Colleagues and Students.* Harvard Ukrainian Studies 7, 276–279. Cambridge, MA, Ukrainian Research Institute, Harvard University.

Harrison, R. M. (1986) *Excavations at Saraçhane in Istanbul 1. The Excavations, Structures, Architectural Decoration, Small Finds, Coins, Bones, and Molluscs.* Princeton, NJ, Princeton University Press and Dumbarton Oaks Research Library and Collection.

Harrison, R. M. (1989) *A Temple for Byzantium. The Discovery and Excavation of Anicia Juliana's Palace-Church in Istanbul.* London, Harvey Miller.

Heck, M. and Hoffmann, P. (2000) Coloured opaque glass beads of the Merovingians. *Archaeometry* 42, 341–357.

Heck, M., Rehren, Th. and Hoffmann, P. (2003) The production of lead-tin yellow at Merovingian Schleitheim (Switzerland). *Archaeometry* 45, 33–44.

Henderson, J. (1985) The raw materials of early glass production. *Oxford Journal of Archaeology* 4, 267–291.

Henderson, J., McLoughlin, S. D. and McPhail, D. S. (2004) Radical changes in Islamic glass technology: Evidence for conservatism and experimentation with new glass recipes from early and middle Islamic Raqqa, Syria. *Archaeometry* 46, 439–468.

James, L. (2006) Byzantine glass mosaic tesserae: some material considerations. *Byzantine and Modern Greek Studies* 30, 29–47.

James, L. (2010) Byzantine mosaics and glass: a problematic relationship. In J. Drauschke and D. Keller (eds.) *Glass in Byzantium – Production, Usage, Analyses.* RGZM – Tagungen 8, 237–243. Mainz, Römisch-Germanisches Zentralmuseum.

Kamber, B. S., Greig, A. and Collerson, K. D. (2005) A new estimate for the composition of weathered young upper continental crust from alluvial sediments, Queensland, Australia. *Geochimica et Cosmochimica Acta,* 69, 1041–1058.

Lahlil, S., Biron, I., Galoisy, L. and Morin, G. (2008) Rediscovering ancient glass technologies through the examination of opacifier crystals. *Applied Physics a-Materials Science & Processing,* 92, 109–116.

Mango, C. and Sevcenko, I. (1961) Remains of the Church of St. Polyeuktos at Constantinople. *Dumbarton Oaks Papers* 15, 243–247.

Marii, F. and Rehren, Th. (2009) Archaeological coloured glass cakes and tesserae from the Petra church. In K. Janssens, P. Degryse, P. Cosyns, J. Caen and L. Van't dack (eds.) *Annales du 17e Congrès de l'Association Internationale pour l'Histoire du Verre,* 295–300. Brussels, University Press Antwerp.

McKenzie, J. (2007) *The Architecture of Alexandria and Egypt 300 BC – AD 700.* New Haven, CT/London, Yale University Press.

Milner, C. (1994) The image of the rightful ruler: Anicia Juliana's Constantine mosaic in the Church of Hagios Polyeuktos. In P. Magdalino (ed.) *New Constantines. The Rhythm of Imperial Renewal in Byzantium, 4th–13th Centuries,* 73–81. Aldershot, Variorum Ashgate.

Mirti, P., Casoli, A. and Appolonia, L. (1993) Scientific analysis of Roman glass from Augusta-Praetoria. *Archaeometry* 35, 225–240.

Mirti, P., Davit, P. and Gulmini, M. (2001) Glass fragments from the Crypta Balbi in Rome: The composition of eighth-century fragments. *Archaeometry* 43, 491–502.

Mirti, P., Lepora, A. and Sagui, L. (2000) Scientific analysis of seventh-century glass fragments from the Crypta Balbi in Rome. *Archaeometry* 42, 359–374.

Mirti, P., Pace, M., Negro Ponzi, M. M. and Aceto, M. (2008) ICP–MS analyses of glass fragments of Parthian and Sasanian epoch from Seleucia and Veh Ardasir (central Iraq). *Archaeometry* 50, 429–450.

Moretti, C. and Gratuze, B. (2002) Vetri romani di Aquileia e di altri siti europei: analisi chimiche e studio comparativo. *Rivista della Stazione Sperimentale del Vetro* 32, 19–28.

Moretti, C. and Hreglich, S. (1984) Opacification and coloring of glass by the use of anime. *Glass Technology* 25, 277–282.

Mundell Mango, M. (1992) The monetary value of silver revetments and objects belonging to churches, A.D. 300–700. In S. A. Boyd and M. Mundell Mango (eds.) *Ecclesiastical Silver Plate in Sixth-Century Byzantium*, 123–136. Washington, D.C., Dumbarton Oaks Research Library and Collection.

Ousterhout, R. (2010) New Temples and new Solomons: the rhetoric of Byzantine architecture. In P. Magdalino and R. Nelson (eds.) *The Old Testament in Byzantium*, 223–253. Washington, D.C., Dumbarton Oaks Research Library and Collection.

Paynter, S. and Kearns, T. (2011) *West Clacton Reservoir, Great Bentley, Essex. Analysis of Glass Tesserae*. Research Department Report Series. Portsmouth, English Heritage.

Picon, M. and Vichy, M. (2003) D'orient en occident: l'origine du verre à l'époque romaine et durant le haute Moyen Âge. In D. Foy and M.-D. Nenna (eds.) *Échanges et commerce du verre dans le monde antique*. Monographies Instrumentum 24, 17–31. Montagnac, Monique Mergoil.

Sayre, E. V. (1963) The intentional use of antimony and manganese in ancient glasses. In F. R. Matson and G. E. Rindone (eds.) *Advances in Glass Technology, Part 2*, 263–282. New York, NY, Plenum Press.

Sayre, E. V. and Smith, R. W. (1961) Compositional categories of ancient glass. *Science,* 133, 1824–1826.

Schibille, N. (2011) Supply routes and the consumption of glass in first millennium CE Butrint (Albania). *Journal of Archaeological Science* 38, 2939–2948.

Schibille, N., Degryse, P., Corremans, M. and Specht, C. G. (2012a) Chemical characterisation of glass mosaic tesserae from sixth-century Sagalassos (south-west Turkey): chronology and production techniques. *Journal of Archaeological Science* 39, 1480–1492.

Schibille, N., Degryse, P., O'Hea, M., Izmer, A., Vanhaecke, F. and McKenzie, J. (2012b) Late Roman glass from the 'Great Temple' at Petra and Khirbet et-Tannur, Jordan - Technology and provenance. *Archaeometry* 54, 997–1022.

Shortland, A. J. (2002) The use and origin of antimonate colorants in early Egyptian glass. *Archaeometry* 44, 517–530.

Shortland, A., Schachner, L., Freestone, I. C. and Tite, M. (2006a) Natron as a flux in the early vitreous materials industry: sources, beginnings and reasons for decline. *Journal of Archaeological Science* 33, 521–530.

Shortland, A. J., Tite, M. S. and Ewart, I. (2006b) Ancient exploitation and use of cobalt alums from the western oases of Egypt. *Archaeometry* 48, 153–168.

Shugar, A. N. (2000) Byzantine opaque red glass tesserae from Beit Shean, Israel. *Archaeometry* 42, 375–384.

Silvestri, A. (2008) The coloured glass of Iulia Felix. *Journal of Archaeological Science* 35, 1489–1501.

Silvestri, A., Molin, G. and Salviulo, G. (2005) Roman and medieval glass from the Italian area: Bulk characterization and relationships with production technologies. *Archaeometry* 47, 797–816.

Silvestri, A., Molin, G. and Salviulo, G. (2008) The colourless glass of Iulia Felix. *Journal of Archaeological Science* 35, 331–341.

Sodini, J.-P. (1993) La contribution de l'archéologie à la connaissance du monde byzantin (IVe–VIIe siècles). *Dumbarton Oaks Papers* 47, 139–184.

Tite, M., Pradell, T. and Shortland, A. (2008) Discovery, production and use of tin-based opacifiers in glasses, enamels and glazes from the late iron age onwards: A reassessment. *Archaeometry* 50, 67–84.

Turner, W. E. S. and Rooksby, H. P. (1959) A study of the opalising agents in ancient opal glasses throughout three thousand four hundred years. *Glastechnische Berichte, Sonderband* 32K, 17–28.

Uboldi, M. and Verità, M. (2003) Scientific analyses of glasses from Late Antique and Early Medieval archaeological sites in northern Italy. *Journal of Glass Studies* 45, 115–137.

Van Der Werf, I., Mangone, A., Giannossa, L. C., Traini, A., Laviano, R., Coralini, A. and Sabbatini, L. (2009) Archaeometric investigation of Roman tesserae from Herculaneum (Italy) by the combined use of complementary micro-destructive analytical techniques. *Journal of Archaeological Science* 36, 2625–2634.

Wedepohl, K. H. and Simon, K. (2010) The chemical composition of medieval wood ash glass from Central Europe. *Chemie der Erde-Geochemistry* 70, 89–97.

Wedepohl, K. H., Simon, K. and Kronz, A. (2011) Data on 61 chemical elements for the characterization of three major glass compositions in Late Antiquity and the Middle Ages. *Archaeometry* 53, 81–102.

Weyl, W. A. (1953) *Coloured Glass*. Sheffield, Society of Glass Technology.

Whitby, M. (2006) The St Polyeuktos epigram (*AP* 1.10): A literary perspective. In S. F. Johnson (ed.) *Greek Literature in Late Antiquity. Dynamism, Didacticism, Classicism*, 159–187. Aldershot, Ashgate.

14

Successors of Rome? Byzantine glass mosaics

Liz James

Byzantine wall and ceiling mosaics are one of the most familiar things about Byzantine art, perhaps the most recognisable aspect of Byzantine art. They were the most elaborate and probably most expensive form of wall decoration used in Byzantium and they survive in churches and mosques across the Mediterranean world from Spain, Italy and Greece in the west, to Syria and Israel in the east, taking in the Ukraine and Georgia to the north and Egypt to the south. But in what ways were Byzantine glass mosaics successors of Roman mosaics? As an art form, they clearly developed from the wall and vault mosaics in use in the Roman period and across the Roman empire. In this context, this paper will briefly look at what is known of the development of wall and vault mosaics in the Roman world and will consider what can be said about the glass used in their manufacture.

In this context, the mosaics of Sta Costanza in Rome and the so-called Mausoleum of Galla Placidia offer an interesting comparison over a period of some one hundred years about the relationships between wall and floor mosaics and the changing nature of the media used in wall mosaics. The building known now as the church of Sta Costanza in Rome is a 4th-century rotunda which was the mausoleum of Constantina, the daughter of Constantine the Great (Stanley 2004). In contrast, the cross-shaped building known as the mausoleum of Galla Placidia in Ravenna was almost certainly not the burial place of the 5th-century western empress Galla Placidia but was more probably built by her as a martyrium or private chapel (Deliyannis 2010, 74–84). Both buildings and indeed both sets of mosaics can be – and are – characterised as late antique or late Roman or even early Christian but the wall mosaics of both offer very different insights into mosaic techniques and media.

The mosaics of the vaults of Sta Costanza are very close to Roman floor mosaics both in design and in medium. The ceiling of the ambulatory of the building is divided into eleven panels which are arranged symmetrically. Six basic mosaic designs were used: geometric shapes (lozenges, octagons, crosses); dolphins 'attacking' octopi; cupids and psyches; inhabited vine scrolls and scenes of putti harvesting grapes; roundels with busts and figures interspersed with floral patterns; and a apparently more random device incorporating scattered plants, birds, fruits and flowers (Stern 1958). The design owes something to stuccoed ceilings but in appearance, in part because of the use of enclosing compartments for the design elements, these mosaics are very strongly reminiscent of the sorts of patterns and motifs found on Roman floor mosaics. Most notably, the formal roundels and geometric designs are a staple of floors, a design that continued in use in Byzantine floor mosaics, and the more scattered scenes, evocative of the well-known 'unswept floor' type of design, are echoed in North African mosaic floors (Dunbabin 1999, 26–27, 248–249). The comparison is maintained because, like floor mosaics, these mosaics are largely made of stone, with glass, including gold glass, used predominantly as highlights.

In contrast, the mosaics of the vaults of Galla Placidia's chapel are closer to what might be conceptualised as 'Byzantine' wall and ceiling mosaics. The vaulting of the north and south arms of the building is decorated with a geometric, but non-compartmentalised, design of large and small rosettes; those of the east and west arms with a vine motif growing from an acanthus with a chi-rho contained in a wreath at the crown of the vault. A series of different borders are used on the arches supporting the central tower. These include a sort of 'fish scale' pattern (north and south), a three-dimensional meander design (east) and garland of fruits and plants (west). In the central vault, a design of gold stars swirl up towards a central cross, with the four evangelist symbols at each corner. These designs are not unique to the chapel or indeed to wall and vault mosaics. Floral wreaths and vine motifs appear on floor mosaics. A blue dome filled with stars is a well-known Roman decorative feature, a version of which is found in Sta Costanza, though here dark blue stars on a white background are used. However, the mosaics in Galla's chapel are less immediately evocative of floor mosaics. What makes them very different to those of Sta Costanza is the extensive use of coloured glass. The use of stone in Sta Costanza creates a static, 'matt' feel in which the coloured and gold glass tesserae glimmer and serve to highlight elements of the design. These elements certainly make the mosaics feel 'richer' in appearance than the stone tesserae of floor mosaics. However, in Galla's chapel, these impressions are pushed much further. Here the quantity of glass used means that the mosaics have a changing, reflective appearance. The tesserae act as a series of mirrors, reflecting and refracting light in different directions and so causing a sense of shifting colour and light. Further, the colours of the two sets of mosaics are quite different. In Sta Costanza, the hues tend to be those of stone: whites, greys and the like. These are relatively dull in comparison to Galla's chapel, where blue, green, gold and red glass tesserae dominate, leading to a brighter, more vivid colouristic effect (Figs. 14.1–14.2).

Sta Costanza is dated to the mid 4th century (Johnson 2009, 139–143); Galla Placidia's chapel to perhaps the mid 430s (Deliyannis, 2010, 74). The contrast between the mosaics of the two buildings reflects something of the development in wall mosaic design and techniques in this period. They also raise questions about relationship between

Fig. 14.1: The mosaics of Sta Costanza, Rome, 4th century (photo Iuliana Gavril).

Fig. 14.2: The mosaics of the 'Mausoleum' of Galla Placidia, Ravenna, 5th century (photo Liz James).

floor and wall mosaics and the transition of media, from stone to glass. In the context of this paper, I will sketch something of the former relationship before moving to look in more detail about the question of media and the growing role of glass in wall and vault mosaics.

It has been believed on the basis of Sta Costanza that wall and vault mosaics were invented in the early 4th century, deriving from floor mosaics, and were first used on a large scale in Christian buildings. It is clear why the mosaics of Sta Costanza, with their repertoire of themes and use of stone could lead to this belief, especially when coupled with what has been seen as an apparent lack of evidence for wall mosaics from before the 4th century. However, as Frank Sear (1977, 29–30) pointed out, it is an idea founded more on a lack of awareness of the evidence than a shortage of actual material. It is true that floor mosaics last better than wall mosaics: floors tend to survive better in the archaeological record than walls, vaults and domes; and glass stuck into plaster on walls is a relatively fragile medium, prone to falling off. Nevertheless, there is a great deal of evidence for Roman wall mosaics; the problem is that it exists mostly in the form of fragments and loose tesserae. Many Roman buildings show traces of mosaic on walls in the form of fragments of mosaic, loose tesserae on the ground and imprints on mortar but it can be the case that these details are not recorded by those working on the buildings. Excavation reports can report simply that tesserae were recovered from a site without being more specific about the type of tesserae and whether they might relate to wall or floor mosaics. One extreme example is a report on a structure on Kos that simply recorded the existence of fifteen loose tesserae (Aleura *et al.* 1990, 356).

In 1977, Sear produced what remains the standard catalogue of Roman wall and vault mosaics with 305 extant examples, dating largely between the 3rd and 4th centuries, but with a few from the 1st century BC and the 1st and 2nd centuries, and a handful going into the 5th century (Sear 1977; but also Stern 1959). The bulk of Sear's examples came from Italy, 162 of the 305, in all. The eastern provinces, by which Sear meant Bulgaria, Cyprus, Greece and Turkey, provided another nine examples, North Africa 60, and Europe 72 across nine countries. Sear's book is an invaluable reference work and my comments here should not be taken as critical of it. Rather, between 1977 and 2012, more examples of early wall and vault mosaics have surfaced, including a 1st-century BC example from Capri (Budetta 2005/06) and a wall mosaic in the Colosseum in Rome (http://www.bbc.co.uk/news/world-europe-14356604; accessed January 31st 2012), and another seventeen 3rd to 4th-century wall mosaics from Turkey, Greece, Israel, Jordan and Italy are listed on the Leverhulme Byzantine Glass Mosaic project website (http://www.sussex.ac.uk/byzantine/research/mosaictesserae). Increasingly, more collections of glass tesserae are being both found and recorded, as for example, the 1268 tesserae excavated at Union Street, London or those found at the West Clacton Reservoir site and dated to the 1st or 2nd centuries (Angela Wardle pers. comm.; Paynter and Kearns 2011). It seems likely that these finds had some connection with mosaic-making.

Significantly, Sear's work made it apparent that mosaics on walls were in existence well before Sta Costanza, from the time of the Roman republic; indeed, Katherine Dunbabin (1999, 236) has suggested that wall mosaics were essentially a Roman invention. These early wall mosaics were, as is well-known, used in the creation of artificial grottoes and nymphaea (Sear 1975, 83–97; Lavagne 1988, 411–37). Such cave-like features were an essential part of the fixtures and fittings of the luxury villa, playing off tensions between rusticity and art whilst providing a shady place for the villa owner to entertain and relax. However, the best-known early wall mosaics are those from Pompeii and Herculaneum and these belong lower down the social scale, from middle and lower middle class settings (Sear 1977, cat. nos. 14, 16, 26, 27, 29, 32, 34–38, 45, 48, 50, 51, 64–69, 71, 72; Dunbabin 1999, 242–243 sets out the evidence for the dating of these mosaics). The location of these mosaics underlines their social significance for the people of Pompeii, where keeping up with the neighbours seems to have been a basic rule of life. They often replace earlier painted decorations, cutting through them, and many are located so that they could be seen from the main door of the house (Dunbabin 1999, 242–243). Although the medium of mosaic, both floor and wall, tends to be associated with large, expensive projects, its use down the social scale should not be overlooked, and this continued to be true in the Byzantine period also. There are quite a few eastern sites where evidence for glass wall mosaics comes from small-scale often anonymous buildings, such as Building 3,5 at Anemurium (Gough *et al.* 1967; Stern 1985) and from relatively small and, relative to Rome, unimportant places: a church with an unknown dedication on Kos (Aleura *et al.* 1990); a church at Çiftlik in the Pontos (Hill 1995); a cave church at Meryemlik in Cilicia (Herzfeld and Guyer 1930), all appear to have traces of 4th-century glass wall mosaics. As the evidence at Pompeii suggested for the 1st century, the use of mosaic was not an automatic sign of status and acculturation, or an indicator of wealth and prestige, or of a medium increasingly restricted to secular and religious rulers.

After Pompeii, the evidence for wall mosaics is patchy and sporadic. It seems they increased in scale and popularity. An increased use of vaulting in Roman architecture, especially in baths, provided another set of locations for wall mosaics, perhaps also as a result of the increased use of concrete. Wall mosaic was an increasingly popular form of decoration among the great imperial builders such as Nero, Domitian and Hadrian and, later in the baths of Caracalla and Diocletian (Lavagne 1988; 1970; Sear 1977, cat. no.

61; DeLaine 1997). By the 2nd century, wall mosaics were also used in Mithraea, where they shared the same cave or grotto theme as those in private nymphaea, and then later, retaining the religious theme, in catacombs, surviving in both Rome and Naples (Sear 1977, cat. nos. 112–118 (Mithraea); 152–162 (catacombs)). A further reciprocal influence between floor and wall mosaics is apparent in, for example, the extension of floor mosaics without a break up the walls of buildings (Dunbabin 1999, 246).

An important consideration in this discussion is how far wall mosaics should be seen as a Roman or Italian preserve or whether they were far more widespread than this would suggest. In this context, the proportion of floor mosaics across the empire would be worth knowing. Sear's figures, with the bulk of his 305 wall and vault mosaics located in Italy, Europe and North Africa, suggests the former. The inferences from this are that wall mosaics were very much a Roman or Italian medium and, potentially, that when mosaic was used as a medium elsewhere in the empire, a centre to periphery model might be envisaged: the weight of numbers suggests a mosaic industry based in Rome or Italy that spread outwards. However, there is a gap in the data about wall mosaics in the eastern empire and some striking absences from the archaeological record. If the western empire used mosaic on a large scale in its houses, fountains, Mithraea and baths, is it not likely that other major cities across the empire, such as Antioch, Alexandria and Ephesos, were following the fashion and doing the same? If they were not, why was this the case?

Almost no evidence survives about the craftsmen who put up wall mosaics. Although it is seems possible that there were two sets of Latin terms reflecting floor and wall mosaicists, *pavimentarii/tesserarii* for the former and *museiarii/musivarii* for the latter, as distinguished in the Price Edict of Diocletian, these may have reflected a difference in types of floor mosaicist (Dunbabin 1999, 275–276, note 39). An implicit assumption in mosaic studies is that the mosaicists themselves must have been based in major cities and that where mosaics are found outside the empire, they must reflect an import or a borrowing of techniques, workmen and material (discussed in James 2006). But this too is questionable in the context of the distribution of wall mosaics and, indeed, in terms of what is known about the manufacture of floor mosaics. For floor mosaics, a model of localised or regionalised workshops in parts of the Roman world is popular (see Dunbabin 1999, 269–278; also Zohar 2006 summarising earlier work), though definitions of the term 'workshop' can vary considerably. Would a similar model work for wall mosaics as they became an increasingly popular art form or were there never enough wall and vault mosaics to suppose anything other than a peripatetic group of artists? Price's (2005, 178) model of itinerant glass workers is one that would, for very similar reasons, work well for wall mosaicists.

What can be concluded at the moment is little more than that between the 1st and 4th centuries, wall mosaic was used alike for secular commissions and religious, public and private in both spheres, and across the social scale. These are all features that continue in its use in Byzantium and that it would also be used in this way in Christian architecture, especially that commissioned by emperors, is unsurprising. Sta Costanza was not a starting point for monumental wall mosaics, but rather a point in their use.

The issue with Sta Costanza and its mosaics, especially in comparison with Galla Placidia's is more to do with the materials used, the emphasis on stone which created the misleading scholarly over-emphasis on floor mosaics. Sear's figures also have implications for the materials of wall mosaic: should it be assumed that the glass for mosaics was made primarily in Italy or even in Rome itself? Further, just as Italy had its glass industry, so too we know that the eastern provinces did and so this raises questions about the type of glass produced in the east; did mosaic tesserae or the glass for tesserae come only from Rome and Italy?

So what of the glass? When did glass begin to be used in wall mosaics and in what form? Threaded glass rods, usually in yellow, white and blue or white and blue, seem to have been used perhaps to middle of 1st century; bits of broken glass vessels and glass disks were also used in the earliest examples (Sear 1977, 39–43; Dunbabin 1999, 238; Boschetti *et al.* 2008 in the context of *opus vermiculatum*). Coloured glass started to appear on walls and vaults perhaps at start of the 1st century, though, obviously, it was used in floor mosaics from much earlier (Sear 1975, 95). Pliny (Natural History 36,189) mentioned that glass mosaics on vaults were a new invention (during the 1st century) and were not present in Agrippa's baths in the Augustan period. The relationship between glass mosaic tesserae and *opus sectile*, however, remains to be discussed (Verità *et al.* 2008a; 2008b). Glass tesserae, which is to say deliberately cut cubes of glass, were used for figured subjects in floor mosaics certainly from the Hellenistic period on; at the moment, their earliest appearance in wall mosaics seems to be in the late Tiberian period, perhaps in the tomb known as the Colombarium of Pomponius Hylas in Rome (Ashby 1910; Sear 1977, cat. no. 25, colour pl. A; Lavagne 1988, 408–409). Here, glass tesserae are used over the entrance to the columbarium on a mosaic plaque with the names of Pomponius Hylas and his wife. The plaque is capped with murex shells and outlined in twisted glass rods. Although most of the decoration is in shell, pumice, white stone and Egyptian blue, glass tesserae in yellow, green and blue are used, for example, in the waves of the border and in details of the griffins at the base of the plaque.

It is from this point, especially with the survivals at Pompeii and Herculaneum, that wall mosaics broke away from the monotone rusticity of the browns, greys and drab stones and shells of the grottoes and expanded into creations of great colour, splendour and fantasy. Increasingly, as the mosaics of Nero's Golden House reveal, glass tesserae were used in the composition of figural images. In the Golden House, green, brown and even gold glass tesserae survive in the composition of Odysseus and the Cyclops (Sear 1977, cat. no. 61; Dunbabin 1999, 241), and what little remain of these mosaics suggest that they must have been spectatcular. A 2nd or early 3rd-century detached mosaic panel now in the Palazzo dei Conservatori in Rome but originally from the nymphaeum of a house attributed to Titus Claudius Claudianus on the Quirinal, shows a scene of a harbour with a ship underway (Sear 1977, cat. no. 123, colour pl. C). It is composed from a mixture of glass, including blue, red and white, and stone, but also shows also how mosaicists used mosaic as if the medium were paint, using small tesserae, and modelling carefully with delicate gradations of colour. Glass, of course, was a wonderful medium to use in the context of water and garden architecture, and the Romans seem to have been well-attuned to this. Even the lower class mosaics in Pompeii display a level of bright colour achievable through a use of glass rather than stone.

After AD 79, the evidence for glass in wall mosaics is more restricted, just as the evidence for wall mosaics themselves is restricted to chance finds, fragments and traces. However, it is clear that glass mosaic tesserae were in use on a large scale on the walls of baths by the 2nd century, at Optis and Leptis Magna (Sear 1977, cat. nos. 177–178), for example, as well as at Carthage (Sear 1977, cat. no. 194), and in the Baths of Caracalla and Diocletian in Rome (DeLaine 1997). By the late 3rd century, and almost certainly earlier, glass tesserae were used in the great halls of imperial palaces, as is the case with Diocletian's Palace in Split (Wilkes 1986). Even then, as at Sta Costanza, a wide range of other materials, including stone and shell, continued to be used in wall mosaics. Indeed, the use of these other media never died out in Byzantine mosaics; it simply diminished in quantity and was used for the creation of deliberate visual effects. What is also apparent in the surviving use of glass in Roman wall and vault mosaics is a developing appreciation of the potential of the medium on a curved surface: of using glass as a sparkling, reflective surface, playing with light and very different to the effect of stone, pottery or shell (James 1996, 19–46). This, of course, was a feature that the Byzantines exploited fully, but the effect of sheets of gold tesserae on the vaulting of, say, the Baths of Caracalla and of Diocletian, suggests that the Romans were not blind to it.

What is known about glass mosaic tesserae from the Roman period and later is limited (James 2006). There is almost no evidence for where the glass tesserae in late antique mosaics came from and it is not clear where the making of coloured tesserae fits into models of primary and secondary glass-making, distribution and trade (see the questions raised in Nenna 2007a and Nenna 2007b).

Evidence suggests that tesserae were cut from sheets or cakes of glass: this is one of the interpretations of these objects at sites such as Philippi (Antonaras 2007, 54–55), Petra (Marii 2001, 379) and Jerash (Baur 1938, 517–518). It is not known, however, whether glass foundries turned out these sheets as a primary process, making coloured glass, or whether raw glass was coloured as a secondary process. Further, it is uncertain whether specialised 'factories', for want of a better word, were responsible for either making coloured raw glass or for colouring raw glass or whether glass was coloured on site (and if so, by whom?). Strabo (16,2,25), writing in the Augustan period, mentioned that glass was produced in Rome during his time (cf. Price 2005, 169) whilst Pliny said that glass was produced in Campania from his own time, the early Flavian period (Natural History 36,194), so there was no real technical reason that tesserae could not have been made in Italy; however, no physical evidence survives about tesserae-making.

As Paynter and Kearns (2011, 5) point out, it has not yet been established exactly how Roman coloured glass was made. Their analysis of tesserae from the West Clacton reservoir site found that most of these tesserae were coloured by the required colourants and opacifiers being added to the natron-base 'colourless' glass (Paynter and Kearns 2011, 37). However, red glass tesserae and some of the green glass tesserae were produced from a plant ash glass. Paynter and Kearns (2011, 37, 38, 42) make it clear that the colouring could have taken place at the stage of manufacture of the raw glass or by mixing colourants (even in the form of recycled vessel glass) with the base glass in a workshop, but propose that the red and green plant ash glasses may have been made at specialised production sites. In a Byzantine context, Ian Freestone et al. (2003) have argued that raw glass was coloured in specialised workshops, an argument that deals effectively with the difficult technical issues involved in colouring glass in the medieval period. This is also a model that Fatma Marii and Thilo Rehren have suggested on a more localised basis at Petra (Marii and Rehren 2009). They propose that transparent glass was collected on site for recycling, re-melted and formed into glass cakes to which colourants were added at a later stage to make the colours for the tesserae. What is crucial here, however, is that this took place on site, implying the manufacture of both cakes and tesserae as required. The same model would seem plausible for the Roman period, but I am unaware of any material evidence that would support it.

How the making of coloured glass tesserae is modelled has implications for how we reconstruct the making of actual mosaics. If mosaicists coloured their glass on site, then it increased the range of colours available to them; if they bought and brought in already coloured tesserae, then the appearance of the actual mosaic was already conditioned by the imported supplies. To use a colour, the artist must be able to make it or have it to hand. Evidence from slightly later, in the 6th-century mosaics of the Euphrasian basilica at Poreć in Croatia, appears to show mosaicists running short of coloured glass tesserae and improvising in other materials (Terry and Maguire 2007). In the apse mosaic, for example, lime green tesserae are used to eke out the gold tesserae; in the side apses, glass is used very sparingly (Terry and Maguire 2007, 79–82). This shows a clear awareness on the part of the mosaicists for what they could get away with visually when the mosaics were viewed from a distance.

It has been said that Roman glass mosaic tesserae came in 'an almost infinite variety of colours' (Sear 1977, 41). On the basis of examining several hundred glass tesserae from about 50 sites in Italy and North Africa between 1st and 3rd centuries, Sear believed that practically any shade of colour could be obtained in glass, and that no colour was exclusive to any period. Whilst it is true that almost any shade of colour could be obtained in glass, in light of what is currently known about Roman and late antique glass technology, its production was more than likely fortuitous than deliberate. This colour range perhaps says more about technical issues than technical skill. The first was knowing what ingredients to add to the raw glass in the first place; the second was knowing how to add it because conditions of manufacture such as the heat of the furnace, the base composition of the glass, the temperature reached in the furnace and the duration of that temperature were all additional factors affecting the colour of the finished product (Henderson 2000, 29–38). Newton (1980, 173–183) argued that it was improbable that ancient glassmakers added small proportions of colourants, suggesting that they did not have the chemical knowledge necessary and Freestone *et al.* (1990) came to a similar conclusion in the specific case of red tesserae.

Sear listed shades of blue and turquoise as the most common colours in his sample, then green, then a range of yellows, browns, purples, reds, oranges, black and white glass. The tesserae were analysed and shown to be a soda-lime-silica glass, opacified with calcium and lead antimonate; copper, cobalt, manganese and chromium are said to have been used as colourants (Sear 1977, 42). The presence of chromium is very odd since it was not used in Roman glass as a colourant; it seems not to have been used before the 19th century. Otherwise the results match with the colourants of Roman glass more generally (Weyl 1953; Gedzevičiūtė *et al.* 2009; Van Der Werf *et al.* 2009; Paynter and Kearns 2011). What is also interesting is that tin began to replace replace antimony as an opacifier at sometime between the 2nd and 5th centuries, but there appears to be no evidence of that in these samples (Turner and Rooksby 1959; Sayre 1963; Tite *et al.* 2008).

Analyses of 5h-century Italian, Jordanian and Syrian glasses suggest that 5th-century glass is generally of the natron-type, probably produced from sands on the Levantine coast, but some variations are apparent. Examples of this Levantine-type glass was identified in Byzantine mosaic assemblages such as the tesserae from 5th-century Shikmona, Israel (Freestone *et al.* 1990), and those from San Vitale in Ravenna, dated to the 6th century (Fiori *et al.* 2003), from the 4th to 6th century in Sagalassos, Turkey (Schibille *et al.* 2012), and from 5th to perhaps 8th-century Petra in Jordan (Marii and Rehren 2009). In terms of successors of Rome, it seems that, unsurprisingly, Roman coloured glass remained fairly consistent. There are cases in this period where cheaper materials were substituted for the transition metals; quartz or bone ash were used in a 5th-century mosaic from Ravenna, for example (Verità 2010). Some of the technological skills of Roman glass workers seem to have been lost during the Middle Ages. For example, marble or stone are usually used for whites and flesh colours in Byzantine mosaics. This was a distinction that Per Jonas Nordhagen saw between medieval mosaics in Rome and Byzantine mosaics and which he identified as a deliberate artistic choice on the part of mosaicists and one of the ways of spotting a Byzantine rather than a Roman mosaic-maker (Nordhagen 1983). Whilst that may well have been the case, the chemical analysis of white and flesh-coloured tesserae, coupled with the analyses of Byzantine glasses, shows that the Byzantines either did not use or did not possess the technology to make white glass because they used quartz to opacify glass (Verità *et al.* 2002; Verità and Rapisarda 2008). Consequently, white glass was in short supply and not ideal for use in mosaics.

It is uncertain when metallic glass tesserae were first made. Sear's catalogue records gold glass in twenty of his 301 sites, and gold tesserae are certainly known from at least the 1st century in Nero's Golden House. Gold tesserae are also known from the Stadium of Domitian (Lavagne 1970, 721; Sear 1977, cat. no. 77). A mid 2nd-century mosaic from the gymnasium baths on Samos employed both gold and silver tesserae (Dunbabin 1999, 245), the earliest example known to me of the use of silver (Roncuzzi-Fiorentini 1983; Fiori *et al.* 1989). Sear notes silver in only one of his wall mosaics, from fragments of mosaics dating perhaps to the 4th century from Sardis now in the museum at Manisa (Sear 1997, cat. no. 171), though silver tesserae are also present in the mosaics of Sta Costanza. In terms of the production of metallic tesserae, Daniel Howells' (2010) research into the making of gold glass has suggested that its manufacture was neither so complex nor so costly as had been supposed, the cost depending on the quantity of gold employed. How well his methods work with mosaic needs more development. Silver leaf tesserae were more problematic. Because gold can be beaten to an almost infinite thinness, considerably more silver is needed to make silver leaf than gold is for gold leaf. Further, because of the relative melting points of silver and glass, the layer of glass (the *cartellino*) placed over the silver leaf tends not to stick very well. As a result, silver tesserae tend to lose their *cartellini* and the silver itself can peel away or tarnish, causing the colour to disappear.

How widespread the use of metallic tesserae was, is also hard to track. Sear recorded the majority of his examples from Italy, Britain, France, Spain, the Balkans and Germany in the 3rd and 4th centuries (Sear 1977 cat. nos. 234 (Britain, though see Leigh *et al.* in preparation, for these as post-Roman), 243 (France), 252, 253, 256, 257, 263 (Germany), 273, 275 (Switzerland), 268 (Spain)), with only one example from North Africa, from baths at Themetra near Sousse in Tunisia (Sear 1977, cat. no. 220) and one from the eastern provinces: the example cited above from Sardis contained both gold and silver tesserae (Sear 1977, cat. no. 171). However, it would seem plausible that gold and silver leaf tesserae were more widespread in the east than this implies. Certainly from the 4th century on, gold, and to a lesser extent silver, was common in eastern wall mosaics, as at the church of St George (the Rotunda) in Thessaloniki, for example (Torp 1963). Examples of gold tesserae are found even in the small churches at Çiftlik and Meryemlik cited above. Considering the extensive use made in Rome in the Baths of Caracalla, for example, it is hard to imagine that the fashion for mosaic would not have taken hold in the east, where aristocratic resources would certainly have allowed for it.

In the case of Sta Costanza, I am not aware that any study of the tesserae exists. However, it can be observed that the palette is quite close to what might be found in a floor mosaic with green and blue glass used as highlights. In Galla Placidia's chapel, the palette is very different, reflecting the change of medium, with an emphasis on blue and green in particular. What developed in Byzantine mosaics was a further shift from the expanses of blue and green seen in Galla's chapel, for example, to the use, or perhaps return, of gold as a background. In terms of the glass used in late antique and Byzantine mosaics, this is the most striking shift. Both gold glass and silver glass tesserae are recorded from both Sta Costanza and Galla Placidia's chapel, but not in anything like the considerable quantity we see later. This change perhaps dates to the 6th and 7th centuries, with a move from what is apparent in 6th-century mosaics in churches in Ravenna such as San Vitale, in Rome (like SS. Cosmas and Damien) and on Mount Sinai towards the scheme of Poreč, also 6th century, and Kiti, in the late 6th or more plausibly 7th century. The continued use of blues and greens in these 6th and 7th-century mosaics suggests that this may well have been an aesthetic shift, a change in taste, first and foremost. What is apparent with Sta Costanza and Galla Placidia's chapel are two trends in the making of wall mosaics: one in which the relationship with floor mosaics is more obvious; and one where the key distinction might be said to be in the nature of the medium employed, the quantity of glass. In other words, the transition to using glass rather than other materials in wall mosaics was a gradual one.

Wall mosaics were in use from the time of the republic and glass tesserae from perhaps the 1st century; neither was a 4th century or a Christian invention; the wall mosaicists of Constantinople were indeed successors of Rome. Byzantine glass wall mosaics, whether like Sta Costanza or like the chapel of Galla Placidia, grew out of Roman practices and Roman glass technologies. The same traditions are visible in later Byzantine mosaics, even the same materials when Roman tesserae were re-used to provide colours no longer made. What is different is the amount of glass used as a matter of course in Byzantine mosaics – the triumph of Galla Placidia over Constantina – the tremendous use of gold, from the apse mosaic and the incredible developments in the manipulation of glass tesserae as a medium. But that is another story.

Acknowledgements

My thanks to Nadine Schibille who updated and advised me on the analytical material.

Bibliography

Aleura, G., Kalopisi, S., Laimou, A. and Panagiotidi, M. (1990) Anaskapphi stin Kardamaina (archaia Alasarna) tis Ko kata ta eti 1988–1990. *Praktika tis en Athinais Arkhaiologikis Etairias* 145, 342–367.

Antonaras, A. (2007) Early Christian glass finds from the Museum Basilica, Philippi. *Journal of Glass Studies* 49, 47–56.

Ashby, T. (1910) The Colombarium of Pomponius Hylas. *Proceedings of the British School at Rome* 5, 463–471.

Baur, P. V. C. (1938) Glassware. In C. H. Kraeling (ed.) *Gerasa. City of the Decapolis*, 505–546. New Haven, CT, American School of Oriental Research.

Boschetti, C. *et al.* (2008) Early evidence of vitreous materials in Roman mosaics from Italy: an archaeological and archaeometric integrated study. *Journal of Cultural Heritage* 9, e21–e26.

Budetta, T. (2005/06) The mosaic-decorated nymphaeum of Massa Lubrense. *Musiva e Sectile. An International Journal for the Study of Ancient Pavements* 2/3, 43–80.

DeLaine, J. (1997) *The baths of Caracalla. A study in the design, construction, and economics of large-scale building projects in imperial Rome.* Journal of Roman Archaeology Supplementary Series 25. Portsmouth, RI, Journal of Roman Archaeology.

Deliyannis, D. M. (2010) *Ravenna in Late Antiquity.* Cambridge, Cambridge University Press.

Dunbabin, K. M. D. (1999) *Mosaics of the Greek and Roman world.* Cambridge, Cambridge University Press.

Fiori, C. *et al.* (1989) Analisi e confront di tesserae vetrose dorate di mosaici bizantini del VI secolo. *Quaderni Istituto di richerce technologiche per la ceramica. Mosaico e restauro musivo* 2, 17–30.

Fiori, C., Vandini, M. and Mazzotti, V. (2003) Colour and technology of mosaic "glazes" in the Justinian and Theodora's panels of the Basilica of San Vitale in Ravenna. *Ceramurgia + ceramic acta* 33, 135–154.

Freestone, I. C., Bimson, M. and Buckton, D. (1990) Compositional categories of Byzantine glass tesserae. In *Annales du 11e Congrès de l'Association Internationale pour l'Histoire du Verre*, 271–279. Amsterdam, Association Internationale pour l'Histoire du Verre.

Freestone, I. C. et al. (2003) Strontium isotopes in the investigation of early glass production: Byzantine and early Islamic glass from the Near East. *Archaeometry* 45, 19–32.

Gedzevičiūtė, V., Welter, N., Schüssler, U. and Weiss, C. (2009) Chemical composition and colouring agents of Roman mosaic and millefiori glass, studied by electron microprobe analysis and Raman microspectroscopy. *Archaeological and Anthropological Science* 1, 15–29.

Gough, M. et al. (1967) Report of the Council of Management and of the Director for Anatolian Studies, 1966. *Anatolian Studies* 17, 3–23.

Henderson, J. (2000) *The science and archaeology of materials. An investigation of inorganic materials.* London, Routledge.

Herzfeld, E. and Guyer, S. (1930) *Meriamlik und Korykos. Zwei christliche Ruinenstätten des rauhen Kilikiens.* Monumenta Asiae Minoris Antiqua 2. Manchester, University Press.

Hill, S. (1995) Çiftlik. *Anatolian Studies* 45, 224–225.

Howells, D. T. (2010) *Late Antique Gold Glass in the British Museum.* Unpublished thesis, University of Sussex.

James, L. (1996) *Light and colour in Byzantine art.* Clarendon studies in the history of art 16. Oxford, Clarendon Press.

James, L. (2006) Byzantine glass mosaic tesserae: some material considerations. *Byzantine and Modern Greek Studies* 30, 29–47.

Johnson, M. J. (2009) *The Roman Imperial Mausoleum in Late Antiquity.* Cambridge, Cambridge University Press.

Lavagne, H. (1970) Le nymphée au Polyphème de la Domus Aurea. *Mélanges d'archéologie et d'histoire* 82, 673–721.

Lavagne, H. (1988) *Operosa Antra. Recherces sur la grotte à Rome de Sylla à Hadrien.* Rome, Ecole française de Rome.

Leigh, G. J., Schibille, N. and James, L. (in preparation) *Gold Glass Tesserae from the Roman Villa site at Southwick, Sussex.*

Marii, F. (2001) Typological and chemical analysis of the glass. In Z. T. Fiema, Ch. Kanellopoulos, T. Waliszewski and R. Schick, *The Petra Church.* American Center of Oriental Research Publications 3, 377–382. Amman, American Center of Oriental Research.

Marii, F. and Rehren, Th. (2009) Archaeological coloured glass cakes and tesserae from the Petra church. In K. Janssens, P. Degryse, P. Cosyns, J. Caen and L. Van't dack (eds.) *Annales du 17e Congrès de l'Association Internationale pour l'Histoire du Verre*, 295–300. Brussels, University Press Antwerp.

Nenna, M.-D. (2007a) La production et la circulation du verre au proche-orient: état de la question. In M. Sarte (ed.) *Production et échanges dans la Syrie grecque et romaine.* Topoi Supplément 8, 123–150. Paris, De Boccard.

Nenna, M.-D. (2007b) Production et commerce du verre à l'époque impériale: nouvelles découvertes et problématiques. *Facta* 1, 125–148.

Newton, R. G. (1980) Recent views on ancient glasses. *Glass Technology* 21, 173–183.

Nordhagen, P. J. (1983) The penetration of Byzantine mosaic technique into Italy in the sixth century AD. In R. Farioli Campanati (ed.) *Atti III colloquio internazionale sul mosaico antico*, 210–222. Ravenna, Lapucci.

Paynter, S. and Kearns, T. (2011) *West Clacton Reservoir, Great Bentley, Essex. Analysis of glass tesserae.* Research Department Report Series. Portsmouth, English Heritage.

Price, J. (2005) Glass-working and glassworkers in towns and cities. In A. Mac Mahon and J. Price (eds.) *Roman working lives and urban living*, 167–190. Oxford, Oxbow Books.

Roncuzzi-Fiorentini, I. (1983) Le smalts à fond d'or et d'argent dans les mosaiques anciennes. In R. Farioli Campanati (ed.) *Atti III colloquio internazionale sul mosaico antico*, 563. Ravenna, Lapucci.

Sayre, E. V. (1963) The intentional use of antimony and manganese in ancient glasses. In F. R. Matson and G. E. Rindone (eds.) *Advances in Glass Technology, Part 2*, 263–282. New York, NY, Plenum Press.

Schibille, N., Degryse, P., Corremans, M. and Specht, Ch. G. (2012) Chemical characterisation of glass mosaic tesserae from sixth-century Sagalassos (south-west Turkey): chronology and production techniques. *Journal of Archaeological Science* 39, 1480–1492.

Sear, F. B. (1975) The earliest wall mosaics in Italy. *Papers of the British School at Rome* 43, 83–97.

Sear, F. B. (1977) *Roman wall and vault mosaics.* Mitteilungen des Deutschen Archäologischen Instituts, Römische Abteilung, Ergänzungsheft 23. Heidelberg, F. H. Kerle.

Stanley, D. J. (2004) Santa Costanza: history, archaeology, function, patronage and dating. *Arte Medievale* 3, 119–140.

Stern, E. M. (1985) Ancient and medieval glass from the Necropolis church at Anemurium. In *Annales du 9e Congrès de l'Association Internationale pour l'Histoire du Verre*, 35–64. Liège, Association Internationale pour l'Histoire du Verre.

Stern, H. (1958) Les mosaiques de l'église de Sainte-Constance à Rome. *Dumbarton Oaks Papers* 12, 158–218.

Stern, H. (1959) Origins et débuts de la mosaïque murale. *Etudes d'Archéologie Classique* 2, 99–121.

Terry, A. and Maguire, H. (2007) *Dynamic Splendor. The Wall Mosaics in the Cathedral of Eufrasius at Poreć.* University Park, PA, Penn State University Press.

Tite, M., Pradell, T. and Shortland, A. (2008) Discovery, production and use of tin-based opacifiers in glasses, enamels and glazes from the late iron age onwards: A reassessment. *Archaeometry* 50, 67–84.

Torp, H. (1963) *Mosaikkene i St. Georg-rotunden i Thessaloniki: et hovedverk i tidlig-bysantinsk kunst.* Oslo, Gyldendal.

Turner, W. E. S. and Rooksby, H. P. (1959) A study of the opalising agents in ancient opal glasses throughout three thousand four hundred years. *Glastechnische Berichte, Sonderband,* 32K, 17–28.

Van Der Werf, I., Mangone, A., Giannossa, L. C., Traini, A., Laviano, R., Coralini, A. and Sabbatini, L. (2009) Archaeometric investigation of Roman tesserae from Herculaneum (Italy) by the combined use of complementary micro-destructive analytical techniques. *Journal of Archaeological Science,* 36, 2625–2634.

Verità, M. (2010) Glass mosaic tesserae of the Neonian Baptistry in Ravenna: nature, origin, weathering causes and processes. In C. Fiori (ed.) *Ravenna Musiva. Conservazione e restauro del mosaico antico e contemporaneo. Atti del del primo convegno internazionale, Ravenna, 22–24 ottobre 2009,* 89–104. Bologna, Ante quem.

Verità, M. and Rapisarda, S. (2008) Studio analitico di materiali vitrei del XII–XIII secolo della Basilica di Monreale a Palermo. *Rivista della Stazione Sperimentale del Vetro* 38.2, 15–28.

Verità, M., Renier, A. and Zechin, S. (2002) Chemical analyses of ancient glass findings excavated in the Venetian lagoon. *Journal of Cultural Heritage* 3, 261–271.

Verità, M., Stella Arena, M., Carruba, A. M. and Santopadre, P. (2008a) Materiali vitrei nell'opus sectile di Porta Marina (Ostia). *Bollettino ICR, Nuova Serie* 16–17, 78–94.

Verità, M., Stella Arena, M., Carruba, A. M. and Santopadre, P. (2008b) Roman glass: art and technology in a fourth-century AD *opus sectile* in Ostia (Rome). *Journal of Cultural Heritage* 9, e16–e20.

Weyl, W. A. (1953) *Coloured Glass*. Sheffield, Society of Glass Technology.

Wilkes, J. J. (1986) *Diocletian's palace, Split*. Sheffield, Dept. of Ancient History and Classical Archaeology.

Zohar, D. (2006) Mosaic artists in the Byzantine east: towards a new definition of workshop construction. *Eastern Christian Art* 3, 141–150.

15

Glass from the Byzantine Palace at Ephesus in Turkey

Sylvia Fünfschilling

The so-called Byzantine Palace (Fig. 15.1) is located near the Arkadiane, the street leading to the port, and quite close to the port itself. Parts of the city, including the large palatial complex, were restructured and rebuilt after a number of major earthquakes in the 4th century. Some of the earlier buildings from the imperial period were levelled, while others were renovated and continued to be used.

Fritz Miltner carried out large-scale excavations in the 1950s during which the large building came to light (http://www.oeaw.ac.at/antike/index.php?id=67), but I am not yet aware where these finds have been stored. The exploration trenches dug between 2005 and 2009 under the direction of Andreas Puelz (*Österreichische Akademie der Wissenschaften*) were planned to broaden knowledge of the constructional history of the buildings gained from the earlier work (http://www.oeaw.ac.at/antike/index.php?id=67). In addition a geophysical survey was carried out, which showed that vast areas of the complex still await discovery below ground.

A large longitudinal hall with two apses, a tetraconch with adjacent apses and a private chapel as well as numerous small connecting rooms and corridors have now been uncovered. The northern section of the complex was taken up by a bathing suite, the rooms of which were arranged in a row, and this building had a different orientation from other sections of the complex. The bathing suite was an earlier, imperial period, construction, which was renovated and incorporated in the new building. It is assumed that a large courtyard was located to the west of the building and that various residential and service rooms were sited to the south.

The palace appears to have been erected in the early 5th century, but it is not known exactly how long it was in use. In the 10th century, however, a lime kiln was installed on its southern edge and there was a cemetery in front of the church between the 12th to the 14th centuries.

As a rule, the exploration trenches provide only preliminary information about the archaeological remains and the stratigraphic sequence of an area that was frequently reconstructed is often difficult to interpret, as the finds assemblages may date from two hundred years or more. Such long periods of time are not helpful for determining the chronological sequence of the finds, particularly in the late phases, when the finds underwent pronounced changes, for example with the introduction of several new types. It is, therefore, necessary to look for similar material from other sites, although comparatively few closely dated contexts are known within the eastern Mediterranean region.

The glass fragments dealt with here all came from the exploration trenches examined between 2005 and 2009. Two of the five boxes, all closely packed with plastic bags, were examined by Daniel Keller before I had access to the material. The material from those two boxes have not been restudied and Daniel Keller has given me permission to use his drawings. While there will be differences between his classification of the material and my own, since researchers pursue their own personal lines of research, this will make very little difference to the overall interpretation of the glass finds.

The exploration trenches contained very different amounts of glass, with the trenches outside of the building producing remarkably large numbers of finds. Residual finds dating from the late Hellenistic and early Roman periods were scarce, and the 1st and 2nd centuries were also not well represented. By contrast, there were many finds dating from the 3rd century, as the earlier buildings were occupied during this period. No contexts definitely dated to the 4th century were recognised,

138   Sylvia Fünfschilling

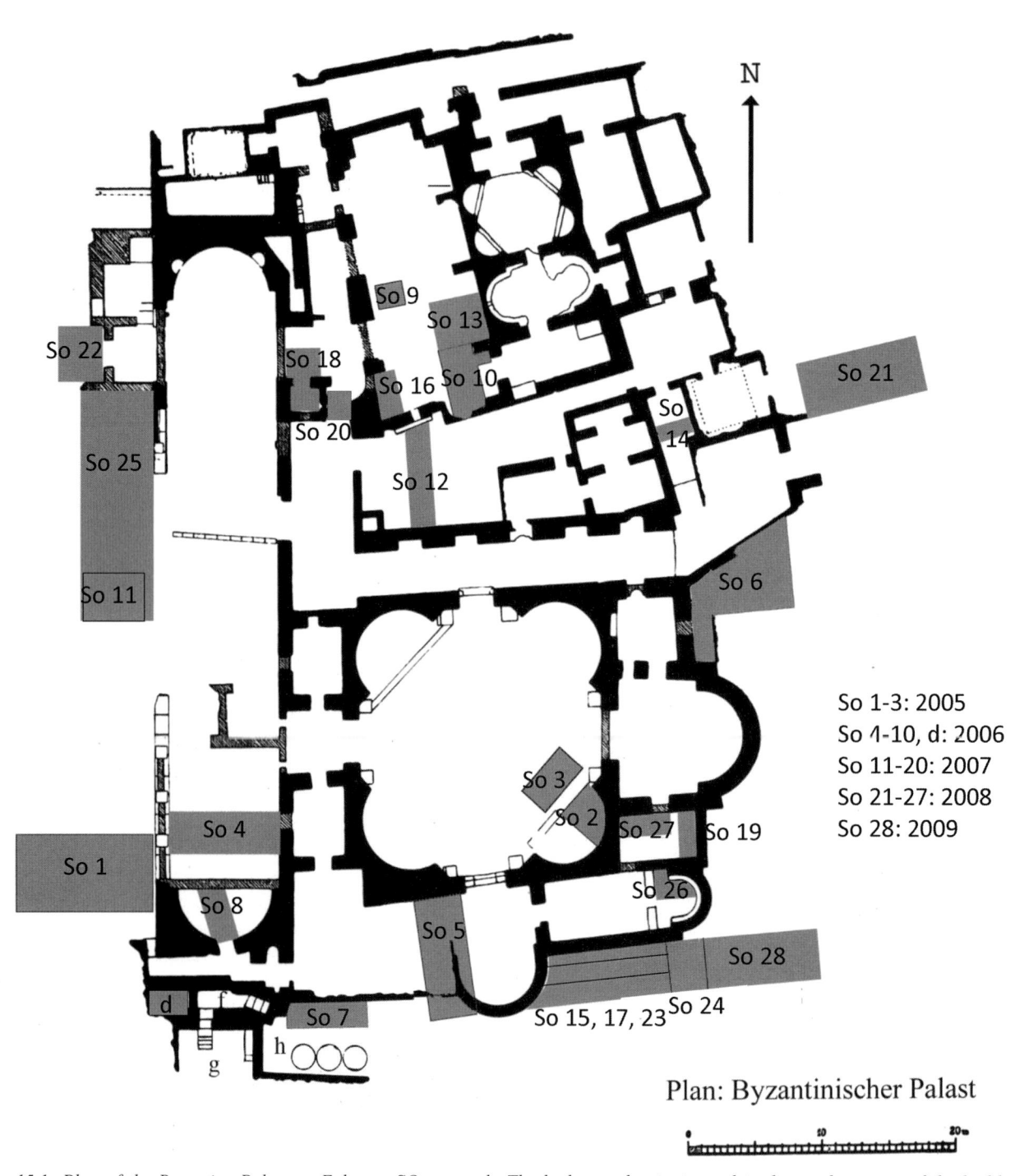

Fig. 15.1: Plan of the Byzantine Palace at Ephesus. SO = trench. The bath complex is situated in the northern part of the building (Andreas Puelz).

but 4th-century forms are found in the finds sequences of the later phases and otherwise date from the 5th century. The actual period of construction of the edifice in the 5th century did not have any stratified contexts with glass, but some of the sequences that covered long periods of time did contain glass vessels from the early 5th century – though these are sometimes difficult to distinguish from 4th-century examples. A particularly large body of finds was recovered from Trench 6, which contained a refuse pit from the 6th and 7th centuries and a small number of earlier finds as well as lead seals from the 6th and 7th centuries. Glass vessels dating from the 8th century or later have not been identified with any degree of certainty, although some fragments appear to be of a later date. Even Trench 5, where the 10th-century lime kiln came to light, has not produced glass fragments which can be dated to that period. I will not deal with the early glass finds here, and will only use the finds from the earlier buildings as reference material.

Window glass was well represented; however, the boxes which I have examined personally did not contain any window glass of the classic western matt/glossy type. Most of the panes were cylinder blown and quite thin with irregular thin edges and smooth surfaces, although they were not as thin and smooth as the examples I was able to examine in Carthage (Bir Messaouda site, unpublished). Beside the cylinder blown window panes, a small number of fragments may have been crown glass, but due to the fragmentation this was difficult to ascertain.

The pieces were generally strongly fragmented, and many of them were also very weathered. The clear glass usually bore a milky white or yellowy layer, while other fragments were covered with a blackish patina. Some of the fragments, in particular the glass tesserae, are covered by thin brownish layer of weathering.

The glass vessels were often naturally coloured. A bluish green hue appears to have become prevalent in the 7th century and there were also many greenish, and fewer yellow-green or olive-green fragments belonging to the 5th/6th century. Colourless or almost colourless pieces occurred in great numbers, while intentionally coloured glass was rare. A few fragments were of a yellow colour also known from other sites of this period in Turkey (Fünfschilling and Laflı 2013, 40, note 41).

The decoration included simple cut bands and lines, some abraded décor (lines and bands as well as shallow facets), and in the 3rd century, some wheel-cut geometric patterns. Applied trailing, usually of the same colour, was also frequent. Pinched decoration and applied blue prunts also occurred, whereas mould-blown decoration was quite rare. Most of the vessels, however, bore no decoration. Mould-formed plates and bowls, usually of colourless glass, or, more rarely, of coloured glass, occurred until the 3rd or 4th century.

The 3rd-century assemblages (Fig. 15.2) contained some earlier finds such as wheel-cut, ribbed and mosaic glass bowls. Colourless moulded plates as well as colourless blown plates/bowls were well represented. Beakers had both cracked-off and fire-rounded rims. Simply cut decoration was characteristic, but complex geometric patterns also occurred. The closed vessels had folded rims typical of the imperial period and also rims with an applied trail. Some polygonal vessels were also found. Many of these shapes continued into at least the first half of the 4th century.

Similar shapes were still in use in the 5th century (Fig. 15.3), including a number of free-blown plates/bowls. Applied thread foot-rings were characteristic, some in a different colour from the vessel itself. There were no large assemblages dating solely from the 5th century.

More finds were detected in the assemblages containing material from the 5th–6th or 5th–7th centuries but the chronological division is based on parallels from other sites (Figs. 15.4–15.5). The mixed contexts produced a number of lamps, which were largely identified because of their characteristic handles or bases. The simple rim fragments were usually not identifiable as belonging to any particular vessel type. Numerous closed vessels with trailing were found, and stemware appeared for the first time, but it was still rare. It would be interesting to know whether these contexts contained more finds from the 5th century than the 6th and 7th century, and the pottery analysis may assist in answering this question. The beaker shapes remained almost unchanged, and cracked-off rims occurred occasionally. It is however, noteworthy that the assemblage dating from the 5th–7th centuries also contained two forms that may have been of a later date.

The refuse pit in Trench 6 that contained 6th and 7th-century lead seals yielded a good range of glass vessels, though it would have been interesting to be able to separate the 6th and 7th-century material (Figs. 15.6–15.7). Close scrutiny of the stratigraphic sequence may perhaps resolve this problem.

Some earlier forms, such as beakers with blue prunts, square vessels and large free-blown plates/bowls, were also found. Most of the fragments, however, came from stemmed glasses and lamps, which were represented in considerable numbers. Vessels with dip-moulded diagonal ribbing and vessels with diagonal ribbing where the points of attachment of the mould at the rims are clearly visible probably date from the 7th century, although this type of decoration appeared earlier as well. The pronounced chalice forms are arguably from the same period.

The closed vessels often had tubular necks, and one large vessel with a wide neck may already point to a date later than the 7th century. Only in this context were small bottles similar to balsamaria found. These often had flattened bodies and were rather carelessly made.

A small number of carefully domed bases, some made of the yellow glass mentioned earlier, are worth mentioning. The wineglass stems were almost invariably folded, but showed a great variety in their folds. Stemmed glasses with bases that appear to have been mould-blown and ribbed knobbed stems appeared to be of 7th-century date. The massive stems probably also date from the 7th century.

The trenches to the south of the church wall contained evidence of large glass sheets that could easily be mistaken for window glass, but were used to manufacture tesserae. Most of these were greenish in colour, but it was often hard to ascertain the exact colour because both the tesserae and the sheets are covered in an earthy crust that is hard to remove. Tesserae covered with gold leaf and obsidian

Fig. 15.2: Characteristic glass vessels dating from the 3rd and early 4th centuries. Earlier finds (heirlooms) in top row, followed by moulded vessels. Bottom left pieces with facet and line cutting (scale 1:2).

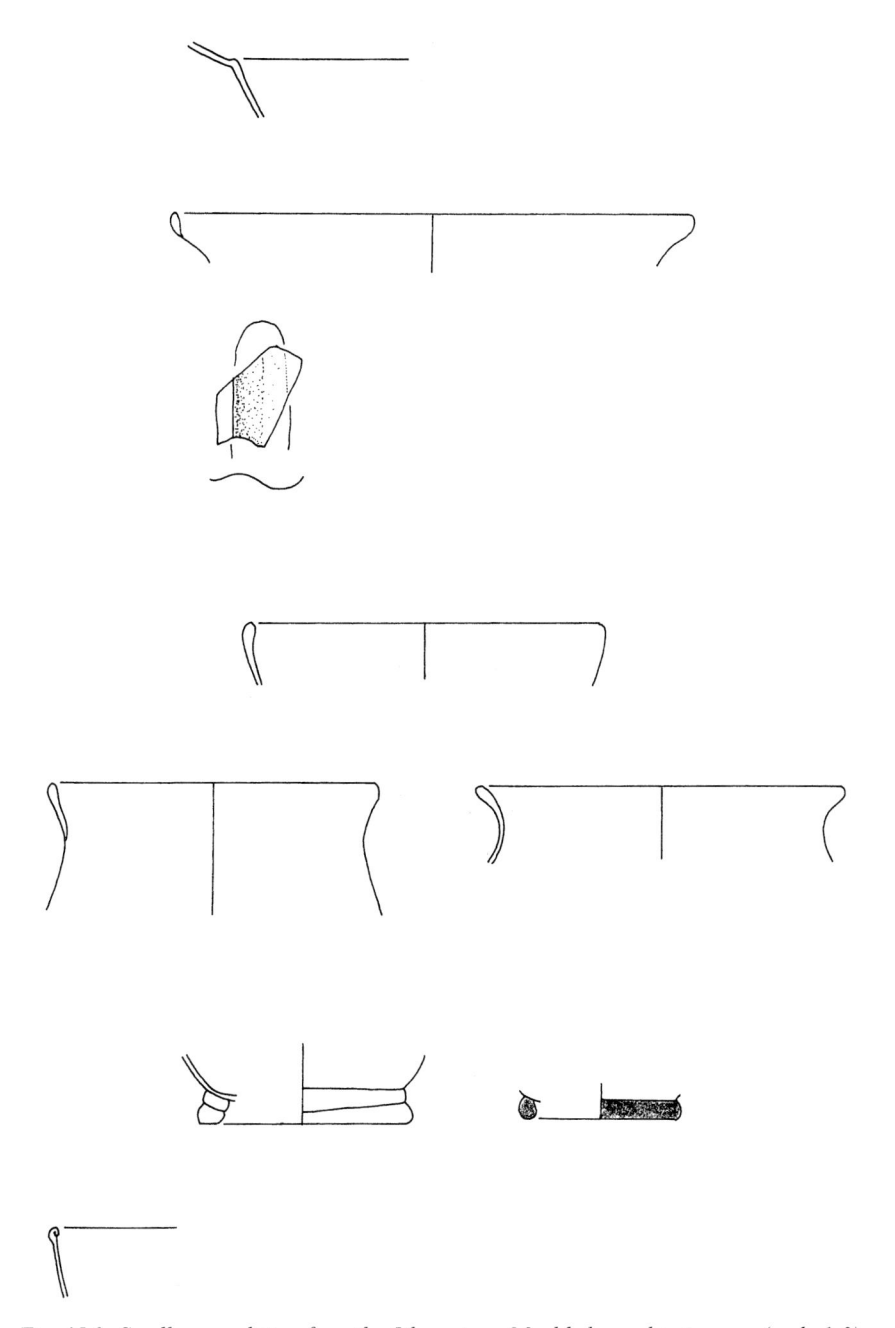

Fig. 15.3: Small group dating from the 5th century. Moulded vessel in top row (scale 1:2).

tesserae were also found. In addition, a number of moils and droplets suggest that some glassworking took place near the palace, and some fragments may be pieces of raw glass.

The late finds from the palace complex at Ephesus have close parallels in the so-called Tunnel of Eupalinos in Samos, a system of channels where the population of the city took refuge and lived at times of danger. The coin sequence continues until the mid 7th century, with the entire assemblage of material probably belonging to the first half and middle of the 7th century (Megow 2004). The main glass finds are lamps and goblets, which probably served a variety of purposes, as well as a number of closed vessels including miniature bottles. Most of the rims were fire-rounded or folded, and the stems of the wineglasses were folded, some of the thin stems being applied separately.

The basilica complex in Kourion in Cyprus has also yielded many similar finds (Young 1993), among them wineglasses with diagonal ribbing. Other parallels for the glass from Ephesus have been found in Istanbul, both in the excavations carried out near Saraçhane (Hayes 1992) and

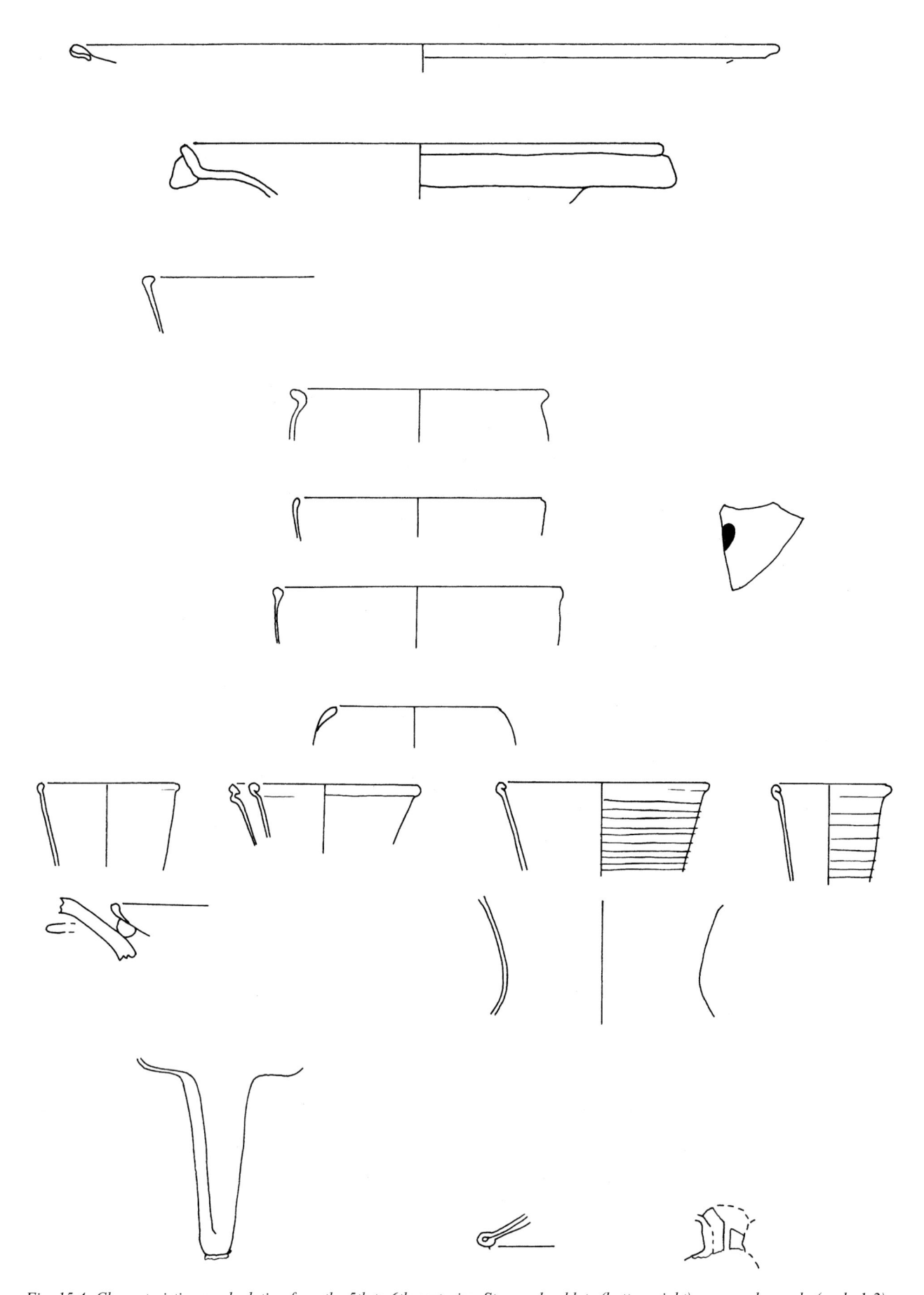

Fig. 15.4: Characteristic vessels dating from the 5th to 6th centuries. Stemmed goblets (bottom right) occur only rarely (scale 1:2).

15 Glass from the Byzantine Palace at Ephesus in Turkey 143

Fig. 15.5: Vessel glass from contexts dating from the 5th to 7th centuries. NB: the vessels in the middle and at the bottom are perhaps later in date. The vessel at the bottom has an impressed pattern on the outside surface, but not inside (scale 1:2).

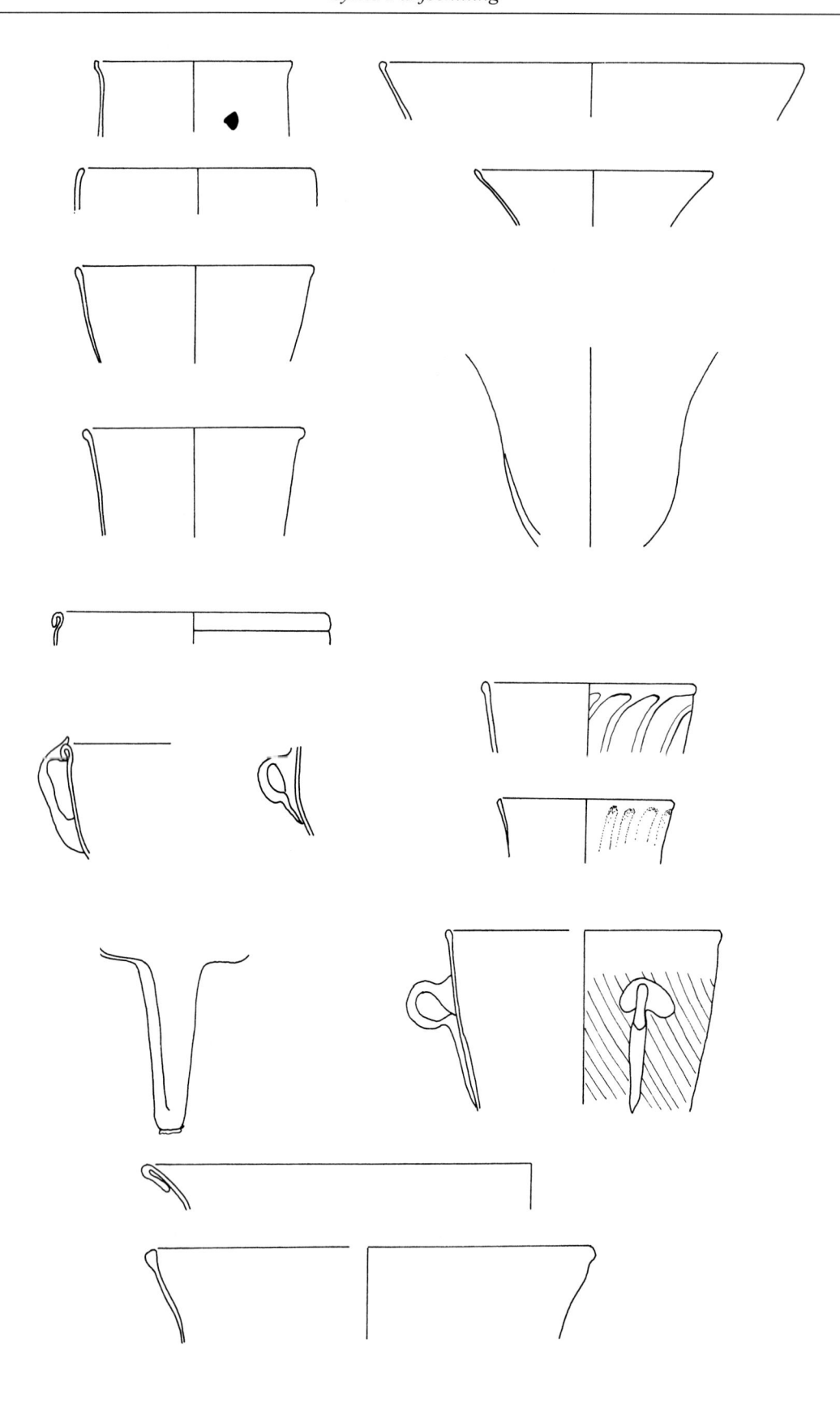

Fig. 15.6: Vessel glass from a pit in Trench 6 with a fill dating from the 6th to 7th centuries (scale 1:2).

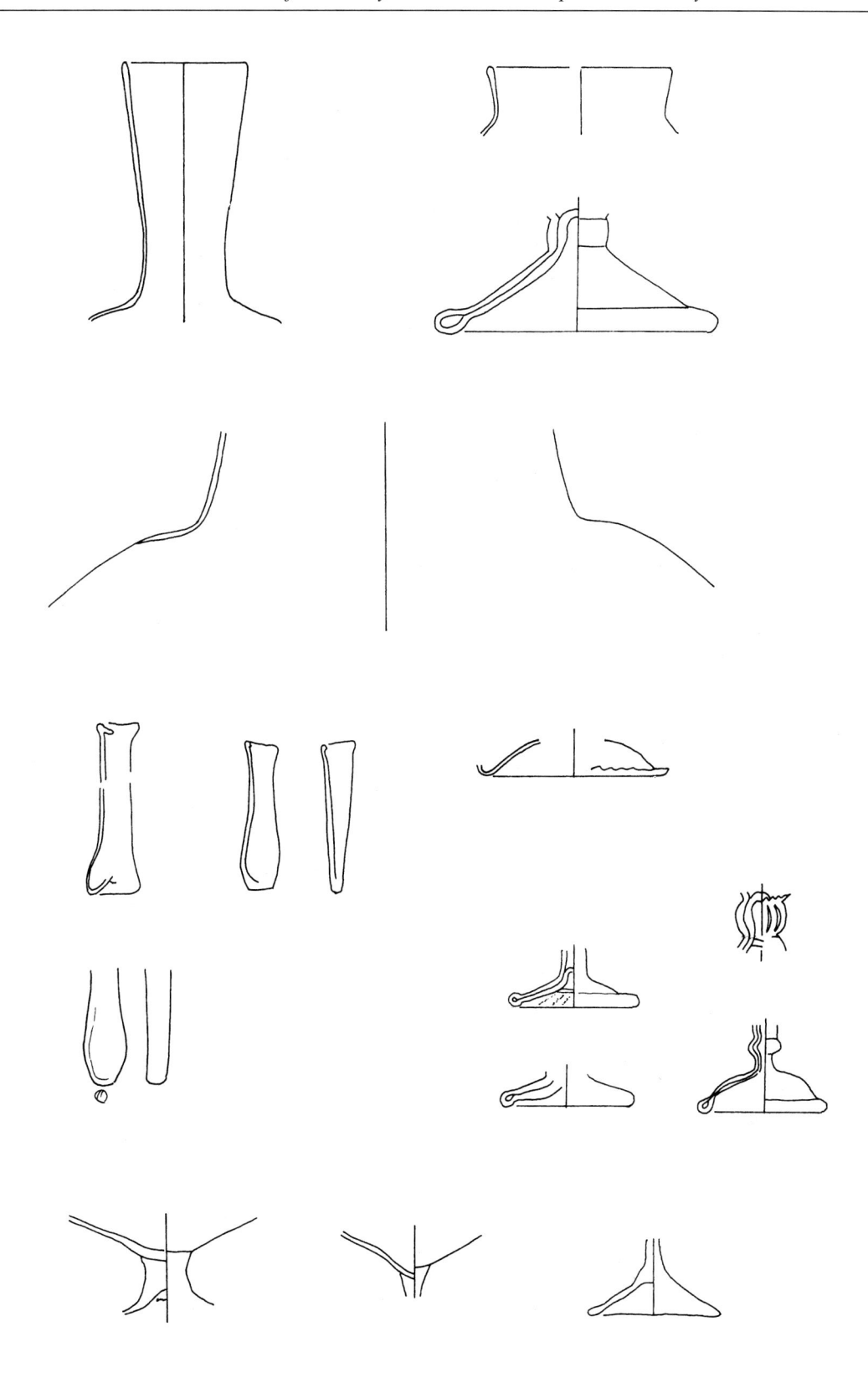

15 Glass from the Byzantine Palace at Ephesus in Turkey — 145

Fig. 15.7: Vessel glass from a pit in Trench 6 with a fill dating from the 6th to 7th centuries. Two vessels, top right and centre, may be later in date (scale 1:2).

in those undertaken during the construction of the city's metro system (Atik 2009; Özgümüs Canav 2009). Close parallels for the late material have also come to light in the city of Hadrianoupolis (Fünfschilling and Laflı 2013) in northern Turkey (Paphlagonia) and also in Pergamon (Schwarzer 2009), Limyra (Baybo 2009), Amorium (Gill 2002) and elsewhere.

The results outlined here are of a preliminary nature, as both the stratigraphic sequence and the ceramic finds have yet to be integrated and closely analysed.

Acknowledgements

I have to thank Laura Rembart and Sabine Ladstätter for their help and Sandy Haemmerle for the English translation.

Bibliography

Atik, S. (2009) Late Roman/Early Byzantine Glass from the Maramaray Rescue Excavations at Yenikapı in Istanbul. In E. Laflı (ed.) *Late Antique/Early Byzantine Glass in the Eastern Mediterranean*. Colloquia Anatolica et Aegaea 2, 1–16. Izmir, Hürriyet Matbaası.

Baybo, S. (2009) Late antique/Early Byzantine Glass from Trench Q 18 at Limyra: Excavation Seasons 2007-2009. In E. Laflı (ed.) *Late Antique/Early Byzantine Glass in the Eastern Mediterranean*. Colloquia Anatolica et Aegaea 2, 189–198. Izmir, Hürriyet Matbaası.

Fünfschilling, S. and Laflı, E. (2013) *Hadrianopolis II. Glasfunde des 6. und 7. Jahrhunderts aus Hadrianopolis, Paphlagonien (Türkei)*. Internationale Archäologie 123. Rahden/Wesfalen, Marie Leidorf.

Gill, M. A. V. (2002) *Amorium Reports, Finds I. The Glass (1987–1997)*. With contributions by C. S. Lightfoot, E. A. Ivison, M. T. Wypyski. British Archaeological Reports International Series 1070. Oxford, Hadrian Books.

Hayes, J. W. (1992) Late Roman and Byzantine Glass. In J. W. Hayes, *Excavations at Saraçhane in Istanbul 2. The Pottery*, 400–409. Princeton, NJ, Princeton University Press.

Megow, W.-R. (2004) Glas. In U. Jantzen, *Die Wasserleitung des Eupalinos. Die Funde*. Samos 20, 51–106. Bonn, Rudolf Habelt.

Özgümuş Canav, Ü. (2009) Late Roman/Early Byzantine Glass from the Marmaray Rescue Excavations at Sirkeci, Istanbul. In E. Laflı (ed.) *Late Antique/Early Byzantine Glass in the Eastern Mediterranean*. Colloquia Anatolica et Aegaea 2, 17–24. Izmir, Hürriyet Matbaası.

Schwarzer, H. (2009) Spätantike, byzantinische und islamische Glasfunde aus Pergamon. In E. Laflı (ed.) *Late Antique/Early Byzantine Glass in the Eastern Mediterranean*. Colloquia Anatolica et Aegaea 2, 85–109. Izmir, Hürriyet Matbaası.

Young, S. H. (1993) A Preview of Seventh-Century Glass from the Kourion Basilica, Cyprus. *Journal of Glass Studies* 35, 39–47.

16

Late Roman and early Byzantine glass from *Heliopolis*/Baalbek

Hanna Hamel and Susanne Greiff

Introduction

The excavations by the German Archaeological Institute, the Brandenburg University of Technology, and the Lebanese Directorate General of Antiquities aim to reconstruct the urban development of *Heliopolis*, modern Baalbek in Lebanon, from the Neolithic to the Ottoman period. The city is located in the Beqaa valley between the Lebanon and Anti-Lebanon Mountains (Fig. 16.1). During the early Roman period, *Heliopolis* was part of the territory of the *Colonia Iulia Felix Berytus* (Beirut). Septimius Severus (AD 193–211) conferred the *ius italicum* on the city which flourished in the following period.

The archaeological work is concentrated in areas with monumental architecture that were excavated from the beginning of the 20th century until the outbreak of the Lebanese Civil War in 1975. The aim of the project was to gain a better understanding of the visible architecture with the help of small sondages (van Ess 2008). Because of this, the excavated material derives from layers of infill from building activities, so the analysis of the finds is limited to basic questions.

All the finds presented in this paper were excavated in the area of Bustan el-Khan in and around the so-called peristyle complex (Fig. 16.2; Burwitz 2008). The building was a big banqueting hall in use from the 1st until at least the later 4th century. In the 5th century, parts of the building were reused and a smaller building was erected in the peristyle complex, using the southern facade and the southern outer wall.

The glass finds

The preservation of the glass is usually quite good in the levels of the Roman and Byzantine period, although the surface often flakes off so that the original thickness and the surface treatment cannot be determined. By contrast, the Islamic glass is heavily weathered and the original colour is usually not visible, and this difference aids the identification of the glass of the different periods. Chemical analysis of the Roman, late Roman, Byzantine and Islamic glass is currently being undertaken by Susanne Greiff (*Römisch-Germanisches Zentralmuseum*, Mainz).

The pottery in the contexts presented here has also been studied by the author. Whereas the ceramic assemblages are almost consistent in quantity throughout the period, the amount of glass varies greatly from century to century. Non-blown ribbed and linear cut bowls are regularly found in contexts of the 1st century (Jennings 2006, 37–45, groups 5–6), while the amount of glass decreases significantly during the 2nd and 3rd centuries. The levels of the late 2nd and first half of the 3rd century were very thin compared to the deep deposits, up to 1.5m thick, for terracing the area of Bustan el-Khan in the 1st century (the northern part) and in the 5th century (the southern part). The quantity of finds in general is smaller in the middle imperial period, but the presence of single fragments of glass in layers containing fairly large amounts of pottery suggests that glass vessels were less common in this period. This phenomenon needs further investigation, but a definitive picture of the early and middle Roman period in *Heliopolis* may be achieved only after finishing the studies of all the contexts.

The peak both in the quality and the quantity of glass tableware was reached in the 4th and 5th centuries. This has been observed at many sites in the eastern Mediterranean and reflects the flourishing late Roman glass production in the Levant (cf. Gorin-Rosen and Katsnelson 2007, 145–147). Glass is also found regularly in the layers of the Byzantine and Islamic periods; the glass of the latter period

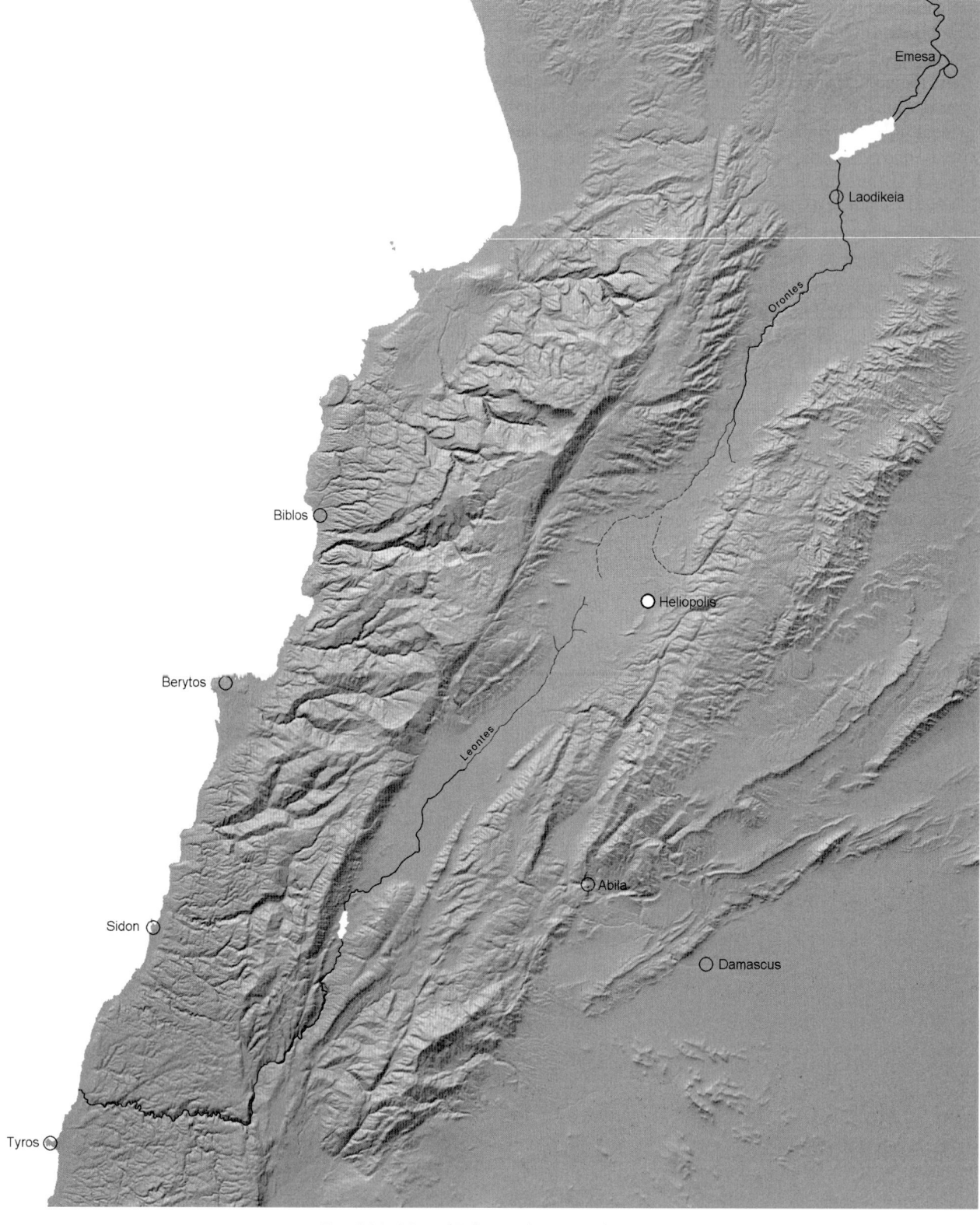

Fig. 16.1: Map of Lebanon (DAI, H. Ehrig).

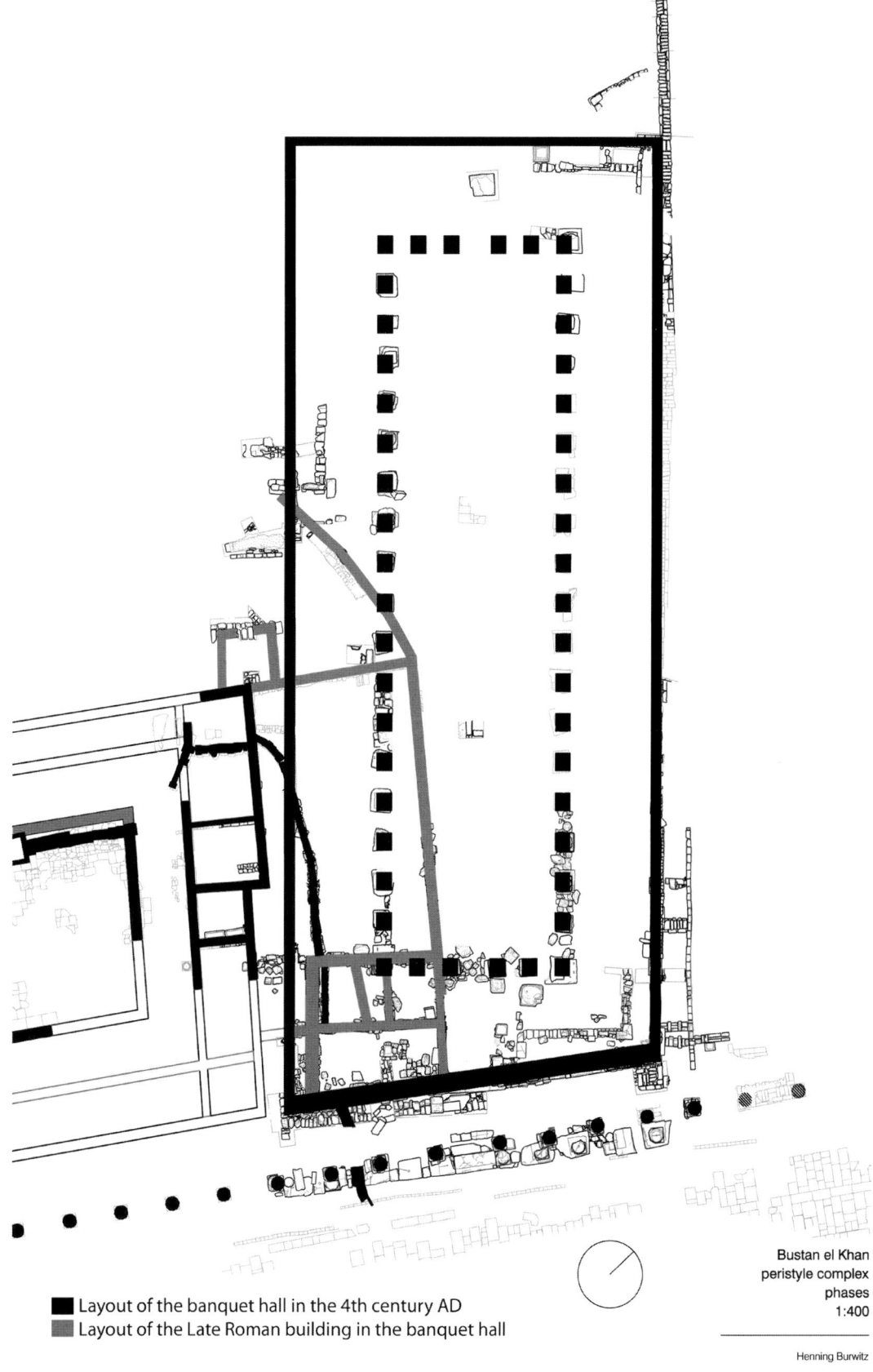

16 *Late Roman and early Byzantine glass from Heliopolis/Baalbek* 149

■ Layout of the banquet hall in the 4th century AD
■ Layout of the Late Roman building in the banquet hall

Bustan el Khan
peristyle complex
phases
1:400

Henning Burwitz

Fig. 16.2: The Peristyle Complex (BTU, H. Burwitz).

is being studied by Bettina Fischer-Genz (Fischer-Genz *et al.* 2010).

In general, the glass found in *Heliopolis* is comparable to that from Beirut studied by Sarah Jennings (2006), although it was found in much smaller amounts and differs in details such as the colours and quantity of certain forms. Parallel assemblages are also found in Galilee and other parts of Israel, where excavations have unearthed large amounts of material from consumption and production sites as well as funerary contexts. Those published groups provide references for almost all vessel types presented in this paper. In addition, certain of the vessel types are better known in Syria and Jordan (Clairmont 1963; Dussart 1998).

The *Heliopolis*/Baalbek research project is still in progress and detailed analysis of all the glass finds is not yet finished, but some principal trends can be discussed. The provenance of the raw glass has not yet been determined and the production centre (or centres) remain unknown for the time being. It seems likely that glass vessels and window panes were produced in the city, but no workshops have been found (see the discussion about the recognition of workshops in Gorin-Rosen and Katsnelson 2007, 73–76).

The first half of the 4th century

A homogeneous group of late 3rd/early 4th-century pottery and glass vessels was excavated next to the banqueting hall. The deposit filled a staircase leading down to the storage cellar of the banqueting hall and contained tablewares as well as vessels for food preparation and storage. This context seems to illustrate the vessels used for feasting in the banqueting hall at the end of the 3rd/beginning of the 4th century. The vessels were intentionally thrown down the stairs and have been found in their primary deposits (Hamel 2008; 2010). The glass in this context is free-blown and made either in shades of natural colour or (nearly) colourless.

Vessels with cracked-off rims

One third of the rims identified were cracked off, and in this context, they were well made with careful finishing of the edges. Most were made in colourless or nearly colourless glass and are very thin-walled; only one complete profile has been found (Fig. 16.3.1). Most of the curved rims belong to conical or cylindrical beakers (Fig. 16.3.2) which are well known forms (*e.g.* Weinberg and Goldstein 1988, 87–94, fig. 4.47; Jennings 2006, 88–92, types 2, 4; Keller 2006, 58, 213, type VII.25a, fig. 20, pl. 13k), but the same distinct S-shaped rim was also found on some hemispherical cups/bowls (Fig. 16.3.3; Weinberg and Goldstein 1988, 94–97, fig. 4.49, nos. 477–479; Jennings 2006, 86–88, type 1; Harden 1949, 152, fig. 1.8). Whereas the latter group were probably used as lamps (Gorin-Rosen and Winter 2010, 173–174, fig. 5.2), the conical beakers with cracked-off polished rims seem to be the preferred form of drinking vessel in this period, at least in the banqueting hall, where luxury tableware was used. Those together with the beakers with fire-rounded rims replace ceramic drinking vessels which were absent in this context in *Heliopolis*.

One vessel with a cracked-off rim is not included in the group above, as it is a bottle. It is the only vessel with an uneven, unfinished rim (Fig. 16.3.4). Parallels for this form which is again typical of the late 3rd/early 4th century are known at Hanita (Barag 1978, 23–27, nos. 45–47). Other vessel forms with cracked-off rim, such as bowls and dishes were introduced later and are absent in this assemblage.

Vessels with fire-rounded rims

The range of shapes with fire-rounded rims is wider than that with cracked-off rims. A group of dishes or shallow bowls with sloping sides (Fig. 16.3.5–6) is typical of the 3rd and early 4th century in the region (Vitto 2010, 69) and in *Heliopolis* these seem to belong to the "dining set", together with the beakers with cracked-off rims. They are made in greenish glass, as are those found in Beirut (Jennings 2006, 105–106, fig. 5.18), Hanita (Barag 1978, 13–17, figs. 7–8) and Khirbat el-Ni'ana (Gorin-Rosen and Katsnelson 2007, 76–78, fig. 1.1–5). Their rim diameters are between 20cm and 25cm. No bases were preserved with the rims. The large pushed-in or, less frequently, solid ring-bases generally associated with this kind of rim, *e.g.* at Hanita and Iqrit (Barag 1978, fig. 7, nos. 10–23; Vitto 2010, 69, fig. 9.1–6; solid base-ring: Gorin-Rosen 2002, 142, fig. 2.7) were not found in the assemblage. No convincing explanation can yet be given for the absence of these bases. It is possible that the bases were not deposited in the same place and that they are absent in this context by chance. On the other hand, another type of base, such as a flat base, may have been made for these 4th-century dishes (cf. Dussart 1998, type BV.2, pl. 12.14; see also Vitto 2010, fig. 9.7 and Barag 1978, no. 29 for bowls with flat bases).

Vessels with fire-rounded and slightly flaring rims are recorded in two sizes: one with diameters around 10cm (Fig. 16.3.7) and the other around 14cm (Fig. 16.3.8). The ones with the smaller diameters were beakers and they have been found in groups of the 3rd and 4th century (*e.g.* Tyre: Harden 1949, fig. 1.1; Jalame: Weinberg and Goldstein 1988, 60–65 [with applied trails]; Khirbet edh-Dharih: Dussart 2007, 210–211, fig. 5.4–4a). The larger vessels are deep bowls rather than beakers and are also well known in Galilee (Vitto 2010, 69–70, fig. 10 with further references; Weinberg and Goldstein 1988, 40–41, fig. 4.2; for a parallel in Jordan cf. Dussart 2007, 210, fig. 4.12). Another group of beakers with rim diameters of 6 to 7cm (Fig. 16.3.9) have sack-shaped bodies. Parallels for this type are to be found in tombs of the 3rd to early 4th century in Galilee (Barag 1978, 28–31, fig. 14; Vitto 2010, 71, fig. 11; cf. a tomb from Tyre: Harden 1949, 152, fig. 1.6; Atallah and Gawlikowska

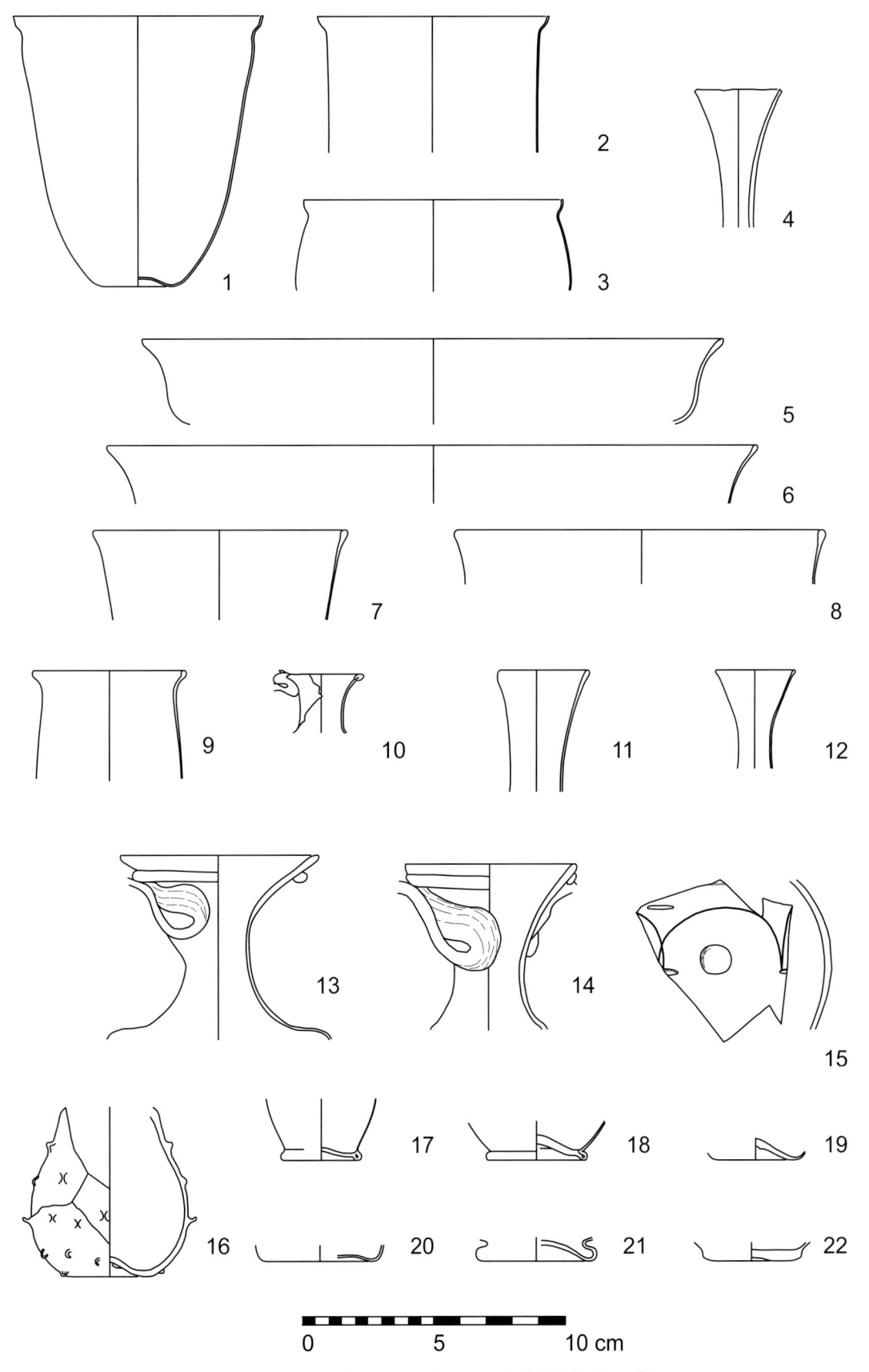

16 *Late Roman and early Byzantine glass from Heliopolis/Baalbek* 151

Fig. 16.3: 4th-century glass vessels (DAI, H. Hamel).

2007, no. 105, pl. 16). Beakers with fire-rounded rims are as common as those with cracked-off rims in *Heliopolis*. They were usually made in naturally coloured glass in shades of blue/green or green.

Some jugs, bottles and flasks were also present in the assemblage. For example there is a juglet with one handle (Fig. 16.3.10; Atallah and Gawlikowska 2007, no. 163) and two rims of flasks or bottles (Fig. 16.3.11–12; Atallah and Gawlikowska 2007, nos. 132–133; Barag 1978, fig. 13, no. 56; Gorin-Rosen and Katsnelson 2007, 99, figs. 11.9, 33.1).

Decorated fragments
Jugs with thick applied trails and handles are well known in the eastern Mediterranean region: *e.g.* in Beirut (Jennings 2006, 113, fig. 5.27), Jalame (Weinberg and Goldstein 1988, 65–67, fig. 4.28) and Petra (Keller 2006, 199, type IV.4b, pl. 5e–h). Two examples were recovered in the 4th-century material at *Heliopolis*. One, a one-handled jug (Fig. 16.3.13; Clairmont 1963, no. 578, pl. 13; Atallah and Gawlikowska 2007, 225, no. 156) made in greenish glass and the other, a two-handled one (Fig. 16.3.14; Clairmont 1963, no. 655, pl. 15) is made in light blue glass (cf. the example from the Athenian Agora: Weinberg and Stern 2009, 146, no. 331). In both cases, the body, trail, and handle were made in glass of the same colour.

One fragment has cut decoration (Fig. 16.3.15), the only identifiable motifs surviving on it being circles surrounded by arcs. Cut decoration is very common in Dura Europos (Clairmont 1963, 56–57; cf. Keller 2006, type VII.84). A fragment of a small flask with pincered decoration around the body is preserved from the shoulder to the base (Fig. 16.3.16), and a pontil scar is clearly visible on the domed base. The glass is light green and the pincered decorations are irregularly set around the body. Parallels for this type of decoration can be found in Dura Europos (Clairmont 1963, 50–53, nos. 214–222) as well as in a Lebanese collection (Atallah and Gawlikoska 2007, nos. 19–20).

Bases
Bases were either pushed in or tubular base-rings (Fig. 16.3.17–22). Pontil scars occur on both forms (Figs. 16.3.16, 16.3.18–19) but the pontil iron was not always used (Fig. 16.3.1). Many fragments, however, were too broken to determine the details of production. As mentioned above, all the hollow ring bases were less than 5cm in diameter (Fig. 16.3.17–18) and may have belonged to either beakers (Vitto 2010, fig. 11) or jugs/bottles (Barag 1978, fig. 13, no. 56; Katsnelson 2010b, 148, fig. 3.12). Most of the plain bases were broken in too many pieces for the exact form and diameter to be identified, so only the better preserved examples are presented here. Bases that were concave or nearly flat (Fig. 16.3.19–20) can be associated with beakers with cracked-off (Fig. 16.3.1) or fire-rounded rims (Weinberg and Goldstein 1988, fig. 4.25) or bottles (Weinberg and Goldstein 1988, fig. 4.36). The cut-out, open base-ring (Fig. 16.3.21) might alternatively belong to a beaker-type (Atallah and Gawlikowska 2007, nos. 100–101, pl. 16; Barag 1978, no. 65, fig. 14). Fig. 16.3.22 is the only fragment of a solid base form generally associated with beakers and produced in large quantities in Jalame during the 4th century (Weinberg and Goldstein 1988, 60–61, fig. 4.23; cf. Gorin-Rosen and Katsnelson 2007, 93, fig. 8.4–9 with further references therein).

The 5th century

The area of Bustan el-Khan was excavated down to the "Roman level" during the 1960s and 1970s so that it is impossible to reconstruct its late Roman and early Islamic layout. Fortunately, some late Roman buildings were built into the banqueting hall re-using the early Roman floor levels (Fig. 16.2). It was there possible to excavate a late Roman filling layer, as this fill elevated the floor outside of the banqueting hall which was left on a lower level until this period.

New forms, including wine-glasses and oil-lamps, were introduced into the standard glass repertoire in the 5th century (Gorin-Rosen and Winter 2010, 165–167), and the largest quantity of glass fragments at *Heliopolis* belongs to this period. Extensive use of window glass can be observed from the 4th/5th century onwards. In addition, a greater number of vessel shapes with cracked-off rims are recognisable than in the 4th century. Decorative elements such as blue blobs and single applied trails appear at this time, although only single sherds have been found.

Vessels with cracked-off rims
The production of conical beakers with curved rims continued (Jennings 2006, 88–90, type 2) though their walls were thicker than in the earlier assemblage and there were no colourless vessels (Fig. 16.4.1; Weinberg and Goldstein 1988, fig. 4.47). By contrast, two of the very rare light yellow coloured fragments (Fig. 16.4.2; cf. Keller 2006, 66, 69–70, 118–119, fig. 28, pl. 14c) were found in this group. One, made in greenish glass with a straight rim and a cut groove below (Fig. 16.4.3) is dated to the late 4th and 5th centuries by Jennings (2006, 90–91, fig. 5.6). It is possible that this form was used as a lamp (Jennings 2006, 91; for further discussion see Gorin-Rosen and Katsnelson 2007, 90–93, fig. 1.1).

Although no hemispherical cups were recognised, different forms of bowls were common. These usually have curved rims and can again be compared to those from Beirut. There are 'medium convex' or segmental bowls (Fig. 16.4.4; Jennings 2006, 93, fig. 5.9; Israeli 2008, 381–382, nos. 140–141; Dussart 1998, type BI.221, pl. 4.22–30; Keller 2006, 205, type VII.9c, pl. 8k), 'large shallow bowls' or cylindrical beakers (Fig. 16.4.5; Jennings 2006, 99–101, fig.

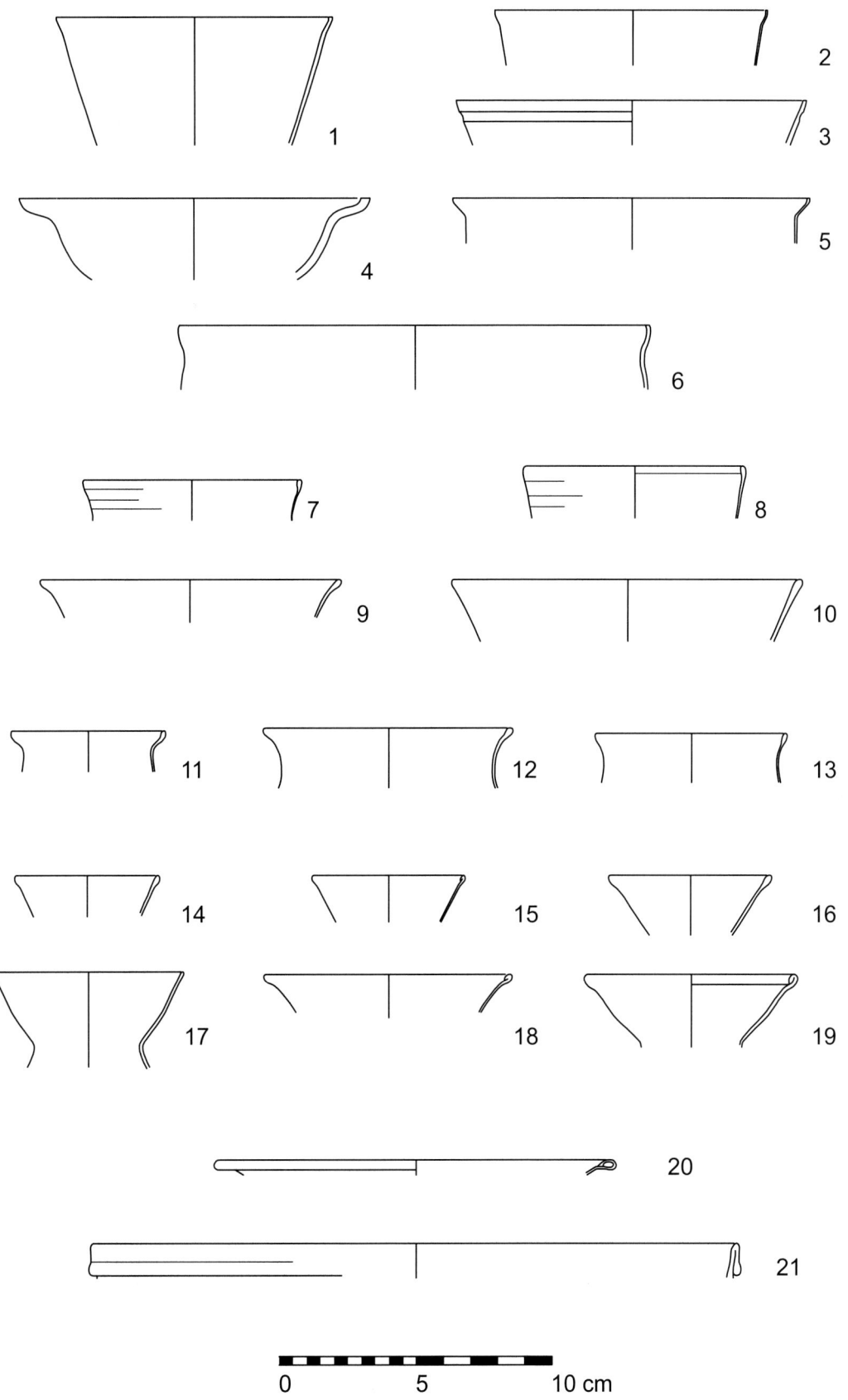

Fig. 16.4: 5th-century glass vessels (DAI, H. Hamel).

5.12), and a bowl shaped oil-lamp (Fig. 16.4.6; see below (lamps); Israeli 2008, 382, nos. 136–139). Their colours range from light blue-green to green.

Vessels with fire-rounded rims
Most of the rims with fire-rounded edges are very difficult to assign to specific forms. Recognition of the distinctions between the rims of beakers, bowls and goblets is not feasible, as the basic shapes are similar although variations in size are noticeable (Fig. 16.4.7–13). The bodies may be flaring or slightly curved. Those with larger diameters might be bowls or goblets (Fig. 16.4.9–10; Weinberg and Goldstein 1988, 40–41, fig. 4.2; Gorin-Rosen and Jackson-Tal 2008, 143, fig. 9.2.9; Gorin-Rosen and Winter 2010, fig. 4.1) while the smaller ones are more likely to be wine-glasses (Fig. 16.4.7–8; Gorin-Rosen and Winter 2010, fig. 2). Fig. 16.4.11 can be compared to Fig. 16.3.9 showing a sack-shaped container (see above). They are naturally coloured in light green, blue-green and blue.

Vessels with funnel-shaped mouths occur in different sizes and are identified as bottles, jugs or flasks (Gorin-Rosen 2009, 94). Most are paralleled by examples from Beirut (Jennings 2006, 176–180, fig. 7.26: 'funnel neck flasks'). Their fire-rounded rims are plain (Fig. 16.4.17), or sometimes rolled-in (Fig. 16.4.18) or folded-in (Fig. 16.4.19). The bodies have not survived so that nothing can be said about their differences in form, but their diameters range from about 5cm (Fig. 16.4.14–16; Gorin-Rosen and Katsnelson 2007, 99, fig. 11.9) to 9cm (Keller 2012, fig. 6.4). Because of their state of preservation it is impossible to show whether the flaring rim has a long neck or is set almost directly above the shoulder, although the date of the deposit and the absence of specimens with long necks suggests that they belong to the group of short necked flasks (Fig. 16.4.17) which Jennings (2006, 177) dates to the 5th century.

Only two bowls with folded rims were found. Both were made of green glass and they are the largest vessels in this assemblage. One has an infolded rim which is very unusual for bowls (Fig. 16.4.20; Gorin-Rosen and Katsnelson 2007, 129, fig. 27.9), while the second (Fig. 16.4.21) has an external closed fold. The larger example is 24cm in diameter. The wall and rim are thick and the rim edge is thickened (Gorin-Rosen and Katsnelson 2007, 129, fig. 27.3–8).

Goblets and lamps
The forms most characteristic of this period, the stemmed goblets and lamps, are recognised by their surviving stems and handles. Unfortunately, neither the stems nor the handles can be securely associated with any of the rims, but as there is only one find of a hollow stem of a lamp (Fig. 16.5.1), it is likely that the preferred lamp form of this period was bowl-shaped (Fig. 16.4.6) with small handles (Fig. 16.5.2–3; Gorin-Rosen and Winter 2010, 173–174, fig. 5.2–6).

The stemmed goblets/wine-glasses are also represented by the surviving stems (Fig. 16.5.4–5). The type is known as 'delicate' with a short stem and a fire-rounded base of the foot (Figs. 16.5.4, 16.5.6–9; Jennings 2006, 127–129, fig. 6.3.6–11, type 2b; Gorin-Rosen 2006, fig. 1.6). Some of the fire-rounded rims already mentioned must belong to these bases, but no complete profile of a goblet has been reconstructed (*e.g.* Gorin-Rosen and Winter 2010, figs. 2, 4). The stems are naturally coloured or colourless, the preferred colour being light blue. They are usually less common than other bases of wine-glasses at sites in the eastern Mediterranean (see Gorin-Rosen and Winter 2010, 169–170 with a discussion of this type) so that their predominance in this context needs further interpretation. It might be due to the specific context and its date, just before the standard Byzantine forms appeared (cf. Gorin-Rosen 2010, 213), which would confirm an early 5th-century date for this assemblage. At the site of a glass workshop in Beirut where this type was not produced, 'delicate' bases were rare and were dated to the 2nd half of the 7th century (Foy 2000, 276–277, fig. 26.3–9). Some of these bases from Beirut were also published by Jennings (2006, 127–129, type 2 goblets) who dated them to the 5th to 7th century, whereas in Caesarea they are frequent finds and have been dated to the 4th to 7th century (Israeli 2008, 385–386, nos. 201–209).

Decorated fragments and bases
Jugs with thick applied trails continued in use, but in the 5th century they have a green body with a blue trail. The rims are plain and no handles have survived. One large jug has a rim diameter of 11cm (Fig. 16.5.10), while the second one is a juglet (Fig. 16.5.11; cf. Jennings 2006, 113–114, fig. 5.27.4–9; Katsnelson 2010a, 139, fig. 4.21; Weinberg and Goldstein 1988, figs. 4.28, 4.31).

One body sherd with blue blobs has been found (Fig. 16.5.12). The fragment does not allow the form of the vessel to be recognised, but analogous pieces are known at Jalame (Weinberg and Goldstein 1988, 87–93) and in Beirut where coloured blob decoration is also rare (Jennings 2006, 102).

As in the 4th century, most of the bases are pushed in or tubular base-rings and if enough of them survives, a pontil scar is often clearly visible. One base (Fig. 16.5.13) is too badly preserved for it to be attributed to a specific type of vessel (cf. Gorin-Rosen and Katsnelson 2007, figs. 8.13, 32.6). Fig 16.5.14 might be the base of a jug or a beaker (Gorin-Rosen 2009, fig. 2.54.15; Weinberg and Goldstein 1988, fig. 4.29). The low ring base (Fig. 16.5.15) possibly belonged to a small bowl (Katsnelson 2010a, 137, fig. 3.12) whereas the pushed-in tubular base (Fig. 16.5.16) is thought to be a jug (Gorin-Rosen 2009, fig. 2.54.13; Weinberg and Goldstein 1988, fig. 4.29). The pushed-in base (Fig. 16.5.17) and the flat base (Fig. 16.5.18) may be from beakers (Gorin-Rosen and Jackson-Tal 2008, 146–147, fig. 9.3.18–19). Bases of larger bowls with a hollow ring base (Fig. 16.5.19; Gorin-Rosen and Katsnelson 2007, 86–88, fig. 6) and a

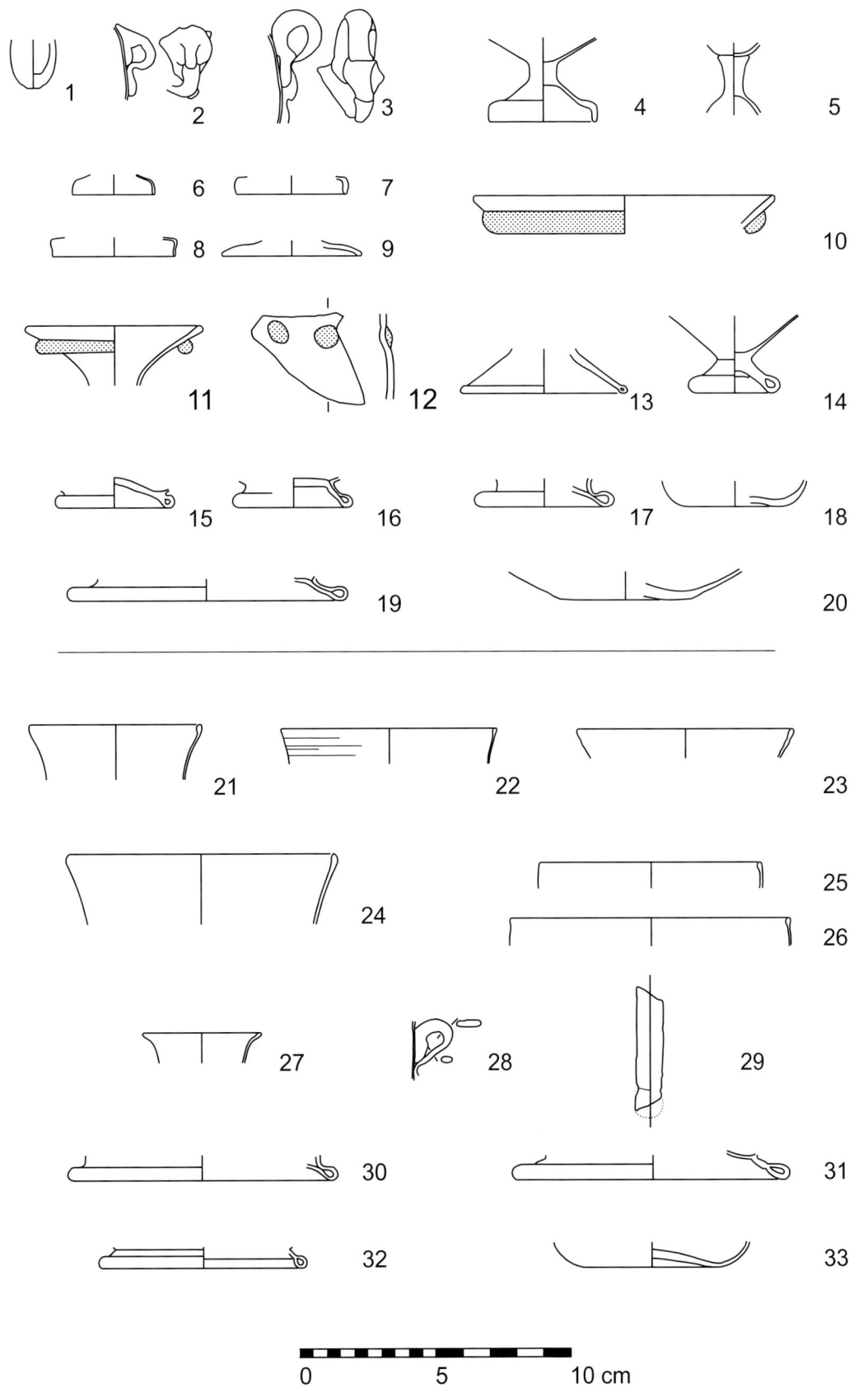

16 *Late Roman and early Byzantine glass from Heliopolis/Baalbek* 155

Fig. 16.5: 5th and 6th-century glass vessels (DAI, H. Hamel).

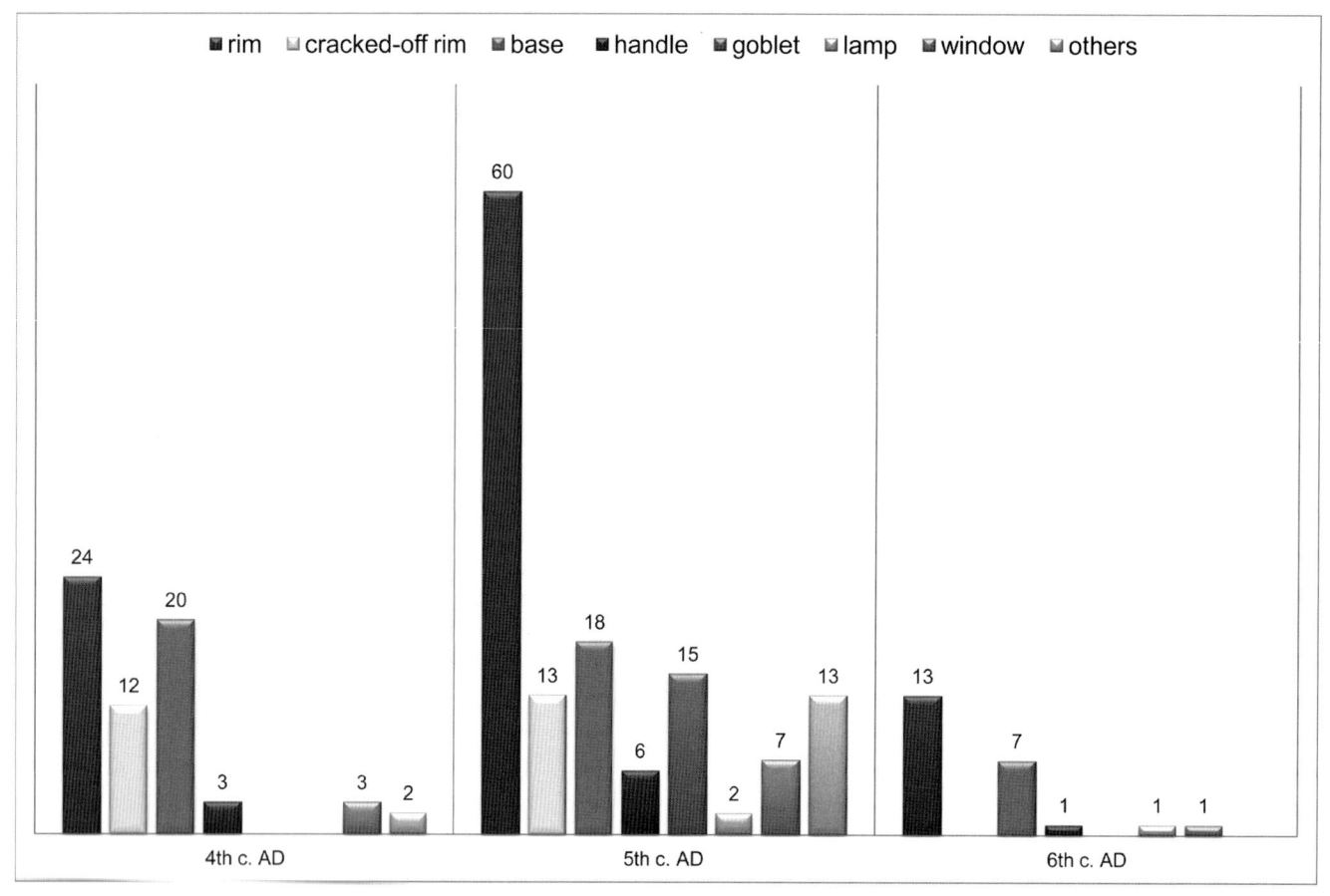

Fig. 16.6: Table showing the glass finds in the Peristyle Complex according to their period (DAI, H. Hamel).

flat base (Fig. 16.5.20; Gorin-Rosen and Katsnelson 2007, 84–85, fig. 5) are also present.

The 6th to 7th century

The layers of the 6th/7th century were excavated in the course of the Lebanese excavations in the 1960s and 1970s. Only a very small area with occupation levels of the 6th century has remained and this cannot be connected to any certain activity in the area of Bustan el-Khan. Nevertheless, the material has characteristics that distinguish it from the vessels of the 5th century.

The most obvious is the absence of beakers with cracked-off rims (Fig. 16.6). These were typical of the contexts of the 4th and 5th centuries, but are not found in the corpus of the 6th century when rims were predominantly fire rounded. Again, this has been observed elsewhere, as for example in Beirut (Jennings 2006, 84). No stems of goblets occur in this context. It seems unlikely that wine-glasses had gone out of fashion in *Heliopolis* by the 6th century because they are still very common at other sites in the area and the fire-rounded rims may belong to wine-glasses. The absence of stems might be because the context has only a limited number of vessel fragments, but fragments of stems usually survive well and are easily recognised. Fragments with trailed decoration were also not found in this context, although this is a common feature in the Byzantine period. More deposits of this period will be needed for further analysis of these phenomena, but because of the earlier excavations this may not be possible in *Heliopolis*.

Vessels with fire-rounded rims

The rims are plain and they range from 6 to 11cm in diameter (Fig. 16.5.21–24). Their colour is usually blue, with some nearly colourless and few green or blue/green examples. Their walls are generally thicker than the earlier vessels, but there are no major differences in form. Their shape is comparable with Byzantine wine-glasses (Gorin-Rosen and Winter 2010, figs. 2–4), so the absence of stems does not prevent their interpretation as stemmed goblets. In Beirut, it was thought statistically probable that these rims were principally from goblets (Jennings 2006, 131; for comparison of rims, see Jennings 2006, fig. 6.8).

Two cups/bowls with straight sides and slightly thickened

Table 16.1: Major and minor elemental composition of two glass samples.

	Na₂O	MgO	Al₂O₃	SiO₂	K₂O	CaO	TiO₂	MnO	FeO
Sample 5	17.49	0.88	2.64	66.64	0.81	10.84	0.07	0.03	0.29
Sample 9	16.10	0.85	2.63	0.14	0.37	8.26	0.09	1.22	0.46

Analytical details: The instrument used was a Micro-XRF Eagle III XXL from Roenalytic GmbH, Taunusstein (Germany) operated with a Rhodium tube (max. 40kV, 1mA), Oxford Instruments Si(Li) detector (resolution 148eV for MnKα). X-ray optics: monocapillary, 0.3mm focus (= analyzed spot size).

Analytical parameters: Vacuum, tube voltage / current: 40kV, 125μA, acquisition time 200Lsec, amplification time 35μs, quantification done by combining fundamental parameter methods and standard aided method with calibration curves based on Corning A, Corning D, NIST 620, NIST 610, BRU7. Values obtained for NIST 620 can be found in Greiff in press. Three points that were thoroughly cleaned from any corrosion layers were analyzed for each sample and the average is given here.

rims were also found (Fig. 16.5.25–26). They are thin-walled and have different rim sizes, one being 8cm in diameter and the other one 11cm. This type is typical for the late Byzantine/Umayyad period (Dussart 1998, BI.31, pl. 5.1–5; Keller 2006, type VII.39, pl. 17g; Dussart 2007, fig. 8.7–7c).

Other elements missing at this period are flasks and jugs, and bottles with funnel mouths, which are also very common in the 5th century, but are represented in *Heliopolis* by only one fragment (Fig. 16.5.27).

Lamps

Two fragments have been classified as lamps. A small loop-handle (Fig. 16.5.28) similar in size and style to those mentioned above is evidence for the continued use of suspension lamps. The second piece is a long solid stem with a constriction on its lower end (Fig. 16.5.29). The fragment is broken on both sides, but the stem can be compared to the 'type 4c solid stem lamps with tooling marks' of Jennings (2006, 145, fig. 6.20.1–7; cf. Foy 2000, fig. 7) which are local to Beirut and dated to the late Byzantine/Umayyad period (Foy 2000, 250).

Bases

The regular form of base is again the tubular base-ring (Fig. 16.5.30–32), but the middle of the base does not survive on any of the examples so it is not clear whether a pontil iron was used. They are large, ranging from 6 to 10cm in diameter and probably belonged to bowls (Foy 2000, fig. 23).

One base is slightly pushed-in (Fig. 16.5.33), and shows no trace of a pontil iron. It is different from the other vessels in many ways: the inner surface is very shiny and smooth and the glass is greenish in colour. This base probably belongs to a bottle (Gorin-Rosen and Katsnelson 2007, fig. 35; cf. Dussart 2007, fig. 7.4–5).

Chemical analysis

Seventeen samples selected from chronologically diverse layers have been analysed by the laboratory of the *Römisch-Germanisches Zentralmuseum* in Mainz. One reason for analysing the fragments was to confirm the preliminary dating of the extensively disturbed layers. This was possible because during the first millennium AD and the Middle Ages major changes in glass compositions occurred with the introduction of new fluxing materials. In addition, small scale compositional variations can be used to assign a certain glass type to one or other of the production centres that were operating at different periods thus giving a rough chronological frame. Another objective of the Micro X-ray Fluorescence analysis was to recognise the nature of some glass-like materials. Two of the samples were categorised as production waste and one was identified as probably being connected to a ceramic production process.

Two of the samples, a bluish-green raw glass chunk (sample no. 5, 5th century) and a piece of flat glass (sample no. 9, 4th century) belong to the layers discussed here, so that their chemical nature will be briefly reviewed. Table 16.1 gives results for major and minor elements. Several chemical glass groups have been identified by different authors (*e.g.* Foy *et al.* 2003, Freestone *et al.* 2000, among others) as being available during the first millennium AD; a short description and discussion of these production groups can be found in Greiff and Keller (this volume). Among the five major groups, there are two potential candidates for the time frames of the contexts for samples 5 and 9. The group of traditional Roman glass compositions was typical for 1st to 4th and even 5th-century glassware, whereas "Levantine I" glass was extensively used between the 5th and the 7th century.

These chemical groups differ in various ways and one distinguishing parameter is the lime (CaO) to alumina (Al₂O₃) ratio (Fig 16.7). For sample 5 (5th-century raw glass chunk) the identification as "Levantine 1" is quite straightforward, whereas sample 9 (4th-century flat glass) needs more careful attention as the data fields for Roman glass and Levantine I compositions overlap for low lime compositions. However, when the other chemical elements such as titanium, manganese and potassium are considered it is clear that sample 9 belongs to the "Levantine I" category.

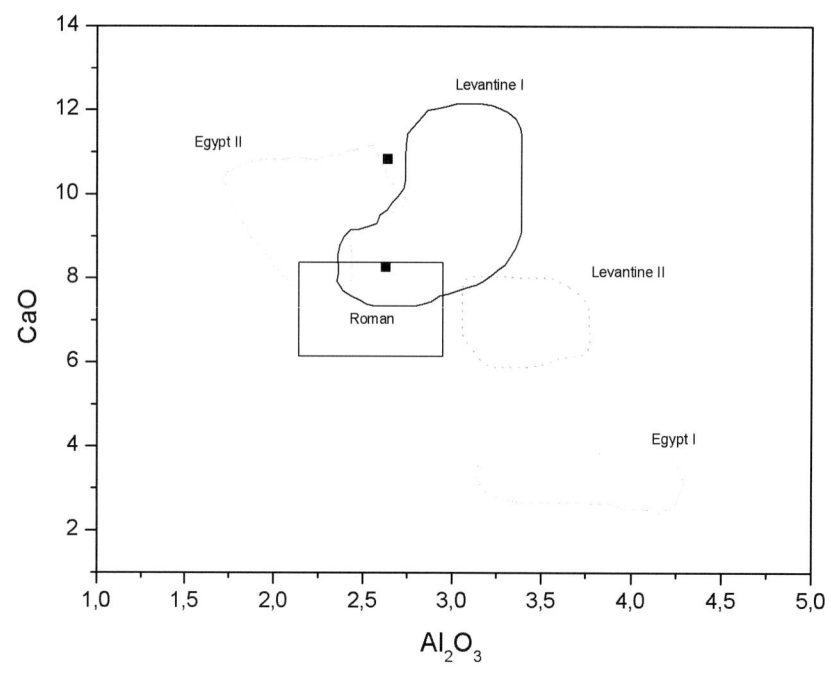

Fig. 16.7: Chemical diagram with lime against alumina and major compositional glass groups of the first millennium AD. The black lined areas of "Roman" and "Levantine I" compositions are potential candidates for the two analyzed Baalbek samples (see text).

Conclusion

The glass vessels from Baalbek are comparable to most other contemporary sites in the eastern Mediterranean region. Neither the quantity nor the forms are significantly different, although decorated and complex forms are almost absent in the assemblage discussed here. The majority of glass finds at all periods were used as drinking vessels, while other forms such as jugs and flasks became more common in the 4th and 5th century than before or after that period. The late Roman period seems to be when the greatest variety and quantity of glass for different forms of storage and the serving and consumption of food and drink was present in Baalbek (Fig. 16.6).

This is evident in the context of the tableware used in the banqueting hall. Ceramic fine wares were only represented by a total of 3 fragments in the infill of the staircase, whereas many glass beakers were present, as well as jugs, bowls, and dishes used to serve the diners at the banquets. The cracked-off rims of the beakers were well finished so that they could be used for drinking. At the beginning of the 4th century glass had replaced pottery for drinking vessels (Figs. 16.3.1–2, 16.3.7, 16.3.9) in the context of "official banquets" in *Heliopolis*, and the food was very probably served in glass dishes/bowls (Fig. 16.3.5–6). Unfortunately, nothing is known about private households from *Heliopolis*, but the general development of domestic glass use may be similar to that shown by Daniel Keller in Petra (2006, 127–130, 135–138, 142–163).

The two glass samples that have been chemically analysed show a composition typical of raw glass produced on the Levantine coast, a finding which is unsurprising in view of the geographical context of the site. More detailed study of other contexts in Baalbek is needed to draw conclusions about a comprehensive typology of glass vessels in *Heliopolis*. The trends presented here should be regarded as preliminary, although other areas in the city studied by the author do not show any major differences.

Acknowledgements

I would like to thank the German Archaeological Institute and the Lebanese Directorate General of Antiquities for the opportunity to study the material from Baalbek. My research was funded by the German Research Foundation for which I am very grateful. All members of the Baalbek-mission provided constant support and help but special thanks must be given to Bettina Fischer-Genz for information on the Islamic glass and Henning Burwitz who provided plans and information on the architectural background. Franziska Jahnke was involved in the fieldwork and Tobias Woskowski supported this work with digital drawings. Special thanks must be extended to the organisers of the meeting in York and Yael Gorin-Rosen for her help with this paper.

Catalogue

4th century

Fig. 16.3.1 Conical beaker, cracked-off rim, nearly colourless, no pontil scar. Dm rim: 9.5cm (no. 316/2010).

Fig. 16.3.2 Cylindrical beaker, cracked-off rim, nearly colourless, leaden weathering. Dm: 8.7cm (no. 303/2010).

Fig. 16.3.3 Hemispherical cup/bowl-shaped lamp, cracked-off rim, colourless, thin silver weathering. Dm: 9.8cm (no. 292/2010).

Fig. 16.3.4 Bottle, unfinished cracked-off rim, light green. Dm: 3.4cm (no. 265/2010).

Fig. 16.3.5 Dish, fire-rounded rim, light green. Dm: 22cm (no. 276/2010).

Fig. 16.3.6 Dish, fire-rounded rim, light green, thin leaden weathering. Dm: 25cm (no. 304/2010).

Fig. 16.3.7 Conical beaker, fire-rounded rim, light green, thin leaden weathering. Dm: 9.4cm (no. 301/2010).

Fig. 16.3.8 Deep bowl, fire-rounded rim, light green, leaden weathering. Dm: 14cm (no. 286/2010).

Fig. 16.3.9 Beaker, fire-rounded rim, light green. Dm: 6cm (no. 293/2010).

Fig. 16.3.10 Juglet, folded-in rim, one handle, blue-green. Dm: 3cm (no.297/2010).

Fig. 16.3.11 Flask/bottle, fire-rounded rim, light green, silver and leaden weathering. Irregular dm: 3.5cm (302/2010).

Fig. 16.3.12 Flask/bottle, fire-rounded rim, colourless, thick white weathering. Dm: 3cm (no. 277/2010).

Fig. 16.3.13 Jug with applied trail, fire-rounded rim, one handle, green. Dm: 7.5cm (no. 279/2010).

Fig. 16.3.14 Jug with applied trail, fire-rounded rim, two handles, blue-green, leaden weathering. Dm: 6.4cm (no. 280/2010).

Fig. 16.3.15 Body sherd, cut decoration, light green (no. 281/2010).

Fig. 16.3.16 Concave base and body with pincers, green, iridescence, pontil scar. Dm: 3cm (no. 278/2010).

Fig. 16.3.17 Tubular base-ring, green, no pontil scar. Dm: 3cm (no. 315/2010).

Fig. 16.3.18 Tubular base-ring, light blue, pontil scar. Dm: 3.8cm (no. 299/2010).

Fig. 16.3.19 Concave base, blue-green, thin leaden weathering, pontil scar. Dm: 3cm (no. 308/2010).

Fig. 16.3.20 Flat base, light green. Dm: 4cm (no. 296/2010).

Fig. 16.3.21 Open base-ring, real colourless, thick white weathering. Dm: 4cm (no. 272/2010).

Fig. 16.3.22 Solid base, green, iridescent. Dm: 3.8cm (no. 298/2010).

5th century

Fig. 16.4.1 Conical beaker, cracked-off rim, blue-green, iridescent. Dm: 10cm (no. 108/2010).

Fig. 16.4.2 Conical beaker, cracked-off rim, pale yellow, iridescent. Dm: 10cm (no.102/2010).

Fig. 16.4.3 Conical beaker, cracked-off rim, cut groove below rim, green, iridescent. Dm: 13cm (no. 98/2010).

Fig. 16.4.4 Segmental bowl, cracked-off rim, blue, iridescent. Dm: 13cm (no. 72/2010).

Fig. 16.4.5 Large shallow bowl/beaker, cracked-off rim, green, iridescent. Dm: 13cm (no. 44/2010).

Fig. 16.4.6 Bowl-shaped lamp, cracked-off rim, blue-green, iridescent. Dm: 17cm (no. 92/2010).

Fig. 16.4.7 Beaker/wine-glass, fire-rounded rim, light blue, iridescent. Dm: 8cm (no. 51/2010).

Fig. 16.4.8 Beaker/wine-glass, fire-rounded rim, light blue. Dm: 8cm (no. 56/2010).

Fig. 16.4.9 Beaker/bowl, fire-rounded rim, green, iridescent. Dm: 11cm (no. 133/2010).

Fig. 16.4.10 Bowl, fire-rounded rim, blue-green, iridescent. Dm: 13cm (no. 81/2010).

Fig. 16.4.11 Beaker, fire-rounded rim, green. Dm: 5.7cm (no. 53/2010).

Fig. 16.4.12 Beaker/wine-glass, fire-rounded rim, green. Dm: 9cm (no. 184/2010).

Fig. 16.4.13 Beaker/wine-glass, fire-rounded rim, green, leaden weathering. Dm: 7cm (no. 231/2010).

Fig. 16.4.14 Jug/flask, fire-rounded rim, pale blue, iridescent. Dm: 5.2cm (no. 413/2010).

Fig. 16.4.15 Jug/flask, rolled-in rim, light blue, iridescent. Dm: 5.5cm (no. 69/2010).

Fig. 16.4.16 Jug/flask, fire-rounded rim, light blue, iridescent. Dm: 6cm (no. 66/2010).

Fig. 16.4.17 Jug/flask, fire-rounded rim, blue-green, iridescent. Dm: 7cm (no. 127/2010).

Fig. 16.4.18 Jug/flask, rolled-in rim, green. Dm: 9cm (no. 130/2010).

Fig. 16.4.19 Jug/flask, folded-in rim, blue-green, iridescent. Dm: 8cm (no. 124/2010).

Fig. 16.4.20 Bowl, folded-in rim, light green. Dm: 15cm (no. 120/2010).

Fig. 16.4.21 Bowl/dish, folded-out rim, green. Dm: 26cm (no. 402/2010).

Fig. 16.5.1 Hollow stem lamp, light blue, iridescent, pontil scar. (no. 64/2010).

Fig. 16.5.2 Loop handle, blue-green. (no. 80/2010).

Fig. 16.5.3 Loop handle, blue-green. (no. 54/2010).

Fig. 16.5.4 'Delicate' base of a wine-glass, light blue, iridescent. Dm: 3.9cm (no. 100/2010).

Fig. 16.5.5 Stem of a wine-glass, light blue, iridescent. (no. 76/2010).

Fig. 16.5.6 'Delicate' base of a wine-glass, light blue, iridescent. Dm: 3cm (no. 126/2010).

Fig. 16.5.7 'Delicate' base of a wine-glass, colourless, iridescent. Dm: 4cm (no. 43/2010).

Fig. 16.5.8 'Delicate' base of a wine-glass, light blue, iridescent. Dm: 4.5cm (no. 42/2010).

Fig. 16.5.9 'Delicate' base of a wine-glass, light blue. Dm: 5cm (no. 48/2010).

Fig. 16.5.10 Jug with applied blue trail, fire-rounded rim, green. Dm: 11cm (no. 125/2010).

Fig. 16.5.11 Juglet with applied blue trail, fire-rounded rim, green. Dm: 6.5cm (no. 139/2010).

Fig. 16.5.12 Body sherd with blue-blob decoration, light green, iridescent. (no. 454/2010).

Fig. 16.5.13 Pushed in base, light blue, iridescent. Dm: 6cm (no. 68/2010).

Fig. 16.5.14 Tubular base-ring, light green. Dm: 3.5cm (no. 73/2010).

Fig. 16.5.15 Tubular base-ring, blue-green, iridescent, pontil scar. Dm: 4.5cm (no. 103/2010).

Fig. 16.5.16 Tubular base-ring, colourless, iridescent, pontil scar, irregular. Dm: 4cm (no. 190/2010).

Fig. 16.5.17 Pushed-in base, light green. Dm: 5cm (no. 99/2010).

Fig. 16.5.18 Flat base, light green, leaden weathering. Dm: 4cm (no. 97/2010).

Fig. 16.5.19 Tubular base-ring, light blue. Dm: 10.4cm (no. 419/2010).

Fig. 16.5.20 Flat base, nearly colourless, iridescent, silver and leaden weathering. Dm: 5cm (no. 86/2010).

6th/7th century

Fig. 16.5.21 Wine-glass, fire-rounded rim, light blue, iridescent. Dm: 6cm (no. 423/2010).

Fig. 16.5.22 Wine-glass, fire-rounded rim, nearly colourless, iridescent. Dm: 7.8cm (no. 427/2010).

Fig. 16.5.23 Wine-glass, fire-rounded rim, light blue, iridescent. Dm: 8cm (no. 390/2010).

Fig. 16.5.24 Wine-glass, fire-rounded rim, blue-green, iridescent. Dm: 9.8cm (no. 426/2010).

Fig. 16.5.25 Bowl/cup, fire-rounded rim, light green. Dm: 8cm (no. 421/2010).

Fig. 16.5.26 Bowl, fire-rounded rim, light green, iridescent. Dm: 10cm (430/2010).

Fig. 16.5.27 Jug/flask, fire-rounded rim, nearly colourless, iridescent. Dm: 4.6cm (no. 399/2010).

Fig. 16.5.28 Loop handle, blue-green (no. 392/2010).

Fig. 16.5.29 Solid stem of a lamp, light blue, tooling marks. Dm: 1cm (no. 424/2010).

Fig. 16.5.30 Pushed-in base, light blue. Dm: 10cm (no. 401/2010).

Fig. 16.5.31 Tubular base-ring, light blue. Dm: 10.4cm (no. 418/2010).

Fig. 16.5.32 Tubular base-ring, light blue. Dm: 8cm (no. 420/2010).

Fig. 16.5.33 Concave base, fire polished, green, iridescent, no pontil scar. Dm: 5.5cm (no. 391/2010).

Bibliography

Atallah, M. and Gawlikowska, K. (2007) The Glass in the Beiteddine Museum (Walid Jumblatt Collection). *Bulletin d'Archéologie et d'Architecture Libanaises* 11, 167–277.

Barag, D. (1978) Ḥanita, Tomb XV. A Tomb of the Third and Early Fourth Century C.E. *'Atiqot* 13, 1–60.

Burwitz, H. (2008) Gelage im großen Stil. Zur Rekonstruktion und Deutung des „Peristylkomplexes" in Heliopolis/Baalbek. In L. Schmidt and A. Bantelman (eds.) *Forschen Bauen und Erhalten*. Jahrbuch 2008/2009, 65–72. Berlin/Bonn, Westkreuz-Verlag.

Clairmont, Ch. W. (1963) *The glass vessels*. The Excavations at Dura-Europos. Final Report 4.5. New Haven, CT, Dura-Europos Publications.

Dussart, O. (1998) *Le verre en Jordanie et en Syrie du sud*. Bibliothèque Archéologique et Historique 152. Beirut, Institut Français d'Archéologie du Proche-Orient.

Dussart, O. (2007) Fouilles de Khirbet edh-Dharih, III. Les verres. *Syria* 84, 205–248.

van Ess, M. (2008) *Baalbek/Heliopolis. Results of Archaeological and Architectural Research 2002–2005*. Bulletin d'Archéologie et d'Architecture Libanaises Hors-Série IV. Beirut, Ministère de la Culture.

Fischer-Genz, B., Lehmann, H. and Vezzoli, V. (2010) Pots in a Corner. Ceramics and glass finds from a closed medieval context in Bustan Nassif (Baalbek). *Bulletin d'Archéologie et d'Architecture Libanaises* 14, 289–306.

Foy, D. (2000) Un atelier de verrier à Beyrouth au débuts de la conquête islamique. *Syria* 77, 239–290.

Foy, D., Picon, M., Vichy, M. and Thirion-Merle, V. (2003) Caractérisation des verres de la fin de l'Antiquité en Méditerranée occidentale: l'émergence de nouveaux courants commerciaux. In D. Foy and M.-D. Nenna (eds.) *Échanges et commerce du verre dans le monde antique*. Monographies Instrumentum 24, 41–85. Montagnac, Monique Mergoil.

Freestone, I. C., Gorin-Rosen, Y. and Hughes, M. J. (2000) Primary glass from Israel and the production of glass in Late Antiquity and the Early Islamic period. In M.-D. Nenna (ed.) *La route du verre. Ateliers primaires et secondaires du second millénaire av. J.-C. au Moyen Âge*. Travaux de la Maison de l'Orient Méditerranéen 33, 65–83. Lyon, Maison de l'Orient Mediterranéen.

Gorin-Rosen, Y. (2002) The Glass Vessel from Burial Cave D at Hurfeish. In Z. Gal (ed.) *Eretz Zafon. Studies in Galilean Archaeology*, *140–*166. Jerusalem, Israel Antiquities Authority.

Gorin-Rosen, Y. (2006) The Glass Finds from Khirbat el-Batiya (Triangulation Spot 819). *'Atiqot* 53, 29*–36* (Hebrew), 198 (English summary).

Gorin-Rosen, Y. (2009) The Glass Vessels from Strata 9–6. In N. Getzov (ed.) *Ḥorbat 'Uẓa. The 1991 Excavations*. Israel Antiquities Authority Reports 42, 78–98. Jerusalem, Israel Antiquities Authority.

Gorin-Rosen, Y. (2010) Glass from the Late Byzantine Remains near Shiqmona. *'Atiqot* 63, 209–218.

Gorin-Rosen, Y. and Jackson-Tal, R. E. (2008) Area F: The Glass Finds. In V. Tzaferis and Sh. Israeli (eds.) *Paneas. The Roman to Early Islamic Periods. Excavations in Areas A, B, E, F, G and H*. Israel Antiquities Authority Reports 37, 141–154. Jerusalem, Israel Antiquities Authority.

Gorin-Rosen, Y. and Katsnelson, N. (2007) Local Glass Production in the Late Roman–Early Byzantine Periods in Light of the Glass Finds from Khirbat el-Ni'ana. *'Atiqot* 57, 73–154.

Gorin-Rosen, Y. and Winter, T. (2010) Selected Insights into Byzantine Glass in the Holy Land. In J. Drauschke and D. Keller (eds.) *Glass in Byzantium – production, usage, analyses*. RGZM – Tagungen 8, 165–181. Mainz, Römisch-Germanisches Zentralmuseum.

Greiff, S. (in press) Chemical glass types used for the production of glassware from late antiquity to the early Islamic period found at Jabal Harun. In Z. T. Fiema and J. Frösén, *Petra – The Mountain of Aaron II. The Nabataean Sanctuary and the Byzantine Monastery*. Helsinki, Societas Scientiarum Fennica.

Hamel, H. (2008) Late 3rd/early 4th century pottery and glass from Baalbek/Heliopolis. *Bulletin d'Archéologie et d'Architecture Libanaises* 12, 203–219.

Hamel, H. (2010) Local Coarse Ware Pottery from 4th Century Baalbek/Heliopolis, Lebanon. In S. Menchelli (ed.) *LRCW 3. Late Roman coarse wares, cooking wares and amphorae in the Mediterranean. Archaeology and archaeometry*. British Archaeological Reports International Series 2185, 877–884. Oxford, Archaeopress.

Harden, D. B. (1949) Tomb-Groups of Glass of Roman Date from Syria and Palestine. *Iraq* 11, 151–159.

Israeli, Y. (2008) The Glass Vessels. In J. Patrich (ed.) *Archaeological excavations at Caesarea Maritima. Areas CC, KK and NN Final Reports I. The Objects*, 367–418. Jerusalem, Israel Exploration Society.

Jennings, S. (2006) *Vessel glass from Beirut. Bey 006, 007, and 045*, Berytus 48–49. Beirut, The American University.

Katsnelson, N. (2010a) Baqa el-Gharbiya Area: The Glass Vessels from Horbat Kosit (East). *'Atiqot* 64, 133–142.

Katsnelson, N. (2010b) Baqa el-Gharbiya Area: The Glass Vessels from Nahal Hadera (North). *'Atiqot* 64, 143–152.

Keller, D. (2006) Die Gläser aus Petra. In D. Keller and M. Grawehr, *Petra ez Zantur III. Ergebnisse der Schweizerisch-Liechtensteinischen Ausgrabungen*. Terra Archaeologica 5, 1–256. Mainz, Philipp von Zabern.

Keller, D. (2012) Pickled eggs and precious spices. Glas in der spätrömischen Küche. In P. Jung and N. Schücker (eds.) *Utere felix vivas. Festschrift für Jürgen Oldenstein*. Universitätsforschungen zur prähistorischen Archäologie 208, 103–112. Bonn, Rudolf Habelt.

Vitto, F. (2010) A Burial Cave from the Third–Early Fourth Centuries CE at Iqrit. *'Atiqot* 62, 59–96.

Weinberg, G. D. and Goldstein, S. M. (1988) The Glass Vessels. In G. D. Weinberg (ed.) *Excavations at Jalame. Site of a Glass Factory in Late Roman Palestine*, 38–102. Columbia, MO, University of Missouri Press.

Weinberg, G. D. and Stern, E. M. (2009) *Vessel Glass*. The Athenian Agora 34. Princeton, NJ, The American School of Classical Studies at Athens.

17

Changes in glass supply in southern Jordan in the later first millennium AD

Susanne Greiff and Daniel Keller

Introduction

The glass finds from the monastery of St Aaron on Jabal Harun near Petra will be used as a case study to explore the supply of glass during the later first millennium AD in southern Jordan. The long-lasting occupation of the monastery with several well defined phases provides a good basis as assemblages associated with the respective phases let to the definition of a glass sequence. The monastery was built in the mid/late 5th century and continued into the early Islamic period and even the Crusader period, although no glass finds younger than the late 9th/early 10th century could be identified. The Byzantine and early Islamic glass finds were grouped according to contexts associated with the subsequent phases of the church and the monastery respectively, thus representing the four phases of the complex (Keller and Lindblom 2008; in press). A monastery/pilgrim hostel with a basilica church and an adjacent chapel was constructed in the mid/late 5th century. After their destruction in the mid/late 6th century, the church and chapel were rebuilt, but on a smaller scale and the pilgrimage centre was reconstructed. In the 7th century, the pilgrimage centre was restored and the church and chapel were remodelled. In the last phase, the complex was reduced to a small fortified monastery with the church being in domestic use while the chapel remained in ecclesiastical use. Of course, the glass finds primarily reflect the history and the status or wealth of the monastery on Jabal Harun (Keller 2010; Keller and Lindblom in press), but secondarily they provide evidence for the glass supply of the wider region of southern Jordan during this period.

Considering ancient glassware from a compositional point of view offers new perspectives for the purpose of discussing and grouping artefacts excavated from a single site such as the monastery on Jabal Harun. First results that focus on the chronological pattern based on the 218 analysed samples were presented in a recent paper (Greiff in press). For the present contribution we aim to compare our results to published data sets of material from the same period derived from other sites in the eastern Mediterranean. This comparison will provide an overview of the way glass trade and commerce evolved in this part of the Near East that would otherwise remain elusive.

Jabal Harun glass groups: chemical categories and chronological evolution

The detailed chronological classification as well as details

Table 17.1: Comparing the listed and measured values of glass standard NIST 620 gives an impression of the data quality attainable by the analytical equipment used. As NIST 620 is a lead-free glass values for lead oxide are based on a glass standard used by Bruker (Bru 7) listed with 0.10 wt.% PbO. Our Micro-XRF results for PbO vary between 0.12 and 0.98%.

	Na_2O	MgO	Al_2O_3	SiO_2	SO_3	K_2O	CaO	TiO_2	FeO	As_2O_3	SrO
Listed	14.39	3.69	1.80	72.08	0.28	0.41	7.11	0.02	0.04	0.06	0.00
Measured	14.73	3.65	1.85	71.86	0.26	0.39	7.07	0.02	0.04	0.07	0.04
Standard deviation	0.29	0.10	0.06	0.35	0.02	0.01	0.13	0.00	0.01	0.00	0.00

of the analytical procedure have been presented in other publications (Keller and Lindblom 2008; in press; Greiff in press). However, the internal structure of the compositional data will be briefly reviewed outlining major conclusions. Furthermore, Table 17.1 presents a comparison between listed and measured values of a standard reference glass in order to inform about the data quality obtained by the instrumentation used. Two hundred thirty-four Micro-XRF-analyses were performed on 218 glass fragments. The fragments had been chosen in order to present a selection that was regarded as representative as possible for the chronological development of glass types and fabrics, including a sufficient number of samples for each vessel type. As might be expected from an ecclesiastical site where lighting played an important role, lighting devices such as polycandelon and single lamps represented the largest group followed by tableware such as goblets, cups, bowls and flasks.

Different groups of glass compositions were established (Fig. 17.1) based on the interpretation of binary diagrams, mainly those depicting the contents of lime versus alumina ($CaO:Al_2O_3$). These two compounds reflect minor mineralogical components depending on the sand used for glass production, which may vary from site to site. Consequently, raw glass produced in Egypt will have a different composition from one produced somewhere on the Levantine coast, despite the glass makers using the same recipe concerning sand versus flux ratios and adding the same amount of sand and soda into their tank furnaces.

Major differences may have also arisen from using different types of soda (plant ash or mineral). The period covered by the objects studied here is important with respect to a change from mineral soda compositions back to plant ash soda use in the eastern Mediterranean. The analyses of the Jabal Harun material, however, have shown that plant ash soda was not extensively used for objects from Jabal Harun. This was a rather astonishing finding because a considerable number of glass from the 8th and 9th centuries was analysed where one expected to see more plant ash based material as it had already become very popular in other parts of the Mediterranean (Henderson *et al.* 2004). Only six objects belong to this particular group, four of them dating to the 8th and 9th centuries (Greiff in press, nos. 137, 157, 159, 194–196).

For the remaining mineral soda samples, according to their respective CaO/Al_2O_3 patterns three separate data clusters and one group with a more linear distribution pattern could be identified (Fig. 17.1). They were labelled according to their CaO contents as "Lower Group", "Middle Group", "Upper Group" and "Line". The average composition of these groups is given in Table 17.2. Object dates and group affiliations were combined in order to investigate whether a time-resolved scheme was behind the identified distribution pattern. This was possible because a large sample set could be studied from the same site. The results clearly demonstrated that the dispersion of the data bear a chronological background with a predominance of objects of a certain period grouped together in one of the four data fields (Greiff in press). Studying the distribution in more detail revealed that objects of a certain vessel

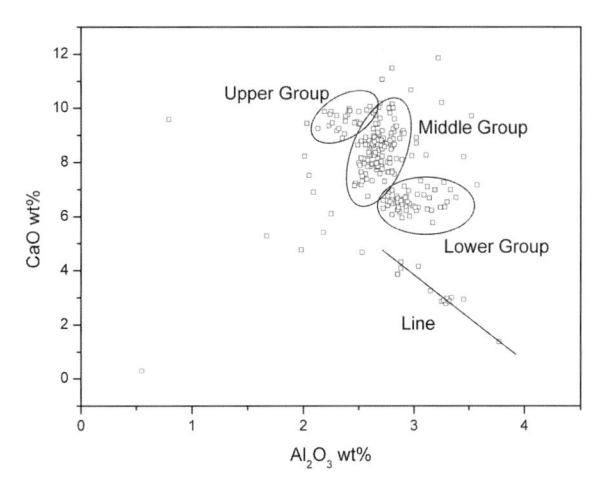

Fig. 17.1: Plotting lime and alumina contents for all Jabal Harun samples indicates that defined chemical groups can be identified that also are of chronological relevance (graph Susanne Greiff).

Table 17.2: Means and standard deviations for selected elements of the different chemical groups defined on the basis of CaO vs Al_2O_3 values (without samples overlapping Upper Group/Middle Group). The overlap between Upper Group and Middle Group compositions becomes obvious by looking at the standard deviations. dl = around detection limit of the method (ca. 0.01 wt% PbO).

Mean Deviation	Na₂O	MgO	Al₂O₃	SiO₂	K₂O	CaO	TiO₂	MnO	FeO	PbO
Upper Group (N = 25)	14.58	0.89	2.40	70.37	0.72	9.51	0.20	0.17	0.75	0.06
	0.70	0.24	0.20	0.63	0.38	0.46	0.08	0.30	0.23	0.10
Middle Group (N = 120)	14.55	0.81	2.69	71.81	0.75	8.52	0.08	0.03	0.39	dl
	1.08	0.12	0.12	1.59	0.27	0.76	0.01	0.02	0.09	-
Lower Group (N = 52)	13.13	0.76	2.97	75.11	0.64	6.56	0.09	0.02	0.44	dl
	1.03	0.09	0.17	1.17	0.10	0.33	0.02	0.00	0.07	-

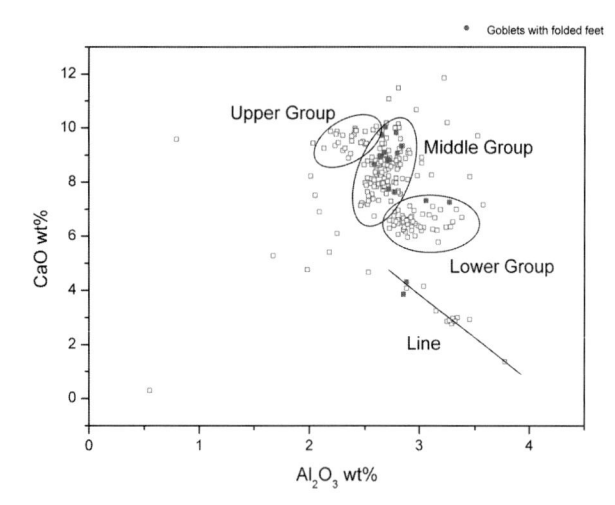

Fig. 17.2: The goblets with folded feet are a good example for demonstrating the fact that a vessel type was available in different chemical group "flavours" (graph Susanne Greiff).

type occupied the same cluster, but with some exceptions: there were always single pieces produced with the same chemical composition as in the preceding period and a few others already made according to a more "modern" glass composition (Fig. 17.2). The logical step is now to explore the data set in a wider regional context comparing it to major glass groups identified and described by several research groups and other contemporaneous data sets.

Classification of late antique and Byzantine compositional groups

During the last 15 years several subsets of late Roman and Byzantine mineral soda glass have been identified, according to their respective contents of alumina and lime (Al_2O_3/CaO) and other compositional features. In several papers Foy and co-workers (2000; 2003) have established four compositional glass groups divided into several subseries for glassware from southern France, Egypt and Tunisia dating from the 5th to the 9th century. Some groups have been already recognised by Sayre and Smith (1961). Similar compositional categories have been defined for the fragments from the Crypta Balbi in Rome analysed by Mirti *et al.* (2001). Based on their work on several primary glass production sites of mineral soda glass Freestone and co-workers (2000; 2002) were able to identify the geographic origin of two of the groups defined by different researchers. The group dominating the 5th and 6th-century assemblages came from sites situated along the Levantine coast. It was named Levantine I and defined by raw glass chunks from Apollonia-Arsuf, Bet She'an, Dor and Jalame, covering 4th to 7th-century assemblages (Apollonia-Arsuf: Freestone *et al.* 2000; 2008; Dor: Freestone *et al.* 2000; Jalame: Brill 1999; detailed Bet She'an data are not published and were extrapolated from graphs documented in different papers). Another group – Levantine II – from the production site of Bet Eli'ezer near Hadera is confined to the early Islamic period. Two primary production sites in Egypt seem to have delivered other large compositional groups to the glass market during the later first millennium AD: Egypt I, a cluster obtained by Gratuze and Barrandon (1990) by statistical analysis of 57 Islamic glass weights and data from Nenna *et al.* (2000); the other is Egypt II an 8th/9th-century group recognised, for example from chunks from El-Ashmunein in Middle Egypt (Bimson and Freestone 1987) but also among the Islamic weights just mentioned. A fifth group called HIMT is characterised by higher levels of transition metals. In the meantime more clusters, but also compositional overlaps have been identified either based on recent excavations of furnace structures of primary glass production as at Apollonia-Arsuf (Freestone *et al.* 2008) or the chemical investigation of larger glass assemblages such as the one from Butrint (Schibille 2011).

Discussing the samples from Jabal Harun in the light of the mentioned glass groups we can state that the composition of the Middle Group corresponds to the compositional range of Levantine I glass except for magnesium oxide (MgO) contents. With an average of 0.81±0.12 MgO is higher than the levels given for the Levantine I sites at Apollonia (0.50–0.70; Freestone *et al.* 2008) or Bet She'an (0.59; Freestone 2006). In terms of lime and alumina the Jabal Harun glassware compares well with the 4th-century site of Jalame that has been incorporated into the Levantine I group (Freestone *et al.* 2000). The earliest objects from Jabal Harun attributed to Levantine I come from mid 5th to 6th-century assemblages, the latest are mid 7th to 8th-century finds but the majority by far are from the earlier category. The Lower Group matches broadly the Levantine II compositions with their lower lime and slightly higher alumina values compared to Levantine I glass. The differences are that alumina is slightly lower (2.97 instead of 3.3 for Bet Eli'ezer) and our potassium oxide (K_2O) values of 0.64wt.% are slightly higher than the 0.46 given for the samples from Israel. This group features late 6th to 8th-century finds with a strong tendency for the 7th/early 8th century. The Upper Group is defined by high lime and low alumina values, both reproduced in the Egypt II group which is based on samples from El Ashmunein. Again, there is a small mismatch for potassium and magnesium values. The entire cluster dates to the 8th and 9th centuries. Elevated lead oxide observed for several examples belonging to this group may indicate a certain degree of recycling (Greiff in press). A smaller number of objects from Jabal Harun with very low lime contents (Line) correspond to glass samples grouped under the term Egypt I. In terms of lime and alumina, many Jabal Harun samples can be found nested

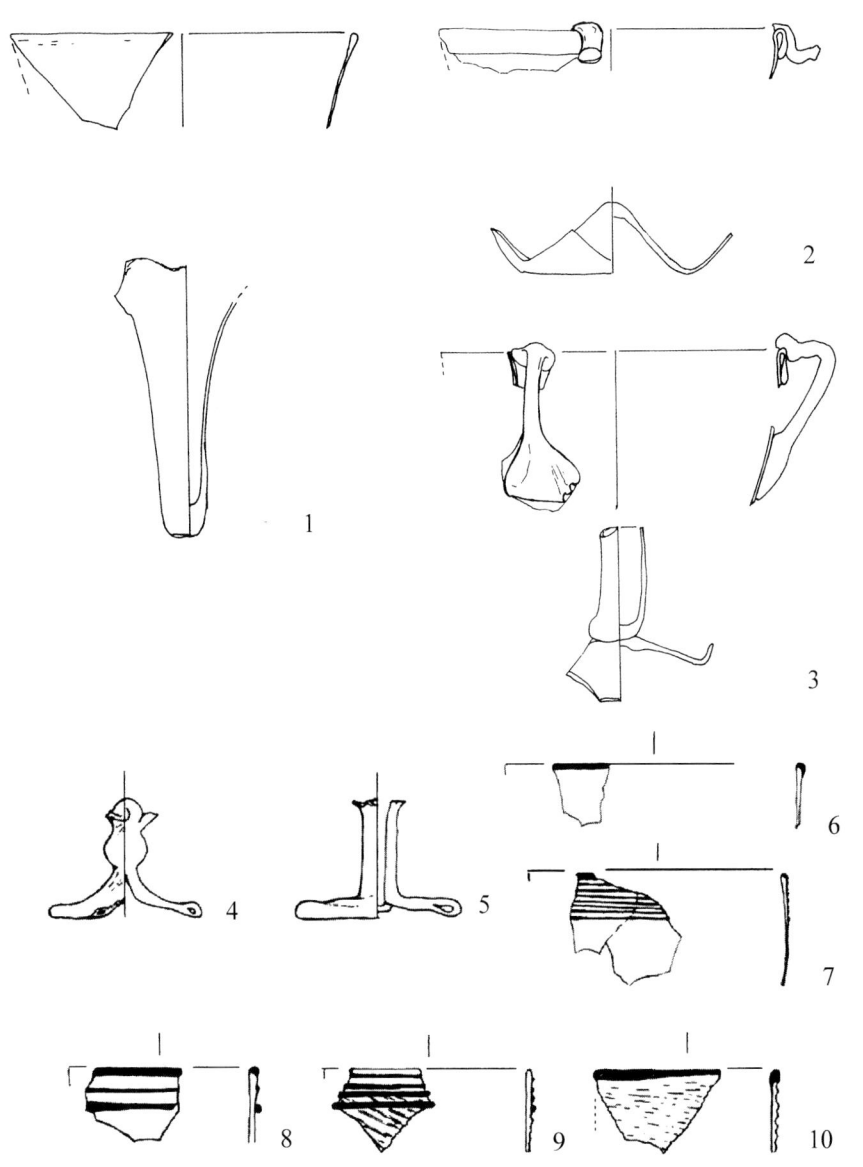

Fig. 17.3: Byzantine blue/green lamps, goblets and flasks of the late 5th–mid 6th century belonging to the Middle Group/Levantine I (scale 1:2; drawings Jeanette Lindblom).

on a line with a negative slope with a Ca:Al ratio of 1.05. A small, well defined group of green bowl-shaped single lamps clusters in an area that corresponds to the low alumina group of Gratuze and Barrandon (1990). The alumina values of 2.7±0.7 given by Nenna *et al.* (2000) only marginally reach the field defined by Gratuze and Barrandon (1990) and their values are lower than any of the Jabal Harun samples. Consequently, the characterisation of the published Egypt I group data as one single production group will need to be discussed.

Chronology and chemical composition of the Jabal Harun assemblage

Byzantine glass of the late 5th–mid 6th century

Several assemblages associated with the first phase of the monastery/pilgrimage hostel and the church could be identified (Keller and Lindblom 2008, 338–340, tables 1–2, fig. 2; in press, tables 1–2, figs. 4–7, 10.1–4). The lamp types in these assemblages are polycandelon lamps (Fig. 17.3.1) and small three-handled single lamps with or without

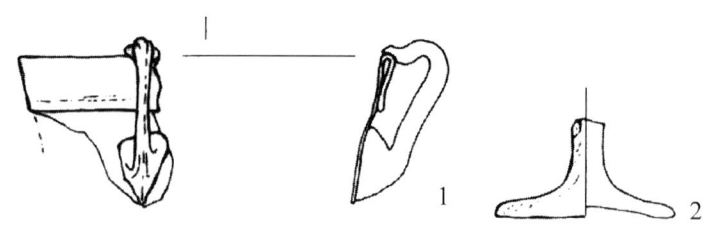

Fig. 17.4: Byzantine blue/green single lamp and stemmed goblet of the late 6th–early 7th century belonging to the Lower Group/Levantine II (lamp) and Middle Group/Levantine I (goblet) respectively (scale 1:2; drawings Jeanette Lindblom).

wick-tube attached to the base (Fig. 17.3.2–3). Both types are made of a clear good quality glass with two variations of strong colours, one blue, the other green (Keller and Lindblom 2008, 338–340; Keller 2010, 185–187, pl. 12.1). Furthermore, these assemblages include goblets with folded feet and fire-rounded rims and blue trails (Fig. 17.3.4–7) and flasks or bottles with fire-rounded rims, cylindrical necks and blue trails, sometimes with mould-blown spiral ribs (Fig. 17.3.8–10). These vessels are made of blue/green glass which is of a lower quality than the one used for the lamps and represents the common naturally coloured glass of the Byzantine period in Petra. The presence of goblets with folded feet and polycandelon lamps indicates that these glass finds can be dated after the mid 5th century representing typical Byzantine glass used in southern Jordan in the late 5th/6th century (Keller and Lindblom in press). Besides the two qualities of blue/green glass very few glass vessels and lamps made of yellow/green glass are also present in these assemblages (Keller and Lindblom in press).

Chemically speaking the vast majority of this material belong to the Middle Group with Levantine I affinities: polycandelon lamps (Fig. 17.3.1; Greiff in press, nos. 1–43), single lamps (Fig. 17.3.2–3; Greiff in press, nos. 44–51), goblets with fire-rounded rims and blue trails (Fig. 17.3.6–7; Greiff in press, nos. 107–116) and flasks with fire-rounded rims, cylindrical necks, blue trails and mould-blown spiral ribs (Fig. 17.3.8–10; Greiff in press, nos. 117–126). The goblets with folded feet (Fig. 17.3.4–5; Greiff in press, nos. 82–97, 217) are more heterogeneous in their chemical make-up (Fig. 17.2) as nos. 94 and 96 are members of the Lower Group (Levantine II) and nos. 86 and 87 are positioned on the Line (probably Egypt I); however, the majority of these goblet feet belong to the Middle Group (Levantine I). Most of the yellow/green Byzantine vessels (Greiff in press, nos. 159–165) are also part of the Middle Group/Levantine I compositions, but here we have an early plant ash glass (Greiff in press, no. 159: coil base; Keller and Lindblom in press, fig. 7.12, no. 123), one with an Egypt II affinity (Greiff in press, no. 162: tube-shaped miniature bottle; Keller and Lindblom in press, fig. 7.9, no. 120) and another one similar to Lower Group/Levantine II samples (Greiff in press, no.

163: tube-shaped miniature bottle; Keller and Lindblom in press, fig. 7.10, no. 121).

Byzantine glass of the late 6th–early 7th century

Only a few glass finds could be associated with the reconstructed pilgrimage centre and the smaller church of the second phase (Keller and Lindblom 2008, 340–341, table 3, fig. 3; in press, table 3, figs. 8–9, 10.5–6). These include larger single lamps with three handles and broader outfolded rims (Fig. 17.4.1) which were made of a blue/green glass with a muddy appearance and lower quality (Keller and Lindblom 2008, 340–341; Keller 2010, 187) as well as goblets with flat feet and solid stems (Fig. 17.4.2) which were made of similar blue/green glass as the goblets of the previous phase. In Israel and Jordan, goblets with flat feet and solid stems begin to replace the goblets with folded feet in the 2nd half of the 6th and the 7th century (Gorin-Rosen and Winter 2010, 167). Although the goblets with flat feet and solid stems remain the predominant goblet type in the Umayyad period, the absence of other Umayyad glass vessel types indicates that these assemblages can be dated to the late 6th/early 7th century (Keller and Lindblom in press).

With regards to their chemical composition the single lamps (Fig. 17.4.1; Greiff in press, nos. 52–61, 218) can be grouped with the Lower Group/Levantine II data cluster. Few exceptions belong to the Middle Group/Levantine I cluster. All goblets with flat feet (Fig. 17.4.2; Greiff in press, nos. 98–106) are also of Levantine I composition.

Umayyad glass of the mid 7th–mid 8th century

More glass finds were associated with the remodelled church and the restored pilgrimage centre of the mid 7th century (Keller and Lindblom 2008, 341–342, table 4, fig. 4; in press, tables 4–6, figs. 11–15). Typical for these assemblages are large single lamps with broad outfolded rims, three handles and wick-tubes (Fig. 17.5.1–2) which are made of a low quality blue/green glass with many bubbles and impurities and occasional wick-tubes of yellow/green glass (Keller and Lindblom 2008, 341–342; Keller 2010,

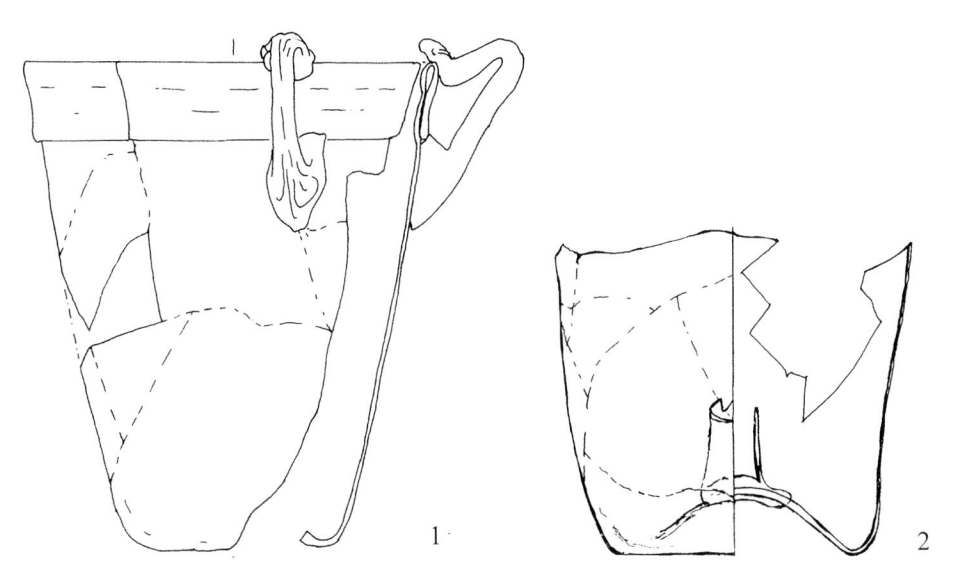

Fig. 17.5: Umayyad blue/green single lamps of the mid 7th–mid 8th century belonging to the Lower Group/Levantine II (scale 1:2; drawings Jeanette Lindblom).

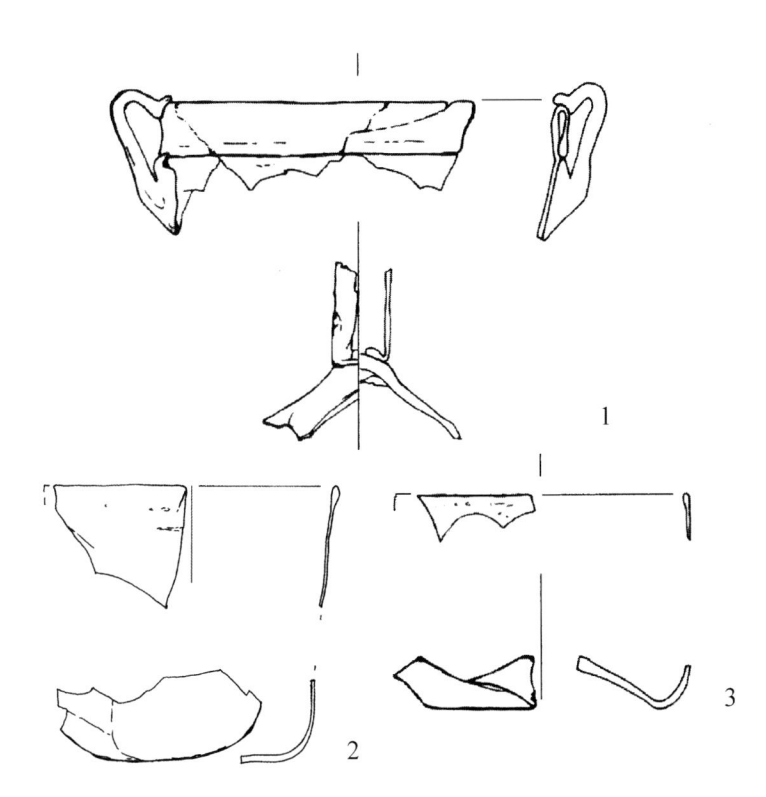

Fig. 17.6: Umayyad yellow/green lamp and cups of the mid 7th–mid 8th century belonging to the Middle Group/Levantine I (scale 1:2; drawings Jeanette Lindblom).

187–188, pls. 12.2, 13.1). Of similar yellow/green glass are single lamps with outfolded rims, three handles and wick-tubes (Fig. 17.6.1) and cylindrical cups with fire-rounded rims and concave bases (Fig. 17.6.2–3). Furthermore, these assemblages yielded bowl-shaped single lamps with three handles (Fig. 17.7.1), cylindrical cups with fire-rounded rims (Fig. 17.7.2) and globular cups with rolled-in rims (Fig. 17.7.3), all made of clear green glass (cf. Keller 2010,

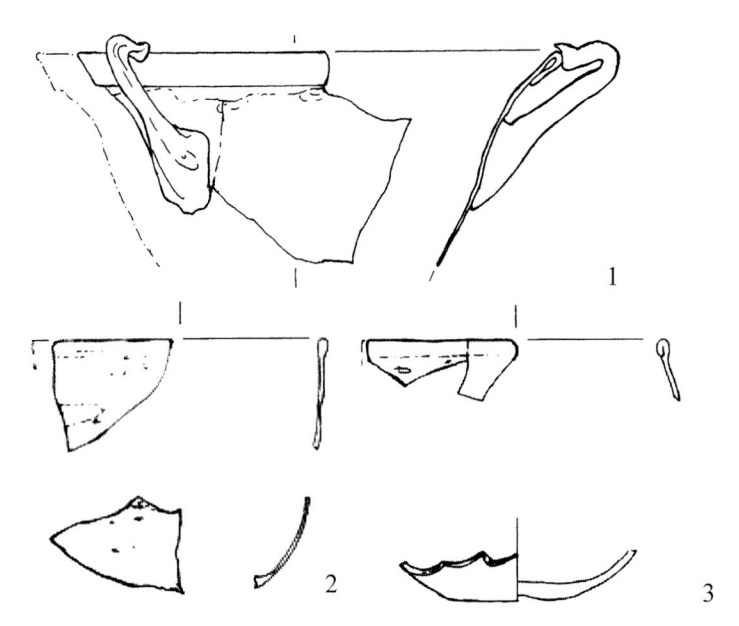

Fig. 17.7: Umayyad green lamp and cups of the mid 7th–mid 8th century belonging to the Line/Egypt I (scale 1:2; drawings Jeanette Lindblom).

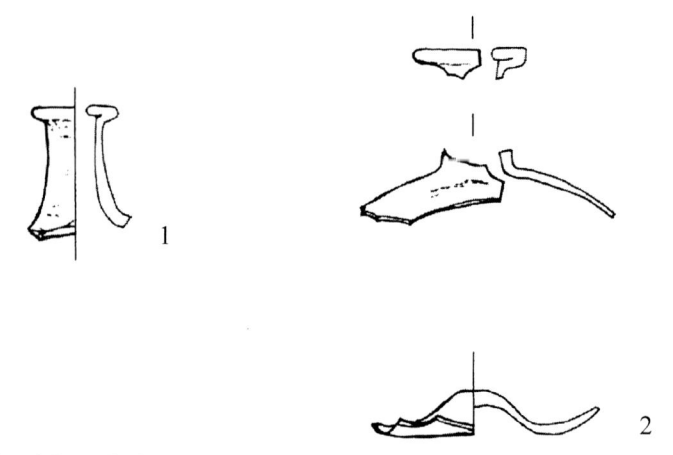

Fig. 17.8: Umayyad green flasks of the mid 7th–mid 8th century made of plant ash glass (scale 1:2; drawings Jeanette Lindblom).

pl. 12.3). Additionally, bottles with infolded flattened rims, short cylindrical necks, squat bodies and concave bases (Fig. 17.8.1–2) made of green glass and covered with a brown enamel-like weathering were present. In Palestine, globular and cylindrical cups replace the stemmed goblets in the Umayyad period (Gorin-Rosen 2008, 124–125). All mentioned vessel types have parallels in contexts dated to the end of the Byzantine or Umayyad period in Palestine and Jordan, thus indicating a date between the mid 7th and mid 8th century (Keller and Lindblom in press).

The vessels of this chronological group show more diverse glass chemistry than the aforementioned earlier examples. The large blue/green single lamps (Fig. 17.5.1–2; Greiff in press, nos. 62–81, 177–178, 215–216) are the typical Lower group/Levantine II representatives except for nos. 63–64 and 215–216 which are part of the Middle Group/Levantine I group. The yellow/green single lamps (Fig. 17.6.1; Greiff in press, nos. 166–173) and the yellow/green cups (Fig. 17.6.2–3; Greiff in press, nos. 174–176) belong to the Middle Group/Levantine I category with two samples that can be found on the Line (Egypt I?). The green bowl-shaped single lamps (Fig. 17.7.1; Greiff in press, nos. 186–190) and two of the green cups (Fig. 17.7.2–3; Greiff in press, nos. 191–193) also belong to this compositional group (Egypt I?) and one is an outlier. To complete the picture of chemical diversity in this period flasks with infolded flattened rims (Fig. 17.8.1–2; Greiff in press, nos. 194–196) are made from plant ash glass.

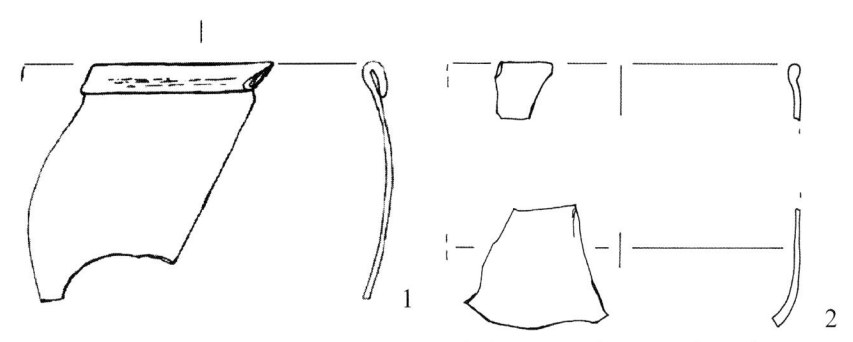

Fig. 17.9: Abbasid blue/green bowl and cup of the mid 8th–9th century belonging to the Lower Group/Levantine II (scale 1:2; drawings Jeanette Lindblom).

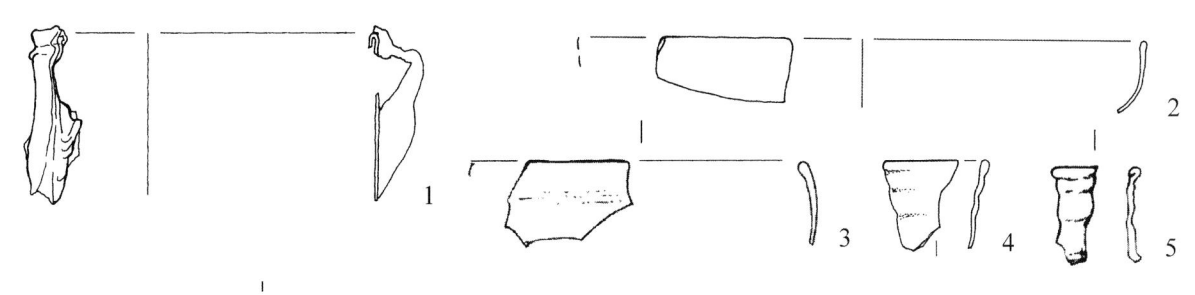

Fig. 17.10: Abbasid light green/turquoise lamp, bowl, cup and bottles of the mid 8th–9th century belonging to the Upper Group/Egypt II (scale 1:2; drawings Jeanette Lindblom).

Abbasid glass of the mid 8th–9th century

The small, perhaps fortified monastery of the last phase also yielded a considerable number of glass finds. Typical for these assemblages (Keller and Lindblom 2008, 342–349, figs. 5–6, 9, 11–12, 14; in press, tables 7–8, figs. 16–17) are blue/green globular bowls or cups with outfolded rims (Fig. 17.9.1), blue/green cylindrical cups with fire-rounded thickened rims (Fig. 17.9.2), light green/turquoise single lamps with three handles and outfolded rims (Fig. 17.10.1), light green/turquoise bowls and globular cups with fire-rounded rims (Fig. 17.10.2–3), light green/turquoise bottles with short-ridged necks (Fig. 17.10.4–5), turquoise cylindrical cups with tonged decoration (Fig. 17.11.1), a dark blue cylindrical cup with tonged and incised decoration (Fig. 17.11.2), a pale purple incised plate (Fig. 17.11.3), yellow/green plates with fire-rounded rims (Fig. 17.12.1–2), yellow/green tonged cups (Fig. 17.12.3), a yellow/green incised cup (Fig. 17.12.4), a yellow/green chalice with a multibeaded stem (Fig. 17.12.5) and a small dark green flask with a short-ridged neck (Fig. 17.13). Parallels for these vessel types are known from late Umayyad and mainly Abbasid contexts thus indicating a date between the mid 8th and the end of the 9th or perhaps the early 10th century (Keller and Lindblom in press).

In the period discussed here plant ash derived glass can be expected and in fact among the bottles with short-ridged necks (Fig. 17.10.4–5; Greiff in press, nos. 155–158) there is one made with a plant ash derived soda (Greiff in press, no. 157) while the rest belongs to the Upper Group/Egypt II compositional group. Most samples of the period are of this Upper Group compositional type: bowls/cups with fire-rounded rims (Fig. 17.10.2–3; Greiff in press, nos. 152–154), yellow/green cups/goblet (Fig. 17.12.3–5; Greiff in press, nos. 183–185), turquoise tonged cups (Fig. 17.11.1; Greiff in press, nos. 201–204), dark blue cups (Fig. 17.11.2; Greiff in press, nos. 206–207) and the incised plate (Fig. 17.11.3; Greiff in press, no. 210). Among the four light green/turquoise single lamps (Fig. 17.10.1; Greiff in press, nos. 145–151) there is one outlier and also the yellow/green plates (Fig. 17.12.1–2; Greiff in press, nos. 179–182) yield one data point on the Line, while the remaining samples are all part of the Upper Group. The globular bowls with outfolded rims (Fig. 17.9.1; Greiff in press, nos. 127–140) are more heterogeneous. Most are associated with the Lower Group/Levantine II cluster, but one is of the Middle Group/Levantine I compositional type and another is on the Line (Egypt I?). Again, one plant ash glass was also identified among those globular bowls. Cups with fire-rounded thickened rims (Fig. 17.9.2; Greiff in press, nos. 141–144) are mainly of Lower Group type

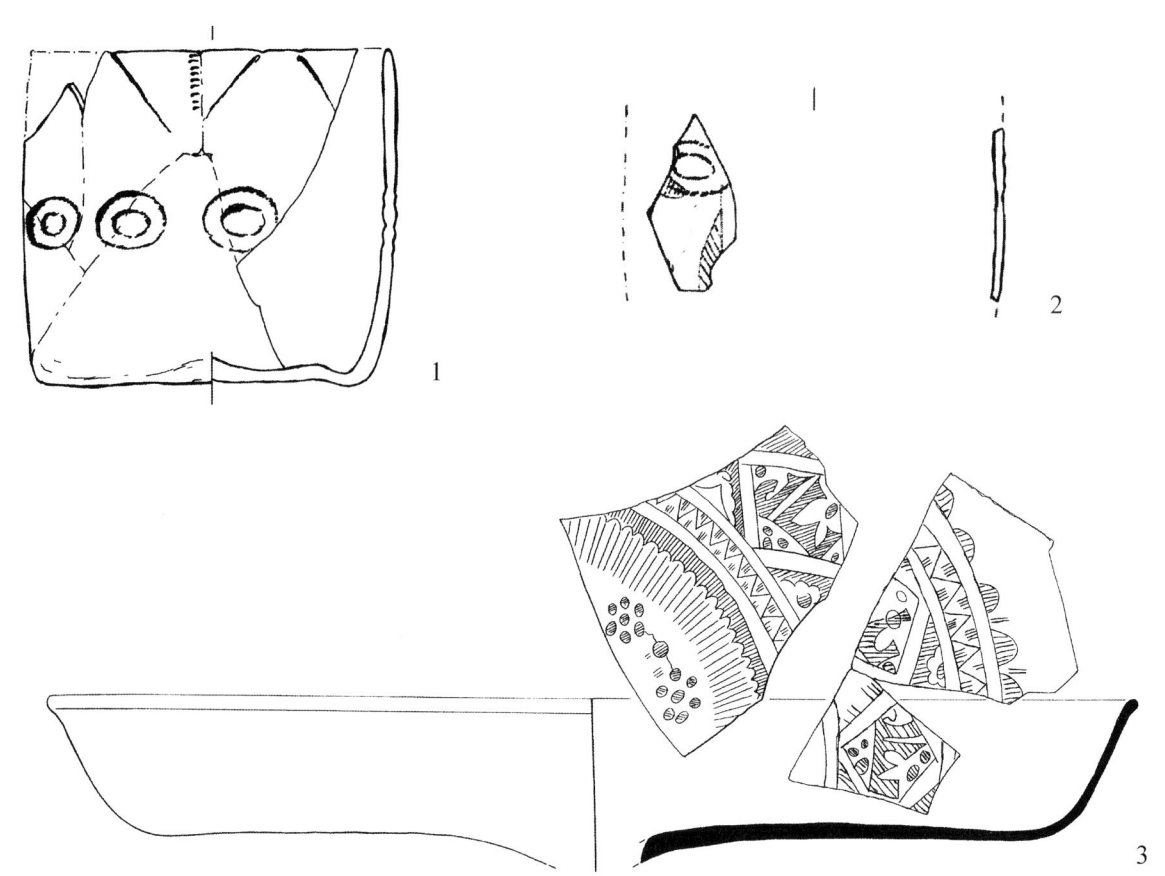

Fig. 17.11: Abbasid turquoise cup, dark blue cup and pale purple plate of of the mid 8th–9th century belonging to the Upper Group/Egypt II (scale 1:2; drawings: Jeanette Lindblom).

composition with one belonging to the Middle Group. The only lead glass identified in the whole data set is a small dark green bottle with short-ridged neck (Fig. 17.13; Greiff in press, no. 198).

Comparing Jabal Harun compositional groups to those from other sites

The analytical data sets suitable for comparison with the results from Jabal Harun were first sought in the geographical vicinity starting with different sites from Jordan. Other sites were chosen because they were monasteries, covered the same chronological range or their geographical position was close to one of the yet identified raw glass production centres. The discussion is confined to mineral soda glass due to the scarcity of plant ash derived glass on Jabal Harun.

Petra and Deir 'Ain 'Abata (southern and central Jordan)

The material most suitable for the purpose of comparison with respect to its chronological range, its geographical proximity to Jabal Harun and the archaeological context is the data set published by Rehren *et al.* (2010). Their study included lamps and window panes from three ecclesiastical contexts from southern and central Jordan. Two assemblages come from churches in Petra, one from the Petra church which was in use from the 5th to the 7th century (34 samples), other from the smaller North Ridge church with finds dating to the 5th and 6th centuries (20 samples). The third glass assemblage was recruited from the site of Deir 'Ain 'Abata, a pilgrimage centre situated near the south-eastern end of the Dead Sea, providing glass finds dating mostly from the 4th to 8th centuries (24 samples).

The entire dataset is clearly dominated by Levantine I glass compositions, in particular the glass supply for the two sites from Petra was furnished with glass from the Syro-Palestinian coast. In the North Ridge church data set one HIMT glass and one sample with a composition similar to Egypt II could be identified. In addition, Petra church analyses exhibit two exceptions from the "Levantine rule" with possible affinities to Roman glass making traditions or a low-lime variety of Egypt II. The Deir 'Ain 'Abata glass

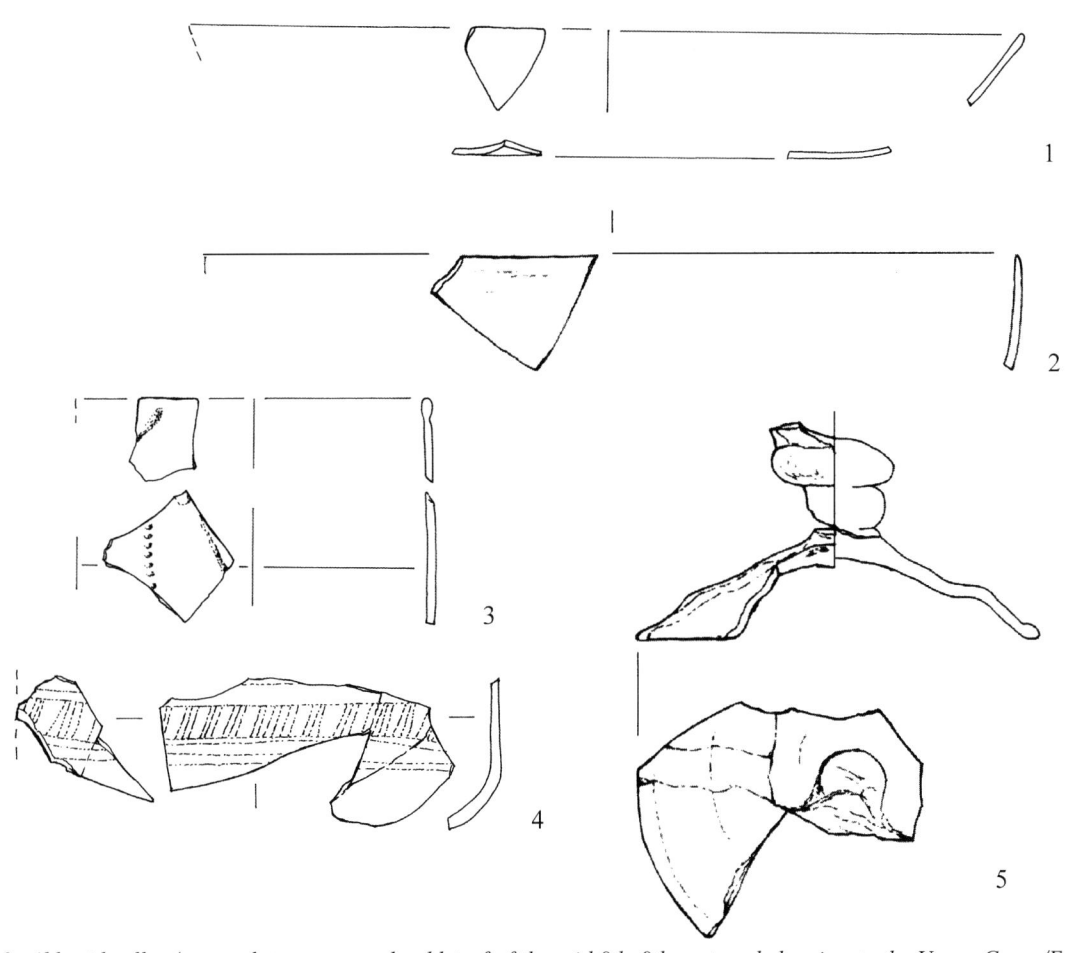

Fig. 17.12: Abbasid yellow/green plates, cups and goblet of of the mid 8th–9th century belonging to the Upper Group/Egypt II (scale 1:2; drawings Jeanette Lindblom).

Fig. 17.13: Abbasid dark green bottle of the 9th/10th century made of lead glass (scale 1:2; drawing Jeanette Lindblom).

assemblage is more heterogeneous. This is not astonishing for a pilgrimage centre. Three samples are of the HIMT composition, two resemble Egypt I, but the predominance of Levantine I is still valid. On the chemical level, the analyses between the three sites differ slightly in terms of lime, alumina, potassium and other elements emphasising the fact that Levantine I in itself consists of compositional sub-groups whose geographical and chronological predominance has not yet been established in a satisfactory manner.

Beit Ras/Capitolias (northern Jordan)

Another Jordanian archaeological complex and its glass (40 samples) were investigated by R. Abd-Allah (2010). At Beit Ras (ancient *Capitolias*) beside vessel remains considerable amounts of working debris such as glass chunks, kiln fragments and fuel ash slag have been identified indicating that Beit Ras was a centre of secondary glass production. The artefacts were excavated from late Roman as well as early Byzantine layers with one set of samples from an area with late Roman structures (3rd to mid 4th century) while the second group was recovered from an area with remains of an early Byzantine church (mid 4th to 5th century). Analyses were preformed both on raw glass chunks and vessel fragments. The compositions of the two groups were found to be practically identical, indicating a continuity of raw glass supply. All samples correspond to the Levantine I glass group.

Maroni Petrera (Cyprus)

Another suitable site for comparison is the church of Ayos Nikolaos at Maroni Petrera on Cyprus with glass finds dating to the 6th to 7th centuries (Freestone *et al.* 2002). Despite having analysed a rather small quantity of glass finds Freestone and his co-workers were able to support the production model of few primary production centres that send their raw glass in form of chunks to many distant secondary workshops. Among the 19 glasses, the majority was of Levantine I composition, whereas the rest was identified as typical HIMT.

Raya and Wadi al-Tur (Sinai)

Another assemblage of glass finds of the periods in question from two sites in the Sinai have been analysed by Kato and co-workers (2009; 2010). Excavated from two well-dated archaeological layers at Raya glass material from the 8th (areas VIII and XXVII) and 9th centuries (Fort of Raya) have been analysed. The material from Wadi al-Tur is less well categorised with a rough dating between the 8th and 13th centuries. The 110 samples can be divided into four clearly distinctive subgroups. N1 corresponds to Levantine I and/or II, N2-a2 to Egypt I and N2-b to Egypt II. For N2-a1 no corresponding groups defined by Freestone *et al.* (2002) could be found. There is a mutual dependence between the date of the archaeological layers and the chemical groups. With regards to provenance groups, we observe a shift between raw glasses originating from the Levantine coast in the 8th century to an Egypt II provenance in the 9th century. In both periods the Egypt I category plays only a minor role. It is difficult to directly compare the values obtained by Kato *et al.* (2009; 2010) with our data as the Japanese colleagues had to restrict themselves to non-destructive analytical procedures with no allowance for any surface preparation. Thus, no values for sodium and silica could be given. As a consequence the dispersion of objects among the groupings is influenced by sample choice.

Butrint (Albania)

The site of Butrint facing the island of Corfu was once a prosperous trading port. The 93 samples from archaeological structures dating from the 1st to the 8th century comprised vessel fragments, window glass, tesserae as well as glass working debris and glass cakes (Schibille 2011). The dating of the four excavation areas where the sampled objects have been found is, however, somewhat uncertain. Two of the total of six sub-groups belonged to Roman glass types while another set (WD1 with 6th to 8th-century samples) could be assigned to Egypt II. Another group (WD2) from the same layers showed chemical characteristics both similar to HIMT and Levantine I glass, thus forming a group comparable to Anglo-Saxon and Merovingian glass types. Only three "real" HIMT compositions, but neither clear Levantine I or Levantine II compositions were present.

Apollonia-Arsuf (Israel)

The primary furnaces discovered during several excavation seasons have been operating during the 6th and 7th centuries (Freestone *et al.* 2000; 2008). The authors used glass from Apollonia-Arsuf to define the Levantine I cluster. However, within both analytical series there are samples that fall into the Levantine II field and in diagrams discussing lime and alumina distributions some are placed between the two areas. According to Freestone *et al.* (2008), the grouping can still be maintained despite the compositional overlap, however, the complex chronological relationships have to be investigated in more detail.

Discussion

The analysis of a representative number of glass objects from dated layers excavated at the monastery of Jabal Harun is a valuable instrument for investigating questions of glass production and trade in the second half of the first millennium AD. The results have shown that most major glass groups formerly identified by other authors were also available at Jabal Harun, such as Levantine I and II as well as Egypt I and II glass groups. However, at Jabal Harun other compositional groups are underrepresented, for example, the complete lack of HIMT glass and the limited number of vessels made from plant ash is worth mentioning.

The lack of HIMT glass

HIMT glass has been identified from 4th to 6th-century contexts from *Augusta Praetoria* (Mirti *et al.* 1993), Carthage (Freestone *et al.* 2005), France and Tunisia (Foy *et al.* 2003), on Mediterranean shipwrecks (Silvestri *et al.* 2005), from Britain (Foster and Jackson 2009), late Roman graves in Germany (Hartmann and Grünewald 2010), Albania (Schibille 2011), Bulgaria (Rehren and Cholakova 2010) and many other sites (Nenna this volume). There are some arguments such as strontium isotope signatures and titanium levels in the sand (Freestone *et al.* 2005; Foy and Picon 2005) that support the idea of Egypt being the most likely production area for this compositional group, more specifically the coastal area between Alexandria and Gaza (Freestone *et al.* 2009, 44) which can be narrowed down to the coast of northern Sinai (Nenna this volume). It is remarkable to find not a single piece of HIMT glass among the Jabal Harun samples taking into consideration the geographical proximity of the site to the northern Sinai and the occurrence of HIMT in other Jordanian contexts of similar date.

Among the Jordanian sites described above, Beit Ras and the Petra church were without any trace of HIMT, while assemblages from the North Ridge church at Petra and the pilgrimage centre of Deir 'Ain 'Abata show at least a small portion of HIMT. In the western part of the Mediterranean, HIMT seems to be the dominating glass group starting from the 4th century, while Levantine I glass reached the more northern areas of the Roman empire to a much lesser extent. The reasons for this contrasting distribution during the 4th to 6th centuries still remain unclear (Foster and Jackson 2009). Judging from the more localised situation in Jordan the distribution network for glassware seemed to be conducted on a dense regional network. This becomes apparent if we take into account the close proximity of Petra and Jabal Harun, finding that within five kilometres distance there is one site without any HIMT glass, while the other site delivers at least a few pieces.

As many of the samples investigated from Jabal Harun come from 5th to 6th-century layers the chronological frame can not be the reason. The absence of HIMT glass could be due to a consumers' choice, *i.e.* the monastery on Jabal Harun could have chosen not to acquire any strongly coloured HIMT glass which was only rarely used in Petra and may therefore have been regarded as a special commodity, whereas the common blue/green glass of this period was preferred. On a wider scale, the rarity of HIMT glass in southern Jordan reflects the isolation of this part of the Near East from the main trade routes of the period (Fiema 2002, 232–234, 238). Although the monastery on Jabal Harun was a pilgrimage centre, it was in an isolated part on the edge of the Byzantine world which was not well linked to the main pilgrimage routes in the Holy Land.

Levantine I characteristics

Judging from the number of analyses from regionally different sites that fit into the Levantine I scheme, it can be confirmed that this area was definitely an important production area in the 5th and 6th centuries, despite its heterogeneous character. The data sets from Apollonia, Dor, Bet She'an and Jalame do not cover the same parts of the Ca/Al data field, but form overlapping fields with distinct compositional core areas. There are also other glass assemblages which seem to hint at a finer compositional distribution of the Levantine I group (Uhlir *et al.* 2010). The Jabal Harun data seem to fit best with the "without MnO" Jalame samples analysed by Brill (1999) for most elements except MgO (0.8 for Jabal Harun, 0.6 for Jalame).

Looking at Levantine I from different sites discussed in this context, for example those from Petra (Petra church and North Ridge church) and Deir 'Ain 'Abata, they do not cover the same corner of the Levantine I data field as the 120 Jabal Harun data points. From the first two assemblages more window glass was analysed, whereas from the excavations from Jabal Harun no window glass was incorporated because secure dating is practically impossible. The 4th to 5th-century material from Beit Ras, however, is compositionally more similar to what we find in Jabal Harun as Levantine I. There are only some objects from Jabal Harun dating to the 7th/early 8th century that conform to Levantine I such as the goblets with flat feet and the yellow/green lamps and cups (Figs. 17.4.2, 17.6), but the majority belongs to 5th and 6th-century material such as the polycandelon lamps, the small single lamps, the goblets with folded feet and blue trails and the flasks with blue trails and mould-blown ribs (Fig. 17.3). Levantine I was the main group used between the mid 5th and the 6th century on Jabal Harun as well as in Petra and central (Deir 'Ain 'Abata) and northern Jordan (Beit Ras). Its predominance in this period confirms the established picture of the glass supply with Levantine raw glass in Jordan during the 5th/6th century.

A Jabal Harun Levantine II variety?

The fact that a clearly defined group of 52 samples shares similarities with Levantine II compositions is astonishing if we look at the other sites discussed here where this compositional type is a rarity; only Deir 'Ain 'Abata features one single sample. Kato *et al.* (2009; 2010) did not discriminate between Levantine I and Levantine II associations in their Egyptian sites, therefore we cannot consider their data set in this context. The overall pattern may be explained by the dating of the glassware of the other sites because few 7th-century glass was analysed. It must be stated that the Jabal Harun Levantine II variety shows considerably less alumina than the Bet Eli'ezer analysis and we cannot be absolutely certain that they actually correspond to the same raw material group. The chronological frame for the Jabal Harun Levantine II glass objects starts in the late 6th century with blue/green single lamps (Fig. 17.4.1) and fades during the 8th/9th century with globular bowls with outfolded rims and cups with thickened rims (Fig. 17.9.1–2), but Levantine II is clearly a typical 7th-century composition as demonstrated by the large blue/green lamps (Figs. 17.5, 17.14). However, it is noteworthy that the single lamps used for the remodelled small church in the late 6th century (Fig. 17.4.1; Keller 2010, 187, fig. 3.3) were the first to be made of Levantine II glass, while the contemporary goblets with solid stems and flat feet (Fig. 17.4.2) were still being made of Levantine I glass. This may suggest that for a large order of glass lamps for a rebuilt church, a new glass composition or newly imported raw glass may have been used, whereas the goblets which probably came to the monastery in smaller amounts on a more regular basis an older glass composition was used. A similar picture emerges with the lamps of the Umayyad period. For the main lighting

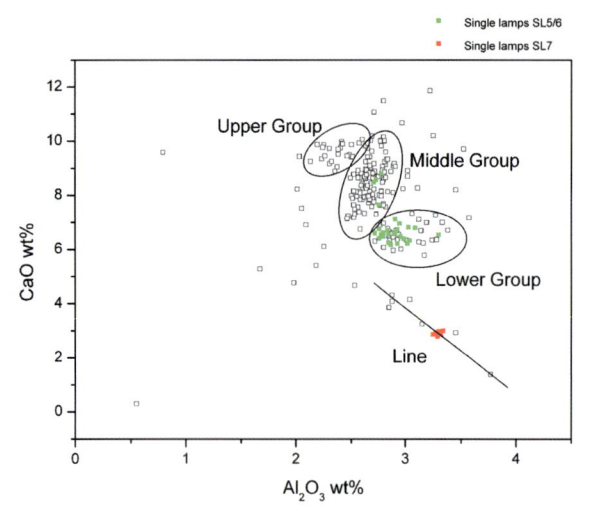

Fig. 17.14: Two types of single lamps covering the same chronological span can be found in different chemical groups. This underlines the heterogeneous distribution system during the Umayyad period (graph Susanne Greiff).

devices for the church of this phase, the large blue/green lamps (Fig. 17.5; Keller 2010, 187–188, fig. 4.2–3; 2011, 262, fig. 7.1–2), Levantine II glass was used, whereas the less frequent yellow/green lamps (Fig. 17.6.1) belong to Levantine I group and the few additional green bowl-shaped lamps (Fig. 17.7.1) belong to Egypt I group, illustrating the predominant use of Levantine II glass for the lamps of this period (Fig. 17.14).

Egypt I: potential subdivisions

The data defining the Egypt I field in the lime/alumina diagrams stretches over a wide range of alumina compositions. In fact, this group seems to consist of two smaller clusters: one at the low and the other at the high alumina end. Taking into account the 10 groups defined by Foy *et al.* (2003), the first one would correspond to Foy's group 9 while the other shows similarities to group 8. The Jabal Harun data belong to the lower alumina end and overlap the field of the data given by Nenna *et al.* (2000). Our data, however, do not form an irregular cluster but are rather positioned on a line with a negative slope. This indicates that the Ca-bearing mineral in the sand did not contribute considerably to the alumina content of the glass batch. As a consequence Ca-feldspar, Ca-micas and other Ca-bearing alumosilicates can be discarded. A rather pure source such as limestone, molluscs and similar fossil organisms should have contributed to the overall composition.

The dating of the glasses positioned along the Egypt I line is characterised by the mid 7th to mid 8th centuries (green lamps and cups; Figs. 17.7, 17.14) with some samples with a late 8th to 9th-century date. However, this "Line-group" is the group with the smallest number of data points. The greatest potential for Egyptian compositions should be found for samples analysed from sites in Egypt or the Sinai. In fact, 13 samples analysed by Kato *et al.* (2009; 2010) were assigned as being related to Egypt I, but they all correspond to the higher alumina end of the group. Another low lime group with low alumina values seem to overlap with the samples found at Jabal Harun. The other glass assemblages discussed above hardly show any glass with Egypt I affinities, although again Deir 'Ain 'Abata is the site with some glass with Egypt I composition. The few lamps and vessels from Jabal Harun confirm the restricted use of Egypt I glass alongside the predominant Levantine glass in the Umayyad period in southern Jordan, where a similar picture to the one from the Sinai emerges.

Egypt II

The last compositional group to be considered here is the one named Egypt II. This, again, is not a coherent cluster, but it is split into two groups differing in their alumina contents. The Egypt II samples recognised among the Jabal Harun glassware belong to those with a higher alumina level, marginally overlapping the Levantine I data field. The latest glass objects dating to the mid 8th and 9th century fall within this compositional category representing the main types of Abbasid glassware on Jabal Harun (Figs. 17.10–17.12). This indicates that Abbasid glass in southern Jordan belongs mainly to the Egypt II composition, which was also observed on sites of this period in the Sinai.

Conclusions

All major compositional groups discussed for the first millennium AD have been identified among the 218 objects analysed from the Jabal Harun material, except HIMT glass. The reasons for this are still unclear, but there is an increasing indication that this type of glass is more often encountered in the western parts of the Mediterranean and Europe. The chronological pattern of the accepted compositional glass groups is confirmed and refined by what we find on Jabal Harun: the 5th to 6th-century material dominates the Middle Group that corresponds to Levantine I assemblages. Very few of the 6th-century glassware can be found on the Line (Egypt I) and the Lower Group data cluster (Levantine II). These two assemblages are dominated by 7th-century samples. The samples of the Upper Group (Egypt II) all belong to the 8th and 9th centuries, where very little 7th-century material can be found. However, the 7th-century glassware is the one with the most heterogeneous distribution pattern (Greiff in press).

Due to the fine chronological framework and a sufficiently representative number of samples, we were able to solidify and refine the evidence for the development of the different glass groups. For example, it was demonstrated that for a certain type of glass vessel different glass compositions were in use (Fig. 17.2). One sort of glass was always dominating, but single pieces still belonged to an older compositional style, whereas other examples were already made from a modern glass type. The chemical distribution pattern of the Jabal Harun samples also indicates that for the major groups subsets with different compositions can be identified. The meaning of these minor differences could be, for example, the existence of small scale regional production series, different kiln technologies, influences of the secondary working procedures, and others. The rather modest amount of plant ash and lead glass shows that these new glass recipes were not yet customarily used in southern Jordan, even in the 9th century.

The main development of compositional glass groups on Jabal Harun changes from Levantine I in the 5th/6th century to Levantine II in the 7th/mid 8th century and to Egypt II from the late 8th to the 9th century. Egypt I was occasionally present, mainly in the 7th/mid 8th century. Levantine I was also the predominant glass composition in southern and central Jordan as well as in Palestine during the Byzantine period. Towards the end of the Byzantine period and into the Umayyad period, Levantine II became predominant not only on Jabal Harun, but also in Palestine, thus reflecting a compositional change in the Levant. On Jabal Harun, the gradual change between these two compositions can be observed, since in the late 6th/early 7th century only new lamp types were made of Levantine II glass while the goblets of that period still belonged to Levantine I glass. The absence of HIMT glass from Jabal Harun and its only occasional presence in Jordan reflects the isolation of this part from the Byzantine trade network and thus from the circulation of HIMT glass from the Sinai which was distributed along these routes. The glass supply of the Byzantine period in southern Jordan depended on the Levantine raw glass production. In the Umayyad period, some Egypt I glass reached Jabal Harun, but Levantine II glass was still predominant. In the Abbasid period Egypt II glass became predominant, providing evidence that raw glass or glass vessels from Egypt now reached the Petra region. This may be due to a change in the trade networks of the early Islamic period or simply because of a chronological change in mineral soda glass from Levantine II to Egypt II. It is noteworthy that the majority of Abbasid glass from Jabal Harun is still mineral soda glass and that there is only a very limited amount of plant ash soda glass. This reflects a consumers' choice or a preference of the secondary glass workshops supplying the monastery on Jabal Harun which preferred to work with Egyptian soda mineral glass instead of the new Levantine plant ash soda glass of the 9th century.

Acknowledgements

The authors would like to thank Jaakko Frösén and Zbigniew T. Fiema for allowing to study, analyse and present glass finds from the Finnish Jabal Hārūn Project (FJHP) in Petra, a project which was supported by the University of Helsinki and the Academy of Finland. Daniel Keller would like to thank Jeanette Lindblom for her support in the research of the glass finds and for providing the drawings and Tina Jakob for checking the English. Susanne Greiff is indebted to Sonngard Hartmann, Dorothea Macholdt and Tobias Eberlei for performing the Micro-XRF analyses.

Bibliography

Abd-Allah, R. (2010) Chemical characterisation and manufacturing technology of late Roman to early Byzantine glass from Beit Ras/Capitolias, Northern Jordan. *Journal of Archaeological Science* 37, 1866–1874.

Bimson, M. and Freestone, I. C. (1987) The discovery of an Islamic glass-making site in Middle Egypt. In *Annales du 10e Congrès de l'Association Internationale pour l'Histoire du Verre*, 237–243. Amsterdam, Association Internationale pour l'Histoire du Verre.

Brill, R. H. (1999) *Chemical analyses of early glasses*. Corning, NY, The Corning Museum of Glass.

Fiema, Z. T. (2002) Late-antique Petra and its hinterland: recent research and new interpretations. In J. H. Humphrey (ed.) *The Roman and Byzantine Near East 3*. Journal of Roman Archaeology Supplementary Series 49, 191–252. Portsmouth, RI, Journal of Roman Archaeology.

Foster, H. E. and Jackson, C. M. (2009) The composition of 'naturally coloured' late Roman vessel glass from Britain and the implications for models of glass production and supply. *Journal of Archaeological Science* 36, 189–204.

Foy, D. and Picon, M. (2005) L'origine du verre en Méditerranée occidentale à la fin de l'Antiquité et dans le haut Moyen Age. In *La Méditerranée et le monde mérovingien. Témoins archéologiques. Actes des XXIIe Journées internationales d'archéologie mérovingienne*. Bulletin archéologique de Provence Supplément 3, 99–110. Aix-en-Provence, Université de Provence.

Foy, D., Vichy, M. and Picon, M. (2000) Lingots de verre en Méditerranée occidentale (IIIe siècle av. J.-C. – VIIe siècle ap. J.-C.). In *Annales du 14e Congrès de l'Association Internationale pour l'Histoire du Verre*, 51–57. Lochem, Association Internationale pour l'Histoire du Verre.

Foy, D., Picon, M., Vichy, M. and Thirion-Merle, V. (2003) Caractérisation des verres de la fin de l'Antiquité en Méditerranée occidentale: l'émergence de nouveaux courants commerciaux. In D. Foy and M.-D. Nenna (eds.) *Échanges et commerce du verre dans le monde antique*. Monographies Instrumentum 24, 41–85. Montagnac, Monique Mergoil.

Freestone, I. C. (2006) Glass production in Late Antiquity and the Early Islamic period: a geochemical perspective. In M. Magetti and B. Messiga (eds.) *Geomaterials in Cultural Heritage*. Geological Society Special Publications 257, 201–216. London, Geological Society.

Freestone, I. C., Gorin-Rosen, Y. and Hughes, M. J. (2000) Primary glass from Israel and the production of glass in Late Antiquity and the Early Islamic period. In M.-D. Nenna (ed.) *La route du verre. Ateliers primaires et secondaires du second millénaire av. J.-C. au Moyen Âge*. Travaux de la Maison de l'Orient Méditerranéen 33, 65–83. Lyon, Maison de l'Orient Méditerranéen.

Freestone, I. C., Jackson-Tal, R. E. and Tal, O. (2008) Raw glass and the production of glass vessels at Late Byzantine Apollonia-Arsuf, Israel. *Journal of Glass Studies* 50, 67–80.

Freestone, I. C., Ponting, P. and Hughes, M. J. (2002) Origins of Byzantine glass from Maroni Petrera, Cyprus. *Archaeometry* 44, 257–272.

Freestone, I. C., Wolf, S. and Thirlwall, M. (2005) The production of HIMT glass: elemental and isotopic evidence. In *Annales du 16e Congrès de l'Association Internationale pour l'Histoire du Verre*, 153–157. Nottingham, Association Internationale pour l'Histoire du Verre.

Freestone, I. C., Wolf, S. and Thirlwall, M. (2009) Isotopic composition of glass from the Levant and the south-eastern Mediterranean region. In P. Degryse, J. Henderson and G. Hodgins (eds.) *Isotopes in Vitreous Materials*, 31–52. Leuven, University Press.

Gorin-Rosen, Y. (2008) The Glass Finds from Khirbat 'Adasa. *'Atiqot* 58, 123–134.

Gorin-Rosen, Y. and Winter, T. (2010) Selected insights into Byzantine glass in the Holy Land. In J. Drauschke and D. Keller (eds.) *Glass in Byzantium – Production, Usage, Analyses*. RGZM – Tagungen 8, 165–181. Mainz, Römisch-Germanisches Zentralmuseum.

Gratuze, B. and Barrandon, J. N. (1990) Islamic glass weights and stamps: analysis using nuclear techniques. *Archaeometry* 32, 155–162.

Greiff, S. (in press) Chemical glass types used for the production of glassware from late antiquity to the early Islamic period found at Jabal Harun. In Z. T. Fiema and J. Frösén, *Petra – The Mountain of Aaron II. The Nabataean Sanctuary and the Byzantine Monastery*. Helsinki, Societas Scientiarum Fennica.

Hartmann, S. and Grünewald, M. (2010) The late antique glass from Mayen (Germany): First results of chemical and archaeological studies. In B. Zorn and A. Hilgner (eds.) *Glass along the Silk Road from 200 BC to AD 1000*. RGZM – Tagungen 9, 15–28. Mainz, Römisch-Germanisches Zentralmuseum.

Henderson, J., McLoughlin, S. D. and McPhail, D. S. (2004) Radical changes in Islamic glass technology: evidence for conservatism and experimentation with new glass recipes from early and middle Islamic Raqqa, Syria. *Archaeometry* 44, 439–468.

Kato, N., Nakai, I. and Shindo, Y. (2009) Change in chemical composition of early Islamic glass excavated in Raya, Sinai Peninsula, Egypt: on-site analyses using a portable X-ray fluorescence spectrometer. *Journal of Archaeological Science* 36, 1698–1707.

Kato, N., Nakai, I. and Shindo, Y. (2010) Transitions in Islamic plant-ash glass vessels: on-site chemical analyses conducted at the Raya/al-Tur area on the Sinai Peninsula in Egypt. *Journal of Archaeological Science* 37, 1381–1395.

Keller, D. (2010) Abbots' orders, pilgrims' donations, glass collection. The supply of glass lamps for a monastic/pilgrimage church in southern Jordan. In J. Drauschke and D. Keller (eds.) *Glass in Byzantium – Production, Usage, Analyses*. RGZM – Tagungen 8, 183–198. Mainz, Römisch-Germanisches Zentralmuseum.

Keller, D. (2011) Glaslampen im frühbyzantinischen Kirchenraum. Künstliche Beleuchtung im Kontext von architektonischen und liturgischen Veränderungen. In P. I. Schneider and U. Wulf-Rheidt (eds.) *Licht – Konzepte in der vormodernen Architektur. Diskussionen zur Archäologischen Bauforschung* 10, 255–270. Regensburg, Schnell & Steiner.

Keller, D. and Lindblom, J. (2008) Glass Finds from the Church and the Chapel. In Z. T. Fiema and J. Frösén, *Petra – The Mountain of Aaron I. The Church and the Chapel*, 331–375. Helsinki, Societas Scientiarum Fennica.

Keller, D. and Lindblom, J. (in press) Glass vessels from the FJHP site. In Z. T. Fiema and J. Frösén, *Petra – The Mountain of Aaron II. The Nabataean Sanctuary and the Byzantine Monastery*. Helsinki, Societas Scientiarum Fennica.

Mirti, P., Casoli, A. and Appolonia, L. (1993) Scientific analysis of Roman glass from Augusta Praetoria. *Archaeometry* 35, 225–240.

Mirti, P., Davit, P., Gulmini, M. and Sagui, L. (2001) Glass fragments from the Crypta Balbi in Rome: the composition of eighth-century fragments. *Archaeometry* 42, 359–374.

Nenna, M.-D., Picon, M. and Vichy, M. (2000) Ateliers primaires et secondaires en Egypte à l'époque hellénistique à l'époque gréco-romaine. In M.-D. Nenna (ed.) *La route du verre. Ateliers primaires et secondaires du second millénaire av. J.-C. au Moyen Âge*. Travaux de la Maison de l'Orient Méditerranéen 33, 97–112. Lyon, Maison de l'Orient Méditerranéen.

Rehren, Th. and Cholakova, A. (2010) The Early Byzantine HIMT glass from Dichin, Northern Bulgaria. *Interdisciplinary Studies* 22/23, 81–96.

Rehren, Th., Marii, F., Schibille, N., Stanford, L. and Swan, C. (2010) Glass supply and circulation in early Byzantine southern Jordan. In J. Drauschke and D. Keller (eds.) *Glass in Byzantium – Production, Usage, Analyses*. RGZM – Tagungen 8, 65–81. Mainz, Römisch-Germanisches Zentralmuseum.

Sayre, E. V. and Smith, R. W. (1961) Compositional categories of ancient glass. *Science* 133, 1824–1826.

Schibille, N. (2011) Supply routes and the consumption of glass in first millennium CE Butrint (Albania). *Journal of Archaeological Science* 38, 2939–2948.

Silvestri, A., Molin, G. and Salviulo, G. (2005) Roman and medieval glass from the Italian area: bulk characterization and relationships with production technologies. *Archaeometry* 47, 797–816.

Uhlir, K., Melcher, M., Schreiner, M., Czurda-Ruth, B. and Krinzinger, F. (2010) SEM/EDX and µ-XRF investigations on ancient glass from Hanghaus 1 in Ephesos/Turkey. In J. Drauschke and D. Keller (eds.) *Glass in Byzantium – Production, Usage, Analyses*. RGZM – Tagungen 8, 47–64. Mainz, Römisch-Germanisches Zentralmuseum.

18

Egyptian glass abroad: HIMT glass and its markets

Marie-Dominique Nenna

Since 2000, archaeometry has played a major role in ancient glass studies, principally in searching for the geographic origins of the products, but also in investigating the technology. For comparison, in the classical world, no more than 20 contributions dealt with glass analyses between 1995–1999 (Nenna 2001, nos. 69–77), around 50 were listed between 2000–2004 (Nenna 2006, nos. 95–124), and around 100 were recorded between 2005–2011 (Nenna 2009, nos. 58–82; 2012, nos. 68–108). The work of the pioneers, such as Sayre and Smith (1961; 1974) and Brill (1988), established the principal compositional differences in ancient glass and showed that glass in classical antiquity was mainly made from sand and mineral soda, *i.e.* natron. This was followed by the development of the hypothesis, now widely accepted, that glass in antiquity was generally produced by two different processes, in primary glass workshops for making raw glass and secondary glass workshops for forming the objects. It implies that searching for the origins of glasses takes place on two levels: one by recognising and characterising the sands used in the primary workshops now known to be situated mainly in the Near East and in Egypt, and the other by identifying glass vessels made in the same secondary workshops, from the same batches of glass. In the same way as metals, glass was recycled during antiquity, and the differences between objects made from fresh glass or recycled glass must also be taken into account. Numerous research teams now explore aspects of the chemistry of ancient glass, but the implications of their results have sometimes been lost for some working in archaeology, as well as for some archaeological scientists, new in the glass domain.

This paper has grown out of reading and trying to understand the increasing number of studies concerned either with one particular glass composition, HIMT glass, or with distinguishing the HIMT glass within the assemblage of glass analysed from a single site. As an archaeologist working on ancient glass production and consumption in Egypt, I was particularly interested when the assumption that HIMT glass could well be Egyptian appeared in the literature, as it adds to the long history of primary and secondary glass production in Egypt, and contributes to the better understanding of commercial exchanges between Egypt and elsewhere in the ancient world in late antiquity. In the paper, I will review the current state of HIMT studies from the point of view of an archaeologist, and will also provide new information about the sands used, the siting of the workshops and the distribution of this particular kind of glass.

HIMT glass: the stages of the study

The term HIMT was invented by Freestone in 1994, in the publication of his analyses of raw glass found in Carthage, where he recognised HIMT, an unusual glass composition with a high iron, manganese and titanium content (Table 18.1). Glass of the same compositional type was isolated by Mirti in 1993 as the 4th century component of the Roman glass vessel assemblage from Aosta in northern Italy (Mirti *et al.* 1993, group E) and by Verità (1995) in vessel glass from Rome and Carthage dated between the end of the 4th and the 7th century. The visual appearance of this glass has been described as "typically transparent and yellowish green to deep olive in colour, as opposed to the more bluish green glass typical of the Roman world in the preceding period" (Freestone *et al.* 2005, 153). In the mid 1990s, no provenance was suggested for this type of raw glass.

The next stage began at the beginning of the 2000s with

Table 18.1: Mean compositions of HIMT glass and related compositions (Foster and Jackson 2009, fig. 2, table 4; Foy et al. 2003b, 83–84).

Source of data and material	Author classification by composition, glass type, date	n	Al2O3	Fe2O3	MgO	CaO	Na2O	K2O	TiO2	MnO	Analytical Method
Mirti et al. 1993, table 2 Aosta, Italy	**Group E** Vessel and window glass 4th century	9	2.56	1.402	0.959	5.88	17.26	1.02	0.514	1.955	ICP-OES
Freestone 1994, table 1 Carthage	**HIMT** Raw glass 4th century	6	2.8	1.89	1.1	6.9	17.9	0.5	0.4	1.7	SEM
Foy et al. 2003b, 83 Various sites in southern and central France, Tunisia and Egypt	*Groupe 1* Vessels, raw glass and glass waste 5th century	43	2.88	2.28	1.23	6.22	19.12	0.41	0.49	2.023	ICP-MS
Foy et al. 2003b, 84 Various sites in southern and central France, Tunisia and Egypt	*Groupe 2, série 2.1* Vessel, raw glass and waste glass Mid 6th–7th century	51	2.54	1.35	1.23	7.78	18.5	0.79	0.16	1.601	ICP-MS
Foy et al. 2003b, 84 Various sites in France and Egypt	*Groupe 2, série 2.2* Vessel and window glass end 7th–8th century	10	2.51	1.13	1.00	7.44	17.68	0.78	0.14	1.001	ICP-MS
Foster and Jackson 2009, table 4 Various Sites in Britain	**HIMT 1** Vessel AD 350–410	123	2.49	1.36	0.98	6.08	19.11	0.50	0.33	1.71	ICP-AES
Foster and Jackson 2009, table 4 Various Sites in Britain	**HIMT 2** Vessel AD 330–410	221	2.25	0.72	0.76	6.00	19.65	0.58	0.12	0.98	ICP-AES

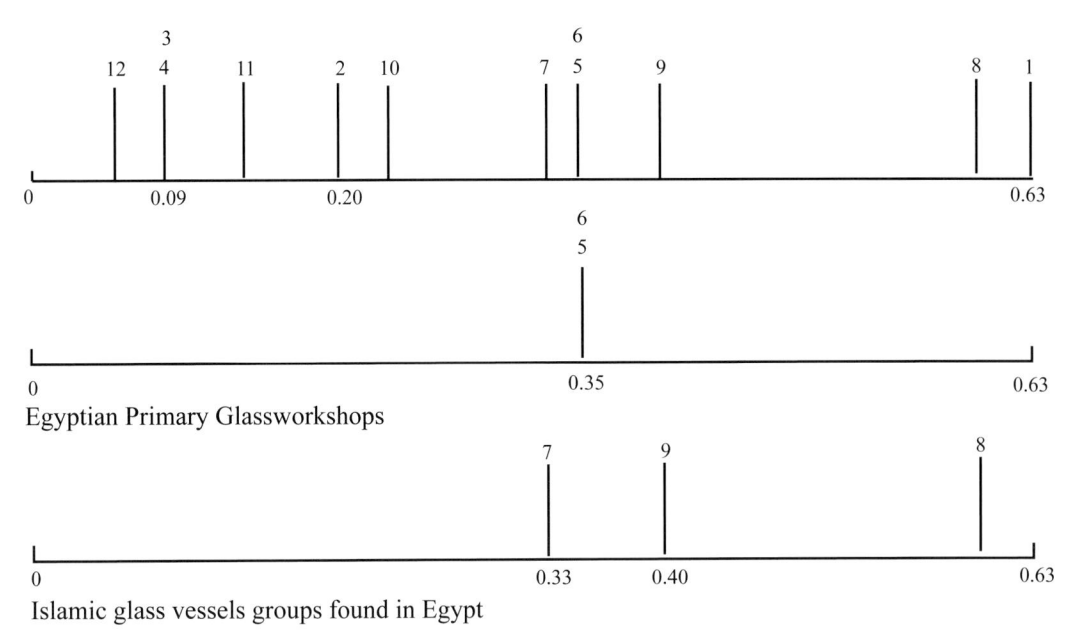

Fig. 18.1: Natron-based glass groups 1–12: percentage of titanium oxyde (TiO$_2$) in the sands (Foy et al. 2003b, fig. 2).

the research of teams of different nationalities who analysed various kinds of material from a wide range of sites. In Britain, Freestone and his co-authors analysed glass from northern Sinai (Freestone *et al.* 2002a), Maroni Petrera on Cyprus (Freestone *et al.* 2002b), and Billingsgate Bath House in London (Freestone *et al.* 2005), and also produced some synthetic and methodological papers (Freestone 2005; 2006). On the other side of the Channel, in France, Picon, Foy, Vichy and later Thirion-Merle worked together to study the raw glass from shipwrecks and secondary workshops (Foy *et al.* 2000a; 2000b) and late antique glass excavated in southern France, Tunisia and northern Egypt (Foy *et al.* 2003b; Foy and Picon 2005). The French research provided a detailed catalogue of samples with drawings and photographs. The samples of raw glass, scrap and vessel glass were all coming from dated sequences based on good archaeological contexts. It distinguished two groups: *Groupe 1*, strongly coloured glass dated to the 5th century, which seems to be equivalent to Freestone's HIMT Group and *Groupe 2* which is related to HIMT and is divided into *série* 2.1, attested in fragments of the mid 6th and 7th century, and *série* 2.2 in fragments dating from the end of the 7th to the end of 8th century. *Groupe 2* has percentages of calcium, aluminium and silica similar to *Groupe 1*, but has lower iron, titanium and manganese contents.

The work of other researchers at roughly the same period, should also be noted. This includes the work of Aerts *et al.* (2003) on vessel glass from Maastricht (Netherlands), Arletti *et al.* (2005) on vessel glass from Emilia-Romagna (Italy), and Degryse *et al.* (2005) on raw glass and vessel fragments from Sagalassos in Turkey.

The suggestion that HIMT glass was made in Egypt emerged independently in British and French publications. Picon and his co-authors (Foy *et al.* 2003b, 47–48) stressed the abundance of this glass in late Roman sites in Egypt and the high content of titanium, specific to Egypt, was shown in their fig. 2, which is reproduced in this paper (Fig. 18.1). This figure presents an overview of the natron glass compositions made in Egyptian primary glass workshops between the 1st and the end of the 9th century. *Groupe 5* is the glass from the primary workshop of Mareotid, dated loosely to the Roman period (Nenna *et al.* 2000). *Groupe 6* is the glass produced in Wadi Natrun and dated by survey and excavation to the 1st–2nd centuries (Nenna *et al.* 2005; Picon *et al.* 2008; Nenna in press a). *Groupe 7* (Foy *et al.* 2003a) is vessel glass dating to the Abbassid period (mid 8th to end of 9th/beginning of 10th century), for which the primary glass workshops have not been located. It is equivalent to Gratuze's Egypt 2 group (Gratuze and Barrandon 1990: Islamic weights), Kato's N2-b group (Kato *et al.* 2009, 1705–1706: vessel glass) and to sherds analyzed in El-Ashumein (Bimson and Freestone 1991: vessel glass). *Groupes 8* and *9* are glass vessels dating to the Umayyad period (mid 7th–mid 8th century), for which the primary glass workshops have not been located (Foy *et al.* 2003a). These two groups are commonly separated on the basis of their different iron, alumina and titanium contents, except in the work of the Japanese team where they both appear in Kato's N2-a2 groups. *Groupe 8*, which has higher levels of iron, alumina and titanium corresponds to Gratuze's Egypt 1B group, while *Groupe 9*, which may pre-date *Groupe 8*, corresponds to Gratuze's 1A group. These two groups (Egypt

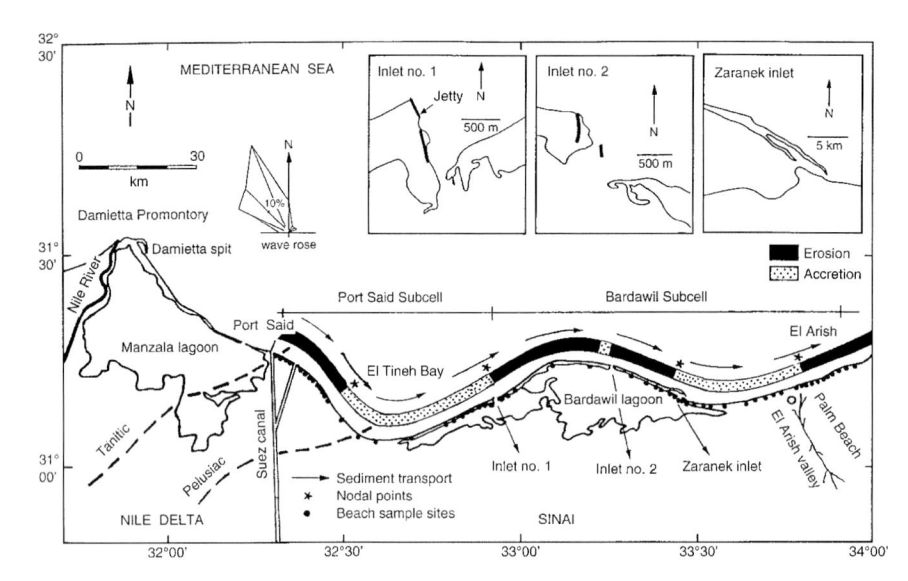

Fig. 18.2: "Generalised map of the study area in the northern Sinai, showing sites of beach samples and trace positions of former channels (long dashes). The large-scale coast-wide erosion/accretion pattern, determined in this study, is schematically depicted parallel to the shoreline. Sediment transport directions are shown by small arrows, based on erosion/accretion patterns, petrologic parameters, and geomorphologic features in this study. The insets show the width of the beach west of the inlet jetties (sand accumulation) and east of jetties (beach erosion), indicating eastward sediment transport; jetties are indicated by dark lines" (O. E. Frihy and M. F. Lotfy (1997) Shoreline changes and beach-sand sorting along the northern Sinai coast of Egypt. Geo-Marine Letters 17, 140–146).

1A et 1B) have been designated as Wadi Natrun in Freestone's articles (Freestone et al. 2002a, *passim*; Freestone 2003, 112, fig. 1; Freestone et al. 2002b, 265, fig. 5; Freestone 2005, figs. 3, 5; 2006, fig. 7; Freestone et al. 2008, 33, fig. 5) as well as in other contributions (Foy et al. 2003a, 141; Rehren and Cholakova 2010, fig. 5). As explained by Freestone et al. (2008, 33), "The Wadi Natrun group is based mainly on analyses of Egyptian Islamic glass coin weights (7th–8th centuries; Gratuze and Barrandon 1990), but is linked to the Wadi by well-provenanced samples of similar low-lime, high-alumina composition from the glassmaking furnaces there (Sayre and Smith 1974; Nenna et al. 2000)", but it should be said that there is to date no archaeological evidence for primary glass workshops in this region of Egypt at this period (Nenna in press a). Some other groups have also been recognised: *Groupe 10* is vessel glass dating to the Umayyad period that may have been manufactured in Egypt, and Kato's N2a-1 group is also dated to 8th century and thought to be Egyptian. All these compositions, in addition to *Groupe 1 and 2*, contain between 0.16 and 0.63 percent of titanium, whereas the glass manufactured in the Syria-Palestine region in the Roman and late Roman period (*Groupes 3* and *4*), as well as *Groupes 11* and *12* (provenance not specified in Foy et al. 2003b), always show under 0.10 percent of titanium.

Some other points were also made by Freestone (Freestone et al. 2005). A high soda content is common in Egyptian glass, thus supporting an origin close to the Egyptian natron deposits, as seen for example in the Wadi Natrun glass of the early Roman period. The complexity of the Sinai coastline (Fig. 18.2) where sandy material with a strong terrestrial component deposited by flooding of the Nile can be found with marine beach sands, suggests an explanation both for the composition of this glass and for its complex strontium isotope signature with both marine and terrigenous origins (summed up recently in Freestone et al. 2009, 42–44). The British and French researchers agree that manganese was intentionally added to provide the strong colour of the glass, and Freestone (2006, 111) has suggested that the high manganese content relates to the proximity of major manganese dioxide (pyrolusite) deposits in Sinai.

The third stage is very recent, with the works of Freestone et al. (2008) on Anglo-Saxon glass (vessel glass in the British Museum), Foster and Jackson (2009: vessel glass from late Roman settlements in Britain), Rehren and Chokalova (2010: waste and vessel glass from Dichin in Bulgaria) and Arletti et al. (2010a; 2010b: vessel glass in Sicily and window glass in central Italy). The growing number of analyses allows researchers to identify and distinguish groups within HIMT glass, according to the composition of the sand, the correlation between the different oxides of high value already cited (iron, titanium, manganese, and also magnesium), and their links with aluminium oxide. Foster and Jackson (2009) identify two groups, HIMT 1 and HIMT 2, and relate them to well dated vessels, suggesting that HIMT 2 (which is yellowish and light in colour) appears around c. AD 330, a little earlier than HIMT 1; both are weakly coloured, compared to Foy *et al. Groupe 1*. Freestone and his co-authors (Freestone *et al.* 2008, 35–36, table 4) label a group of vessel glass dated between AD 400–550 as Saxon I. This falls within the HIMT spectrum but has lower levels of iron and titanium and higher calcium, which makes it similar to the Frankish glass from Krefeld-Gellep, Merovingian glass from Vicq and the slightly later, 7th-century glass from Crypta Balbi in Rome. Rehren and Cholakova (2010) distinguish between three groups, all within the HIMT spectrum: Dichin Group I dated to the end of the 5th century is called HIT because of its low percentage of manganese, and Dichin Groups IIa and IIb, both of which were worked locally.

Very recent work using absorption spectroscopy has concentrated on the origin of the colour of HIMT glass which may be a more objective way to define the colours, as well as providing information about the furnace atmosphere (Cosyns 2011, 355–399; De Ferri *et al.* 2011).

Terminology and sampling strategies

In Table 18.2, I have summarised most of the publications in which samples of the HIMT glass composition have been recognised, using the following nine fields: modern countries, place of finding, the general character of the site, the chronology of the context in which the samples were found, the term used to define the glass composition, the colour of the glass as described by the authors, the nature of the samples, the presence/absence of drawings and of indications of typology, and the published references.

The first point to make about Table 18.2 is that, despite 86 groups of analyses being listed, this research is still in its early phases. Some regions, such as southern France (Foy *et al.* 2003b) and Britain (Freestone *et al.* 2008; Foster and Jackson 2009) have been studied in depth, whereas in most of the others we have only case-studies where the glass of one or two sites have been examined. Moreover, countries such as Spain and Greece and the eastern Adriatic coastal region are not represented.

The identification of the character of the find spots is broad. I have described the sites where raw glass, moils or defective pieces have been found as glass workshops, and all the sites where no traces of glassworking have been identified as consumption sites. For the sake of clarity, I think the latter term should be reserved to that kind of site and not include glass workshop sites even though, strictly speaking, they are also consumers. The other categories are very small: they are one shipwreck and one harbour deposit.

For the chronology, I have chosen, whenever possible to use the centuries rather than the name of the culture, *e.g.* Byzantine, Merovingian or Anglo-Saxon. In eastern Mediterranean studies, classical glass specialists are accustomed to their period of study continuing until the Arab conquest in the mid 7th century, although the term 'Byzantine' is not always used for a specific political context with well defined range of dates. By contrast, in western Europe, there is often a "human" gap between historians and archaeologists studying Roman material and with those dealing with the material of the post-Roman political entities from the early 5th century onwards, such as the Anglo-Saxon, Frankish or Merovingian kingdoms. This means, in the case of Britain, for example, that to understand the composition of glass in circulation between the 4th and 9th centuries, we must consult both the work of Foster and Jackson (2009) for the material dated up to c. AD 410 and that of Freestone and his co-authors (2008) for glass after that date.

As explained above, the term HIMT for this glass composition was first used by Freestone (1994) and all publications since then, except the French ones, have used the same term, although within the case-studies, other terms are also used.

The colour of the glass is a particularly relevant issue, as it often points archaeological glass specialists towards the recognition of HIMT glass. The work done by French researchers has highlighted the predominance of HIMT glass (*Groupe 1*) in southern France in the 5th century (Foy *et al.* 2003b), while Foster and Jackson (2009) show that glass of the same composition appeared in Britain in the second quarter of the 4th century. Since the same term (HIMT) is used for both assemblages of material, this might be seen to imply a chronological difference in the distribution of HIMT glass within the western provinces, but this is not the case, as there is little or no overlap in date between them. The French researchers have concentrated their sampling strategy on olive-green glass of deep colour from contexts dating mainly to the 5th century, and have not analysed much material from well-dated earlier (*i.e.* 4th century) contexts (Foy *et al.* 2003b, 48), whereas the British research team has concentrated on 4th and early 5th-century glass which is mainly olive and yellowish-green to greenish. The appearance of pale coloured HIMT glass by the mid 4th century at the latest is confirmed by the chronology of the objects analysed from burials in Hambach Forest near Cologne (Wedepohl and Hartmann 2000), for example in tomb 166: 4th century, tombs 165, 182, 188: second half of 4th century, tomb 189, HA381, tombs 1, 2: end of 4th century). As has been stressed in more than one publication, most recently by Freestone *et al.* (2009, 44), there were no primary workshops in Hambach Forest, contrary to Wedepohl's suggestion, as the glass composition thought to be of local production matches HIMT glass very closely.

Table 18.2: List of analyses performed on HIMT glass and related compositions, sorted by country and site, with information on the site context, the chronology, the name given to the glass group and the colour described in bibliography, the nature of the sample, the presence/ absence of typology indications or drawings and the bibliography (in grey: analyses of raw glass chunks).

Country	Site	Nature of site	Chronology of site	Glass Group
Belgium	Vieux-Ville	Consumption	End 4th–early 5th c.	HIMT (vase) + Levantine I (decor)
Belgium	Crupet	Consumption	4th c.	HIMT
Belgium	Maastricht	Consumption	4th–5th c.	HIMT
Britain	Barton Court Farm (Oxfordshire)	Consumption	4th–beg. 5th c.	HIMT 1 and 2
Britain	Barnsley Park (Gloucestershire)	Consumption	4th c.	HIMT 2
Britain	Beadlam Villa (North Yorkshire)	Consumption	4th–beg. 5th c.	HIMT 1 and 2
Britain	Canterbury (Kent)	Consumption	4th–beg. 5th c.	HIMT 1 and 2
Britain	Caister on-sea (Norfolk)	Consumption	4th–beg. 5th c.	HIMT 1 and 2
Britain	Castle Eden (Co. Durham)	Consumption	AD 400–550	Related to HIMT
Britain	Dalton Parlours (West Yorkshire)	Consumption	4th c.	HIMT 2
Britain	Dorchester (Dorset)	Consumption	4th–beg. 5th c.	HIMT 1 and 2
Britain	Dorchester-on-Thames (Oxfordshire)	Consumption	4th–beg. 5th c.	HIMT 1 and 2
Britain	Droxford (Hampshire)	Consumption	AD 400–550	Related to HIMT
Britain	East Shefford (Berkshire)	Consumption	AD 400–550	Related to HIMT
Britain	Faversham (Kent)	Consumption	AD 400–550	Related to HIMT
Britain	Frocester Court (Gloucestershire)	Consumption	4th c.	HIMT 1 and 2
Britain	Great Chesterford (Essex)	Consumption	AD 400–550	Related to HIMT
Britain	Howletts (Kent)	Consumption	AD 400–550	Related to HIMT
Britain	Jarrow (Tyne and Wear)	Consumption	7th–early 8th c.	HIMT
Britain	Billingsgate Bath House, London	Consumption	4th–beg. 5th c.	HIMT
Britain	Billingsgate Bath House, London	Consumption	4th–beg. 5th c.	HIMT 1 and 2
Britain	Longbridge (Warwickshire)	Consumption	AD 400–550	Related to HIMT
Britain	Lullingstone Villa (Kent)	Consumption	4th–beg. 5th c.	HIMT 1 and 2
Britain	Mucking (Essex)	Consumption	AD 400–550	Related to HIMT
Britain	Portchester Castle (Hampshire)	Consumption	4th c.	HIMT 1 and 2
Britain	Shakenoak Villa (Oxfordshire)	Consumption	4th–beg. 5th c.	HIMT 1 and 2
Britain	Bath (Somerset)	Consumption	4th–beg. 5th c.	HIMT 1 and 2
Britain	Sittingbourne (Kent)	Consumption	AD 400–550	Related to HIMT
Britain	Towcester (Northampton)	Consumption	4th–beg. 5th c.	HIMT 1 and 2
Britain	York (North Yorkshire)	Consumption	4th–beg. 5th c.	HIMT 1 and 2
Bulgaria	Dichin	Consumption	AD 470–490	Dichin Group I
Bulgaria	Dichin	Workshop	AD 410–470	Dichin Group IIa and IIb
Cyprus	Maroni Petrera	Consumption	*tpq* mid 7th c.	HIMT
Egypt	Tebtynis	Consumption	Surface / 6th c.	*Groupe 1*
Egypt	Tebtynis	Consumption	Second half of 6th c.	*Groupe 2 série 2.1*
Egypt	Taposiris	Consumption	Surface	*Groupe 1*
Egypt	Fostat	Consumption	Islamic context	*Groupe 1*
Egypt	Fostat	Consumption	Umayyad	*Groupe 2 série 2.2*
Egypt	Northern Sinai	Consumption	4th–5th c. (survey)	HIMT
France	Arles	Workshop	Beginning 5th c.	Visual
France	Béziers	Consumption	10th–11th c. residual	*Groupe 2 série 2.2*
France	Bordeaux	Workshop	7th–8th c.	*Groupe 2 série 2.1*
France	Éauze (Gers)	Workshop	Beginning 5th c.	Visual

Colour	Nature of samples	Remarks	Bibliography
"verdâtre"	Vessel (Is. 129)	Drawing	Fontaine-Hodiamont and Wouters 2004/05
"verdâtre"	Vessel (Is. 122)	Drawing	Fontaine-Hodiamont and Wouters 2004/05
[No indication]	Vessel	No drawing	Aerts *et al.* 2003
"Yellowish-green, colourless"	Vessel	Typology	Foster and Jackson 2009
"Yellowish-green, colourless"	Vessel	Typology	Foster and Jackson 2009
"Yellowish-green, colourless"	Vessel	Typology	Foster and Jackson 2009
"Yellowish-green, colourless"	Vessel	Typology	Foster and Jackson 2009
"Yellowish-green, colourless"	Vessel	Typology	Foster and Jackson 2009
"Light green"	Vessel (claw beaker)	Drawing	Freestone *et al.* 2008
"Yellowish-green, colourless"	Vessel	Typology	Foster and Jackson 2009
"Yellowish-green, colourless"	Vessel	Typology	Foster and Jackson 2009
"Yellowish-green, colourless"	Vessel	Typology	Foster and Jackson 2009
"Redbrown"	Vessel (cone beaker)	Drawing	Freestone *et al.* 2008
"Redbrown"	Vessel (claw beaker)	Drawing	Freestone *et al.* 2008
"Light green, olive green"	Vessel (claw beaker)	Drawing	Freestone *et al.* 2008
"Yellowish-green, colourless"	Vessel	Typology	Foster and Jackson 2009
"Redbrown"	Vessel (claw beaker)	Drawing	Freestone *et al.* 2008
"Lightly blue-green, lightly green, lightly olive, green-brown"	Vessel (cone beaker, claw beaker)	Drawing	Freestone *et al.* 2008
"Colourless, weakly coloured"	Window	Typology	Freestone 2003
?	Vessel	Typology	Freestone *et al.* 2005
"Yellowish-green, colourless"	Vessel	Typology	Foster and Jackson 2009
"Light green"	Vessel (cone beaker)	Drawing	Freestone *et al.* 2008
"Yellowish-green, colourless"	Vessel	Typology	Foster and Jackson 2009
"Light green, light green brown"	Vessel (claw beaker)	Drawing	Freestone *et al.* 2008
"Yellowish-green, colourless"	Vessel	Typology	Foster and Jackson 2009
"Yellowish-green, colourless"	Vessel	Typology	Foster and Jackson 2009
"Yellowish-green, colourless"	Vessel	Typology	Foster and Jackson 2009
"Redbrown"	Vessel (claw beaker)	Drawing	Freestone *et al.* 2008
"Yellowish-green, colourless"	Vessel	Typology	Foster and Jackson 2009
"Yellowish-green, colourless"	Vessel	Typology	Foster and Jackson 2009
Transparent green glass	Vessel	Drawing	Rehren and Cholakova 2010
"Yellow/dark yellow/amber/olive"	Vessel + Refuse	Drawing	Rehren and Cholakova 2010
"Clear, green"	Vessel	No drawing	Freestone *et al.* 2002b
"olive"	Vessel	Drawing	Foy *et al.* 2003b, 52
"incolore, jaunâtre, bleuté, vert-jaune"	Vessel	Drawing	Foy *et al.* 2003b, 59–60
"brun"	Vessel	No drawing	Foy *et al.* 2003b, 52
"olive"	Vessel	Drawing	Foy *et al.* 2003b, 52
Violet	Window	No drawing	Foy *et al.* 2003b, 61
"Yellow green to olive"	Vessel	No drawing	Freestone *et al.* 2002a
vert olive	Raw glass	No drawing	Foy 2009, 126
bleuâtre	Vessel	Drawing	Foy *et al.* 2003b, 61
"olive jaunâtre… incolore jaunâtre"	Raw glass	No drawing	Foy *et al.* 2003b, 56
"vert olive"	Raw glass	No drawing	Foy 2009, 126

Country	Site	Nature of site	Chronology of site	Glass Group
France	Jouars-Pontchartrain	Consumption	Mid 5th–mid 6th c.	HIMT
France	Jouques	Consumption	7th c. ?	*Groupe 2 série 2.2*
France	Le Bouquet (Var)	Consumption	Beginning 8th c.	*Groupe 2 série 2.2*
France	Loupian	Consumption	Beginning 5th c.	*Groupe 1*
France	Lyon	Consumption	Beginning 5th c.	*Groupe 1*
France	Maguelonne	Workshop	End 6th c.	*Groupe 2 série 2.2*
France	Marseille	Workshop	5th–beg. 6th c.	*Groupe 1 and 2.1*
France	Narbonne	Consumption	Beginning 5th c.	*Groupe 1*
France	Port-Vendres	Harbour deposit	5th–6th c.	*Groupe 1 and 2.1*
France	Port-Vendres	Shipwreck Redoute béar	Beginning 5th c.	*Groupe 1*
France	Roquebrune (Var)	Consumption	8th c. ?	*Groupe 2 série 2.2*
France	St Come et Damien (Var)	Consumption	8th–9th c.	*Groupe 2 série 2.2*
France	St-Jean de Garguier (Var)	Consumption	Beginning 5th c.	*Groupe 1 and 2.1*
France	Toulouse	Workshop	5th c. ?	*Groupe 1*
France	Vaison	Consumption	Not mentionned	*Groupe 2 série 2.2*
France	Vitry-sur-Orne	Consumption	7th c.	*Groupe 2 série 2.2*
Germany	Hambach	Workshop	4th c.	HIMT
Germany	Mayen	Consumption	Mid 4th–mid 5th c.	HIMT
Italy	Aoste	Consumption	4th c.	Group E
Italy	Aquileia	Consumption	4th c.	HIMT
Italy	Catania	Workshop	4th–7th c.	HIMT
Italy	Ganzirri (Sicily)	Consumption	4th–7th c.	HIMT
Italy	Galeata	Consumption	6th c.	HIMT
Italy	Grado	Consumption	5th–8th c.	*Groupe 2 (A2/2)*
Italy	Modena Region	Consumption	4th c.	HIMT
Italy	Mevaniola	Consumption	4th c.	HIMT
Italy	Rome	Consumption	4th–5th c.	*Gruppi I, II*
Italy	Rome	Consumption	End 5th–7th c.	*Gruppo IV*
Italy	Rome (Crypta Balbi)	Consumption	7th c.	*Groupe 2*
Italy	Sevegliano	Workshop ?	4th–6th c.	Related to HIMT
Italy	Vicenza	Consumption	5th–8th c.	*Groupe 2 (A2/2)*
Jordan	Deir Ain Abata	Consumption	"Early Byzantine"	HIMT
Jordan	Petra	Consumption	"Early Byzantine"	HIMT
Serbia	Caricin Grad	Workshop	Mid 6th–early 7th c.	related to HIMT
Tunisia	Carthage	Workshop		HIMT
Tunisia	Carthage	Consumption	End 4th–5th c.	*Gruppo I*
Tunisia	Carthage	Consumption	End 5th–7th c.	*Gruppo IV*
Tunisia	Nabeul	Consumption	Early 5th–6th/7th c.	*Groupe 1 / 2.1*
Tunisia	Sidi Jdidi	Consumption	Second half 6th c.	*Groupe 2.1*
Tunisia	Oued R'mel	Consumption	6th c.	*Groupe 2.1*
Turkey	Ephesos	Consumption	4th c.	HIMT
Turkey	Pergamon	Consumption	4th–5th c.	HIMT
Turkey	Sagalassos	Workshop	AD 450–650	HIMT

Colour	Nature of samples	Remarks	Bibliography
"vert olive"	Window	No drawing	Blin *et al.* 2006
"bleuâtre"	Vessel	Drawing	Foy *et al.* 2003b, 61
"bleuâtre"	Vessel	Drawing	Foy *et al.* 2003b, 61
"olive"	Vessel	Drawing	Foy *et al.* 2003b, 49–50
"olive"	Vessel	Drawing	Foy *et al.* 2003b, 49–50
"jaunâtre"	Raw glass + refuse + vessel	Drawing	Foy *et al.* 2003b, 56–57
"verdâtre, brun ambre, olive"	Raw glass/vessel	Drawing	Foy *et al.* 2003b, 49–50, 53, 57
"olive"	Vessel	Drawing	Foy *et al.* 2003b, 50, 53
"olive" / "olive jaunâtre"	Raw glass/vessel	Drawing	Foy *et al.* 2003b, 49–50
"vert-jaune"	Vessel	Drawing	Foy *et al.* 2003b, 53
"bleuâtre"	Vessel	No drawing	Foy *et al.* 2003b, 61
"bleuâtre"	Vessel	Drawing	Foy *et al.* 2003b, 61
"olive"	Vessel	Drawing	Foy *et al.* 2003b, 49–50, 57
"olive, vert-jaune"	Raw glass	Drawing	Foy *et al.* 2003b, 49
"bleuâtre"	Vessel	Drawing	Foy *et al.* 2003b, 61
Not mentionned	Vessel	Drawing	Foy *et al.* 2003b, 61
?	Raw glass + vessel	Drawing	Wedepohl and Hartmann 2000; Freestone *et al.* 2009, 44
"Olive green"	Vessel	No drawing	Hartmann and Grünewald 2010
?	Vessel/window	No drawing	Mirti *et al.* 1993
"Light green, Green"	Vessel (Is. 106, 116)	Typology	Arletti *et al.* 2008
"Green-grey"	Raw glass	No drawing	De Ferri *et al.* 2011
"Deep olive-green"	Vessel	No drawing	Arletti *et al.* 2010a
"Light green, light green-olive, colourless"	Window	No drawing	Arletti *et al.* 2010b
"Yellow"	Vessel	No drawing	Silvestri *et al.* 2005
"Pale Yellow green, olive, yellow green, green"	Vessel (Is. 106)	Typology	Arletti *et al.* 2005
"Light green, green-yellow, green"	Window	No drawing	Arletti *et al.* 2010b
"giallo intenso, verde giallastro, incolore verdastro"	Vessel	Typology, drawing	Verità 1995
"incolore giallastro, giallastro intenso …"	Vessel	Typology, drawing	Verità 1995
?	Vessel/window	No drawing	Mirti *et al.* 2000
?	Vessel (atypical)	No drawing	Verità and Vallotto 1998
"Yellow"	Vessel	No drawing	Silvestri *et al.* 2005
Not mentionned in detail	Vessel	No drawing	Rehren *et al.* 2010
Not mentionned in detail	Vessel	No drawing	Rehren *et al.* 2010
"Greenish, blue"	Raw Glass	No drawing	Drauschke and Greiff 2010
?	Raw glass	No drawing	Freestone 1994; Freestone *et al.* 2005
"giallo intenso"	Vessel	Typology, drawing	Verità 1995
"verde giallastro, giallo"	Vessel	Typology, drawing	Verità 1995
"olive" /jaunâtre, vert jaune"	Vessel	Drawing	Foy *et al.* 2003b, 51–53
verdâtre	Vessel	Drawing	Foy *et al.* 2003b, 58
jaunâtre	Vessel	Drawing	Foy *et al.* 2003b, 58
"Olive green"	Vessel (square bottles, cups)	No drawing	Uhlir *et al.* 2010
"Greenish"	Window	No drawing	Schibille 2011
"Yellow green"	Vessel/raw glass	No drawing	Degryse *et al.* 2005

The chronology of the use of HIMT glass

Taking a broad view, it can be said that HIMT glass was in competition with Near Eastern glass (Freestone's Levantine I) from the middle of the 4th to the middle or end of the 7th century, when the workshops producing HIMT glass in northern Sinai closed and were replaced by other workshops in Egypt. These have not yet been located but they continued to use mineral soda with different sands, which are characterized by low levels of calcium. HIMT glasses competed for its markets throughout the Mediterranean world and Europe, except in the Near Eastern region, as has been shown by Freestone in numerous works on glass in Israel (for example, Freestone *et al.* 2000). The case of Jordan is interesting: in northern Jordan, only Levantine I glass is attested (Abd Allah 2010), while in southern Jordan, where Egyptian objects are known from the early imperial period onwards, a small quantity of HIMT glass is also present (Rehren *et al.* 2010). When the number of sherds analysed is substantial or general discussion is included in publications, it can be seen that this competition leads, at least in some regions, to a predominance of Egyptian glass. For example, in Britain in the 4th and early 5th century, HIMT glass represents 66% of the glass analysed (344 of 517 analyses, see Foster and Jackson 2009, 191–192) and in Britain between AD 400–550 when there appears to be a drastic reduction in glass vessel consumption, as the 29 samples analysed represent 5% of the total vessel glass recovered from early Anglo-Saxon England, the composition related to HIMT (Anglo-Saxon 1) is the only one attested (Freestone *et al.* 2008, 32–37). Similarly, in Marseille, southern France, 90% of the material dating from the second quarter of the 5th century belongs to *Groupe 1* (Foy *et al.* 2003b, 48).

Over such a long period of time, around 300 years, it is reasonable to expect changes of location of the workshops, changes in the tastes of the customers, changes in the distribution networks, and also differences in the glass itself because of recycling. Visually the colour of the vessel glass is typically as it was described by Freestone *et al.* (2005, 153) but it varies from what Foster and Jackson call "weak HIMT" (which is nearly colourless) to "strong HIMT" (which is olive green), with different shades of yellowish, yellowish green, greenish, and green between these extremes. Therefore, the connection that archaeological glass specialists sometimes try to make between the different shades and fabrics and their chronology is not sustainable. When Foster and Jackson (2009) in their fig. 1, note chemical similarities between their HIMT 1 group and *Groupe 2* of Picon and co-authors, they are making the correlation solely on a compositional level, without reference to colour and chronology. It should also be noted that in addition to the range of shades of HIMT glass used in vessels, black glass of similar composition was used in jewellery, as shown by the work of Cosyns on the bangles dated to the mid 4th–5th century (Cosyns 2011, 411–412).

This means that if an Egyptian provenance for this glass is accepted, the primary glass workshops were not concentrated in one place, but must have been more widely distributed and active over a long period. These workshops were able to produce a range of different colours, by adding or omitting manganese for olive-green or "naturally coloured" glass, or by adding iron to produce 'black' glass, according to the requirements of their customers.

It is not possible to explain why this new glass appeared in the mid 4th century, any more than it is possible to understand the beginning of the taste for colourless glass at the end of the 1st century, though the latter may be the result of new technology, or a return to the value placed on colourless glass as an imitation of rock crystal, or a question of cost (Freestone 2008; Nenna in press b). As Foster and Jackson have pointed out (2009, 195–196), there is no evidence for a reduction of glass production in the Near Eastern region, as there was population growth and economic prosperity in Syria-Palestine in the 4th century and the glass industry in the region was flourishing. The regular occurrence of Levantine vessel glass on the same sites as HIMT vessel glass, though in smaller quantities, clearly shows that this glass was coming from Syria-Palestine, and was being distributed to the same markets. Moreover, raw glass chunks of Levantine origin are also attested in secondary glass workshops, and sometimes in the same ones as HIMT glass (see, for example Foy *et al.* 2003b, 67, 70, 72). One reason why HIMT glass is more dominant than Levantine glass may be because of the cost. As Foster and Jackson (2009; 2010) have shown, Levantine I and Colourless 1 vessel glass show no traces of recycling and they appear to be higher quality glasswares than the objects produced in HIMT 2 and Colourless group 3. This could well be because the quality of the technology of HIMT glass was lower than that of Levantine glass, much more variable and also less expensive than Levantine I glass (see Verità 1995, 294). Egyptian glassworkers did not hesitate to introduce recycled glass into the primary batch to aid the fusion of the sand and the flux (Foy *et al.* 2003b, 46), without concerning themselves about the consistency of the colour, and this practice seems to have increased over time.

The location of the primary glass workshops producing HIMT

Returning to the question of the provenance of HIMT glass, I have included the unpublished information from a sand survey that Maurice Picon, Valérie Thirion-Merle, Michèle Vichy and I conducted in 2002 in this section of the paper. Sands were sampled from four areas: at Aboukir, from the dunes situated between Aboukir and Rosetta, at the mouth of the Nile at Rosetta as well as near Baltim and Gamasa (Fig. 18.4).

TiO$_2$

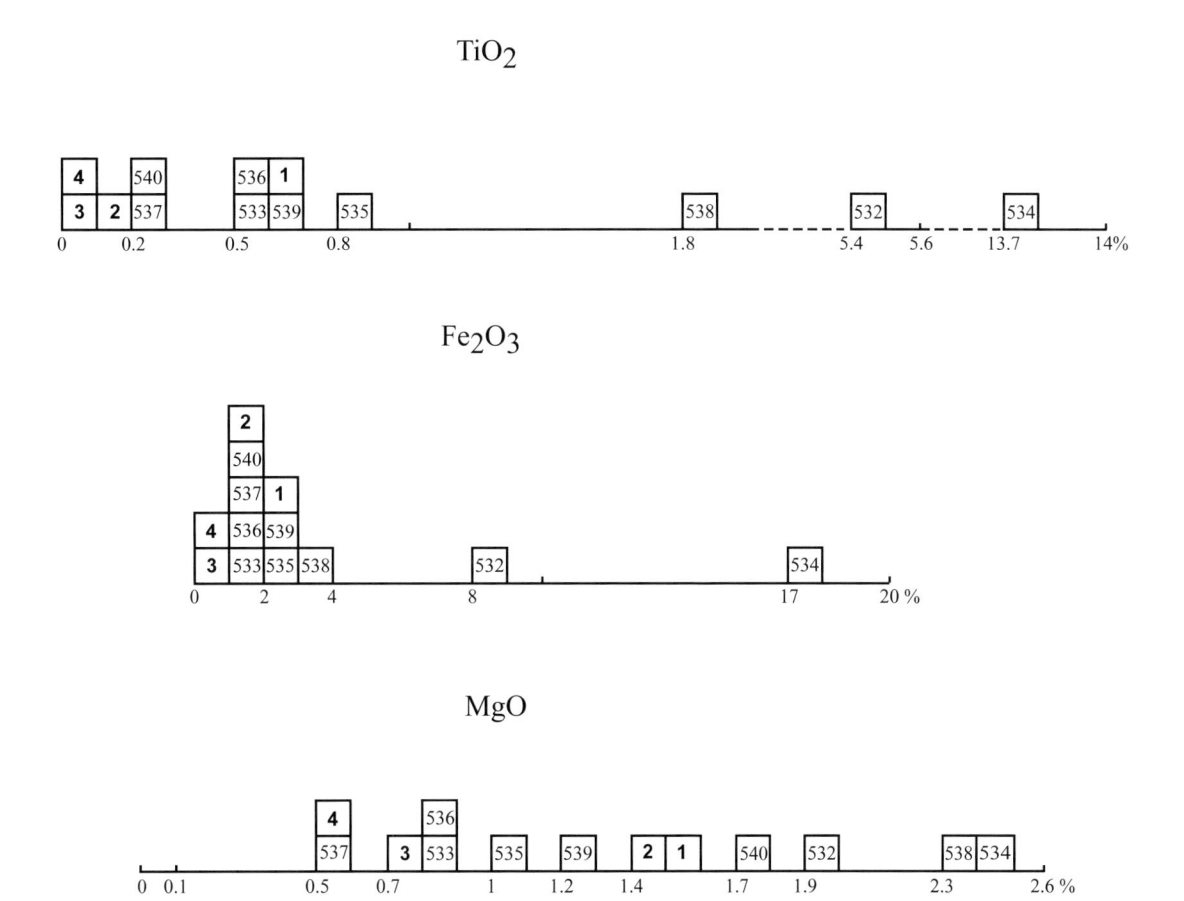

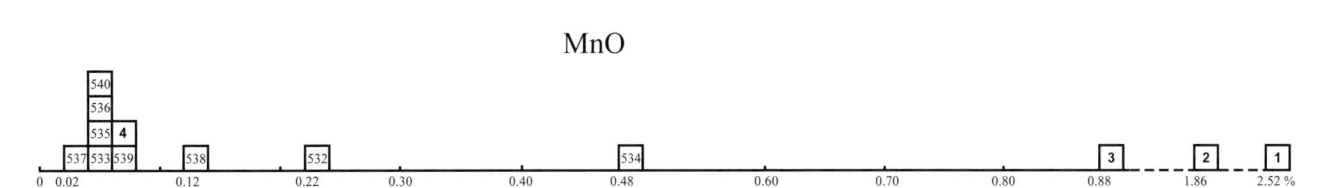

Fe$_2$O$_3$

MgO

MnO

Fig. 18.3: Histogramm of the percentages of titanium oxyde (TiO$_2$), iron oxyde (Fe$_2$O$_3$), magnesium oxyde (MgO) and manganese oxyde (MnO) for the sand samples collected in Egypt and the sands from Groupes 1 to 4 (indicated in bold). Analyses by M. Picon, V. Thirion-Merle and M. Vichy.

On these shores the separation by aeolian activity between the silts and the sands brought by the Nile has resulted in the building up of the largest deposits of Nilotic sands. The histogram of the percentages of titanium oxide, iron oxide and magnesium oxide of the sands sampled in Egypt and of the sands from Picon's *Groupes 1* to *4* (Fig. 18.3), shows that the sand used in the manufacture of *Groupe 1* and *Groupe 2* glasses is similar to Nilotic sand, as they present a similar level of concentration of titanium, iron and magnesium as the sands used to manufacture *Groupes 1* and *2*. For titanium oxide, the sands sampled show concentrations between 0.2% and 13.7%, *Groupe 1* averaging 0.6% and *Groupe 2* averaging 0.2%. For iron oxide they show concentrations between 1% and 17.8%, *Groupe 1* averaging 2.85% and *Groupe 2* averaging 1.65%. For magnesium oxide, the concentrations range from 0.5 to 2.6%, *Groupe 1* averaging 1.53%, and *Groupe 2* averaging 1.5%. For manganese oxide, the histogram shows very clearly that this was deliberately added by the glassworkers as the Nilotic sands have lower levels of manganese than the sands used in *Groupes 1* and *2*.

It should be noted that there are no important settlements on the coast between Rosetta and Port Said, and that significant changes have occurred in the region since

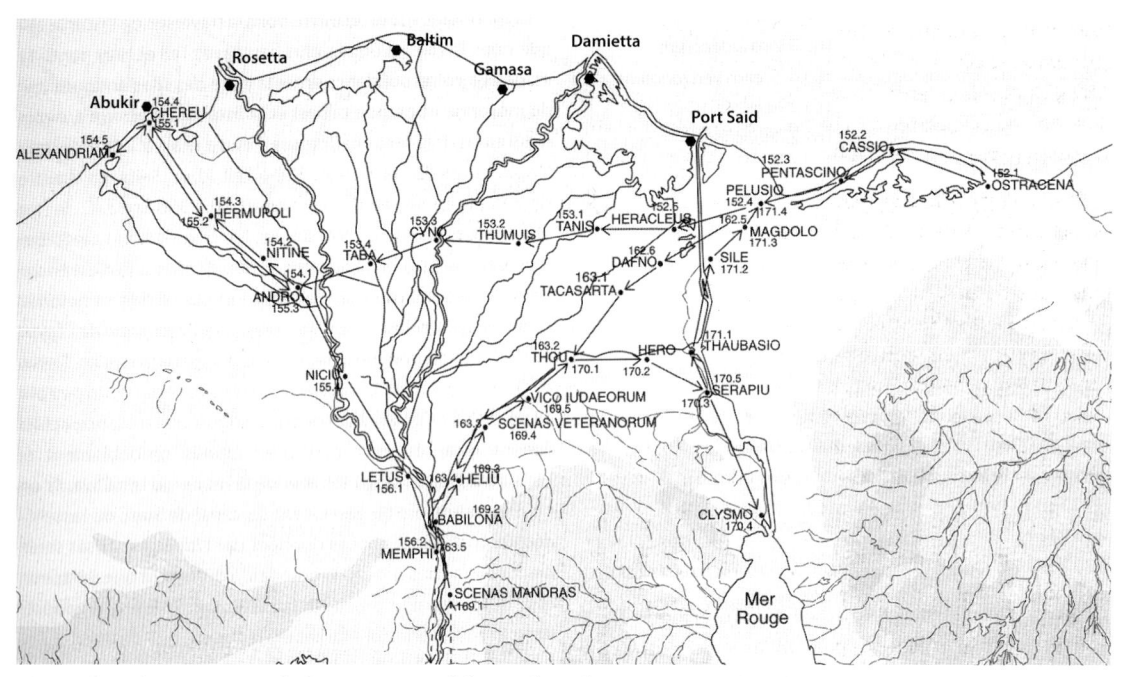

Fig. 18.4: Map of northern Egypt with the restitution of the roads and cities presented in the Itinerarium Antonini Augusti (D. Valbelle and J.-Y. Carrez-Maratray (2000) Le camp romain du Bas-Empire à Tell el-Herr, *8–10, fig. 2. Paris, Errance).*

antiquity, with the disappearance of Nile mouths and the Canopic, Tanitic and Pelusiac branches. The coast is now affected by recession of the shoreline. The map of northern Egypt showing the roads and cities present in the *Itinerarium Antonini Augusti* dating to the beginning of the 4th century (Fig. 18.4), clearly demonstrates the absence of settlements along the coastline of the delta. It must be added that the sands collected between Aboukir and Port Said were too heavily loaded with black particles (pyroxenes), to be used in glassmaking. For geological as well as historical reasons, the hypothesis of production in northern Sinai is more convincing, despite the fact that no ancient texts mention the glass production in Sinai, as is shown by the work of Verreth (2006). This is perhaps not very surprising, in view of the general dearth of references to craftmanship in ancient sources.

The site of Ostrakine (*Ostracena*) must be considered as a possible production centre (Ian Freestone, pers. comm.). Ostrakine, the modern town of El-Felusyat, is situated at the eastern end of lake Bardawil, the ancient lake Sirbonis, 30km west of El-Arish and 3km from the Mediterranean coast, and it was mentioned in ancient texts at the end of the 1st century BC. It was sited at the junction of two important ancient roads connecting Palestine and Egypt: the coastal road is shown in the *Itinerarium*, and the inland road was the ancient Way of Horus. It also had a well-protected inland harbour, situated near one of the natural outlets connecting the lake with the sea. Although never a military site, it was on the border between Egypt and Arabia in the ancient world. The city enjoyed prosperity from the 3rd century onwards, was one of the principal towns of *Provincia Augustamnica* created during the 5th century and appears on the Madaba mosaic which is dated to c. AD 560–565. Part of the town is today under water due to rising sea levels, and the site consists of four islands emerging from the salt marsh, although ruins also appear in the water between the islands. The area of the ancient site is c. 1200m north-south and east-west (Clédat 1910) or two square km (Oren 1993b). The geological report of D. Neev states that El-Felusyat was flooded at the end of the Byzantine period or in the early Islamic period because of tectonic movements (Verreth 2006, 389, note 1588, quoting Oren), and until the 9th century there are no written references to sites in this region. Among the surviving ancient remains, two basilicas and a fortified monastery were excavated by Clédat in 1914 (Clédat 1916) and the Israeli expedition in 1976–1977 unearthed a third basilica as well as a "commercial center" (Oren 1993a; 1993b). The Israeli reports mention that "the area west of the fortified monastery was occupied by various industrial installations for manufacturing glass and metal objects" (Oren 1993a, 308) and that "an industrial site in which metal and glass objects were produced, was recorded north of the fortified monastery, it contained large quantities of glass, broken vitrified materials, copper refuse and fragments of metal vessels" (Oren 1993b, 1172). Whether this industrial activity was sited to the west or north, or to the east as suggested by a British surveyor in the early 20th century who wrote "fragments of pottery and glass of all colours, with shapeless lumps of copper, cover the salt-pan between this (the island with Clédat's south basilica) and the larger mound" (*i.e.* the one with the fortified monastery) (Anonymous 1920), the quantity of glass impressed the different expeditions. The Israeli expedition has not yet published its full results, but Yael Gorin-Rosen confirmed during the York conference in 2011 that she and Tamar Winter have established that finds of glass vessels and raw glass were abundant in most of the sites surveyed by the Israeli expedition in Sinai.

Another good candidate would be Pelusium (*Pelusio*) and its region. Pelusium is the eastern counterpart of Alexandria, with an important maritime and river harbour developing mainly from the 4th century onwards, and travellers and archaeologists working here have been impressed by the quantity of glass found on the surface: "*La vocation industrielle de Péluse, dans ce domaine, comme dans ceux de la céramique, de la verrerie ou de la métallurgie du bronze, éclate à chaque pas qu'impriment le visiteur moderne dans le sol de ses tells aujourd'hui désolés*" (Carrez-Maratray 1999, 431). Surveys and excavations in this huge city have been focussed on the monumental buildings, and no surveys have been undertaken with the participation of glass specialists. Nevertheless, in the survey undertaken in the mid 1990s in the eastern suburbs of Pelusium, glass associated with scoria is mentioned (Jaritz *et al.* 1996, 34, île 9a, île 10); the toponym of one of the areas, Tell el-Zugag (hill of glass), is evocative (Jaritz *et al.* 1996, 49–51) and the drawings of two items coming from this site (Jaritz *et al.* 1996, 73, nos. 314–315, fig. 28) are more likely to be glass waste than toilet bottles as suggested in the report. Like Ostrakine, Pelusium has been affected by very important changes since antiquity, such as the disappearance of the Pelusiac branch of the Nile and more recently the changes connected to the establishment of the Peace Canal and the agricultural development of the region.

The question of the primary materials for glass making must be addressed. If the sands are easily available, the question of the natron can be solved, either by transporting it from the Wadi Natrun, Barnughi (Nitria) region, or from closer deposits known in the eastern part of the delta in Wadi Tumilat (Lucas 1912), or by producing it on the spot. Ostrakine and Pelusium were known in antiquity for the salt industry based on deposits in lake Bardawil (Carrez-Maratray 1999, 429–430; Verreth 2006, vol. 1, 115), and it would be interesting to know whether the recent suggestion of Shortland and his co-authors (2011) that sulphate-rich materials were processed to convert them into a usable glass-making flux might be applicable in this case. For fuel, the situation would have been similar to that in Wadi Natrun, where rushes and reeds, together with palm trees and may be acacia and tamarisks were used (Nenna in press a). Rushes and reeds are known to have been present at lake Bardawil in antiquity (Verreth 2006, vol. 1, 115, 257). One could wonder if bones, especially vertebrae with cartilage which have a good combustible potential, were used, as they are attested in a ceramic kiln at Pelusium dated to the 9th century (Delahaye *et al.* 2009). The use of rushes and reeds as principal fuel, of which the calorific potential is different from hard wood and less easily domineable, is well attested in pottery and amphora production in Egypt. It is responsible of many failed amphorae batches (see for example in Mareotid region, Empereur and Picon 1998) and could be also the reason for the poor quality of some of the HIMT glass.

The precise location of the places where HIMT glass was manufactured is not yet established, and the full publication of the Israeli expedition is eagerly awaited as, since the beginning of 2011, the Sinai has become a very unstable political region and foreign missions are not permitted to work there.

The distribution of HIMT glass

The trade in HIMT glass can be traced archaeologically, in the same way as other categories of glass, through the studies of three different kinds of artefacts: raw glass chunks, containers, and luxury wares. Trade in common kinds of vessel glass is also attested (see for example Foy 2009, 124, fig. 19: Egyptian oval plate), but the state of regional studies in glass is not sufficiently advanced for it to be possible to distinguish between locally produced and imported vessels made from the same kind of glass. The high percentage of common vessel glass made from recycled rather than fresh HIMT glass, as seen in the samples from Britain or from Dichin in Bulgaria, introduces a further level of complexity.

At present, we do not have the equivalent of the raw glass cargos in the shipwrecks of the Roman period for HIMT glass, except perhaps in the shipwreck "Orsi" of Scifo, near Crotone in Calabria dated c. AD 200 (Pensabene 1978; Spadea 2006, 69–71: the raw glass is only mentioned in the publications, but the chunks exhibited in the Museum of Capo Colonna show that one is blue-green in colour, and the other is a deep green olive colour, very similar to the colour of HIMT glass, and it would be most interesting to analyse this piece, not least because of its early date), but chunks of raw glass of HIMT have been identified in various places (listed in Table 18.2). Apart from the harbour deposit of Port-Vendres, chunks from glass workshop contexts have been analysed in Germany (Hambach), in southern France (Maguelonne, Marseille, Bordeaux, Toulouse, and visually identified in Arles and Éauze), Sicily (Catania), Tunisia (Carthage), Serbia (Caricin Grad) as well as in the eastern Mediterranean (Sagalassos in Turkey).

The containers circulating for their contents may show either the distribution patterns connected to the routes of travellers/pilgrims or a "true" trade of the contents. The two-headed flasks which are common in Egypt and widespread around the Mediterranean may belong to the first group, as suggested by Foy (2009, 123; see also Foy 2010 for a wider study of their distribution). The analyses of two examples from Narbonne and Ephesos show that some of them were made in HIMT glass. Some bear Christian symbols and their contents may have been holy water, or sacred oils connected to the cults of saints, as is the case for the ceramic flasks of St Menas. It is certain, if the places where these glass flasks have been found were to be recorded systematically, that the distribution would be similar to that of the pottery flasks of St Menas produced in the St Menas religious complex 45km south-west of Alexandria (90 sites listed recently; see Pichot 2011, 184–187).

The second group, that is, the vessels traded for their contents, includes the deep olive green containers for wine or garum such as the rare glass imitations of the spatheion amphora, very probably of Egyptian production and known in Egypt, Italy, Turkey (Nenna 2003a, fig. 4.4; Czurda-Ruth 2007, 186, nos. 827–828) and Spain (Foy 2009, 123, fig. 18), and the two-handled cylindrical bottles with abraded geometric decoration, also very probably of Egyptian production, known in Egypt, Italy, Germany and southern France (Foy *et al.* 2003b, 54–55; Nenna 2003b, 371, fig. 32). However, in the case of some other very specific products, such as square bottles made with HIMT glass with base-marks bearing a Greek inscription (for analyses of examples from Ephesos, see Uhlir *et al.* 2010), the composition of the glass does not seem to be a good clue for determining the place of production. None of these bottles have been recorded in Egypt and most have been discovered in Asia Minor, the rest being distributed in small numbers around the Mediterranean, mainly in harbour settlements (Nenna 2011).

The circulation of the Egyptian glass containers may be compared to the one of the pottery amphorae of Egyptian production, recently studied by Dixneuf (2011). Egyptian wines were considered to be luxury products, as were other oriental wines. Even though the distribution of these wine amphorae is a reflection of the current state of research, it is important to stress that they have been recorded in all parts of the ancient world, and that except for the Rome-Pozzuoli area, the North Adriatic and southern France, they are found in small numbers. The chronological sequence in Rome shows that they were imported from the 1st century BC to the 1st century AD, then decreasd between the 2nd and the 4th century, with a new impetus in the 5th century.

For the period under consideration, the middle of the 4th century to the middle/end of the 7th century, the status of glass varies in the different regions of the ancient world and thus the use of the term "luxury glass", referring to special techniques and decoration, must be used cautiously. While vessel glass was widely used in everyday life around the Mediterranean, consumption was reduced and followed a different pattern in the north-western provinces, so glass was in itself a luxury product, whether the vessels and objects were simple or sophisticated. Even around the Mediterranean, luxury glass is seldom encountered after the beginning of the 5th century, when the art of engraving declined, and painted glass, mosaic glass and elaborate mould-blown vessels disappeared.

To sum up, recent research in archaeometry has demonstrated the appearance in the 4th century of a new kind of glass in the glass workshops of the Roman empire, which had previously been supplied mainly with Levantine glass. This new glass was manufactured in northern Sinai from at least the middle of the 4th century until the middle of the 7th century, when the primary workshops in Sinai stopped making glass and were replaced by other primary glass workshops in Egypt which supplied mainly the eastern Mediterranean region. During these three centuries, the primary glass workshops in Sinai provided raw glass of different colours and hues – from yellowish to black – to all parts of the ancient world (*i.e.* Europe and the Mediterranean), but more assessment of the degree and the importance of recycling in the secondary glass workshops and more detailed archaeological studies of the artefacts are now needed, so that the chronological phases of this trade, and the range of activities of the secondary glass workshops can be defined more precisely. As the broad glass compositions are now well defined, to progress in the understanding of the distribution of HIMT raw glass and finished objects from Egypt, and its recycling in secondary workshops, we must, as archaeological glass researchers, ensure that the forms of glass selected for analysis are identified and dated correctly, and provide as much information as possible about the sherds selected. As has already been explained this research is still developing and many aspects remain to be investigated, to produce a fuller and more detailed assessment of the impact of HIMT glass on glass industry and trade in late antiquity.

Bibliography

Abd-Allah, R. (2010) Chemical characterisation and manufacturing technology of late Roman to early Byzantine glass from Beit Ras/Capitolias, Northern Jordan. *Journal of Archaeological Science* 37, 1866–1874.

Aerts, A., Velde, B., Janssens, K. and Dijkman, W. (2003) Change in Silica Sources in Roman and Post Roman Glass. *Spectrochimica Acta Part B* 58, 659–667.

Anonymous (1920) Antiquities on the Desert Coast between Egypt and Palestine. *The Geographical Journal* 55, 464–467.

Arletti, R., Giordani, N., Tarpini, R. and Vezzalini, G. (2005) Archaeometrical analysis of glass of Western Emilia Romagna (Italy) from the Imperial age. In *Annales du 16e Congrès de l'Association Internationale pour l'Histoire du Verre*, 80–84. Nottingham, Association Internationale pour l'Histoire du Verre.

Arletti, R., Vezzalini, G., Biaggio Simona, S. and Maselli Scotti, F. (2008) Archaeometrical studies on Roman Imperial age glass from Canton Ticino. *Archaeometry* 50, 606–626.

Arletti, R., Giaccobe, C., Quartieri, S., Sabatino, G., Tigano, G., Triscari, M. and Vezzalini, G. (2010a) Archaeometrical investigation of Sicilian early Byzantine glass: chemical and spectroscopic data. *Archaeometry* 52, 99–114.

Arletti, R., Vezzalini, G., Benati, S., Mazzeo Saracini, L. and Gamberini, A. (2010b) Roman window glass: a comparison of findings from three different Italian sites. *Archaeometry* 52, 252–271.

Bimson, M. and Freestone, I. C. (1991) Appendix 3: Glassmaking on the Komasterion site: The discovery of an Islamic glass-making site in middle Egypt. In D. M. Bailey, *Excavations at El-Ashmunein IV. Hermopolis Magna. Buildings of the Roman Period*, 64–65. London, British Museum Press.

Blin, O., Vanpeene, N. and Velde, B. (2006) Les verres de vitrage du bâtiment à plan basilical de Jouars-Pontchartrain (Yvelines). *Bulletin de l'Association Française pour l'Archéologie du Verre*, 46–49.

Brill, R. H. (1988) Scientific Investigations of the Jalame Glass and Related Finds. In G. D. Weinberg (ed.) *Excavations at Jalame. Site of a Glass Factory in Late Roman Palestine*, 257–294. Columbia, MO, University of Missouri Press.

Carrez-Maratray, J.-Y. (1999) *Péluse et l'angle oriental du Delta égyptien aux époques grecque, romaine et byzantine*. Cairo, Institut Français d'Archéologie Orientale.

Clédat, J. (1910) Notes sur l'isthme de Suez. *Annales du Service des Antiquités de l'Égypte* 10, 209–237.

Clédat, J. (1916) Fouilles à Khirbet el-Flousiyat (janvier–mars 1914). *Annales du Service des Antiquités de l'Égypte* 16, 16–32.

Cosyns, P. (2011) *The production, distribution and consumption of black glass in the Roman Empire during the 1st – 5th century AD. An archaeological, archaeometric and historical approach.* Unpublished PhD. Brussels, Vrije Universiteit.

Czurda-Ruth, B. (2007) *Hanghaus 1 in Ephesos. Die Gläser.* Forschungen in Ephesos VIII/7. Vienna, Österreichische Akademie der Wissenschaften.

Degryse, P., Schneider, J., Poblome, J., Waelkens, M., Haack, U. and Muchez, P. (2005) A Geochemical Study of Roman to Early Byzantine Glass from Sagalassos, South-West Turkey. *Journal of Archaeological Science* 32, 287–299.

Delahaye, F., Dixneuf, D. and Chaix, L. (2009) Un four de potier arabe at Tell el-Farama. *Geneva* 57, 152–158.

Dixneuf, D. (2011) *Amphores égyptiennes. Production, typologie, contenu et diffusion (IIIe siècle avant J.-C. – IXe siècle après J.-C.).* Etudes Alexandrines 22. Alexandria, Centre d'Études Alexandrines.

Drauschke, J. and Greiff, S. (2010) Chemical aspects of Byzantine glass from Caricin Grad/Iustiniana Prima (Serbia). In J. Drauschke and D. Keller (eds.) *Glass in Byzantium – Production, Usage, Analyses.* RGZM – Tagungen 8, 25–46. Mainz, Römisch-Germanisches Zentralmuseum.

Empereur, J.-Y. and Picon, M. (1998) Les ateliers d'amphores du lac Mariout. In J.-Y. Empereur (ed.) *Commerce et artisanat dans l'Alexandrie hellénistique et romaine.* Bulletin de Correspondance Hellénique Supplément 33, 75–91. Athens, Ecole Française d'Athènes.

De Ferri, L., Arletti, R., Ponterini, G. and Quartieri, S. (2011) XANES, UV-VIS and luminescence spectroscopic study of chromophores in ancient HIMT glass. *Journal of European Mineralogy* 23, 969–980.

Fontaine-Hodiamont, C. and Wouters, H. (2004/05) Le diota de Vieuxville et la cruche de Crupet, Approche technologique, analyses et restauration de deux verres romains tardifs. *Revue de l'Institut royal du patrimoine artistique* 31, 19–38.

Foster, H. E. and Jackson, C. M. (2009) The composition of "naturally coloured" late Roman vessel glass from Britain and the implications for models of glass production and supply. *Journal of Archaeological Science* 36, 189–204.

Foster, H. E. and Jackson, C. M. (2010) The composition of late Romano-British colourless vessel glass: glass production and consumption. *Journal of Archaeological Science* 37, 3068–3080.

Foy, D. (2009) Les apports de verres de Méditerranée orientale, en Gaule méridionale, aux IVe et Ve siècles ap. J.-C. In K. Janssens, P. Degryse, P. Cosyns, J. Caen and L. Van't dack (eds.) *Annales du 17e Congrès de l'Association Internationale pour l'Histoire du Verre*, 121–129. Brussels, University Press Antwerp.

Foy, D. (2010) Fioles bicéphales de la fin de l'Antiquité en Narbonnaise. In C. Fontaine-Hodiamont (ed.) *D'Ennion au Val Saint-Lambert. Le verre soufflé-moulé. Actes des 23es Rencontres de l'Association française pour l'archéologie du Verre.* Scientia Artis 5, 261–266. Brussels, Institut Royal du Patrimoine Artistique.

Foy, D. and Picon, M. (2005) L'origine du verre en Méditerranée occidentale à la fin de l'Antiquité et dans le Haut Moyen âge. In *La Méditerranée et le monde mérovingien.* Bulletin archéologique de Provence Supplément 3, 99–110. Aix-en-Provence, Université de Provence.

Foy, D., Picon, M. and Vichy, M. (2000a) Les matières premières du verre et la question des produits semi-finis, Antiquité et Moyen âge. In P. Pétrequin *et al.* (eds.) *Arts du Feu et productions artisanales. XXes rencontres internationales d'Archéologie et d'Histoire d'Antibes*, 420–432. Antibes, Association pour la Promotion et la Diffusion des Connaissances Archéologiques.

Foy, D., Picon, M. and Vichy, M. (2003a) Verres omeyyades et abbassides d'origine égyptienne: les témoignages de l'archéologie et de l'archéométrie. In *Annales du 15e Congrès de l'Association Internationale pour l'Histoire du Verre*, 138–143. Nottingham, Association Internationale pour l'Histoire du Verre.

Foy, D., Picon, M., Vichy, M. and Thirion-Merle, V. (2003b) Caractérisation des verres de la fin de l'Antiquité en Méditerranée occidentale: l'émergence de nouveaux courants commerciaux. In D. Foy and M.-D. Nenna (eds.) *Échanges et commerce du verre dans le monde antique.* Monographies Instrumentum 24, 41–85. Montagnac, Monique Mergoil.

Foy, D., Vichy, M. and Picon, M. (2000b) Lingots de verre en Méditerranée orientale (IIIe siècle av. J.-C. – VIIe siècle apr. J.-C. Approvisionnement et mise en oeuvre. Données archéologiques et données de laboratoire. In *Annales du 14e Congrès de l'Association Internationale pour l'Histoire du Verre*, 51–57. Amsterdam, Association Internationale pour l'Histoire du Verre.

Freestone, I. C. (1994) Chemical analysis of "raw" glass fragments. In H. R. Hurst (ed.) *Excavations at Carthage II, 1. The Circular*

Harbour, North Side, 290. Oxford, Oxford University Press for British Academy.

Freestone, I. C. (2003) Primary glass sources in the mid first millenium AD. In *Annales du 15e Congrès de l'Association Internationale pour l'Histoire du Verre*, 111–115. Nottingham, Association Internationale pour l'Histoire du Verre.

Freestone, I. C. (2005) The provenance of ancient glass through compositional analysis. In P. B. Vandiver, J. L. Mass and A. Murray (eds.) *Materials Issues in Art and Archaeology VII*, 195–208. Warrendale, PA, Materials Research Society.

Freestone, I. C. (2006) Glass production in late Antiquity and the early Islamic period. A geochemical perspective. In M. Magetti and B. Messiga (eds.) *Geomaterials in Cultural Heritage*. Geological Society Special Publications 257, 201–216. London, Geological Society.

Freestone, I. C. (2008) Pliny on Roman glassmaking. In M. Martinon-Torres and T. Rehren (eds.) *Archaeology, History and Science: Integrating Approaches to Ancient Materials*. UCL Institute of Archaeology Publications, 77–100. Walnut Creek, CA, Left Coast Press.

Freestone, I. C., Gorin-Rosen, Y. and Hughes, M. J. (2000) Primary glass from Israel and the production of glass in late Antiquity and the early Islamic period. In M.-D. Nenna (ed.) *La route du verre. Ateliers primaires et secondaires de verriers du second millénaire av. J.-C. au Moyen Âge*. Travaux de la Maison de l'Orient Méditerranéen 33, 65–83. Lyon, Maison de l'Orient Méditerranéen.

Freestone, I. C., Greenwood, R. and Gorin-Rosen, Y. (2002a) Byzantine and early Islamic glassmaking in the Eastern Mediterranean, production and distribution of primary glass. In G. Kordas (ed.) *First International Conference Hyalos, Vitrum, Glass. History, Technology and Conservation of Glass and Vitreous Materials in the Hellenic World*, 167–174. Athens, Alphanet.

Freestone, I. C., Hughes, M. J. and Stapleton, C. P. (2008) The composition and production of Anglo-Saxon glass. In V. Evison, *Catalogue of Anglo-Saxon Glass in the British Museum*. British Museum Research Publication 167, 29–46. London, British Museum Press.

Freestone, I. C., Ponting, M. and Hughes, M. J. (2002b) The origins of Byzantine glass from Maroni Petrera, Cyprus. *Archaeometry* 44, 257–272.

Freestone, I. C., Wolf, S. and Thirlwall, M. (2005) The production of HIMT glass, elemental and isotopic evidence. *Annales du 16e Congrès de l'Association Internationale pour l'Histoire du Verre,* 153–157. Nottingham, Association Internationale pour l'Histoire du Verre.

Freestone, I. C., Wolf, S. and Thirlwall, M. (2009) Isotopic composition of glass from the Levant and the south-eastern Mediterranean region. In P. Degryse, J. Henderson and G. Hodgins (eds.) *Isotopes in Vitreous Materials*. Studies in Archaeological Sciences 1, 31–52. Leuven, Leuven University Press.

Gratuze, B. and Barrandon, J.-N. (1990) Islamic glass weights and stamps: analysis using nuclear techniques. *Archaeometry* 32, 155–162.

Hartmann, S. and Grünewald, M. (2010) The late antique glass from Mayen (Germany): first results of chemical and archaeological studies. In B. Zorn and A. Hilgner (eds.) *Glass along the Silk Road from 200 BC to AD 1000*. RGZM – Tagungen 9, 15–28. Mainz, Römisch-Germanisches Zentralmuseum.

Jaritz, H. (ed.) (1996) *Pelusium. Prospection archéologique et topographique de la région de Kana'is 1993 et 1994*. Stuttgart, Franz Steiner.

Kato, N., Nakai, I. and Shindo, Y. (2009) Change in chemical composition of early Islamic glass excavated in Raya, Sinai Peninsula, Egypt: on-site analyses using a portable X-ray fluorescence spectrometer. *Journal of Archaeological Science* 36, 1698–1707.

Lucas, A. (1912) *Natural Soda Deposits in Egypt*. Cairo, Government Press.

Mirti, P., Casoli, A. and Appolonia, L. (1993) Scientific analysis of Roman glass from Augusta Praetoria. *Archaeometry* 35, 225–240.

Mirti, P., Lepora, A. and Saguì, L. (2000) Scientific Analysis of Seventh-Century Glass Fragments from the Crypta Balbi in Rome. *Archaeometry* 42, 359–374.

Nenna, M.-D. (2001) Verres de l'antiquité gréco-romaine: cinq ans de publication (1995–1999). *Revue archéologique*, 303–342.

Nenna, M.-D. (2003a) Verreries de luxe de l'antiquité tardive découvertes à Douch (oasis de Kharga, Égypte). In *Annales du 15e Congrès de l'Association Internationale pour l'Histoire du Verre*, 93–97. Nottingham, Association Internationale pour l'Histoire du Verre.

Nenna, M.-D. (2003b) Verres gravés d'Égypte du Ier siècle au Ve siècle apr. J.-C. In D. Foy and M.-D. Nenna (eds.) *Échanges et commerce du verre dans le monde antique*. Monographies Instrumentum 24, 359–375. Montagnac, Monique Mergoil.

Nenna, M.-D. (2006) Verres de l'antiquité gréco-romaine: cinq ans de publication (2000–2004). *Revue Archéologique*, 83–166.

Nenna, M.-D. (2009) Verres de l'antiquité gréco-romaine: trois ans de publication (2005–2007). *Revue Archéologique*, 281–336.

Nenna, M.-D. (2011) Marques en grec. In D. Foy and M.-D. Nenna (eds.) *Corpus des signatures et marques sur verre 3. Grande Bretagne et addenda: Pays-Bas, France, Allemagne, Suisse, Croatie, Espagne, Portugal, Grèce, Turquie, mer Noire, Proche-Orient*, 257–273. Lyon/Aix-en-Provence, Association Française pour l'Archéologie du Verre.

Nenna, M.-D. (2012) Verres de l'antiquité gréco-romaine: trois ans de publication (2008–2010). *Revue Archéologique*, 63–129.

Nenna, M.-D. (in press a) Primary glass workshops in Graeco-Roman Egypt: preliminary report on the excavations on the site of Beni Salama (Wadi Natrun). In I. C. Freestone, J. Bailey and C. M. Jackson (eds.) *Glass in the Roman Empire. In honour of Jennifer Price*. Oxford, Oxbow.

Nenna, M.-D. (in press b) Le verre incolore dans l'Antiquité: de l'histoire de la production à l'histoire du goût. In P. Jockey (ed.) *Les arts de la couleur en Grèce et ailleurs*. Bulletin de Correspondance Hellénique Supplément. Athens, École Française d'Athènes.

Nenna, M.-D., Picon, M. and Vichy, M. (2000) Ateliers primaires et secondaires de verriers en Égypte à l'époque gréco-romaine. In M.-D. Nenna (ed.) *La route du verre. Ateliers primaires et secondaires de verriers du second millénaire av. J.-C. au Moyen Âge*. Travaux de la Maison de l'Orient Méditerranéen 33, 97–112. Lyon, Maison de l'Orient Méditerranéen.

Nenna, M.-D., Picon, M., Vichy, M. and Thirion-Merle, V. (2005) Ateliers primaires du Wadi Natrun: nouvelles découvertes.

In *Annales du 16e Congrès de l'Association Internationale pour l'Histoire du Verre*, 56–63. Nottingham, Association Internationale pour l'Histoire du Verre.

Oren, E. (1993a) A Christian Settlement at Ostrakine in North Sinai. In Y. Tsafrir (ed.) *Ancient Churches Revealed*, 305–314. Jerusalem, The Israel Exploration Society.

Oren, E. (1993b) Ostrakine. In E. Stern (ed.) *The New Encyclopedia of Archaeological Excavations in the Holy Land 3*, 1171–1173. Jerusalem, The Israel Exploration Society.

Pensabene, P. (1978) A cargo of marble shipwrecked at Punta Scifo near Crotone (Italy). *International Journal of Nautical Archaeology* 7, 105–178, 233–234.

Pichot, V. (2011) La Maréotide: histoires en eaux troubles. In I. Hairy (ed.) *Du Nil à Alexandrie. Histoires d'eaux*, 162–193. Alexandria, Centre d'Etudes Alexandrines.

Picon, M., Thirion-Merle, V. and Vichy, M. (2008) Les verres au natron et les verres aux cendres du Wadi Natrun (Égypte). *Bulletin de l'Association Française pour l'Archéologie du Verre*, 36–41.

Rehren, Th. and Cholakova, A. (2010) The early Byzantine HIMT glass from Dichin, Northern Bulgaria. *Interdisciplinary Studies (Archaeological Institute of Sofia)* 22/23, 81–96.

Rehren, Th., Marii, F., Schibille, N., Stanford, L. and Swan, C. (2010) Glass supply and circulation in early Byzantine southern Jordan. In J. Drauschke and D. Keller (eds.) *Glass in Byzantium – Production, Usage, Analyses*. RGZM – Tagungen 8, 65–81. Mainz, Römisch-Germanisches Zentralmuseum.

Sayre, E. V. and Smith, R. W. (1961) Compositional categories of ancient glass. *Science* 133, 1824–1826.

Sayre, E. V. and Smith, R. W. (1974) Analytical studies of ancient Egyptian glass. In A. Bishay (ed.) *Recent advances in the science and technology of materials 3*, 47–70. New York, NY, Plenum Press.

Schibille, N. (2011) Late Byzantine mineral soda high alumina glasses from Asia minor. A new primary glass production group. *PLoS ONE* 6(4): e18970.doi:10.1371/journal.pone.0018970.

Shortland, A. J., Degryse, P., Walton, M., Geer, M., Lauwers, V. and Salou, L. (2011) The evaporitic deposits of Lake Fazda (Wadi Natrun, Egypt) and their use in Roman glass production. *Archaeometry* 53, 916–929.

Silvestri, A., Molin, G. and Salviulo, G. (2005) Roman and Medieval glass from the Italian area, bulk characterization and relationships with production technologies. *Archaeometry* 47, 797–816.

Spadea, R. (2006) *Il Museo archeologico del Parco Archeologico di Capo Colonna a Crotone*. Reggio Calabria, Soprintendenza per i Beni Archaeologici della Calabria.

Uhlir, K., Melcher, M., Schreiner, M., Czurda-Ruth, B. and Krinzinger, F. (2010) SEM/EDX and -XRF investigations on ancient glass from Hanghaus 1 in Ephesos/Turkey. In J. Drauschke and D. Keller (eds.) *Glass in Byzantium – production, usage, analyses*. RGZM – Tagungen 8, 47–64. Mainz, Römisch-Germanisches Zentralmuseum.

Verreth, H. (2006), *The northern Sinai from the 7th century BC till the 7th century AD. A guide to the sources*. Leuven (http://www.trismegistos.org).

Verità, M. (1995) Le analisi di vetri. In D. Foy (ed.) *Le verre de l'antiquité tardive et du haut moyen âge. Typologie, chronologie, diffusion*, 291–300. Guiry-en-Vexin, Musée archéologique départemental du Val-d'Oise.

Verità, M. and Vallotto, M. (1998) Analisi chimica di reperti vitrei del IV secolo D.C. rinvenuti a Sevegliano. *Quaderni Friulani di Archeologia* 8, 7–19.

Wedepohl, K. H. and Hartmann, G. (2000) Die chemische Zusammensetzung der spätkaiserzeitlichen Gläser. In W. Gaitzsch, K. H. Wedepohl, A.-B. Follmann-Schulz, G. Hartmann and U. Tegtmeier, Spätrömische Glashütten im Hambacher Forst-Produktionsort der ECVA-Fasskrüge, *Bonner Jahrbücher* 200, 131–147, 223–231.

19

Continuity and change in Byzantine and early Islamic glass from *Syene*/Aswan and Elephantine, Egypt

Daniel Keller

Introduction

Glass finds of the late antique and early Islamic periods from Upper Egypt are relatively unknown. Only a few Byzantine glass finds from the province *Thebais Superior* have been presented so far. From north to south, the published material was found from Coptos to Edfu. Some glass finds from Coptos come from an excavation undertaken in the early 20th century and can therefore only be generally dated to the period of the 4th–7th centuries (Nenna 2000, 23–24, figs. 9–10). The late antique glass finds from the Coptic monastery of Epiphanius at Thebes were only briefly described, but not illustrated in the report on this excavation (Winlock 1926, 94–95). Some glass finds from the Coptic hermitages at Esna which were occupied during the 6th/7th century have been published (Jacquet-Gordon 1972, 92–96, pl. 233.1–14; Mossakowska-Gaubert 2012, 361–362, fig. 4). A few glass finds of the late antique period from Edfu were found in contexts of the 9th/10th century, but are residual and date to the 4th–7th centuries (Henne 1924, 29, 39, 42, pls. 24–25; Arveiller-Dulong and Nenna 2005, 486–491, nos. 1329, 1331–1333, 1337, 1339–1341, 1343–1344). Recently, a single rim sherd of a glass bowl with a fire-rounded rim from a context of the mid 5th century was included in the presentation of pottery from a stratified sequence at Edfu (Gascoigne 2005, 179, no. 19, fig. 13.19). Early Islamic glass from southern Egypt is so far completely unknown.

Since 1969, the German Archaeological Institute Cairo and the Swiss Institute of Architectural and Archaeological Research Cairo have been excavating the Egyptian town of Elephantine on an island at the 1st cataract of the Nile. The late antique and early medieval occupation of Elephantine is well documented in the area around the Khnum temple which was originally established in the early 2nd millennium BC, continuously renewed and extended until the Graeco-Roman period, and destroyed at the end of the 4th century (Arnold 2008, 80–84). A domestic quarter was then established around the remains of the temple in the late antique period and the occupation of the area continued in the early Islamic period. The occupation is divided into three phases, the first belonging to the 5th/6th century, the second to the 7th century and the third to the 9th century (Arnold 2003, 29–37, 47–130; 2008, 84–85). Since 2000, the joint mission of the Swiss Institute of Architectural and Archaeological Research Cairo and the Inspectorate of Aswan of the Supreme Council of Antiquites conducted salvage excavations in the neighbouring town of Aswan (ancient *Syene*), on the right bank of the Nile. Several areas with remains of the late antique and medieval periods were excavated and provide a sequence of glass finds from the 4th to the 14th century (von Pilgrim *et al.* 2004, 129–136, 140–148; 2006, 243–253, 257–264; 2008, 338–340, 344; 2010, 179–181). The glass finds from *Syene*/Aswan have been recorded but, with the exception of a bowl and two goblet feet from the fill of a crypt dating to the 7th century (Keller 2009, 281, fig. 2), their contextual study remains to be completed and a detailed stratigraphical analysis is still outstanding.

On the other hand, the stratigraphy and the phasing of the glass finds from Elephantine was already included in the preliminary glass studies, thus providing the first chronological information on the development of some late antique and early Islamic glass drinking vessels at the 1st cataract (Keller 2008; 2012). Therefore, only some observations on the shape, colour and fabric of the predominant drinking vessels of the Byzantine (6th/7th century) and early Islamic period (8th/9th century) from both sites will be discussed in this short contribution to

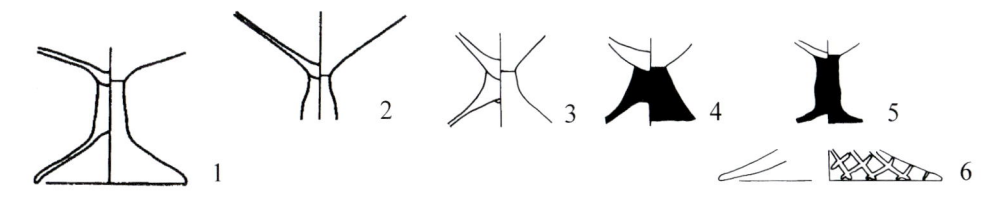

Fig. 19.1: Byzantine stemmed goblets from Elephantine and Aswan (scale 1:2; drawings Daniel Keller).

demonstrate change and continuity in glass working in Upper Egypt. For the Byzantine period, *i.e.* the 6th/7th century, stemmed goblets are the commonest and most typical form of drinking vessel (Keller 2008, 142–144, fig. 22.7–12; 2012, 481, 486, fig. 2.8–13), whereas the cylindrical cups with tonged decoration are the most characteristic glass vessel of the early Islamic period of the late 8th/9th century (Keller 2008, 145–146, fig. 24).

Byzantine stemmed goblets

Stemmed goblets are the predominant drinking vessel of the Byzantine period. An estimated minimum number of 257 such goblets was recorded, 123 from Elephantine and 134 from *Syene*/Aswan (for the method of establishing the estimated minimum number of glass vessels in an assemblage: Cool and Price 1995, 9–10). Most of the stemmed goblets have delicate applied conical feet with short stems and fire-rounded vertical lower ends (Fig. 19.1.1–4). On Elephantine, such goblets are present in contexts from the mid 6th century to the 7th century (Keller 2008, 142–143, fig. 22.7–9; 2012, 481, 486, fig. 2.8–10) and in *Syene*/Aswan they occur in contexts dating between the late 6th and mid/late 7th centuries (Keller 2008, 143, note 352; 2009, 281, fig. 2.2–3). A 6th/7th-century date for such goblets in Egypt is confirmed by relevant finds from Esna (Jacquet-Gordon 1972, 96, pl. 233.12–13; Mossakowska-Gaubert 2012, 361, fig. 4.12–13), Alexandria (Rodziewicz 1984, 240–241, fig. 262, pl. 73.372–379) and Coptos (Nenna 2000, 24, fig. 10). They represent a major type of Byzantine stemmed goblets in Egypt. Another type, namely goblets with long solid stems and flat feet, are less frequent on Elephantine and in *Syene*/Aswan (Fig. 19.1.5–6). They have a slightly later start date in the mid or 2nd half of the 6th century and occur frequently in Egypt until the late 7th/early 8th century, *i.e.* the Umayyad period judging by finds from Elephantine (Keller 2008, 143, fig. 22.10–12; 2012, 481, 486, fig. 2.11–13), *Syene*/Aswan (Keller 2008, 143–144, note 358), Esna (Jacquet-Gordon 1972, 93, pl. 233.3; Mossakowska-Gaubert 2012, 361, fig. 4.3), el-Ashmunein (Bailey 1998, 153, nos. Y66–Y66bis, pl. 93.Y66–Y66bis), Naqlun (Mossakowska-Gaubert 2004, 1447–1448, fig. 2.I.3–I.5; Mossakowska-Gaubert 2012, 358,

Fig. 19.2: Blue/green Byzantine goblet from Aswan (photo Swiss Institute of Architectural and Archaeological Research Cairo).

fig. 2.3–4), Tebtynis (Nenna 2000, 14, fig. 10; Foy 2001, 469–470, nos. 33–46, fig. 2.33–46) and Fustat (Foy 2000, 154, fig. 1.4–11). Thus, they represent a Byzantine/Umayyad stemmed goblet type.

The fabric is generally of a good quality with few bubbles and impurities. The predominant colour of the stemmed goblets is blue/green (Fig. 19.2) with almost 40% of the goblets at Elephantine and almost 70% of the goblets at *Syene*/Aswan being made of different shades of blue/green glass (Table 19.1). Green goblets are the second largest colour group, consisting of more than 30% of the goblets at Elephantine and slightly more than 20% at *Syene*/Aswan.

Table 19.1: Colours of Byzantine stemmed goblets from Elephantine and Aswan.

Colour	Elephantine	Aswan	Total
Blue/green	49	93	142
Green	39	29	68
Yellow/green	28	3	31
Colourless	5	6	11
Blue	1	3	4
Purple	1	0	1
Total	123	134	257

Table 19.2: Colours of Abbasid tonged cups from Elephantine and Aswan.

Colour	Elephantine	Aswan	Total
Blue/green	13	44	57
Green	8	17	25
Yellow/green	2	6	8
Colourless	1	8	9
Purple	0	2	2
Amber	0	1	1
Total	24	78	102

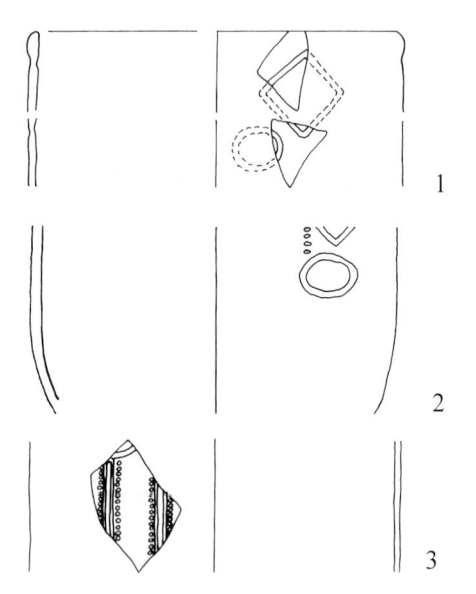

Fig. 19.3: Early Islamic tonged cups from Elephantine (scale 1:2; drawings Daniel Keller).

Yellow/green goblets are also frequent at Elephantine (totalling almost 23%), but they are rare at *Syene*/Aswan; colourless, blue and purple goblets were rare at both sites (Table 19.1). The most obvious difference between the goblets from Elephantine and those from *Syene*/Aswan is the larger amount of yellow/green goblets from the former site. This may be explained by the larger amount of 6th-century glass from Elephantine compared to the goblets from *Syene*/Aswan which seem to belong mostly to the 7th century (or even first half of the 8th century). While the latter represent the typical Byzantine/Umayyad fabrics, the yellow/green goblets from Elephantine reflect the continuation of a late Roman fabric which was predominant in the 4th/5th century as demonstrated by the typical conical beakers which are in Egypt usually made of yellow/green glass (Arveiller-Dulong and Nenna 2005, 429).

Abbasid tonged cups

During the late 8th/9th century the Byzantine tradition of goblets was finally replaced by cylindrical cups with tonged decoration (Fig. 19.3.1–3). A minimum number of 102 cups was found at both sites: 24 at Elephantine and 78 at *Syene*/Aswan. The use of tongs to decorate glass vessels is a new technique of the early Islamic period. Such cups are typical for the Abbasid period in Egypt as demonstrated by finds from Abbasid contexts at Elephantine (Keller 2008, 145–146, fig. 24), el Ashmunein (Bailey 1998, 150, nos. Y28–Y30, pls. 92.Y28, 92,Y30), Tebtynis (Foy 2001, 474–475, nos. 84–101), Fustat (Scanlon and Pinder-Wilson 2001, 80–82, fig. 38) and Alexandria (Rodziewicz 1984, 347, fig. 348.1–12).

The colour, quality and fabric of the glass used for the tonged cups is the same as that previously used for the stemmed goblets. There is no visible difference to the eye and the glass is still of a good quality with few bubbles and impurities. Apart from the tonged decoration the only difference is the thickness of the cups as they have thicker walls compared to the thin-walled goblets. Regarding the colours, blue/green is still the predominant colour (Fig. 19.4), with about 55% of the cups from both sites belonging to this group (Table 19.2). Green is the next most frequent colour, with 33% of the cups from Elephantine and slightly more than 20% from *Syene*/Aswan. 10% of the cups from *Syene*/Aswan are colourless, while about 8% from both sites are yellow/green. Colourless cups are rare in Elephantine and purple and amber cups occur occasionally in *Syene*/Aswan (Table 19.2). The slightly larger amount of colourless glass at *Syene*/Aswan may indicate that the relevant cups are the latest among the tonged vessels, already belonging to the late Abbasid/early Fatimid period, when new colours and fabrics such as colourless glass with wheel-cut decoration appeared, in addition to emerald green bottles with short-ridged necks, dark blue elongated bottles with cracked-off rims and purple mould-blown vessels. This would be a reasonable explanation given the fact that glass of the Fatimid period was found at *Syene*/Aswan in considerable numbers whereas the glass sequence on Elephantine ends in the Abbasid period.

Continuity in colour and fabric

The colours and fabrics remained the same from the Byzantine to the Abbasid period which suggests a continuous use of the same or similar raw glass from the 6th to the 9th century. Unfortunately, it was not possible to perform chemical analysis of the glass finds from *Syene*/Aswan and Elephantine, hence this statement has to remain hypothetical for the time being and needs to be tested in the future. However, no difference in the colours and fabrics between the Byzantine/Umayyad goblets (Fig. 19.2) and the Abbasid tonged cups (Fig. 19.4) is visible to the naked eye, which suggests the use of similar glass for both types and in both periods. Tonged cups similar to those from *Syene*/Aswan and Elephantine were found on Jabal Harun in southern Jordan (Keller and Lindblom 2008, 342, 344, 349 nos. 101–102, 125, 153–155, figs. 5.3, 6.9, 11.2, 14.2–5; in press, no. 386, fig. 17.9). They are still made of natron glass (Greiff in press, nos. 183, 201–204) which is of Egyptian origin and belongs to the Egypt II compositional group (Greiff and Keller this volume). This suggests a continuation of the use of natron glass in Egypt for the tonged cups of the Abbasid period of the late 8th/9th century. Only in the late 9th/10th century glass of different quality, fabrics and colours appeared which may reflect the change from natron to plant ash glass. However, this assumption needs to be tested by chemical analysis in the future. A different picture emerges in the Levant, *i.e.* in Israel and Jordan where a difference between the colours and fabrics used in the Byzantine/Umayyad period and those predominant in the Abbasid period is clearly recognisable to the naked eye (Gorin-Rosen 2010, 213; Keller and Lindblom in press) as well as traceable by chemical analysis (Greiff in press; Greiff and Keller this volume).

Change in shape

The shape of the drinking vessels changed from stemmed goblets used during the Byzantine and Umayyad periods to cylindrical cups during the Abbasid period and this was accompanied by the appearance of a new decorative technique with tonged patterns. The latter reflects the emergence of new fashions in glass working in the early Islamic period (Gorin-Rosen 2010, 214, 228). The change in shape from stemmed goblets to cylindrical cups is not a regional phenomenon limited to the 1st cataract but represents a general change in the preferred glass drinking vessel from the Byzantine/Umayyad to the Abbasid period. This change can also be observed at other sites in Egypt such as Alexandria, el-Ashmunein, Tebtynis and Fustat where goblets are predominant in the Byzantine/Umayyad period whereas cups occur in the Abbasid period (Rodziewicz 1984, 240–241, 347; Bailey 1998, 150, 153; Foy 2001, 469–470, 474–475; Foy *et al.* 2003, 138–140). Furthermore, this change also occurs in Palestine as demonstrated by the finds from Beth Shean (Hadad 2005, 28, 37–38) and Ramla (Gorin-Rosen 2010, 221, 242–245), in southern Jordan as the finds from Jabal Harun indicate (Keller and Lindblom in press; Greiff and Keller, this volume) and in northern Jordan and Syria as observed by the finds from Jerash, Pella and Qasr el Hayr esh-Sharqi (presented by M. O'Hea at the 17th congress of the *Association Internationale pour l'Histoire du Verre* in Antwerp in 2006). Thus we are looking at a general change in the preferred drinking vessel in Egypt and the Near East which occurred during the 8th century.

The typological change in glass working reflects a cultural change in the drinking habits, as the Abbasid cylindrical cups with tonged decoration usually have a capacity of more than 500ml and are thus considerably larger than the smaller Byzantine/Umayyad goblets which usually have a capacity of less than 250ml. The preference for larger drinking vessels in the early Islamic period is unlikely to have been caused by a change from wine to water, but rather by a change in the way of drinking from individual goblets being used in the Byzantine and Umayyad periods when every guest had his/her own drinking vessel to large cups being passed around from one guest to the next in the Abbasid period. What inspired this cultural change in the preferred drinking vessel is difficult to determine. Perhaps it was a Mesopotamian or Persian influence, as bowls of a larger size than the Byzantine goblets were already the predominant drinking vessel in Sasanian glass (Simpson 2003, 363; Keller 2010, 75). The Abbasid court inherited the culinary culture of its Sasanian counterpart (Simpson 2003, 370), thus the concept of using bowls or large cups rather than small goblets for drinking may have also been inspired by a Mesopotamian or Persian tradition inherited from the Sasanians. However, there is a difference between the hemispherical Sasanian facet-cut bowls and the large cylindrical cups with tonged decoration of the Abbasid period. The former could stand well on their own as the pontil was neatly removed by a deep hemispherical facet which created a secure resting point, but they were also comfortable for holding in the hand because of their faceted walls (Simpson 2003, 361; this volume; Keller 2010, 75). The latter can stand perfectly on their flat bases, but were more difficult to hold because of their large diameter and their cylindrical shape. Furthermore, the large cylindrical cups of the Abbasid period are of a larger size and capacity (500ml) than the Sasanian bowls which only had a capacity of around 250–350ml (Keller 2010, 75). Therefore, another concept of dining may be behind this change in the preferred glass drinking vessel. The small Byzantine goblets and the medium sized Sasanian bowls were often refilled by servants (Simpson 2003, 367), but the Abbasid cups once filled could be put in front of the guest and lasted for a long time of drinking and thus needed to be refilled less frequently.

Fig. 19.4: Blue/green early Islamic tonged cup from Aswan (photo Swiss Institute of Architectural and Archaeological Research Cairo).

Summary

On the one hand, the Byzantine/Umayyad stemmed goblets and Abbasid tonged cups from the 1st cataract demonstrate a continous use of similar glass without any difference at least to the naked eye in colours and fabrics. On the other hand, the shape of the preferred glass drinking vessel changed and a new decorative technique emerged in the Abbasid period. Whether the continuity of colours and fabrics reflects a continous use of the same or similar raw glass or whether different raw glass was used to produce glass vessels of the same or similar appearance, remains to be tested by chemical analysis. Regardless whether the same or different raw glass was used, a change in colours and fabrics and thus also in the glass working tradition occurred at the 1st cataract in the late 9th/early 10th century only with the emergence of colourless glass with wheel-cut decoration, purple mould-blown vessels and emerald green as well as dark blue bottles.

The change from stemmed goblets to cylindrical cups with tonged decoration reflects a technological change in glass working and a new fashion in the decoration of glass, but also a cultural change of dining traditions. The different shape and larger size of the preferred glass drinking vessel of the Abbasid period suggests a change from small individual goblets to large cups which were either passed around or which were still used as individual drinking vessels, but placed on their flat bases in front of the guests and refilled less frequently compared to the smaller goblets of the earlier period.

Acknowledgements

I would like to thank Cornelius von Pilgrim (Swiss Institute of Architectural and Archaeologcal Research Cairo) for allowing me to study and present the glass finds from Elephantine and *Syene*/Aswan. Furthermore, I am thankful to Wolfgang Müller (Swiss Institute of Architectural and Archaeological Research Cairo) for providing information on the stratigraphy and contexts from *Syene*/Aswan and Felix Arnold (German Archaeological Institute Cairo) for explanations of the stratigraphy and the phasing of the late antique and early Islamic strata at Elephantine. I am grateful to Yael Gorin-Rosen (Glass Department, Israel Antiquities Authority) for discussing many aspects of Byzantine and early Islamic glass and I would like to thank Tina Jakob (Department of Archaeology, Durham University) for checking and correcting my English.

Bibliography

Arnold, F. (2003) *Die Nachnutzung des Chnumtempelbezirks. Wohnbebauung der Spätantike und des Frühmittelalters*. Elephantine 30. Archäologische Veröffentlichungen 116. Mainz, Philipp von Zabern.

Arnold, F. (2008) Der Bezirk des Chnumtempels: Stratigraphische Untersuchungen südlich des Tempelhauses. In G. Dreyer *et al.*, Stadt und Tempel von Elephantine. 33./34./35. Grabungsbericht. *Mitteilungen des Deutschen Archäologischen Institutes Abteilung Kairo* 64, 78–86.

Arveiller-Dulong, V. and Nenna, M.-D. (2005) *Les verres antiques du Musée du Louvre II. Vaiselle et contenants du Ier siècle au début du VIIe siècle après J.-C.* Paris, Somogy.

Bailey, D. M. (1998) *Excavations at el-Ashmunein V. Pottery, Lamps and Glass of the Late Roman and Early Arab Periods*. London, British Museum Press.

Cool, H. E. M. and Price, J. (1995) *Roman vessel glass from excavations in Colchester 1971–85*. Colchester Archaeological Report 8. Colchester, Colchester Archaeological Trust.

Foy, D. (2000) L'héritage antique et byzantin dans la verrerie islamique: exemples d'Istabl 'Antar-Fostat. *Annales Islamologiques* 34, 151–178.

Foy, D. (2001) Secteur nord de Tebytnis (Fayoum). Le verre byzantine et islamique. *Annales Islamologiques* 35, 465–489.

Foy, D., Picon, M. and Vichy, M. (2003) Verres omeyyades et abbassides d'origine égyptienne: les témoignages de l'archéologie et de l'archéometrie. In *Annales du 15e Congrès de l'Association Internationale pour l'Historie du Verre*, 138–143. Nottingham, Association Internationale pour l'Historie du Verre.

Gascoigne, A. (2005) Dislocation and Continuity in Early Islamic Provincial Urban Centres: the Example of Tell Edfu. *Mitteilungen des Deutschen Archäologischen Institutes Abteilung Kairo* 61, 153–189.

Gorin-Rosen, Y. (2010) The Islamic Glass Vessels. In O. Gutfeld, *Ramla. Final Report on the Excavations North of the White Mosque.* Qedem 51, 213–264. Jerusalem, The Hebrew University of Jerusalem.

Greiff, S. (in press) Chemical glass types used for the production of glassware from late antiquity to the early Islamic period found at Jabal Harun. In Z. T. Fiema and J. Frösén, *Petra – The Mountain of Aaron II. The Nabataean Sanctuary and the Byzantine Monastery.* Helsinki, Societas Scientiarum Fennica.

Hadad, Sh. (2005) *Islamic Glass Vessels from the Hebrew University Excavations at Bet Shean.* Excavations at Bet Shean 2. Qedem Reports 8. Jerusalem, The Hebrew University of Jersualem.

Henne, H. (1924) *Rapport sur les fouilles de Tell Edfou 1921–1922.* Cairo, Institut Français d'Archéologie Orientale.

Jacquet-Gordon, H. (1972) *Les ermitages chrétiens du désert d'Esna III. Céramique et objects.* Cairo, Institut Français d'Archéologie Orientale.

Keller, D. (2008) Preliminary report on the Late Roman, Byzantine and Early Islamic glass finds. In G. Dreyer *et al.*, Stadt und Tempel von Elephantine. 33./34./35. Grabungsbericht. *Mitteilungen des Deutschen Archäologischen Institutes Abteilung Kairo* 64, 137–148.

Keller, D. (2009) Deposition, disposal and re-use of broken glass from early Byzantine churches. In K. Janssens, P. Degryse, P. Cosyns, J. Caen and L. Van't dack (eds.) *Annales du 17e Congrès de l'Association Internationale pour l'Histoire du Verre*, 281–288. Brussels, University Press Antwerp.

Keller, D. (2010) Functional and economic aspects of late Sasanian and early Islamic glass from Kush, United Arab Emirates. In B. Zorn and A. Hilgner (eds.) *Glass along the Silk Road from 200 BC to AD 1000.* RGZM – Tagungen 9, 71–80. Mainz, Römisch-Germanisches Zentralmuseum.

Keller, D. (2012) Context, stratigraphy, residuality. Problems of establishing a chronology of Early Byzantine glass in Southern Egypt. In B. Böhlendorf-Arslan and A. Ricci (eds.) *Byzantine Small Finds in Archaeological Contexts.* Byzas 15, 477–488. Istanbul, Ege Yayinlari.

Keller, D. and Lindblom, J. (2008) Glass Finds from the Church and the Chapel. In Z. T. Fiema and J. Frösén, *Petra – The Mountain of Aaron I. The Church and the Chapel*, 331–375. Helsinki, Societas Scientiarum Fennica.

Keller, D. and Lindblom, J. (in press) Glass vessels from the FJHP site. In Z. T. Fiema and J. Frösén, *Petra – The Mountain of Aaron II. The Nabataean Sanctuary and the Byzantine Monastery.* Helsinki, Societas Scientiarum Fennica.

Mossakowska-Gaubert, M. (2004) La verrerie utilisée par les anachorètes: l'ermitage no. 44 à Naqlun (Fayyoum). In M. Immerzeel and J. Van der Vliet (eds.) *Coptic studies on the threshold of a new Millennium II. Proceedings of the seventh International Congress of Coptic Studies, Leiden 2000.* Orientalia Lovaniensia Analecta 133, 1443–1469. Leuven/Paris, Peeters.

Mossakowska-Gaubert, M. (2012) Verres de l'époque byzantine – début de l'époque arabe (Ve–VIIIe siècle): objects provenant des ermitages en Égypte. In D. Ignatiadou and A. Antonaras (eds.) *Annales du 18e Congrès de l'Association Internationale pour l'Histoire du Verre*, 357–366. Thessaloniki, Association Internationale pour l'Histoire du Verre.

Nenna, M.-D. (2000) Ateliers de production et sites de consummation en Égypte. In *Annales du 14e Congrès de l'Association Internationale pour l'Histoire du Verre*, 20–24. Lochem, Association Internationale pour l'Histoire du Verre.

von Pilgrim, C. *et al.* (2004) The Town of Syene. Preliminary Report on the 1st and 2nd Season in Aswan. *Mitteilungen des Deutschen Archäologischen Institutes Abteilung Kairo* 60, 119–148.

von Pilgrim, C. *et al.* (2006) The Town of Syene. Report on the 3rd and 4th Season in Aswan. *Mitteilungen des Deutschen Archäologischen Institutes Abteilung Kairo* 62, 215–277.

von Pilgrim, C. *et al.* (2008) The Town of Syene. Report on the 5th and 6th Season in Aswan. *Mitteilungen des Deutschen Archäologischen Institutes Abteilung Kairo* 64, 305–356.

von Pilgrim, C. *et al.* (2010) The Town of Syene. Report on the 7th Season in Aswan. *Mitteilungen des Deutschen Archäologischen Institutes Abteilung Kairo* 66, 179–224.

Rodziewicz, M. (1984) *Les habitations romaines tardives d'Alexandrie à la lumière des fouilles à Kôm el-Dikka.* Alexandrie 3. Warsaw, Ed. Scient. de Pologne.

Scanlon, G. T. and Pinder-Wilson, R. (2001) *Fustat Glass of the Early Islamic Period. Finds excavated by The American Research Center in Egypt 1964–1980.* London, Altajir World of Islam Trust.

Simpson, St J. (2003) From Mesopotamia to Merv: reconstructing patterns of consumption in Sasanian households. In T. Potts, M. Roaf and D. Stein (eds.) *Culture through Objects. Ancient Near Eastern Studies in Honour of P. R. S. Moorey*, 347–375. Oxford, Griffith Institute.

Winlock, H. E. (1926) *The monastery of Epiphanius at Thebes 1. The Archaeological Material.* Publications of the Metropolitan Museum of Art, Egyptian Expedition 3. New York, The Metropolitan Museum of Art.

20

Sasanian glass: an overview

St John Simpson

Introduction

The Sasanian empire stretched over 2,000 kilometres at its greatest extent from northern Mesopotamia to the edge of Central Asia, and lasted over four hundred years from the early 3rd to mid 7th centuries. Its capital was Ctesiphon, at its western end in present-day central Iraq, and this must have created a strong sense of patronage in a region which was not only home to deep-seated technologies and traditions but also much more open to the flow of ideas and technologies from Roman Syria than the more conservative Iranian plateau (Fig. 20.1).

Sasanian glass vessels, whether complete or fragmentary, have been known from archaeological excavations in Iraq for over 150 years, and in small numbers from the art market as early as the 1890s, but in the absence of any other evidence all were assumed to be the work of late Assyrian, Roman, Byzantine or early Islamic workshops (*e.g.* Layard 1853, 597 [= BM N.833–834]; Harden 1932). This began to change in 1934 with the circulation of a dissertation on the glass recently excavated by the *Deutsche Orient-Gesellschaft* at Ctesiphon (Puttrich-Reignard 1934) and the illustration of elaborate facet-cut glass found in a series of small palatial residences at Kish (Harden 1934, 131–136).

From 1958 onwards, the reported discoveries of large numbers of facet-cut hemispherical bowls and a small number of other decorated types in the Dailaman region of north-west Iran raised the profile of a possible Sasanian glass industry (von Saldern 1963; Fukai 1977). Almost all major western museums soon acquired a selection of these types and Corning Museum of Glass acquired its first examples (a faceted beaker, a bottle with relief-cut bosses and a faceted tube) as early as 1959. This is so far the only public collection to be published in full (Whitehouse 2005), although a catalogue of the British Museum collection is well advanced (Barag and Simpson in preparation) and the small number in the Khalili collection has been published (Goldstein *et al.* 2005). Many other vessels entered collections in Japan where interest was fuelled by their connection between the country's imperial history and the so-called "Silk Road" concept of east/west trade first coined by the 19th-century German geographer Ferdinand von Richthofen (Fukai 1977; Taniichi 2010). Fakes and pastiches also began to appear as demand exceeded supply; they include some very crudely moulded imitations in composite materials where the tell-tale mould seams can still be seen (*e.g.* Goldstein 1978, 133–134).

Items on the art market skewed perception: assumptions that Sasanian glass was produced within Iran as part of a long tradition extending from the Achaemenid period began to enter the secondary literature. However there is no evidence for either and there is a common confusion between findspot and place of production (Riazi 2010; cf. Ignatiadou 2010). Moreover, several influential comments have been made about the organisation of Sasanian glass production. Following Ghirshman's statement (1954, 343) that it was a state monopoly, Wenke (1987, 256) commented that the "production of glass, metalwork, and many other crafts ... under imperial control required thousands of craftsmen, administrators, and other specialists whose activities could most effectively be co-ordinated in large cities". Lamm (1939, 2596) suggested that itinerant Jewish glass workers played an important role in the development of this industry, whereas others have seen it as the work of deported Roman craftsmen (Fukai 1960, 176; Harper 1974; von Saldern 1963, 15). The result, according to the *Encyclopedia Iranica*, was that glass was rather commonly used (Huff 1987), and the *Cambridge History of Iran* goes further by stating that "the principal Sasanian centres of glass production were in

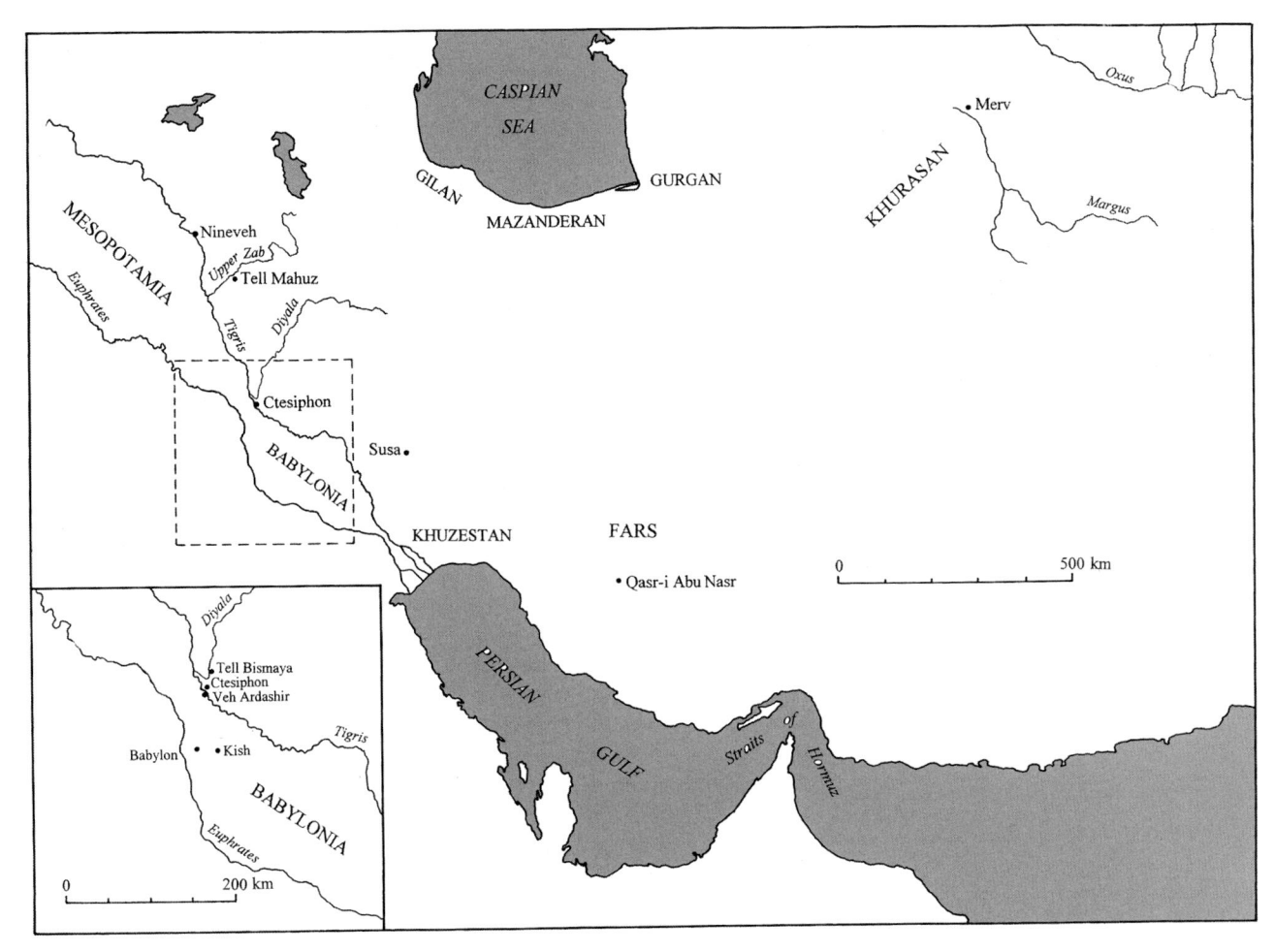

Fig. 20.1: Map showing some of the main Sasanian sites mentioned.

northern Mesopotamia and north-west Iran ... The identity of shapes suggests that these vessels, whether glass or silver, served the same mortuary and perhaps ritual purposes. It would seem, therefore, that the art of the Sasanian glassmaker must have held a position of pre-eminence perhaps not inferior to that of the silver- or goldsmith" (Shepherd 1986, 1105). More recently, it has been claimed that "some areas of Gilan were glassmaking centres in the Sasanian period and that Sasanian glass was traded westwards as far as the Mediterranean, Europe and North Africa" (Riazi 2010, 108). All of these statements are open to question.

One of the key Iranian sites traditionally used to illustrate patterns of cultural connection between ancient Iran and Mesopotamia is Susa, situated as it is in lowland south-west Iran. However, it does not appear to have produced much Sasanian glass, let alone the evidence for production claimed by one author (Shepherd 1986, 1105), and even the extent of Sasanian occupation at the city is unclear (Boucharlat 1987).

During the 1960s and 1970s excavations were carried out by an Italian expedition at Veh Ardashir, the "new town" founded by Ardashir I (c. 224–240) on the site of an older settlement known in Aramaic as Coche across the Tigris from the capital at Ctesiphon (Fig. 20.2). The published preliminary reports suggested the existence of glass-working in a lengthy sequence from the 3rd to the 5th or 6th century in the so-called "Artisans' Quarter" in the southern part of the city, and from the end of the 6th century onwards at the site of Tell Baruda near the ancient city centre. The full range of types represented included not only cut glass but also mass-produced plain and mould-blown forms which hitherto have attracted less attention (Negro Ponzi 1966; 1984; 1987; 2002; 2005). This evidence was the first to suggest that Mesopotamia was a major producer and consumer of glass in the Sasanian period and this assemblage, although still only partially published, remains fundamental.

Production

Large-scale production of glass in Iraq during the Sasanian

Fig. 20.2: Plan of the excavated quarters in the southern portion of the Sasanian city of Veh Ardashir; note that the partially excavated mound at the top produced evidence for glass furnaces. The shading indicates streets, alleys and open courtyards.

20 Sasanian glass: an overview   203

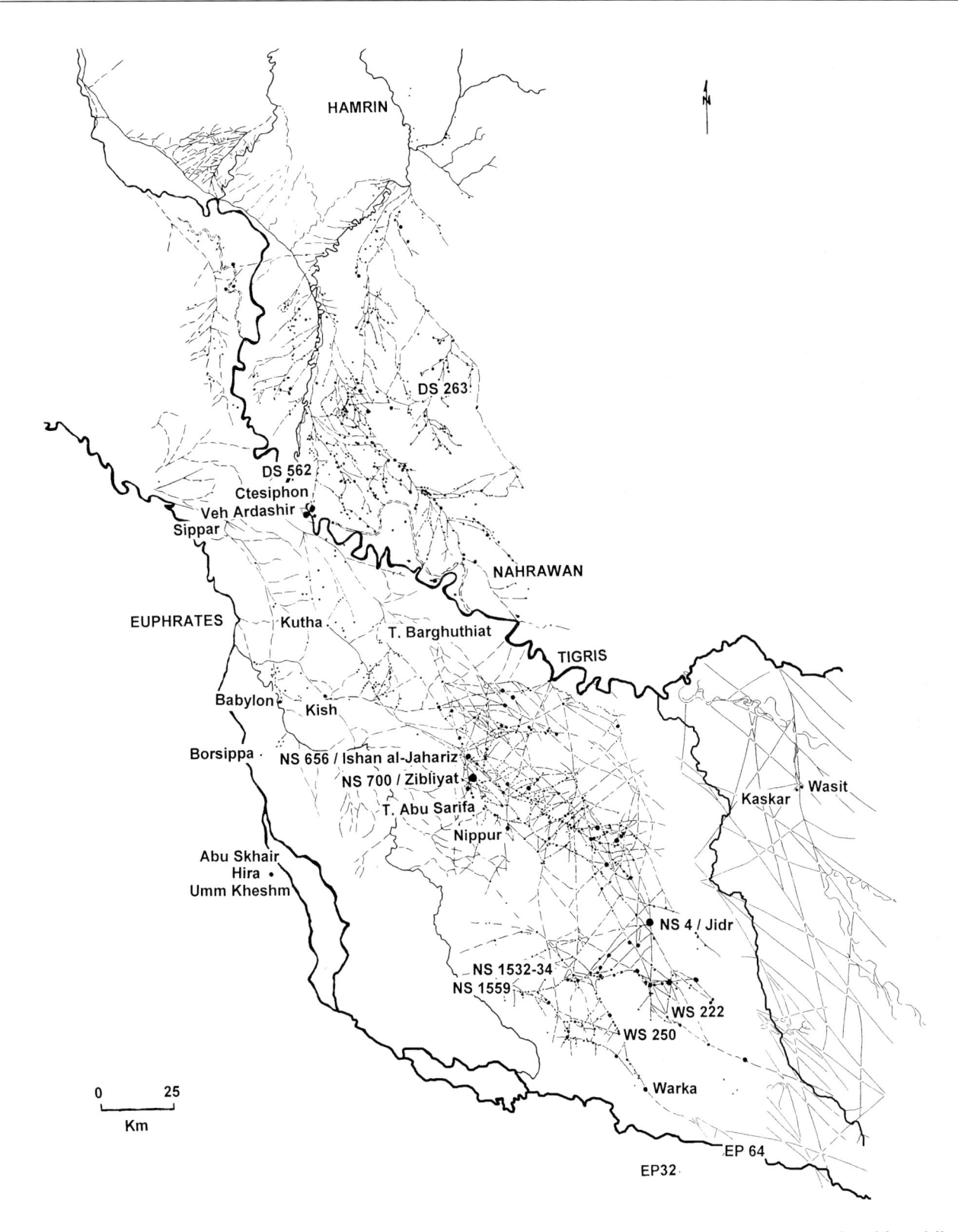

Fig. 20.3: Map showing the distribution of Sasanian archaeological sites and canals in central and southern Iraq combined from different surveys of varying intensity (after Adams 1965, fig. 5; Adams 1972, map 8; Gibson 1972, fig. 16; Adams 1981, figs. 44–45; Wright 1981, fig. 1; Gwon-Gu Kim 1989, fig. 2; note that the date of the watercourses marked east of Jidr are uncertain as these based purely on LANDSAT imagery as this region remains unsurveyed on the ground yet some clearly represent a continuation of the Sasanian canal network recorded upstream).

period is indicated through archaeological surface surveys which have revealed ten Sasanian or Sasanian – early Islamic sites in the central and southern parts of the country (Fig. 20.3; Table 20.1). The dating criteria appear mostly to have been based on associated pottery. The sites can be up to several hundred metres across and are covered with glass manufacturing waste (although no moils or trails from blowing have been recognised), and in some cases have the remains of what may be tank-furnaces with possible evidence of fritting (Brill 2005, 66–67, 71). This suggests that there was a very important rural yet industrial scale component to the glass industry whose location was dictated by easier access to raw materials (either sand or good quality alkali) or fuel. It is not clear whether these industrial centres simply supplied the urban glass-houses with their raw material in the form of chunks or ingots, or whether a range of vessels were also shipped out along the canal waterways on which most were located. Moreover, how the production was organised is unknown, let alone the ethnicity or faith of those involved. The excavation of one of these sites would undoubtedly yield a great deal of important information.

There is also evidence for glass-working within an urban Sasanian context. Furnaces used in glass production were reported from one area of Veh Ardashir; the preliminary excavation reports indicate the construction of consecutive furnaces on top of one another, implying continuity of workshop production (Cavallero 1966, 63, 77–78, fig. 24). Manufacturing waste and cullet have also been reported from here and Uruk/Warka (Negro Ponzi 1984, 33; 1987, 265; Boehmer 1991, 475–477). In addition, a fragmentary plaster dip-mould, cullet and glass-making waste were recovered during the earlier German investigations at Ctesiphon (Kröger 1985; forthcoming). The presence of moulds should be an indication for on-site production but as they are easily and cheaply reproduced, and more robust than the vessels they were designed to make, their discovery is not always proof that they were made in the place they were found (Rogers 2005, 19).

Until recently, only a small number of compositional analyses of Sasanian glass had been published, namely two deep bowls with short necks decorated with shallow circular facets separated by wheel-abraded horizontal lines. These were found in early 4th-century tombs at Echeng (China) and Tatetsuka (Japan). Four other vessels derived from the Iranian art market have also been published: these indicate use of plant ash with high levels of magnesium and potassium but the significance of this has been overlooked (Fukai 1968; An 1987, 30, notes 12–13).

In the past decade a growing number of other studies has been carried out based on finds from Ctesiphon, Veh Ardashir and three glass-making sites in southern Iraq (Brill 2005), Veh Ardashir (Mirti *et al*. 2008; 2009), other Mesopotamian sites (British Museum, in progress), a settlement at Kush in south-east Arabia (Freestone and Lambarth forthcoming) and the city site of Merv in modern Turkmenistan (Roehrs forthcoming). These confirm the manufacture and use of different varieties of glass made using plant ash as a flux which later formed a major group of early Islamic glass industries represented at Raqqa although interpreted there as an experimental composition (Freestone 2006; cf. Henderson and McLoughlin 2003, Type 4) (Fig. 20.4). In addition to Salsola (Arabic *khurrait*), there is no shortage of alkali-rich plants in southern Iraq including various Chenopodiaceae known locally by their Arabic name of *shinan* or *shinaf*: these were a traditional source of alkali for soap factories (Forbes 1839, 428; Guest 1933, 87, 92). Compositional analyses of green/yellowish-green and blue-green chunks of raw glass and waste material, as well as vessel fragments excavated at Veh Ardashir indicate they are silica-soda-lime glass with elevated magnesium (MgO) and potassium (K_2O), the latter in the range of 3.2–8.4% (HMG glass). The variation in magnesium to potassium ratios and amount of phosphorus content were interpreted as indicating two major (and possibly other minor) recipes using more than one kind of plant ash: the first type (Sasanian 1) characterised by a MgO content of mainly 3.0–5.0% and a phosphorus content generally between 900 and 1800 µg g^{-1}, and the second (Sasanian 2) with an even higher MgO content (6–8%) but lower phosphorus (500–800 µg g^{-1}). The first type contrasts with the composition of Parthian glass from neighbouring Seleucia but is present at Veh Ardashir from the beginning of the Sasanian period, implying that the city's glass industry was founded by workers coming from elsewhere in southern Mesopotamia. The second type appears in the 4th century. Both types were made (or worked) at Veh Ardashir but varying aluminium and calcium contents suggest that different sands might have been used to prepare different compositions. However glass recycling might also account for this (Mirti *et al*. 2008; 2009). The Veh Ardashir analyses also indicate varying amounts of copper, lead and tin: the likely source of this is recycled scrap bronze and the same explanation has been given for similar traces in Sasanian glazes from the same site (Mirti *et al*. 2008, 442; Pace *et al*. 2008). The Babylonian Talmud contains numerous allusions to recycling and the relative scarcity of metal fragments from the excavations at this site might reflect this, as was independently suggested for Sasanian Merv (cf. Simpson 2005b, 235; 2008, 70). Some of these passages specifically refer to glass as the rabbis debated the implications of recycling on the ritual purity of the material (Grossmark 2010). Moreover, the purchase of scrap metal recurs as legal cases in Avodah Zarah 71b and Bechorot 13b where it was sold by non-Jews and found to contain an idol (cf. also Bava Metzia 73a). The reuse of metal is also implied in a statement in the Mishna Kelim which compares it with the recycling of glass: "Why did the Rabbis impose purity upon glassware? ... Since it is manufactured from sand, the

Table 20.1: Published descriptions of Sasanian and/or early Islamic glass-producing and/or working sites located on archaeological surface surveys in southern Iraq, ranked in ascending order of size.

Survey site nmber	Name (if known)	Site description	Approx size in metres (L × W × ht)	Approx area in hectares	Attributed period	Publication reference
Nippur Survey 700	Zibliyat	Area south of the tower, near the western edge of the site where "much melted glass and slag from kilns" was reported	70 × 70 × 4.5	0.49	Sasanian-Islamic [but more likely early Islamic as only c. 9th century pottery has been noted from the site]	Adams 1981, 259.
Diyala Survey 263 (nearest)	Tell Umm Jirin (nearest)	Site located one km north of T. Umm Jirin where "great quantities of molten glass refuse" were reported	?	0.50	Sasanian	Adams 1965, 146; Brill 2005, 66.
Eridu Survey 64	Tell Umm Ghemimi	Site was "covered with glass sherds and glass cullet"; there were "few potsherds but much glass cullet and two current basins"	100 NW × 60 × 2	0.60	Cullet probably Sasanian according to Brill	Wright 1981, 335, 341; Brill 2005, 66–67.
Warka Survey 250	?	Site was covered with "much glass, including slag fragments"	140 NW × 110 × 1.8	1.54	Sasanian	Adams and Nissen 1972, 250.
Nippur Survey 1559	?	Site was "bisected by an ancient canal-bed from NW. Many glass kiln wasters"	240 NW × 100 × 2	2.40	Sasanian	Adams 1981, 289.
Warka Survey 222	?	Site was characterized by "much glass, some glass slag"	180 N × 140 × 0.5	2.52	Sasanian and recent	Adams and Nissen 1972, 228.
-	Tulul Jezzaz (part)	Site located 400 m east-south-east of Nippur Survey 1532. "Much glass slag occurs here also, but with a greater proportion of chunks of glass without furnace-lining adhesions as well as with greater numbers of glass vessels of various kinds and with more occupational debris [than Nippur Survey 1532]"	180 × 180 × 2.5	3.24	Sasanian – early Islamic	Adams 1981, 288–289.
Nippur Survey 1532	Tulul Jezzaz (part)	The site is "seemingly composed in very large part of slag from glass furnaces. There are great numbers of irregular chunks of glass adhering to clay furnace lining, colourless or in green, brown, blue, and violet hues … It seems possible that we have here the remains of a specialized glass-producing unit"	240 NW × 140 × 4	3.36	Sasanian – early Islamic	Adams 1981, 288.
Nippur Survey 1533	Tulul Jezzaz (part)	Located immediately east of Nippur Survey 1532, the site is covered "with almost as much evidence of glass production" [as Nippur Survey 1532]	280 × 280 × 3	7.84	Sasanian – early Islamic	Adams 1981, 289.
Nippur Survey 1534	Tulul Jezzaz (part)	This site "extends irregularly for about 1.5 km ENE along an ancient canal levee. Average width appears to be about 230 m. Some elevation of debris continuous and many individual mounds. Towards the ENE end is the most prominent mound in the group, 50 [m] diameter × 4 [m], with the well-preserved bases of three glass kilns forming its summit. Kiln debris and other evidence of extensive glassmaking is very plentiful on all parts of the site"	1.5 km ENE × 230	34.50	Sasanian, probably also early Islamic	Adams 1981, 289; Brill 2005, 66.

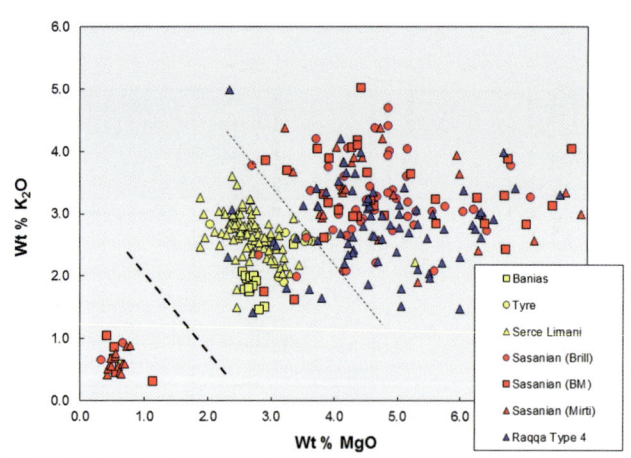

Fig. 20.4: Plotting potassium (K_2O) and magnesium (MgO) of Sasanian and Islamic glass (graph I. C. Freestone).

flaked away to expose the original colour and enhance any decoration but this has significantly thinned the vessel walls. The true appearance of the glass is given by the exceptionally preserved examples excavated in sealed stone sarcophagi in tombs in China (Watt *et al.* 2004, 156, 211, 258–259, cat. nos. 65, 117, 158–159) or preserved in storage in the Shōsō-in at Nara (Taniichi 1986a). Weathering may have led to the under-representation or even disappearance from the archaeological record of some thin-walled plain shapes, such as open plates or window-glass, and it is significant that footed goblets found at Kish are only represented by their folded feet (*e.g.* Harden 1934, 134, fig. 5, cat. no. 16).

Rabbis declared it the same as earthenware ... since they can be repaired when broken, they were considered as metal utensils" (Levene and Rothenberg 2007, 137).

Sasanian glass fabrics are often slightly bubbly, perhaps because cullet was regularly used in its manufacture (cf. Mirti *et al.* 2009, 1067). They are typically tinged because of the iron content in the sand. Most common are pale greenish (representing between 73.8 and 77.8% of the glass from graves at Abu Skhair and Tell Mahuz) or yellow tinges, but yellowish green, light greenish blue and light brownish fabrics are also described in the literature. Although pale greenish fabrics were employed for blowing the blanks supplied to glass cutters, much late Sasanian cut glass is characterised by a light brownish (manganese) tinge, and when recovered from an archaeological context is almost invariably covered with a thick layer of enamel-like gunmetal-grey weathering which reflects its high magnesium content. Some turquoise to deep blue glass with milky white weathering was also found in late and post-Sasanian contexts at Ctesiphon, Kush and Merv, but where this was actually produced is unknown (*e.g.* Keller 2010, 73–75, 78, fig. 4.1–4). Deliberately coloured glass vessels are rare and the small number of red and purple wares found at Tell Mahuz may have been imported from Roman Syria (Negro Ponzi 1968/69). There is no evidence for the production or circulation of cameo glass and evidence for gold-glass is limited to tesserae found near a bath-house behind the Taq-i Kisra; these may have been imported from Roman Syria along with the porphyry and other marble decoration used here (cf. Reuther 1929, 443–445). A small number of allegedly Sasanian gold-glass personal ornaments known from the Iranian art market are probably also Roman (Simpson 2005a).

The weathering typical of excavated Sasanian glass often conceals the true colour of the underlying fabric: on many art market pieces the weathering has been deliberately

Forms and decorative techniques

The principal forms of Sasanian glassware are bowls, beakers, stemmed goblets, small bottles and a wide variety of small unguentaria but, unlike the Roman glass tradition, large storage vessels are almost totally absent and those published from Nippur, along with most of the other associated pieces, are likely to be 8th century and later rather than Sasanian (cf. Meyer 1996).

Sasanian glassware was invariably blown, often using small simple dip moulds to help create and combine subtle decoration with a tactile surface. Some types were mass-produced but others appear relatively rare. However there is enough information from excavated contexts to create a working typology into which the unprovenanced pieces can be fitted. Dating is supplied by a combination of the sequence from Veh Ardashir, short-lived single-period assemblages, *terminus post quem* dates from sealed tombs and treasuries in the Far East and judicious comparison with eastern Roman typologies.

Hot working

Excavations reveal a range of undecorated free-blown forms. Small unguentaria occur in both domestic and funerary contexts and include barely inflated tubes (Fig. 20.5.1–3), tall-necked with rounded or pushed-up bases (Fig. 20.5.4–25) and short-necked rounded versions with short (Fig. 20.6.1–19) or cylindrical necks (Fig. 20.6.20–27). Other forms include miniature bottles with rounded bodies and a variety of forms of neck and opening (Figs. 20.7–20.8), straight-sided bowls (Fig. 20.9.1–8), footed bowls (Fig. 20.9.9–10), bowls with cracked-off rims (Fig. 20.10.1–3), conical and rounded beakers (Fig. 20.10.4–12), stemmed goblets (Fig. 20.10.13–18) and footed chalices (Fig. 20.10.19–20). The walls and feet of some bowls and miniature bottles were pinched with pincers to create low relief warts (Figs. 20.11–20.12), a feature also found on some Syrian Roman glass and which make for easy handling and support (Whitehouse 2005, 25–26).

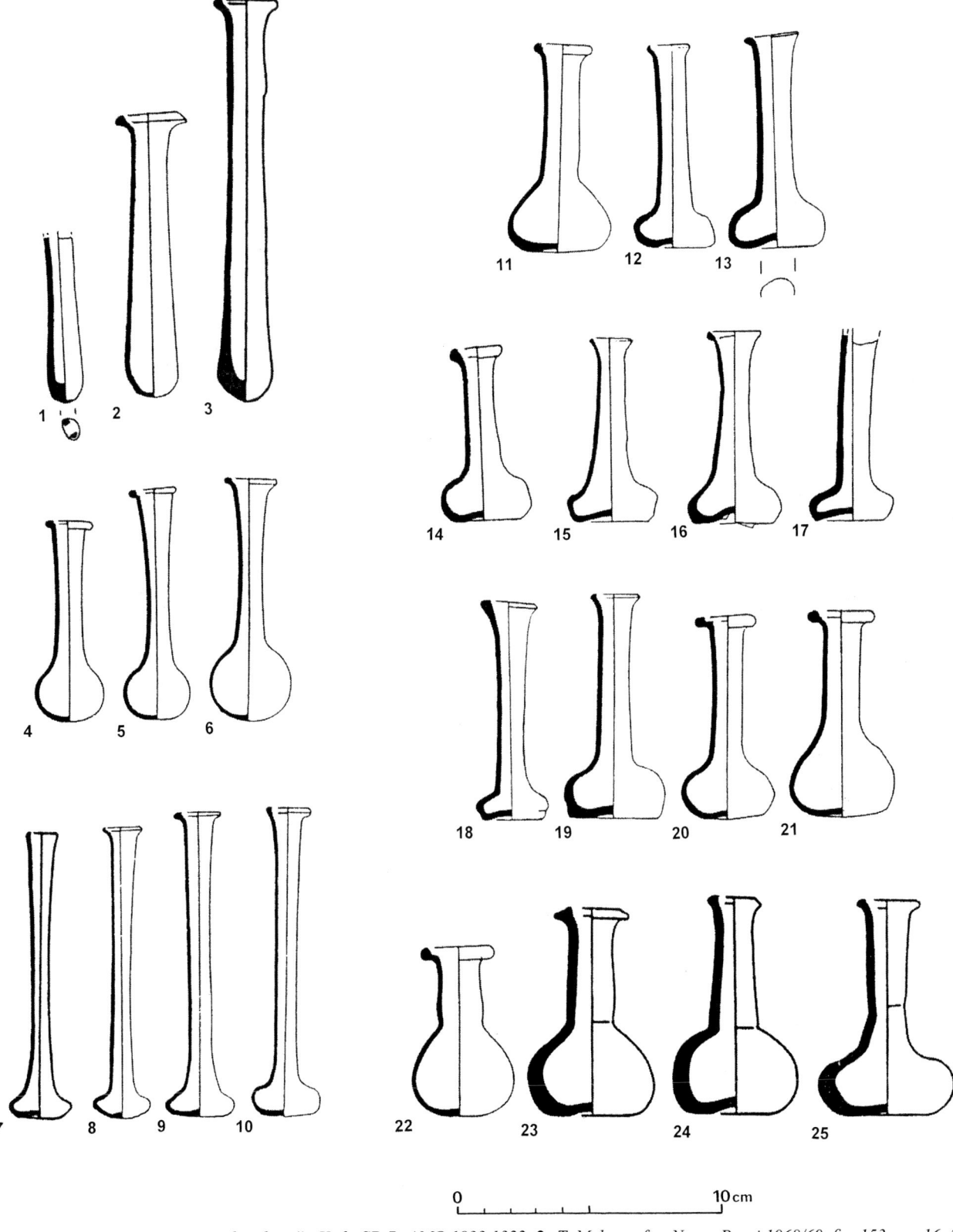

*Fig. 20.5: Plain unguentaria: single tubes (**1**: Kish, SP-7; AMO 1933.1322; **2**: T. Mahuz, after Negro Ponzi 1968/69, fig. 153, no. 16; **3**: Veh Ardashir, after Negro Ponzi 1984, fig. 1.21); tall-necked (**4–6, 8–12, 14, 19–22**: T. Mahuz, after Negro Ponzi 1968/69, fig. 153, nos. 2–4, 12–14, 7, 10, 8, 11, 9, 5; **7, 23–25**: Veh Ardashir, after Negro Ponzi 1984, fig. 1.9, 19, 18, 20; **8–10**: **13**: Abu Habba, BM 91530; **15–17**: T. Barghuthiat, AMO 1933.1392, 1391, 1393; **18**: Nineveh, BM 99435).*

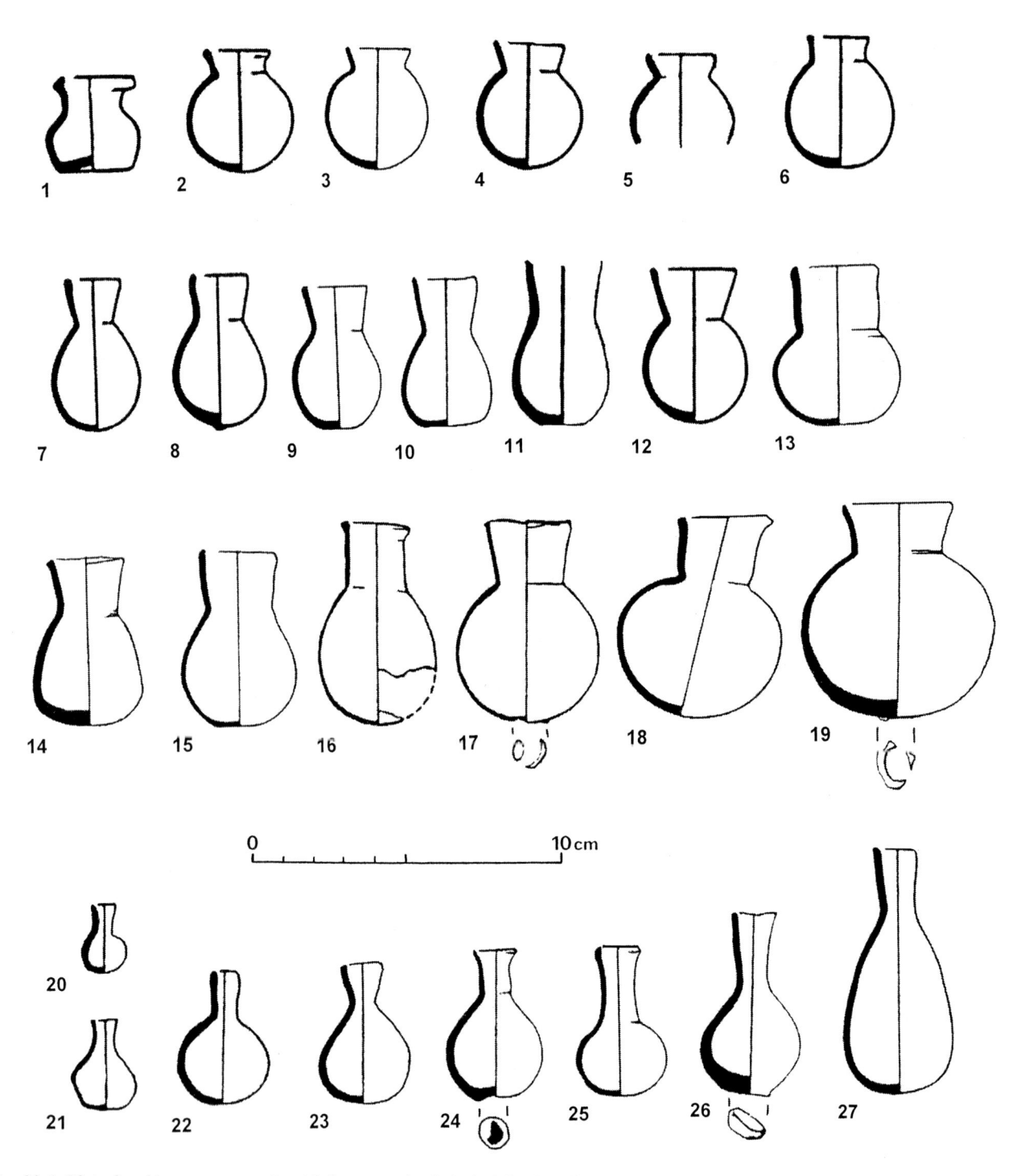

*Fig. 20.6: Plain free-blown unguentaria with flaring necks (**1–2, 4, 6–8, 12**: Veh Ardashir, after Negro Ponzi 1984, fig. 1.1, 4, 2–3, 6–8; **3, 9–10, 13, 15, 18, 25, 27**: Abu Skhair, after Negro Ponzi 1972, fig. 20, nos. 1, 3–4, 6, 5, 8, fig. 21, nos. 25, 30; **5, 20, 22**: Qasr-i Abu Nasr, after Whitcomb 1985, fig. 58.d, b, a; **11, 16–17**: T. Mohammed Arab; **14, 23**: T. Barghuthiat, AMO 1933.1394, 1395; **19**: Mesopotamia, BM 91489; **21**: Qal'eh-i Dukhtar, after Huff 1978, fig. 22; **24, 26**: Kish, SP-7, AMO 1933.1318, 1320).*

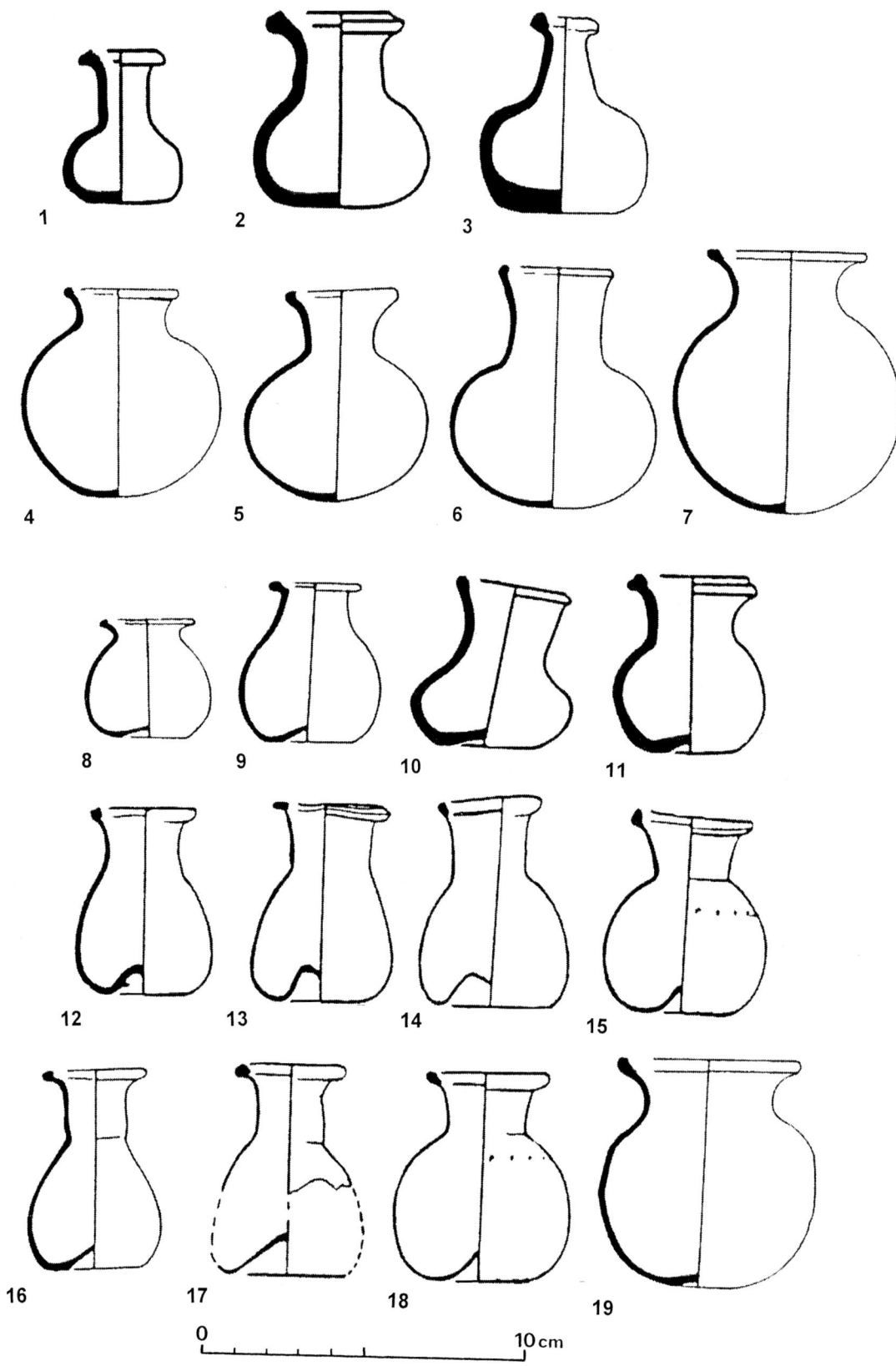

*Fig. 20.7: Plain free-blown unguentaria with folded-in lips (**1–2, 10–11**: Veh Ardashir, after Negro Ponzi 1984, fig. 1.10, 13, 11–12; **3**: Nineveh, BMAG 71'43; **4–9, 16**: Abu Skhair, after Negro Ponzi 1972, fig. 20, nos. 21, 10–11, 22, 12, 19, 21; **12–15, 17–18**: T. Mohammed Arab; **19**: T. Mahuz, after Negro Ponzi 1968/69, fig. 153, no. 23).*

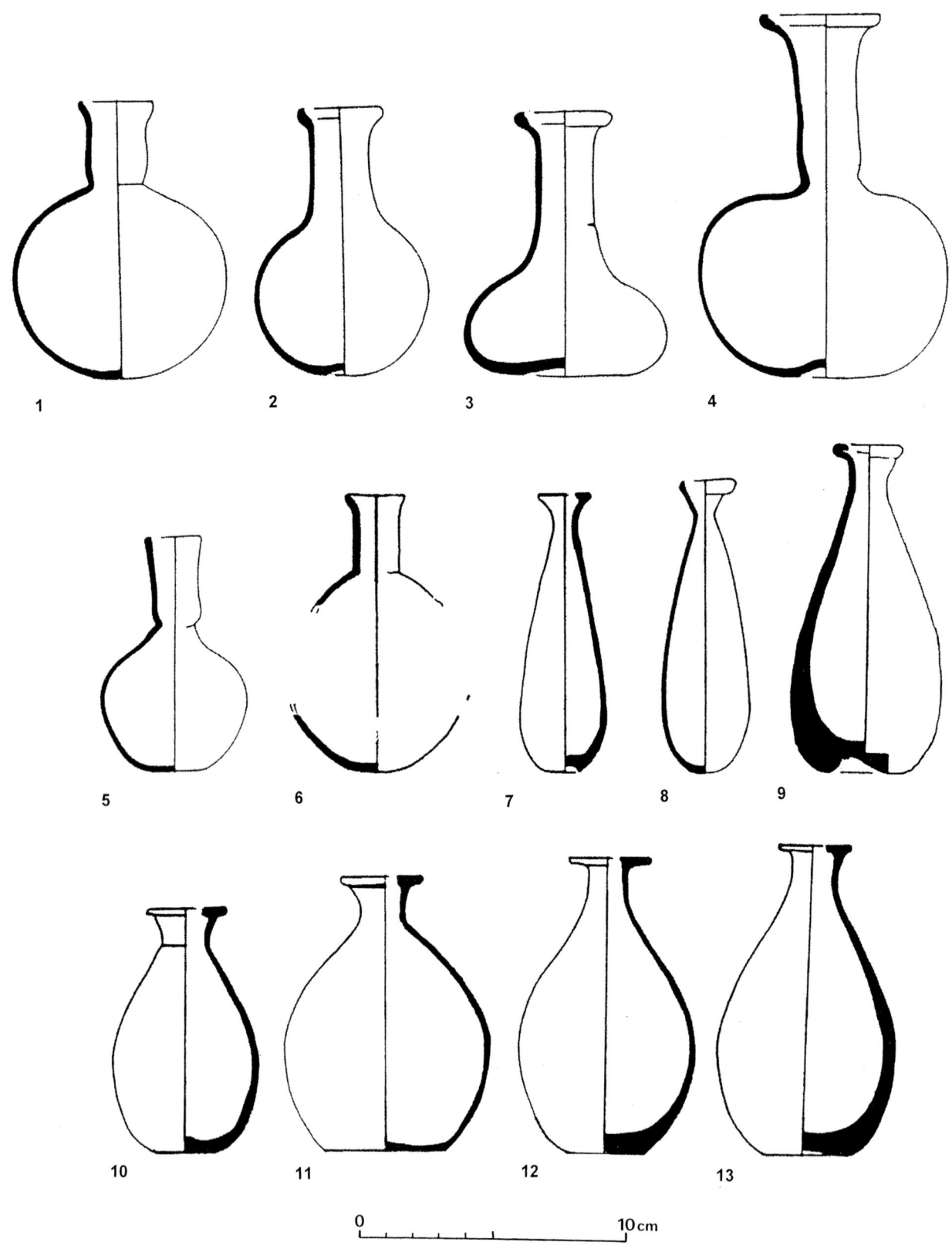

*Fig. 20.8: Plain free-blown bottles (**1–5**: T. Mahuz, after Negro Ponzi 1968/69, fig. 154, nos. 27, 26, 24, 30, 29; **6**: T. Mohammed Arab; **7, 10–13**: T. Bismaya = Diyala Survey 562, after Khairi 1987/88, 19; **8**: Abu Skhair, after Negro Ponzi 1972, fig. 21, no. 32; **9**: Nineveh, BM 91467).*

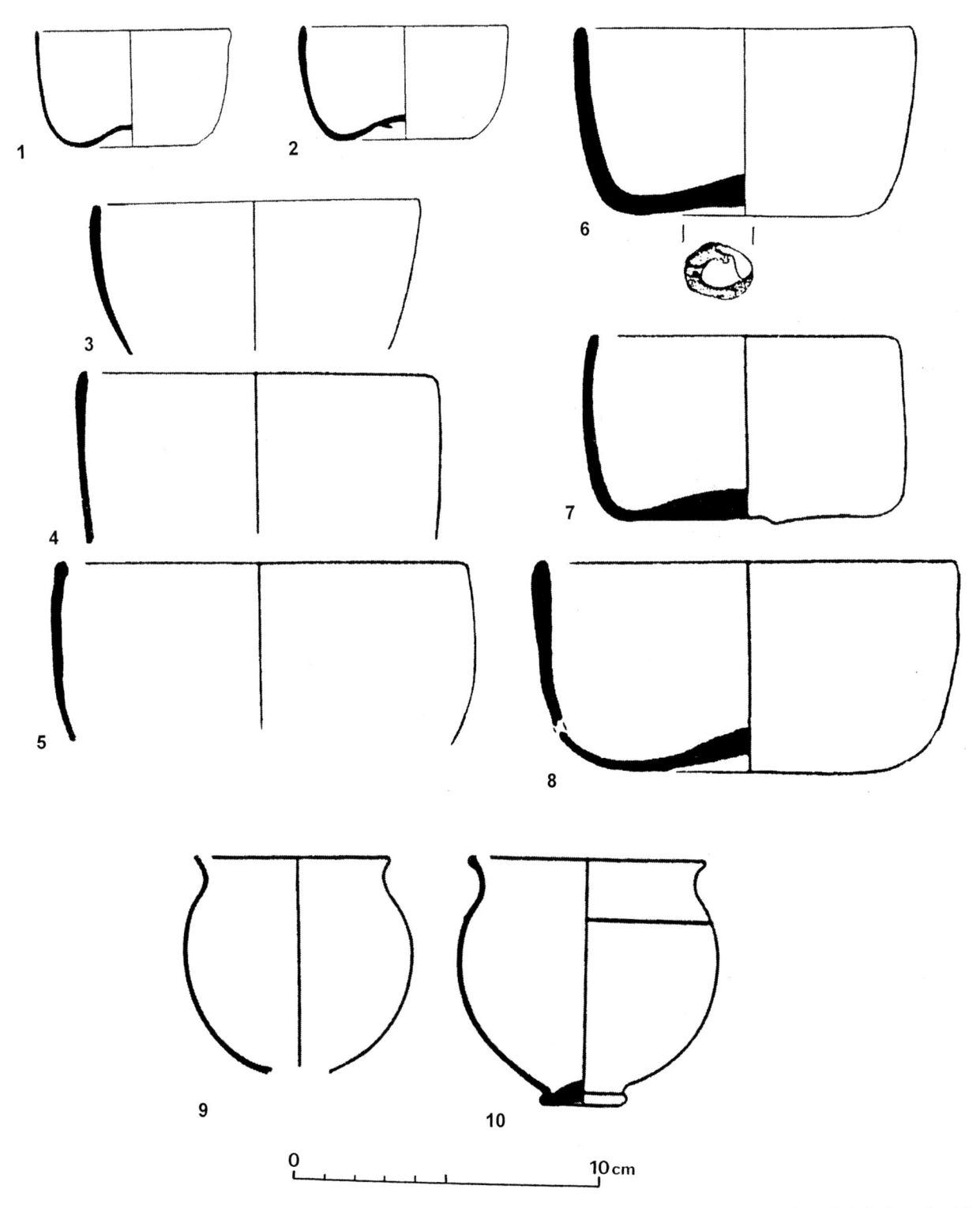

*Fig. 20.9: Plain free-blown bowls with straight sides (**1–3**: Kish, SP-6, AMO 1933.1328, 1621, 620; **4–5, 7–8**: Veh Ardashir, after Negro Ponzi 1987, fig. A, nos. 318, 381, 149, 521/522; **6**: T. Barghuthiat, AMO 1933.1397); plain deep bowls with rounded sides (**9–10**: Veh Ardashir, after Negro Ponzi 1984, fig. 2.7, 6).*

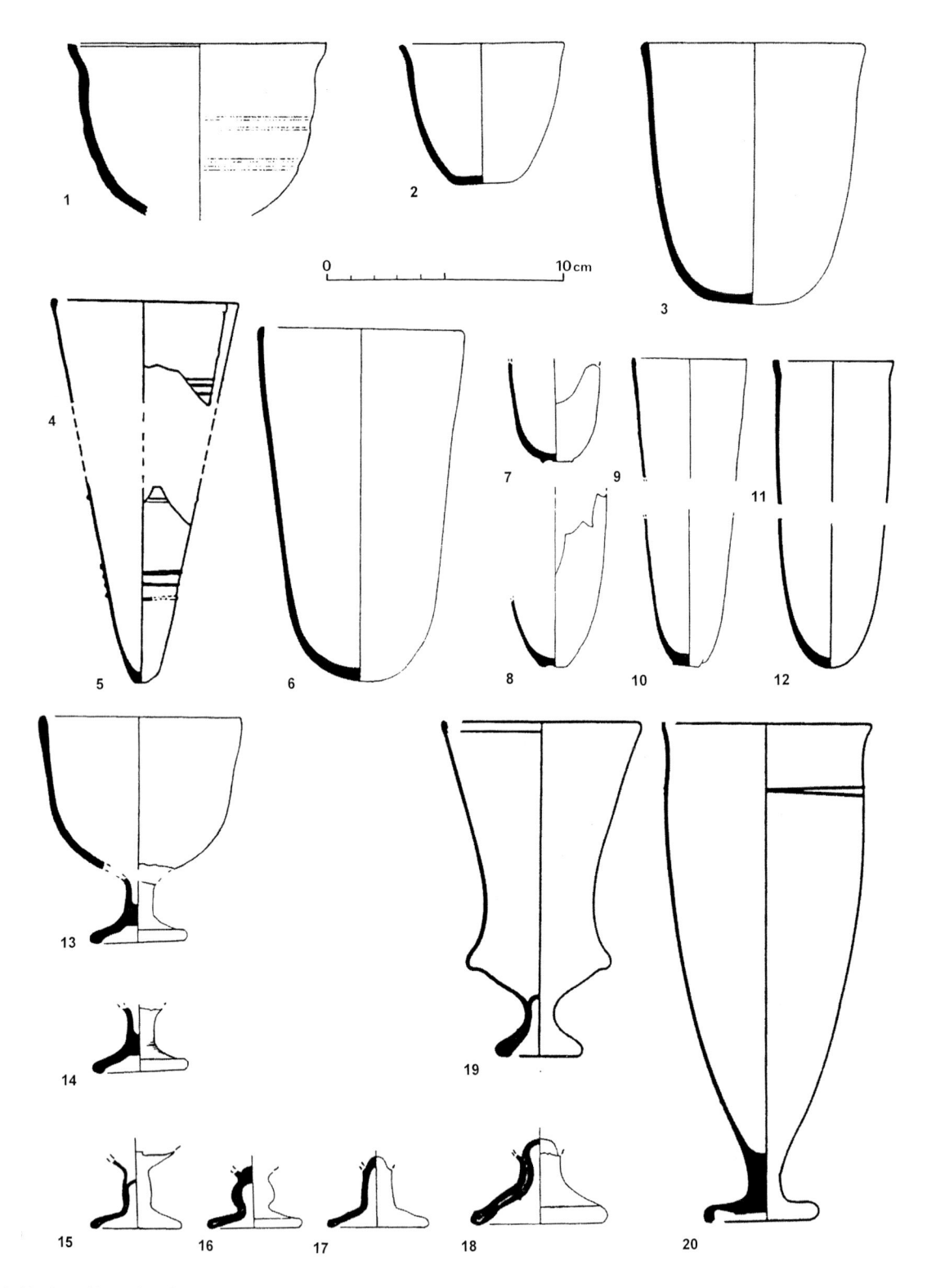

*Fig. 20.10: Free-blown bowls, beakers, stemmed goblets and chalices. Bowl with cracked-off rim and wheel-abraded lines (**1**: Nineveh, BM 91559); plain rounded base beakers (**2–3**: T. Mahuz, after Negro Ponzi 1968/69, fig. 157, nos. 62–63); plain conical beakers with wheel-abraded lines (**4–5**: Veh Ardashir, after Negro Ponzi 1984, fig. 2.10); plain conical beakers (**6**: T. Mahuz, after Negro Ponzi 1968/69, fig. 157, no. 64; **7–10**: Kish, SP-7, AMO 1969.618a, 622, 597a, 597b; **11–12**: Veh Ardashir, after Negro Ponzi 1984, fig. 2.2); plain stemmed goblets (**13**: T. Ajaja, BM N.1517; **14**: Nimrud, BM N.1042; **15–18**: Kish, SP-7, AMO 1969.611, 610b, 613c, 614); plain footed chalices (**19–20**: Veh Ardashir, after Negro Ponzi 1984, fig. 2.1, 5).*

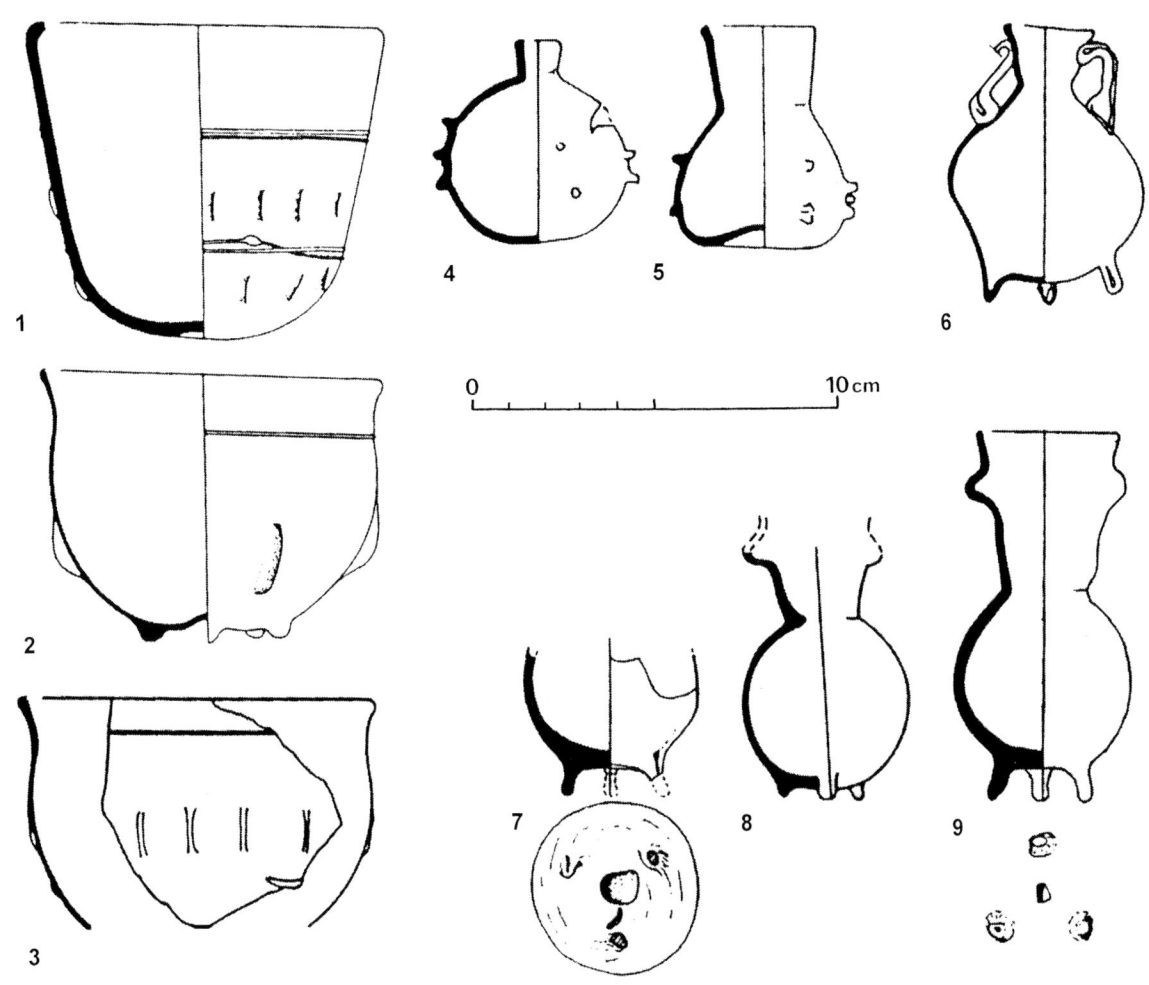

*Fig. 20.11: Pinched glassware: deep bowls with pinched out fins (**1**: Veh Ardashir, after Negro Ponzi 1984, fig. 3.12; **2–3**: T. Mahuz, after Negro Ponzi 1968/69, fig. 157, nos. 68–69); bottles with warts (**4–5**: Abu Skhair, after Negro Ponzi 1972, fig. 21, nos. 40–41); bottle with pulled out feet and trailed-on handles (**6**: Abu Skhair, after Negro Ponzi 1972, fig. 21, no. 39); bottles with pulled out feet and necks (**7**: Kish, SP-7, AMO 1969.625; **8**: Abu Skhair, after Negro Ponzi 1972, fig. 21, no. 38; **9**: Mesopotamia, BM 91475).*

Trailed handles were added to some of these types as well as to a distinctive class of (usually dark green) plain or mould-blown re-blown ribbed juglets (Fig. 20.13): the necks of these were constricted with pincers and the bottom pushed in with the blowpipe to leave a hollow pontil mark (Fig. 20.14.14–16). The use of pincers to constrict the neck also occurs on a small globular form of bottle with a cylindrical neck. Some were left plain (Figs. 20.14.1–9; 20.15) but others were dipped into moulds to create decorative vertical ribs (Figs. 20.14.10–13; 20.16). Mould-blown ribbing was also used on other types of bottle or small jar (Fig. 20.17.1–3), deep footed bowls (Fig. 20.17.4–6), rounded bowls (Fig. 20.17.7–9), taller beakers (Figs. 20.17.10–11; 20.18), conical beakers (Fig. 20.17.12–14) and tall-necked candle-stick unguentaria (Fig. 20.19.15–17). This tradition of optic-blown ribbing is one of the characteristics of Sasanian glass which has been rather overlooked in studies based on collections biased towards cut glass. It nevertheless exerted a major influence on early Islamic glass production when the honeycomb effect of cut glass bowls was imitated more cheaply by using patterned moulds.

Applied trailing other than for handles is uncommon, particularly adding glass of a different colour to the main body, and those published from early Sasanian graves at Tell Mahuz in northern Iraq may represent imports from Roman Syria (Negro Ponzi 1968/69). Trailing was added to the necks and bodies of some bottles and mini-juglets (Figs. 20.19.11–12, 20.19.14; 20.20.1–2) and double-tube unguentaria (Fig. 20.20.3–6); the latter represent a local version of the better-known eastern Roman type but are clearly distinguishable by their fabric and trailing technique. An alternative form of hot applied decoration was in the form of flattened circular blobs added to the bodies of small bottles (Fig. 20.20.7–9); this tradition continues into the early Islamic period (Negro Ponzi 2005, 143–144, figs. 4.16, 25).

Fig. 20.12: Pinched bowl, BM 134374.

Fig. 20.13: Juglet with trailed handle, BM 91472.

There is no evidence for influence from metalwork apart from the similarity in profile of one form of plain-footed bowl represented by two blue examples, one excavated at Susa and the second from the Iranian art market (Demange (ed.) 2006, 153, cat. no. 99; Newby 1995, 9, cat. no. 37).

Cold worked decoration

The origins of Sasanian cut glass are unclear but it first appears at Veh Ardashir during the early 4th century (Negro Ponzi 1984; 1987). Glass of any sort appears to have been rare at Parthian Seleucia (and compositional analyses indicate that some of this is silica-soda-lime glass with a low magnesium content probably imported from the eastern Roman world; cf. Mirti *et al.* 2008); as the earliest Sasanian cut glass is related to Roman types, western inspiration seems most likely for the style of cutting although the compositional analyses indicate the hot working was based within a traditional Mesopotamian cultural context. It then becomes increasingly elaborate with a shift from rice facets or isolated circular facets to more heavily cut and closely set or overlapping circular facets, sometimes combined with pseudo-architectural arcading, which may come from a single workshop (cf. Braat 1964). The aesthetic of these later pieces relied on multiple reflections combined with a reassuring sense of weight and belongs to the world of the lapidary, although surprisingly none of the known Sasanian pieces were decolourised to imitate rock crystal (unless one includes the so-called "vase d'Elinor", cf. Simpson 2007). In a few cases the finished items may have been supplemented with metal mounts and several tubes have silver or copper alloy caps (*e.g.* Oliver Jr. 1980, 137).

Unsurprisingly, cut-glass vessels usually had thicker walls than plain ware (although no thicker than some mould-blown glass), and this relative robustness undoubtedly contributes to their preferential preservation and recognition. Open bowls are the commonest form. In the early/mid 4th century these have cracked-off rims and are decorated on the exterior with equally spaced shallow circular facets (Figs. 20.21.11–13; 20.22) (Goldstein *et al.* 2005, 51, cat. no. 37). These are followed by examples with flaring walls and deeper oval facets, the rims again being cracked-off and left unfinished (Figs. 20.21.8–10; 20.23) (Whitehouse 2005, 46–47, cat. no. 53). The fabrics of all these are typically pale greenish.

During the 6th century these forms were replaced by hemispherical bowls with rows of deeper closely set or partially overlapping facets, sometimes overlapping to the extent that they resemble a polygonal honeycomb or tortoise-shell pattern (Whitehouse 2005, 42–44, cat. nos. 46–48) (Figs. 20.24–20.26). They were produced from both light green and light brownish fabrics; the latter tend to be thicker and heavier. Shallow bowls decorated on the outside in the same way are a less common type but nevertheless attested from excavations as well as the art market, and there is one famous example in the San Marco Treasury (Simpson 2007) (Fig. 20.25.17). As with other types of cut glass, these bowls appear to have been cut from bottom to top, as the facets decrease in depth as they near the rim. As with their earlier predecessors, they fit comfortably in the hand and the grip is improved by the increased number and depth of the facets.

The same type of hemispherical cut facets was used to

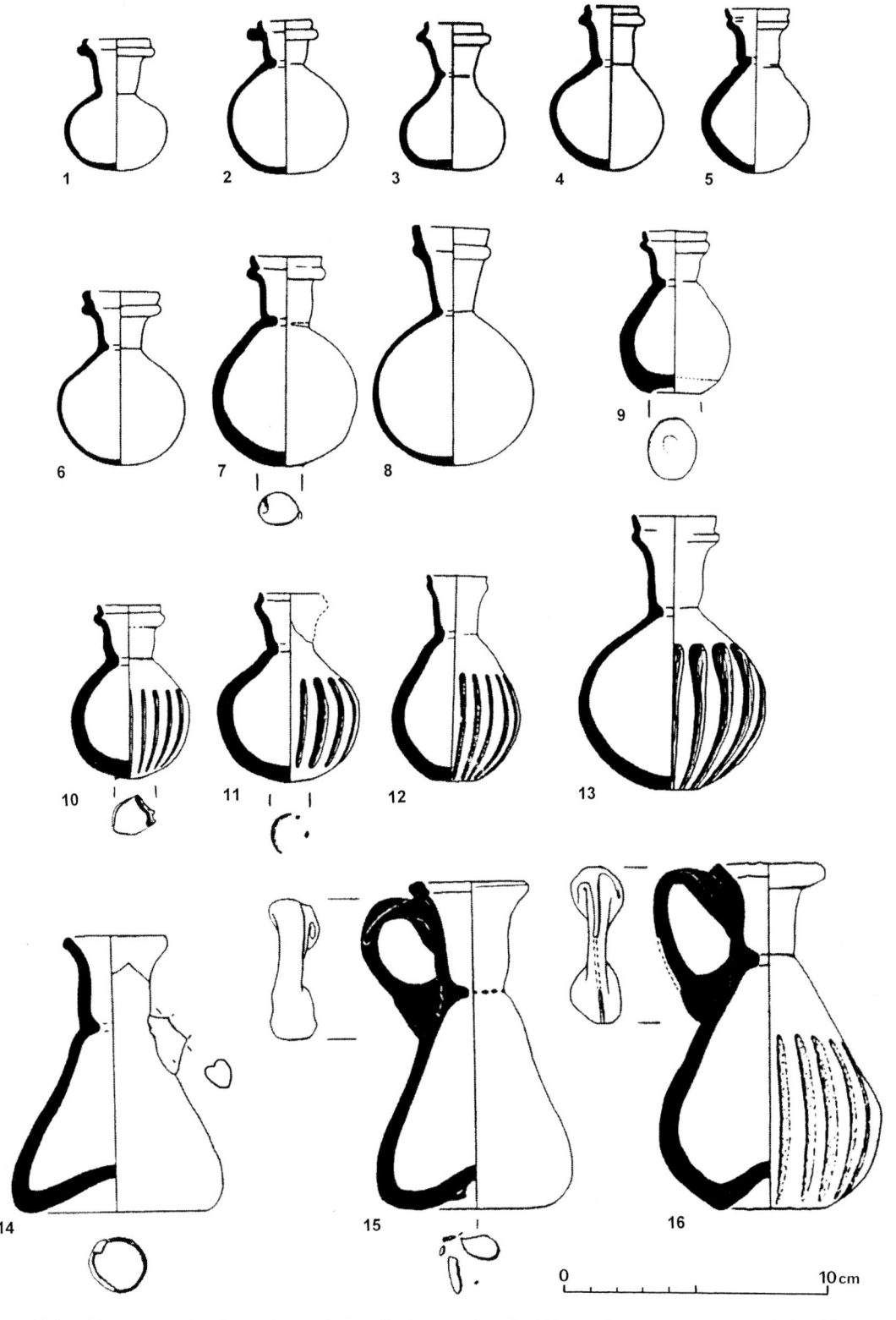

*Fig. 20.14: Small free-blown plain bottles with pinched necks (**1–2, 6, 8**: Abu Skhair, after Negro Ponzi 1972, fig. 21, nos. 34–37; **3–4**: Veh Ardashir, after Negro Ponzi 1984, fig. 1.16–17; **5, 7**: Nineveh, BMAG 694'61, BM 99433); small plain bottle with finished pontil (**9**: Nimrud, BM 91490); small mould-blown re-blown bottles with pinched necks (**10–11**: Babylon, BM 91491, 91483; **12–13**: Nineveh, BM 91539, BMAG 555'61); small juglets with trailed-on handles and pinched necks (**14**: Kish, SP-7/8, AMO 1933.1321; **15–16**: Abu Habba, BM 91472, 91471).*

decorate other forms of container, for instance pear-shaped jars (Figs. 20.27.9–10; 20.28) and amphora-like pourers (Fig. 20.29) and, from the early 7th century, tall cylindrical tubes (Figs. 20.27.11–12; 20.30) (Pinder-Wilson 1963; Harper et al. 1978, 153, cat. no. 76; Whitehouse 2005, 54–57, cat. nos. 65–66). These must have been designed for specific functions and all appear to be quite rare as only some twenty tubes, about a dozen pear-shaped jars and six amphora-shaped rhyta are known from publications or major museum collections, and only facet-cut versions have been recognised. A small number of facet-cut stemmed goblets (Figs. 20.21.1; 20.31), miniature bottles (Fig. 20.21.2–3) and beakers (Fig. 20.21.5–10) possibly represent the working of blanks imported from glass-houses more accustomed to selling them as plain versions. Squarish facets were normally placed as the uppermost row on other bowls and goblets (Fig. 20.21.14–17) (e.g. Boucharlat and Lecomte 1987, pl. 99.9; Braat 1964). More elaborate double-faceting and/or plain protruding knobs are found on some other deep bowls (Fig. 20.27.1–8) (Whitehouse 2005, 45–46, cat. nos. 50–52). These must have required an exceptional investment of time and care and it is perhaps not surprising that they are rarer than the normal hemispherical faceted bowls. In all cases there is a very high degree of finish and polish, extending to the removal of any traces of hot working, the rounding of the rims and the typical replacement of the pontil mark with a neatly cut facet which enhanced the resting position of the vessel.

Circulation and deposition

The built environment

There are no contemporary depictions of glass from within the Sasanian empire, although a number of pieces are depicted on Central Asian wall-paintings, notably from Dunhuang (e.g. Taniichi 1986b), and neither the names nor the organisation of the craftsmen involved are known. Contemporary written sources on the use of glass in the Sasanian empire are scarce and limited to occasional references in the Babylonian Talmud. One passage referring to the consumption of roast goose describes the clarity of the gravy as being "as clear as white glass" (Pesachim 74b) and another passage states:

> "Originally, when they would serve drinks in a house of mourning, the wealthy would serve in vessels of white glass, and the poor in vessels of coloured glass, and the poor would feel ashamed. [The rabbis] therefore instituted that all who serve drinks at the mourners' home should serve them in vessels of coloured glass, out of concern for the honour of the poor" (Moed Katan 27a; Schottenstein edition).

It is unclear from this whether the drinks were served in bowls or goblets, or whether the vessels were disposed of after the wake, but the passage does show that clear glass was regarded as more valuable than coloured glass (which in the case of Babylonia means naturally rather than artificially coloured glass).

Glass was relatively common at Sasanian sites in Mesopotamia but not as common as in the early Islamic period when finds increase here and across Iran and Central Asia. There is little quantified evidence, however, and better recording in future would enable a greater understanding of the relative frequency, comparative value and scale of production. At Veh Ardashir, some 8,800 fragments are reported from the Italian excavations of two residential insulae in the southern portion of the site (Negro Ponzi 1984, 33). The proportion to pottery is unrecorded but (fragmented) faceted as well as plain hemispherical bowls are represented even at small rural sites in the upper Tigris valley such as Seh Qubba, Qara Dere and Khirbet Deir Situn where glass formed between 0.6 and 4.9% of the combined pottery/glass sherd total. At the small settlement mound of Tell Abu Sarifa, near Nippur in south-central Iraq, glass formed 2.0% of the combined sherd total from the late Sasanian period (level II), rising to 6.35% in level IV (c. 9th century). Analysis of collections from older excavations at Kish and Nineveh confirm consistent numbers of cut glass vessels, including different varieties of hemispherical bowls, tubes and miniature flasks, and prove the circulation of these alongside Roman bowls, lamps and square bottles within different residential contexts in both northern and south-central Iraq (Simpson 1992; 1996; 2005c).

The other region where there is a growing body of excavated material is the southern Caucasus. The largest quantity of published pieces come from Azerbaijan, then part of the Sasanian empire, and includes almost all the main types known from Mesopotamia including plain, pinched, mould-blown and facet-cut varieties (Nuriijev 1981; also Efendi 1976, fig. 9). In addition, hemispherical bowls decorated with circular and double-circular facets were found in 6th century and later occupation layers in the cities of Dvin (Armenia), Urbnisi and Rustavi (Georgia) (Djanpoladian and Kalantarian 1988, 42–43, pls. I–II; Džanpoladjani 1974, 47, 57, pl. I.1–3; Chilashvili 1964, 119, fig. 53), and another was found in a grave at Komunt in North Ossetia (Loukonine and Ivanov 2003, 92); a deep beaker bowl decorated with "nip't diamond waies" is illustrated from Djinbaliskaya in Georgia (Ramishvili et al. 1984, 82, pl. LXXXIX.2), and the lower part of a faceted tube of late Sasanian or early Islamic date is published from Dvin (Džanpoladjani 1974, pl. II.1). Moreover, evidence for glassworking of this period is also reported from Dvin. These finds suggest that the importance of the Caucasus may have been underestimated in much of the literature, and this region may have been the source of production for Sasanian glass reportedly found in graves in the Gilan region of neighbouring north-west Iran (see below).

Fig. 20.15: Plain globular bottle, BM 99433.

Fig. 20.16: Plain mould-blown re-blown ribbed bottle, BM 1929,1012.290.

The pattern is more ambiguous for other regions, but glassware seems scarce and so presumably relatively highly prized on the Iranian plateau. Only a few pieces are reported from the fully cleared standing remains of a 3rd-century palatial residence at Qal'eh-i Dukhtar (Huff 1978, figs. 20–23) or extensive excavations at the late Sasanian fire-temple complex at Takht-i Sulaiman. Semi-quantified data come from Tureng Tepe, where excavation of the 6th-century fort on the summit produced six sherds, including fragments of three separate facet-cut bowls, and apparently constituting 1% of the combined total of pottery/glass diagnostics (Boucharlat and Lecomte 1987, 172–73, pls. 99.6–9, 156a–c). The number and proportion of glass to pottery sherds climbs slightly during the 7th–8th century occupation in Period VII A–B and appears to peak at 5.6% in the 9th century phase of Period VII C (Boucharlat and Lecomte 1987, 176, 178–182, pls. 100, 102–103). A relatively large number of types is represented from the (complete) excavation of the small town citadel at Qasr-i Abu Nasr, near Shiraz, but the late and post-Sasanian levels are unfortunately mixed and the state of preservation implied by the drawings suggests that the published selection is biased towards complete or semi-complete vessels (Whitcomb 1985, 154–160, figs. 58–59). There is also evidence for glass circulating along the Persian Gulf: no sites of this period have yet been excavated on the Iranian side but the small settlement site of Kush in modern Ras al-Khaimah produced 50 sherds in the first two phases, which probably date between the 5th and early 7th centuries, and represent 0.7% of the combined glass/pottery sherd assemblage (Keller 2010, tab. 1; in press).

Different excavation and recovery techniques yield different results, site formation processes differ and few of the excavated assemblages are quantified. Before the 1992–2000 excavations at the site of Merv, evidence for Sasanian glass from a half-century of almost continuous excavation was effectively limited to rare vessels found in Rooms VI, VIII and XXII in YuTAKE Trench 6 (and probably dating to the later 4th century), one of which was a Mesopotamian mould-blown re-blown ribbed bottle with

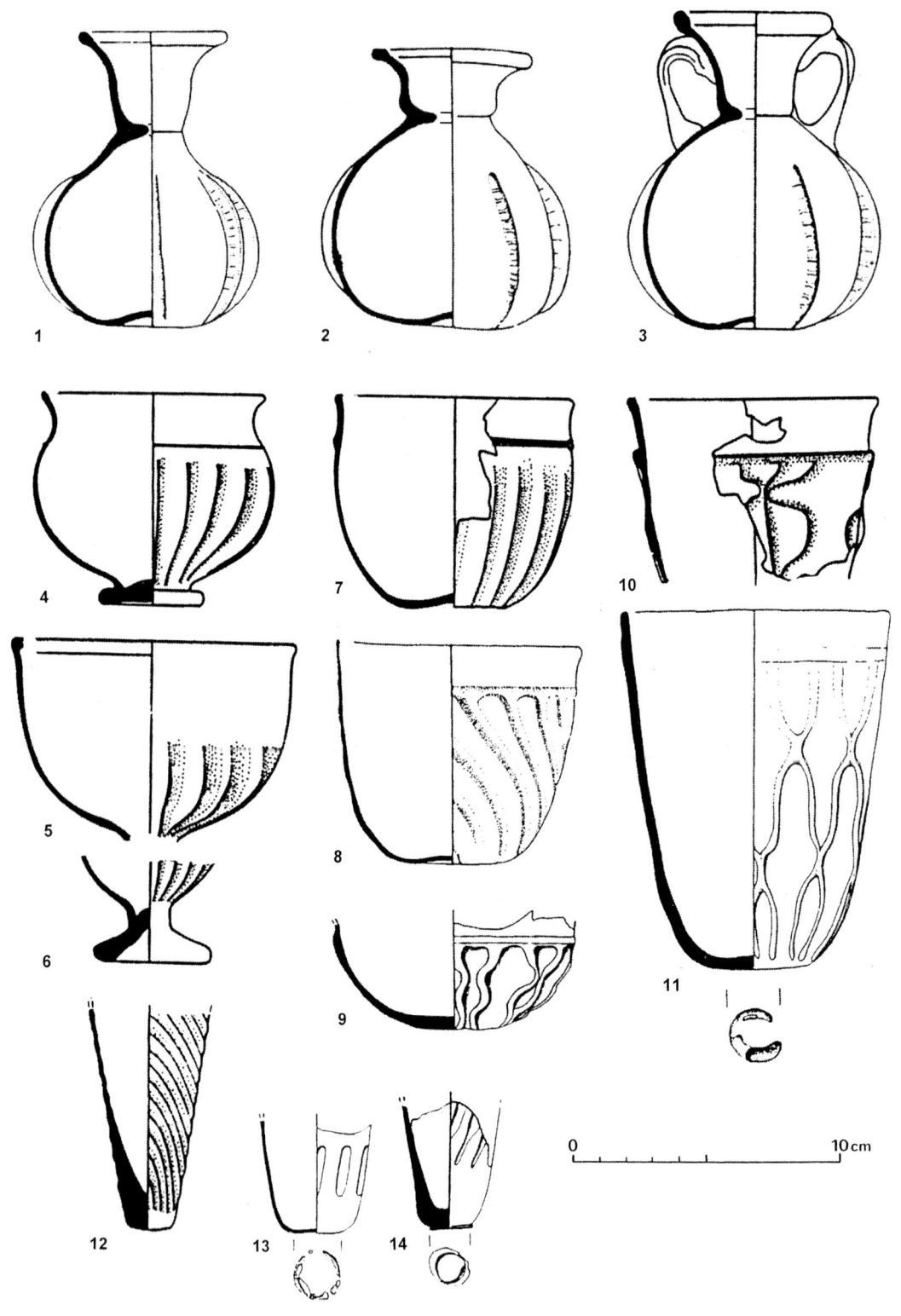

*Fig. 20.17: Pear-shaped bottles with pinched necks and probably mould-blown fins (**1–3**: T. Mahuz, after Negro Ponzi 1968/69, fig. 156, nos. 51–53); deep footed bowls with straight mould-blown ribs (**4–6**: Veh Ardashir, after Negro Ponzi 1984, figs. 2.9, 3.6–7); deep bowls and beakers with lightly pushed in bases and straight, twisted or pinched mould-blown ribs (**7, 10**: Veh Ardashir, after Negro Ponzi 1984, figs. 2.8, 3.11; **8**: T. Mahuz, after Negro Ponzi 1968/69, fig. 157, no. 70; **9**: Kish, SP-7, AMO 1969.605; **11**: unprovenanced, BM 135208); conical beakers with mould-blown decoration (**12**: Veh Ardashir, after Negro Ponzi 1984, fig. 3.9; **13**: Mesopotamia, BM 91556; **14**: Nimrud, BM N.1040).*

Fig. 20.18: Tall beaker with pincered mould-blown ribs, BM 135208.

constricted neck which was said to contain traces of oil (Katsuris and Buryakov 1963); another vessel, reportedly "in the shape of an antique aryballos", was found in the "Oval Building" which probably dates to the 6th century (Dresvyanskaya 1974). However, the subsequent excavation of part of a single residence in the citadel yielded a total of 89 sherds of glassware, several of which belonged to cut glass vessels; material was also recovered from 4th/5th-century contexts within a modest residential quarter in the lower city. This disparity arises from the very heavy fragmentation; also some pieces were in such a poor state of preservation that it is doubtful that they would have been recognised as glass were it not for careful hand recovery and the presence of a glass specialist in the field (Simpson 2005b). Nevertheless, a simple comparison of frequency of glass sherds with pottery indicate that glassware constituted only 0.15% of the combined assemblage, and thus is even scarcer than the figures recorded from Iraq, the Persian Gulf or Tureng Tepe. Only a single sherd of Mesopotamian glazed pottery was found at Merv, so here it was even scarcer than glass; this suggests increasing rarity with greater distance from places of production at the opposite end of the Sasanian empire.

Funerary contexts

Sasanian glass vessels were regularly interred with the dead. 3rd–4th-century cemeteries excavated at Tell Mahuz in northern Iraq (Negro Ponzi 1968/69), and Abu Skhair (Negro Ponzi 1972) and Umm Kheshm in the south (al-Shams 1987/88; al-Haditti 1995; Negro Ponzi 2005) have produced large assemblages of complete vessels, mostly small flasks and unguentaria. At Abu Skhair these constituted 46.3% of the combined total of pottery and glass grave-goods. They were only slightly less common at Tell Mahuz where they constituted 41.8% of the combined total. These vessels presumably originally contained scented oils, perfumes or powders intended to accompany the deceased to the afterlife; the excavator of Umm Kheshm offered us the possibility of analysing the contents of vessels from his excavations: sadly the Gulf War intervened during which he died of natural causes and most of his finds were lost when the dig-house storerooms were looted in 1991.

Small bottles were also placed in inhumation graves in western and north-west Iran. Evidence for this comes from a re-used cairn at War Kabud in Luristan (Vanden Berghe 1972) and several burials excavated on the summit of Haftavan tepe, near Lake Urmia (Burney 1973, pl. VIII.d). Graves are the likely origin for some of the complete glass vessels known from the Iranian art market. Art market reports suggest that Gilan province (including the Dailaman district) in north-west Iran was the principal source for these, as well as other finds such as swords and high-tin bronze vessels. Limited re-investigation by a Japanese expedition in 1964 confirmed in spite of heavy looting of hill-top cemetery sites of all periods the occasional interment of glassware, swords and metal vessels with inhumation burials placed inside subterranean graves (Sono and Fukai 1968; cf. Akira 1981). These finds suggest the choice of costly drinking vessels to accompany the burials of elite, probably male, individuals. However they do not provide evidence for local glass production: instead it seems more likely that they originate from the neighbouring southern Caucasus, and continue a pattern of close cultural connection which extends back for at least 1500 years before the Sasanian period (cf. Moorey 1971, 17).

There is also evidence for placing glass bowls and small bottles with the dead in eastern Arabia, near Dhahran and on Bahrain: these finds further support the circulation and prizing of small amounts of Sasanian glass by some communities along the Persian Gulf (Zarins, Mughannam and Kamal 1984, 42, pl. 50.10; Andersen 2007). This practice continued after the Islamic conquest, both in the Persian Gulf and in Iraq. On Bahrain a small number of inhumation graves at al-Hajjar and al-Muqsha contained small greyish bottles decorated with trails (Andersen 2007, 85–90): although originally dated to the 6th–7th centuries, the close typological parallels from Sir Bani Yas and Kharg

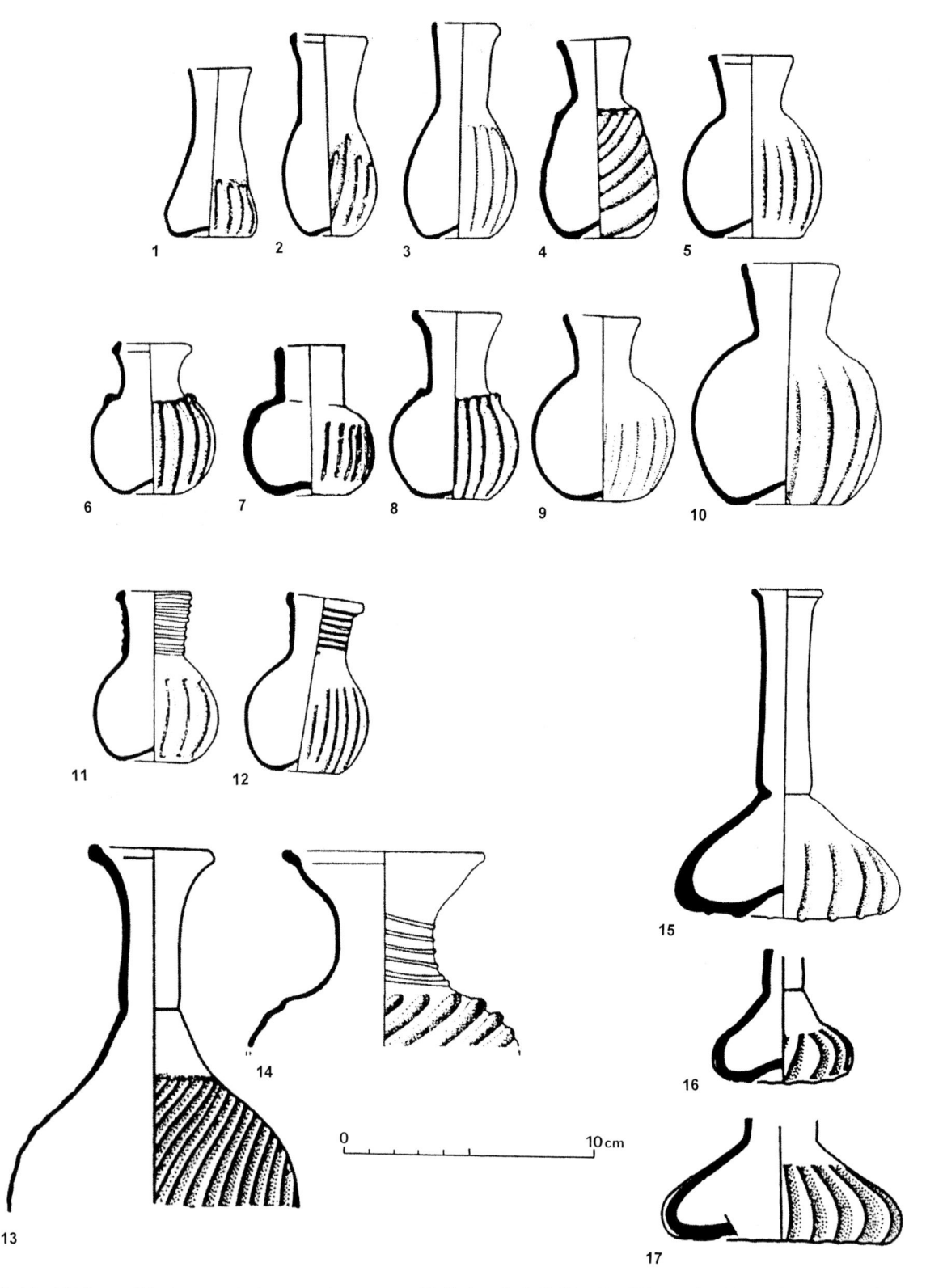

*Fig. 20.19: Mould-blown ribbed unguentaria at varying stages of inflation (**1–6, 8–10***: Abu Skhair, after Negro Ponzi 1972, fig. 22, nos. 48, 50, 52, 63, fig. 21, nos. 45, 60, fig. 22, no. 62, fig. 21, no. 44, fig. 22, no. 46;* **7***: T, Mohammed Arab); mould-blown ribbed unguentaria with trailed necks (***11–12***: Abu Skhair, after Negro Ponzi 1972, fig. 22, nos. 53–54); mould-blown ribbed bottles with plain or trailed necks (***13***: Veh Ardashir, after Negro Ponzi 1984, fig. 3.3;* **14***: T. Mahuz, after Negro Ponzi 1968/69, fig. 155, no. 48); candlestick unguentaria with mould-blown ribs (***15***: T. Mahuz, after Negro Ponzi 1968/69, fig. 155, no. 47;* **16–17***: Veh Ardashir, after Negro Ponzi 1984, fig. 3.4–5).*

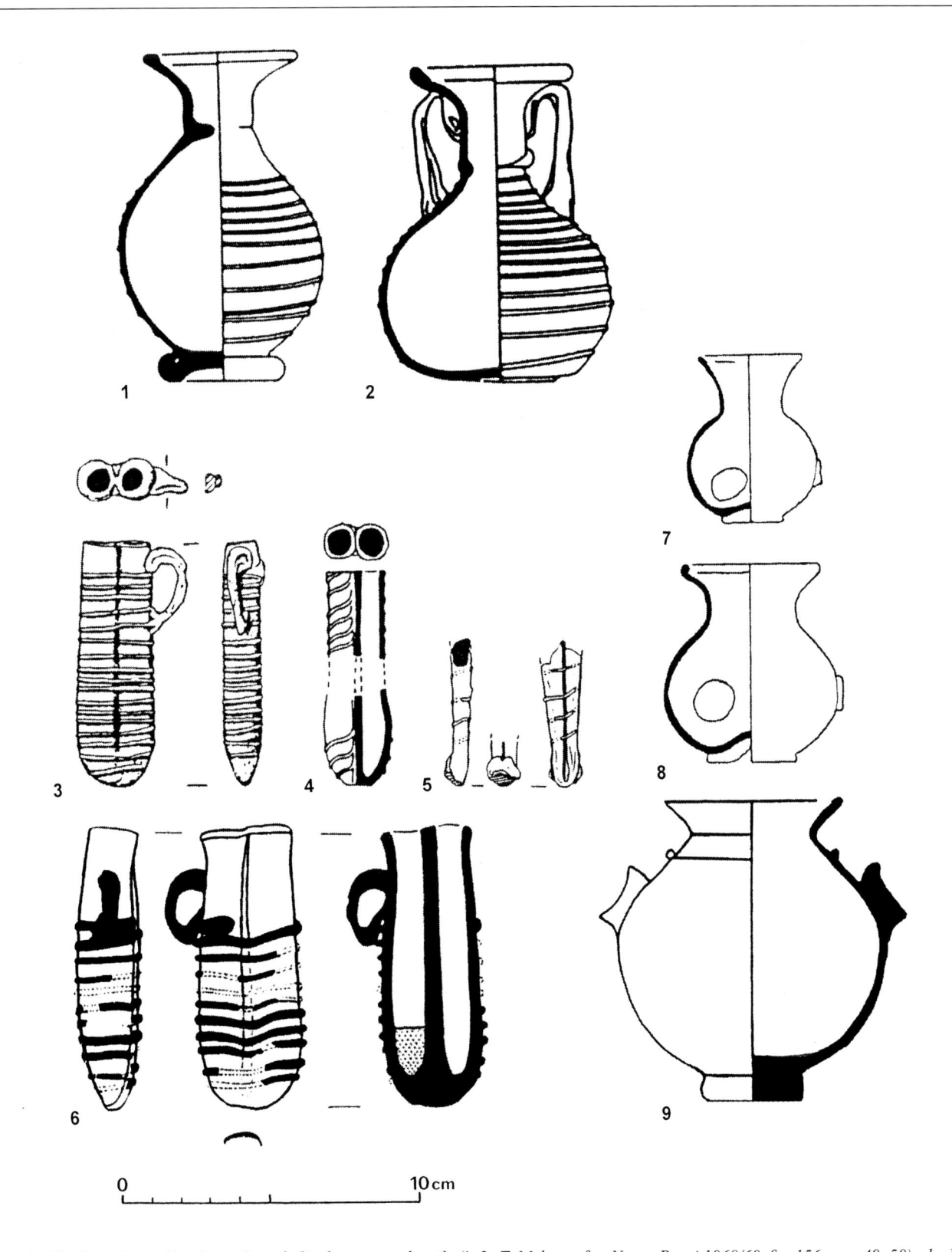

*Fig. 20.20: Pear-shaped bottles with neck diaphragms and trails (**1–2**: T. Mahuz, after Negro Ponzi 1968/69, fig. 156, nos. 49–50); double tube unguentaria with trails (**3**: T. Mohammed Arab; **4**: Qasr-i Abu Nasr, after Whitcomb 1985, fig. 58.i; **5**: Nineveh, BMAG 1989.A.323; **6**: Mesopotamia, BM 91502); small bottles with circular applied blobs (**7–8**: Bahrain, Budaiya Road Cemetery, after Lombard and Kervran (eds.) 1989, 112, nos. 197, 196; **9**: T. Bismaya = Diyala Survey 562, after Khairi 1987/88, 19).*

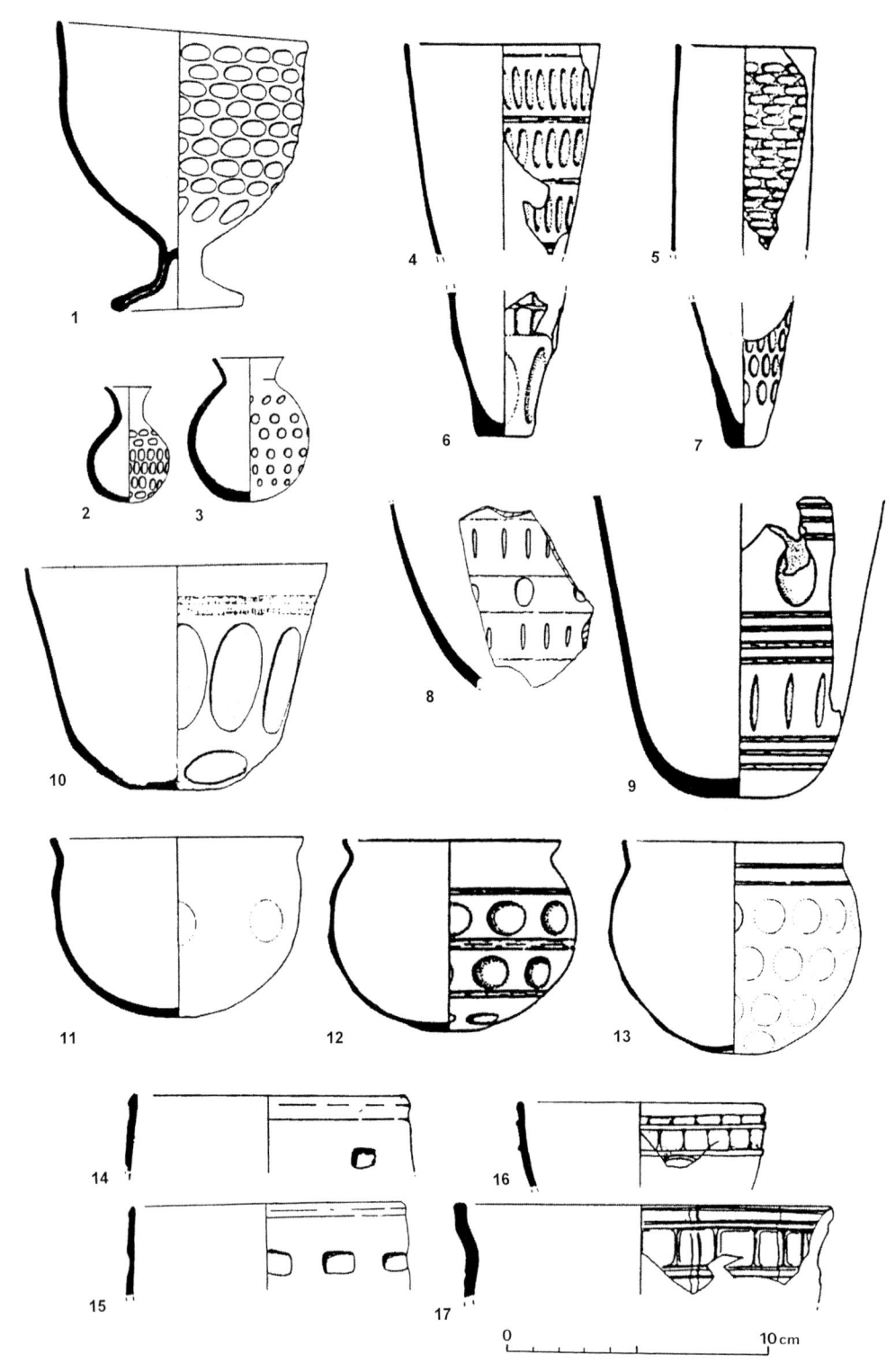

*Fig. 20.21: Facet-cut stemmed goblet (**1**: unprovenanced, BM 135713); facet-cut unguentaria (**2–3**: Nineveh, BM 91519, 91544); facet-cut conical beakers (**4-7**: Veh Ardashir, after Negro Ponzi 1984, figs. 4.2–3, 5–6); facet-cut rounded beakers (**8**: Nineveh, BM N.1395; **9**: Veh Ardashir, after Negro Ponzi 1984, fig. 4.4); bowl with cracked-off rim and shallow oval facets below wheel-abraded line (**10**: unprovenanced, BM 135304); deep bowls with short necks, separated facets and some with wheel-abraded lines (**11, 13**: T. Mahuz, after Negro Ponzi 1968/69, fig. 157, nos. 71–72; **12**: Veh Ardashir, after Negro Ponzi 1984, fig. 4.1); bowls with squarish facets placed below the rim (**14–15**: Warka, after Finster 1983, pl. 48.15, 17; **16**: Qasr-i Abu Nasr, after Whitcomb 1985, fig. 59.v; **17**: Tureng Tepe, after Boucharlat and Lecomte 1987, pl. 99.6).*

20 Sasanian glass: an overview 223

Fig. 20.22: Bowl with cracked-off rim and separated shallow facets, BM 135854.

Fig. 20.23: Flaring bowl with oval facets, BM 135304.

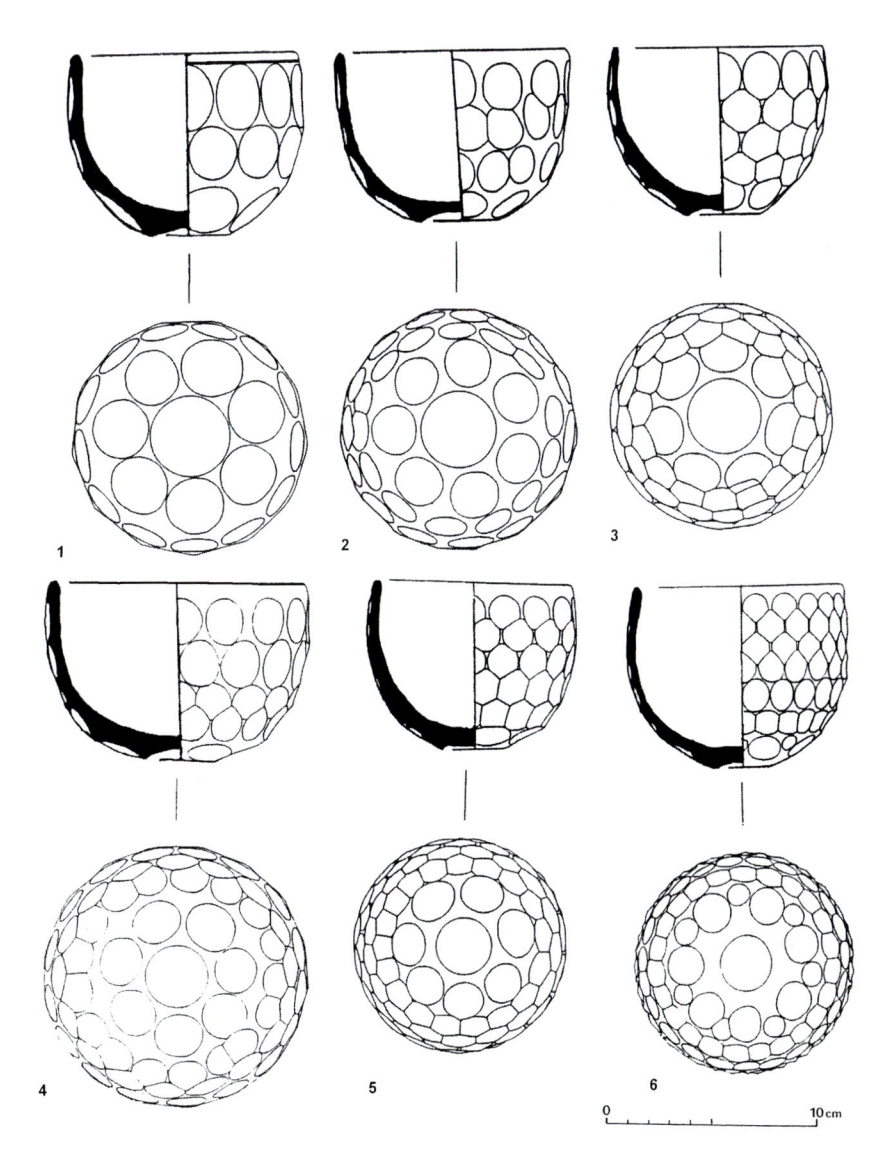

Fig. 20.24: Facet-cut hemispherical bowls (unprovenanced, after Fukai 1968, nos. 11–12, 14–15, 18–19).

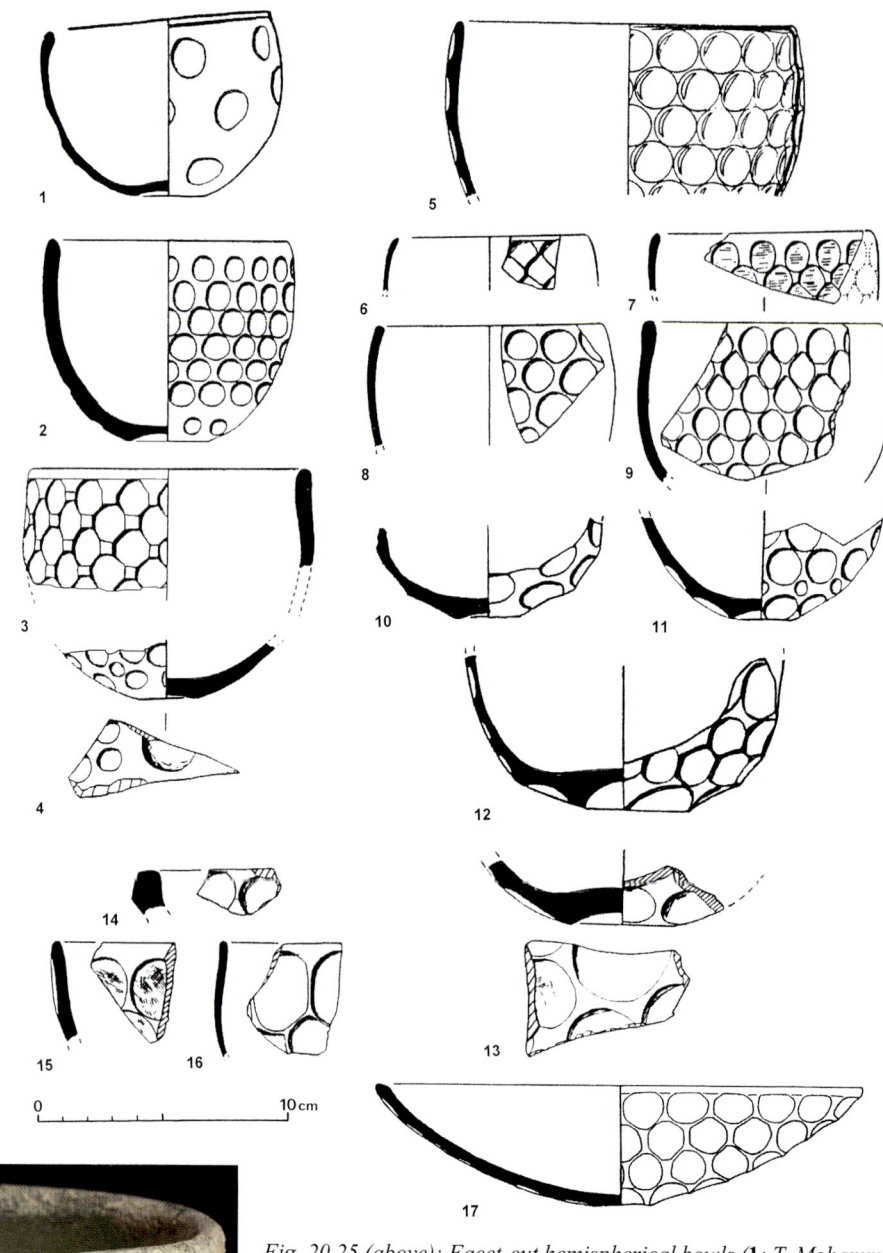

Fig. 20.25 (above): Facet-cut hemispherical bowls (1: T. Mohammed Arab; 2: possibly Telloh, BM 134915; 3–4: Telul Hamediyat, Iraq, after Kawamata 1991, figs. 26.5, 12.1; 5: Tureng Tepe, after Boucharlat and Lecomte 1987, pl. 99.9; 6: Qara Dere; 7, 9: Nineveh, BM SM.2424, BMAG 555'61; 8: Khirbet Aqar Babireh; 10: Urbnisi, after Chilashvili 1964, 119, fig. 53; 11, 16: Kish, SP-7, AMO 1933.1323, 1969.628j; 12: Veh Ardashir, after Negro Ponzi 1984, fig. 4.7; 13, 15: T. Ajaja, BM N.1510, N.1512; 14: Seh Qubba); facet-cut shallow bowl (17: Kish, SP-7, AMO 1969.592).

Fig. 20.26 (left): Hemispherical bowl with overlapping facets, BM 134915.

20 Sasanian glass: an overview

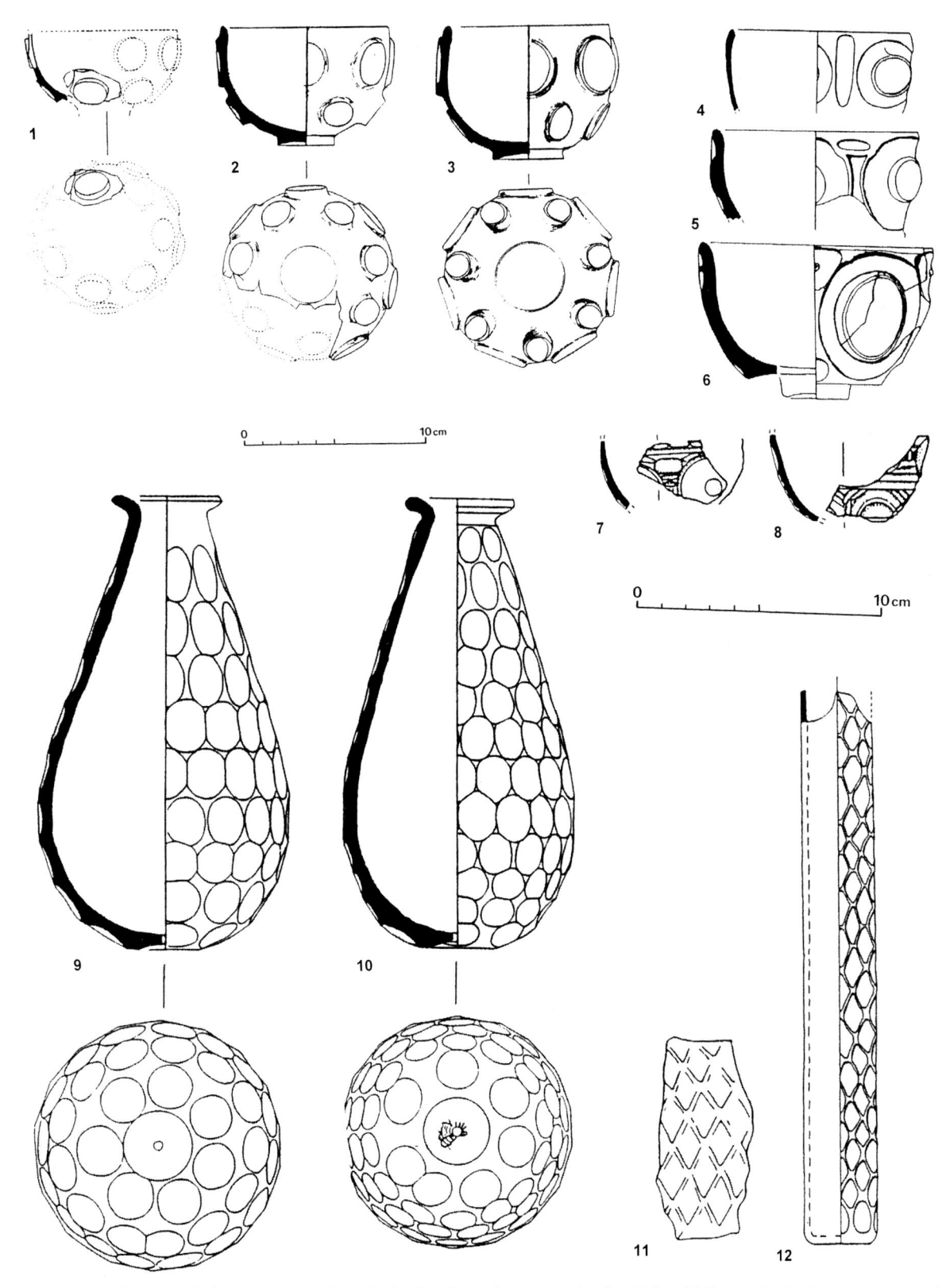

*Fig. 20.27: Footed bowls with facet-cut protruding knobs (**1**: Okinoshima island, after Fukai 1968, no. 24; **2–3**: unprovenanced, after Fukai 1968, nos. 26, 25); footed bowls with double circular facets (**4–6**: Kish, SP-7, AMO 1969.595-596, 116; **7-8**: Veh Ardashir, after Negro Ponzi 1984, fig. 4.13, 12); facet-cut pear-shaped jars (**9–10**: unprovenanced, after Fukai 1968, nos. 34–35); facet-cut tubes (**11**: Qasr-i Abu Nasr, after Whitcomb 1985, fig. 59.e; **12**: Nineveh, BM 91498a).*

Fig. 20.28: Pear-shaped jar with overlapping facets, BM 135711.

Fig. 20.29: Amphora-like pourer with overlapping facets, BM 135712.

island suggest a slightly later date extending into the 8th century (Steve *et al.* 2003, 79–83, pls. 44–50) and similar examples reported from Umm Kheshm have been dated too early (cf. Negro Ponzi 2005, 144). Moreover, graves excavated by the University of Baghdad at Sippar in central Iraq, contained trailed double unguentaria supported on quadrupeds – a distinctive type also known further east from Susa and Qasr-i Abu Nasr usually regarded as dating to about the 8th century (al-Jadir and Abdullah 1988, pls. 5.3–4, 19.2–3; cf. Lamm 1931, 361, pl. LXXVII.4; Whitcomb 1985, 154, 158–159, fig. 591). Finally, a single inhumation grave excavated on the summit of Tell Razuk in the Hamrin basin of east central Iraq contained the flexed body of an adult male buried with a copper alloy oval drinking bowl of a type known in Middle Persian as a *makog* (literally: "boat-vessel"). He also possessed a squat green glass bottle belonging to a well-known type thought to date to the 7th century in China but also attested from 8th-century contexts at Fustat and Jebel Sais and the 6th–early 8th-century site of Kafyr-kala in southern Tajikistan (Gibson (ed.) 1981, 81, pl. 101; cf. Watt *et al.* 2004, 324–325, cat. no. 220; Litvinskij and Solovjev 1985, 70–72, fig. 23.12). So, not all glass described in the archaeological literature as Sasanian is correctly attributed and the advent of Islam did not result in a sudden termination of customs and funerary practices which had their roots in the preceding period.

Imports and exports

The import of small numbers of Roman glass lamps, bowls and bottles is illustrated by finds excavated at Nineveh (Simpson 2005c) and Veh Ardashir (Negro Ponzi 1984, 34, fig. 2.10) and compositional analysis confirms some of the latter – including deep cut bowls and a conical lamp decorated with blue prunts – to be natron glass (Mirti *et al.*

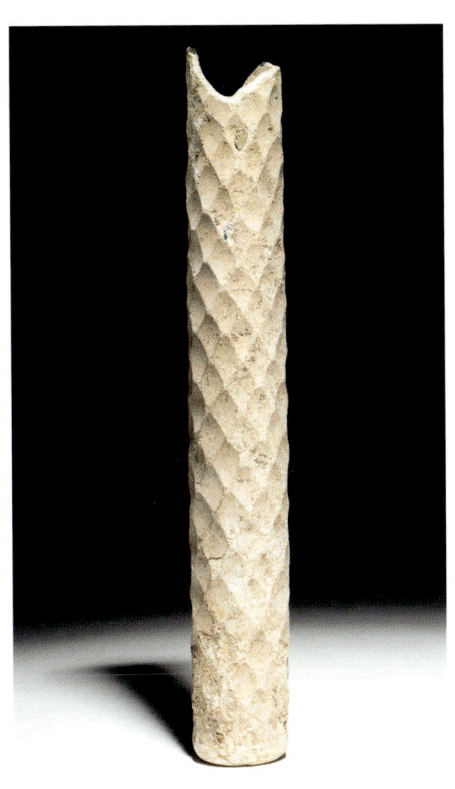

Fig. 20.30: Cylindrical tube with overlapping facets, BM N.833.

Fig. 20.31: Stemmed goblet with overlapping facets, BM 135713.

2008, 438, VA 07, 11, 13, 20–21, 28 = Negro Ponzi 1984, fig. 4.11, 13). Natron glass is also represented from Sasanian domestic contexts at Merv, although the small size of the fragments made it impossible to match the chemical analyses to vessel forms (Roehrs forthcoming). No Sasanian glass has yet been recognised from archaeological contexts from the Roman world although one faceted shallow bowl did make its way into the San Marco treasury after the sack of Constantinople during the Fourth Crusade (Simpson 2007).

Nevertheless, small amounts of Sasanian glass did trickle overland to the east and via maritime trade into the Indian Ocean. The most famous illustration of the eastward trade is the spectacularly well-preserved hemispherical bowl with circular facets deposited in the Shōsō-in at Nara in Japan (Fukai 1960). This treasure-house was sealed in AD 756 when Emperor Shomu died but the bowl itself was much older. There are a number of other finds from across China (*e.g.* Watt *et al.* 2004, 156, 210–211, 258–259, 324–325, cat. nos. 65, 116–117, 158–159, 219–220), Korea (Whitfield (ed.) 1984, 93) and Japan (Taniichi 1986a; 2010), and many from dated tombs, although whether they arrived by land, sea or, as seems increasingly likely, a combination of both has excited different ideas within Silk Road studies (*e.g.* Bivar 1970; Raschke 1978; Taniichi 2010).

There is growing archaeological evidence for Sasanian maritime trade via the Persian Gulf with the Indian Ocean. Torpedo jars, glazed Mesopotamian pottery and a Sasanian bulla are known from western India and Sri Lanka although no Sasanian glass has yet been recognised (*e.g.* Coningham *et al.* 2006, 107–111, fig. 5.2; Tomber 2007). Two pieces of Sasanian cut glass have been published recently from Yemen: one is a bowl of the same type as that from San Marco (Simpson 2007) and the second was excavated at the Indian Ocean port of Qana (Salles and Sedov 2010, 148, fig. 64, no. 590). A small number of free-blown bottles with pinched walls is also attested from southern Arabia, whence they were presumably exported for their contents (Simpson (ed.) 2002, 136–137, cat. nos. 170–174). All of these may have come overland but are more likely to represent maritime trade as there are also numerous fragments of bitumen-lined Sasanian torpedo jar amphorae from lower Mesopotamia and/or south-west Iran (Salles and Sedov 2010, 42–46, fig. 16: nos. 149–155; 154–159, fig. 68: nos. 608–611), south-east Iranian Fine Orange Painted Ware beakers (Simpson (ed.) 2002, 101, cat. no. 117; Salles and Sedov 2010, 46–48, fig. 17: no. 176; 74, 82–83, fig. 34: nos. 376–382; 95–97, fig. 42: no. 402; 254–255, fig. 108: no. 1073), and probable Mesopotamian glazed wares (*e.g.* Salles and Sedov 2010, 18, 24–25, fig. 8, no. 37, mis-identified as Chinese porcelain). In any case the finds reopen the question of how far this route played a role in the transmission of Sasanian goods to south-east Asia and the Far East.

Conclusions

The general development of Sasanian glass is now becoming clearer; it possessed its own distinctive range of forms, fabrics and manufacturing characteristics which distinguishes it as a local industry. Its origins are less well understood yet the combination of plant ash compositions, distinctive forms and techniques, and the scale of manufacture attested from surveys in southern Iraq, suggest that it developed in Mesopotamia, used local resources and primarily catered for local patrons. The foundation of Veh Ardashir in the early 3rd century was accompanied by new glass workshops there, suggesting mobility of glassworkers familiar with producing and working plant ash glass and probably coming from elsewhere within southern Mesopotamia. The development of different plant ash glass recipes and the adoption of new forms of cut glass at this city in the 4th century may suggest greater experimentation, or a further influx of glass-workers influenced to some degree by contemporary eastern Roman forms. This may have been because of imports; the circulation of small numbers of Roman glass vessels is archaeologically and analytically proven not only from Mesopotamia, but even as far as Merv at the opposite end of the Sasanian empire. This adds to a growing picture of close cultural interaction between the eastern Roman and Sasanian empires during the 4th century which extended beyond material culture and fashion to encompass religious belief and intellectual thought.

Although the evidence is still limited, there are hints at differential patterns of circulation across the Sasanian empire, but a great deal more archaeological research is required before we begin to understand the reasons. Whether any glassware was produced on the Iranian plateau remains uncertain as no evidence for production or working has been found there. In contrast, evidence for large-scale production has been reported from surveys in central and southern Iraq; the southern Caucasus also appears to have been an important region, and the number of published vessels found in excavations is also highest in these two western regions. Sasanian glass was produced to different standards: some was mass-produced, is relatively common and was also placed in graves. Other forms are scarce and took many hours to produce. These are not found in graves in Mesopotamia although hundreds of complete examples from the Iranian art market probably derive from graves in Iran. They also circulated beyond the empire and have been excavated in graves in Arabia, the northern Caucasus and Far East where they were particularly highly treasured.

The Sasanian glass industry influenced subsequent early Islamic glass-working, not only in the choice of composition but also in the continuing prevalence of dip moulds and the liking for heavy cutting, albeit applied to new forms. The greater mobility of craftsmen and wider horizons of patronage after the Islamic conquest accelerated earlier trends and new workshops began to be founded deeper into Iran and Central Asia by the 9th century.

Acknowledgements

This paper is dedicated in memory of Mariamaddalena Negro Ponzi who passed away just before this volume was sent to press. Her pioneering research on Sasanian glass from Iraq remains of fundamental importance and following her recent retirement she was set to complete the final publication of the glass from Veh Ardashir. Unless otherwise credited to publications, drawings are usually by the author and all have been amended for consistency of style; photographs are reproduced by courtesy of the Trustees of the British Museum; pieces in the British Museum are cited by their BM number, others in the Ashmolean Museum and Birmingham Museum & Art Gallery are cited by their AMO and BMAG numbers respectively.

Bibliography

Adams, R. McC. (1965) *Land Behind Baghdad. A History of Settlement on the Diyala Plains*. Chicago, IL, University of Chicago Press.

Adams, R. McC. (1972) Settlement and irrigation patterns in ancient Akkad. In McG. Gibson (ed.) *The City and Area of Kish*, 182–208. Miami, FL, Field Research Project.

Adams, R. McC. (1981) *Heartland of Cities. Surveys of Ancient Settlement and Land Use on the Central Floodplain of the Euphrates*. Chicago, IL, University of Chicago Press.

Adams, R. McC. and Nissen, H. J. (1972) *The Uruk Countryside. The Natural Setting of Urban Societies*. Chicago, IL, University of Chicago Press.

Akira, H. (1981) Dailaman ai Shahpir. Re-examinations of their Chronology. *Bulletin of the Ancient Orient Museum* 3, 43–61.

Andersen, S. F. (2007) *The Tylos Period Burials in Bahrain 1. The Glass and Pottery Vessels*. Manama, Culture and National Heritage, Kingdom of Bahrain in association with Moesgard Museum and Aarhus University.

An, Jiayao (1987) *Early Chinese Glassware*. Chinese Translations 12. Hong Kong, Millennia.

Barag, D. and Simpson, St J. (in preparation) *Catalogue of Western Asiatic Glass in the British Museum 2. The Eastern Roman and Sasanian Glass*.

Bivar, A. D. H. (1970) Trade between China and the Near East in the Sasanian and early Muslim periods. In W. Watson (ed.) *Pottery and Metalwork in T'ang China: their chronology and external relations*. Colloquies on Art and Archaeology in Asia 1, 1–11. London, Percival David Foundation of Chinese Art, University of London.

Boehmer, R. M. (1991) Uruk 1980–1990: a progress report. *Antiquity* 65, 465–478.

Boucharlat, R. (1987) Suse à l'époque sasanide. *Mesopotamia* 22, 357–366.

Boucharlat, R. and Lecomte, O. (1987) Les petits objets. In R. Boucharlat and O. Lecomte *et al.*, *Fouilles de Tureng Tepe 1. Les périodes Sassanides et Islamiques*. Recherche sur les Civilisations, Mémoire 74, 171–186. Paris, Editions Recherche sur les Civilisations.

Braat, W. C. (1964) Three Sassanian glass vessels, recently acquired by the Museum. *Oudheidkundige Mededelingen uit het Rijksmuseum van Oudheden te Leiden* 45, 115–116.

Brill, R. H. (2005) Chemical Analyses of Some Sasanian Glasses from Iraq. In D. Whitehouse, *Sasanian and Post-Sasanian Glass in The Corning Museum of Glass*, 65–88. Corning, NY, The Corning Museum of Glass.

Burney, C. A. (1973) Excavations at Haftavan Tepe 1971: Third Preliminary Report. *Iran* 11, 153–172.

Cavallero, M. (1966) The excavations at Choche (presumed Ctesiphon) – Area 2. *Mesopotamia* 1, 63–81.

Chilashvili, L. (1964) *Nakalari Urbnisi (istorikal-arkeologinri gemokvlevr) [The city site of Ubnisi (historical and archaeological study)]*. Tbilisi.

Coningham, R. *et al.* (2006) *Anuradhapura. The British-Sri Lankan Excavations at Anuradhapura Salgaha Watta 2. II. The Artefacts*. British Archaeological Reports International Series 1508 = Society for South Asian Studies Monograph 4. Oxford, Archaeopress.

Demange, F. (ed.) (2006) *Les Perses sassanides. Fastes d'un empire oublié (224–642)*. Paris, Editions Findakly.

Djanpoladian, R. M. and Kalantarian, A. A. (1988) *Trade relations of Medieval Armenia in the VI–XIIIth Centuries (According to glass-work data)*. Arkeologicheskie Pamyatniki Armenii 14, Part VI. Erevan, Akademiia Nauk Armenskoi SSR.

Dresvyanskaya, G. Y. (1974) Oval'nyi' dom khristianskoi obshchiny v starom Merve [The 'Oval' Building of the Christian Community at Ancient Merv]. In *Trudy YuTAKE* 15, 155–181. Ashkhabad.

Džanpoladjani, R. M. (1974) *[Srednevekovoe steklo Dvina IX–XIII vv.]*. Erevan, Akademiia Nauk Armenskoi SSR.

Efendi, R. (1976) *Decorative and Applied Arts of Azerbaijan (middle ages)*. Baku, Išyğ.

Finster, B. (1983) Grabungen in der Sasanidenstadt (B'XX). In J. Schmidt, *XXXI–XXXII. Vorläufiger Bericht über die von dem Deutschen Archäologischen Institut aus Mitteln der Deutschen Forschungsgemeinschaft unternommenen Ausgrabungen in Uruk-Warka (1973, 1973/74)*, 36–53. Berlin, Gebr. Mann.

Forbes, F. (1839) A Visit to the Sinjar Hills in 1838, with some account of the Sect of Yazidis, and of various places in the Mesopotamian Desert, between the Rivers Tigris and Khabur. *Journal of the Royal Geographical Society* 9, 409–430.

Freestone, I. C. (2006) Glass production in late antiquity and the early Islamic period: a geochemical perspective. In M. Maggetti and B. Messiga (eds.) *Geomaterials in Cultural Heritage*. Geological Society Special Publication 257, 201–216. London, Geological Society.

Freestone, I. C. and Lambarth, S. (forthcoming) Scientific analyses of selected glass compositions. In St J. Simpson *et al.*, *Excavations at Kush: A Sasanian and Islamic site in Ras al-Khaimah, United Arab Emirates II. The Small Finds and Glassware: Catalogue, Discussion and Scientific Analyses*. Oxford, Archaeopress.

Fukai, S. (1960) A Persian Treasure in the Shoso-in Repository. *Japan Quarterly* 7, 169–176.

Fukai, S. (1968) *Study of Iranian art and archaeology. Glass and metalwork*. Tokyo, Yoshikawa Kobunkan.

Fukai, S. (1977) *Persian Glass*. New York/Tokyo/Kyoto, Weatherhill/Tankosha (translated E. B. Crawford).

Ghirshman, R. (1954) *Iran from the earliest times to the Islamic conquest*. Harmondsworth, Penguin.

Gibson, McG. (1972) *The City and Area of Kish*. Miami, FL, Field Research Project.

Gibson, McG. (ed.) (1981) *Uch Tepe. Tell Razuk, Tell Ahmed al-Mughir, Tell Ajamat*, Chicago, IL, University of Chicago.

Goldstein, S. M. (1978) Fakes and Forgeries of Ancient Glass. In *Annales du 7e Congrès Internationale d'Etude Historique du Verre*, 129–136. Liège, Edition du Secrétariat Général.

Goldstein, S. M. *et al.* (2005) *The Nasser D. Khalili Collection of Islamic Art XV. Glass from Sasanian antecedents to European imitations*. London, Nour Foundation.

Grossmark, T. (2010) "And He Decreed that Glassware is Susceptible to Becoming Unclean": The Application of the Laws of Ritual Purity to Glassware Reconsidered. *Jewish Studies Quarterly* 17, 191–212.

Guest, E. (1933) *Notes on plants and plant products with their colloquial names in 'Iraq*. Department of Agriculture, Bulletin 27. Baghdad, Government Press.

Gwon-Gu Kim (1989) *Diachronic analysis of changes in settlement patterns of the Hamrin region*. Unpublished M.Phil thesis, University of Cambridge.

Al-Haditti, A-M. M. A. R. (1995) Umm Keshm – summary report. *Mesopotamia* 30, 217–239.

Harden, D. (1932) Report on Glass-ware found at Nineveh in the season 1927–1928. Unpublished manuscript, dated December 1932.

Harden, D. (1934) Excavations at Kish and Barghuthiat 1933. II. The Pottery. *Iraq* 1, 124–136.

Harper, P. O. (1974) Cat. No. 168: Rhyton. In O. W. Muscarella, *Ancient Art. The Norbert Schimmel Collection*. Mainz, Philipp von Zabern.

Harper, P. O. *et al.* (1978) *The Royal Hunter. Art of the Sasanian Empire*. New York, NY, The Asia Society.

Henderson, J. and McLoughlin, S. D. (2003) Glass Production in Al-Raqqa: Experimentation and Technological Changes. In *Annales du 15e Congrès de l'Association Internationale pour l'Histoire du Verre*, 144–148. Nottingham, Association Internationale pour l'Histoire du Verre.

Huff, D. (1978) Ausgrabungen auf Qal'a-ye Dukhtar bei Firuzabad 1976. *Archäologische Mitteilungen aus Iran* 11, 117–150.

Huff, D. (1987) Archaeology, IV. Sasanian. In *Encyclopaedia Iranica* II, 302–308. London, Routledge.

Ignatiadou, D. (2010) Achaemenid and Greek Colourless Glass. In J. Curtis and St J. Simpson (eds.) *The World of Achaemenid Persia*, 419–426. London, I. B. Tauris.

al-Jadir, W. and Abdullah, Z. R. (1988) *Sippar 1. Excavations of the 1985 Season*. Baghdad [Arabic text].

Katsuris, K. and Buryakov, Y. F. (1963) Izuchenie remeslennogo kvartala antichnogo Merva u severnykh vorot Gyaur-kaly [A study of the craft area of ancient Merv near the north gate of Gyaur-Kala]. In *Trudy YuTAKE* 12, 119–163. Ashkhabad.

Kawamata, M. (1991) Telul Hamediyat near Tells Gubba and Songor: Part III. *Al-Rafidan* 12, 249–259.

Keller, D. (2010) Functional and economic aspects of Late Sasanian and Early Islamic glass from Kush, United Arab Emirates. In B. Zorn and A. Hilgner (eds.) *Glass along the Silk Road from 200 BC to AD 1000*. RGZM – Tagungen 9, 71–80. Mainz, Römisch-Germanisches Zentralmuseum.

Keller, D. (in press) Glass vessels. In St J. Simpson *et al., Excavations at Kush: A Sasanian and Islamic site in Ras al-Khaimah, United Arab Emirates II. The Small Finds and Glassware: Catalogue, Discussion and Scientific Analyses*. Oxford, Archaeopress.

Khairi, A. H. (1987/88) Tell Besmayeh. *Sumer* 45, 9–32, 105 (English abstract).

Kröger, J. (1985) Some remarks on the glass finds of the Ctesiphon excavations 1928/29 and 1931/32. Unpublished paper presented in Torino July 1985.

Kröger, J. (forthcoming) *Parthisches, sasanidisches und islamisches Glas: Die Glasfunde von Ktesiphon (Iraq) nach den Ausgrabungen der Ktesiphon-Expedition 1928–29 und 1931–32*.

Lamm, C. J. (1931) Les verres trouvés a Suse. *Syria* 12, 358–367.

Lamm, C. J. (1939) Glass and hard stone vessels. In A. U. Pope (ed.) *A Survey of Persian Art III*, 2592–2606. Oxford, Oxford University Press.

Layard, A. H. (1853) *Discoveries in the ruins of Nineveh and Babylon*. London, John Murray.

Levene, D. and Rothenberg, B. (2007) *A Metallurgical Gemara. Metals in the Jewish Sources*. London, Institute for Archaeo-Metallurgical Studies/Institute of Archaeology/University College London.

Litvinskij, B. A. and Solovjev, V. S. (1985) *Kafyrkala. Frühmittelalterliche Stadt im Vachs-Tal, Süd-Tadzikistan*. Materialien zur allgemeinen und vergleichenden Archäologie 28. Munich, C. H. Beck.

Lombard, P. and Kervran, M., (eds.) (1989) *Bahrain National Museum Archaeological Collections. A Selection of Pre-Islamic Antiquities*. Manama, Directorate of Museum and Heritage/Ministry of Information.

Loukonine, V. and Ivanov, A. (2003) *Persian Art*. London, Sirocco.

Meyer, C. (1996) Sasanian and Islamic glass from Nippur, Iraq. In *Annales du 13e Congrès de l'Association Internationale pour l'Histoire du Verre*, 247–255. Lochem, Association Internationale pour l'Histoire du Verre.

Mirti, P., Pace, M., Negro Ponzi, M. M. and Aceto, M. (2008) ICP–MS analysis of glass fragments of Parthian and Sasanian epoch from Seleucia and Veh Ardašīr (Central Iraq). *Archaeometry* 50, 429–450.

Mirti, P., Pace M., Malandrino, M. and Negro Ponzi, M. (2009) Sasanian glass from Veh Ardašīr: new evidences by ICP-MS analysis. *Journal of Archaeological Science* 36, 1061–1069.

Moorey, P. R. S. (1971) *Catalogue of the ancient Persian bronzes in the Ashmolean Museum*. Oxford, Clarendon Press.

Negro Ponzi, M. M. (1966) The excavations at Choche (the presumed Ctesiphon). Area 2. *Mesopotamia* 1, 63–88.

Negro Ponzi, M. M. (1968/69) Sasanian Glassware from Tell Mahuz (North Mesopotamia). *Mesopotamia* 3/4, 293–384.

Negro Ponzi, M. M. (1972) Glassware from Abu Skhair (Central Iraq). *Mesopotamia* 7, 215–237.

Negro Ponzi, M. M. (1984) Glassware from Choche (Central Mesopotamia). In R. Boucharlat and J.-F. Salles (eds.) *Arabie Orientale, Mésopotamie et Iran méridional de l'age du fer au début de la periode islamique. Recherche sur les Civilisations*, Mémoire 37, 33–40. Paris, Editions Recherche sur les Civilisations.

Negro Ponzi, M. M. (1987) Late Sasanian Glassware from Tell Baruda. *Mesopotamia* 22, 265–275.

Negro Ponzi, M. M. (2002) The glassware from Seleucia (Central Iraq). *Parthica* 4, 63–156.

Negro Ponzi, M. M. (2005) Mesopotamian Glassware of the Parthian and Sasanian Period: Some notes. In *Annales du 16e Congrès de l'Association Internationale pour l'Histoire du Verre*, 141–145. Nottingham, Association Internationale pour l'Histoire du Verre.

Newby, M. (1995) *The Beauty of Ancient Glass*. London, Hadji Baba Ancient Art.

Nuriiyev, A. B. (1981) *Gafqaz Albaniijasynyn shushǎ mǎ'mulaty vǎ istehsaly tarikhi*, Baku, Elm.

Oliver Jr., A. (1980) *Ancient Glass in the Carnegie Museum of Natural History, Pittsburgh*. Pittsburgh, PA, Carnegie Institute.

Pace, M., Bianco Prevot, A., Mirti, P. and Venco Ricciardi, R. (2008) The technology of production of Sasanian glazed pottery from Veh Ardašīr. *Archaeometry* 50, 591–608.

Pinder-Wilson, R. (1963) Cut-Glass Vessels from Persia and Mesopotamia. *British Museum Quarterly* 27, 33–39.

Puttrich-Reignard, O. H.-W. (1934) *Die Glasfunde von Ktesiphon*. Kiel, Christian-Alberts Universität zu Kiel.

Ramishvili, R. M. *et al.* (1984) [Work of the Djinbaliskaya Complex archaeological expedition]. In O. Lordkipanidze *et al., Polevye Archeologičeskie Issledovaniya v. 1981 God*, 59–68. Tbilisi.

Raschke, M. G. (1978) New Studies in Roman Commerce with the East. In H. Temporini (ed.) *Aufstieg und Niedergang der Römischen Welt II.9.2*, 604–1378. Berlin/New York, Walter de Gruyter.

Reuther, O. (1929) The German Excavations at Ctesiphon. *Antiquity* 3, 434–451.

Riazi, M. (2010) Glass along the Silk Road in the Near East from the Persian Empire to the Middle Ages. In B. Zorn and A. Hilgner (eds.) *Glass along the Silk Road from 200 BC to AD 1000*. RGZM – Tagungen 9, 105–113. Mainz, Römisch-Germanisches Zentralmuseum.

Roehrs, S. (forthcoming) Compositional analyses of glass beads. In St J. Simpson *et al. Excavations at Merv. Investigations of a Sasanian residential quarter*. Louvain, Peeters.

Rogers, J. M. (2005) Problems in the study of Islamic glass. In S. M. Goldstein *et al., The Nasser D. Khalili Collection of Islamic Art XV. Glass from Sasanian antecedents to European imitations*, 18–25. London, The Nour Foundation.

von Saldern, A. (1963) Achaemenid and Sassanian Cut Glass. *Ars Orientalis* 5, 7–16.

Salles, J.-F. and Sedov, A. V. (2010) *Qāni'. Le port antique du Hadramawt entre la Méditerranée, l'Afrique et l'Inde. Fouilles Russes 1972, 1985–89, 1991, 1993–94. Preliminary reports of the Russian Archaeological Mission to the Republic of Yemen*. Turnhout, Brepols.

al-Shams, M. A. (1987/88) The excavations of the Hira cemetery. *Sumer* 45, 42–56 [Arabic section].

Shepherd, D. G. (1986) Sasanian art. In E. Yarshater (ed.) *Cambridge History of Iran 3.2. The Seleucid, Parthian and Sasanian Periods*, 1055–1112. Cambridge, Cambridge University Press.

Simpson, St J. (1992) *Aspects of Archaeology of the Sasanian Period in Mesopotamia*. Unpublished DPhil. thesis, University of Oxford (three volumes).

Simpson, St J. (1996) From Tekrit to the Jaghjagh: Sasanian sites, settlement patterns and material culture in Northern Mesopotamia. In K. Bartl and S. R. Hauser (eds.) *Continuity and change in northern Mesopotamia from the Hellenistic to the Early Islamic period*, 87–126. Berlin, Dietrich Reimer.

Simpson, St J. (ed.) (2002) *Queen of Sheba. Treasures from ancient Yemen*. London, British Museum Press.

Simpson, St J. (2005a) Review: David Whitehouse, Sasanian and Post-Sasanian Glass in The Corning Museum of Glass. *Bead Study Trust Newsletter* 46, 8–10.

Simpson, St J. (2005b) Glass and small finds from Sasanian contexts at the ancient city-site of Merv: understanding patterns of circulation and retrieval of ancient material culture at a multi-period mudbrick site. In V. P. Nikonorov (ed.) *Central Asia from the Achaemenids to the Timurids. Archaeology, history, ethnology, culture. Papers from an International Scientific Conference dedicated to the Centenary of Alexander Markovich Belenitsky*, 232–238. St Petersburg, Institute of the History of Material Culture of the Russian Academy of Sciences and State Hermitage.

Simpson, St J. (2005c) Sasanian glass from Nineveh. In *Annales du 16e Congrès de l'Association Internationale pour l'Histoire du Verre*, 146–151. Nottingham, Association Internationale pour l'Histoire du Verre.

Simpson, St J. (2007) From San Marco to South Arabia: observations on Sasanian cut glass. In A. Hagedorn and A. Shalem (eds.) *Facts and Artefacts. Art in the Islamic World. Festschrift for Jens Kröger on his 65th Birthday*, 59–88. Leiden, Brill.

Simpson, St J. (2008) Suburb or slum? Excavations at Merv (Turkmenistan) and observations on stratigraphy, refuse and material culture in a Sasanian city. In D. Kennet and P. Luft (eds.) *Recent advances in Sasanian Archaeology and History*, 65–78. Oxford, Archaeopress.

Sono, T. and Fukai, S. (1968) *Dailaman III. The excavations at Hassani Mahale and Ghalekuti 1964*. Tokyo University Iraq-Iran Archaeological Expedition, Report 8. Tokyo, University of Tokyo/Institute of Oriental Culture.

Steve, M.-J. *et al.* (2003) *L'Île de Khārg. Une page de l'histoire du Golfe Persique et du Monachisme Oriental*. Neuchâtel, Recherches et Publications.

Taniichi, T. (1986a) The Origin of the Cut Glass Bowl in Shosoin Treasure. *Bulletin of the Okayama Orient Museum* 5, 35–46.

Taniichi, T. (1986b) Roman and Post-Roman Glass Vessels Depicted in Asian Wall Paintings. *Orient* 22, 128–142.

Taniichi, T. (2010) Sasanian and post-Sasanian plant ash glass vessels delivered to Japan. In B. Zorn and A. Hilgner (eds.) *Glass along the Silk Road from 200 BC to AD 1000*. RGZM – Tagungen 9, 239–46. Mainz, Römisch-Germanisches Zentralmuseum.

Tomber, R. (2007) Rome and Mesopotamia – importers into India in the first millennium AD. *Antiquity* 81, 972–988.

Vanden Berghe, L. (1972) Recherches archéologiques dans le Luristan. Cinquieme Campagne: 1969. Prospections dans le Pusht-i Kuh Central (Rapport Préliminaire). *Iranica Antiqua* 9, 1–48.

Watt, J. C. Y. *et al.* (2004) *China, Dawn of a Golden Age, 200–750 AD*. New York, NY, The Metropolitan Museum of Art.

Wenke, R. J. (1987) Western Iran in the Partho-Sasanian Period: The Imperial Transformation. In F. Hole (ed.) *The Archaeology of Western Iran. Settlement and Society from Prehistory to the Islamic Conquest*, 251–281. Washington D.C., Smithsonian Institution.

Whitcomb, D. S. (1985) *Before the Roses and Nightingales. Excavations at Qasr-i Abu Nasr, Old Shiraz*. New York, NY, The Metropolitan Museum of Art.

Whitehouse, D. (2005) *Sasanian and Post-Sasanian Glass in the Corning Museum of Glass*. Corning, NY, The Corning Museum of Glass.

Whitfield, R. (ed.) (1984) *Treasures from Korea. Art through 5000 Years*, London, British Museum Publications.

Wright, H. T. (1981) The Southern Margins of Sumer. Archaeological Survey of the Area of Eridu and Ur. In R. Mc. Adams, *Heartland of Cities. Surveys of Ancient Settlement and Land Use on the Central Floodplain of the Euphrates*, 295–345. Chicago, IL, University of Chicago.

Zarins, J., al-Mughannam, A. S. and Kamal, M. (1984) Excavations at Dhahran South – The Tumuli Field (208–92), 1403 AH / 1983. A Preliminary Report. *Atlal* 8, 25–54.